CLIMATE AND DEVELOPMENT

World Scientific Series on Environmental, Energy and Climate Economics

Series Editor: Richard S J Tol (*University of Sussex, UK*)

Published

Vol. 1 *Climate and Development*
edited by Anil Markandya and Dirk T G Rübbelke

Volume 1 World Scientific Series on Environmental, Energy and Climate Economics

CLIMATE AND DEVELOPMENT

Editors

Anil Markandya
Basque Centre For Climate Change, Spain

Dirk Rübbelke
Technische Universität Bergakademie Freiberg, Germany

World Scientific

NEW JERSEY • LONDON • SINGAPORE • BEIJING • SHANGHAI • HONG KONG • TAIPEI • CHENNAI • TOKYO

Published by

World Scientific Publishing Co. Pte. Ltd.
5 Toh Tuck Link, Singapore 596224
USA office: 27 Warren Street, Suite 401-402, Hackensack, NJ 07601
UK office: 57 Shelton Street, Covent Garden, London WC2H 9HE

Library of Congress Cataloging-in-Publication Data
Names: Markandya, Anil, 1945– editor. | Rübbelke, Dirk T. G., 1972– editor.
Title: Climate and development / editors Anil Markandya, Basque Centre For Climate Change, Spain, Dirk Rübbelke, Technische Universität Bergakademie Freiberg, Germany.
Description: New Jersey : World Scientific, [2022] | Series: World scientific series on environmental, energy and climate economics ; volume 1 | Includes bibliographical references and index.
Identifiers: LCCN 2021035794 | ISBN 9789811240546 (hardcover) | ISBN 9789811240553 (ebook for institutions) | ISBN 9789811240560 (ebook for individuals)
Subjects: LCSH: Environmental economics. | Climatic changes--Economic aspects. | Environmental policy--Economic aspects.
Classification: LCC HC79.E5 C5929 2022 | DDC 333.7--dc23
LC record available at https://lccn.loc.gov/2021035794

British Library Cataloguing-in-Publication Data
A catalogue record for this book is available from the British Library.

For any available supplementary material, please visit
https://www.worldscientific.com/worldscibooks/10.1142/12376#t=suppl

Desk Editors: Aanand Jayaraman/Laul Bhakti/Sylvia Koh

Typeset by Stallion Press
Email: enquiries@stallionpress.com

https://doi.org/10.1142/9789811240553_fmatter

Preface

This book is concerned with the twin challenges of human development and climate change. It aims to provide the reader with a panorama of the different ways in which climate affects development and how the expected changes in climate over the next century are likely to influence the development paths of both rich and poor countries.

For many years already, we — the editors of the book — had dedicated much of our research effort to climate and development challenges for humanity. It was in 1989 that Anil Markandya co-authored "Blueprint for a Green Economy" with David Pearce and Edward Barbier. The "Blueprint" was a pioneering contribution to greening economies, leading them toward sustainable development. Edward Barbier is also a contributor of a chapter in this book.

More recently, we addressed issues of co-benefits of climate policy in our book "Ancillary Benefits of Climate Policy" that we edited jointly with Wolfgang Buchholz and Stefan Vögele, both of whom also contribute essays to the present volume. The book on ancillary benefits presents the state of the art in the research of effects jointly generated by climate policy and illustrates links to development issues.

In the process of drafting, compiling, and publishing this book, many people were involved. We owe our special thanks to Theresa Stahlke who supported us in organizing the submission and review process. Her comments on several parts of the book helped to improve it significantly. Furthermore, there were also several anonymous referees who reviewed the essays included in this volume and we are also grateful to them.

Last but not least, we are indebted to Richard Tol, the editor of the book series including this volume, who gave us invaluable advice in framing our book project.

https://doi.org/10.1142/9789811240553_fmatter

About the Editors

Anil Markandya graduated from the London School of Economics with a Master of Science in Econometrics and was awarded his Ph.D. from the same institution on the Economics of the Environment in 1976. He has worked extensively on environmental problems from an economic viewpoint. He was a lead author for Chapters of the third and fourth IPCC Assessment Reports on Climate Change (which were awarded a share of the Nobel Peace Prize in 2007) and a Lead Author for the fifth Assessment Report.

In 2008, he was nominated by Cambridge University as one of the top 50 contributors to thinking on sustainability in the world. From 2000 to 2006, he was a Lead Economist at the World Bank. He has acted as advisor to several governments and international organizations over the last 30 years.

Professor Markandya was President of the European Association of Environmental and Resource Economics from 2014 to 2015. Currently, he is Distinguished Ikerbasque Professor at the Basque Centre for Climate Change in the Basque Country, Spain, and Honorary Professor of Economics at the University of Bath, UK.

Dirk T. G. Rübbelke is Professor of Economics at the Technische Universität Bergakademie Freiberg, Germany. Before he joined Technische Universität Bergakademie Freiberg, he was IKERBASQUE Research Professor at the Basque Centre for Climate Change (2010–2014), Senior Research Fellow at the Center for International Climate and Environmental Research, Oslo, Norway (2008–2010), and Junior Professor at Chemnitz University of Technology, Germany (2002–2008). He is also Research Associate at the Centre for European Economic Research (ZEW), Mannheim, and Fellow Member of the CESifo Research Network, Munich. Prof. Rübbelke has pursued research and taught at internationally renowned universities and research centers, including the Australian National University in Canberra, Hebrew University Jerusalem, Jadavpur University in Kolkata, Makerere University in Kampala, Max Planck Institute for Tax Law and Public Finance in Munich, and the University of Nottingham.

https://doi.org/10.1142/9789811240553_fmatter

Contents

Preface v

About the Editors vii

Introduction xiii

Part 1: What are the Prospects for Development in the Face of Climate Change? 1

Chapter 1: The Economic Impact of Climate in the Long Run 3
Richard S. J. Tol

Chapter 2: Balancing the Distribution Across Generations: Putting the Horse Before the Cart 37
Wolfgang Buchholz and Dirk Rübbelke

Chapter 3: Climate and Development: The Role of the Sustainable Development Goals 67
Edward B. Barbier and Joanne C. Burgess

Chapter 4: Losing and Gaining Freedom Due to Climate Change 91

Evert Van de Vliert and Mohsen Joshanloo

Chapter 5: Economic Damage of Climate Change: How Far is it From the Physical Damage? 115

Taoyuan Wei and H. Asbjørn Aaheim

Chapter 6: Climate Change Impacts and Market-Driven Adaptation: The Costs of Inaction Including Market Rigidities 137

Francesco Bosello and Ramiro Parrado

Chapter 7: Agricultural TFP Under a Changing Climate: Evidence from High, Middle, and Low-Income Countries 177

Sevil Acar and Simay Kızılkaya

Part 2: Pathways Through Which Climate Change Can Cause Harm (or Benefit) to Development 219

Chapter 8: The Climate–Conflicts Nexus and the Role of Geographical Spillovers 221

Federica Cappelli, Valeria Costantini, Elena Paglialunga, Giorgia Sforna and Anil Markandya

Chapter 9: A Subscription vs. Appropriation Framework for Natural Resource Conflicts 257

Dripto Bakshi and Indraneel Dasgupta

Chapter 10: Climate and Migration 309
Katrin Millock and Cees Withagen

Part 3: How Climate Policy Can be Designed to Aid Development? 343

Chapter 11: Smart and Sustainable Cities in the MENA Countries: Combining Sustainable Growth and Climate Adaption? 345
Jan Friesen and Marc Ringel

Chapter 12: Negative Emissions in Climate Policy — Scenarios, Governance, and Challenges 367
Joahnnes Pfeiffer and Karen Pittel

Chapter 13: Can Blue Carbon Initiatives Help Conserve Mangroves in Developing Countries? 415
Christa Brunnschweiler and Tiziana Luisetti

Chapter 14: The Fight Against Deforestation of Tropical Forests — The Contribution of the Blockchain-Based Contract Management Method to Minimize Illegal Logging 439
Elena Mechik and Michael von Hauff

Chapter 15: Impact of Germany's Phase Out of Coal Power Plants on Developing Countries 465
Stefan Vögele and Kristina Govorukha

Index 501

https://doi.org/10.1142/9789811240553_fmatter

Introduction

1. Preamble

One of the world's greatest challenges is to raise living standards for everyone so that they have a life free from hunger and as free from disease as possible. This means improving the conditions under which some people live in all countries, but particularly those in the group often referred to as developing countries. Progress along several indicators of well-being have been recorded in the post-war period, although there have been setbacks, sometimes the result of conflict, sometimes poor governance, and sometimes natural disasters. Nevertheless, in general, things have moved in a positive direction for most of humanity for the past 70 years, and even longer for some countries.

This picture has been complicated by the phenomenon of climate change, which has already made its impact during the last three decades or so, through extreme weather events that have increased the frequency and intensity of both floods and droughts, higher incidence of certain diseases, shifts in the productivity of land for crops and livestock, and (mostly negative) changes in marine and terrestrial ecosystems. The extent of climate change experienced so far is relatively small compared to what can be expected if the underlying forces that propel it (an increase in the emission of greenhouse gases (GHGs)) continue at anything like the current levels. The global community is wrestling with the challenge of how much these emissions can be reduced to stabilize climate without imposing too high a cost on the present generation, in particular on those in the present generation least able to bear that cost. The 2015 Paris Accord stated the aim to limit the increase in global mean temperatures to 2°C compared to pre-industrial levels and if possible keep it down to 1.5°C. Achieving this is possible, but at what cost and to whom? Furthermore, even if the goal is realized, significant impacts from climate change can be expected. Evidence indicates that these will be felt most severely in countries that are relatively poor. These effects of climate change will be added to by the measures taken to reduce GHGs. Together, they will determine how climate change affects the prospects for development across the globe. These complex and difficult questions are what the present volume seeks to address.

2. What are the Prospects for Development in the Face of Climate Change?

The first part of the book sets the scene in the context of the wider debate of how much climate matters for a country's prospects for a stable and prosperous economy and society. Richard Tol reminds the readers how early scholars were convinced that geography was destiny, that climate, a key part of geography, determined the human condition. He notes that current economists by and large argue against that and take the view that the quality of institutions is more important in determining the prospects of a country. He argues that neither position is tenable on its own. His chapter reviews the literature and presents new empirical evidence to show that climate does have a significant effect on development, but that this effect is mediated by institutions, and that the effect shrinks with affluence. So, to the extent that countries can raise their levels of wealth, they will be able to overcome (or at least reduce) the difficulties climate change will pose. That leaves open the question of whether they will grow in the present and future circumstances; so far, COVID-19 notwithstanding, growth does not appear to have fallen for most of the world in spite of the climate change experienced.

Action to reduce GHGs implies a cost to present generations and a benefit to future generations. So, it involves an intergenerational transfer. Much of the discussion about how much the GHGs should be reduced now has revolved around trade-offs between the well-being of present and future generations. In many climate economics studies like the Stern Review[1] or that by Nordhaus (2007),[2] this trade-off is represented by an intertemporal social welfare function (SWF) of the utilitarian type and its key parameters, i.e., the social discount rate and the degree of concavity of the underlying utility function.[3] The lower these parameters are, the higher the desirable level of current reductions in GHGs. The technological conditions for GHG abatement, however, are quite uncertain so the question arises whether a certain fixed SWF is able to imply a balanced intergenerational distribution of well-being under different technological circumstances. Wolfgang Buchholz and Dirk Rübbelke look at this question of robustness of social evaluation by formulating three normative postulates that an SWF should fulfill: One is that welfare of future generations should not be lower than that of the present, i.e., development should be sustainable. The second is that the sacrifices of present generations should not become unduly high and the third is that distribution of welfare across generations should not become too uneven. They conclude that by choosing a SWF with a zero social discount rate, the first condition can be met quite easily. The second can be met by assuming a sufficiently high elasticity of the marginal utility of income and thus by a large enough concavity of the utility function. The third condition cannot be guaranteed under their modeling assumptions. This leads perhaps to the conclusion that discussion of the normative aspects of intergenerational distribution in the case of climate change may need to be conducted using an alternative non-utilitarian objective

---

[1]Stern, N. H., *et al.* (2006). *Stern Review: The Economics of Climate Change*. Cambridge University Press, Cambridge.

[2]Nordhaus, W. D. (2007). A review of the Stern review on the economics of climate change. *Journal of Economic Literature*, 45(3), 686–702.

[3]On utility discounting, also see: Weitzman, M. L. (2007). A review of the Stern Review on the economics of climate change. *Journal of Economic Literature*, 45(3), 703–724.

function — perhaps one of a maximin nature as suggested by John Roemer (2011).[4]

The consequences of climate change on development in the recent past and in the coming decades are examined in the chapter by Edward Barbier and Joanne Burgess. They do it through tracking progress on the Sustainable Development Goals (SDGs). Globally, the loss from the rise in CO_2 per capita over 2000–2016 amounted to $311 per person. But, as indicators for eleven other SDGs improved, there was an overall net gain of $12,737 per capita. For low-income countries, however, CO_2 emissions decline actually resulted in a benefit of only $31 per person. Once positive and negative interactions with other SDGs were taken into account, the net welfare gain in poor economies was only $244 per person. Thus, progress in terms of development was highly skewed against the poor countries, even though they did not lose out because of climate change policy in the recent past. The chapter also examines the implications of the SDG analysis for climate and development objectives beyond 2030. Current trends suggest that increased growth in per capita incomes in low- and middle-income countries has been accompanied by worsening future climate scenarios, which may seriously undermine other development goals. Ensuring these scenarios are not realized in the coming decades will be important in meeting the development goals of these countries.

A different perspective of climate change on development is offered by Evert Van de Vliert and Mohsen Joshanloo. They argue that the climatic demands and stresses of cold and heat are more threatening for the poor, but more beneficial for the rich, gradually resulting in lower freedom for the poor, but higher freedom for the rich. Freedom in this context relates to freedom from want, freedom from fear, freedom of expression and participation, freedom from discrimination, freedom to realize one's human potential, and freedom to function effectively. The chapter makes country-level forecasts of freedom by around the year 2100 on the basis of climato-economic livability under current

[4]Roemer, J. E. (2011). The ethics of intertemporal distribution in a warming planet. *Environmental and Resource Economics*, 48(3), 363–390.

projections of global warming and economic development. The emerging picture is mixed and not immediately self-evident. It indicates that especially poor populations in Asia whose habitats will become less threatening may gain, whereas other populations in Asia and the great majority of Africa faced with more threatening habitats will lose rather than gain freedom. Finally, inhabitants of several rich countries will have to defend current freedom rankings against relative decreases. A focus of new effort for development should, they argue, seek measures that will counter the negative developments of freedom resulting from climate change, wherever they occur.

An important part of the research on climate change seeks to estimate the damages that will be caused by the change in different parts of the world. It is mostly forward looking and based on complex Integrated Assessment Models. Damage estimates vary in the literature, with most models coming up with relatively small percentages of current GDP; amounts that would become even smaller relative to what GDP would be if expected trends in growth were realized. There are, however, considerable differences in damages between different countries. The chapter by Taoyuan Wei and Asbjørn Aaheim goes even further. Through a detailed modeling of the agricultural sector, they show how these effects depend on the extent of adaptation. For average 2100 climate scenarios, the economic impacts of a 2.3% reduction in the productivity of grain under present economic conditions range between 0% and 2.3% of the sum of global GDP. However, it ranges between 25% and 70% of the GDP across regions. They conclude that previous studies may be too optimistic in indicating the economic damages, particularly in developing countries. The regions depending heavily on agriculture need to reduce their dependence on agriculture during the economic development to be better prepared for the potential economic consequences of climate change. Overall, the paper emphasizes the importance of granularity in the study of climate effects.

A second paper by Francesco Bosello and Ramiro Parrado addresses this question of the size of the damages caused by climate change to economic output and economic growth. They focus their attention on the criticism that previous estimates of the damages have been too low because they have assumed highly flexible market responses in shifting resources, including labor and capital away, from sectors that are negatively impacted and toward ones that can operate effectively with climate change. They show that introducing rigidities in the adjustment processes does raise economic damage assessments, but not substantively. They demonstrate that while more difficult adjustment increases damages globally by about 20% at high-temperature levels, this is not sufficient to drastically change the overall picture. They note further that the autonomous market adjustment mechanisms embedded in Computable General Equilibrium (CGE) models explain only marginally the low climate change costs. These are in fact due to omission of other impacts because of their proven difficulty to be modeled, such as extreme weather events, damages due to ecosystem services' losses, as well as major disruptions due to the existence of tipping points. It is these that could change the picture drastically about the possible consequences of climate change for future development.

The last paper in this section is the one by Sevil Acar and Simay Kızılkaya. It has some similarities to the one by Wei and Aaheim in looking at the effects of climate change, especially extreme weather events, on agricultural total factor productivity over the period 1995–2015 for 137 countries. The authors find the impacts of climate change to be negative only in the case of low- and middle-income countries. This partly reflects differential climate impacts for these countries, but, to a large extent, it also reflects their income levels. These play a major role in how the countries cope with the effects of such changes or shocks in order to maintain their productivity levels. It underscores the finding that the level of development is a major factor in a country's ability to respond to climate change.

3. Pathways Through Which Climate Change Can Cause Harm (or Benefit) to Development

Discussions in the popular press as well as academic journals have focused on two pathways for climate change to result in disruption to economic and social stability. One is an increase in physical conflict and violence as available land and water resources become scarce and the other is migration. In this book, there are three chapters that have something to say about these.

The chapters by Federica Cappelli, Valeria Costantini, Elena Paglialunga, Giorgia Sforna, and Anil Markandya and Dripto Bakshi and Indraneel Dasgupta address the question of conflict. The Cappelli *et al.* chapter focuses on Africa. Other researchers have noted how in the last decades the disruptive effects of climate change have been manifesting themselves at a far greater pace and with a stronger intensity. A review of 50 independent studies examining the impacts of climate change on conflicts found strong support for a causal link ranging across regions, time intervals, and spatial scales. This chapter reports on a more detailed assessment of Africa, which supports these conclusions. The main routes through which climate changes result in such conflicts are pressures in agriculture, scarcity of water and other resources, and migration. At the same time, there are several other aspects that could offset the local conditions, eventually degenerating in armed conflicts. The analysis finds some support for factors such as GDP per capita, natural resources and infrastructure availability, and quality of institutions in reducing the link between climate change and violence.

The chapter by Dripto Bakshi and Indraneel Dasgupta examines the issue of conflict in a theoretical model in which actions taken by one group spillover to other groups. In many cases, these spillovers increase social conflict, but it is also possible that they could increase aggregate income. As long as channels exist for all parties to benefit from that aggregate increase, such actions may reduce conflict. In many different developing country contexts, climate change can increase the costs imposed on one ethnic group due to another group's exploitation of some natural resource. This generally increases inter-group competition over natural resources and often triggers persistent and widespread social conflict. Such conflict in turn affects decentralized community-level mechanisms for the maintenance and augmentation of the contested natural resource, which feeds back into the original conflict. This feedback can work in either direction: to reduce the conflict or increase it. The key is to find ways to ensure that the ones that decrease pressures for conflict are chosen.

The third paper in this section by Katrin Millock and Cees Withagen looks in more detail at migration. They review recent estimates of the effect of weather and climate on migration and identify some issues that have been relatively understudied. One is the general equilibrium effects of climate change and migration. As a result of the movement of people, the economies in both the receiving origin and destination communities will adjust, with effects on many groups other than the migrants. A second concerns thresholds in the climate–migration relationship. These have been studied mainly in terms of the links between income and migration, and weather, climate, and migration. Other thresholds are only starting to become incorporated in the literature. In particular, the link between sea-level rise and migration in coming decades is likely to be important, and it is a subject of some recent papers. A third issue where much work remains to be done relates to climate change and conflict, and their influence on migration. The papers on conflict in this volume look at this to some extent. There is no doubt that the response of people through migration is already an important adaptation mechanism and is likely to become more so. It will be critical to develop the right kinds of support to ensure that it is used to increase well-being and not diminish it.

4. How Can Climate Policy Be Designed to Aid Development?

The last part of the book consists of chapters that study how climate policy can be made more development compatible.

The chapter by Jan Friesen and Marc Ringel looks at how cities combine sustainable growth and climate adaptation in the Middle East and North Africa (MENA) region. Five MENA cities have been surveyed and analyzed in detail and have been juxtaposed to a comparison group of European cities. They start by noting that evidence supports the observation that smart city programs can deliver economic growth and climate protection at the same time. Their main goal is to analyze the combination of economic, technological, and climate action in smart city projects in the MENA region in comparison to a group of European cities. Findings show that regional context plays a clear role in the design and the governance of many of these projects. Governance of smart city projects is a pivotal aspect, which deserves further examination. Key factors in success are (i) information and communication technologies (ICT) and smart network infrastructure; (ii) energy efficiency; (iii) renewable energies; and, to a lesser extent, (iv) sustainable mobility. MENA region programs would also benefit from an enhanced dialogue between national governments and universities and research bodies on this topic.

If the Paris Accord targets mentioned earlier are to be met, it seems very likely that later in this century the planet will have to move to net-negative emissions of GHGs, i.e., measures will have to be taken to absorb more carbon from the atmosphere than is generated in any year. The paper by Johannes Pfeiffer and Karen Pittel goes into the contribution of such emissions from a governance and implementation perspective. Their chapter gives an overview of the literature on this topic, which focuses predominantly on technical aspects, potentials for deployment, and costs. It contributes further to addressing questions regarding (a) impacts of negative emissions technologies on sustainable development that go beyond carbon dioxide removal and (b) the design of climate policy frameworks needed to foster the deployment of carbon dioxide removal (CDR).

Given their prominent role in many climate change mitigation scenarios, negative emissions technologies can substantially contribute to sustainable development by mitigating risks and impacts from more severe climate change. The interlinkage between sustainable development and CDR, however, is more complex and more ambiguous. In particular, CDR and its integration in long-term sustainable mitigation strategies involve a broad range of questions about how costs and risks of climate change, climate change mitigation, and CDR deployment itself are distributed geographically between different countries and intertemporally between different generations.

CDR can provide co-benefits in addition to its contribution to climate change mitigation, but it also comes with negative external costs. Ecosystem-based approaches like the restoration of wetlands or forests combine the generation of CDR with the protection of biodiversity, for example, the application of biochar and methods of soil carbon sequestration can contribute to soil fertility and an increase in food security. Afforestation and reforestation may positively affect local temperature and precipitation patterns and improve local water systems. Even more technical approaches like bioenergy with carbon capture and storage (BECCS) have positive co-benefits, for example, by providing energy services or fostering local (rural) employment and income. Substantial negative external costs of CDR can arise from the demand for water (e.g., for forest plantations), the increased use of fertilizers for the fast growth of biomass (for bioenergy or biochar generation), or indirectly via large energy demand. Another major sustainability concern arises from the land area which some methods of removal require. These co-benefits and external costs will have to be taken into account in the design and implementation of measures for CDR.

A number of policies linked to carbon capture also have co-benefits for terrestrial and marine ecosystems. One such area is with respect to mangroves, studied in the chapter by Christa Brunnschweiler and Tiziana Luisetti. Mangrove forests are important global carbon sinks and offer other local ecosystem services such as fish nurseries and sources of firewood and building materials. Most mangroves are located in developing countries, where — despite widespread legal protection — they are in severe decline mainly due to human pressure. The authors conclude that blue carbon projects can indeed help meet the terrestrial targets for these ecosystems better if three conditions are met. First, in the design phase, large-scale projects should combine the use of qualitative, participatory methods, which have proved effective for stakeholder involvement in small projects, with more quantitative, survey and experimental methods for faster, evidence-based solutions. Second, the financial product chosen for a blue carbon project must be supported by local communities. And third, bundling ecosystem services together is more likely to achieve financial returns that are high enough to facilitate the crucial stakeholder support at community and higher levels.

A more technical policy that could reduce GHGs while simultaneously contributing to better forest management in developing countries, through reducing illegal logging and raising more fiscal resources, is elaborated in the paper by Elena Mechik and Michael von Hauff.

Despite the importance of tropical forests, they continue to be devastated, causing 17% of global carbon emissions, loss of biodiversity, and climate change. Decades of efforts by governmental, nongovernmental, and international organizations to reduce illegal deforestation worldwide have had limited success. The authors analyze the opportunities to develop administrative methods for forest conservation based on the blockchain technology in combination with the economic activities of forest communities. The aim is to reduce the sale of illegally logged timber, to contribute to the reduction of illegal logging, and thereby to the mitigation of climate change. Based on this analysis, they propose a concept for tropical forest preservation through a blockchain-based contract management platform. This concept is based on field research of economic activities in Brazilian, Indian, and Thai forest communities.

Some concern has been expressed in the climate policy debate on whether measures taken to reduce GHGs in developed countries could have a detrimental impact on the economies of developing countries. One such pathway is examined in the paper by Stefan Vögele and Kristina Govorukha in the context of Germany's phase out of hard-coal-fired power plants. The impacts are assessed by applying the list of SDGs of the UN to spillovers in Colombia and South Africa as important coal suppliers and to China as a supplier of photovoltaic (PV) modules that will partially substitute coal-fired power plants. Their study shows that a reduction of mining activities due to phase out of coal-fired power plants could be helpful in reaching SDGs in developing countries. However, the impacts are small as Germany imports a relatively small share of coal. Hence, the phase out of coal-fired power in Germany will not have a significant impact on developing countries' mining industries, as well as on the PV industry of China.

5. Final Thoughts

This book has a rich and complex set of messages on the links between climate change and development. The historic evidence so far points to differential impacts of changes in the climate on countries according to their level of development, with the poorer ones being more affected.

While all countries are likely to be more affected as changes become more severe, the difference is also likely to grow. Development, therefore, is an important part of adapting to climate change. At the same time, climate-related events will make this more difficult, at least in some areas. The challenge is to overcome these new constraints on sustainable development. The chapters in this volume offer some suggestions for how this can be done. But, it is only a start: many gaps remain in our knowledge about possible impacts, their human and social consequences, and on how they might be addressed.

PART 1

WHAT ARE THE PROSPECTS FOR DEVELOPMENT IN THE FACE OF CLIMATE CHANGE?

https://doi.org/10.1142/9789811240553_0001

Chapter 1

The Economic Impact of Climate in the Long Run

Richard S. J. Tol

*Department of Economics, University of Sussex, Falmer, United Kingdom**
Institute for Environmental Studies, Vrije Universiteit, Amsterdam, The Netherlands
Department of Spatial Economics, Vrije Universiteit, Amsterdam, The Netherlands
Tinbergen Institute, Amsterdam, The Netherlands
CESifo, Munich, Germany
Payne Institute for Earth Resources, Colorado School of Mines, Golden, CO, USA
r.tol@sussex.ac.uk

Early scholars were convinced that geography is destiny and that climate determines the human condition. Current economists by and large argue that institutions are destiny, and that the only thing that matters to humans is other human beings. Neither position is tenable. I review the literature and present new empirical evidence that shows that climate does have a significant effect on development, that this effect is mediated by institutions, and that the effect shrinks with affluence.

1. Introduction

Poverty is concentrated in the tropics and subtropics. The correlation is clear, but causation is disputed. This matters, for if a warm

*Jubilee Building, BN1 9SL, UK.

climate prevents or slows economic development, then a warming climate would hurt economic growth. I assess the literature on climate and development, and present new empirical evidence.

The literature on climate and development is vast, spanning almost three millennia, going back to Guan (c780 BC). I cannot present a comprehensive survey in a limited space. See Castells-Quintana *et al.* (2017) for an attempt. Instead, I highlight the two extreme positions, environmental determinism and institutional determinism, that dominate the earlier and later literature, respectively. I take an intermediate position, but one that is closer to institutionalism. The empirical evidence — both from the literature and new material presented below — supports that position: Climate matters, but is not dominant, it is mediated by institutions, and its impact weakens over time.

This chapter continues as follows. Section 2 reviews the literature, focusing on patterns of development in 2, natural disasters in 2.1, and weather in 2.2. Section 3 presents new regression results, for population density in 3.1 and for per capita income in 3.2. Section 4 concludes.

2. Previous Literature

There are three schools of thought on the impact of geography and climate on human development: (*i*) climate is destiny; (*ii*) climate is important; and (*iii*) climate used to be important but is no longer.

Environmental determinism was a popular theory in centuries past. Guan (c780 BC) posits that water is the root from which beauty and ugliness, worthiness and unworthiness, stupidity and giftedness are produced. A people's character was determined by the rivers on whose shores they dwelt. Hippocrates (400 BC) argued that pronounced seasons cause savagery and courage, while weather that changes little breeds indolence and cowardice. Aristotle (350 BC) goes further, writing that "[t]hose who live in a cold climate and in Europe are full of spirit, but wanting in intelligence and skill [...] [w]hereas the natives of Asia are intelligent and inventive, but they are wanting in spirit, and therefore they are always in a state of subjection and slavery." Ibn Khaldun (1377) contradicts Aristotle, arguing that *heat* makes one merry and stupid, and cold air gloomy and overly concerned for the future. These sentiments lasted. Huntington (1915) claims that heat makes for lack of industry, an irascible temper, drunkenness, and sexual indulgence.[1]

Febvre (1922) was one of the first to argue against environmental determinism, emphasizing that social forces are at least as important. He of course had the benefit of hindsight against Aristotle's claim that Europeans would be incapable of ruling over others and Hippocrates' prediction that Europe would never have absolute monarchs. Environmental determinism is now often seen as a historical rather than a contemporary view (Lewthwaite, 2001), a view that is tainted by post-hoc justifications of the position of the hegemon (Blaut, 1999).[2] However, environmental determinism lives on. Diamond (1998) is the main current proponent of this hypothesis. Diamond argues that the current distribution of income across the world can be explained by a few factors of geography. The orientation of the axis of the Eurasian continent is East-West. That implies that areas with similar climates are connected. An innovation in one place — say, a newly domestic animal or a newly bred crop — can be used in a large area. This is not the case on continents with a North—South orientation, that is, Africa and the Americas. The distribution of domesticable plants and animals is also supposed to have been more favorable in Eurasia. Europe got ahead of China because its geography was conducive to many small kingdoms, competing for supremacy and thus innovative; China's geography, instead, invited a uniform empire. Diamond's grasp of history is not without blemish, and his notion that human history is shaped by geographic factors beyond our control is in contrast with the facts. Diamond's hypothesis could be dismissed when comparing the two halves of Hispaniola and Korea. Nevertheless, Olsson and Hibbs (2005) find empirical

---

[1]Huntington (1917) even argues that climate change caused the collapse of the Roman Empire, a theme picked up later by Harper (2017). The causal chains in Harper's book are long and fragile.

[2]Robert Rankin duly places the Garden of Eden in Brentford, London.

support: Diamond's drivers do have explanatory power for the distribution of income.[3]

Landes (1998) argues that its cool summers, mild winters, and regular rains gave Europe an advantage over other places. Others, including Sachs (2003, see also Gallup *et al.* (1999)), argue that climate and geography are contributing factors to (under)development, influential but not dominant. Diseases such as malaria and diarrhea impair children's cognitive and physical development. This leads to poverty in their later life so that there are limited means to protect their own children against these diseases. Furthermore, high infant mortality may induce parents to have many children, and risk-averse parents to have more children than they really want. As a result, investment in the children's health and education is spread thin and the children are likely to grow up to a life of poverty. Infectious diseases are more virulent and prevalent in warmer and wetter climates. Unlike Diamond, Landes and Sachs are not determinists. Sachs indeed calls for active measures to suppress tropical diseases, not just to alleviate the immediate suffering but also to overcome the economic impact in the long run.

Infrastructure also affects economic development (Bougheas *et al.*, 1999; Fernald, 1999; Morrison and Schwartz, 1996; Röller and Waverman, 2001). Travel and transport allow for trade (Ricardian growth) and specialization (Smithian growth). Infrastructure is more expensive in some climates than in others, for example, because of repairs after floods (Schweikert *et al.*, 2014). Disasters have other effects on development too. Saving rates would be higher without disasters (Skidmore, 2001). Households and companies trade off returns to investment against its safety. In a high-risk environment, safe assets with a low return would be preferred, particularly if insurance or asset diversification is expensive or unavailable — as is often the case in poor countries (Bénabou, 1996). Slow growth is the result.

Some have argued that highly volatile environments induce a feast-and-famine culture. A rational response to the risk of losing it all,

---

[3]Andersen *et al.* (2016) argue that it is not climate, but rather UV-radiation that explains incomes, through its impact on the probability of going blind and hence the incentive to learn a craft or trade. Their order of magnitude seems off.

whether to a drought or a warlord, could indeed be to enjoy the good times while they last and hope to make it through the bad times. If such an investment-is-pointless attitude becomes ingrained, people may be slow to escape poverty even if volatility falls (Filipski *et al.*, 2019). van de Vliert (2008) documents many other examples of how climate may have affected culture.

Others, including Acemoglu *et al.* (2001, 2002), take a different position: Climate used to matter, but no longer. They argue that climate and geography were important in the past in shaping institutions (education, rule of law, etc.), but that institutions explain the current pattern of development. Tropical diseases determined the pattern of European colonization. Some parts of the world were hospitable to Europeans, who settled there (often after removing or killing the natives) and established schools and universities, courts, and representative government. Europeans could not cope with the diseases prevalent in other parts of the world, and therefore raided rather than settled. The plunder, pillage, and rape that followed destroyed native societies. This historical divide, which is due to climate through the spread of tropical diseases, explains the current income distribution rather well. Alsan (2015) argues that the tsetse fly, which is confined to certain climates, plays an important role in Africa's poverty, as it prevents the use of animals for milk, meat, transport, and traction, and indirectly leads to more political fragmentation, which in turn hampers economic growth.

Easterly and Levine (2003) and Rodrik *et al.* (2004) agree that institutions are the only thing that matter *now*: Climate and geography have no power to explain the current distribution of income across the nations of the world once the effects of education, the rule of law and the quality of governance have been accounted for. They also find that climate does explain the strength of institutions.

This extreme position — that the only thing that nowadays matters to humans is other humans — can not seriously be maintained. Climate indisputably affects agriculture, energy, health, and tourism. Geography incontrovertibly affects transport. Nordhaus (2006) and Henderson *et al.* (2018) use subnational rather than national data. Climate matters in their analyses, but as they do not control for institutional variables, instead of relying on country fixed effects, they do not refute the earlier findings of Acemoglu, Easterly, and Rodrik.

All three schools of thought — climate is destiny, climate is important and climate was important but is no longer — have empirical support. See Table 1. This reflects the difficulty of establishing causality in a cross-section when there are many confounding factors — including, to confuse the institutional determinists, evidence that climate shapes culture.

Unfortunately, the current state of knowledge is that we do not know. I think we can safely exclude the two extreme positions, but it is too early to say whether climate played a minor or major role in determining why some people are poor and others rich — and hence under what circumstances climate change would prevent certain economies from growing.

If the climate is a contributing factor to the probability that people are trapped in poverty, the impacts of climate change may be (much) larger than commonly believed (Tol, 2018). The welfare impacts of growing at a small rate versus not growing at all are large when compounded over a century or more.

2.1. *Natural disasters*

Natural disasters have a number of effects on the economy (Albala-Bertrand, 1993). When disaster strikes, economic activity is disrupted and input factors are destroyed. Some disasters, such as floods and storms, particularly affect physical capital, such as buildings, roads, and bridges. Other disasters, such as epidemics, primarily affect people and thus the labor force. After the disaster, there is recovery. The dead are buried, debris cleared away. Savings are mobilized, and insurance payouts and charity received to rebuild houses and roads. These are economic activities and thus contribute to Gross Domestic Product (GDP). Natural disasters thus neatly illustrate the *broken window fallacy* of Bastiat (1850): Destruction of the capital stock is not measured by GDP (but rather by Net Domestic Product). Repair of the capital stock is included in GDP. A naive look at GDP growth rates may thus lead one to conclude that natural disasters are good for short-term

Table 1. Empirical evidence of the impact of climate on economic development and growth

Study	Data	Dependent variable	Findings
Gallup *et al.* (1999)	Cross-section	Per capita income growth	A climate suitable for malaria affects development and growth; controlled for institutions.
Acemoglu *et al.* (2001)	Cross-section	Per capita income	Protection against the risk of expropriation is the key predictor of development. Expropriation risk is best explained by the mortality of European settlers at the onset of colonialization.
Bloom *et al.* (2003)	Cross-section	Per capita income	Development in poor countries and the chance of being poor are affected by temperature and precipitation.
Easterly and Levine (2003)	Cross-section	Per capita income	Geography and climate explain a broad range of institutions. Institutions in turn explain development.
Rodrik *et al.* (2004)	Cross-section	Per capita income	Geography and climate explain a broad range of institutions. Institutions in turn explain development.
Olsson and Hibbs (2005)	Cross-section	Per capita income	Climate, latitude, continental size and orientation, and domesticable plants and animals significantly influence development; controlled for institutions.
Nordhaus (2006)	Cross-section	Income	The relationship between temperature and output is negative when measured per capita and positive per area.
Barrios *et al.* (2010)	Panel	Growth	The secular decline in rainfall in sub-Saharan Africa explains slow economic growth.

(*Continued*)

Table 1. (*Continued*)

Study	Data	Dependent variable	Findings
Dell *et al.* (2012)	Panel	Growth	Temperature shocks affect economic growth, but only in poor countries.
Alsan (2015)	Cross-section	Night lights, number of cattle	Climate limits the spread of the tse-tse fly, which affected pre-colonial agriculture and political centralization, and hence current development.
Andersen *et al.* (2016)	Cross-section	Per capita income	Not climate but ultraviolet radiation explains disease ecology and hence development.
Henderson *et al.* (2018)	Cross-section	Night lights	Temperature, rainfall, growing days and malaria suitability all affect development.

economic growth. This is not the case. Natural disasters stimulate economic activity. Natural disasters do not improve welfare. GDP is a measure of economic activity. It is not a welfare indicator. In cases like these, we should focus on NDP growth rates, but data availability is limited.

Natural disasters have different impacts at different phases of the business cycle (Tol and Leek, 1998). During a recession, the loss of input factors is less problematic as there is overcapacity anyway. The recovery phase, if it materializes, is a Keynesian economic stimulus. During a boom, capacity is tight and lost inputs cannot readily be replaced. The demand stimulus from recovery may drive up inflation rather than output. Recovery replaces destroyed capital goods with new ones. Although the initial response is often to restore things *exactly as they were*, in fact, replacements are often superior: New machinery would be state-of-the-art, new buildings better designed, new roads without previous bottlenecks, and so on. This does not accelerate economic growth in the long run: The capital stock would be replaced anyway. Natural disasters force the hand of economic agents with regard to the timing of replacement investment. Discretionary timing would be preferred. There is a chance that a natural disaster destroys an entrenched monopoly or topples a corrupt government — this would accelerate economic growth — but a natural disaster is just as likely to entrench corruption or destroy market challengers.

The impact of natural disasters on the economy in the short term is therefore mixed, but probably negative on net. The same is true in the long term. If there is a risk of natural disasters, resources are diverted to protective measures, be they financial (e.g., insurance) or physical (e.g., dykes). Insurance premiums are invested in liquid assets with a low return. The return on dykes is essentially zero. If the disaster risk were zero, those resources could be used for consumption or for investment in productive assets.

Natural disasters have different impacts on different economies (Cavallo and Noy, 2011, Kellenberg and Mobarak, 2011). Recovery requires resources. In developed economies, recovery is paid for by insurance, from household and company reserves, by the government, or by new loans from commercial lenders. In developing economies, contributions from these sources are limited, and recovery depends on support from informal networks and charity. Recovery from natural disasters is therefore slower, and sometimes much slower in developing countries than in developed economies. There may be hysteresis if customers switch to new suppliers. For instance, it takes several years to establish a banana plantation. Bananas are often sold on multi-year contracts. A new contract need not be on offer for a plantation restored after a hurricane.

The empirical evidence on the impact of natural disasters has grown rapidly, revealing heterogeneity in many dimensions (see Table 2). Earlier studies used the EM-DAT data,[4] which only report natural disasters when they cause substantial damage to humans.[5] This compounds the endogeneity of richer societies being better able to shield themselves from natural disasters. There is now a substantial body of literature that shows that natural disasters indeed slow down economic growth (Klomp and Valckx, 2014, Lazzaroni and van Bergeijk, 2014). This negative effect is stronger in poorer countries, probably because of financial underdevelopment, which may itself be caused by natural disasters (McDermott *et al.*, 2013, Klomp, 2014, 2015, 2017, 2018, 2020, Keerthiratne and Tol, 2017). That is, natural disasters slow economic growth and more so in poorer countries. In other words, areas which are more prone to extreme weather are more likely to be trapped in poverty.

2.2. *The impact of weather on the economy*

Natural disasters apart, there is a recent and increasing interest in studying the economic impact of weather (see Dell *et al.*, 2014, for an early review). Many of these studies are cast as relevant to climate change, but that is a bit of a stretch: Weather shocks are not climate change. Deryugina and Hsiang (2017) set out the conditions under which a weather impact equals a climate impact. These conditions are rather

[4] See https://public.emdat.be/.

[5] The data by Felbermayr and Gröschl (2013) do not suffer this problem. See https://www.ifo.de/en/ebdc-data/ifo-game.

Table 2. Studies of vulnerability to natural disasters.

Study	Hazard	Region	Explanatory variables
Yohe and Tol (2002)	Natural disasters	World	Poverty (+), inequality (+), population density (+)
Kahn (2005)	Natural disasters	World	Poverty (+), democracy (−), institutions (−)
Toya and Skidmore (2007)	Natural disasters	World	Poverty (+), institutions (−)
Escaleras *et al.* (2007)	Earthquakes	World	Corruption (+)
Kellenberg and Mobarak (2008)	Natural disasters	World	Poverty (− then +)
Price (2008)	Hurricanes	USA	Poverty (+), black (+)
Raschky (2008)	Natural disasters	World	Poverty (− then +), institutions (−)
Zhang *et al.* (2009)	Drought	China	Poverty (+)
Yamamura (2010)	Natural disasters	Japan	Poverty (+), social capital (−)
Keefer *et al.* (2011)	Earthquakes	World	Poverty (+), democracy (−)
Escaleras and Register (2012)	Natural disasters	World	Decentralization (−)
Hu *et al.* (2012)	Earthquakes	China	Poverty (+)
Rubin and Rossing (2012)	Natural disasters	Latin America	Poverty (+), inequality (+)
Wamsler *et al.* (2012)	Natural disasters	Brazil, El Salvador	Education (−)
Ward and Shively (2012)	Natural disasters	World	Poverty (+)
Yamamura (2012)	Natural disasters	World	Ethnic polarization (+)
Chen *et al.* (2013)	Natural disasters	China	Poverty (+)
Ferreira *et al.* (2013)	Floods	World	Poverty (+), institutions (?)
Ji and Ying (2013)	Natural disasters	World	Poverty (+), medical services (−)
Padli *et al.* (2013)	Natural disasters	World	Poverty (+), education (−)
Skidmore and Toya (2013)	Natural disasters	World	Decentralization (−)
Fankhauser and McDermott (2014)	Hurricanes, floods	World	Poverty (+), institutions (?)

(*Continued*)

Table 2. (*Continued*)

Felbermayr and Gröschl (2014)	Natural disasters	World	Poverty (?), institutions (+), trade (+)
Huang (2014)	Floods	China, Japan	Poverty (− then +)
Iwata *et al.* (2014)	Natural disasters	Japan	Institutions (+)
Muttarak and Lutz (2014)	Natural disasters	Case studies	Education (−)
Rubin (2014)	Natural disasters	Vietnam	Poverty (+), inequality (+)
Zhang *et al.* (2014)	Natural disasters	China	Poverty (+)
Zhou *et al.* (2014)	Natural disasters	China	Poverty (+), education (−), young (+), old (+)
Jongman *et al.* (2015)	Floods	World	Poverty (+)
Lim *et al.* (2015)	Heat waves	East Asia	Poverty (+)
Lin *et al.* (2015)	Earthquakes	Taiwan	Poverty (+), female (+), young (+), old (+)
Lin (2015)	Natural disasters	World	Democracy (−), institutions (−)
Park *et al.* (2015)	Hurricanes	South Korea	Poverty (+), building codes (−)
Toya and Skidmore (2015)	Natural disasters	World	ICT (−)
Wen and Chang (2015)	Natural disasters	World	Right-wing government (−)
Austin and McKinney (2016)	Natural disasters	World	Poverty (+), democracy (−), women's rights (−)
Breckner *et al.* (2016)	Natural disasters	World	Insurance (−), institutions (−)
Dresser *et al.* (2016)	Hurricanes	Atlantic	Poverty (+)
Escaleras and Register (2016)	Natural disasters	World	Corruption (+)[a]
Klomp (2016)	Natural disasters	World	Poverty (+)
Peregrine (2017)	Natural disasters	Ancient societies	Democracy (−)
Persson and Povitkina (2017)	Natural disasters	World	Democracy (−), institutions (−)
Tselios and Tompkins (2017)	Natural disasters	World	Decentralization (+)

(*Continued*)

[a]Escaleras and Register further find that natural disasters increase corruption.

Table 2. (*Continued*)

Villagra and Quintana (2017)	Tsunami	Chile	Institutions (−)
Ward and Shively (2017)	Natural disasters	World	Poverty (+)
Zuo *et al.* (2017)	Natural disasters	World	Institutions (−)
Albuquerque Sant'Anna (2018)	Floods	Rio de Janeiro	Urban infrastructure (−)
Enia (2018)	Natural disasters	World	Rule of law (−)
Hu *et al.* (2018)	Floods	World	Population density (+), poverty (+)
Liu *et al.* (2018)	Earthquakes	China	Public infrastructure (−), insurance (−)
Peregrine (2018)	Natural disasters	Ancient societies	Democracy (−)
Winsemius *et al.* (2018)	Floods and droughts	World	Poverty (+)
Wu *et al.* (2018)	Natural disasters	China	Poverty (+)
Yonson *et al.* (2018)	Hurricanes	Philippines	Poverty (+), institutions (−), urbanization (+)
Formetta and Feyen (2019)	Natural disasters	World	Wealth (−)

strict. Lemoine (2018) adds rational expectations. If these conditions are not met, a weather impact is to a climate impact as a short-term elasticity is to a long-term elasticity: perhaps an upper bound.

This is even more so for the impact of weather on development in the long-term. Weather extremes may well preclude certain options — a small chance of frost puts an end to non-hardy perennials, for instance. But weather extremes are part of climate. You need hysteresis for weather to matter in the long run. Had the sun not shone that day, this country would have been much poorer. Such an argument can be made for certain aspects of political and military history, but it is much harder to maintain for economic development.

Dell *et al.* (2012) show that temperature affects economic growth, and more so in *poorer* countries. Burke *et al.* (2015) also find that temperature affects economics, and more so in *hotter* countries. Testing Dell's hypothesis against Burke's, Letta and Tol (2018) find in favor of Dell: Poverty rather than heat makes a country more vulnerable to heat.[6] This cannot explain the correlation between climate and development, but it does again suggest path dependence and poverty traps. Countries that had the good fortune of a long sequence of mild weather became less vulnerable to the bad weather that inevitably followed. Barrios *et al.* (2010) find that the seminal drying of Sub-Saharan Africa largely explains its lackluster economic growth in the second half of the 20th century.

3. New Evidence

3.1. *Climate in the age of Malthus*

Malthus (1798) is one of the fathers of environmentalism, noting that a geometric increase in population combined with an arithmetic increase in food supply would lead to famine. His ideas have echoed through the ages, most prominently in the 20th century in the works of the Club

[6]These studies find no impact of rainfall. Damania *et al.* (2020) shows that rainfall does have an effect on subnational economic growth rates.

of Rome (Meadows *et al.*, 1972) and, more recently, in the activism of Extinction Rebellion (Westwell and Bunting, 2020).

Malthus is also one of the great Classical economists. The modern incarnation of his theory of economic development is that technological progress is not used to improve living standards, but rather to increase population growth so that more people live at a subsistence level (Eckstein *et al.*, 1988). While usually considered as a model that describes changes over time, it can be applied over space as well: In a Malthusian equilibrium, areas with better technologies are more densely populated.

The standard Malthusian model is limited to fertility and mortality. Boustan *et al.* (2020) show that, for the USA between 1920 and 2010, natural disasters led people to leave the affected area, echoing an earlier finding by Strobl (2011). If these results are representative, migration thus reinforces the Malthusian model, with high (low) population densities in (un)favorable areas.

Klein Goldewijk *et al.* (2010) have estimated human population densities for the whole world, at a $5' \times 5'$ grid, for the last 12,000 years.[7] I regress the natural logarithm of population density on the current climate to discern its influence on spatial differences in technology, as follows:

$$\begin{aligned}\ln D_{i,j,t} &= \alpha_{0,t} + \alpha_{1,t} T_{i,j,t} + \alpha_{2,t} T^2_{i,j,t} + \alpha_{3,t} P_{i,j,t} \\ &\quad + \alpha_{4,t} P^2_{i,j,t} + \alpha_{5,t} T_{i,j,t} P_{i,j,t} + \alpha_{6,t} \ln D_{i,j,t-1} + u_{i,j,t} \qquad (1)\end{aligned}$$

where $D_{i,j,t}$ is population density for latitude i, longitude j, and time t, $T_{i,j}$ is temperature, $P_{i,j}$ is precipitation, and $u_{i,j}$ are IID errors. Observations are for 10,000BC, 9,000BC,... ,0AD, 100AD,... ,2,000AD. For the oldest observations, the lagged dependent variable is omitted.

There are many observations. In 10,000BC, 228,563 grid cells were occupied by humans, increasing to 277,987 grid cells in 2000. It is therefore no surprise that the estimated coefficients are highly significant.

---

[7] See https://themasites.pbl.nl/tridion/en/themasites/hyde/.

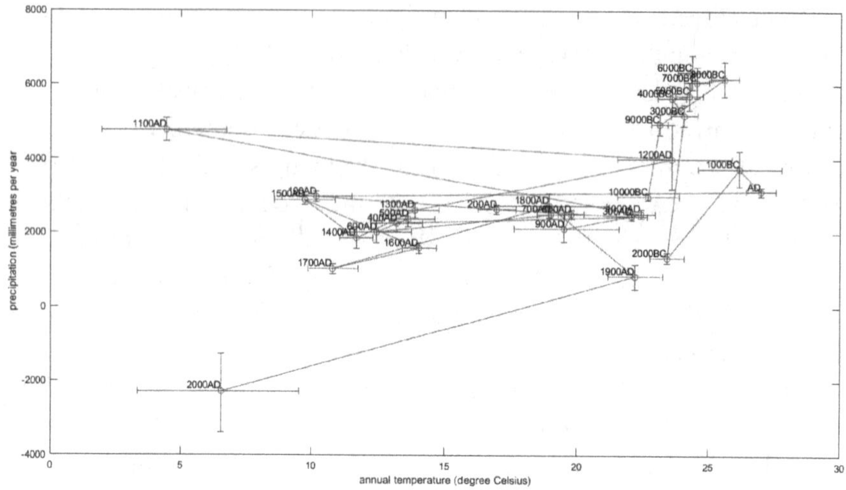

Fig. 1. Highest potential population density by annual rainfall and temperature over time.

Figure 1 summarizes the results. It shows the temperature and rainfall for which population density would be highest if climate were the only thing that mattered:

$$P_t^* = \frac{2\alpha_3\alpha_2 - \alpha_1\alpha_5}{4\alpha_3\alpha_2 - \alpha_5^2} \tag{2}$$

$$T_t^* = -\frac{\alpha_1 + \alpha_5 P_t^*}{2\alpha_{2,t}} \tag{3}$$

The 90% confidence intervals in Figure 1 were derived by simulating 10,000 draws for the parameter estimates.

Figure 1 shows that the area with the highest potential population density in 10,000BC had a temperature of 23°C and 3,000 mm/year rainfall. Early humans liked it warm and wet. With primitive heating and clothing, cold winters were deadly. High net primary production in the tropics meant abundant food.

For later years, the interpretation of the numbers in Figure 1 changes, as we condition on population density in the previous period. The regression coefficients should be interpreted as deviations from the trend in population growth. From 9,000BC to 3,000BC, population density grew fastest in areas that are hot and wet. The optimum climate is close to the hottest (30°C) and wettest (8,000 mm/year) places in the sample.

In 2,000BC, we see a marked shift toward dryer conditions, presumably as irrigation improves. In 100AD, we observe a large push toward temperate climates. In the centuries that follow, the optimal temperature for population growth shifts around a lot, while the best precipitation stays in a narrower range. 1,100AD stands out with rapid population growth in Scandinavia. In the 19th century, we observe human colonization of the drylands. This continues in the 20th century when also Siberia and Canada are populated.

The key insight of Figure 1 is that, over time, the link between climate and human life weakened. This is highlighted in Figure 2, which shows the adjusted R^2 and the Wald statistic for joint significance of the climate parameters, two measures of the explanatory power of temperature and precipitation. As agriculture, irrigation, clothing, heating, and cooling improved, humans moved into hitherto inhospitable

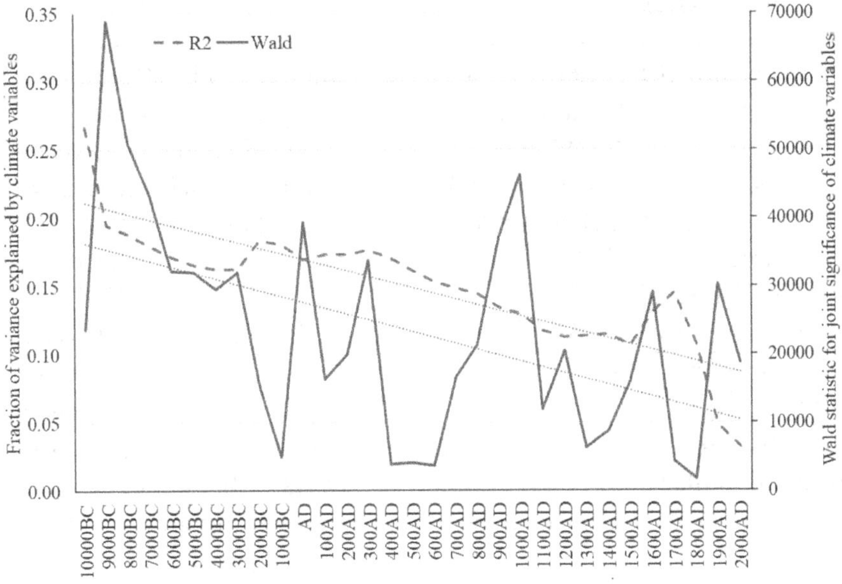

Fig. 2. The explanatory power of climate for population density.

areas. We now have bustling cities in the rainforest, the desert, and the Arctic — while humans continue to dream of moving to even more hostile places, such as Mars.

Xu *et al.* (2020) study the same data, arguing that human life is fragile to climate change. Their estimate of the human climate envelope is unfortunately biased since they top-censored the data, did not correct their estimates for censoring, and extrapolated into the censored part of the data domain.

3.2. *Climate in the age of Solow*

Maddison (2010) has gathered reconstructions of income in the past.[8] I use a regression identical to Eq. (1), with the log of population density replaced by the log of per capita income, and grids replaced by countries. I do so for the years 1820, 1850, 1870, 1890, 1900, 1910, 1913, 1929, 1938, 1950, 1960, . . . ,2010. Before 1950, the temporal spacing is determined by data availability. After 1950, in order not to overwhelm the analysis with recent data, I kept roughly the same frequency of observation.

The quadratic terms of temperature and precipitation are never significant. For 1820, the linear terms for temperature (0.29 (0.02) ln($/person/year)/Kelvin)) and precipitation (0.0079 (0.0005) ln($/person/year)/(mm/year)) are highly significant as is the cross-term (−0.00033 (0.00005) ln($/person/year)/Kelvin/(mm/year)). Together, these coefficients imply that, if annual rainfall exceeds 905 (77) mm/year, colder is better; in dryer places, hotter is better. If the temperature exceeds 23.9 (2.0)°C, dryer is better; in cooler places, wetter is better.

However, in later years, only the lagged dependent variable is significant, with the exception of 1990 (wetter countries are richer) and 2000 (wetter, hotter countries are richer). Those results disappear again in 2010. However, without the lagged dependent variable, temperature and rainfall and their interaction are always highly significant. This analysis thus confirms the earlier findings of Acemoglu *et al.* (2001),

[8] See https://www.rug.nl/ggdc/historicaldevelopment/maddison/.

Easterly and Levine (2003), and Rodrik *et al.* (2004). Climate appears to have a significant effect on development until you control for confounding factors. Climate may have a significant impact on those confounding factors, in which case climate may have had a significant impact on development in the past. Then again, that past impact may be apparent for lack of proper, indeed any, controls in the past.

Galor and Weil (2000) unify models of Malthusian stagnation and Solowian growth; see also Galor (2005, 2011). Dalgaard and Strulik (2013) show that these demo-economic models can be simplified to history-augmented Solow models. The augmentation is the time that has passed since take-off. They use this model to successfully explain the income distribution in the year 2000: Countries where the demographic transition started later are significantly poorer. They control for climate — tropical countries are significantly poorer — but do not test whether climate is correlated with the start year of the fertility decline.

Figure 3 does that, plotting the year of the start of demographic transition according to Reher (2004) against the average temperature.

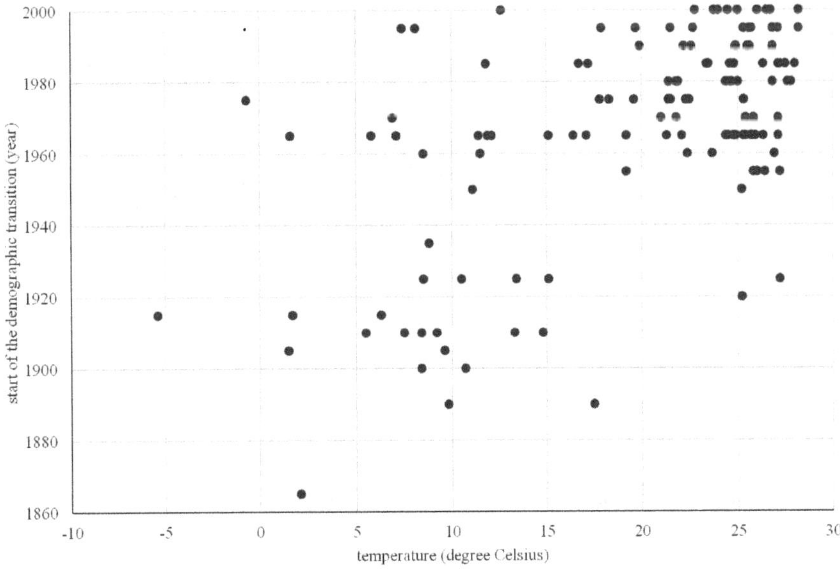

Fig. 3. The start year of the demographic transition as a function of the average annual temperature.

There is a clear correlation. Colder countries saw fertility fall earlier. For every degree warmer, the demographic transition is postponed by 2.18 (0.26) years. However, Fig. 3 also shows that the correlation is far from perfect — other factors than temperature are important too. $R^2 = 0.34$. We cannot learn much from a relatively small cross-section.

Brückner and Ciccone (2011, see also Cáceres and Malone (2015)) find that, in the second half of the 20th century, rainfall shocks affect democratization in Subsaharan Africa. This matters, because democracy does cause growth (Acemoglu *et al.*, 2019). Figure 4 plots the year of the start of democracy, here defined as the year in which the Polity IV indicator turns positive,[9] against the average temperature. There is a positive correlation. Colder countries have been democracies for longer. One degree warmer means that democracy is delayed by 1.57 (0.50) years. However, the relationship is weak. $R^2 = 0.34$. And, of

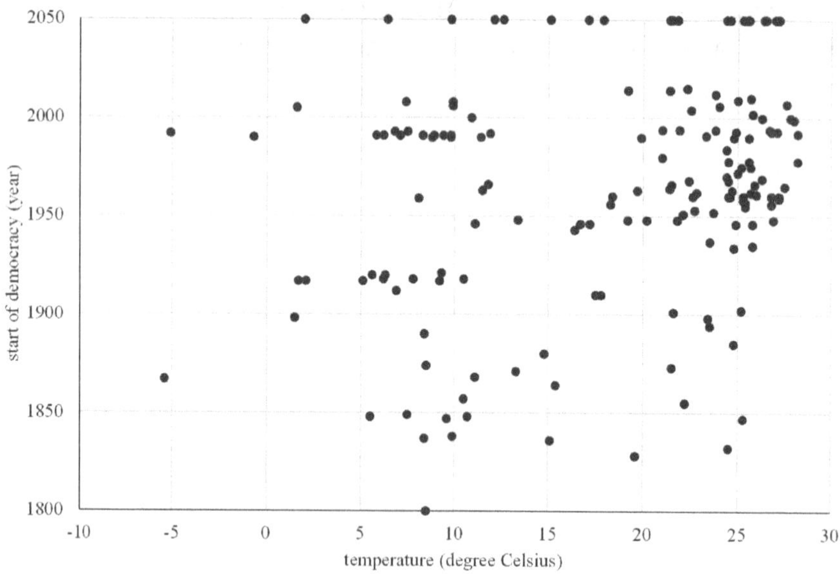

Fig. 4. The start year of democracy as a function of the average annual temperature.

[9]See https://www.systemicpeace.org/inscrdata.html.

course, a small cross-section cannot teach us much. Furthermore, this simple model ignores that democracy is sometimes reversed.

3.3. *Subnational data*

The Global Data Lab has put together a dataset of per capita income at the subnational level for almost all countries in the world. Figure 5 plots this against the average temperature for the period 1981–2010. There is a clear correlation. For every increase in the temperature by 1°C, the natural logarithm of per capita income falls by 0.0921 (0.0029); this is the naïve prediction shown in Fig. 5. If we control for non-climatic influences by introducing country dummies, the impact of temperature falls to 0.0118 (0.0026). That is, warmer regions within countries are statistically significantly poorer than the country average. The effect is small, 1.2% per Kelvin.

Figure 5 shows something else too. In cold and cool places, no region is poor (income below $1000/person/year). In warm and hot

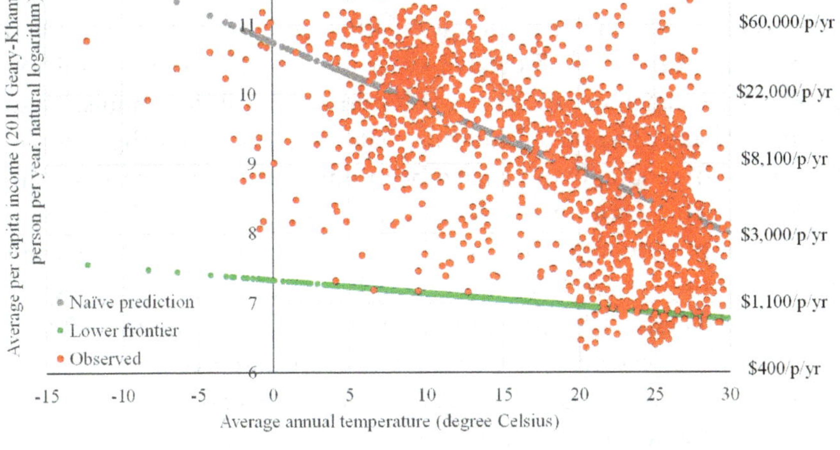

Fig. 5. Per capita income at the subnational level as a function of the average annual temperature.

places, some regions are rich, but most regions are poor. I therefore estimated a stochastic frontier using the command in S. When controlling for country dummies, temperature has no statistically significant effect on the maximum attainable per capita income, but hotter countries are likely to fall further below the frontier. Reversing the sign, I also estimated the lower bound. This is shown in Fig. 5. The minimum attainable per capita income increases by 1.87% (0.32) per Kelvin. The floor placed under income is a weak one, ranging from $850/person/year in the hottest countries to $1900/p/yr in the coldest. Efficiency increases with temperature: Hotter countries can be further away from the lower bound than colder countries.

Figure 5 is consistent with the box-plots shown by Nordhaus (2006). Nordhaus' data are economic output, rather than income, and per grid cell, rather than administrative unit. Nordhaus' data also reveal that affluence can be found anywhere, regardless of climate, while absolute poverty is absent in temperate climates.

4. Conclusion

For many centuries, environmental determinism was the majority view. Climate and geography are destiny. The then-dominant economic and military power was in the leading position because (the) God(s) had granted them the most favorable environment. This view prevails in a minority of analysts. In recent years, institutional determinism had the upper hand. The only thing that matters to people is other people. Climate and geography may have been important in the past but are no longer. There is a third school of thought that argues that climate and geography are influential but not dominant. Natural disasters and infectious diseases are both a cause and consequence of underdevelopment. Analysis of human population density over the last 12,000 years reveals a weakening effect of temperature and precipitation and a persistence of population in place. Analysis of the national average per capita income over the last 200 years reveals a climate impact in 1820, but not later, although persistence is strong. Colder regions may have started growing their economies earlier. Analysis of regional per capita income reveals that temperature hardly limits affluence, but cold limits poverty.

These findings need to be revisited as finer-grained data become available for recent years and as historical observations come online. While it is unlikely that the main thrust of the current research will be overturned — there are too many studies already, with different methods applied to different data — new research should shed light on how and to what extent climate affects economic activity and human well-being, and how institutions and technologies mediate and shape these effects and in turn are shaped by climate. The existence, or not, of climate-related poverty traps requires particular attention, both because it is methodologically challenging and because it matters most to the people affected. The analysis above ignores the many interactions between population and economic growth. As climate is projected to change, it is particularly important to investigate how policy interventions can help to alleviate the negative impacts of climate change and enhance its positive impacts.

Acknowledgments

Theodoros Chatzivasileiadis helped with the construction of Table 2. An anonymous referee had excellent comments.

References

Acemoglu, D., Johnson, S., and Robinson, J. A. (2001). The colonial origins of comparative development: An empirical investigation. *American Economic Review*, 91(5), 1369–1401, doi: 10.1257/aer.91.5.1369.

Acemoglu, D., Johnson, S., and Robinson, J. A. (2002). Reversal of fortune: Geography and institutions in the making of the modern world income distribution. *The Quarterly Journal of Economics*, 117(4), 1231–1294.

Acemoglu, D., Naidu, S., Restrepo, P., and Robinson, J. A. (2019). Democracy does cause growth. *Journal of Political Economy*, 127(1), 47–100, doi: 10.1086/700936.

Albala-Bertrand, J. (1993). *Political Economy of Large Natural Disasters*, Oxford University Press, Oxford.

Albuquerque Sant'Anna, A. (2018). Not so natural: Unequal effects of public policies on the occurrence of disasters. *Ecological Economics*, 152, 273–281, doi: 10.1016/j.ecolecon.2018.06.011.

Alsan, M. (2015). The effect of the tsetse fly on African development. *American Economic Review*, 105(1), 382–410, http://www.aeaweb.org/articles?id=10.1257/aer.20130604.

Andersen, T. B., Dalgaard, C.-J., and Selaya, P. (2016). Climate and the emergence of global income differences. *The Review of Economic Studies*, 83(4), 1334–1363, http://dx.doi.org/10.1093/restud/rdw006.

Aristotle (350 BC). *Politics*, http://classics.mit.edu/Aristotle/politics.7.seven.html.

Austin, K. and McKinney, L. (2016). Disaster devastation in poor nations: The direct and indirect effects of gender equality, ecological losses, and development. *Social Forces*, 95(1), 355–380, doi: 10.1093/sf/sow056.

Barrios, S., Bertinelli, L., and Strobl, E. (2010). Trends in rainfall and economic growth in Africa: A neglected cause of the African growth tragedy. *The Review of Economics and Statistics*, 92(2), 350–366, doi: 10.1162/rest.2010.11212, https://doi.org/10.1162/rest.2010.11212.

Bastiat, F. (1850). *Ce qu'on voit et ce qu'on ne voit pas*, Guillaumin, Paris.

Bénabou, R. (1996). Inequality and growth. *NBER Macroeconomics Annual*, 11, X1–74.

Blaut, J. (1999). Environmentalism and eurocentrism. *Geographical Review*, 89(3), 391–408.

Bloom, D. E., Canning, D., and Sevilla, J. (2003). Geography and poverty traps. *Journal of Economic Growth*, 8(4), 355–378.

Bougheas, S., Demetriades, P., and Morgenroth, E. (1999). Infrastructure, transport costs and trade. *Journal of International Economics*, 47(1), 169–189, doi: 10.1016/S0022-1996(98)00008-7.

Boustan, L. P., Kahn, M. E., Rhode, P. W., and Yanguas, M. L. (2020). The effect of natural disasters on economic activity in US counties: A century of data. *Journal of Urban Economics*, 118(C), 103257 http://www.sciencedirect.com/science/article/pii/S0094119020300280.

Breckner, M., Englmaier, F., Stowasser, T., and Sunde, U. (2016). Resilience to natural disasters — insurance penetration, institutions, and disaster types. *Economics Letters*, 148, 106–110, doi: 10.1016/j.econlet.2016.09.023.

Brückner, M. and Ciccone, A. (2011). Rain and the democratic window of opportunity. *Econometrica*, 79(3), 923–947, http://www.jstor.org/stable/41237773.

Burke, M., Hsiang, S. M., and Miguel, E. (2015). Global non-linear effect of temperature on economic production. *Nature*, 527(7577), 235–239.

Cáceres, N. and Malone, S. W. (2015). Optimal weather conditions, economic growth, and political transitions. *World Development*, 66, 16–30, http://www.sciencedirect.com/science/article/pii/S0305750X14002137.

Castells-Quintana, D., del Pilar Lopez-Uribe, M., and McDermott, T. K. (2017). Geography, institutions and development: A review of the long-run impacts of climate change. *Climate and Development*, 9(5), 452–470, https://doi.org/10.1080/17565529.2016.1167665.

Cavallo, E. and Noy, I. (2011). Natural disasters and the economy - a survey. *International Review of Environmental and Resource Economics*, 5(1), 63–102, doi: 10.1561/101.00000039.

Chen, S., Luo, Z., and Pan, X. (2013). Natural disasters in China: 1900-2011. *Natural Hazards*, 69(3), 1597–1605, doi: 10.1007/s11069-013-0765-0.

Dalgaard, C.-J. and Strulik, H. (2013). The history augmented solow model. *European Economic Review*, 63, 134–149, http://www.sciencedirect.com/science/article/pii/S0014292113000871.

Damania, R., Desbureaux, S., and Zaveri, E. (2020). Does rainfall matter for economic growth? Evidence from global sub-national data (1990–2014). *Journal of Environmental Economics and Management*, 102, p. 102335, http://www.sciencedirect.com/science/article/pii/S0095069620300589.

Dell, M., Jones, B. F., and Olken, B. A. (2012). Temperature shocks and economic growth: Evidence from the last half century. *American Economic Journal: Macroeconomics*, 4(3), 66–95, doi: 10.1257/mac.4.3.66, http://www.aeaweb.org/articles?id=10.1257/mac.4.3.66.

Dell, M., Jones, B. F., and Olken, B. A. (2014). What do we learn from the weather? the new climate-economy literature. *Journal of Economic Literature*, 52(3), 740–798.

Deryugina, T. and Hsiang, S. (2017). The marginal product of climate. Working Paper 24072, National Bureau of Economic Research, doi: 10.3386/w24072, http://www.nber.org/papers/w24072.

Diamond, J. (1998). *Guns, Germs and Steel: A Short History of Everybody for the Last 13,000 Years*, Macmillan, London.

Dresser, C., Allison, J., Broach, J., Smith, M.-E., and Milsten, A. (2016). High-amplitude atlantic hurricanes produce disparate mortality in small, low-income countries. *Disaster Medicine and Public Health Preparedness*, 10(6), 832–837, doi: 10.1017/dmp.2016.62.

Easterly, W. and Levine, R. (2003). Tropics, germs, and crops: How endowments influence economic development. *Journal of Monetary Economics*, 50(1), 3–39, doi: https://doi.org/10.1016/S0304-3932(02)00200-3.

Eckstein, Z., Stern, S., and Wolpin, K. (1988). Fertility choice, land, and the malthusian hypothesis. *International Economic Review*, 29(2), 353–361, doi: 10.2307/2526671.

Enia, J. (2018). Do contracts save lives? The relationship between contract intensive economies and natural disaster fatalities. *Risk, Hazards and Crisis in Public Policy*, 9(1), 60–81, doi: 10.1002/rhc3.12130.

Escaleras, M., Anbarci, N., and Register, C. (2007). Public sector corruption and major earthquakes: A potentially deadly interaction. *Public Choice*, 132(1-2), 209–230, doi: 10.1007/s11127-007-9148-y.

Escaleras, M. and Register, C. (2012). Fiscal decentralization and natural hazard risks. *Public Choice*, 151(1–2), 165–183, doi: 10.1007/s11127-010-9740-4.

Escaleras, M. and Register, C. (2016). Public sector corruption and natural hazards. *Public Finance Review*, 44(6), 746–768, doi: 10.1177/1091142115613155.

Fankhauser, S. and McDermott, T. (2014). Understanding the adaptation deficit: Why are poor countries more vulnerable to climate events than rich countries? *Global Environmental Change*, 27(1), 9–18, doi: 10.1016/j.gloenvcha.2014.04.014.

Febvre, L. (1922). *La Terre et l'Évolution Humaine: Introduction Géographique à l'Histoire*, La Renaissance du Livre, Paris.

Felbermayr, G. and Gröschl, J. (2013). Natural disasters and the effect of trade on income: A new panel IV approach. *European Economic Review*, 58, 18–30, doi: https://doi.org/10.1016/j.euroecorev.2012.11.008.

Felbermayr, G. and Gröschl, J. (2014). Naturally negative: The growth effects of natural disasters. *Journal of Development Economics*, 111, 92–106, doi: https://doi.org/10.1016/j.jdeveco.2014.07.004, special Issue: Imbalances in Economic Development.

Fernald, J. (1999). Roads to prosperity? assessing the link between public capital and productivity. *American Economic Review*, 89(3), 619–638, doi: 10.1257/aer.89.3.619.

Ferreira, S., Hamilton, K., and Vincent, J. (2013). Does development reduce fatalities from natural disasters? new evidence for floods. *Environment and Development Economics*, 18(6), 649–679, doi: 10.1017/S1355770X13000387.

Filipski, M., Jin, L., Zhang, X., and Chen, K. (2019). Living like there's no tomorrow: The psychological effects of an earthquake on savings and spending behavior. *European Economic Review*, 116, 107–128, doi: 10.1016/j.euroecorev.2019.04.004.

Formetta, G. and Feyen, L. (2019). Empirical evidence of declining global vulnerability to climate-related hazards. *Global Environmental Change*, 57, p. 101920, http://www.sciencedirect.com/science/article/pii/S0959378019300378.

Gallup, J. L., Sachs, J. D., and Mellinger, A. D. (1999). Geography and economic development. *International Regional Science Review*, 22(2), 179–232.

Galor, O. (2005). From stagnation to growth: Unified growth theory. 171–293, Elsevier, http://www.sciencedirect.com/science/article/pii/S157406840501004X.

Galor, O. (2011). *Unified Growth Theory*, Princeton University Press, Princeton.

Galor, O. and Weil, D. N. (2000). Population, technology, and growth: From malthusian stagnation to the demographic transition and beyond. *American Economic Review*, 90(4), 806–828, https://www.aeaweb.org/articles?id=10.1257/aer.90.4.806.

Guan, Z. (c780 BC). *Guanzi*, http://www.gutenberg.org/ebooks/7483.

Harper, K. (2017). *The Fate of Rome: Climate, Disease, and the End of an Empire*, Princeton University Press, Princeton.

Henderson, J. V., Squires, T., Storeygard, A., and Weil, D. (2018). The global distribution of economic activity: Nature, history, and the role of trade. *The Quarterly Journal of Economics*, 133(1), 357–406, doi: 10.1093/qje/qjx030.

Hippocrates (400 BC). *On Airs, Waters, Places*, http://classics.mit.edu/Hippocrates/airwatpl.23.23.html.

Hu, P., Zhang, Q., Shi, P., Chen, B., and Fang, J. (2018). Flood-induced mortality across the globe: Spatiotemporal pattern and influencing factors. *Science of the Total Environment*, 643, 171–182, doi: 10.1016/j.scitotenv.2018.06.197.

Hu, Y., Wang, J., Li, X., Ren, D., Driskell, L., and Zhu, J. (2012). Exploring geological and socio-demographic factors associated with under-five mortality in the wenchuan earthquake using neural network model. *International Journal of Environmental Health Research*, 22(2), 184–196, doi: 10.1080/09603123.2011.613113.

Huang, G. (2014). Does a Kuznets curve apply to flood fatality? A holistic study for China and japan. *Natural Hazards*, 71(3), 2029–2042, doi: 10.1007/s11069-013-0994-2.

Huntington, E. (1915). *Civilization and Climate*, Yale University Press, New Haven, https://archive.org/details/civilizationand01huntgoog/page/n60/mode/2up.

Huntington, E. (1917). Climatic change and agricultural exhaustion as elements in the fall of rome. *The Quarterly Journal of Economics*, 31(2), 173–208, doi: 10.2307/1883908, http://dx.doi.org/10.2307/1883908.

Ibn Khaldun, A. (1377). *Muqaddimah*, https://asadullahali.files.wordpress.com/2012/10/ibn_khaldun-al_muqaddimah.pdf.

Iwata, K., Ito, Y., and Managi, S. (2014). Public and private mitigation for natural disasters in japan. *International Journal of Disaster Risk Reduction*, 7, 39–50, doi: 10.1016/j.ijdrr.2013.12.005.

Ji, L. and Ying, W. (2013). Study on relevance between social economic environment and resistance to disasters. *Research Journal of Applied Sciences, Engineering and Technology*, 6(6), 1030–1034, doi: 10.19026/rjaset.6.4008.

Jongman, B., Winsemius, H., Aerts, J., Coughlan De Perez, E., Van Aalst, M., Kron, W., and Ward, P. (2015). Declining vulnerability to river floods and the global benefits of adaptation. *Proceedings of the National Academy of Sciences of the United States of America*, 112(18), E2271–E2280, doi: 10.1073/pnas.1414439112.

Kahn, M. (2005). The death toll from natural disasters: The role of income, geography, and institutions. *Review of Economics and Statistics*, 87(2), 271–284, doi: 10.1162/0034653053970339.

Keefer, P., Neumayer, E., and Plümper, T. (2011). Earthquake propensity and the politics of mortality prevention. *World Development*, 39(9), 1530–1541, doi: 10.1016/j.worlddev.2011.02.010.

Keerthiratne, S. and Tol, R. (2017). Impact of natural disasters on financial development. *Economics of Disasters and Climate Change*, 1, 33–54.

Kellenberg, D. and Mobarak, A. (2008). Does rising income increase or decrease damage risk from natural disasters? *Journal of Urban Economics*, 63(3), 788–802, doi: 10.1016/j.jue.2007.05.003.

Kellenberg, D. and Mobarak, A. (2011). The economics of natural disasters. *Annual Review of Resource Economics*, 3, 297–312, doi: 10.1146/annurev-resource-073009-104211.

Klein Goldewijk, K., Beusen, A., and Janssen, P. (2010). Long-term dynamic modeling of global population and built-up area in a spatially explicit way: Hyde 3.1. *The Holocene*, 20(4), 565–573, https://doi.org/10.1177/0959683609356587.

Klomp, J. (2014). Financial fragility and natural disasters: An empirical analysis. *Journal of Financial Stability*, 13, 180–192, doi: 10.1016/j.jfs.2014.06.001.

Klomp, J. (2015). Sovereign risk and natural disasters in emerging markets. *Emerging Markets Finance and Trade*, 51(6), 1326–1341, doi: 10.1080/1540496X.2015.1011530.

Klomp, J. (2016). Economic development and natural disasters: A satellite data analysis. *Global Environmental Change*, 36, 67–88, doi: 10.1016/j.gloenvcha.2015.11.001.

Klomp, J. (2017). Flooded with debt. *Journal of International Money and Finance*, 73, 93–103, doi: 10.1016/j.jimonfin.2017.01.006.

Klomp, J. (2018). Do natural catastrophes shake microfinance institutions? using a new measure of mfi risk. *International Journal of Disaster Risk Reduction*, 27, 380–390, doi: 10.1016/j.ijdrr.2017.10.026.

Klomp, J. (2020). Do natural disasters affect monetary policy? a quasi-experiment of earthquakes. *Journal of Macroeconomics*, 64, 103164, doi: 10.1016/j.jmacro.2019.103164.

Klomp, J. and Valckx, K. (2014). Natural disasters and economic growth: A meta-analysis. *Global Environmental Change*, 26(1), 183–195.

Landes, D. (1998). *The Wealth and Poverty of Nations*, Abacus, London.

Lazzaroni, S. and van Bergeijk, P. A. G. (2014). Natural disasters' impact, factors of resilience and development: A meta-analysis of the macroeconomic literature. *Ecological Economics*, 107, 333–346.

Lemoine, D. (2018). Sufficient statistics for the cost of climate change. Working Paper 25008, National Bureau of Economic Research, doi: 10.3386/w25008, http://www.nber.org/papers/w25008.

Letta, M. and Tol, R. S. J. (2018). Weather, climate and total factor productivity. *Environmental and Resource Economics*, 73, 283–305, https://doi.org/10.1007/s10640-018-0262-8.

Lewthwaite, G. (2001). Environmental determinism. in Smelser, N. J. and Baltes, P. B., eds., *International Encyclopedia of the Social & Behavioral Sciences*, Pergamon, Oxford, pp. 4607–4611, http://www.sciencedirect.com/science/article/pii/B0080430767024967.

Lim, Y.-H., Bell, M., Kan, H., Honda, Y., Guo, Y.-L., and Kim, H. (2015). Economic status and temperature-related mortality in Asia. *International Journal of Biometeorology*, 59(10), 1405–1412, doi: 10.1007/s00484-014-0950-1.

Lin, K.-H., Chang, Y.-C., Liu, G.-Y., Chan, C.-H., Lin, T.-H., and Yeh, C.-H. (2015). An interdisciplinary perspective on social and physical determinants of seismic risk. *Natural Hazards and Earth System Sciences*, 15(10), 2173–2182, doi: 10.5194/nhess-15-2173-2015.

Lin, T.-H. (2015). Governing natural disasters: State capacity, democracy, and human vulnerability. *Social Forces*, 93(3), 1267–1300, doi: 10.1093/sf/sou104.

Liu, Y., Wei, J., Xu, J., and Ouyang, Z. (2018). Evaluation of the moderate earthquake resilience of counties in China based on a three-stage DEA model. *Natural Hazards*, 91(2), 587–609, doi: 10.1007/s11069-017-3142-6.

Maddison, A. (2010). *The World Economy: Volume 1: A Millennial Perspective and Volume 2: Historical Statistics*, Organization for Economic Cooperation and Development, Paris.

Malthus, T. (1798). *An Essay on the Principle of Population*, J. Johnson in St Paul's Church-yard, London.

McDermott, T. K., Barry, F., and Tol, R. S. (2013). Disasters and development: natural disasters, credit constraints, and economic growth. *Oxford Economic Papers*, 66(3), 750–773, https://doi.org/10.1093/oep/gpt034.

Meadows, D. H., Meadows, D. L., Randers, J., and Behrens III, W. W. (1972). *The Limits to Growth*, Universe Books, New York.

Morrison, C. and Schwartz, A. (1996). State infrastructure and productive performance. *American Economic Review*, 86(5), 1095–1111.

Muttarak, R. and Lutz, W. (2014). Is education a key to reducing vulnerability to natural disasters and hence unavoidable climate change? *Ecology and Society*, 19(1), doi: 10.5751/ES-06476-190142.

Nordhaus, W. D. (2006). Geography and macroeconomics: New data and new findings. *Proceedings of the National Academy of Science*, 103(10), 3510–3517, www.pnas.org/cgi/doi/10.1073/pnas.0509842103.

Olsson, O. and Hibbs, J., D. A. (2005). Biogeography and long-run economic development. *European Economic Review*, 49, 909–938.

Padli, J., Habibullah, M., and Baharom, A. (2013). Determinants of flood fatalities: Evidence from a panel data of 79 countries. *Pertanika Journal of Social Science and Humanities*, 21, September, 81–98.

Park, D.-S., Ho, C.-H., Nam, C., and Kim, H.-S. (2015). Evidence of reduced vulnerability to tropical cyclones in the Republic of Korea. *Environmental Research Letters*, 10(5), doi: 10.1088/1748-9326/10/5/054003.

Peregrine, P. (2017). Political participation and long-term resilience in pre-columbian societies. *Disaster Prevention and Management*, 26(3), 314–329, doi: 10.1108/DPM-01-2017-0013.

Peregrine, P. (2018). Social resilience to climate-related disasters in ancient societies: A test of two hypotheses. *Weather, Climate, and Society*, 10(1), 145–161, doi: 10.1175/WCAS-D-17-0052.1.

Persson, T. and Povitkina, M. (2017). "Gimme shelter": The role of democracy and institutional quality in disaster preparedness. *Political Research Quarterly*, 70(4), 833–847, doi: 10.1177/1065912917716335.

Price, G. (2008). Hurricane Katrina: Was there a political economy of death? *Review of Black Political Economy*, 35(4), 163–180, doi: 10.1007/s12114-008-9033-z.

Raschky, P. (2008). Institutions and the losses from natural disasters. *Natural Hazards and Earth System Science*, 8(4), 627–634, doi: 10.5194/nhess-8-627-2008.

Reher, D. S. (2004). The demographic transition revisited as a global process. *Population, Space and Place*, 10(1), 19–41, https://onlinelibrary.wiley.com/doi/abs/10.1002/psp.313.

Rodrik, D., Subramanian, A., and Trebbi, F. (2004). Institutions rule: The primacy of institutions over geography and integration in economic development. *Journal of Economic Growth*, 9(2), 131–165, https://doi.org/10.1023/B:JOEG.0000031425.72248.85.

Röller, L.-H. and Waverman, L. (2001). Telecommunications infrastructure and economic development: A simultaneous approach. *American Economic Review*, 91(4), 909–923, doi: 10.1257/aer.91.4.909.

Rubin, O. (2014). Social vulnerability to climate-induced natural disasters: Cross-provincial evidence from Vietnam. *Asia Pacific Viewpoint*, 55(1), 67–80, doi: 10.1111/apv.12037.

Rubin, O. and Rossing, T. (2012). National and local vulnerability to climate-related disasters in Latin America: The role of social asset-based adaptation. *Bulletin of Latin American Research*, 31(1), 19–35, doi: 10.1111/j.1470-9856.2011.00607.x.

Sachs, J. D. (2003). Institutions don't rule: Direct effects of geography on per capita income. Working Paper 9490, National Bureau of Economic Research, doi: 10.3386/w9490, http://www.nber.org/papers/w9490.

Schweikert, A., Chinowsky, P., Espinet, X., and Tarbert, M. (2014). Climate change and infrastructure impacts: Comparing the impact on roads in ten countries through 2100. *Procedia Engineering*, 78, 306–316, doi: 10.1016/j.proeng.2014.07.072.

Skidmore, M. (2001). Risk, natural disasters, and household savings in a life cycle model. *Japan and the World Economy*, 13(1), 15–34, doi: 10.1016/S0922-1425(00)00056-6.

Skidmore, M. and Toya, H. (2013). Natural disaster impacts and fiscal decentralization. *Land Economics*, 89(1), 101–117, doi: 10.3368/le.89.1.101.

Strobl, E. (2011). The economic growth impact of hurricanes: Evidence from U.S. coastal counties. *Review of Economics and Statistics*, 93(2), 575–589, doi: 10.1162/REST_a_00082.

Tol, R. and Leek, F. (1998). *Economic Analysis of Natural Disasters*, Routledge, London, pp. 308–327.

Tol, R. S. J. (2018). The economic impacts of climate change. *Review of Environmental Economics and Policy*, 12(1), 4–25, doi: 10.1093/reep/rex027.

Toya, H. and Skidmore, M. (2007). Economic development and the impacts of natural disasters. *Economics Letters*, 94(1), 20–25, doi: 10.1016/j.econlet.2006.06.020.

Toya, H. and Skidmore, M. (2015). Information/communication technology and natural disaster vulnerability. *Economics Letters*, 137, 143–145, doi: 10.1016/j.econlet.2015.10.018.

Tselios, V. and Tompkins, E. (2017). Local government, political decentralisation and resilience to natural hazard-associated disasters. *Environmental Hazards*, 16(3), 228–252, doi: 10.1080/17477891.2016.1277967.

van de Vliert, E. (2008). *Climate, Affluence and Culture*, Cambridge University Press, Cambridge.

Villagra, P. and Quintana, C. (2017). Disaster governance for community resilience in coastal towns: Chilean case studies. *International Journal of Environmental Research and Public Health*, 14(9), doi: 10.3390/ijerph14091063.

Wamsler, C., Brink, E., and Rentala, O. (2012). Climate change, adaptation, and formal education: The role of schooling for increasing societies' adaptive capacities in el salvador and brazil. *Ecology and Society*, 17(2), doi: 10.5751/ES-04645-170202.

Ward, P. and Shively, G. (2012). Vulnerability, income growth and climate change. *World Development*, 40(5), 916–927, doi: 10.1016/j.worlddev.2011.11.015.

Ward, P. and Shively, G. (2017). Disaster risk, social vulnerability, and economic development. *Disasters*, 41(2), 324–351, doi: 10.1111/disa.12199.

Wen, J. and Chang, C.-P. (2015). Government ideology and the natural disasters: A global investigation. *Natural Hazards*, 78(3), 1481–1490, doi: 10.1007/s11069-015-1781-z.

Westwell, E. and Bunting, J. (2020). The regenerative culture of extinction rebellion: Self-care, people care, planet care. *Environmental Politics*, 29(3), 546–551, https://doi.org/10.1080/09644016.2020.1747136.

Winsemius, H., Jongman, B., Veldkamp, T., Hallegatte, S., Bangalore, M. and Ward, P. (2018). Disaster risk, climate change, and poverty: Assessing the global exposure of poor people to floods and droughts. *Environment and Development Economics*, 23(3), 328–348, doi: 10.1017/S1355770X17000444.

Wu, J., Han, G., Zhou, H., and Li, N. (2018). Economic development and declining vulnerability to climate-related disasters in China. *Environmental Research Letters*, 13(3), doi: 10.1088/1748-9326/aaabd7.

Xu, C., Kohler, T. A., Lenton, T. M., Svenning, J.-C., and Scheffer, M. (2020). Future of the human climate niche. *Proceedings of the National Academy of Sciences*, 117(21), 11350–11355, https://www.pnas.org/content/117/21/11350.

Yamamura, E. (2010). Effects of interactions among social capital, income and learning from experiences of natural disasters: A case study from Japan. *Regional Studies*, 44(8), 1019–1032, doi: 10.1080/00343400903365144.

Yamamura, E. (2012). The death toll from natural disasters: The role of income, geography and institutions: Comment. *Economics Bulletin*, 32(2), 1545–1554.

Yohe, G. W. and Tol, R. S. J. (2002). Indicators for social and economic coping capacity — moving towards a working definition of adaptive capacity. *Global Environmental Change*, 12(1), 25–40.

Yonson, R., Noy, I., and Gaillard, J. (2018). The measurement of disaster risk: An example from tropical cyclones in the philippines. *Review of Development Economics*, 22(2), 736–765, doi: 10.1111/rode.12365.

Zhang, H.-M., Yue, X.-P., and Zhou, S.-Q. (2009). Impact of local economic development on drought risks: A case of north China. 974–977, doi: 10.1109/GSIS.2009.5408027.

Zhang, Y., Zheng, Y., and Zhang, B. (2014). Socioeconomic factors that influence the natural disasters: Empirical analysis based on provincial panel data. *Journal of Natural Disasters*, 23(2), 15–20, doi: 10.13577/j.jnd.2014.0203.

Zhou, Y., Li, N., Wu, W., Liu, H., Wang, L., Liu, G., and Wu, J. (2014). Socioeconomic development and the impact of natural disasters: some empirical evidences from China. *Natural Hazards*, 74(2), 541–554, doi: 10.1007/s11069-014-1198-0.

Zuo, W., Zhu, W., Wang, F., Wei, J., and Bondar, A. (2017). Exploring the institutional determinants of risk governance: A comparative approach across nations. *International Journal of Disaster Risk Reduction*, 24, 135–143, doi: 10.1016/j.ijdrr.2017.05.022.

https://doi.org/10.1142/9789811240553_0002

Chapter 2

Balancing the Distribution Across Generations: Putting the Horse Before the Cart

Wolfgang Buchholz[*,‡] **and Dirk Rübbelke**[†,§]

[*] *University of Regensburg and CESifo Munich 93040 Regensburg, Germany*

[†] *TU Bergakademie Freiberg 09599 Freiberg, Germany*

[‡] *wolfgang.buchholz@ur.de*

[§] *dirk.ruebbelke@vwl.tu-freiberg.de*

In a productive economy, there is a generic conflict of interest between generations: On the one hand, there should be savings to achieve economic progress and at least to ensure sustainability, i.e., to avoid a decline of well-being over time. On the other hand, the burden that is inflicted on earlier generations through their savings in favor of the future generations should not become excessive. Against this background, the question arises whether a unique utilitarian social welfare function (SWF) is capable of taking these two ethical postulates into account for any given technology and thus there is flexibility in the sense of Asheim (2017). In a simple two-generation model, we first of all show that the answer to this question is ambiguous. While SWFs can be found that ensure sustainability in any case, excessive savings cannot be prevented by the same SWF for all, but in the two-generation case at least for linear and concave technologies. In this context, we in particular highlight that the elasticity of marginal utility of the utility function that underlies the SWF is of much more importance for avoiding overburdening of the early generation than the social discount rate. We also note that inequality of well-being between generations cannot be kept within a limit by a single SWF for any given technology. Extending the analysis to the multi-period case provides analogous results.

1. Motivation

The damage caused by global warming will mostly affect future generations. Climate change thus poses a serious ethical question, i.e., a problem of distributive justice across generations: In order to protect future generations from the adverse consequences of climate change and thus to secure or even foster their well-being, the current generation has to mitigate its greenhouse gas emissions, which requires costly abatement measures and thus reduces the well-being today. Therefore, a generic trade-off between well-being of the present and that of future generations arises, which has been a basic issue in the discussion on the appropriate social discount rate (Hepburn, 2006, 2007, Stern, 2007, Stern, 2015, Ch. 5) and in a more general perspective on intergenerational equity (Broome, 2012, Greaves, 2017, Kelleher, 2017). The double-sided fairness problem that is caused in this way is reflected by two conflicting normative postulates, the first of which pertains to the interests of the future generations and hence is dominating the climate change debate.

Postulate 1. Later generations should not have a lower welfare than the earlier ones, and if possible, a higher one. There should be human development ("growth of well-being") despite ecological restrictions. This requires investment by the earlier generations and thus transfer (or "gifts") from the earlier to the later generations.

That later generations should not be worse off than the earlier ones, which is the minimum condition for fulfilling Postulate 1, is tantamount to the *sustainability postulate*: "(T)he no-gift baseline is pure sustainability" (Llavador *et al.*, 2015, p. 38, Cowen, 2018).

Yet, fairness across generations also requires that the interests of the earlier generations have to be taken into account, too. This means that they should not be overburdened through their investments in favor of the later generations. This leads to the second postulate, which states that *excessive savings* should be prevented — and which has been a main motivation for giving future generations less weight in social evaluation than present ones (e.g., Arrow, 1999a,b, Dasgupta, 2008).[1]

Postulate 2. The savings and the associated transfers to the later generations should not become unduly high and not lead to excessive sacrifices of the earlier generations.

In addition, following the standard ideas on distributional equity, one could impose another postulate that directly refers to the degree of inequality of well-being across generations.

Postulate 3. Distribution of well-being should not become too unequal between generations.

Postulates 1 and 2 become particularly meaningful when the available production technology is *productive* so that savings of an earlier generation increase welfare of the later generations by a higher amount. Then, literally speaking, there is an "incubation bucket" for the intergenerational transfers (Schelling, 1995, Asheim *et al.*, 2001 in the context of sustainability). If the bucket would be leaky instead, a sustainable development would not be feasible. The productivity condition usually is assumed to hold in reality — with "doomsday prophets" as the exception.

Against the background of these three normative postulates, the following question arises: How to meet them through applying certain social preferences over streams of well-being across generations?[2]

[1]Referring to Koopmans (1960), Arrow (1999a) has dubbed this the "weak Koopmans argument" for discounting future utilities. In contrast, the "strong Koopmans argument" (Chichilnisky *et al.*, 2020) deals with the logical necessity of discounting as part of preference orderings on infinite-dimensional consumption streams if certain conditions (as the Pareto principle and continuity) are to be fulfilled. The deep specific problems that stem from infinity are not relevant for the results of our paper and therefore are neglected (see Kamaga, 2020, for an extensive treatment of this issue).

[2]The problem of finding an ethically appealing balance of interests between generations satisfying the two postulates listed above was already addressed by the philosophers Kant (1784) and Rawls (1972).

This question, in particular, means that it has to be examined in the framework of ethical or "prescriptive" social choice theory (Chichilnisky *et al.*, 2020), which intertemporal social welfare functions may be capable of ensuring distributions of well-being between generations that are skewed in favor of the future generations but not skewed too much. Thus, on the one hand, transfers from the earlier to the later generations should be made so that the welfare gains that arise from productivity of investment are not given away. Yet, on the other hand, these transfers should not become too high in order to prevent an overcharging of the earlier generations and a too imbalanced distribution of well-being across generations.

A simple approach for satisfying these postulates is to adapt the social preferences to the given technology. In this vein, Rawls (1971, p. 262) has stated that *we may obtain a more plausible result if the welfare of future generations is weighted less heavily*; *and the most suitable discount rate may depend upon ...productivity of capital* .... In the following, we will, in contrast, analyze whether it is possible to find social welfare functions, which satisfy these postulates not only for a particular technology but *for all productive technologies.* In this way, we in particular assess the robustness of ethically grounded intertemporal social evaluation against unexpected changes of technological environments, which are likely in the case of climate change.

If social preferences would instead have to depend on the specifically given technology to attain an ethically sensible balance of interest between generations, this would — metaphorically speaking — mean putting *the cart before the horse*: *Our ethics should (instead, the authors) be stated prior to knowledge of what ... the constraints defining the feasibility set* (*are, the authors*) (Llavador *et al.*, 2015, p. 47). According to the usual view in economics, such a way of proceeding, i.e., to choose the evaluation criterion after the technology has come to be known, is not considered as legitimate.

Focusing on the standard case in which intertemporal evaluation is done by an utilitarian social welfare function,[3] it will be shown in

[3]It can be shown that the main results also continue to hold when more general intertemporal social preferences are considered.

this paper

- that it is easy to find social welfare functions that avoid violation of Postulate 1 for any productive technology, i.e., to exclude a non-sustainable development;
- that it is possible to some extent to find social welfare functions that satisfy Postulate 2, but that it is not possible to satisfy Postulate 3.

The chapter will be organized as follows: In Section 2, our main arguments will be presented in an elementary, two-period model similar to the one in Buchholz (2003), Llavador *et al.* (2015, pp. 44–47), and Roemer (2019). In Section 3, it will then be briefly considered how our basic results can be generalized to a multi-period setting. Section 4 concludes, drawing also attention to some non-utilitarian criteria for intertemporal social evaluation.

2. The Two-Period Setting

2.1. *The framework*

There are two generations, 1 and 2, of equal size. Consumption, which is understood in a quite comprehensive sense as an indicator of well-being, including the benefits provided by environmental quality, medical services, and quality of education, is denoted by c_1 for generation 1 and by c_2 for generation 2. The technology, which determines the feasible consumption profiles (or "paths") (c_1, c_2), is given by $F(c_1, c_2) \leq w$, where F is a (weakly) concave production function that is twice differentiable and strictly monotone increasing in both variables and which is defined for $c_1 \geq 0$ and $c_2 \geq 0$. The variable w denotes the initial endowment given to generation 1, which is measured in units of the consumption good. Generation 1's maximal consumption then is w, which is attained if generation 2's consumption is zero, i.e., $F(w, 0) = w$. Given a fixed initial endowment w, the upper boundary of the convex set of feasible consumption profiles is described by a decreasing and weakly concave (and differentiable) transformation curve $c_2 = T(c_1)$, which is given by $F(c_1, T(c_1)) = w$. The function $T(c_1)$ is defined on the interval $[0, w]$, and $T(w) = 0$ holds (see Fig. 1).

The technology is called *productive* if the marginal rate of transformation between consumption in period 1 and consumption in period

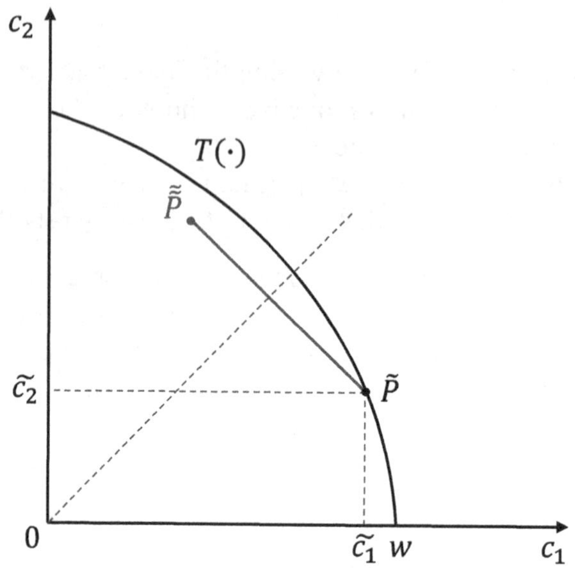

Fig. 1. The non-optimality of non-sustainable paths in a productive economy.

2 exceeds 1 everywhere, i.e., if $-T'(c_1) = \frac{\partial F/\partial c_1}{\partial F/\partial c_2} > 1$ holds for all $c_1 \in [0, w]$. Then, an additional marginal consumption sacrifice by generation 1, i.e., a marginal increase of savings, raises consumption of generation 2 by more than this additional investment. The difference between generation 1's endowment w and its actual consumption c_1 can be interpreted as this generation's total savings or investments.

In the following, we will often consider the case in which the technology is linear so that $F(c_1, c_2) = c_1 + \frac{c_2}{m}$ holds. The transformation curve then is $T(c_1) = -mc_1 + mw$, where $m > 1$ is the constant marginal rate of transformation between consumption of generation 1 and that of generation 2. The transformation curve thus is a falling straight line with slope $-m$ and has the axis intercepts w and mw.

Consumption paths will be assessed by an intertemporal utilitarian *Social Welfare Function (SWF)* of the type

$$W(c_1, c_2) = u(c_1) + \delta u(c_2), \tag{1}$$

where $u(c_i)$ is a strictly monotone increasing, twice-differentiable, and concave utility function that evaluates consumption of each generation

$i = 1, 2$. Note that from the viewpoint of "prioritarianism", $u(c)$ is not a "utility function" in the true sense of the word that measures the generations' satisfaction, but plays a purely instrumental role expressing an "ethical observer's" (Llavador *et al.*, 2015) or "social benefactor's" (Chichilnisky *et al.*, 2020) preferences for equality of distribution (Atkinson, 1970, Adler, 2012). Yet, in the context of this paper, this otherwise important conceptual distinction concerning the meaning of $u(c)$ (Kaplow, 2010) is of no importance, so we will use the notion "utility function" throughout.

The parameter δ is the utility discount factor, which indicates the ratio by which the utility levels of both generations enter the SWF $W(c_1, c_2)$ and for which usually $\delta \leq 1$ is assumed: If $\delta < 1$, the future generation has less weight in social evaluation than the present one. Consequently, in this case, a systematic bias for the present generation is incorporated in the SWF, which thus shows *pure time preference*.[4] If instead $\delta = 1$, both generations are treated equally by $W(c_1, c_2)$. In any case — due to the concavity of the utility function $u(c)$ — the social indifference curves, along which the level of intertemporal social welfare is constant, are concave (and clearly falling).

An important special sub-class of SWFs of type (1) is given when the underlying utility function $u(c_i)$ is iso-elastic, so that (1) becomes

$$W(c_1, c_2) = \frac{c_1^{1-\eta}}{1-\eta} + \delta \frac{c_2^{1-\eta}}{1-\eta}, \tag{2}$$

where $\eta > 0$ and $\eta \neq 1$. The parameter η is the *elasticity of marginal utility* $\eta = -\frac{u''(c)c}{u'(c)}$, which indicates the degree of inequality aversion in social evaluation. For $\eta = 1$, by observing $\lim_{\eta \to 1} \frac{c^{1-\eta}}{1-\eta} = \ln c$, one has $W(c_1, c_2) = \ln c_1 + \delta \ln c_2$.

Given a SWF of type (1) for any concave transformation curve $T(c_1)$, there exists a unique optimal consumption path (c_1^*, c_2^*), which

[4]Even if generations, in principle, are treated equally in social evaluation, pure time discounting can be justified through the possibility that future generations might not exist (Sidgwick, 1907). For a theoretical elaboration on this "extinction discounting," see Chichilnisky *et al.* (2020).

maximizes $W(c_1, c_2)$ over all feasible consumption paths (c_1, c_2), i.e., $u(c_1^*)+\delta u(c_2^*) \geq u(c_1)+\delta u(c_2)$ holds for all $c_2 = T(c_1)$. Applying the Lagrange method, it directly follows that a W-optimal consumption path (c_1^*, c_2^*) is characterized by the first-order condition

$$u'(c_1^*) = \delta T'(c_1^*)u'(T(c_1^*)). \tag{3}$$

Condition (3) shows that (c_1^*, c_2^*) crucially depends on the interplay between the discount factor δ and the marginal productivities $T'(c_1)$ that result for the given technology.

2.2. *Ensuring fulfillment of Postulate 1 by treating generations equally*

The minimum condition for the fulfillment of Postulate 1 is that the W-optimal paths for all productive technologies be sustainable, which means that they are non-decreasing, i.e., $c_2^* \geq c_1^*$ holds for any productive technology. According to condition (3), this can be ensured by assuming $\delta = 1$, i.e., by equal treatment of both generations and thus by an undiscounted utilitarian SWF $W(c_1, c_2) = u(c_1) + u(c_2)$. Such impartiality, and thus anonymity, of intergenerational social evaluation is a fundamental moral requirement through which a fair and non-discriminatory treatment of generations is attained. Equal treatment of different generations in social evaluation has not only been postulated by many philosophers but also by economists such as Pigou (1920) and Ramsey (1928), and more recently, e.g., by Stern (2007), Roemer (2011, 2019), Adler and Treich (2015), and Chichilnisky *et al.* (2020).

Proposition 1. *If* $\delta = 1$, *the* W*-optimal consumption path* (c_1^*, c_2^*) *for any given productive technology is sustainable and even increasing for productive economies.*

Proof. From (3), we have $u'(c_1^*) = T'(c_1^*)u'(T(c_1^*))$ if $\delta = 1$. Since $T'(c_1^*) > 1$ from the productivity assumption, this implies $u'(c_1^*) > u'(T(c_1^*))$ so that concavity of the utility function $u(c_i)$ gives $c_2^* = T(c_1^*) > c_1^*$. □

In the c_1-c_2-diagram (see Fig. 1), productivity of the technology implies that — given some consumption profile $\tilde{P} = (\tilde{c}_1, \tilde{c}_2)$ with $\tilde{c}_1 > \tilde{c}_2$ — the permuted consumption path $\tilde{\tilde{P}} = (\tilde{c}_2, \tilde{c}_1)$ lies below the transformation curve $T(c_1)$. This shows in an alternative way that any $\tilde{P} = (\tilde{c}_1, \tilde{c}_2)$ lying below the 45°-line cannot be W-optimal.

Having $\delta = 1$, i.e., no pure time discounting, is not only sufficient but also necessary for satisfying Postulate 1 since for any discounted utilitarian SWF with $\delta < 1$, Postulate 1 will be violated by some productive technology.

Proposition 2. *If $\delta < 1$, there exist productive technologies for which the W-optimal path is not sustainable, i.e., $c_2^* < c_1^*$ holds.*

Proof. For a linear technology, the first-order condition (3) becomes $u'(c_1^*) = \delta m u'(c_2^*)$ (with $c_2^* = T(c_1^*) = -mc_1^* + mw$). As $\frac{1}{\delta} > 1$, we can choose a productivity parameter m for which $1 < m < \frac{1}{\delta}$. Then, $\delta m < 1$, which gives $u'(c_1^*) < u'(c_2^*)$ and consequently $c_1^* > c_2^*$ since the utility function $u(c)$ is concave. □

The intuition behind Proposition 2 is that for a productivity m, which is low as compared to the given discount factor δ, total welfare will not increase if investment by generation 1 is so high that generation 2 becomes better off.

2.3. *Ensuring Postulate 1 through amending discounted utilitarian SWFs*

Starting from an SWF $W(c_1, c_2)$ with $\delta < 1$, Postulate 1 can also be ensured by constructing new "hybrid" SWFs, which leave the ranking of all sustainable consumption paths (c_1, c_2) unchanged, i.e., for which $\breve{W}(c_1, c_2) = u(c_1) + \delta u(c_2)$ holds if $c_1 \leq c_2$. For a non-sustainable path (c_1, c_2) where $c_1 > c_2$, social welfare is, as in Zuber and Asheim (2012), instead defined as $\breve{W}(c_1, c_2) = u(c_2) + \delta u(c_1)$, which means that any non-sustainable consumption path is permuted before the original SWF $W(c_1, c_2)$ is applied. Consequently, for this "rank discounted utilitarian approach" only the ranking of consumption profiles given by $W(c_1, c_2)$ in the region $\{(c_1, c_2) : c_2 \geq c_1\}$ is relevant for social evaluation.

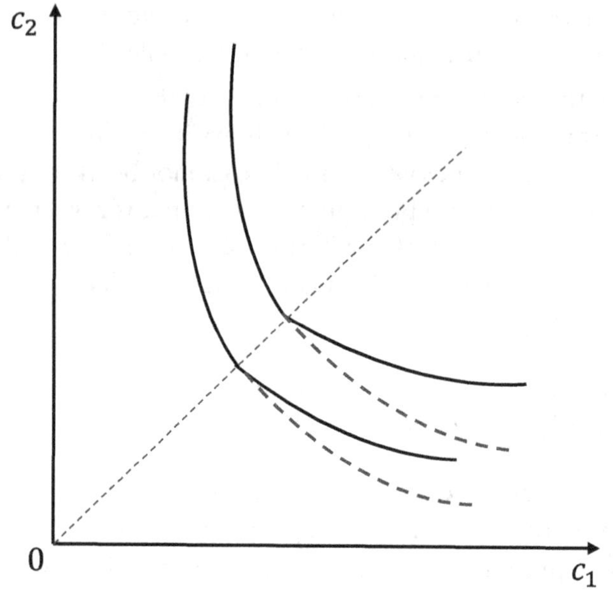

Fig. 2. Indifference curves for the rank discounted utilitarian approach.

The indifference curves for $\breve{W}(c_1, c_2)$ are obtained by mirroring the upper part of the social indifference curves of the original SWF $W(c_1, c_2)$ on the 45°-line at which the new $\underset{\smile}{W}$-indifference curves now have a kink (see Fig. 2).

A second approach for ensuring Postulate 1 starting from some given discounted SWF $W(c_1, c_2)$ is based on a partial inclusion of the maximin criterion leading to an amended SWF $\underset{\smile}{W}(c_1, c_2)$ (see Asheim and Mitra, 2010). Again, we have $\underset{\smile}{W}(c_1, c_2) = u(c_1) + \delta u(c_2)$ if $c_1 \leq c_2$, but now, $\underset{\smile}{W}(c_1, c_2) = c_2$ if $c_1 > c_2$. The social indifference curves for $\underset{\smile}{W}(c_1, c_2)$ (see Fig. 3) coincide with those of $W(c_1, c_2)$ above the 45°-line and are flat straight lines right of the 45°-line, which reflect the maximin component in the new SWF $\underset{\smile}{W}(c_1, c_2)$.

On a given transformation curve $T(c_1)$, we now define $\hat{c}$ as the constant consumption level that is technically feasible for both generations,

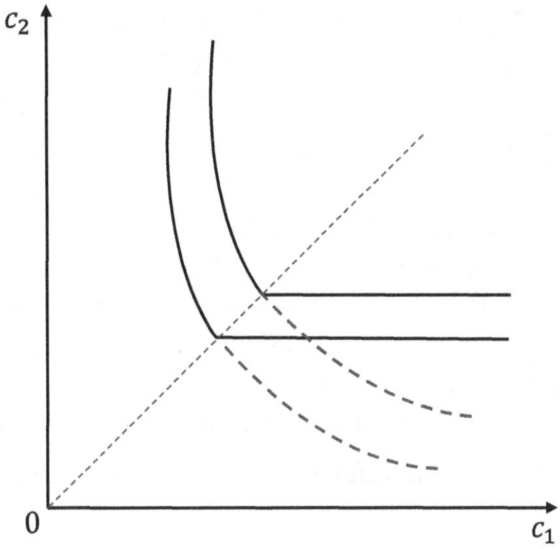

Fig. 3. Combining discounted utilitarianism with maximin.

i.e., for which $\hat{c} = T(\hat{c})$ holds. The $\breve{W}$- and $\underset{\smile}{W}$-optimal consumption paths then can be characterized as follows:

Proposition 3.

(i) *If the W-optimal consumption path (c_1^*, c_2^*) is sustainable, then it is also $\breve{W}$-optimal and $\underset{\smile}{W}$-optimal.*

(ii) *If the W-optimal consumption path (c_1^*, c_2^*) is non-sustainable, then the equal consumption profile $(\hat{c}, \hat{c})$ is both $\breve{W}$-optimal and $\underset{\smile}{W}$-optimal.*

Proof. At any point (c, c) on the 45°-line, the original W-indifference curves have a slope with absolute value $\frac{u'(c)}{\delta u'(c)} = \frac{1}{\delta} \geq 1$. Since the W-indifference curves are concave, the $\breve{W}$-indifference curves below the 45°-line then have a slope whose absolute value is smaller than 1. Thus, they are flatter there than the transformation curve $T(c_1)$ for which $-T'(c_1) > 1$ holds everywhere due to the productivity assumption. This gives $\breve{W}(\hat{c}, \hat{c}) > \breve{W}(c_1, T(c_1))$ for all

$c_1 > \hat{c}$. If now $c_1^* \leq c_2^*$ holds for the W-optimal path, then $\breve{W}(c_1^*, c_2^*) = W(c_1^*, c_2^*) > W(\hat{c}, \hat{c}) = \breve{W}(\hat{c}, \hat{c}) > \breve{W}(c_1, T(c_1))$ for all $c_1 > \hat{c}$ and, clearly, $\breve{W}(c_1^*, c_2^*) = W(c_1^*, c_2^*) > W(c_1, T(c_1)) = \breve{W}(c_1, T(c_1))$ for all $c_1 \leq \hat{c}$. Hence, (c_1^*, c_2^*) is $\breve{W}$-optimal in this case, which shows (i).

If instead $c_1^* > c_2^*$, we only have to show that $\breve{W}(\hat{c}, \hat{c}) = W(\hat{c}, \hat{c}) > W(c_1, T(c_1)) = \breve{W}(c_1, T(c_1))$ holds for all $c_1 < \hat{c}$: Otherwise the W-indifference curve through $(\hat{c}, \hat{c})$ would be flatter there than $T(c_1)$. Due to its concavity, the whole part of $T(c_1)$ right of $(\hat{c}, \hat{c})$ and thus in particular (c_1^*, c_2^*) would lie below this convex indifference curve. Hence, $W(c_1^*, c_2^*) < W(\hat{c}, \hat{c})$ which would contradict the W-optimality of (c_1^*, c_2^*). This shows (ii). The proof for $\underset{\smile}{W}$-optimality is analogous as the slope of the $\underset{\smile}{W}$-indifference curve is zero to the right of the 45°-line. □

The reasoning so far has provided a positive result: Violation of Postulate 1 can be avoided for any given productive technology by applying a fixed SWF $W(c_1, c_2)$ — either by dispensing with utility discounting or by amending discounted utilitarian SWFs in an appropriate way. This means that the class of standard intertemporal SWFs exhibits "flexibility" in the sense of Asheim (2017).

2.4. *Ensuring Postulate 2*

Unlike Postulate 1, there is no clear and unambiguous specification of Postulate 2. In the following, we will use a rather weak criterion by saying that Postulate 2 is satisfied if there exists a SWF $W(c_1, c_2)$ so that for any productive technology $T(c_1)$, the associated W-optimal consumption path (c_1^*, c_2^*) has $c_1^* \geq \underline{\alpha} w$ for some "protection level" $\underline{\alpha} > 1$. In relation to its endowment w, generation 1's consumption sacrifice for the benefit of the future generation then is limited by $1 - \underline{\alpha} < 1$ so that extremely excessive savings and complete immiseration of generation 1 are avoided.

In order to find SWFs that give such protection for the earlier generation, we make the W-optimal consumption path that specifically results for a linear technology $T(c_1) = -mc_1 + mw$ (with a fixed endowment w) dependent on the underlying productivity parameter m, i.e.,

$(c_1^*(m), c_2^*(m))$. Based on the linear case, we now show that there are SWFs even in the specific class given by (2), which are able to satisfy Postulate 2.

Proposition 4. *Any SWF of type* (2) *with* $\eta > 1$ *ensures a protection level* $\alpha = \frac{1}{1+\delta^{\frac{1}{\eta}}}$ *for generation* 1 *for all concave and productive technologies.*

Proof. Take any SWF of type (2) with $\eta > 1$. (i) For a linear technology with the productivity parameter m, we have

$$c_1^*(m) = \frac{w}{1 + \delta^{\frac{1}{\eta}} m^{\frac{1}{\eta}-1}} \tag{4}$$

which is shown by an easy application of the Lagrange method to the maximization of (2) subject to $c_1 + \frac{c_2}{m} = w$. If $\eta > 1$, we get that $c_1^*(m)$ is increasing in m and thus $c_1^*(m) > c_1^*(1) = \frac{w}{1+\delta^{\frac{1}{\eta}}}$ holds for all linear technologies and $m > 1$. In this special case, the result of Proposition 4 holds.

(ii) For a given general technology with the W-optimal consumption path $P^* = (c_1^*, c_2^*)$, we now define a hypothetical linear technology by $\tilde{T}(c_1) := -\tilde{m}c_1 + \tilde{m}c_1^* + c_2^*$, where $\tilde{m}$ is the marginal rate of substitution between c_1 and c_2 and thus the absolute value of the slope of $T(c_1)$ in the point P^*. Then, the W-optimal consumption path for the linear technology $\tilde{T}(c_1)$ is also P^*. Concavity of $T(c_1)$ implies that generation 1's hypothetical endowment $\tilde{w} = c_1^* + \frac{c_2^*}{\tilde{m}}$ under $\tilde{T}(c_1)$ is larger than its actual endowment w (see Fig. 4). Thus, $\frac{c_1^*}{w} > \frac{c_1^*}{\tilde{w}} \geq \frac{1}{1+\delta^{\frac{1}{\eta}}}$, so that $\underline{\alpha} = \frac{1}{1+\delta^{\frac{1}{\eta}}}$ also gives the protection level that is guaranteed for all concave technologies. □

According to Proposition 4, any desired protection level α for generation 1 in the range between $\frac{1}{2}$ and 1 can be achieved by appropriate choices of δ. It follows from Eq. (4) that in any case the protection level converges to 1 if productivity m goes to infinity, i.e., generation 1 will benefit to a high degree from increases of productivity. This also holds if $\delta = 1$, i.e., if generations are treated equally and Postulate 1 is

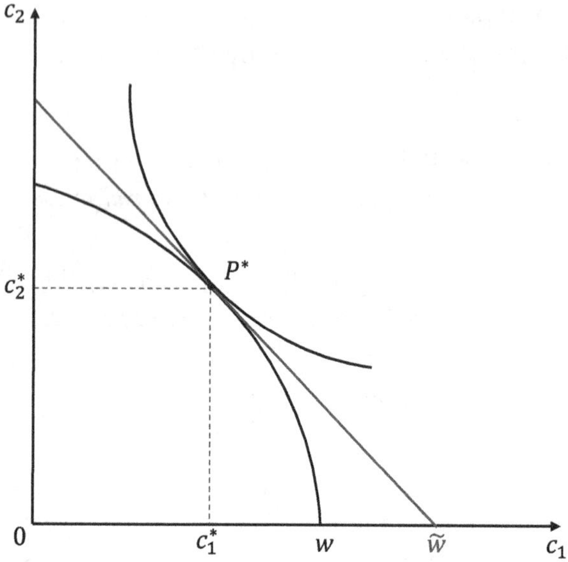

Fig. 4. Protecting generation 1 in case of a concave technology.

respected. Then, in particular, we get $\underline{\alpha} = \frac{1}{2}$ for all $\eta > 0$, which shows that Postulate 1 and Postulate 2 can be satisfied simultaneously.

Choosing $\delta < 1$ to get a broader range for the protection level, however, comes at a price since, according to Proposition 2, for any $\delta < 1$, there exist technologies for which the W-optimal paths are non-sustainable. Moreover, $\delta < 1$ would imply that in the pure distribution scenario with a linear technology and $m = 1$ (and also for values of m being close to 1), generation 1 could appropriate a larger share of the cake than generation 2, which seems unfair even without reference to the sustainability postulate.

Figure 5 describes how — for some given $\eta > 1$ — consumption $C^*(m) = (c_1^*(m), c_2^*(m))$ of both generations develops if the productivity parameter m varies in the interval $[1, \infty)$ where the path that results for $\delta = 1$ is marked in green: For $m = 1$, such a path starts in the point $(\frac{w}{2}, \frac{w}{2})$ on the 45°-line, and — as directly follows from (4) — it bends upwards and falls nowhere below the 45° -line. Finally, $C^*(m)$ approximates the vertical line through the endowment point $(w, 0)$ if productivity m goes to infinity. If the inequality aversion parameter η

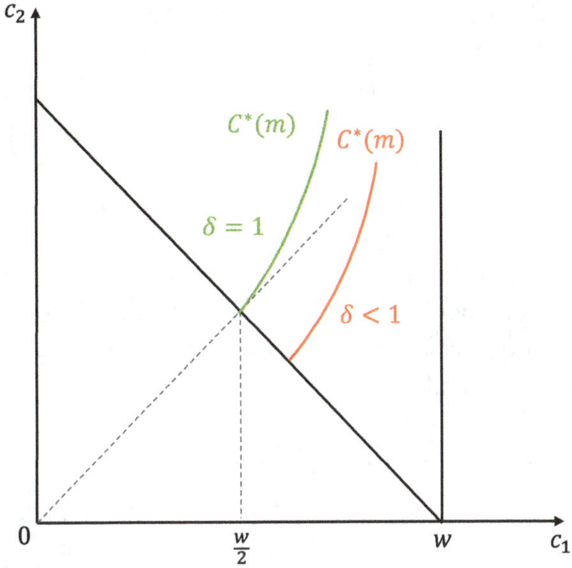

Fig. 5. Consumption paths for varying productivities in case of a linear technology.

increases, the path $C^*(m)$ would be shifted leftward to the right, which is in line with the fact that a higher inequality aversion η is of advantage for generation 1. If instead $\delta < 1$, then the path $C^*(m)$ starts (for $m = 1$) at the point $\left(\frac{w}{1+\delta^{\frac{1}{\eta}}}, \frac{\delta^{\frac{1}{\eta}} w}{1+\delta^{\frac{1}{\eta}}}\right)$ below the 45°-line. In Fig. 5, such a path is marked in red.

In Fig. 5, both consumption levels, $c_1^*(m)$ and $c_2^*(m)$, are increasing in m. The increase of $c_2^*(m)$ follows from additive separability and concavity of the SWF and the ensuing non-Giffen property of c_2. The increase of $c_1^*(m)$, however, requires that — in the terminology of microeconomics — c_1 and c_2 are gross complements, which in the special case visualized by Fig. 5 is implied by $\eta > 1$. In ethical social choice theory, this complementarity corresponds to "circumstance solidarity" (Fleurbaey, 2008, Buchholz and Schumacher, 2010), which means that an improvement of the technology should not only benefit the future generation but also the present one. In the context of this paper, circumstance solidarity as implied by $\eta > 1$ provides a sufficient condition for satisfying Postulate 2, i.e., for giving protection to the present by applying the same SWF to all concave technologies.

If instead $\eta < 1$, so that consumption in period 1 is a gross substitute to consumption in period 2, Eq. (4) shows that $c_1^*(m)$ goes to zero if m goes to infinity for all $\delta \leq 1$. Then, Postulate 2 is clearly violated. Hence, a certain strictly positive protection level for generation 1 cannot be guaranteed through the discount factor δ alone if the elasticity of marginal utility η has not been chosen appropriately, i.e., if $\eta < 1$. Therefore, we can conclude that — as compared to the discount factor δ — the inequality aversion parameter η is of superior importance w.r.t. the fulfillment of Postulate 2.

2.5. *The limits of ensuring Postulate 2*

Until now, we have restricted attention to the important class of (weakly) concave technologies. If one drops this assumption, the fulfillment of Postulate 2 is no longer guaranteed.

Proposition 5. *For any given SWF W of type* (1), *there exists a non-concave technology $T(c_1)$ with the optimal consumption path (c_1^*, c_2^*) so that $\alpha = \frac{c_1^*}{w}$ becomes arbitrarily low.*

Proof. Take any $m > 1$ and consider the linear technology $T(c_1) = -mc_1 + mw$. Now, choose a welfare level $\bar{W}$ which is represented by a social indifference curve that lies everywhere above the transformation curve $T(c_1)$. For any $\tilde{c}_1 \in]0, w[$, we determine the straight line which passes through the point $\tilde{P} = (\tilde{c}_1, T(\tilde{c}_1))$ and which is tangential to the indifference curve corresponding to $\bar{W}$. This straight line, whose slope is denoted by $-\tilde{m}$, is now interpreted as a second transformation curve $\tilde{T}(c_1) = -\tilde{m}c_1 + T(\tilde{c}_1) + \tilde{m}\tilde{c}_1$ and which for any $\tilde{c}_1$ is steeper than $T(.)$, i.e., $\tilde{m} > m$ (see Fig. 6).

A combination of these two linear transformation curves gives a transformation curve $\hat{T}(\cdot)$ with a kink in point $\tilde{P} = (\tilde{c}_1, \tilde{c}_2)$, which is defined by $\hat{T}(c_1) = \tilde{T}(c_1)$ for $c_1 \leq \tilde{c}_1$ and by $\hat{T}(c_1) = T(c_1)$ for $c_1 > \tilde{c}_1$ (and marked in green). The W-optimal point $\hat{P}^* = (\hat{c}_1^*, \hat{c}_2^*)$ on the convex transformation curve $\hat{T}(\cdot)$ is given by the point of tangency between $\tilde{T}(\cdot)$ and the social indifference curve $\bar{W}$. Since clearly $\hat{c}_1^* < \tilde{c}_1$,

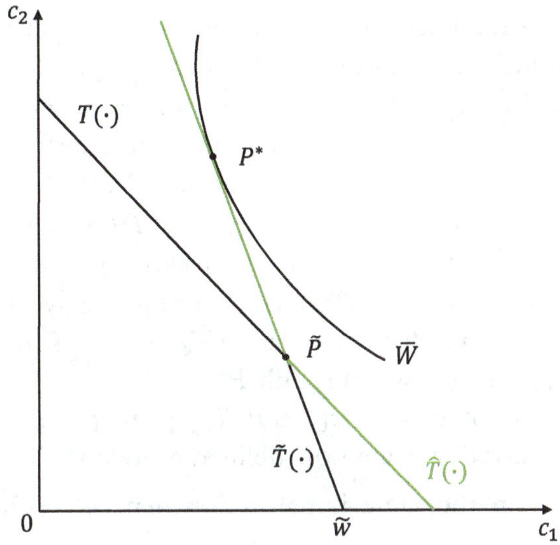

Fig. 6. Violation of Postulate 2 in case of a non-concave technology.

the consumption level that generation 1 attains in $\hat{P}^* = (\hat{c}_1^*, \hat{c}_2^*)$ will come arbitrarily close to zero if $\tilde{c}_1$ is chosen small enough — irrespective of which utility function $u(\cdot)$ and which discount factor $\delta \leq 1$ had been chosen as components of the SWF $W(c_1, c_2)$. □

Proposition 5 shows that no definite protection level for generation 1 can be guaranteed and thus Postulate 2 cannot be satisfied by applying a unique SWF $W(c_1, c_2)$ if the class of admitted technologies is expanded beyond the weakly concave technologies.

But, even for the class of concave technologies, circumstance solidarity as a more stringent condition for the protection of the present cannot not be ensured with the same SWF.

Proposition 6. *For any given SWF $W(c_1, c_2)$of type* (1), *there exist concave technologies $T_a(c_1)$ and $T_b(c_1)$ with optimal consumption paths (c_1^{a*}, c_2^{a*}) and (c_1^{b*}, c_2^{b*}), respectively, so that $T_b'(c_1) \geq T_a'(c_1)$ for all and $T_b'(c_1) > T_a'(c_1)$ holds for some $c_1 \in (0, w)$, but $c_1^{b*} < c_1^{a*}$.*

Proof. (i) Take some $\tilde{P}^a = (\tilde{c}_1^a, \tilde{c}_2^a)$ at which we have $\tilde{m}_a > 1$ for the marginal rate of substitution between c_1 and c_2 given a SWF $W(c_1, c_2)$

of type (1). On the linear transformation curve $\tilde{T}_a(c_1) := -\tilde{m}_a c_1 + \tilde{m}_a \tilde{c}_1^a + \tilde{c}_2^a$, which passes through $\tilde{P}^a$ and has slope $-\tilde{m}_a$, we choose a point $\tilde{P}^b = (\tilde{c}_1^b, \tilde{c}_2^b)$ to the right of $\tilde{P}^a$ and some marginal rate of transformation $\tilde{m}_b > \tilde{m}_a$ and then consider the transformation curve $\tilde{T}_b(c_1) := -\tilde{m}_b c_1 + \tilde{m}_b \tilde{c}_1^b + \tilde{c}_2^b$ passing through $\tilde{P}^b$. If $\tilde{P}^b$ lies sufficiently close to $\tilde{P}^a$, the optimum $Q = (\tilde{c}_1^{b*}, \tilde{c}_2^{b*})$ on $\tilde{T}_b(c_1)$ lies to the left of P^a, i.e., $\tilde{c}_1^{b*} < \tilde{c}_1^a$ holds (see Fig. 7). This follows from continuity as Q clearly would lie to the left of $\tilde{P}^a$ if, as a limiting case, we had $\tilde{P}^b = \tilde{P}^a$. Now, define a third transformation curve $\tilde{T}_d(c_1) := -\tilde{m}_d c_1 + \tilde{m}_d \tilde{c}_1^b + \tilde{c}_2^b$ with $\tilde{m}_d > \tilde{m}_b$, which passes through P^b.

(ii) Two technologies $T_a(c_1)$ and $T_b(c_1)$ with the properties as required in Proposition 6 are now defined as follows: Both technologies are based on the same initial endowment $w = \tilde{c}_1^b + \frac{\tilde{c}_2^b}{\tilde{m}_d}$ and $T_a(c_1) = T_b(c_1) := \tilde{T}_d(c_1)$ holds for all $c_1 \in [\tilde{c}_1^b, w]$. For all $c_1 \in [0, \tilde{c}_1^b]$, we set $T_a(c_1) = \tilde{T}_a(c_1)$ and $T_b(c_1) = \tilde{T}_b(c_1)$. As $\tilde{m}_d > \tilde{m}_b > \tilde{m}_a > 1$, the technologies $T_a(c_1)$ and $T_b(c_1)$ are concave and productive. $T_b(c_1)$

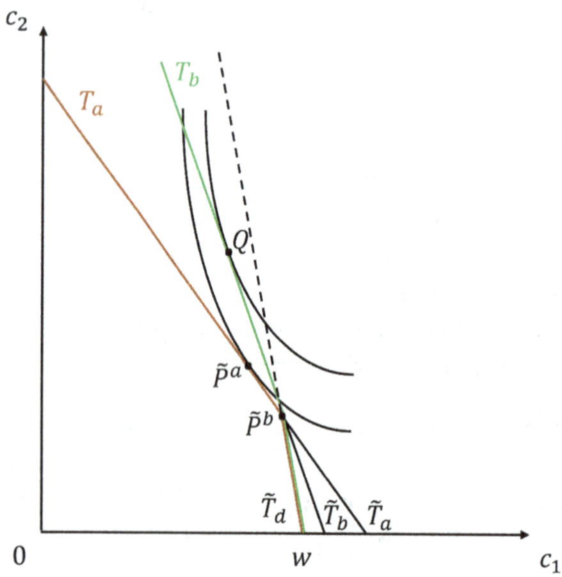

Fig. 7. The violation of the circumstance solidarity postulate for concave technologies.

has the same marginal productivity as $T_a(c_1)$ on $[\tilde{c}_1^b, w]$ and a higher marginal productivity on $[0, \tilde{c}_1^b]$. Yet, for the W-optima for the two technologies, we have $c_1^{b*} = \tilde{c}_1^{b*} < \tilde{c}_1^a = c_1^{a*}$ by construction. □

2.6. *The impossibility of satisfying Postulate 3*

We now ask whether it is possible to satisfy Postulate 3, which refers to the case where "the ethical observer (...) (is, WB and DR) interested in reducing intergenerational inequality" (Llavador *et al.*, 2015, p. 47). The question thus is whether an uneven distribution of consumption can be avoided for any given productive technology by a unique and fixed SWF $W(c_1, c_2)$. The answer to this question is negative even for the class of concave technologies.

Proposition 7. *For any given SWF $W(c_1, c_2)$ of type (1), there is a linear technology $T(c_1)$ so that for the W-optimal consumption path (c_1^*, c_2^*), the ratio $\rho^* = \frac{c_2^*}{c_1^*}$, i.e., the degree of inequality of consumption between the two generations, becomes arbitrarily large.*

Proof. Take any consumption levels $\tilde{c}_1$ and $\tilde{c}_2$ with some arbitrarily low ratio $\tilde{\rho} = \frac{\tilde{c}_1}{\tilde{c}_2}$ and consider the linear technology $\tilde{T}(c_1) := -\tilde{m}c_1 + \tilde{w}$, for which $\tilde{w} = \tilde{c}_1 - \frac{\tilde{c}_2}{\tilde{m}}$, and — given some SWF $W(c_1, c_2)$ — $\tilde{m}$ is the marginal rate of substitution between c_1 and c_2 in the point $\tilde{P} = (\tilde{c}_1, \tilde{c}_2)$ (see Fig. 8). The W-optimal solution for this technology is $(\tilde{c}_1, \tilde{c}_2)$, since the transformation curve $\tilde{T}(c_1)$ is tangential to the social indifference curve passing through $(\tilde{c}_1, \tilde{c}_2)$. Moving along the social indifference curve through $\tilde{P}$ to the left, e.g., from $\tilde{P}$ to $\tilde{\tilde{P}}$ in Fig. 8, leads to a technology $\tilde{\tilde{T}}(\cdot)$ for which inequality in the W-optimum is still higher. □

Proposition 7 says that no standard utilitarian SWF, i.e., neither a specific utility function $u(c)$ nor a utility discount factor δ, is able to avoid an extremely unequal distribution of well-being in any case even in the two-period case.

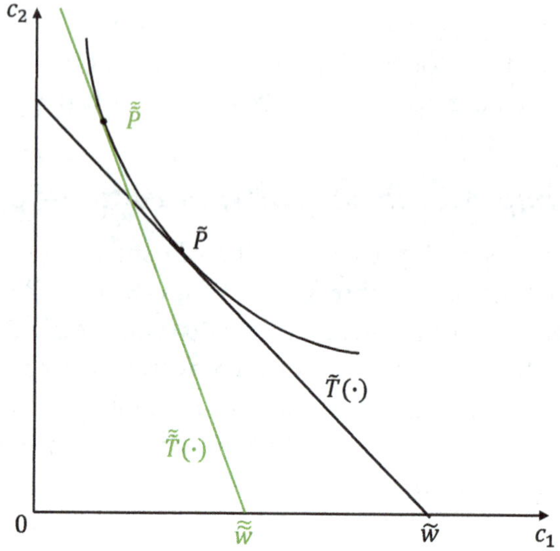

Fig. 8. Violation of Postulate 3.

3. The Case of Multiple Periods

We now generalize the linear model of the two-period case to the case of an arbitrary number T of generations $t = 1, 2, \ldots, T$, where T may also be infinite. Consumption of generation t is denoted by c_t and consumption paths over the entire time horizon by $C = (c_1, c_2, \ldots)$. As a generalization of (1), the intertemporal utilitarian SWF is given by

$$W(C) = \sum_{t=1}^{T} \delta^{t-1} u(c_t), \tag{5}$$

where $u(c_i)$ again is a strictly monotone increasing, twice-differentiable, and concave utility function and $\delta \leq 1$ is a constant social utility discount factor. In the case of an iso-elastic utility function $u(c) = \frac{c^{1-\eta}}{1-\eta}$, Eq. (2) turns into

$$W(C) = \sum_{t=1}^{T} \delta^{t-1} \frac{c_t^{1-\eta}}{1-\eta}. \tag{6}$$

3.1. *The linear model in the multi-period case*

In this case, marginal productivity of investment is constant within each generation t, but may vary between periods. A technology thus is given by the initial endowment w of generation 1 and a non-decreasing sequence $\tau = (m_t)_{t=1,\dots,T}$ of productivity parameters for which $m_1 = 1$ and $m_t \geq 1$ hold for all periods t. Each m_t is the marginal rate of transformation between consumption in period 1 and consumption in period t. The production function then becomes

$$F_\tau(C) = \sum_{t=1}^{T} \frac{c_t}{m_t}. \tag{7}$$

Furthermore, we set $\mu_t = \frac{m_{t+1}}{m_t}$ to indicate "immediate" productivity of investment from period t to the next period $t+1$, i.e., the marginal rate of transformation between consumption in these two periods.

Quite analogous to the two-period case, the first-order condition that characterizes an optimal consumption path for a general SWF of type (5) becomes $\delta\mu_t u'(c^*_{t+1}) = u'(c^*_t)$ and, consequently, $\delta^{t-1} m_t u'(c^*_t) = u'(c^*_1)$. Optimal consumption paths thus are non-decreasing and thus sustainable if and only if $\delta\mu_t \geq 1$ or, equivalently, if $\delta \geq \frac{1}{\mu_t}$ holds for all $t \geq 1$. Consequently, just in the two-period case, Postulate 1 is satisfied for all productive technologies if and only if $\delta = 1$, i.e., if and only if all generations are treated equally.

If, in particular, the SWF is of type (6), we get $\delta^{t-1} m_t c_t^{*-\eta} = c_1^{*-\eta}$, which gives

$$c^*_t = (\delta^{t-1} m_t)^{\frac{1}{\eta}} c^*_1. \tag{8}$$

Plugging (8) into the production function (7) and observing the general feasibility constraint $F_\tau(C) = \sum_{t=1}^{T} \frac{c_t}{m_t} = w$, we obtain

$$c^*_1 = \frac{w}{\sum_{t=1}^{T} \delta^{\frac{t-1}{\eta}} m_t^{\frac{1}{\eta}-1}}. \tag{9}$$

The characterization of initial consumption by equation (9) clearly requires that $\sum_{t=1}^{T} \delta^{\frac{t-1}{\eta}} m_t^{\frac{1}{\eta}}$ is finite, which is always the case if $T < \infty$. Yet, in the case of an infinite time horizon, $T = \infty$, additional assumptions are needed for that, especially if the productivity parameters m_t are increasing fast enough.[5]

If $T < \infty, \delta = 1$, and $m_t = 1$ for all $t = 1, \ldots, T$, then (9) implies that $c_1^* = \frac{w}{T}$ and, by observing (8), that $c_t^* = \frac{w}{T}$ also holds for any $t = 2, \ldots, T$, i.e., the cake of fixed size w is distributed equally among the finite T generations in this special case. A technological improvement in the multi-period scenario occurs if, at least, in one period $\tilde{t}$, the productivity parameter $\mu_{\tilde{t}}$ (and thus all m_t for $t \geq \tilde{t}$) increases. If $\eta > 1$, then it directly follows from (9) that consumption c_1^* of the first generation and thus of all generations will increase. This shows that circumstance solidarity holds. Given $T < \infty$ and $\delta = 1$, the protection level that is ensured for generation 1 (and thus for each generation) then is $\alpha = \frac{1}{T}$. Choosing a discount factor $\delta < 1$ would again provide a higher protection level, but would — as in the two-period case — lead to non-sustainability for some productive technologies. Hence, Postulate 2 can be fulfilled also in the multi-period case with linear technologies when the underlying SWF has $\eta > 1$. If $T = \infty$, we still have circumstance solidarity, but no generation can be guaranteed a certain share of the initial endowment w as protection level: If productivity m_t goes to one for each period of time t, the same is true for sustainable consumption that is accessible to each generation.

Moreover, with improving technology, inequality of consumption will go to infinity for any general SWF $W(c_1, c_2)$ of type (5) if the utility function has $\lim_{c \to \infty} u'(c) = 0$. To show this, assume some period $\tilde{t}$

---

[5]If $T = \infty$ and especially $\mu_t = \mu$ are the same in all periods t, an optimal path exists if and only if $\delta < \mu^{\eta-1}$. Since $\mu > 1$, this condition is fulfilled if $\eta > 1$ for any $\delta \leq 1$ and hence particularly for $\delta = 1$. If, however, $\eta < 1$ and thus, $\mu^{\eta-1} < 1$, existence of an optimal path requires that δ must lie sufficiently close to zero. Consequently, a fixed discount factor cannot ensure the existence of optimal paths for all productivity parameters. Therefore, the inequality aversion parameter η is of outstanding importance also w.r.t. the existence of optimal paths when the time horizon is infinite.

and let μ_t go to infinity. As the productivities in the previous periods are bounded and optimal consumption c_1^* of generation 1 is bounded by its endowment w, we get from (8) that consumption in period $\tilde{t}$ is bounded, too. From the first-order condition $\delta\mu_t u'(c_{t+1}^*) = u'(c_t^*)$, it follows that marginal utility in period $t+1$ must go to zero if μ_t approaches infinity. Consequently, consumption c_{t+1}^* goes to infinity and, due to the boundedness of c_t^*, this is also true for the ratio $\frac{c_{t+1}^*}{c_t^*}$ between consumption in period $t+1$ and consumption in period t.

3.2. *General production functions*

In the general case, the consumption possibilities are described by a general function $F(C)$, which is twice differentiable, strictly monotone increasing in all arguments $c_1, c_2, \ldots,$ and concave. That a technology is productive now means that along any feasible consumption path $C = (c_1, c_2, \ldots)$, we have $mc(t_1, t_2) := \frac{\partial F/\partial c_{t_1}}{\partial F/\partial c_{t_2}} > 1$ for the marginal rate of transformation of consumption between any two periods t_1 and t_2 with $t_2 > t_1$. Then, additional savings by an earlier generation can increase consumption of each later generation by a higher amount. Along an optimal path, the first-order condition

$$u'(c_{t_1}^*) = \delta^{t_2 - t_1} m_{C^*}(t_1, t_2) u'(c_{t_2}^*) \tag{10}$$

holds for all periods t_1 and t_2 with $t_2 > t_1$. Concerning Postulate 1, condition (10) immediately provides a result that generalizes Propositions 1 and 2.

Proposition 8. *In the multi-period setting, Postulate* 1 *is satisfied for all productive technologies by an SWF of type* (5) *if and only if* $\delta = 1$.

For a consideration of Postulate 2 in the multi-period case, we focus on circumstance solidarity. This makes it possible to include the case $T = \infty$, where a fixed protection level $\underline{\alpha} > 0$ for each generation's consumption cannot be guaranteed for all productive technologies. To this end, we now make the consumption paths that are optimal for a given SWF of type (5) dependent on a parameter τ, which may take values in an interval $\Gamma \subseteq \mathbb{R}^+$ and which characterizes a class of technologies, i.e.,

$$C^*(\tau) = (c_1^*(\tau), c_2^*(\tau), c_3^*(\tau), \ldots). \tag{11}$$

We assume that a higher τ implies a higher productivity, which makes it technically possible to increase consumption of each generation given a constant initial endowment w. In the case of linear technologies as treated before, τ could be identified with one or several productivities μ_t.

We now infer when it is possible to have circumstance solidarity with the same SWF of type (5) for all technologies in such a class Γ, i.e., to ensure that an increase of τ raises consumption of all generations on an optimal path. To this end, we set $m_t^*(\tau) = m_{C^*(\tau)}(1, t)$ for the marginal rates of transformation between period 1 and any period $t \geq 2$ along the optimal path corresponding to τ. To make things easier, we assume that a technological improvement that follows from an increase of τ raises *all* marginal rates of transformation along an optimal path, i.e., $\frac{\partial m_t^*}{\partial \tau} > 0$ holds for all $t \geq 2$ and all $\tau \in \Gamma$. We now take the derivative of the first-order condition (10) w.r.t. τ when $t_1 = 1$ and $t_2 = t$. Omitting the argument τ, this yields

$$u''(c_1^*)\frac{dc_1^*}{d\tau} = \delta^{t-1}\left(m_t^* u''(c_t^*)\frac{dc_t^*}{d\tau} + \frac{dm_t^*}{d\tau}u'(c_t^*)\right) \tag{12}$$

If $\frac{dc_1^*}{d\tau} > 0$, then — due to $u''(c_1^*) < 0$ — the left-hand side of (12) is negative, so the right-hand side must be negative, too. Since $\frac{dm_t^*}{d\tau} > 0$, $u'(c_t^*) > 0$, and $u''(c_t^*) < 0$, this, however, can only be achieved if $\frac{dc_t^*}{d\tau} > 0$. As this holds for any period $t \geq 2$, we therefore have the following result:

Proposition 9. *If along a consumption path that is optimal for some given SWF $W(C)$ of type* (5), *an improvement of technology increases consumption of generation* 1, *then it must also increase consumption of all subsequent generations.*

This result says that under quite general conditions, the entire optimal consumption path will be shifted upward when productivity τ

grows if and only if the first generation's consumption is increased by this technological improvement.

Moreover, condition (9) shows that $\frac{dc_1^*}{d\tau} > 0$ holds if the right-hand side of (12) is negative at least for one period $t \geq 2$. Then, it is also negative for all periods $t \geq 2$. By transforming the term within the bracket of the right-hand side of (12), we get the following result.

Proposition 10. *Circumstance solidarity, i.e.,* $\frac{dc_1^*}{d\tau} > 0$, *holds if*

$$\eta(c_t^*) = -\frac{u''(c_t^*)c_t^*}{u'(c_t^*)} > \frac{\frac{dm_t^*}{d\tau}c_t^*}{m_t^*\frac{dc_t^*}{d\tau}} = \frac{\frac{dm_t^*}{d\tau}}{m_t^*} / \frac{\frac{dc_t^*}{d\tau}}{c_t^*} \tag{13}$$

for some $t \geq 2$.

Condition (13) again highlights the crucial importance that the elasticity of marginal utility, i.e., inequality aversion, plays for the fulfillment of Postulate 2, which confirms the insight that has been obtained in the two-period case. In contrast, the discount factor δ does not play any role in this context.

Finally, concerning Postulate 3, we have already shown that it cannot be fulfilled in the multi-period case even in the sub-case with linear technologies.

4. Conclusion

On the one hand, it is possible to satisfy Postulate 1 and to ensure sustainability for any productive technology by applying utilitarian SWFs that are treating all generations equally from the outset or, alternatively, through modifying the standard discounted utilitarian SWFs. On the other hand, as has been shown in this paper, it is not possible to satisfy Postulate 2, for which circumstance solidarity provides a sufficient condition, through the same SWF for *all* technologies. Yet, fortunately, it is possible to protect the early generations from excessive savings at least for some specific classes of technologies and particularly for the linear ones. In this context, we have, above all, highlighted the outstanding importance the elasticity of marginal utility η (compared with the often invoked utility discount rate δ) plays for the fulfillment of Postulate 2.

To this end, an adequate choice of η in the range $\eta > 1$ is completely sufficient, while an unequal treatment of generations, i.e., $\delta < 1$, is not required. This, in a certain sense, extends the result in Asheim and Buchholz (2003), who have shown the redundancy of discounting at least for the case of a single given technology. Finally, it is never possible to find standard utilitarian SWFs that are able to fulfill Postulate 3, i.e., to prevent extremely uneven distributions of consumption between the generations for any given productive technology. So, utilitarianism and prioritarianism show limitations when equality of well-being between generations is at stake. For even more fundamental reasons, the utilitarian approach has been criticized by Rawls especially in the intergenerational context: *(T)his calculus of advantages, which balances the losses of some against benefits of others, appears even less justified in the case of generations than among contemporaries* (Rawls, 1971, p. 253). This supports the view that "goodness orderings" given by utilitarian SWFs[6] are not able to satisfy ethical intuition in any situation.

As an alternative to the standard utilitarian criteria for intertemporal evaluation, Llavador *et al.* (2011, 2015) have developed the "growth sustainability approach," which they have also applied to determine growth paths that are optimal in a world with climate change.[7] The SWFs that underlie this "sustainabilitarian approach" are given by $W(c_1, c_2, \dots) = \inf \left(\frac{c_t}{g^{t-1}}\right)_{t=1,2,\dots}$, where the parameter $g \geq 0$ as the desired factor for economic growth serves as the normative objective. For the special case $g = 1$ the standard maximin criterion results through which, however, growth and economic progress are precluded. If instead, as suggested by Llavador *et al.* (2011, 2015), $g > 0$ is assumed, along an optimal path $(c_1^*, c_2^*, \dots)$ we have $\frac{c_t^*}{g^{t-1}} = const.$ and $\frac{c_{t+1}^*}{c_t^*} = g$ for all $t = 1, 2, \dots$, i.e., constant growth with the growth rate $\rho = g - 1$. Hence, all three postulates are ensured from the very

---

[6]For a discussion of "goodness orderings" in the intergenerational context, see Broome (2012) and Greaves (2017) and especially for an assessment of their appropriate scope, Kelleher (2017).

[7]For a general review of other approaches in moral and political philosophy, see Stern (2015, Ch. 6).

beginning by applying this non-utilitarian criterion. But also this class of intertemporal evaluation criteria suffers from severe limitations, too. So, if in the linear case productivity m becomes very small and $m < g$ holds, an optimal growth sustainabilitarian path will not exist. This means that g, which is the normative objective in this approach, cannot be chosen independently of the technology. Hence, a problem that is pertinent w.r.t. the standard utilitarian criteria also arises in the context of the sustainabilitarian approach. This reinforces the impression that it may be very hard and even impossible to find criteria for intertemporal evaluation that can fulfill all sensible requirements at the same time.

Yet, for reasons that lie completely outside the scope of social choice theory, the severity of conflicts between the different normative postulates that are guiding the assessment of economic development may decline over time. In the case of global warming, the distributional conflict between generations is somewhat defused since, through "green" technological progress, abatement of greenhouse gases has become much cheaper. So, in particular, the costs of solar and wind energy have fallen dramatically in the past few decades, which has made more ambitious mitigation policies more viable (e.g., Buchholz *et al.*, 2019). This means that it has now become easier to reconcile Postulate 1 on the one hand with Postulates 2 and 3 on the other. This might give some hope for a more successful climate policy in the future (Chichilnisky *et al.*, 2020).

Acknowledgments

Previous versions of this paper have been presented at workshops at the TU Bergakademie Freiberg and at the PET conference in Strasbourg in July 2019. We thank the participants of these events for their helpful comments and suggestions. Special thanks to Anja Brumme and Theresa Stahlke for their technical assistance.

References

Adler, M. (2012). *Well-being and Fair Distribution — Beyond Cost-benefit Analysis*, Oxford University Press, Oxford and New York.

Adler, M. and Treich, N. (2015). Prioritarianism and climate change. *Environmental and Resource Economics*, 6, 279–308.

Arrow, K. J. (1999a). Discounting, morality, and gaming, in Portney, P. R. and Weyant, J. P. (eds), *Discounting and Intergenerational Equity*, Resources for the Future, Washington, DC, 14–21.

Arrow, K. J. (1999b). Intergenerational equity and the rate of discount in long-term social investment, in Sertel, M. R. (ed), *Contemporary Economic Issues. International Economic Association Series*, Palgrave Macmillan, London, 89–102.

Asheim, G. B. (2003). The malleability of undiscounted utilitarianism as a criterion of intergenerational justice. *Economica*, 70, 405–422.

Asheim, G. B. (2017). Sustainable growth. *Social Choice and Welfare*, 49, 825–848.

Asheim, G. B. and Mitra, T. (2010). Sustainability and discounted utilitarianism in models of economic growth. *Mathematical Social Sciences*, 59, 148–169.

Asheim, G. B., Buchholz, W., and Tungodden, B. (2001). Justifying sustainability. *Journal of Environmental Economics and Management*, 41, 252–268.

Atkinson, A. (1970). On the measurement of inequality. *Journal of Economic Theory*, 2, 244–263.

Broome, J. (2012). *Climate Matters: Ethics in a Warming World*, W.W. Norton, New York.

Buchholz, W. (2003). Balancing the interests of the present and the future, in Böhringer, C. and Löschel, A. (eds), *Empirical Modelling of the Economy and the Environment. ZEW Economic Studies Vol.* 20, Physica, Heidelberg, 315–326.

Buchholz, W. and Schumacher, J. (2010). Discounting and welfare analysis over time: Choosing the η. *European Journal of Political Economy*, 26, 372–385.

Buchholz, W., Dippl, L., and Eichenseer, M. (2019). Subsidizing renewables as part of taking leadership in international climate policy: The case of Germany. *Energy Policy*, 129(C), 765–773.

Chichilnisky, H., Hammond, P., and Stern, N. (2020). Fundamental discounting and intergenerational equity with extinction discounting. *Social Choice and Welfare*, 54, 397–424.

Cowen, T. (2018). *Stubborn Attachments: A Vision for Society of Free, Prosperous and Responsible Individuals*, Stripe Press, San Francisco.

Dasgupta, P. (2008). Discounting climate change. *Journal of Risk and Uncertainty*, 37, 141–169.

Fleurbaey, M. (2008). *Fairness, Reciprocity, and Welfare*, Oxford University Press, Oxford and New York.

Greaves, H. (2017). Discounting for public policy: A survey. *Economics and Philosophy*, 33, 1–49.

Hepburn, C. (2006). 'Discounting climate change damages: Working note for the Stern Report', *Working Note*, University of Oxford.

Hepburn, C. (2007). Valuing the far-off future: Discounting and its alternatives, in Atkinson, G. and Dietz, S. (eds), *Handbook of Sustainable Development*, Chapter 7, Edward Elgar.

Kamaga, K. (2020). *Social Welfare Evaluation and Intergenerational Equity*, SpringerBriefs in Economics, Development Bank of Japan Research Series, Springer Nature, Singapore.

Kant, I. (1784). Idee zu einer allgemeinen Geschichte in weltbürgerlicher Absicht. *Berlinische Monatsschriften* IV, 385–411.

Kaplow, L. (2010). Concavity of utility, concavity of welfare, and redistribution of income. *International Tax and Public Finance*, 17, 25–42.

Kelleher, P. J. (2017). Pure time preference in intertemporal welfare economics. *Economics and Philosophy*, 33, 441–473.

Koopmans, T. (1960). Stationary ordinal utility and impatience. *Econometrica*, 28, 287–309.

Llavador, H., Roemer, J. E., and Silvestre, J. (2011). A dynamic analysis of human welfare in a warming planet. *Journal of Public Economics*, 95, 1607–1620.

Llavador, H., Roemer, J. E., and Silvestre, J. (2015). *Sustainability for a Warming Planet*, Harvard University Press, Cambridge, MA.

Pigou, A. C. (1920). *The Economics of Welfare*, Macmillan and Co., London, England.

Ramsey, F. P. (1928). A mathematical theory of saving. *Economic Journal*, 38, 543–559.

Rawls, J. (1971). *A Theory of Justice*, Harvard University Press, Cambridge, MA.

Roemer, J. E. (2011). The ethics of intertemporal distribution in a warming planet. *Environmental and Resource Economics*, 48, 363–390.

Roemer, J. E. (2019). Utilitarianism, the discounting of future welfare levels, and sustainability, in Gardiner, S. (ed), *The Oxford Handbook of Intergenerational Ethics*, Oxford University Press, Oxford and New York.

Schelling, T. (1995). Intergenerational discounting. *Energy Economics*, 23, 395–401.

Sidgwick, H. (1907). *The Methods of Ethics*, Macmillan, London.

Stern, N. (2007). *The Stern Review on the Economics of Climate Change*, Cambridge University Press, Cambridge, UK.

Stern, N. (2015). *Why Are We Waiting? The Logic, Urgency, and Promise of Tackling Climate Change*, The MIT Press, Cambridge, MA and London, UK.

Zuber, S. and Asheim, G. B. (2012). Justifying social discounting: the rank discounted utilitarian approach. *Journal of Economic Theory*, 147, 1572–1601.

https://doi.org/10.1142/9789811240553_0003

Chapter 3

Climate and Development: The Role of the Sustainable Development Goals

Edward B. Barbier* **and Joanne C. Burgess**

Department of Economics, Colorado State University, Fort Collins, CO 80523-1771, USA
**edward.barbier@colostate.edu*

This chapter explores climate-related trade-offs and synergies in meeting development objectives, as reflected by the 17 Sustainable Development Goals (SDGs). Using Climate Action (SDG 13) as our benchmark indicator, we estimate the per capita welfare change associated with achieving this goal net of any gains or losses in attaining the other SDGs. We conduct this analysis for the world and for low income countries. Globally, the loss from the rise in CO_2 per capita over 2000–2016 amounts to \$311 per person. But, as indicators for eleven other SDGs improved, there was an overall net gain of \$12,737 per capita. For low-income countries, CO_2 emissions declined over 2000–2016 with an estimated benefit of \$31 per person. However, once positive and negative interactions with other SDGs are taken into account, the net welfare gain in poor economies is only \$244 per person. This chapter also examines the implications of our SDG analysis for climate and development objectives beyond 2030. Current trends suggest that increased growth in per capita incomes in low- and middle-income countries has been accompanied by increasing emissions and worsening future climate scenarios, which may seriously undermine other development goals. Addressing this trade-off is critical over the coming decades.

1. Introduction

In 2015, the General Assembly of the United Nations (UN) formally adopted "The 2030 Agenda for Sustainable Development." This provides a framework for "peace and prosperity for people and the planet, now and into the future" (United Nations, 2015). The centerpiece of Agenda 2030 involves the 17 Sustainable Development Goals (SDGs). As emphasized by Sachs (2012, p. 2206), the SDGs "aim for a combination of economic development, environmental sustainability, and social inclusion." Attaining the SDGs can be viewed as sustainable development in its broadest sense, that is, achieving progress across economic, social, and environmental systems simultaneously (Barbier, 1987, Barbier and Burgess, 2019).

The various SDGs are interlinked and integrated by design. To ensure sustainable development, countries need to make progress on all of the 17 goals simultaneously and to take account of possible trade-offs and synergies across the different goals (Sachs *et al.*, 2019, United Nations, 2015, 2019). It is important to determine whether progress toward achieving one goal will come at the sacrifice or improvement of other goals (Barbier and Burgess, 2019, Costanza *et al.*, 2016, Gupta and Vegelin, 2016, Moyer and Hedden, 2020, Sachs, 2012). For example, we may have reduced poverty or hunger over recent years, but the way in which this progress has been achieved — e.g., through economic expansion and industrial growth — may have come at the cost of attaining some environmental or social goals, such as action on climate. Similarly, action on climate may benefit goals such as good jobs and economic growth, and life on land and below sea, but constrain other goals such as responsible consumption and production.

Analyzing progress toward the various SDGs while accounting for the trade-offs and synergies between climate and development objectives is especially important. For example, von Stechow *et al.* (2016) maintain that sustainable development considerations are central for choosing socially acceptable pathways for limiting global warming to 2°C. It is critical that such pathways ensure that other SDGs are met through appropriate climate policy. Thus, the authors argue that progress on the climate policy and SDG agendas should be tracked within a unified framework.

Developing such a framework for analyzing progress toward both SDG 13 Climate Action and the other 16 SDGs has become more essential since the COVID-19 pandemic. Although global carbon dioxide (CO_2) emissions have fallen sharply during the pandemic, the trend in recent years has been rising emissions as growth in energy use from fossil fuel sources outpaced the rise of low-carbon sources and activities, especially in developing countries (Peters *et al.*, 2020). The pandemic could further undermine progress toward SDG 13, by reducing the commitment to global climate action (United Nations, 2020).

This chapter develops one unified framework for exploring how progress toward climate action yields trade-offs and complementarities with other SDGs. In order to do this, we utilize a methodological approach developed by Barbier and Burgess (2019) to estimate the welfare effects of progress in attaining one SDG while accounting for interactions in achieving other SDGs. We use Climate Action (SDG 13) as our benchmark indicator, and we estimate the per capita welfare change of achieving this goal net of any gains or losses in attaining the other SDGs. We conduct this analysis for the world and for low-income countries. This framework allows us to explicitly examine the net gains and losses for key trade-offs as well as important synergies, or "win-wins," among progress on Climate Action and other SDGs. By applying our analysis globally and for low income countries, we are able to see if there are significant differences in attaining SDG 13 and other sustainable development goals for poor economies as compared to the world as a whole. Such a framework can make a significant contribution to assessing possible trade-offs and synergies in achieving the Climate Action and the other 16 SDGs, which is essential for evaluating progress toward the UN's 2030 sustainability agenda (Nilsson *et al.*, 2016, United Nations, 2019, 2020, von Stechow *et al.*, 2016).

This chapter also examines the implications of our SDG analysis for climate and development objectives beyond 2030. For example, current global trends suggest that it is unlikely that the SDG 1 objective of ending extreme poverty will be attained by 2030 (Moyer and Hedden, 2020, United Nations, 2019). Equally, global greenhouse gas (GHG) emissions have been increasing, not declining, in recent years (Peters *et al.*, 2020). These trends indicate that the principle means for alleviating poverty in most of the world has been to increase growth in per capita incomes in low- and middle-income countries, but this has been accompanied by increasing emissions and worsening future climate scenarios. This implies that in the future there could be an even greater conflict between attaining SDG 1 and ensuring that SDG 13 Action on Climate and other environmental SDGs are met. Clearly, addressing this trade-off in coming decades is critical for global economic development to be sustainable.

2. Progress in Attaining the Sustainable Development Goals

Assessing progress in attaining the SDGs is challenging, in part because of data constraints. First, there is no single universally accepted data source representing each of the 17 SDGs. In addition, these goals comprise 169 different targets and 231 possible indicators to choose from United Nations (2015). Although such a proliferation of indicators suggests that it might be relatively easy to choose one or more representative indicators for each goal, their usefulness is limited by poor data quality and coverage over countries and sufficient years (Dang and Serajuddin, 2020, United Nations, 2019).

Table 1 depicts the 17 SDGs of Agenda 2030 along with our choice of representative indicator over the period from 2000 to 2016. Although the SDGs were only ratified in 2015, it is standard in the literature to analyze the SDG indicators from the year 2000 onward. First, many of the SDGs evolved from the previous Millennium Development Goals for which data series were collected, and the United Nations Statistical Database for the SDG indicators provides data starting at the year 2000.[1] Furthermore, other studies examining the SDGs typically start their analyses in the year 2000, see, for example, Moyer and Hedden (2020), Sachs (2012), and Dang and Serajuddin (2020).

---

[1] https://unstats.un.org/sdgs/indicators/database/.

Table 1. The 17 sustainable development goals.

Goal[a]	Indicator[b]
1. No Poverty	Poverty headcount ratio at $1.90 a day (2011 PPP) (% of population)
2. Zero Hunger	Prevalence of undernourishment (% of population)
3. Good Health and Well Being	Births attended by skilled health staff (% of total)
4. Quality Education	Adolescents out of school (% of lower secondary school age)
5. Gender Equality	Proportion of seats held by women in national parliament (%)
6. Clean Water and Sanitation	People using at least basic drinking water services (% of population)
7. Affordable and Clean Energy	Access to clean fuels and technologies for cooking (% of population)
8. Good Jobs and Economic Growth	Adjusted net national income per capita (annual % growth)
9. Industry, Innovation and Infrastructure	Manufacturing, value added (% of GDP)
10. Reduced Inequalities	GINI Index (World Bank estimates)
11. Sustainable Cities and Communities	PM2.5 air population, population exposed to levels exceeding WHO guideline value (% of total)
12. Responsible Consumption and Production	Adjusted net savings: excluding particulate emissions damage (% of GNI)
13. Climate Action	CO_2 emissions (metric tons per capita)
14. Life Below Water	Total fisheries production (10^6 metric tons)
15. Life on Land	Forest area (10^6 km^2)
16. Peace, Justice and Strong Institutions	Completeness of birth registration (%)
17. Partnerships for the Goals	Debt service to exports (%)

Notes: [a]United Nations (2015).
[b]World Bank, *World Development Indicators*. Available at http://databank.worldbank.org/data/.

As far as possible, we have chosen the primary indicator listed by the United Nations (2015) for each goal. For example, for Goal 1, No Poverty, Target 1.1 is to eradicate extreme poverty for all people everywhere by 2030 (UN, 2017). The primary indicator for Target 1.1 is the "proportion of population below the international poverty line, by sex, age, employment status and geographical location (urban/rural)," which is listed as Indicator 1.1.1 (UN, 2017). Our representative indicator is the "Poverty headcount ratio at $1.90 a day (2011 PPP) (% of population)," which is the current UN international poverty line (United Nations, 2019). In other cases, such as Goal 13 Climate Action, there is insufficient data on the indicators for the first target listed, which is to "strengthen resilience and adaptive capacity to climate-related hazards and natural disasters in all countries" (Target 13.1) (UN, 2017). We therefore employ an alternative indicator, CO_2 emissions (metric tons per capita), for which a more comprehensive and complete data series is available.

The data for each of our representative SDG indicators are taken from the World Bank's World Development Indicators, which provide a relatively complete and reliable set of data at the country level for our chosen indicators over the period from 2000 to 2016. Data beyond 2016 were either extremely limited or not available. The data were selected to ensure adequate coverage both globally and for the special case of low-income countries, which consist of a subset of global countries with an income per capita of $1,005 or less in 2017.[2] Providing a focus on the most vulnerable countries, in comparison to all economies in the world, is of particular concern for the international development community.

Using the representative indicator for each goal depicted in Table 1, it is possible to conduct a quantitative assessment of current progress over 2000–2016 for each of the 17 SDGs. This assessment is applied to all countries of the world and to low-income countries, which are economies in which the 2017 per capita income was $1,005 or

[2]The World Bank lists 31 low-income economies, defined as those with a GNI per capita, calculated using the World Bank Atlas method, of $1,005 or less in 2017. https://datahelpdesk.worldbank.org/knowledgebase/articles/906519-world-bank-country-and-lending-groups.

less. We estimate both actual changes in value in the original units of each indicator from 2000 to 2016, and also the percentage change in these values over this period, using averages derived at the world and low-income country level. Based on the latter change, we then assess whether the representative indicator for each of the 17 SDGs has been improving or declining over 2000 to 2016. Table 2 depicts the results of this analysis for the world.

The benchmark indicator in our analysis is SDG 13 Climate Action, which is represented by per capita CO_2 emissions. Table 2 indicates that, for the world between 2000 and 2014, these emissions increased by 4.7%, which suggests that global progress toward this goal has been declining over this period.

Table 2 shows that eleven other SDG indicators did improve over 2000–2016 for the world, i.e., the indicators for SDG 1 No Poverty, SDG 2 Zero Hunger, SDG 3 Good Health and Well Being, SDG 4 Quality Education, SDG 5 Gender Equality, SDG 6 Clean Water and Sanitation, SDG 7 Affordable and Clean Energy, SDG 10 Reduced Inequalities, SDG 11 Sustainable Cities and Communities, SDG 12 Responsible Consumption and Production, and SDG 17 Partnerships for the Goals. However, five SDG indicators also declined, i.e., for SDG 8 Good Jobs and Economic Growth, for SDG 9 Industry, Innovation and Infrastructure, SDG 14 Life Below Water, SDG 15 Life on Land, and SDG 16 Peace, Justice and Strong Institutions.

Table 3 summarizes the analysis of the SDGs over 2000–2016 for low-income countries. For these poor economies, per capita CO_2 emissions declined by 6.9% from 2000–2014. Thus, progress by low-income countries toward SDG 13 Climate Action has occurred over this period. Table 3 also shows that poor economies achieved a similar pattern of improvement and decline in other SDG indicators over 2000–2016 as the world did, with two exceptions. For low-income countries, the indicators for SDG 11 Sustainable Cities and Communities and SDG 12 Responsible Consumption and Production declined from 2000 to 2016.

In sum, our quantitative assessment of changes in representative SDG indicators from 2000–2016 identifies a number of possible trade-offs and synergies in attaining climate and development objectives. The most interesting finding is that, for the world, there

Table 2. SDG indicators, world, 2000–2016.

SDG Indicator	Actual Value 2000	Actual Value 2016	2000–2016 % Change	2000–2016 Outcome
1. Poverty headcount ratio at $1.90 a day (2011 PPP) (% of population)	20.8	3.0	−85.5	Improving
2. Prevalence of undernourishment (% of population)[a]	15.8	11.2	−29.2	Improving
3. Births attended by skilled health staff (% of total)[b]	80.9	86.1	6.4	Improving
4. Adolescents out of school (% of lower secondary school age)	16.2	11.6	−28.5	Improving
5. Proportion of seats held by women in national parliament (%)	11.7	20.8	77.0	Improving
6. People using at least basic drinking water services (% of population)[a]	81.7	87.4	7.0	Improving
7. Access to clean fuels and technologies for cooking (% of population)[b]	55.8	65.0	16.5	Improving
8. Adjusted net national income per capita (annual % growth)[b]	1.7	0.8	−52.0	Declining
9. Manufacturing, value added (% of GDP)	13.0	11.4	−11.8	Declining
10. GINI Index (World Bank estimates)[a]	43.8	36.3	−17.2	Improving
11. PM2.5 air population, population exposed to levels exceeding WHO guideline value (% of total)[b]	91.1	89.3	−1.9	Improving
12. Adjusted net savings: excluding particulate emissions damage (% of GNI)[b]	6.9	7.6	10.8	Improving
13. CO_2 emissions (metric tons per capita)[b]	4.7	5.0	4.7	Declining
14. Total fisheries production (10^6 metric tons)	136.5	199.7	49.1	Declining
15. Forest area (10^6 km^2)[a]	40.6	40.0	−1.4	Declining
16. Completeness of birth registration (%)	73.8	67.1	−9.1	Declining
17. Debt service to exports (%)[a]	12.1	7.3	−40.1	Improving

Notes: [a]2015; [b]2014.

Source: World Bank, *World Development Indicators*. Available at http://databank.worldbank.org/data/.

Table 3. SDG indicators, low-income countries, 2000–2016.

	Actual Value		2000–2016	
SDG Indicator	2000	2016	% Change	Outcome
1. Poverty headcount ratio at $1.90 a day (2011 PPP) (% of population)	81.3	28.1	−65.4	Improving
2. Prevalence of undernourishment (% of population)[a]	34.0	27.7	−18.6	Improving
3. Births attended by skilled health staff (% of total)[b]	38.3	61.5	60.8	Improving
4. Adolescents out of school (% of lower secondary school age)	45.9	37.3	−18.9	Improving
5. Proportion of seats held by women in national parliament (%)	10.3	20.3	96.9	Improving
6. People using at least basic drinking water services (% of population)[a]	49.9	61.3	22.7	Improving
7. Access to clean fuels and technologies for cooking (% of population)[b]	9.4	13.7	44.8	Improving
8. Adjusted net national income per capita (annual % growth)[b]	−0.3	−0.8	−146.7	Declining
9. Manufacturing, value added (% of GDP)	8.9	8.2	−7.0	Declining
10. GINI Index (World Bank estimates)[a]	42.9	40.0	−6.8	Improving
11. PM2.5 air population, population exposed to levels exceeding WHO guideline value (% of total)[b]	99.1	100.0	0.9	Declining
12. Adjusted net savings: excluding particulate emissions damage (% of GNI)[b]	−0.3	−5.6	−1894.9	Declining
13. CO_2 emissions (metric tons per capita)[b]	0.4	0.3	−6.8	Improving
14. Total fisheries production (10^6 metric tons)	2.9	4.1	46.5	Declining
15. Forest area (10^6 km^2)[a]	4.0	3.8	−6.3	Declining
16. Completeness of birth registration (%)	93.3	32.1	−65.6	Declining
17. Debt service to exports (%)[a]	15.4	6.4	−58.5	Improving

Notes: [a]2015; [b]2014. Low-income countries are economies in which 2017 per capita income was $1,005 or less.
Source: World Bank, *World Development Indicators.* Available at http://databank.worldbank.org/data/.

has been a setback since 2000 in achieving SDG 13 Climate Action, whereas for low-income countries there has been some progress.

It also appears that progress has occurred simultaneously toward goals that are largely associated with "economic" or "social" aims (e.g., SDGs 1–7, 10, and 17), whereas there has been less success in attaining other "environmental" goals (e.g., SDGs 11, 12, 14, and 15). Based on the declines in the indicators for SDG 8 and SDG 10, and in SDG 12 for low-income countries, there should also be concern about the "sustainability" of some of the economic progress that has occurred from 2000 to 2016. For instance, some SDG indicators have declined significantly for low-income countries (e.g., SDGs 8, 12, 16, 14, 9, 15, and 11) compared to all countries in the world (see Tables 2 and 3). This suggests that the modest progress over 2000–2016 in achieving SDG 13 as well as other important SDGs in poor economies may have come at significant trade-offs for attaining other goals that are essential to the sustainability of these economies.

3. Welfare Effects

In addition to identifying possible trade-offs and synergies in attaining the different SDGs and quantifying the magnitude of these changes, it is also useful to estimate the welfare implications of these changes. A standard method in economics for addressing such a welfare effect is to estimate the "willingness to pay" (WTP) by a representative individual for an improvement in one SDG indicator, taking into account possible simultaneous changes — positive or negative — in other SDG indicators. For example, Barbier and Burgess (2019) show that the basic methodology to analyze choice and welfare under imposed quantities (Freeman, 2003, Lankford, 1988) can be adapted to measure the welfare effects of an increase in one SDG that reflects any interactions with any other SDG. Such an approach uses the compensating surplus measure of the welfare gain (or loss) associated with changes in the various SDG indicators.

Here, the methodological framework for the welfare analysis developed by Barbier and Burgess (2019) is applied to the quantitative assessment of the net changes in SDG indicators over 2000 to 2016 presented in Tables 2 and 3, for the world and low-income countries, respectively. We outline briefly the approach and then discuss the results. Full details of the methodology can be found in Barbier and Burgess (2019).

In this analysis, we derive an estimate of the "willingness to pay" for an improvement in a benchmark SDG, while taking into account any negative and positive changes in other SDG indicators. We use Climate Action (SDG 13) as our benchmark indicator. We estimate the change in per capita welfare over 2000–2016 toward this goal net of any gains or losses in attaining each of the remaining 16 goals. We conduct this analysis for the world and for low-income countries. Following Barbier and Burgess (2019), we choose the world's adjusted net national income (ANNI) per capita in 2000 as the proxy for the income necessary to compensate the average individual in the global economy for a change in the indicator level of any SDG. Using the world's ANNI per capita in 2000 as our numeraire allows us to assume that an individual would be willing to pay \$1 of this sustainable income for a 1% improvement in each SDG indicator for the Climate Action goal from 2000 to 2016. Equally, if an SDG indicator declines from 2000 to 2016, then the individual would accept an additional \$1 ANNI to compensate for the trade off of a 1% loss in this indicator.

Table 4 depicts the results of this analysis applied at the world level. The first row shows that, in the absence of trade-offs or complementarities with attaining any other SDG, the compensation for the rise in per capita CO_2 emissions that occurred globally over 2000 to 2014 amounts to \$311 per person. However, over the 2000–2016 period, indicators for eleven other SDGs improved. Our analysis shows that the WTP for the total gains from these additional improvements amounts to an additional \$15,564 per capita. But, over this same period, the indicators for five other SDGs declined, and the welfare estimate of these total losses is \$8,188. Thus, for the world, we estimate the per capita welfare change of all these climate and development interactions over 2000–2016 is a net gain of \$12,737 per capita. This is almost double the value of the numeraire level of income, real adjusted net national income per capita, which was \$6,635 in 2000. Despite the loss in welfare due to failure to make progress on SDG 13 Climate Action, the world appears to have experienced an overall net welfare gain through its progress toward most SDGs over 2000 to 2016.

Table 4. Welfare analysis of climate and development SDG interactions, world, 2000–2016.

Sustainable Development Goal	Change (%) in Indicator 2000–2016	WTP ($) per capita
13. Climate Action	−4.7	−311
Gains in other SDGs		
1. No Poverty	85.5	5,671
5. Gender Equality	77.0	5,111
17. Partnership for the Goals	40.1	2,661
2. Zero Hunger	29.2	1,935
4. Quality Education	28.5	1,890
10. Reduced Inequalities	17.2	1,141
7. Affordable and Clean Energy	16.5	1,095
12. Responsible Consumption and Production	10.8	716
6. Clean Water and Sanitation	7.0	462
3. Good Health and Well Being	6.4	426
11. Sustainable Cities and Communities	1.9	127
Total Gains	320.1	21,326
Losses in other SDGs		
8. Good Jobs and Economic Growth	−52.0	−3,453
14. Life Below Water	−49.1	−3,258
9. Industry, Innovation and Infrastructure	−11.8	−780
16. Peace, Justice and Strong Institutions	−9.1	−604
15. Life on Land	−1.4	−93
Total Losses	−123.4	−8,188
Net Welfare Change	192.0	12,737

Notes: WTP = Willingness to pay.
Numeraire: Adjusted net national income per capita (constant 2010 US$), 2000 $6,635.
Adjusted net national income is gross national income (GNI) minus consumption of fixed capital and net depletion of natural resources, from World Development Indicators. Available at http://databank.worldbank.org/data/.

Table 5 shows the results of our welfare analysis for low-income countries. The willingness to pay for the reduction in per capita CO_2 emission that occurred over 2000–2014 in these poor economies is estimated to be $31 per person. This benefit is complemented by

Table 5. Welfare analysis of SDG climate and development interactions, low-income countries, 2000–2016.

Sustainable Development Goal	Change (%) in Indicator 2000–2016	WTP ($) per capita
13. Climate Action	6.8	31
Gains in other SDGs		
1. No Poverty	65.4	299
5. Gender Equality	96.9	442
3. Good Health and Well Being	60.8	277
17. Partnership for the Goals	58.5	267
7. Affordable and Clean Energy	44.8	204
6. Clean Water and Sanitation	22.7	104
4. Quality Education	18.9	86
2. Zero Hunger	18.6	85
10. Reduced Inequalities	6.8	31
Total Gains	393.4	1,795
Losses in other SDGs		
8. Good Jobs and Economic Growth	−146.7	−669
12. Responsible Consumption and Production	−73.7	−336
16. Peace, Justice and Strong Institutions	−65.6	−299
14. Life Below Water	−46.5	−32
9. Industry, Innovation and Infrastructure	−7.0	−780
15. Life on Land	−6.3	−29
11. Sustainable Cities and Communities	−0.9	−4
Total Losses	−346.7	−1,582
Net Welfare Change	53.5	244

Notes: WTP = Willingness to pay.
Numeraire: Adjusted net national income per capita (constant 2010 US$), 2000 $456.
Adjusted net national income is gross national income (GNI) minus consumption of fixed capital and net depletion of natural resources, from World Development Indicators. Available at http://databank.worldbank.org/data/. Low-income countries are economies in which 2017 per capita income was $1,005 or less.

improving indicators for nine other SDGs, which leads to total welfare gains of an additional $1,582 per person. However, the latter gains are more than canceled out by the welfare losses associated with the decline in seven SDG indicators for low-income countries over

2000–2016, which amounts to \$1,582 per person. Overall, once these interactions are taken into account, the net welfare change for climate and development interactions in poor economies from 2000 to 2016 is \$244 per person. This is considerably lower than the net welfare gain at the global level (see Table 4) and nearly half of the numeraire level of income, real adjusted net national income per capita, which was \$456. Despite the modest progress toward SDG 13 Climate Action, it appears that over 2000 to 2016 low-income countries have experienced an overall net welfare loss in achieving most SDGs.

In sum, our welfare analysis reveals a disturbing trend in progress toward climate and development actions since 2000. Whereas the world appears to have experienced a significant net welfare gain overall, even after taking account of compensation for the rise in per capita CO_2 emissions, the lack of progress in achieving many SDGs in poor economies means that they have experienced a net per capita welfare loss. This is despite the fact that, compared to the world at large, low-income countries attained some gains toward SDG 13 Climate Action.

4. Toward 2030 and Beyond

The climate and development trade-offs identified in our analysis are worrisome for the coming decades, especially given recent trends. Although global CO_2 emissions have fallen sharply during the COVID-19 pandemic, they have risen by 1% annually over the past decade as growth in energy use from fossil fuels outpaced the rise of low-carbon sources and activities (Peters *et al.*, 2020). The decline in emissions during COVID-19 has resulted mainly from a slowdown in the global economy, rather than from a decoupling of economic growth from carbon emissions. The main factor is the growth in fossil fuel CO_2 emissions in China, India, and most low- and middle-income countries, which have dominated global emission trends over the past 20 years (Peters *et al.*, 2020).

Consequently, the 2020 fall in global CO_2 emissions of around 2–7% over 2019 levels is likely to be temporary, as the world economy recovers (Le Quéré *et al.*, 2020). There is also concern that the pandemic will further undermine the commitment to global action on climate, biodiversity, and other environmental issues (United Nations, 2020). Evidence is emerging that the crisis has led to weakening of environmental and climate regulations and their enforcement worldwide, with consequences for CO_2 emissions in the near term and even the long run (Helm, 2020).

Given these recent trends, it appears that the predictions of the UN's 2019 *Emissions Gap Report* are still relevant (United Nations Environment Program, 2019). Even if countries meet commitments made under the 2015 Paris Agreement, the world is heading for a 3.2°C global temperature rise over pre-industrial levels, which would lead to wide-ranging and destructive climate impacts in the coming decades. Instead, global emissions need to fall by 7.6% each year over the next decade, if the world is to get back on track toward the goal of limiting temperature rises to close to 1.5°C (United Nations Environment Program, 2019).

At the same time, the growing global financial burden of the world economic downturn and the financial commitments made during the pandemic will impact strategies for attaining sustainability and development objectives during the post COVID recovery. In the aftermath of the pandemic, it will be difficult for the international community to mobilize "maximum financial and technical support for the poorest and most vulnerable people and countries hardest hit," as urged by the United Nations (2020, p. 1). This will especially be the case for any additional support for low-income countries to spur greater progress toward the SDGs by 2030 as well as assist them in mitigating climate emissions.

The impact of COVID-19 could further undermine progress toward the SDGs by 2030, especially in poor economies (United Nations, 2020). This will occur at a critical juncture for some of the SDGs. The United Nations (2019) *Sustainable Development Goals Report* acknowledges, with 736 million people living in extreme poverty in 2015, the world is not on track to end poverty by 2030. There were 821 million undernourished people in 2017, up from 784 million in 2015. Around 785 million people lack even basic drinking water services, and 673 million still practice open defecation. About

3 billion people lack clean cooking fuels and technology, and of the 840 million people without electricity, 87% live in rural areas. Projections suggest that 28 poor countries will not achieve any of the nine human development-related target values associated with SDGs 1–4, 6, and 7 (Moyer and Hedden, 2020). And, as the analysis of this chapter has shown, progress to date in achieving the SDGs is largely associated with "economic" or "social" aims (e.g., SDGs 1–7, 10, and 17), whereas there has been less success in attaining other "environmental" goals (e.g., SDGs 11–15).

There are two areas for urgent progress toward achieving both climate and development objectives toward 2030 and beyond.

First, all countries must follow up their Nationally Determined Contributions (NDCs) pledged under the Paris Climate Change Agreement with policy commitments and actual carbon abatement implementation. As Roelfsema *et al.* (2020) show, if the Paris Agreement NDCs were fully implemented, the gap between current policies and the Paris goals would be reduced by as much as a third. But, more importantly, there must be global action at the next UN Climate Conference of the Parties (COP 26) for all countries to significantly step up their climate commitments as well as assistance to low-income countries to make sure that the aim of limiting temperature rises to 1.5°C is still feasible.

Second, in the absence of additional financial support, it is critical that developing countries find innovative policy mechanisms to simultaneously achieve climate and development aims in a cost-effective manner. This requires identifying affordable policies that can yield immediate progress toward several SDGs together, rather than sacrificing some goals to achieve others, and aligns economic incentives for longer-term sustainable development. For example, Barbier and Burgess (2020) suggest two policies that meet these criteria with respect to climate and development objectives: (i) a fossil fuel subsidy swap to fund clean energy investments and dissemination of renewable energy in rural areas; and (ii) a tropical carbon tax, which is a levy on fossil fuels that funds natural climate solutions. Such innovative and cost-effective policy mechanisms do not require substantial external support, and they foster greater progress toward achieving the SDGs in poorer economies.

A "subsidy swap" for fossil fuels reallocates the savings from subsidy reform for coal, oil, and natural gas consumption to fund clean energy investments (International Institute for Sustainable Development, 2019a). In 2018, fossil fuel consumption subsidies reached $427 billion annually, of which nearly $360 billion were in developing countries.[3] International Institute for Sustainable Development (2019a) maintains that a 10–30% subsidy swap from fossil fuel consumption to investments in energy efficiency and renewable energy electricity generation could substantially improve the transition to a low-carbon economy. Already, some progress along these lines has been made in India, Indonesia, Morocco, and Zambia. A study of 26 countries — 22 of which are low and middle income — found that the removal of fossil fuel subsidies on its own reduces greenhouse gas emissions by 6 percent on average for each country from 2018 until 2025 (International Institute for Sustainable Development, 2019b).

A fossil fuel subsidy swap should also be used to facilitate greater dissemination and adoption of renewable energy and improved energy efficiency technologies in rural areas. This is critical for reducing energy poverty across developing countries (Barbier, 2020, Casillas and Kammen, 2010, Pahle *et al.*, 2016, Rogelj *et al.*, 2013). Morocco, Kenya, and South Africa illustrate how other public policy approaches can also facilitate the adoption and deployment of renewable energy and improved energy efficiency technologies in rural areas (Barbier, 2020, Pahle *et al.*, 2016).

Using this policy to support energy efficiency and renewable energy in rural areas would also have important equity gains. In low- and middle-income economies, it is mainly wealthier, urban households that benefit from fossil fuel consumption subsidies, whereas it is rural households that increasingly comprise the extremely poor (Castañeda *et al.*, 2018). Across 20 developing countries, the poorest fifth of the

---

[3]From https://www.iea.org/topics/energy-subsidies. Accessed on May 8, 2020.

population received on average just 7% of the overall benefit of fossil fuel subsidies, whereas the richest fifth gained almost 43% (del Granado *et al.*, 2012).

Developing countries should also consider adopting a "tropical carbon tax" (Barbier and Burgess, 2020). This is a levy on fossil fuels that is invested in natural climate solutions (NCSs) aimed at conserving, restoring, and improving land management to protect biodiversity and ecosystem services. NCSs are a relatively inexpensive way of reducing tropical land use change, which is a major source of greenhouse gas emissions. For example, cost-effective tropical NCSs can mitigate 6,560 10^6 tonnes of CO_2e in the coming decades at less than \$100 per 10^3 tonnes of CO_2e, which is about one-quarter of emissions from all tropical countries (Griscom *et al.*, 2020). Costa Rica and Colombia have already adopted a tropical carbon tax strategy. If 12 other megadiverse countries roll out a policy similar to Colombia's, they could raise \$1.8 billion each year between them to invest in natural habitats that benefit the climate (Barbier *et al.*, 2020). A more ambitious policy of taxation and revenue allocation could yield nearly \$13 billion each year for natural climate solutions.

Moreover, such a strategy can be "pro-poor." Ecosystem services such as drinking water supply, food provision, and cultural services are estimated to contribute between 50% and 90% of income and subsistence among the rural poor and those who live in forests (Convention on Biological Diversity, 2019). Such services can make an important contribution to ending extreme poverty (SDG 1), achieving zero hunger (SDG 2), improving health (SDG 3), and meeting many of the other 14 SDGs.

Together, these policies can make an important contribution toward meeting immediate SDG objectives in low-income countries, such as boosting economic activity, job creation, poverty reduction, environmental improvement, and support of health care needs. Moreover, they do so in a cost-effective manner that raises rather than requires scarce financial resources. These policies also provide strategic support for the development of a solid framework of incentives for long-term sustainable development.

5. Conclusion

Climate action is one of the 17 Sustainable Development Goals (SDGs) included in the UN's Agenda 2030. As von Stechow *et al.* (2016) argue, progress on climate policy and SDG agendas should be tracked within a unified framework. Developing such a framework for analyzing progress toward both SDG 13 Climate Action and the other 16 SDGs is especially vital, given that the COVID-19 pandemic could be undermining progress and commitments to global climate action (United Nations, 2020).

This chapter develops one unified framework for exploring how progress toward climate action yields trade-offs and complementarities with other SDGs. We assess quantitatively progress in the SDGs over 2000–2016 at the global level and for low-income countries, using a representative indicator for each goal. Following the approach developed by Barbier and Burgess (2019), we then estimate the welfare changes for improvements in Climate Action (SDG 13) net of any welfare gains and losses in attaining each of the remaining 16 goals.

For the world, the per capita welfare change of these climate and development interactions over 2000–2016 is a net gain of $12,737 per capita. This is almost double the value of the numeraire level of income, real adjusted net national income per capita, which was $6,635 in 2000. Despite lack of progress in SDG 13 Climate Action, the world appears to have experienced an overall net welfare gain through its progress toward most SDGs over 2000 to 2016.

For low-income countries, the net welfare change for climate and development interactions in poor economies from 2000 to 2016 is $244 per person. This is considerably lower than the net welfare gain at the global level, and nearly half of the numeraire per capita income, which was $456 in 2000. Despite the modest progress toward SDG 13 Climate Action, it appears that over 2000 to 2016 low-income countries have experienced an overall net welfare loss in achieving most SDGs.

We note two additional concerns about these climate–development trade-offs. First, for both the world and low-income countries, most of declining indicators are associated with other "environmental" goals (e.g., SDGs 11, 12, 14, and 15). Second, there should also be concern about the "sustainability" of some of the economic progress that has occurred from 2000 to 2016, especially for low-income countries, which have experienced large declines over this period in indicators for SDG 8 Good Jobs and Economic Growth, SDG 12 Responsible Consumption and Production, SDG 16 Peace, Justice and Strong Institutions, and SDG 14 Life Below Water. The decline in these environmental goals may constrain or undermine progress in achieving improvements in other economic and social goals in the future (Costanza *et al.*, 2016, Gupta and Vegelin, 2016).

Consequently, our analysis suggests that progress toward important social and economic SDGs over 2000–2016 may have come at the expense of making our economies less sustainable, especially with respect to "environmental" goals, and certainly climate action at the global level. Lack of progress in attaining any one of these latter goals, and especially global climate action, may on its own be sufficient to constrain future progress toward all other SDGs goals. To ensure a sustainable future to 2030 and beyond, we strongly urge global action on climate that leads to a significant increase in climate commitments and assistance to low-income countries with the aim of limiting global warming to 1.5°C.

In addition, low-income countries should be a priority in policy efforts to improve global sustainability. As our analysis shows, the SDG indicators that improved for poor economies over 2000–2016 generally increased less than for the world. However, the declines in SDG indicators were substantially much larger for low-income countries, and the aggregate effect of the interactions across all SDGs was to lower the overall net benefits.

The current COVID-19 pandemic has led to a slowing down of the world economy. Looking to the future, the growing global financial burden of the world economic downturn will impact strategies and financial support for attaining sustainability and development objectives during the post-COVID recovery, particularly in the low-income countries (United Nations, 2020). The slowdown in the world economy has also led to a decline in global CO_2 emissions, but this is likely to be a temporary remission, and global CO_2 emissions are expected to revert to previous higher levels once the world economy recovers. Furthermore, the essential need to address COVID-19 may have undermined the commitment to global action on climate, biodiversity, and other environmental issues and resulted in a relaxation of environmental and climate regulations worldwide (United Nations, 2020). This could further undermine progress toward the SDGs by 2030, especially in poor economies (United Nations, 2020).

Thus, future international development policies should focus on the specific sustainability challenges faced by poor economies in implementing the 2030 sustainable development agenda. In addition, low-income countries must also develop their own innovative, workable, and cost-effective policies to secure multiple SDGs and achieve sustainable economic development. Here, we have recommended two such policies with respect to climate and development objectives: a fossil fuel subsidy swap to fund rural clean energy, and a tropical carbon tax to finance natural climate solutions. Such initiatives could achieve important environmental and climate objectives, as well as address equity concerns in a cost-effective manner that raises rather than requires scarce financial resources. Together, these policies can make an important contribution toward simultaneously meeting a number of SDG objectives in low-income countries, such as boosting economic activity, job creation, poverty reduction, environmental improvement, and support of health care needs. In this way, low-income countries can develop a solid framework of incentives for long-term sustainable development.

References

Barbier, E. B. (1987). The concept of sustainable economic development. *Environmental Conservation*, 14(2), 101–110.

Barbier, E. B. (2020). Is green rural transformation possible in developing countries? *World Development*, 131, 104955.

Barbier, E. B. and Burgess, J. C. (2019). Sustainable development goal indicators: Analyzing trade-offs and complementarities. *World Development*, 122, 295–305.

Barbier, E. B. and Burgess, J. C. (2020). Sustainability and development after COVID-19. *World Development*, 135, 105082.

Barbier, E. B., Lozano, R., Rodríguez, C. M., and Troëng, S. (2020). Adopt a carbon tax to protect tropical forests. *Nature*, 578.

Casillas, C. E. and Kammen, D. M. (2010). The energy-poverty-climate nexus. *Science*, 330(6008), 1181–1182.

Castañeda, A., Doan, D., Newhouse, D., Nguyen, M. C., Uematsu, H., and Azevedo, J. P. (2018). A new profile of the global poor. *World Development*, 101, 250–267.

Convention on Biological Diversity (CBD). (2019). *Biodiversity and the 2030 Agenda for Sustainable Development: Technical Note*. Secretariat of the Convention on Biological Diversity, Montreal, https://www.cbd.int/development/doc/biodiversity-2030-agenda-technical-note-en.pdf.

Costanza, R., Daly, L., Fioramonti, L., Giovannini, E., Kubiszewski, I., Mortensen, L. F., Pickett, K. E., Ragnarsdottir, K. V., De Vogli, R., and Wilkinson, R. (2016). Modelling and measuring sustainable wellbeing in connection with the UN Sustainable Development Goals. *Ecological Economics*, 130, 350–355.

Dang, H. A. H. and Serajuddin, U. (2020). Tracking the sustainable development goals: Emerging measurement challenges and further reflections. *World Development*, 127(C), 104570.

del Granado, F. J. A., Coady, D., and Gillingham, R. (2012). The unequal benefits of fuel subsidies: A review of evidence for developing countries. *World Development*, 40(11), 2234–2248.

Freeman, A. M. III. (2003). *The Measurement of Environmental Values: Theory and Methods*, 2nd ed. Resources for the Future, Washington, D.C.

Griscom, B. W., Busch, J., Cook-Patton, S. C., Ellis, P. W., Funk, J., Leavitt, S. M., Lomax, G., Turner, W. R., Chapman, M., Engelmann, J., and Gurwick, N. P. (2020). National mitigation potential from natural climate solutions in the tropics. *Philosophical Transactions of the Royal Society B*, 375(1794), 20190126.

Gupta, J. and Vegelin, C. (2016). Sustainable development goals and inclusive development. *International Environmental Agreements: Politics, Law and Economics*, 16(3), 433–448.

Helm, D. (2020). The environmental impacts of the coronavirus. *Environmental and Resource Economics*, 76, 21–38, https://doi.org/10.1007/s10640-020-00426-z.

International Institute for Sustainable Development (IISD). (2019a). *Fossil Fuel to Clean Energy Subsidy Swaps: How to Pay for and Energy Revolution*, IISD, Winnipeg, Canada.

International Institute for Sustainable Development (IISD). (2019b). Raising Ambition Through Fossil Fuel Subsidy Reform: Greenhouse Gas Emissions Modelling Results from 26 Countries. IISD, Winnipeg, Canada.

Lankford, R. H. (1988). Measuring welfare changes in settings with imposed quantities. *Journal of Environmental Economics and Management*, 15(1), 45–63.

Le Quéré, C., Jackson, R. B., Jones, M. W., Smith, A. J., Abernethy, S., Andrew, R. M., De-Gol, A. J., Willis, D. R., Shan, Y., Canadell, J. G., and Friedlingstein, P. (2020). Temporary reduction in daily global CO_2 emissions during the COVID-19 forced confinement. *Nature Climate Change*, 10(7), 1–7.

Moyer, J. D. and Hedden, S. (2020). Are we on the right path to achieve the sustainable development goals? *World Development*, 127, 104749.

Nilsson, M., Griggs, D., and Visbeck, M. (2016). Policy: Map the interactions between sustainable development goals. *Nature*, 534(7607), 320–322.

Pahle, M., Pachauri, S., and Steinbacher, K. (2016). Can the Green Economy deliver it all? Experiences of renewable energy policies with socio-economic objectives. *Applied Energy*, 179, 1331–1341.

Peters, G. P., Andrew, R. M., Canadell, J. G., Friedlingstein, P., Jackson, R. B., Korsbakken, J. I., Le Quéré, C., and Peregon, A. (2020). Carbon dioxide emissions continue to grow amidst slowly emerging climate policies. *Nature Climate Change*, 10(1), 3–6.

Roelfsema, M., van Soest, H. L., Harmsen, M., van Vuuren, D. P., Bertram, C., den Elzen, M., Höhne, N., Iacobuta, G., Krey, V., Kriegler, E., and Luderer, G. (2020). Taking stock of national climate policies to evaluate implementation of the Paris Agreement. *Nature Communications*, 11(1), 1–12.

Rogelj, J., McCollum, D. L. and Riahi, K. (2013). The UN's 'Sustainable Energy for All' initiative is compatible with a warming limit of 2°C. *Nature Climate Change*, 3(6), 545–551.

Sachs, J. D. (2012). From millennium development goals to sustainable development goals. *The Lancet*, 379(9832), 2206–2211.

Sachs, J. D., Schmidt-Traub, G., Kroll, C., Lafortune, G., and Fuller, G. (2019). Sustainable development Report 2019. Bertelsmann Stiftung and Sustainable Development Solutions Network (SDSN). *Report*. New York.

United Nations (UN). (2015). Transforming Our World: The 2030 Agenda for Sustainable Development. *Report*. United Nations, New York.

United Nations (UN). (2017). Sustainable Development Goals: 17 Goals to Transform our World. Available at http://www.un.org/sustainabledevelopment/sustainable-development-goals/ Accessed May 26, 2017.

United Nations (UN). (2019). The Sustainable Development Goals Report 2019. *Report.* United Nations, New York.

United Nations (UN). (2020). Shared responsibility, global solidarity: Responding to the socio-economic impacts of COVID-19. *Report.* UN Secretary General, New York, March 2020, https://www.un.org/sites/un2.un.org/files/sg_report_socio-economic_impact_of_covid19.pdf.

United Nations Environment Program (UNEP). (2019). *Emissions gap report 2019. Report.* UNEP, Nairobi, https://www.unenvironment.org/resources/emissions-gap-report-2019.

von Stechow, C., Minx, J. C., Riahi, K., Jewell, J., McCollum, D. L., Callaghan, M. W., Bertram, C., Luderer, G., and Baiocchi, G. (2016). 2°C and SDGs: United they stand, divided they fall? *Environmental Research Letters*, 11(3), 034022.

https://doi.org/10.1142/9789811240553_0004

Chapter 4

Losing and Gaining Freedom Due to Climate Change

Evert Van de Vliert*,‡ and Mohsen Joshanloo†,§

**Faculty of Behavioural and Social Sciences, University of Groningen Groningen, The Netherlands*
†Department of Psychology, Keiymyung University, Deagu, South Korea
‡e.van.de.vliert@rug.nl
§mjoshanloo@hotmail.com

Global cooling and global warming are reset buttons for all life on Earth. No continent, no country, no creature is immune. To better understand these reset buttons, scholars need to divert their concentration away from average annual temperatures toward winter and summer deviations from livable temperatures. To this end, we introduce and apply a novel thermometer for measuring local livability. The measured climatic demands and stresses of cold and heat are next interpreted as being more detrimentally threatening for the poor, but more beneficially challenging for the rich, gradually resulting in lower freedom for the poor, but higher freedom for the rich. This climato-economic theory of freedom has been empirically supported for freedom from want, freedom from fear, freedom of expression and participation, freedom from discrimination, freedom to realize one's human potential, and free and effective functioning. Poor people tend to lose freedom under climatic threats, whereas rich people tend to gain freedom under climatic challenges. The results allow country-level forecasts of freedom by around the year 2100 on the basis of climato-economic livability under current projections of global warming and economic development.

1. Introduction

For more than a century, each world citizen has had a free pass to travel by air and, thus, by implication, to contribute to greenhouse gas emissions. This unlimited freedom is bound to change now that governing bodies are starting to place judicial and financial restrictions on commercial and private flights. The unfolding web of limitations and regulations will inevitably discriminate between winners and losers, and between economic classes and age cohorts. This is only one example of how global warming is gradually changing the global distribution of freedoms defined here as "opportunities to be able to make and implement autonomous choices of goals, means, and outcomes" (Van de Vliert, 2013a, p. 465).

In addressing freedoms of choice, human development and human rights organizations share basically the same objectives (United Nations Development Programme, 2000). Notably, both reflect a common motivation to advocate and secure worldwide freedom from want, freedom from fear, freedom of expression and participation, freedom from discrimination, and freedom to realize one's human potential. More or less all of these freedoms may be gradually redistributed by global warming, which is a real challenge for human development and human rights initiatives and projects (United Nations Development Programme, 2007). As a consequence, the fight for freedom for all and the fight against global warming must be seen as interrelated efforts.

This chapter explores the impacts of global cooling and global warming on fundamental freedoms worldwide while making three basic assumptions. First, plants, animals, and humans react and adapt to winter and summer deviations from livable temperatures rather than annual averages of local temperatures (Cline, 2007, Parsons, 2003, Scholander *et al.*, 1950). Second, humans use cash and other assets to modify the impacts of adverse winters and summers (Parker, 2000). Climate-compensating goods and services include clothing, shelter structures, warming and cooling systems, meals, and medical cure and care. Third, larger deviations from livable temperatures decrease people's freedoms to the extent that they are poorer, but increase people's freedoms to the extent that they are richer (Conway *et al.*, 2017, Van de Vliert, 2009, Van de Vliert, 2013a, Zhang *et al.*, 2015).

These assumptions reject both climatic and economic determinism. Instead, in synthesis, they constitute a climato-economic theory of freedom outlined in the next section and then applied throughout this chapter. The next section also discusses the extant evidence supporting the theory for separate fundamental freedoms and for an overarching configuration of free and effective functioning. Subsequent sections broaden the evidence: low freedom is associated with tightness under climatic threats, high freedom with creativity under climatic challenges, and varying freedom as in the case of the Greenland Norse facing the Little Ice Age following the Medieval Warming Period. The final section contains country-level forecasts of freedom by around the year 2100 on the basis of projected global warming and economic development.

2. Climato-Economic Theory of Freedom

No plant, animal, or human is impervious to the problems posed by bitter winters and scorching summers. Colder winters and hotter summers entail larger deviations from physiological homeostasis, fewer nutritional resources, greater health problems, and more adaptations as a natural result. For plants and animals, cold- and heat-induced demands are threatening. For humans, with greater mental abilities, however, extreme temperatures can be either detrimentally threatening or beneficially challenging in the end. This is so because demands placed on people are a double-edged sword (Bandura, 1997, Lazarus and Folkman, 1984). Greater thermal demands in interaction with insufficient wealth resources to meet the demands promote unfree choices that are mandatory and routinized, whereas greater thermal demands in interaction with sufficient wealth resources promote free choices that are autonomous and adventurous (Conway *et al.*, 2017, Karwowski and Lebuda, 2013, Kong, 2013, Robbins, 2015, Van de Vliert, 2013a, Zhang *et al.*, 2015).

This climato-economic explanation of spatial and temporal variations in freedom is presented here in subsections describing a novel thermometer for measuring livability (Fig. 1; subsection 2.1), the main effects of climatic temperatures of cold and heat on local cultures (2.2),

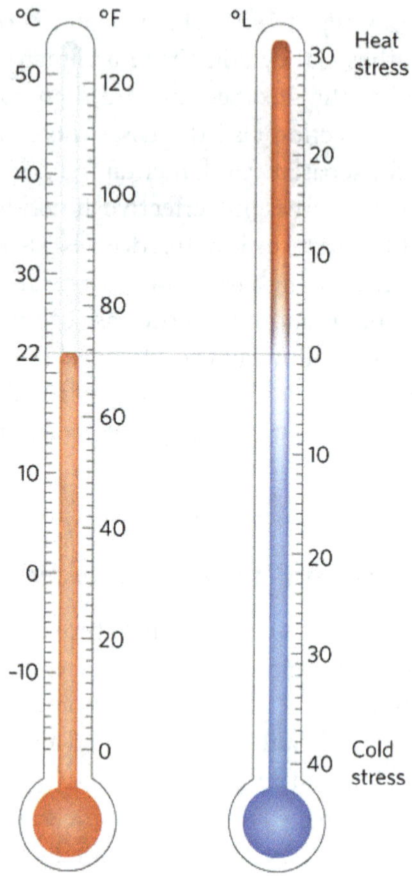

Fig. 1. Thermometer for measuring livability (°L).
Source: Van de Vliert (2017).

interactive effects of the economic resources of liquid cash and illiquid assets (2.3), and ultimately the resulting freedom, subdivided into components of separate fundamental freedoms (2.4) and a configuration of free and effective functioning (2.5).

2.1. *Thermometer for livability*

The use of average annual temperature as a predictor of national culture (e.g., Georgas *et al.*, 2004, Hofstede, 2001, Vanhanen, 2009, Xu *et al.*,

2020) is at odds with the fact that warm-blooded humans are adversely affected by both extreme cold and extreme heat. Indeed, an appropriate indicator of the relevance of stressful thermal demands for humans should take account of winter and summer deviations from a biologically optimal point of reference. Therefore, in current climate culture research, 22°C (~72°F) is adopted as a benchmark from which measurements of societal livability are made (e.g., Conway *et al.*, 2017, Chen *et al.*, 2015, Kong, 2013, 2016, Kusano and Kemmelmeier, 2018, Robbins, 2015, Van de Vliert, 2013a,b, 2017, Van de Vliert and Tol, 2014, Wei *et al.*, 2017).

A country's thermal climate, assessed across major cities and weighted by population size, is considered more demanding and stressful to the extent that winters are colder than 22°C and summers are hotter than 22°C. Specifically, thermal demands are the sum of the absolute centigrade deviations from 22°C for the average lowest temperature in the coldest month; the highest temperature in the coldest month; the lowest temperature in the hottest month; and the highest temperature in the hottest month. Indices for the sum of these cold and heat demands are available for 230 independent countries and dependent territories (Van de Vliert, 2013b; http://www.rug.nl/staff/e.van.de.vliert/projects). In South Africa, for example, with its cold winters (|−2°C − 22°C|+ |7°C 22°C|) and hot summers (|29°C − 22°C|+ |39°C − 22°C|), cold demands (39°L) and heat demands (24°L) add up to a total demands score of 63°L.

2.2. *Main effects of climatic temperatures*

A casual glance at the thermometer for livability makes clear that the impacts of climatic temperatures on local cultures cannot be accurately studied by concentrating on either colder-than-temperate or hotter-than-temperate demands. Like separated upstream rivers having additive downstream effects, colder-than-temperate and hotter-than-temperate demands and stresses supplement each other's impact in affecting the cultural fabric of daily life. It is, however, an incomplete and painfully misleading story that climatic temperatures determine who we are and what we do and believe in. For more than 25 centuries, scholars have told that fallacious story over and over again (Feldman, 1975, Jankovic, 2010).

Even in the 20th century, proponents of the geographical school still studied how climatic cold and heat determine our mental and behavioral existence (Sorokin, 1928, Tetsuro, 1971), sometimes with horrifying overtones of the superiority of some races and inferiority of others (Huntington, 1945, Taylor, 1937). It is of course true that more extreme ambient temperatures can lead to cognitive demands, affective stress responses, and conative attempts to cope with cold or heat. But, it is a terribly mistaken idea that humankind has no other option than to adapt passively to a fixed climatic habitat. On the contrary, our ancestors have invented and developed not only a rainbow of counteractions against climatic problems but also property and money as tools that can particularly help to shape our destiny and help us thrive during bitter winters, scorching summers, or both.

2.3. *Interactive effects of wealth resources*

Owning, earning, saving, and trading can help minimize discomfort and improve the quality of life in cold and hot areas and seasons. Economic modeling of climatic cold and heat as cost-raising factors (Burke *et al.*, 2015, Jankovic, 2010, Rehdanz and Maddison, 2005) leads to the conclusion that both colder-than-temperate winters and hotter-than-temperate summers generate less income and are more expensive. As a rule, economic wealth resources can provide all the necessities of life in these more stressfully demanding circumstances, including heat and cold, food and drink, and cure and care. Articulating the way that this is visible in modern communities, families in richer countries spend up to 50% of their household income on climate-compensating goods and services, a figure that rises up to 90% in poorer countries (Parker, 2000).

Our central tenet is that the same climatic temperatures can be appraised as either threatening or challenging depending upon the wealth resources available for handling the problems. The greater economic costs of living in colder or hotter places evoke stronger threat appraisals in case of poverty, but stronger challenge appraisals in case

	Four climato-economic habitats			
Climatic demands	Cold or hot	Temperate	Temperate	Cold or hot
Wealth resources	Poor	Poor	Rich	Rich
Cultural adaptations	↓	↓	↓	↓
Stress appraisals	Threatening	Unthreatening	Unchallenging	Challenging
Fundamental freedoms	Low	Intermediate	Intermediate	High

Fig. 2. Climato-economic theory of freedom.

of wealth. Figure 2 further clarifies how climatic demands and wealth resources interact in shaping cultural adaptations. The columns above the arrows sketch four prototypical circumstances of livability, and the columns below the arrows relate them to two domains of cultural adaptation — stress appraisals and fundamental freedoms. As can be seen, more threatening habitats are thought to incur greater losses of freedom, whereas more challenging habitats produce greater gains in freedom.

2.4. *Fundamental freedoms*

Freedoms of choice are fundamental to the extent that they are dealing with meeting basic human needs for surviving and thriving. Human development organizations are driven by an action perspective on freedoms to meet basic needs, whereas human rights organizations are driven by a normative perspective on freedoms to meet basic needs (United Nations Development Programme, 2000, 2007). The arrows in Fig. 2 add a supplementary ecological perspective by emphasizing the interface between climato-economic habitats and freedoms to meet basic needs. Greater climatic deviations from 22°C (Fig. 1) are expected to lead to greater losses of freedom in poor populations, but to greater gains of freedom in rich populations.

Ample empirical evidence supports this theory. Freedom from want, freedom from fear, freedom of expression and participation, freedom from discrimination, and freedom to realize one's human potential appear to decrease in countries with more threatening climato-economic habitats, but to increase in countries with more challenging habitats (for overviews, see Conway *et al.*, 2017, Kong, 2013, Van de Vliert, 2009, Van de Vliert, 2013a, Zhang *et al.*, 2015). For example, greater climatic demands come with greater press repression in poorer countries (e.g., Russia and Turkmenistan), but greater press freedom in richer countries (e.g., Canada and Finland). Similarly, freedom from discrimination is lower in poorer Chinese provinces with more demanding climates such as Heilongjiang and Jilin, but higher in richer Chinese provinces with more demanding climates such as Ningxia and Tianjin (Van de Vliert *et al.*, 2013). This is a remarkable finding because the provincial level of wealth, as such, has no association with freedom from discrimination.

2.5. *Free and effective functioning*

An alternative test of the climato-economic theory concentrated not on separate freedoms but on the overarching configuration of components of free and effective thinking and behaving. In a multi-level study (Van de Vliert and Joshanloo, 2020), we analyzed Gallup World Poll data gathered from 393,948 individuals nested in 145 countries. Care was taken to control for confounding influences of gender, age, secondary education, tertiary education, adequacy of one's household income, and overall life satisfaction.

Building on a preceding study (Joshanloo, 2018), the broad domain of free and effective functioning was captured by averaging such fundamental experiences as making free choices, learning, getting ahead, volunteering, giving or getting help, and receiving respectful treatment. A country's climatic demands were represented by the common factor (eigenvalue $\lambda = 2.65$, $R^2 = 0.66$) of the variation in cold stress (negative loading), heat stress, rainfall stress, and pathogen stress (positive loadings). The linear term of this bipolar scale refers to cold-induced versus heat-induced ecostress, and its quadratic term to overall temperature-induced ecostress. Wealth resources were proxied by the average log-transformed income per head.

The multi-level findings suggest that both colder-than-temperate and hotter-than-temperate climates are negatively linked to the free and effective functioning of poorer people, but positively associated with the free and effective functioning of richer people. In addition, poorer people tend to live less free and effective lives in colder than in hotter climates. These interactive effects of temperature-induced stresses and wealth-induced resources on free and effective functioning were cross-validated at individual and collective levels. Finally, similar north–south patterns of distribution of free and effective functioning robustly occurred for inhabitants of eastern and western parts of the Earth.

3. Tightness under Climatic Threats

Although common sense dictates that tight bureaucratic control and creativity are not on friendly terms, scientific caution dictates that one should not jump to the assumption that tightness and creativity are mutually exclusive dimensions. Therefore, the interactive effect of climatic demands and poverty on tight bureaucratic control (reflecting low freedom) and the interactive effect of climatic demands and riches on creativity (reflecting high freedom) are treated here in subsequent sections. The following is an overview of how cultural manifestations of tightness have been related to threatening climato-economic habitats.

3.1. *Contextualizing tightness*

National cultures vary along a dimension ranging from loose to tight modes of control, that is, from weak to strong rules, roles, and sanctions (Gelfand *et al.*, 2011, Triandis, 1995). These varying modes of control apply to ingroups and outgroups who can be, and often are, people with lower or higher status at the same time (Triandis, 1995). Thus, the cultural dimension of tightness overarches and synthesizes the dimensions of increasing differentiation and discrimination between familiars and strangers (individualism/collectivism) and increasing power distance or hierarchism (lower-downs versus higher-ups) (Van de Vliert, 2020).

Tight bureaucratic control is anything but context-free (Gelfand *et al.*, 2011).

When confronted by a threatening loss of control over their environment, people will first attempt to restore control, using cash and other assets as major tools to do so. If such wealth resources are lacking, however, as is the case in threatening climato-economic habitats, control mechanisms in the form of formalization and centralization often serve as back-up tools (Kong, 2013, 2016, Van de Vliert, 2009, Van de Vliert, 2013a). More formalization ties group members more securely to behavioral prescriptions that guide and control goals, means, and outcomes. More centralization places the power of decision-making and control in the hands of fewer people higher up in the hierarchy.

Formalization and centralization in conjunction lead to tightness and unfree bureaucratic choices that are mandatory and routinized (Mintzberg, 1979, Morgan, 1986) at the expense of individual and collective freedom. Putting these considerations together, it makes sense to expect that freedom-restricting tightness will peak in threatening climato-economic habitats, will be intermediate in unthreatening and unchallenging habitats, and will be minimal in challenging climato-economic habitats where people prefer to take their own fate into their own hands (cf. Fig. 2).

3.2. *Test of the hypothesis*

The relationship between tightness and climatic threats was tested in a secondary analysis of survey data gathered among about 17,000 middle managers from over 900 organizations in 61 societies throughout the world (House *et al.*, 2004). Tightness was tapped by eight 7-point value questions, four about the extent to which people "seek orderliness, consistency, structure, formalized procedures, and laws to cover situations in their daily lives" (formalization) and four about the extent to which people "expect and agree that power should be shared unequally" (centralization) (for details, see House *et al.*, 2004).

A country's climatic demands were measured with the thermometer for livability (Fig. 1), and local wealth resources were again proxied by the average log-transformed national income per head. As discussed in the next subsection, tightness was regressed on climatic demands, wealth resources, and their interaction. This analysis was repeated to exclude rival explanations in terms of the economic sector (i.e., agriculture, industry, and service) and religion (i.e., Islamic, Protestant, and Roman Catholic).

3.3. *Regression results*

Wealth resources accounted for 21% of the variation in tightness. In additive (5%) and interactive (11%) combination with climate-induced demands, however, the percentage of predicted variation in tightness increased from 21% to 37%. Inhabitants endorsed tight formalization and centralization most in threatening climato-economic habitats (e.g., Iranians and Kazakhstanis), less in unthreatening and unchallenging habitats (e.g., Filipinos and Taiwanese), and least in challenging habitats (e.g., Austrians and Finns). Cold demands and heat demands are both important, although colder winters contribute more to the results than hotter summers (Van de Vliert, 2009). The supplementary analyses further revealed that the results held after controlling for variations in economic activities and religious differences.

Although the middle managers in this sample function in both superior and subordinate roles, some concern is warranted that superiors rather than subordinates are more likely to approve tight control behavior. In two other studies, the endorsement of control mechanisms was compared across habitats to address these concerns (Van de Vliert and Postmes, 2012, 2014). Inhabitants of more threatening climato-economic habitats were found to be more satisfied and happier if they were controlled by autocratic governments; inhabitants of more challenging climato-economic habitats were found to be more satisfied and happier under democratic rule. In short, populations in more threatening climato-economic habitats tend to endorse tighter formal rules and hierarchical roles, most likely to avoid ambiguity and risk (Kong, 2013, 2016).

4. Creativity under Climatic Challenges

4.1. *Climato-economic prediction*

Creativity may be seen as freedom in disguise. Indeed, it is difficult to imagine creativity without free choices inherent in inventive idea generation and innovative idea implementation. In consequence, the climato-economic theory of freedom in Fig. 2 predicts that creativity will be minimal in threatening habitats, intermediate in unthreatening and unchallenging habitats, and maximal in challenging habitats where people are in a position to make autonomous and adventurous choices of their own. Here, we present renewed analyses to test this prediction.

4.2. *Test of the prediction*

Murray (2014), Van de Vliert and Murray (2018) worldwide measures of invention and innovation allowed the construction of a 155-country index of creativity based on data from five different sources: (1) rates of Nobel Prize laureates per country of birth, (2) the technology index of the United Nations, (3) country rates of patent applications from the World Intellectual Property Organization, (4) Cornell University's global innovation index, and (5) a measure of invention versus innovation from the World Economic Forum. The one-component solution ($R^2 = 0.85$) is a good representation of the five measures ($0.85 < r < 0.96$). Extensive evidence of the internal consistency, cross-cultural equivalence, and construct validity of the index has been reported elsewhere (Van de Vliert and Murray, 2018).

Each country's climato-economic conditions were assessed as in Section 3.2 above. The first control variable entered into the regression analysis was the prevalence of human-to-human transmitted or non-zoonotic parasitic diseases such as measles, cholera, leishmaniasis, and leprosy. This particular index, compiled by Fincher and Thornhill (2012), was chosen as these non-zoonotic diseases are preeminently the ones that motivate people to avoid potentially infectious contact with others, thus inhibiting social network structures that are conducive to creativity. Non-zoonotic diseases served as a competitive predictor because disease-causing pathogens are known to reduce invention and innovation (Murray, 2014).

Current points of historical trajectories of national IQ, industrialization, and urbanization were also controlled for as these processes are so entwined with increasing material wealth that they might unintentionally confirm the prediction of creativity as freedom in disguise. National IQ — the average intelligence of a country's inhabitants relative to other countries' inhabitants — is available from Lynn and Vanhanen (2006). Industrialization (United Nations Development Programme, 2004, 2007) is each country's position on the historical continuum from agriculture to industrial and service employment (based on national percentages of employment in the three sectors). Urbanization (Parker, 1997) is the percentage of the country's total population living in urban areas.

4.3. *Regression results*

National IQ and urbanization together account for 60% of the variation in creativity, leaving no significant traces for the prevalence of non-zoonotic diseases and industrialization. Climatic demands ($b = 0.17$, $p < 0.01$) and wealth resources ($b = 0.65$, $p < 0.001$) account for an extra 11% of the variation over and above the positive impact of national IQ ($b = 0.02$, $p < 0.01$). Finally, and most importantly, the interaction of climatic demands and wealth resources also reaches significance ($b = 0.28, p < 0.001$), increasing the total effect size from 71% to 77%.

The plot of the interaction effect provides full support for the idea that Nobel laureates, technological pioneers, and innovative entrepreneurs are underrepresented in populations with poorer income, poorer health, and poorer education, but more so to the extent that these populations reside in more threatening habitats. Also, nobel laureates, technological pioneers, and innovative entrepreneurs are overrepresented in richer populations with a better income, health, and education, but more so to the extent that these populations reside in more challenging habitats. Supplementary analyses suggest that imperfect sampling of small and adjacent countries within the same climatic subzone, and of large countries with different climatic subzones, has biased the results only to a trivial extent.

5. The Climato-Economic Case of the Greenland Norse

Most likely, the Norse communities in medieval Greenland collapsed because climatic and economic hardships pushed them on a slippery slope toward extinction. As reported elsewhere (Van de Vliert, 2013c) and summarized here, historical and archaeological studies (e.g., Diamond, 2005, Dugmore *et al.*, 2007, Fagan, 2008, Seaver, 1996) converge in a picture of Norse and Inuit societies inhabiting southwest Greenland during the 13th and 14th centuries and coping with the same climatic demands in different economic ways. The Norse had a sedentary lifestyle and agricultural economies, whereas the Inuit had a nomadic lifestyle and aquacultural economies. For example, Norse but not Inuit boys and girls learned in their youth to tend and milk cattle and sheep, to churn butter and make cheese, and to spin and weave wool. The Norse imported tar, lumber, and iron from Europe in exchange for locally woven cloth, arctic furs, and, above all, walrus ivory; but, the self-supporting Inuit did not rely on imported goods.

When the Little Ice Age gradually replaced the Medieval Warm Period, increasingly long and bitter winters reduced crop and livestock production, increased overgrazing and deforestation, caused malnutrition, weakened immunity to a variety of illnesses, and brought trade with Europe to a virtual standstill. Whereas the colder climate was tolerable or even beneficial for the Inuit with their fishing economy, it was a full-blown disaster for the Norse, whose agricultural economy was too dependent on pasturing animals, growing hay, and long-distance trading by boat. Increasingly, this situation must have resulted in threat appraisals and discrimination between higher-ups and lower-downs: "There were many innovations that might have improved the material conditions of the Norse ... but those innovations could have threatened the power, prestige, and narrow interests of the chiefs. In the tightly controlled, interdependent society of Norse Greenland, the chiefs were in a position to prevent others from trying out such innovations" (Diamond, 2005, p. 276).

The most counterproductive adaptation seems to have been the entwinement of hierarchical and ingroup–outgroup discrimination. Perceived threat, common survival goals, power politics, and ingroup love are the ideal seedbed for outgroup hate (Brewer, 1999). More and more, the Christian Norse began to see the Inuit as despicable and mean pagans. This prevented the Norse from freely trading with the Inuit and learning from them how to build fast kayaks by stretching sealskins over frameworks, how to make harpoons and other whale-hunting equipment, and how to sophisticatedly hunt ringed seals, fish, and whales. Climato-economically reinforced ingroup–outgroup discrimination seems to have pushed away the very lifebelt of liberal intergroup cooperation with the Inuit that could have saved the Norse from downward roads to rack and ruin. Around 1450, the "superior" Norse died out, literally through starvation or Inuit aggression or figuratively through migration, abandoning exhausted lands, farm buildings, and churches to the hands of the "inferior" Inuit.

6. Forecasted Freedom by 2112

So far, this chapter has introduced a novel thermometer for measuring livability, outlined a climato-economic theory of freedom, and discussed quantitative and qualitative evidence in support of that theory. So far, the contextualization of freedom has been based on observations, not projections. So far, predictions have been used to describe and explain the past and the present, not to forecast the future. The current section shifts the time perspective from what we know about the impact of climato-economic habitats to what we do not know by reporting on a study conducted in 2012 to forecast freedom changes in the next 100 years (Van de Vliert, 2013a).

This forward-looking study was undertaken to clarify the possible long-term impacts of two huge threats humanity faces today: global warming and local poverty. Evidently, the accuracy of the forecasts of freedom depends on the quality of the climatic and economic projections, with the consequence that forecasts had to be made cautiously and that the results should not be overinterpreted. Against this background, the worldwide distribution of freedom in 2112 was estimated for 104 relatively small countries for which climato-economic projections and subsequent freedom forecasts could be made. Sections 6.1 to 6.3 are adapted from the original publication in *Behavioral and Brain Sciences* (Van de Vliert, 2013a).

6.1. *Climato-economic projections*

A country's livability under future conditions of global warming and economic development was derived from information provided by the Intergovernmental Panel on Climate Change (IPCC, 2001). This was done in three steps. First, building on IPCC data, Cline (2007) has developed temperature projections for the 21st century, broken down by month and country. With the help of the thermometer for livability (Fig. 1), the average temperatures for the coldest and hottest months over the 2070–2099 period were converted into an indicator of a country's climatic demands by around the year 2100. Second, likewise building on IPCC assessments, Van Vuuren *et al.* (2008) have estimated national wealth resources around 2100. Specifically, they have estimated each country's income per head based on algorithms that take into account base year, relation between level of income and economic growth rate, regional income convergence, population size, and age profile of the population.

Third, in agreement with the climato-economic theory (Fig. 2), the product of the standardized climatic demands and the standardized wealth resources around 2100 served as a statistical indicator of a country's livability around 2100. In order to increase accuracy, livability was computed for four future scenarios, emphasizing globalization and economic prioritization (A1), regionalization and economic prioritization (A2), globalization and environmental prioritization (B1), and regionalization and environmental prioritization (B2) (IPCC, 2001). This created four simulations of each country's climato-economic livability at the beginning of the 22nd century.

6.2. *Assessment of freedom*

6.2.1. *Measured freedom in 2012*

Each country's overall level of freedom in 2012 was represented by "opportunities to be able to make and implement autonomous choices," grouped into freedom from discrimination (Van de Vliert, 2011a), press freedom (Van de Vliert, 2011b), and political freedom from autocracy (Pemstein *et al.*, 2010). These indicators were chosen because they had strong climato-economic linkages: climatic demands (CD), wealth resources (WR), and their interaction (CD × WR) predicted considerable variation in freedom from discrimination (47%), press freedom (36%), and political freedom (35%) in 2012. The three sets of three regression coefficients (CD, WR, CD × WR) predicting the three components of freedom in 2012 were next applied to the climato-economic livability at the beginning of the 22nd century.

6.2.2. *Forecasted freedom in 2112*

Twelve estimates of the level of a country's freedom in 2112 were made by applying the three regression equations (freedom in 2012: no discrimination, no press repression, no political autocracy) to the four climato-economic simulations (scenarios for 2100: A1, A2, B1, B2). Despite the differences between the four simulations, the four averages for freedom from discrimination, press freedom, and political freedom were not significantly different from each other (paired-samples tests, $ts \leq \pm 1.27$, $df = 103$, $ps \geq 0.21$), and were highly intercorrelated ($0.87 \leq r \leq 0.97$). The 12 estimates were therefore standardized and then combined into a single cross-national index of freedom in 2112.

6.3. *Relative changes in freedom: 2012–2112*

To visually explore the changes in freedom, measured freedom in 2012 was plotted against forecasted freedom in 2112. Because of the way they were constructed, the unstandardized indices approximated a standardized distribution, with the consequence that it made no difference whether unstandardized or standardized indices were plotted. In the plot with standardized indices, included as Fig. 3, countries on

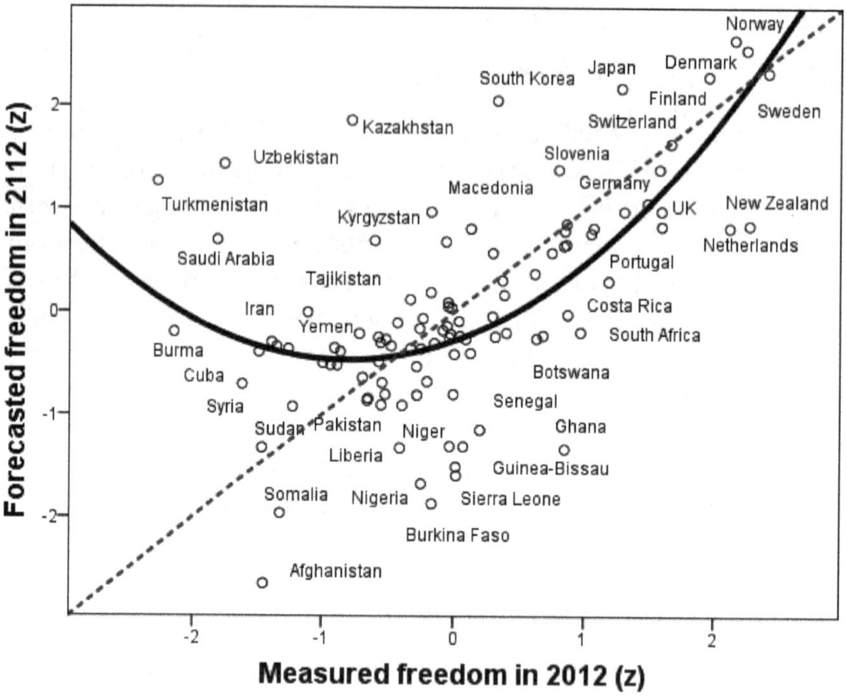

Fig. 3. Relative changes in freedom between 2012 and 2112 forecasted for 104 countries on the basis of their livability under current projections of global warming and economic development.

Source: Van de Vliert (2013a).

the dotted diagonal undergo no relative changes in freedom, whereas countries above or below the diagonal move up or down on the international ladder of freedom, respectively. Overall, a significantly hockey-stick-shaped curve of relative increases in freedom surfaced that accounted for 45% of the changes, and generally indicated that populations with little freedom in 2012 are expected to have moved up the ladder of freedom by the year 2112.

The left part of the curve in Fig. 3 indicates that especially poor populations in Asia whose habitats will become less threatening will gain relative levels of freedom. The Turkmens, the Uzbeks, and the Kazakhstanis, for example, will even surpass the Britons, the New Zealanders, and the Dutch in freedom. The lower middle part of the curve predicts that Afghans and Pakistanis, and the great majority of Africans (e.g., Somalis, Nigerians, Burkinabe, and Sierra Leoneans) will lose rather than gain freedom. Finally, the right part of the curve visualizes the slightly worrying prospect of inhabitants of several rich countries who have to defend current freedom rankings against relative decreases in both climatic demands and wealth resources during the remainder of this century. In increasingly less challenging climato-economic habitats, their predispositions to freedom tend to weaken.

Self-evidently, these forecasts of freedom on the basis of the estimates of climato-economic livability 100 years from now are informed guesses at best. Freedom from discrimination, press freedom, and political freedom are influenced by multiple factors outside the IPCC scenarios, including unforeseen discoveries, major disasters, mass violence, and public health emergencies. What Section 6 does suggest, however, is that creeping changes in climato-economic habitats may well drive creeping changes in freedom, with the possible consequence that scientific engineering of freedom comes within reach.

7. Conclusions and Implications

Whether global cooling or warming is a curse or a blessing depends on the winters and summers of one's place of residence. More specifically, it depends on the extent to which winter and summer temperatures deviate from the optimal point of livability at 22°C ($\sim 72°F$). Larger downward or upward deviations from 22°C are more demanding and stressful. Cold or heat stresses appraised as more threatening go hand in hand with greater reductions in free courses of action, until zero degrees of freedom will bring starvation, ill health, and death. By contrast, cold or heat stresses appraised as challenging go hand in hand with higher degrees of freedom and better psychosocial functioning.

This main conclusion raises the collateral question of what force may be responsible for turning climatic threats into climatic challenges. The answer provided in this chapter is that people use wealth resources to turn threatening winters and summers with lower degrees of freedom into challenging winters and summers with higher degrees of freedom. Indeed, cash and other assets can make the difference between whether global cooling or warming is a curse or a blessing. The same downward or upward deviations from 22°C can work as a curse for the poor, but as a blessing for the rich. Losing and gaining freedom have climato-economic rather than either climatic or economic roots.

This chapter opened with two converging perspectives on the promotion of fundamental freedoms: the human development perspective of economists and the human rights perspective of lawyers. Scholars and practitioners with human development or human rights agendas could probably benefit from the reported research results, illustrated with forecasts of freedom in the year 2112. The theory-based empirical evidence seems to be leaning toward the following recommendation: To promote fundamental freedoms throughout the world, we need to empower people to generate more wealth if they are living in a more demanding cold or hot climate.

Such targeted economic development of climatically deprived populations compares favorably with other worldwide interventions. For example, Figs. 1–3 imply that carbon dioxide (CO_2) strategies, which aim to minimize global warming by removing CO_2 from the atmosphere, create both winners and losers. Similarly, solar radiation strategies that aim to stimulate global cooling by reflecting or blocking sunlight also create both winners and losers. Targeted economic development, by contrast, aims to turn climatic losers into climatic winners.

References

Bandura, A. (1997). *Self-efficacy: The Exercise of Control*, Freeman, New York.

Brewer, M. B. (1999). The psychology of prejudice: Ingroup love and outgroup hate. *Journal of Social Issues*, 55, 429–444.

Burke, M. Hsiang, S. M., and Miguel, E. (2015). Global non-linear effect of temperature on economic production. *Nature*, 527, 235–239.

Chen, L., Hsieh, J. J. P.-A., Van de Vliert, E., and Huang, X. (2015). Cross-national differences in individual knowledge-seeking patterns: A climato-economic contextualization. *European Journal of Information* Systems, 24, 314–336.

Cline, W. R. (2007). *Global Warming and Agriculture: Impact Estimates by Country*, Center for Global Development, Peterson Institute for International Economics, Washington, DC.

Conway, L. G., Bongard, K., Plaut, V., Gornick, L. J., Dodds, D. P., Giresi, T., Tweed, R. G., Repke, M. A., and Houck, S. C. (2017). Ecological origins of freedom: Pathogens, heat stress, and frontier topography predict more vertical but less horizontal government restriction. *Personality and Social Psychology Bulletin*, 43, 1378–1398.

Diamond, J. (2005). *Collapse: How Societies Choose to Fail or Survive*, Allen Lane, London.

Dugmore, A. J., Keller, C., and McGovern, T. H. (2007). Norse Greenland settlement: Reflections on climate change, trade, and the contrasting fates of human settlements in the North Atlantic islands. *Arctic Anthropology*, 44, 12–36.

Fagan, B. (2008). *The Great Warming: Climate Change and the Rise and Fall of Civilizations*, Bloomsbury Press, New York.

Feldman, D. A. (1975). The history of the relationship between environment and culture in ethnological thought: An overview. *Journal of the History of the Behavioral Sciences*, 11, 67–81.

Fincher, C. L. and Thornhill, R. (2012). Parasite-stress promotes in group assortative sociality: The cases of strong family ties and heightened religiosity. *Behavioral and Brain Sciences*, 35, 61–79.

Gelfand, M. J. *et al.* (2011). Differences between tight and loose cultures: A 33-nation study. *Science*, 332, 1100–1104.

Georgas, J., Van de Vijver, F. J. R., and Berry J. W. (2004). The ecocultural framework, ecosocial indices, and psychological variables in cross-cultural research. *Journal of Cross-Cultural Psychology*, 35, 74–96.

Hofstede, G. (2001). *Culture's Consequences: Comparing Values, Behaviors, Institutions, and Organizations Across Cultures*, Sage, Thousand Oaks, CA.

House, R. J., Hanges, P. J., Javidan, M., Dorfman, P. W., and Gupta, V., (eds.) (2004). *Culture, Leadership, and Organizations: The GLOBE Study of 62 Societies*, Sage, Thousand Oaks, CA.

Huntington, E. (1945). *Mainsprings of Civilization*, Wiley, New York.

IPCC (Intergovernmental Panel on Climate Change). (2001). *Climate Change 2001: The Scientific Basis*, Cambridge University Press, Cambridge, UK.

Jankovic, V. (2010). Climates as commodities: Jean Pierre Purry and the modelling of the best climate on Earth. *Studies in History and Philosophy of Science Part B: Studies in History and Philosophy of Modern Physics*, 41, 201–207.

Joshanloo, M. (2018). Optimal human functioning around the world: A new index of eudaimonic well-being in 166 nations. *British Journal of Psychology*, 109(1), doi: 10.1111/bjop.12316.

Karwowski, M. and Lebuda, I. (2013). Extending climato-economic theory: When, how, and why it explains differences in nations' creativity. *Behavioral and Brain Sciences*, 36, 493–494.

Kong, D. T. (2013). Examining climato-economic contextualization of generalized social trust mediated by uncertainty avoidance. *Journal of Cross-Cultural Psychology*, 44, 574–588.

Kong, D. T. (2016). A gene-dependent climato-economic model of generalized trust. *Journal of World Business*, 50, 226–236.

Kusano, K. and Kemmelmeier, M. (2018). Ecology of freedom: Competitive tests of the role of pathogens, climate, and natural disasters in the development of socio-political freedom. *Frontiers in Psychology*, 9, 954, doi: 10.3389/fpsyg.2018.00954.

Lazarus, R. S. and Folkman, S. (1984). *Stress, Appraisal and Coping*, Springer, New York.

Lynn, R. and Vanhanen, T. (2006). *IQ and Global Inequality*, Washington Summit, Augusta, GA.

Mintzberg, H. (1979). *The Structuring of Organizations: A Synthesis of the Research*, Prentice-Hall, Englewood Cliffs, NJ.

Morgan, G. (1986). *Images of Organization*, Sage, Beverly Hills, CA.

Murray, D. R. (2014). Direct and indirect implications of pathogen prevalence for scientific and technological innovation. *Journal of Cross-Cultural Psychology*, 45, 971–985.

Parker, P. M. (1997). *National Cultures of the World: A Statistical Reference*, Greenwood Press, Westport, CT.

Parker, P. M. (2000). *Physioeconomics: The Basis for Long-run Economic Growth*, MIT Press, Cambridge, MA.

Parsons, K. C. (2003). *Human Thermal Environments: The Effects, of Hot, Moderate, and Cold Environments on Human Health, Comfort, and Performance* (2nd ed.), Taylor and Francis, London.

Pemstein, D., Meserve, S. A., and Melton, J. (2010). Democratic compromise: A latent variable analysis of ten measures of regime type. *Political Analysis*, 18, 426–449.

Rehdanz, K. and Maddison, D. (2005). Climate and happiness. *Ecological Economics*, 52, 111–125.

Robbins, B. G. (2015). Climate, affluence, and trust: Revisiting climato-economic models of generalized trust with cross-national longitudinal data, 1981–2009. *Journal of Cross-Cultural Psychology*, 46, 277–289.

Scholander, P. F., Hock, R., Walters, V., Johnson, F., and Irving L. (1950). Heat regulation in some arctic and tropical mammals and birds. *The Biological Bulletin*, 99, 237–258

Seaver, K. A. (1996). *The Frozen Echo: Greenland and the Exploration of North America ca. A.D. 1000–1500*, Stanford University Press, Stanford, CA.

Sorokin, P. A. (1928). *Contemporary Sociological Theories*, Harper, New York.

Taylor, T. G. (1937). *Environment, Race, and Migration*, University of Chicago Press, Chicago, IL.

Tetsuro, W. (1971). *Climate and Culture: A Philosophical Study*, Hokuseido Press, Tokyo, Japan.

Triandis, H. C. (1995). *Individualism and Collectivism*, Westview, Boulder, CO.

United Nations Development Programme. (2000). *Human Development Report 2000*. Oxford University Press, New York.

United Nations Development Programme. (2004). *Human Development Report 2004*. Oxford University Press, New York.

United Nations Development Programme. (2007). *Human Development Report 2007/2008: Fighting Climate Change*. Palgrave Macmillan, New York.

Van de Vliert, E. (2009). *Climate, Affluence, and Culture*, Cambridge University Press, New York.

Van de Vliert, E. (2011a). Climato-economic origins of variation in ingroup favoritism. *Journal of Cross-Cultural Psychology*, 42, 494–515.

Van de Vliert, E. (2011b). Bullying the media: Cultural and climato-economic readings of press repression versus press freedom. *Applied Psychology: An International Review*, 60, 354–376.

Van de Vliert, E. (2013a). Climato-economic habitats support patterns of human needs, stresses, and freedoms. *Behavioral and Brain Sciences*, 36, 465–480.

Van de Vliert, E. (2013b). White, gray, and black domains of cultural adaptations to climato-economic conditions. *Behavioral and Brain Sciences*, 36, 503–521.

Van de Vliert, E. (2013c). Creating cultures between arctics and deserts. *Advances in Culture and Psychology*, 3, 227–282.

Van de Vliert, E. (2017). Climatic imprints on personality. *Nature Human Behaviour*, 1, 864–865.

Van de Vliert, E. (2020). The global ecology of differentiation between us and them. *Nature Human Behaviour*, 4, 270–278.

Van de Vliert, E. and Joshanloo, M. (2020). Impacts of colder and hotter climates on richer and poorer people's daily functioning. *Climate Research*, 82, 137–148.

Van de Vliert, E. and Murray, D. R. (2018). Climate and creativity: Cold and heat trigger invention and innovation. *Creativity Research Journal*, 30, 17–28.

Van de Vliert, E. and Postmes, T. (2012). Climato-economic livability predicts societal collectivism and political autocracy better than parasitic stress does. *Behavioral and Brain Sciences*, 35, 94–95.

Van de Vliert, E. and Postmes, T. (2014). Democracy does not promote well-being except in rich countries with demanding climates. *Journal of Cross-Cultural Psychology*, 45, 1179–1195.

Van de Vliert, E. and Tol, R. S. J. (2014). Harsh climate promotes harsh governance (except in cold-dry-wealthy environments). *Climate Research*, 61, 19–28.

Van de Vliert, E., Yang, H., Wang, Y., and Ren, X. (2013). Climato-economic imprints on Chinese collectivism. *Journal of Cross-Cultural Psychology*, 44, 589–605.

Vanhanen, T. (2009). *The Limits of Democratization: Climate, Intelligence, and Resource Distribution*, Washington Summit Publishers, Augusta, GA.

Van Vuuren, D. P., Lucas, P. L., and Hilderink, H. (2007). Downscaling drivers of global environmental change: Enabling use of global SRES scenarios at the national and grid levels. *Global Environmental Change*, 17, 114–130.

Wei, W., Lu, J. G., Galinsky, A. D., Wu, H., Gosling, S. D., Rentfrow, P. J. *et al.* (2017). Regional ambient temperature is associated with human personality. *Nature Human Behaviour*, 1, 890–895.

Xu, C., Kohler, T. A., Lenton, T. M., Svenning, J.-C., and Scheffer, M. (2020). Future of the human climate niche. *Proceedings of the National Academy of Sciences of the United States of America*, 117(21), 11350–11355, doi: 10.1073/pnas.1910114117.

Zhang, J., Reid S. A., and Xu, J. (2015). Predicting attitudes toward press- and speech freedom across the U.S.A.: A test of climato-economic, parasite stress, and life history theories. *PLoS ONE*, 10(6), e0125241, doi: 10.1371/journal.pone.0125241.

https://doi.org/10.1142/9789811240553_0005

Chapter 5

Economic Damage of Climate Change: How Far is it From the Physical Damage?

Taoyuan Wei* and H. Asbjørn Aaheim†

CICERO Center for International Climate Research, P.O. Box 1129, Blindern, NO-0318 Oslo, Norway
**taoyuan.wei@cicero.uio.no*
†asbjorn.aaheim@cicero.oslo.no

Costs of climate change in integrated assessment models (IAMs) are in most cases based on a fixed relationship between a change in mean temperature and a change in the value added. The consequences of economic behavior, measures taken to adapt specifically to expected climatic changes, and resulting market effects are thereby omitted. This chapter shows how attention to these factors affects estimates of the costs of climate change. With a given physical effect on grain yield as the point of departure, we show how the economic impacts depend on assumptions related to adaptation within the agricultural sector throughout the world. In an average 2100 climate, the economic impacts of a 2.3% reduction in the productivity of grain under present economic conditions ranges between 0 to 2.3% of the sum of GDP in all world regions, depending on opportunities for adaptation, but between −25 and 70% of the GDP on regional levels. Changes in relative prices across sectoral products modify considerably the economic damage estimated at constant prices. The regional GDP calculated at purchasing power parities (PPP) used in many studies tends to be too optimistic to indicate the economic damages, particularly in developing countries. Hence, GDP deflated at local consumer price index is recommended to indicate the regional rather than global economic damages in these countries. The regions depending heavily on agriculture are suggested to reduce their dependence on agriculture during the economic development to be better prepared for the potential economic consequences of climate change.

1. Introduction

In the integrated assessment models (IAMs) like DICE (Nordhaus, 1993) and FUND (Tol, 1997), the optimal paths of emissions and social cost of carbon are sensitive to the specification of climate damage functions (Botzen and Van Den Bergh, 2012, Dayaratna *et al.*, 2017), which show the impact on an economic aggregate (e.g., value added) of increasing changes in temperature. The functions are usually calibrated under a given change in temperature or concentrations of CO_2. The impacts follow a choice of functional form under increasing climate change, e.g., the quadratic form proposed by Nordhaus (2008) or a highly nonlinear form proposed by Weitzman (2012), where the latter is more sensitive to high temperature increases.

The damage functions are, in principle, based on quantifications of the physical impacts of climate change. They can be estimated by statistical methods (Mendelsohn *et al.*, 2000, Nordhaus, 2006, Lemoine and Kapnick, 2016) or meta-analysis (Fankhauser, 1995, Tol, 2002). Regardless of method, the fixed linkage between indicators for a change in climate and an economic aggregate is subject to a range of assumptions, which implies considerable uncertainty related to the estimates of economic impacts of climate change (Hertel *et al.*, 2016, Van Den Bergh *et al.*, 2015). The impact on an economic aggregate due to a change in grain yield caused by climate change, for example, can be estimated as the physical effect on grain yield multiplied by a constant price. This estimation implies that the impacts on grain yields do not affect the production or consumption of grain products in any way. The following possibilities are thereby excluded:

1. If the physical damage implies a change in the productivity of land, the economic damage will depend on how the producers adapt, with further consequences for the use of other input factors.
2. How the producers adapt depends on their possibilities to compensate a reduction in the productivity of land with more work or with alternative technologies.
3. Adaptation implies that producers of grain will use more (or less) labor and other production factors, with consequences for other production activities in the economic system.

4. A damage in the production of grain will enforce a reduction in the consumption of grain products, and the economic impacts will depend on how consumers replace their use of grain products.

This chapter addresses what these factors imply for assessments of the economic impacts of climate change. For illustration, we take given estimates of the impacts on grain yields in physical terms in different world regions as a point of departure and estimate the economic impacts under different assumptions. Particular attention is paid to the impacts on relative prices, which help to explain the drivers behind the differences in the impact estimates.

Notably this study finds that, among others, the regional gross domestic product (GDP) calculated at purchasing power parities (PPP) used in many studies tends to be too optimistic to indicate the regional economic damages in developing countries although it is plausible for estimating the global damages. Hence, GDP deflated at local consumer price index, as a better indicator of regional welfare, is recommended to indicate the regional rather than global economic damages in developing countries.

The chapter is organized as follows. Section 2 presents the methods used in this study. Section 3 reports results and provides further discussion. Section 4 concludes the chapter.

2. Methods

First, we use a simple theoretical model to highlight the assumptions underlying different estimates of the economic impacts of a given physical effect of climate change in one sector, grain production, in a closed economy. Next, we present the numerical global model used to quantify the economic impacts of climate change on grain production under alternative assumptions of production and consumption functions in different world regions.

2.1. *The theory underlying cost estimates*

To show the implications of alternative quantifications of the economic consequences of climate change, we take the intuitive definition of the economic impact, where all prices are assumed constant, as our point of departure. Then, we simplify the description of the economy by assuming a closed economy with a fixed capital stock without depreciation. In that case, the value added across all sectors (Y) or GDP, equals consumption (C). The value of physical quantities produced in an economy that is divided into two sectors, grain production (Y_G) and production of other goods (Y_N), for example, is found by the quantities multiplied with their respective prices, P_G and P_N, which thereby applies as a measure of welfare:

$$C = P_G C_G + P_N C_N = P_G Y_G + P_N Y_N = Y. \tag{1}$$

Climate change will affect both the production of grain and the production of other goods. If there are no ways to reallocate the resources needed to produce the two goods and the market prices remain unaffected, the economic impacts of climate change, and thereby the change in consumption, can be estimated as

$$dC = P_G dY_G + P_N dY_N, \tag{2}$$

which corresponds to the intuitive estimate of economic impacts.

If the impacts cause a reallocation of resources used to produce grain and other goods, for example because production of grain implies that some farmers have to close down and are employed in production of other goods, and preferences of consumers may adapt to the impacts, then the physical impacts will also lead to a change in prices. Hence, the economic impact of climate change must include the real price change effect besides the physical damage impacts (Asheim and Wei, 2009),

$$dC = \underbrace{Y_G dP_G + Y_N dP_N}_{\text{price change effect}} + \underbrace{P_G dY_G + P_N dY_N}_{\text{physical quantity effect}}. \tag{3}$$

In practice, the price change effect can be considerable and even greater than the physical quantity effect for grain products since the majority of grain products are food to satisfy the sustained demand of consumers, which is necessary even if prices become very high, i.e., the demand is price-inelastic. Hence, estimates of the economic impacts of climate change must take the impacts on prices into account, to include the socioeconomic consequences of adaptation to climate change among economic agents.

To illustrate the economic mechanisms underlying the socio-economic impacts of climate change, we assume that production of grain and other goods are subject to the following production functions:

$$Y_G = f(K_G, \bar{L}, T);\ Y_N = g(K_N) = g(\bar{K} - K_G), \tag{4}$$

where K_G and K_N are capital inputs covering all productive resources in production of grain and other goods, respectively, excluding land used for grain production ($\bar{L}$), and T is an indicator for the climate, which is often represented by mean temperature. Here, the physical effects of climate change are limited to grain production, while the production of other goods is affected only indirectly by the realloca-tion of productive resources between the two sectors that follows from the impacts on the production of grain. To get as much as possible out of the productive resources assuming constant prices, the marginal productivity of these resources will be equalized in the two sectors, meaning that $P_G f_1 = P_N g_1$ in the optimal case. Then we have

$$\begin{aligned} P_G dY_G + P_N dY_N &= P_G(f_1 dK_G + f_3 dT) - P_N g_1 dK_G \\ &= P_G f_3 dT, \end{aligned} \tag{5}$$

which seems to justify that the economic damage at constant prices can be assessed by the cost of the physical damage of climate change, dT, as assumed in (2). However, the grain price (P_G) would not keep constant since grain output is damaged by climate change. In addi-tion, the condition of equalized marginal productivity of all resources ($P_G f_1 = P_N g_1$) is unrealistic when an economy is disturbed by the impact of climate change on grain production. Climate change may imply a change in the variability of weather over the seasons, with new challenges to the planning of the timing of sawing and choice of equipment. The equipment cannot be reallocated to production of other goods overnight, however, meaning that the marginal produc-tivity of capital in grain production will differ from that of capital assets in other sectors at least in the short run. Then, the second equation of

Eq. (5) is no longer valid. To capture the economic damage in such sub-optimal cases, the calculations that follow assume there is no substitution between capital assets in production of grain and in other production activities, while there is full substitution between labor in the two sectors.

To adapt to changes in long-term trends in climate, producers will try to adjust their use of input factors in the production of grain. This implies that all the resources used in production will be reallocated between grain production and other sectors, until the marginal productivity of all resources is the same in both sectors in the optimal case. There are at least two ways to represent this adjustment in the modeling. One is based on Hicksian neutral technology and the other on attaching the impacts to the productivity of land, i.e.,

$$Y_G = A(T)h(K_G, \bar{L}) \quad \text{or} \quad Y_G = Ah(K_G, \tau(T)\bar{L}). \tag{6}$$

The first alternative (Hicksian) reflects the case where producers of grain apply the same production method and technology from the existing one, regardless of climate. In that case, producers find it unnecessary to adapt to climate change by adjusting the composition of input factors. The only change is the scale of production. For example, if an extreme event like a flood occurs just before the harvest of grain, no adaptation measures would help to reduce the damage on the grain yields. Another example is if climate change implies a reduction in the production of grain, the number of farms may be reduced, but the remaining farms continue as before, without any adjustments in the way they produce grain, e.g., by investments in irrigation and other machinery. In such cases, the Hicksian production form is plausible.

The second alternative applies if climate change motivates measures to adapt to new constraints related to impacts on the productivity and availability of land, such as the use of labor, machinery, and irrigation systems. While the means of production other than land are unaffected by the climatic changes themselves, producers will adapt to a change in the productivity of land by changing the use of the other means of production. As the adaptation can be reflected by the technology options described by the production functions in the model, the impact of climate change can be attached to the productivity of land in this case. Then, the model allocates other means of production according to the availability of all the resources, which reflects adaptation in a broad, socioeconomic context. In the next section, we estimate the socioeconomic impacts of climate change on grain production in both cases assuming fully mobile labor and still immobile capital assets across sectors in a static numerical model. Note that we do not simulate the fully optimal case since the reallocation of capital assets across sectors is not considered although it might happen to some extent in the longer run.

The changes in grain production will affect the production of other goods as well, due to less available grain products as intermediate inputs and the reallocation of labor and other intermediate inputs, although the reallocation of capital assets is not allowed in our following numerical simulation. This leads to a change in prices, which also depends on consumers' demand. This demand is derived from the utility function of consumers, which in this simplified illustrative model is a function of the two aggregated goods,

$$U = u(C_G, C_N). \tag{7}$$

Utility maximization yields

$$P_G = \frac{\partial u(C_G, C_N)}{\partial C_G}, \quad P_N = \frac{\partial u(C_G, C_N)}{\partial C_N}. \tag{8}$$

The impacts on prices thereby depend on the choice of functional form of the utility functions. To capture the influence of this choice, we will, in the numerical model that follows, consider three types of utility functions: constant elasticity of substitution (CES), Cobb–Douglas (elasticity of substitution = 1), and Leontief (elasticity of substitution = 0).

To sum up, the calculations address the economic impacts of a given physical impact of climate change on the productivity of land in production of grain by using two different grain production functions, and three alternative consumption functions.

2.2. *The numerical model*

We examine how the different assumptions affect the estimates of economic damage due to climate change by using a static multi-sector, multi-regional, global computable general equilibrium (CGE) model GRACE (Aaheim and Rive, 2005, Aaheim *et al.*, 2018, Carattini *et al.*, 2019, Wei *et al.*, 2019). The model has been applied to studies on climate impact, adaptation, mitigation, and related policy analysis (Aaheim *et al.*, 2012, Glomsrød *et al.*, 2013, Underdal and Wei, 2015, Glomsrød *et al.*, 2016, Wei *et al.*, 2017, Orlov *et al.*, 2020, e.g.). In this study, we adopt the version of GRACE in Wei *et al.* (2019), which is based on the 2011 global economic data from the Global Trade Analysis Project (GTAP) database v.9 Aguiar *et al.* (2016). In the model, the world is divided into 140 regions and a regional economy consists of 14 production sectors including four agricultural sectors, two food sectors, one manufacturing sector, one transport sector, one services sector, and five energy sectors.

The four agricultural sectors produce wheat, rice, maize, and other agricultural products, respectively. In this study, the default production functional form for these agricultural sectors is a nested CES function described in Fig. 1. The top-level combines land (RES) with an

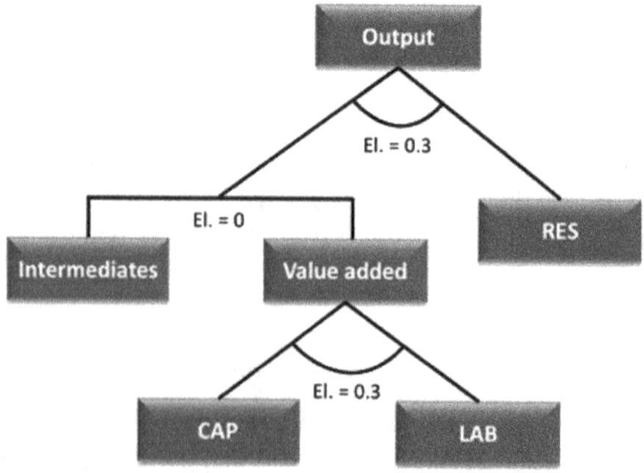

Fig. 1. Default production structure of agricultural sectors in GRACE. "El." refers to the chosen elasticities of substitution for the components in each aggregate.

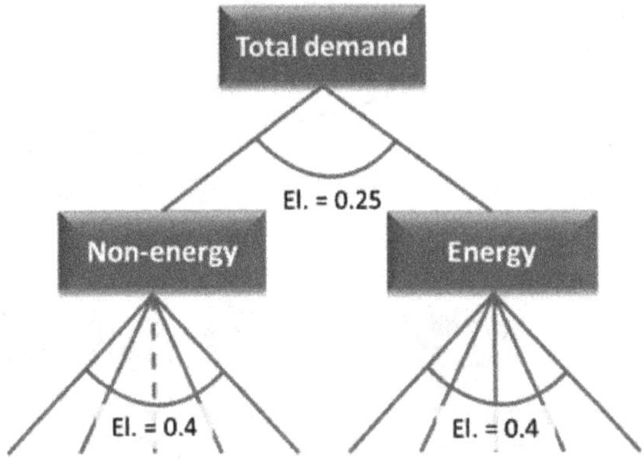

Fig. 2. Default final demand structure in GRACE. "El." refers to the chosen elasticities of substitution for the components in each aggregate.

aggregate of all other input factors, which are divided into a Leontief composite of intermediate goods and value added, where the value added combines capital (CAP) and labor (LAB).

This study also addresses the implications of alternative demand structures for consumers. The default demand structure in GRACE is shown in Fig. 2. At the top level, substitution can be made between energy and the other goods (non-energy). At the bottom level, the energy combines five energy goods (i.e., coal, crude oil, gas, refined oil and electricity) and the non-energy combines all the other goods.

To examine the effect of alternative demand structures of households, we introduce the other demand structure by moving the aggregated agricultural products to the top level combined with the other products (Fig. 3). If the substitution elasticity of this level is 1 corresponding to the Cobb–Douglas combination, consumers will spend the same share of their total income on agricultural products and the other goods. If the elasticity is 0 corresponding to the Leontief combination, then consumers prefer to consume the same combination of agricultural products and the other goods in physical terms, rather than monetary terms. The demand for the other consumer goods follows the same structure as shown in Fig. 2.

The other settings of the model are the same as in the version described in detail in Aaheim *et al.* (2018), which shows the structure

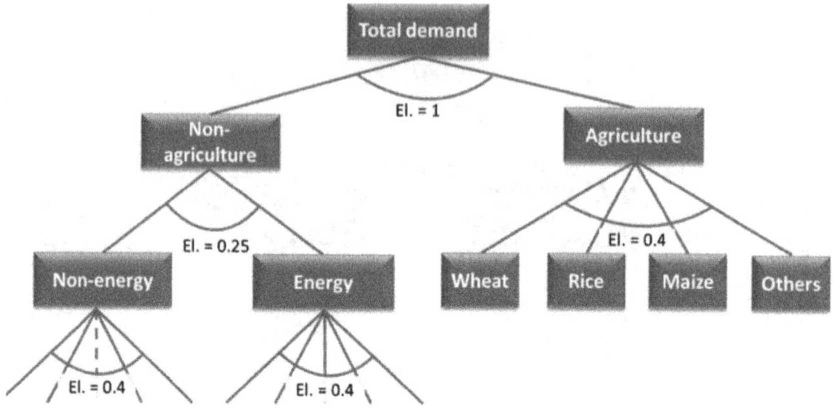

Fig. 3. Alternative final demand structure in GRACE. "El." refers to the chosen elasticities of substitution for the components in each aggregate.

of the model, how the parameters are calibrated, and specifications of the preferences and technologies in GRACE.

2.3. *Alternative cases to estimate economic damage*

We calibrate GRACE to the 2011 global economic data described in the GTAP database v.9 (Aguiar *et al.*, 2016), which gives a reference case that corresponds to the current climate situation. The alternative cases show the socioeconomic impacts on grain production of climate change, indicated by projected changes in average temperatures in 2050 and 2100. The immediate impact on grain production is estimated based on assessments of the physical impacts on the growth of grains. The GRACE model then shows how these impacts penetrate further to the economic system before an estimate of the economic impacts is provided.

The key assumptions in the alternative cases are listed in Table 1. All share the same assumptions related to the economic system. The reference case represents the 2011 economy, which is unaffected by climate change by assumption. The alternatives introduce the same physical damage of climate change on grain yields. What differs is the alternative production and demand structures described above. Climate change is represented by regional average temperature in 2050

Table 1. Assumptions for alternative cases.

		Average temperature 2050 (or 2100)			
Scenarios	Reference	Output	Land	LandCD	LandLf
The reference year	2011	2011	2011	2011	2011
External shock	NA	The same physical impact on grain yield			
Trigger point in grain production	NA	Output	Land	Land	Land
Consumption function	Default (CES)	Default	Default	Cobb–Douglas	Leontief

and 2100. Following Wei *et al.* (2019), we use the average temperature under the Representative Concentration Pathway 8.5 (RCP8.5) scenario generated from an ensemble of 32 climate models participating in the Coupled Model Intercomparison Project — Phase 5 (CMIP5) (Taylor *et al.*, 2012). The temperature change has a direct effect on grain yields, which is estimated in physical terms by a statistical model presented in Moore *et al.* (2017).

There are two ways to introduce the physical impact on grain yields in the economic system. One is to interpret the physical impact as the impact on the total output of grain. This means that a 5% physical damage on yields reduces the output of grain at the same rate of 5%. Hence, producers have no possibilities to adapt to climate change by changing the composition of input factors to limit the losses, such as if an unexpected flood driven by global warming destroys a part of the grain plants just before harvest. The "Output" alternative thereby represents a worst case showing the economic impacts of climate change.

The other way to integrate the physical impact is linking it to a reduction in the productivity of land. Then, the physical impact of climate change is considered isolated to the contributions to grain production from land. Other production factors, such as labor and capital, may compensate some of the losses related to the physical effect on the grain growth, e.g., by a change in production methods or intensified nutrition. The impacts in this case are shown in the "Land" alternative.

We also calculate the implications of flexibility in consumers' demand, expressed by the elasticities of substitution. The "LandCD" alternative replaces the default choice of CES demand-functions by Cobb–Douglas functions, which implies more flexibility and higher ability to adapt the consumption patterns (Fig. 3). The "LandLf" alternative applies Leontief functions to describe an inflexible consumption pattern, where substitution is disregarded. It must be added that the grain land is assumed as given and unaffected by climate change in all alternatives.

We emphasize that the objective of this study is to show the uncertainties related to assessments of economic damages of climate change if based on deterministic estimates of physical effects. Hence, the study does not project future economic impacts of climate change. These will depend on many other factors, which add to the climatic changes, such as population growth, technological changes, capital accumulation, income distribution, and changes in lifestyle. All these factors may affect the capacity to adapt to the impacts of climate change in a future economy, and there are reasons to believe that the RCP8.5 gives an overly pessimistic projection of the future. The question is rather what role different socioeconomic factors play for assessments of the impacts of climate change.

3. Results and Discussion

For each scenario, we calculate GDP at constant prices (GDP_CP), GDP deflated by global consumer price index (GDP_GCPI), and GDP deflated by national consumer price index (GDP_NCPI), respectively. According to Asheim and Wei (2009), GDP deflated by national consumer price index (CPI) considers the price change effect, and can be taken as an indicator of the regional welfare.

3.1. *Price change effect*

Our results show that the price change effect is considerable for the estimated economic damage. As shown in Fig. 4, global GDP calculated by all the three approaches indicates the same direction of the climate change damage for each of the scenarios. GDP_GCPI and GDP_NCPI

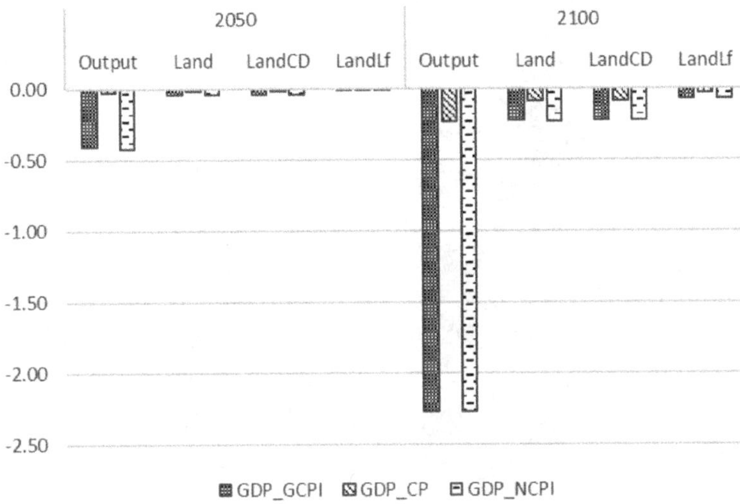

Fig. 4. Damages to global GDP due to impacts of climate change on production of main grains including wheat, rice, and maize under various assumptions in 2050 and 2100. In the "Output" cases, physical damage is assumed the same as damage on total production of grains in percentage. In other cases, physical damage is assumed the same as reduction in land productivity of grains in percentage where the "LandCD" cases further assume constant share of grains in total spending of households through a Cobb–Douglas consumption function and the "LandLf" cases assume constant ratio between grains and other goods in real terms through a Leontief consumption function.

are identical at the global level although they differ at national level (Fig. 5). Damages in terms of GDP_CP are much smaller than the other two in all cases (Fig. 4). The largest economic damage indicated by GDP_NCPI occurs in the 2100 "Output" alternative when the total grain production suffers the same as the physical damage in percentage terms by assumption, nearly ten times the damage indicated by the global GDP_CP. In other scenarios, the damages are modest although the global GDP_CPs are still much smaller than the other two indicators. These results imply that GDP_CP considerably underestimates the economic damages since the real price change effect is not included as done by the other two indicators.

The explanation to the large difference between the physical effects and the economic impacts is that grain products are largely necessary

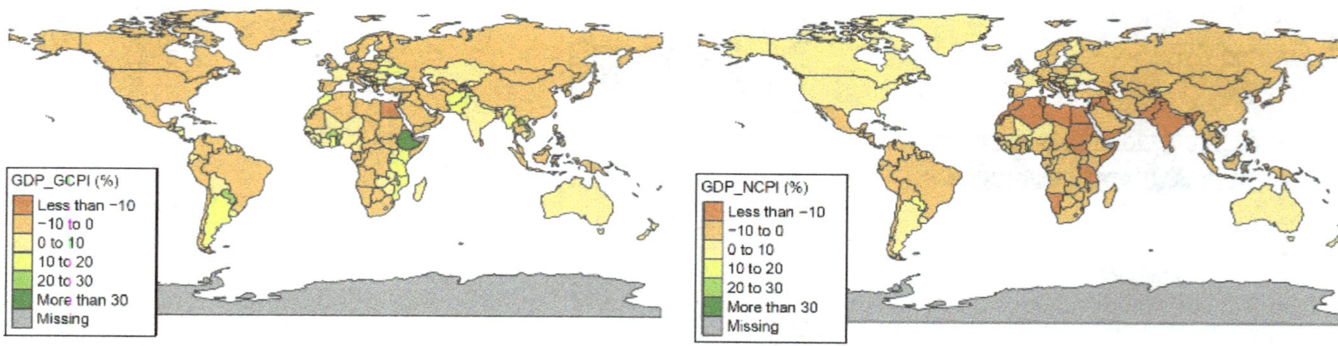

Fig. 5. Damages on national GDP at current price deflated by Global CPI (GDP_GCPI, in the left panel) and national CPI (GDP_NCPI, in the right panel) in the 2100 "Output" case (corresponding to average global warming in RCP8.5).

consumer goods and inelastic to a change in prices. Hence, damage on grain production leads to grain prices' increase at a higher rate than the physical damage. In what follows, we will focus on the GDP deflated by CPI rather than that at constant price.

3.2. *Adaptation*

As shown in Fig. 4, the "Output" alternative implies much stronger damage estimates than the "Land" interpretation. With climate change impacts corresponding to those in 2100, the economic damage in the "Output" alternative is 2.27% of GDP_NCPI (or 0.23% of GDP_CP) while that in the "Land" alternative is less than 0.23% of GDP_NCPI (or 0.09% of GDP_CP).

The explanation for the dramatic difference between the two alternatives is related to the possibilities for grain producers to adapt the production methods that avoid the negative physical damage of climate change. For example, if grain producers observe (or are warned about) negative impacts of climate change in advance, at least some of them will adjust their input to the production, e.g., by increasing the use of labor to offset the reduction in the productivity of land. If there is no way to limit the damages, the demand for labor in grain production will decrease and some of the workers in grain production will be employed in other sectors, and thereby limit the economic impacts at the regional level. The "Output" alternative excludes both adjustments. This alternative can, therefore, be considered as a worst-case estimate of the economic damage. The "Land" alternative includes both adjustments. It therefore gives much lower estimates of the economic damage and illustrates the considerable potential of adaptation measures of grain producers to mitigate the negative physical damage of climate change.

Note that the adjustment cost of the adaptation measures is not included in the "Land" alternative, meaning that the reduced economic damages resulting from these adaptation measures is somewhat over-estimated in this alternative. The over-estimation then depends on whether the assumed adaptation measures are feasible in terms of both economic and technical terms. In any case, the potential benefit of the adaptation measures to reduce the economic damage as shown in our study would motivate the producers to take a large range of adaptation measures, as long as the adaptation cost is lower than the potential benefit from the avoided physical damage.

3.3. *Consumer preferences*

The assumptions related to consumer behavior may also contribute to mitigate the economic damage, especially under the Leontief demand assumption. In the 2100 climate scenario, the estimated economic damage under the Leontief demand assumption ("LandLf") is only 0.08% of GDP_NCPI, while it is about 0.23% in the CES/CD demand assumption ("Land" or "LandCD"). Following the Leontief demand assumption, households cannot substitute grain products with other goods. Households will, therefore, spend a higher share of their income on grain products as the physical damage on grain production results in higher grain prices, compared to the cases of CES (or CD) demand assumption, where households can substitute gain products with other products. The relatively inelastic demand for grain products in households, on the one hand, motivate more grain production and supply. On the other hand, the demand for other products than grain is relatively reduced, allowing more resources to be used for grain production at relatively lower costs. Both channels result in less economic damage.

3.4. *Impacts on regional GDP*

Although all the alternatives imply negative economic impacts at the global level in terms of GDP_GCPI and GDP_NCPI, there are positive impacts at the national level even in the worst "Output" case for 2100, as shown in Fig. 5. The figure also shows that GDP_GCPI underestimates the regional variations compared to GDP_NCPI. In some cases, GDP_GCPI indicates the wrong direction of the economic damages of a country since the impacts on prices are much stronger at the regional level than the global average.

As measured by GDP_NCPI, North American countries enjoy economic benefits rather than suffering economic damage as indicated by GDP_GCPI. More African countries suffer economic damage compared to that indicated by GDP_GCPI. Particularly, the economic damage in Ethiopia is 6% of GDP_NCPI rather than a benefit equal to 41% of GDP_GCPI, indicating how high prices at local level compared to the global average dramatically change the estimated economic impact.

As indicated by GDP_NCPI in Fig. 5, most countries in Africa, Asia, and Latin America suffer economic damages, particularly India and North African countries. On the contrary, Canada, US, Australia, Argentina, and several European countries enjoy certain economic benefits rather than damages.

GDP_GCPI in this study can be taken as an approximate of GDP calculated at PPP, when the basket of consumer goods is assumed to include all consumer goods in the world. It is well known that such an indicator tends to overestimate the GDP of developing countries while being proper for developed countries since much more consumer goods in the PPP basket are from developed countries. According to Asheim and Wei (2009), GDP deflated at local CPI can serve as an indicator of welfare by taking price change effects into account to avoid counter-intuitive results. Hence, it is more plausible to use GDP_NCPI to indicate economic damage resulting from climate change at national and regional levels.

3.5. *The choice of price index in IAMs*

GDP_CP is commonly used by statistical offices of a country and by researchers to measure economic damages associated with physical damages of climate change by assuming constant prices. The results above show problems in using this index because the effects of changes in relative prices are excluded. Climate change will typically imply different damages across sectors, which cause changes in relative prices across sectors. This study shows that changes in relative prices may modify the estimated economic damage considerably, which should not be omitted.

Most IAMs represent damages of climate change by the reduction in an economic aggregate, usually GDP. The question arises, which GDP indicator should be used to measure the damages of climate change? As shown above, it depends on how the adaptation of producers and consumers is modeled in the IAMs. For example, if the utility is linked to an aggregate of consumption as the only independent variable, a CPI-deflated GDP should be used since in this case the utility function does not capture effects of changes in relative prices among products. If the utility function is based on individual products as separate independent variables, the indicator calculated at constant price seems more plausible, since the effect of relative price changes is partially captured by the utility function although the adaptation of producers is still excluded. The results above show that the difference may be large.

If the aim is to compare economic damages across regions or countries, then GDP deflated by local CPI is recommended rather than GDP at PPP as illustrated by GDP_GCPI in this study, although GDP at PPP is widely adopted by international organizations such World Bank and International Monetary Fund, and many IAMs.

4. Conclusions

This chapter shows how alternative assumptions related to adaptation may modify estimates of the economic damage caused by climate change. The main message is the need to specify assumptions underlying estimates of the economic damages due to climate change. We show that adaptation among economic agents implies that a physical effect of climate change on grain yield at 2.3% on the world scale in 2100 is modified to a reduction in costs between 0 and 2.3%, depending on the assumptions related to adaptation.

The economic impacts vary considerably across regions, however. In an average 2100 climate, the economic impacts due to a given physical impact on grain production range from −25% to 70% of the GDP at the regional level, although only 0–2.3% at the global level. Not surprisingly, developing countries depending heavily on agriculture would suffer more economic damages due to climate change. It is important for these countries to adjust industrial structure and develop diverse income sources to be better prepared for the much stronger regional damages resulting from climate change than the global average.

A main reason why economic damages estimated at constant prices provide a poor indicator of the economic impacts is that the price effects are omitted. GDP deflated at local or regional CPI is the most plausible indicator of economic damage resulting from climate change to measure the changes in local or regional welfare, although GDP at constant prices and PPP is widely adopted to represent economic damage resulting from climate change in most IAMs and previous studies.

Since GDP is widely taken as an indicator of economic growth, the choice of a price index in the GDP calculation is crucial to properly evaluate the climate change impact on economic growth, particularly in the cases of large changes in relative prices due to climate change. This is particularly important for developing countries as GDP at PPP tends to underestimate the damages due to climate change to the local economy.

References

Aaheim, A., Amundsen, H., Dokken, T., and Wei, T. (2012). Impacts and adaptation to climate change in European economies. *Global Environmental Change-Human and Policy Dimensions*, 22, 959–968.

Aaheim, A., Orlov, A., Wei, T., and Glomsrød, S. (2018). GRACE model and applications. *Report.* Oslo, Norway: CICERO.

Aaheim, A. and Rive, N. (2005). A model for global responses to anthropogenic changes in the environment (GRACE). *Report.* Oslo, Norway: CICERO.

Aguiar, A., Narayanan, B., and Mcdougall, R. (2016). An overview of the GTAP 9 data base. *Journal of Global Economic Analysis*, 1, 181–208.

Asheim, G. B. and Wei, T. (2009). Sectoral income. *Environmental and Resource Economics*, 42, 65–87.

Carattini, S., Kallbekken, S., and Orlov, A. (2019). How to win public support for a global carbon tax. *Nature*, 565, 289–291.

Dayaratna, K., Mckitrick, R., and Kreutzer, D. (2017). Empirically constrained climate sensitivity and the social cost of carbon. *Climate Change Economics*, 08, 1750006.

Fankhauser, S. (1995). Protection versus Retreat: The economic costs of sea-level rise. *Environment and Planning A: Economy and Space*, 27, 299–319.

Glomsrød, S., Wei, T., and Alfsen, K. (2013). Pledges for climate mitigation: The effects of the Copenhagen accord on CO_2 emissions and mitigation costs. *Mitigation and Adaptation Strategies for Global Change*, 18, 619–636.

Glomsrød, S., Wei, T., Aamaas, B., Lund, M. T., and Samset, B. H. (2016). A warmer policy for a colder climate: Can China both reduce poverty and cap carbon emissions? *Science of The Total Environment*, 568, 236–244.

Hertel, T. W., Baldos, U. L. C., and van der Mensbrugghe, D. (2016). Predicting long-term food demand, cropland use, and prices. *Annual Review of Resource Economics*, 8, 417–441.

Lemoine, D. and Kapnick, S. (2016). A top-down approach to projecting market impacts of climate change. *Nature Climate Change*, 6, 51–55.

Mendelsohn, R., Morrison, W., Schlesinger, M. E., and Andronova, N. G. (2000). Country-specific market impacts of climate change. *Climatic Change*, 45, 553–569.

Moore, F. C., Baldos, U., Hertel, T., and Diaz, D. (2017). New science of climate change impacts on agriculture implies higher social cost of carbon. *Nature Communications*, 8, 1607.

Nordhaus, W. D. (1993). Optimal greenhouse-gas reductions and tax policy in the "DICE" model. *The American Economic Review*, 83, 313–317.

Nordhaus, W. D. (2006). Geography and macroeconomics: New data and new findings. *Proceedings of the National Academy of Sciences of the United States of America*, 103, 3510–3517.

Nordhaus, W. D. (2008). *A Question of Balance: Weighing the Options on Global Warming Policies*, Yale University Press.

Orlov, A., Sillmann, J., Aunan, K., Kjellstrom, T., and Aaheim, A. (2020). Economic costs of heat-induced reductions in worker productivity due to global warming. *Global Environmental Change*, 63, 102087.

Taylor, K. E., Stouffer, R. J., and Meehl, G. A. (2012). An overview of CMIP5 and the experiment design. *Bulletin of the American Meteorological Society*, 93, 485–498.

Tol, R. S. J. (1997). On the optimal control of carbon dioxide emissions: An application of FUND. *Environmental Modeling & Assessment*, 2, 151–163.

Tol, R. S. J. (2002). Estimates of the damage costs of climate change. Part 1: Benchmark estimates. *Environmental and Resource Economics*, 21, 47–73.

Underdal, A. and Wei, T. (2015). Distributive fairness: A mutual recognition approach. *Environmental Science & Policy*, 51, 35–44.

Van Den Bergh, J. C. J. M., and Botzen, W. J. W. (2015). Monetary valuation of the social cost of CO_2 emissions: A critical survey. *Ecological Economics*, 114, 33–46.

Wei, T., Glomsrød, S., and Zhang, T. (2017). Extreme weather, food security and the capacity to adapt — the case of crops in China. *Food Security*, 9, 523–535.

Wei, T. Y., Zhang, T. Y., Cui, X. F., Glomsrod, S., and Liu, Y. (2019). Potential influence of climate change on grain self-sufficiency at the country level considering adaptation measures. *Earths Future*, 7, 1152–1166.

Weitzman, M. L. (2012). GHG targets as insurance against catastrophic climate damages. *Journal of Public Economic Theory*, 14, 221–244.

Wouter Botzen, W. J. and Van Den Bergh, J. C. J. M. (2012). How sensitive is Nordhaus to Weitzman? Climate policy in DICE with an alternative damage function. *Economics Letters*, 117, 372–374.

https://doi.org/10.1142/9789811240553_0006

Chapter 6

Climate Change Impacts and Market-Driven Adaptation: The Costs of Inaction Including Market Rigidities

Francesco Bosello[*,‡] **and Ramiro Parrado**[†,§]

[*]Department of Environmental Sciences, Informatics and Statistics, University Ca' Foscari of Venice, Italy; RFF-CMCC European Institute on Economics and the Environment (EIEE) and Centro Euro-Mediterraneo sui Cambiamenti Climatici (CMCC), Italy

[†]RFF-CMCC European Institute on Economics and the Environment (EIEE) Centro Euro-Mediterraneo sui Cambiamenti Climatici (CMCC), Italia, and Università Ca' Foscari, Venezia, Italia

[‡]francesco.bosello@unive.it

[§]ramiro.parrado@cmcc.it

In this paper, we present a simple impact assessment exercise conducted with a CGE model with two purposes. First, we address a specific criticism raised against IAMs: that of "overly optimistic" representation of adaptation processes that brings, as a consequence, the implicit conclusion of a tendency to underestimate climate change damages. We show that by introducing rigidities in adaptation processes, the general results of the economic damage assessment performed do change, but not substantively. We conclude that although a more difficult adaptation increases the damages as expected (in our specific case, globally by 20%, but at high-temperature levels), this is not sufficient to drastically change the overall picture. On the one hand, this highlights robustness of the results obtained with respect to adaptation processes. On the other hand, it shows that the autonomous market adaptation mechanisms embedded in CGE models explain only marginally low climate change costs. These are in fact due to omission of other impacts because of their proven difficulty to be modeled, such as extreme events, damages due to ecosystem services' losses, as well as major disruptions due to the existence of tipping points.

Second, we also verify whether the assessments performed with CGE models produce lower climate change cost estimates than IA models using reduced-form climate change damage functions. We show that, in fact, when the same impact categories are considered across the two methodologies, damage estimates do not differ significantly at the global level.

1. Introduction and Background

To manage the complexity of economic assessments of climate change impacts, climate change research has depended on increasing development and application of integrated assessment models (IAMs). Their distinctive feature is to describe in a controlled environment the "climate change issue" in its entirety, i.e., connecting the climatic, environmental, and social components.

Two broad approaches can be identified in the economic quantification of climate change damages with IAMs. One makes ample use of reduced-form climate change damage functions (CCDFs). Basically, a more or less sophisticated functional form translates temperature increases into GDP losses (Nordhaus, 1991, Nordhaus and Yang, 1996, Nordhaus and Boyer, 2000, Popp, 2004, Manne and Richels, 2004, Edenhofer *et al.*, 2005, Bosello *et al.*, 2006, Gerlagh, 2007, Ortiz *et al.*, 2011, Tol, 2014, Ignjacevic *et al.*, 2020). Parameterization of these functions derives from an extrapolation of the impact literature, econometric analyses, and/or qualified expert opinions. A different approach, often coupled with the use of Computable General Equilibrium (CGE) models, consists in translating climate change pressures into changes in quantity/quality of factors of production and/or in agents' preferences driving demand and supply behavior in the models. GDP losses (climate change costs) then are the direct outcome of the simulation and do not stem from an explicit function and its *ad hoc* parameterization (see, e.g., Tsigas *et al.*, 1997, Darwin and Tol, 2001, Deke *et al.*, 2001, Bosello *et al.*, 2007, 2008, 2012; Aaheim *et al.*, 2009; Eboli *et al.*, 2010, Roson and Van der Mensbrugghe, 2010, Ciscar *et al.*, 2011, Parrado and De Cian, 2013, Dellink *et al.*, 2019, Szewczyk *et al.*, 2020).

Results from IAMs and IAMs, however, have been subjected to many criticisms: The following are their "recognized" limitations: the difficulty to capture many social facts like the role of institutions, conflicts, disruption of knowledge, learning, and social capital potentially triggered by climate change (Anthoff and Tol, 2013, Stern, 2013); the still weak empirical foundation of damage functions (Pindyck, 2017, 2019); and the complexity to include risk, irreversibility, and catastrophic events (Weitzman, 2007, 2008, 2009, 2010, Ackerman and Stanton, 2012). One particular criticism refers to over-simplified modeling of adaptation processes that disregards the fact that, while adapting, agents may not use perfect information and, for technological, economic, psychological, and cultural characteristics, may be resistant to some changes (Patt *et al.*, 2010).

All this suggests quite clearly an underestimation of climate change costs. This idea seems somehow supported by comparing the outcomes of IAMs with alternative assessment methods, like econometric approaches or semi-qualitative techniques (Howard and Sterner, 2017). The former, in particular, received a recent push by numerous papers developing a country-level analyses that investigates the relation across many social, economic, and climatic variables (see Carleton and Hsiang (2016) for a survey and Auffhammer (2018) for discussion) and highlights impacts an order of magnitude larger than IAMs, especially at relatively moderate temperature increases (Burke *et al.*, 2015).

This paper contributes to this debate from two perspectives. First, it tests if and how introducing rigidities, i.e., "more realism," in autonomous adaptation processes influences the final economic evaluation of climate change impacts. The exercise starts from a "standard" climate change impact assessment developed with a CGE model. The choice of the CGE methodology, rather than the use of an IAM applying a reduced-form CCDF, has two main motivations. On the one hand, the former, more than the latter, features explicitly many different parameters and equations that represent technological or behavioral adaptation processes. On the other hand, climate change impact assessments conducted with CGE models seem to highlight lower losses also compared with hard-linked IAMs.

In the exercise, the primary factors' substitution in the production function, the substitutability of domestic with imported intermediates, and, finally, the sectoral workforce mobility in the model are reduced from their baseline level. It is demonstrated that, while these frictions in adaptation increase the cost of climate change impacts, they neither change substantively the qualitative nor the quantitative results. The first conclusion is thus partly upsetting. On the positive side, one can conclude that results from these kinds of assessments are robust to assumptions on adaptation. More on the negative side, it might be recognized that these models have only limited possibilities, i.e., are too "rigid," to realistically capture adaptation processes.

Second, the exercise proposes a comparison of economic damages estimated with the CGE model with reduced-form CCDFs from well-established IAMs. It does so extrapolating, from the damage estimates, its own reduced-form CCDF. It is shown that, at the global level, reduced forms are not significantly different when the comparison is even, i.e., when the same impact categories are included.

In what follows, Section 2 describes the ICES CGE model used and the scenario calibration, Section 3 the derivation and implementation of climate change impacts, Section 4 presents the impact estimates for different temperature increase scenarios, extrapolates a reduced-form climate change damage function with "model baseline" market-driven adaptation, and compares it with the results from reduced forms used in other well-established IA models, Section 5 analyzes the effects of introducing rigidities in adaptation processes, and finally Section 6 concludes.

2. The ICES CGE Model and Benchmark

ICES is a recursive-dynamic computable general equilibrium (CGE) model based on the GTAP 8 database (Narayanan *et al.*, 2012). The ICES simulation period is 2007–2050 resolved in one-year time steps, with 2007 as the calibration year. Compared to the standard GTAP database and model, in addition to the dynamic in capital stock, it includes renewable energy production. Different versions of the ICES model have been extensively used in past exercises to assess many different kinds of climate change impacts for different climatic scenarios and regional aggregations from an economic viewpoint (for extended

Table 1. Regional and sectoral details of the ICES model applied in this study.

Regional detail				
Europe	*Africa/Middle East*	*Americas*	*Asia*	*Oceania*
North Europe	North Africa	USA	Japan	Australia
North_EU15	Sub-Saharan Africa	Canada	South Korea	New Zealand
Med_EU15	South Africa	Rest of LACA	South Asia	
Med_EU12	Middle East	Brazil	India	
East_EU12		Mexico	China	
Rest of Europe			East Asia	
Russia				
Rest of FSU				

Sectoral detail	
Sectors	*Energy sectors*
Agriculture	Coal
Forestry	Oil
Fishing	Gas
Energy sectors (see right column) →	NuclearFuel
Energy Intensive Industries	Oil_Pcts
Other Industries	Ely_Nuclear
Transport	Ely_Biomass
Market services	Ely_Hydro
Public services	Ely_Solar
	Ely_Wind
	Ely_Other

model description and reference, the interested reader is addressed to www.icesmodel.org). For the sake of the present analysis, the world economic system has been specified into 25 regions and 19 representative industries (see Table 1).

The socio-economic reference for the analysis is the SSP2 — "Middle of the Road or Dynamics as Usual" scenario of the Shared Social Economic Pathways (O'Neill *et al.*, 2014). This scenario assumes socio-economic development in line with that of recent decades, with reductions in resource and energy intensity at historic rates and a slowly

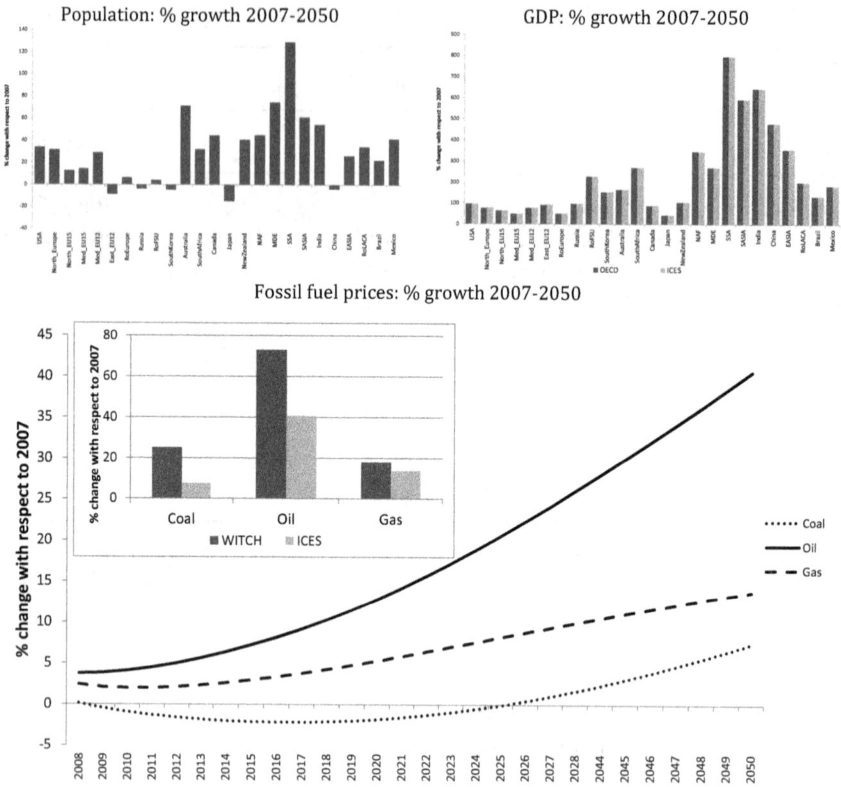

Fig. 1. Population, GDP, and fossil fuel price trends for the ICES baseline.

decreasing fossil fuel dependency. Quantitatively, the ICES reference baseline assumes the following (see Fig. 1):

- GDP and population growths as those reported for the SSP2 in the "OECD version."[1]
- Labor force growth the same as that of population.

[1]The SSPs database is available at: https://secure.iiasa.ac.at/web-apps/ene/SspDb/.

- Fossil fuel price growth trends of 25%, 73%, and 18% for coal, oil, and gas, respectively, within the period 2007–2050.[2]
- Energy efficiency yearly increases between 0.28% and 0.56% in developed countries and 0.63 % in developing countries.[3]

3. Economic Assessment of Climate Change Impacts

This exercise considers an extended set of climate change impacts. They refer to the consequences of changes in sea level, in fish stock productivity, in land productivity, in tourism flows, in energy demand, in health status, and in ecosystem services. Source information is based on bottom-up partial-equilibrium exercises performed within the framework of recently concluded and ongoing EU Sixth and Seventh Framework Program (FP6 and FP7) research projects: ClimateCost, SESAME, and Global-IQ. The impact literature and the methodology applied by dynamic optimization hard-linked integrated assessment models supported the computations of impacts on health and ecosystem services. Table 2 provides a summary of the impacts considered as well as their sources. All studies have a global coverage. Most of them they come from grid-based datasets and models and report data with a high spatial resolution. When necessary, results have been aggregated to match the geographical resolution of the CGE model.

Impacts are computed for temperature increases consistent with the Representative Concentration Pathways (RCPs) 2.6, 6.0, and 8.5 (Van Vuuren *et al.*, 2012). Nonetheless, only crop yield changes are

---

[2]These price trends are derived from simulations performed with the WITCH integrated assessment dynamic optimization model (Bosetti *et al.*, 2009) applied to the SSP2. WITCH, among other features, offers a detailed description of the energy system and therefore an endogenous energy price formation.

[3]We set these average growth rates for energy efficiency based on information from (IEA, 2011, 2012). For 2011, the World Energy Outlook 2011 shows an annual average reduction of energy intensity of about 1.3% and almost 1.5 % for OECD and non-OECD countries, respectively, in the period 1985–2009. In the following edition of the WEO 2012, the annual average percentage change of world energy intensity is reported to be only -0.5% for the period 2000–2010. Accordingly, we impose higher growth rates of energy efficiency for developing countries (0.63%) and lower rates for developed countries (between 0.28% and 0.56%).

Table 2. Summary of climate change impacts considered and source models.

CC Impact	Source	Project	Time frame	Scenarios/reduced form	
				AR5	SRES
Sea level rise	DIVA model — Vafeidis *et al.* (2008)	ClimateCost	2001–2100		A1B, E1
Fisheries	Cheung *et al.* (2010)	SESAME	2000–2060		A1
Agricult.	PIK — LPJmL model ISIP-MIP runs	GLOBAL-IQ	2007–2100	RCP 8.5 RCP 6.0 RCP 2.6	
Ecosyst.	Warren *et al.* (2006), Manne *et al.* (1995)	—	2000–2060	***Reduced form***	
Tourism	Tol (2002a,b) — HTM Bigano *et al.* (2007)	ClimateCost	2005–2100		A1, B2
Energy demand	POLES — Criqui (2001), Criqui *et al.* (2009)	ClimateCost	2000–2050		A1
Health	Tol (2002a,b)	—	2008–2060	***Reduced form***	

explicitly related to those scenarios. The other source studies quantify impacts in the A1B and/or B2 IPCC SRES scenarios (Nakicenovic and Swart, 2000). This introduces a relatively minor approximation problem in specifying the RCP 8.5 reference, as until 2050 its temperature profile and that of A1B are reasonably close. Larger differences characterize RCP 8.5, RCP 6.0, and RCP 2.6. Thus, when necessary, impacts consistent with the RCP 6.0 and RCP 2.6 have been reconstructed mapping the temperature of A1B and B2 scenarios to that of RCP 6.0 following Rogelj *et al.* (2012) and the average trend of temperature changes for each RCP. Then, impacts have been translated from a temperature increase scenario to the other proportionally. They have not been obtained by direct re-running of the sectoral/bottom-up impact models. The outcomes of our elaborations are reported in the next subsections.

3.1. *Sea level rise*

Estimates of coastal land lost to *sea level rise* are based upon the Dynamic Integrated Vulnerability Assessment (DIVA) model outputs (Vafeidis *et al.*, 2008) applied in the FP7 ClimateCost project (Brown *et al.*, 2011). DIVA is an engineering model designed to address the vulnerability of coastal areas to sea level rise. The model is based on a world database of the natural system and socio-economic factors for world coastal areas reported with a spatial resolution of 0.5°. The temporal resolution is 5-year time steps until 2100 and 100-year time steps from 2100 to 2500. Changes in natural as well as socio-economic conditions of possible future scenarios are implemented through a set of impact-adaptation algorithms. Impacts are then assessed both in physical (i.e., sq. km of land lost) and economic (i.e., value of land lost and adaptation costs) terms. The Met Office Hadley Centre generated the sea level rise scenarios for Climate Cost.

3.2. *Fisheries*

Climate change-induced changes in global catch potential derive from the FP6 SESAME project and are based upon Cheung *et al.* (2010). Basically, the changes in future catch potential are calculated considering (i) species distribution and (ii) the primary production of oceans:

1. Species distribution depends on species' maximum and minimum depth limits, and northern and southern latitudinal range limits, an index of association with major habitat types.
2. Primary production has been predicted following published algorithms and empirical models, according to two climate scenarios.

By combining this kind of information for each spatial cell, the empirical model (Cheung *et al.*, 2008a) computes the maximum catch potential. The specific details are described in Cheung *et al.* (2010). They applied an empirical model Cheung *et al.* (2008a) that predicts maximum catch potential depending upon the primary production and distribution range of 1,066 species of exploited fish and invertebrates. Distribution of each species on a 30′ latitude 30′ longitude grid is derived from an algorithm (**?**) including the species' maximum and minimum depth limits, northern and southern latitudinal range limits, an index of association with major habitat types, and known occurrence boundaries as input parameters. Future changes in species distribution are simulated by using a dynamic bioclimate envelope model (Cheung *et al.*, 2008a, 2010). The model associates species' preference profiles with environmental conditions: seawater temperature (bottom and surface), salinity, distance from sea ice, and habitat types (coral reef, estuaries, seamounts, coastal upwelling, and a category that includes all other habitat types). Preference profiles consider the suitability of environmental conditions to each species. Then, these are linked to the expected carrying capacity in a population dynamic model. The model assumes that carrying capacity varies positively with habitat suitability of each spatial cell. Finally, aggregating spatially and across species, the related change in total catch potential can be determined.

3.3. *Agriculture*

Climate change impacts on crop yield (physical production per hectare) derive from the output of the LPJmL Dynamic Global Vegetation Model (Bondeau *et al.*, 2007) developed at PIK and applied within the FP7 Global-IQ project. The LPJ model endogenously determines spatially explicit transient vegetation composition and the associated carbon and water budgets for different land uses. It can estimate potential yield and its changes for many crops with a global resolution of 0.5 degree grid cells (roughly 50 km^2). In Global-IQ, yield data for the different crops have been aggregated into just one weighted average value for the agricultural sector as a whole. The data hereby estimated do not consider the carbon fertilization effects on vegetation.

3.4. *Ecosystems*

To estimate losses in ecosystem services, a modified Willingness to Pay (WTP) approach has been used. The starting assumption is that these services are largely non-marketed and non-directly marketable. Accordingly, their value can be only extracted through elicitation of preferences. In particular, the WTP to avoid a given loss in ecosystems is used to approximate the lost value in case they are not protected. This is for instance the methodology applied in the MERGE model (Manne *et al.*, 1995) where the monetized ecosystem losses related to a 2.5°C temperature increase above preindustrial levels are set equal to the 2% of GDP when per capita income is above $40,000. The 2% figure is the US EPA expenditure on environmental protection in 1995. The implicit assumptions are that what is actually paid is reasonably close to the WTP, and also roughly sufficient to preserve ecosystems and their services in a world warming moderately.

This approach has been applied here, but by rescaling all to the more recent data of the EU 2007 expenditure on environmental protection by the public sector (0.62% of GDP, EUROSTAT, 2013), and assuming more conservatively than Manne *et al.* (1995) that the observed expenditure allows protection against 2°C warming. Then, to derive WTP in non-EU countries, the logistic function proposed by Manne *et al.* (1995) is used (see also Warren *et al.*, 2006):

$$WTP_{n,t|t=2^\circ\mathrm{C}} = \gamma \Delta T^{\varepsilon}_{n,t|t=2^\circ\mathrm{C}} \times \frac{1}{1 + 100e^{(-0.23 * GDPn,t|t=2^\circ\mathrm{C}/POPn,t|t=2^\circ\mathrm{C})}}. \quad (1)$$

While ε is set at the original value of 2, γ is calibrated from EU data in order to give exactly 0.62% of GDP when per capita income is the

2007 EU average ($34,262), and $\Delta T = 2°C$. The last step is to use the WTP to measure the direct cost of losses in the ecosystem and their services.

3.5. *Tourism*

Changes in *tourism flows* induced by climate change are derived from simulations based on the Hamburg Tourism Model (HTM, Bigano *et al.*, 2006, 2007) amply used in EU research projects like FP6 CIRCE, ClimChalp, and more recently the FP7 ClimateCost project. HTM is an econometric simulation model, estimating the number of domestic and international tourists by country, the share of international tourists in total tourists, and tourism flows between countries. The model runs in time steps of 5 years. First, it estimates the total tourists in each country, depending on the size of the population and of average income per capita. Then, it divides tourists between those that travel abroad and those that stay within the country of origin. In this way, the model provides the total number of holidays as well as the trade-off between holidays at home and abroad. The share of domestic tourists in total tourism depends on the climate in the home country and on per capita income. International tourists are then allocated to all other countries based on a general attractiveness index, climatic characteristics, per capita income in the destination countries, and the distance between origin and destination. Climate is proxied by the annual mean temperature which enters among the explanatory variables with a quadratic form. This is to capture the fact that warmer climate can indeed be more attractive, but just up to a given "optimal level." Then, further increases are negative for tourism.

The model is calibrated to 1995 data, and as in Berrittella *et al.* (2006) and Bigano *et al.* (2008), estimations of tourism flows by region are obtained from version 1.2 of the Hamburg Tourism Model (HTM).

3.6. *Residential energy demand*

Responses of *residential energy demand* to increasing temperatures derive from the POLES model (Criqui, 2001, Criqui *et al.*, 2009) which was also used in the FP7 ClimateCost project. POLES is a bottom-up partial-equilibrium model of the world energy system.

It determines future energy demand and supply for different energy vectors (coal, oil, natural gas, electricity) according to energy price trend, technological innovation, and climate impacts through their effects on heating and cooling degree days.

3.7. *Health*

Impacts on human health are expressed by changes in mortality and morbidity associated with malaria, schistosomiasis, dengue, diarrhea, cardiovascular, and respiratory diseases applying the same methodology of Bosello *et al.* (2006). Estimates of the change in mortality due to vector-borne diseases (malaria, schistosomiasis, dengue fever) as the result of a one-degree increase in the global mean temperature are taken from Tol (2002a,b). To account for changes in vulnerability possibly induced by improved access to health care facilities associated with improvement in living standards (read GDP growth), Tol (2002a,b) applies the relationship between per capita income and disease incidence developed by Tol and Dowlatabadi (2001).[4] We use the same relationship applying the projected per capita regional income growth of the ICES model.

For diarrhea, we follow Link and Tol (2004), who report the estimated relationship between mortality and morbidity on the one hand and temperature and per capita income on the other hand using the WHO Global Burden of Disease data (Murray and Lopez, 1996). Martens (1998) reports the results of a meta-analysis of the change in cardiovascular and respiratory mortality for 17 countries. Tol (2002a,b) extrapolates these findings to all other countries, using the current climate as the main predictor. Cold-related cardiovascular, heat-related cardiovascular, and (heat-related) respiratory mortality are specified separately, as are the cardiovascular impacts on the population below 65 and above. Heat-related mortality is assumed to only affect the urban population. We use this model directly on a country basis, before aggregating to the ICES regions.

[4]Vulnerability to vector-borne diseases strongly depends on basic health care and the ability to purchase medicine. Tol and Dowlatabadi (2001) suggest a linear relationship between per capita income and health. In this analysis, vector-borne diseases have an income elasticity of −2.7.

Changes in health care expenditures are also estimated. The literature on the costs of diseases is thin and few papers can be used as reference. The costs of vector-borne diseases are taken from Chima *et al.* (2003), who report the expenditure on prevention and treatment costs per person per month.

Figure 2 reports the data computation for 2050 referring to the RCP 2.6, 6.0, and 8.5 (respectively, associated with a temperature increase of 1.76°C, 1.91°C, and 2.52°C with respect to preindustrial level).

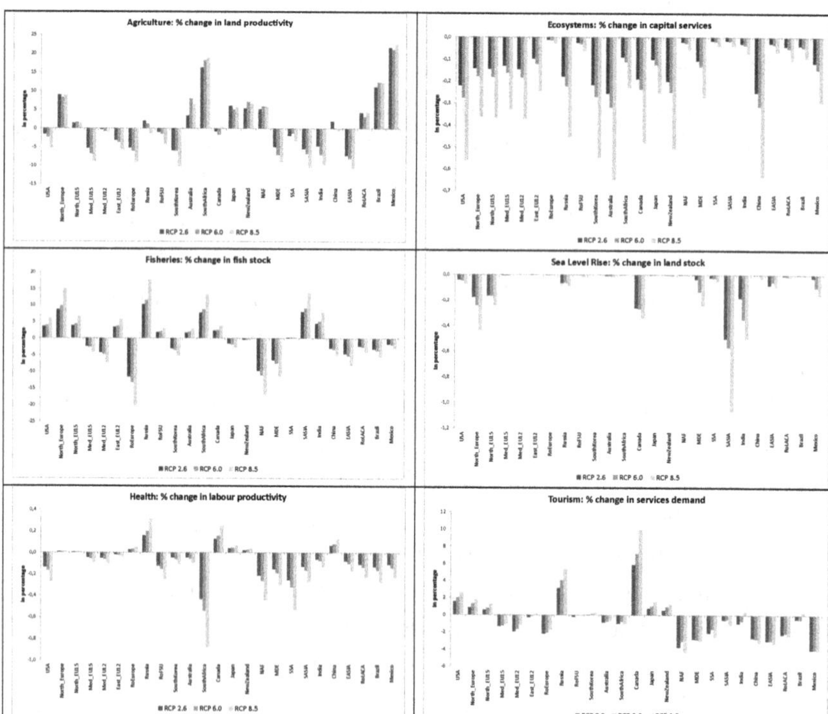

(a)

Fig. 2. Direct impacts of climate change, inputs to the ICES CGE model (ref. year 2050).

Source: Our elaborations from quoted studies reported in Section 3.

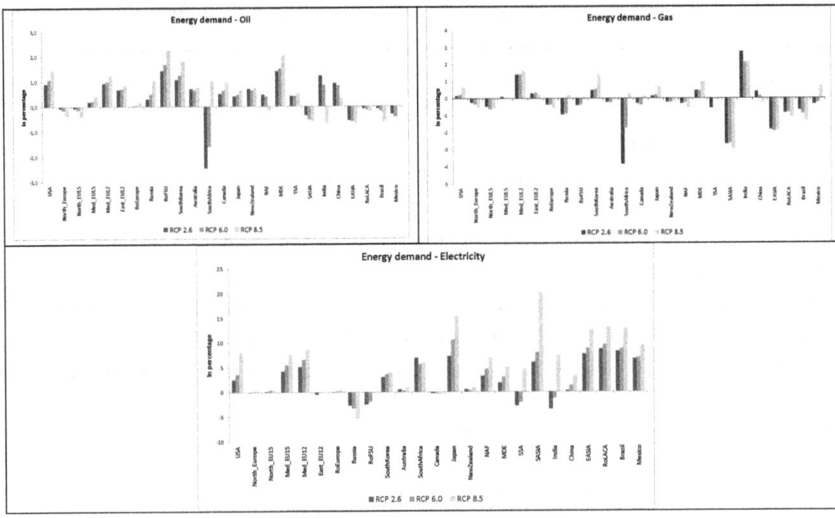

(b)

Fig. 2. (*Continued*)

3.8. *Including climate change impacts in the CGE model*

Once the impacts have been quantified, they need to be translated into a format compatible with that of the ICES model, i.e., accordingly, into changes of those factors driving demand and supply patterns inside the model. The impacts on supply and demand are summarized in Table 3.

Two broad categories of impacts can be distinguished in Table 3. The first affects the supply side of the economic system and concerns variables that are typically exogenous in CGE models, namely, quantity or productivity of primary factors. Changes in these variables can be thus easily accommodated. Impacts on sea level rise, agriculture, and human health belong to this category and they do not require any substantial change in the basic structure of the model to be implemented.

The second affects changes in the demand side. Impacts on tourism and on energy consumption are of this kind. This implies the need to intervene on variables which are endogenous to, or the output of, the model. The technicality involved is more complex than in the case of

Table 3. Climate-change impacts modelled in ICES.

Supply-side impacts
Impacts on land quantity (land loss due to sea level rise)
Impacts on capital stock (assumed to be equal in % to land loss due to sea level rise)
Impacts on fisheries (changes in fish stock available to the fishing industry)
Impacts on land productivity (yield changes due to temperature changes)
Impacts on ecosystem services (assumed to reduce capital stock according to the willingness to pay to avoid the impacts due to an increase in temperature)
Impact on labor productivity (changes in morbidity and mortality — health effect of climate change)
Demand-side impacts
Impacts on energy demand (change in households energy consumption patterns for heating and cooling purposes)
Impacts on recreational services demand (change in tourism flows induced by changes in climatic conditions)
Impacts on health care expenditure

exogenous variables and the following procedure has been adopted. The computed percentage variations in the demands are imposed as exogenous shifts in the respective demand equations. The implicit assumption is that the starting information refers to partial equilibrium assessments, thus with *all prices and income levels held ideally constant*. The model is then left free to determine the *final* demand adjustments. Modification in demand structure is imposed, however, to comply with the budget constraint, so the changed consumption of energy and tourism services is compensated by opposite changes in expenditure for all the other commodities.

In what follows, we briefly discuss the procedures adopted to implement each of the impacts considered inside the ICES model.

Land losses to sea level rise have been modeled as percent decreases in the stock of productive land and capital by region. Both modifications concern land and capital stocks variables, which are exogenous to the model and therefore can be straightforwardly implemented. As information on capital losses is not readily available, in the ICES simulations, it is assumed that they exactly match land losses.[5]

Changes in *potential fish catches* have been modeled as percent reductions in the natural resource stock (primary factor of production) available to the countries' fishing sectors.

Changes in *crop yields* have been modeled through exogenous changes in land productivity. Due to the nature of source data, land productivity varies by region, but is uniform across all crop types present in ICES.

Impacts on *ecosystems* have been modeled as a loss of physical capital stock. In ICES, the capital stock does not enter directly in the production function, rather capital services do. Nonetheless, in the model, there is a one-on-one relationship between capital stock and capital services as any change in the former implies an equal change in the latter. The assumption thus made is that ecosystems offer a set of support services to the production activity, which are all embedded in capital services. When the ecosystem deteriorates, its production support services deteriorate, and thus, (through deterioration of the capital stock) capital services deteriorate. The amount of the deterioration corresponds to the WTP assessed following the procedure in Section 3.4.

Changes in *tourists' flows* have been modeled as changes in (rescaled) households' demand addressing the market services sector, which includes recreational services. In addition, changes in monetary flows due to variations in tourism demand are simulated through a direct correction of the regional income of each region.

Changes in regional *households' demand for oil, gas, and electricity* have been modeled as changes in households' demand for the output of the respective industries.

[5]We could have avoided including capital losses, however, they are an important part of sea level rise costs; therefore, we prefer to have a rough even though arbitrary estimation of this component rather than none. We are not including displacement costs.

Changes in labor productivity are also considered as the channel to account for *health* impacts. Lower mortality translates into increased labor productivity which is one on one proportional to the change in the total population. The underlying assumption is that health impacts affect active population, disregarding the age characteristic of cardiovascular and respiratory diseases. This information is complemented with health expenditures as percentage of GDP.

4. Climate Change Impacts in a Context of "Standard" Market Adaptation

Results refer to the economic effects of all the impacts mentioned above when they are jointly imposed over the model baseline. These could be referred as market impacts or damages given that they do not consider any other kind of damage estimation such as catastrophic ones. Figure 3 reports climate change impacts on GWP. As expected, RCP 2.6, which is a stabilization scenario, produces the lower costs, while RCP 6.0 is in the middle of the range. In 2050, total costs remain small even in RCP 8.5 reporting the higher CO_2 concentrations. In that year, temperature increase is just slightly beyond the 2.5°C increase. In this context, impacts are still manageable and roughly amount to 0.64% of GDP.

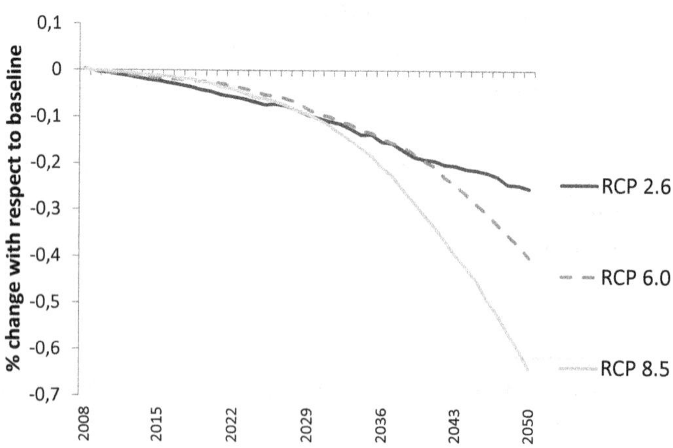

Fig. 3. Climate change impacts on Gross World Product (GWP).

These aggregate figures however hide important regional asymmetries revealed by Figure 4.[6] This highlights, on the one hand, the huge differentiation in regional exposure, sensitivity, and adaptive capacity and, on the other hand, the usefulness of a disaggregated assessment. The clear insight emerging is the higher vulnerability of developing countries to climate change impacts, particularly regions like South Asia and India losing more than 4% of their GDP, and Eastern Asia and Sub-Saharan Africa losing roughly 2% of their GDP in 2050 in the RCP 8.5 scenario.

Figure 5 disentangles the different drivers of GDP impacts at the regional level.[7] It highlights two main points: (i) The final effect (All impacts) results from the interaction of pressures exerted by several single impacts which could be either positive or negative, and that may compensate each other up to a certain extent; and (ii) vulnerability is

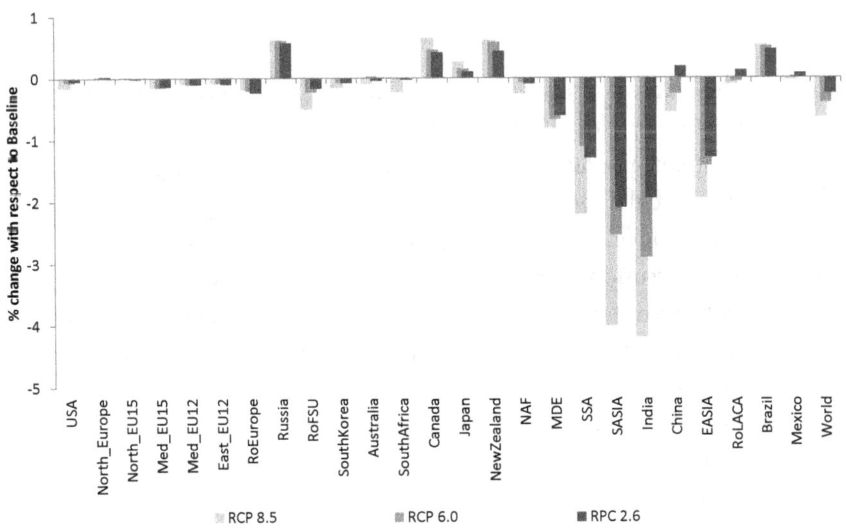

Fig. 4. Climate change impacts on regional GDP in 2050.

[6]The trend of impacts from 2007 to 2050 for each region and each RCP scenario is in Fig. A.1 of the Annex at the end.

[7]This is done for RCP 8.5; the other concentration scenarios are qualitatively similar.

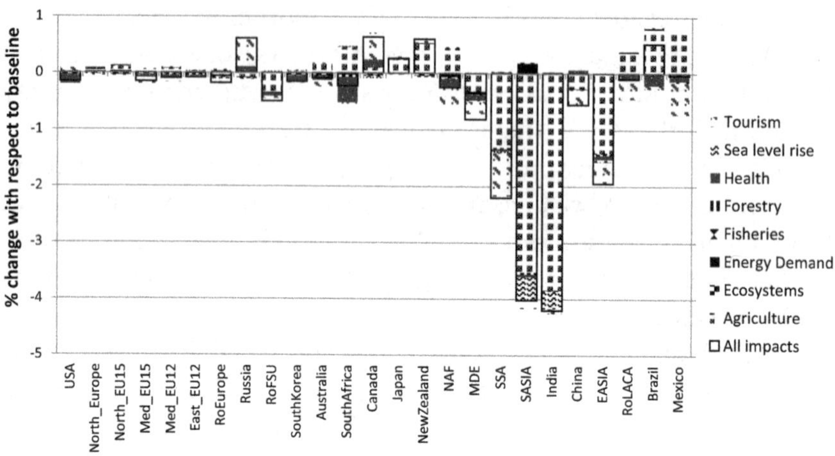

Fig. 5. Decomposition of climate change effects on regional GDP by type of impact (ref. RCP 8.5).

not the same across countries and it depends on economic and geographical characteristics. The most significant effects come from agriculture, tourism, sea level rise, and health. Impacts on agriculture and sea level rise reveal a higher vulnerability in developing countries, while tourism affects developed countries also but mostly in a positive way. An interesting outcome for most of the world, including most developed regions, is the vulnerability arising from health impacts from climate change, which, for instance, is very important in the USA as well as in other Annex 1 countries.

These results are quite well established in the literature.

Taken as they are, they may convey the following implications: climate change is of concern just in the longer term; it can be a relevant issue for developing but is much less for developed countries; and without "low-probability catastrophic losses," it remains basically a distributional/equity rather than a "scale" issue.

What kind of reduced-form climate change damage functions could these results produce? Would they differ substantively from the functions existing in the literature?

4.1. *Reduced-form climate change damage functions*

The GDP losses quantified in Section 4 can offer a basis for estimating a reduced-form CCDF for each of the ICES region. This reduced-form damage function embeds the effect of market-driven adaptation (or said differently the "endogenous price effect") that the CGE model can capture. The procedure is the following. For each year, the different RCPs produce three sets of impacts linked to three different temperature increases and consequently three GDP effects. We selected as reference one single year, specifically 2050, which is the year with the strongest temperature–GDP signals (we recall that impacts are defined for a temperature increase of 1.76°C, 1.91°C, and 2.52°C with respect to preindustrial level). Then, we apply exactly the same functional form used by Nordhaus and Boyer (2000) and Nordhaus (2007) in the RICE model to extrapolate the damage-temperature trend out of sample:

$$D_r(t) = \theta_{1,r}T(t) + \theta_{2,r}T(t)^2$$

where D_r is the regional damage at time t, T is the change in temperature, while $\theta_{1,r}$ and $\theta_{2,r}$ are fitted parameters for each region. The outcome of the procedure for the world and some representative regional aggregates is represented in Fig. 6.

At the world level, a temperature increase of 5°C would produce a GDP loss of roughly 2.75%. This value is close to what is reported for similar temperature increases for instance by the FUND model (roughly 3% of global GDP loss), but lower than in the PAGE (5% world GDP loss) and DICE (7% world GDP loss) models according to the values used in IWGSCC (2010).[8,9]

However, these figures computed by ICES do not account for some important damage components. One that, for instance, in the Nordhaus work, is a major driver of economic losses refers to "catastrophic events." These are defined as severe events such as sharp sea

[8]To be precise, this document reports GDP losses referring in fact to 2100.

[9]Incidentally, it is worth noting the huge GDP losses in India and the Sub-Saharan Africa, both larger than the 7%.

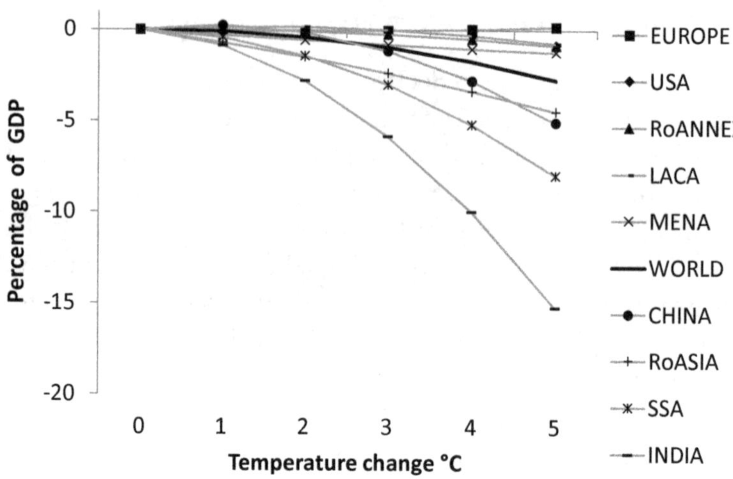

Fig. 6. Regional reduced-form damage functions for market impacts.

level rise, a shutdown of the thermohaline circulation, a runaway greenhouse effect, shifting monsoons, a collapse of the West Antarctic Ice Sheet, and are quantified in terms of percentage of GDP following an approach of willingness to pay to avoid catastrophic risk (Nordhaus and Boyer, 2000).

To allow a more even comparison, we include thus a catastrophic damage component in our reduced-form CCDF following the same methodology and quantification of Nordhaus (2007).[10] The total damages that we are finally able to extrapolate are represented in Fig. 7.

As shown by Fig. 7, the reduced-form climate change damage function enhanced with catastrophic damages reports GWP losses of 6.09% for a 5°C, comparable with those of DICE 2007.[11] This points out, once again, the particular relevance of low-probability high-damage events, and of their modeling, in determining the final economic impact. Given the few points available for the extrapolation, also the

---

[10]In fact, the regional detail between ICES and Nordhaus (2007) is slightly different. When the regions do not perfectly match, we used simple averaging techniques to derive the appropriated catastrophic losses.

[11]This stresses a particular vulnerability for India, the Sub-Saharan Africa, the Rest of Asia, and China, all with losses higher than 7% of GDP for a 5°C temperature increase.

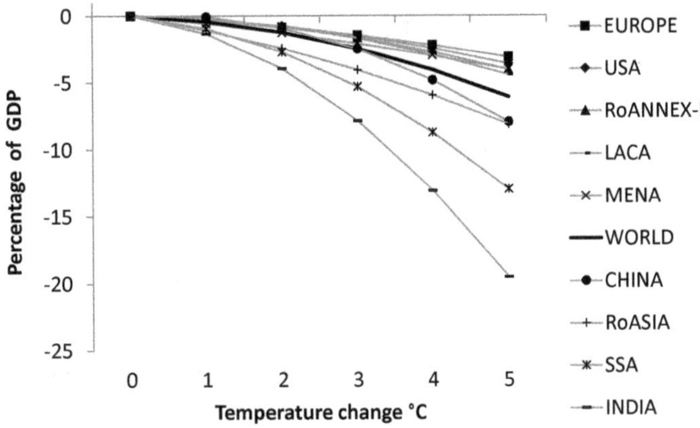

Fig. 7. Regional reduced-form damage functions for market impacts corrected with catastrophic losses.

choice of the particular functional form for the damage function is crucial in determining the economic losses for high-temperature increases.

In summary, when the comparison is even, damage information extracted from the ICES CGE model does not result in CCDFs sensibly different from those obtained with other methodologies, even though the first, differently from the latter, incorporates explicitly endogenous market reactions.

Anyway, the objection to CGE models concerning their potentially overly optimistic view of market-driven adaptation due to the absence of frictions and instantaneous adjustments after a shock still applies. What is the role of these features in the final determination of climate change costs? This question is addressed in the next sections.

5. Introducing Rigidities in Market-driven Adaptation

As standard in CGE models, ICES adopts the Walrasian perfect competition paradigm to simulate adjustment processes. Industries are modeled through representative firms, minimizing costs while taking prices as given. The production functions are specified via a series of nested CES functions as shown in Fig. 8. Final output is the result of the combination of a Value-Added-Energy composite with other intermediate

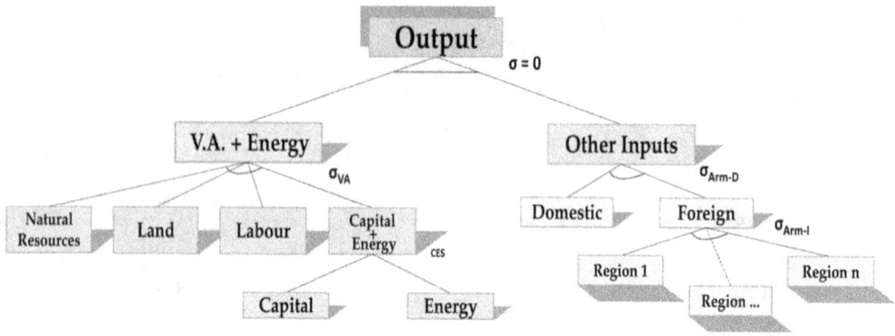

Fig. 8. A reduced representation of the production functions in ICES.

inputs in a Leontief technology production function. The value-added nest is a particularly important node as it governs the substitutability across primary factors, in order to produce the final output. The key parameter is the elasticity of substitution σ_{VA}. Furthermore, intermediate inputs can be produced domestically or imported. Domestic and foreign inputs are imperfect substitutes according to the so-called "Armington" assumption, which accounts for — among others — product heterogeneity. Armington elasticities ($\sigma_{Arm-D}, \sigma_{Arm-I}$) specify this substitutability.

Sectoral mobility of primary inputs within a region can be perfect or sluggish. In the standard ICES version labor and capital are perfectly mobile across sectors within a region, and accordingly there is just one wage economy-wide.

We model a more difficult market-driven adaptation working on these three different "stages" of the production activity. We reduce by a quarter the degree of substitutability between primary factors (σ_{VA}); between domestic and imported intermediates (σ_{Arm-D} and σ_{Arm-I}); then, we abandon the assumption of perfect sectoral mobility of the labor force transforming labor into a sluggish factor of production.

The idea behind the first experiment is to explore the effect of a less optimistic assumption on the technological options available to substitute inputs. The 25% reduction of the initial calibrated value is inspired by Jomini *et al.* (1991), according to whom in the short term substitution elasticities are roughly 60% of the long-term ones. We thus used the slightly higher estimate of 75% to represent a more rigid system.

The rationale of the second experiment is to simulate a more difficult substitutability of domestic with foreign inputs. In principle, this could be driven by both technological reasons or by a more difficult trade. The 25% reduction derives from comparing the GTAP 8 Armington elasticities (on average 7) with the old GTAP 5 elasticity (on average 5.3).

The third experiment aims to remove the particularly unrealistic assumption of frictionless and instantaneous labor mobility from a shrinking to an expanding sector. Sluggishness implies that labor is an imperfect substitute across sectors. It can still move from one sector to another depending on wage differentials, but now its allocation depends upon a constant elasticity of transformation (CET) function which is set to −0.5

In a final experiment, we combine all these three rigidities in a worst-case scenario. The climate change impacts are those calculated for the RCP 8.5.

5.1. *Results*

The inclusion of the rigidities mentioned above in the production process induces an increase in the costs of climate change as shown in Fig. 9. GWP losses rise from roughly 0.64% to almost 0.87%.[12]

The major drivers of these higher costs are the lower degree of substitution across primary factors and the reduced Armington elasticity. The first pushes losses to more than 0.73% of Global GDP in 2050. Facing a reduced ability to recombine primary factors intensifies the initial negative impact on the supply side of the economy. For instance, reduced land productivity can be only partly compensated by using more of the remaining primary factors. Limiting the model's flexibility related to international trade increases climate change costs also to

[12]Note that in this comparison, we are not using the values corrected with catastrophic losses, but those stemming from smooth climate change.

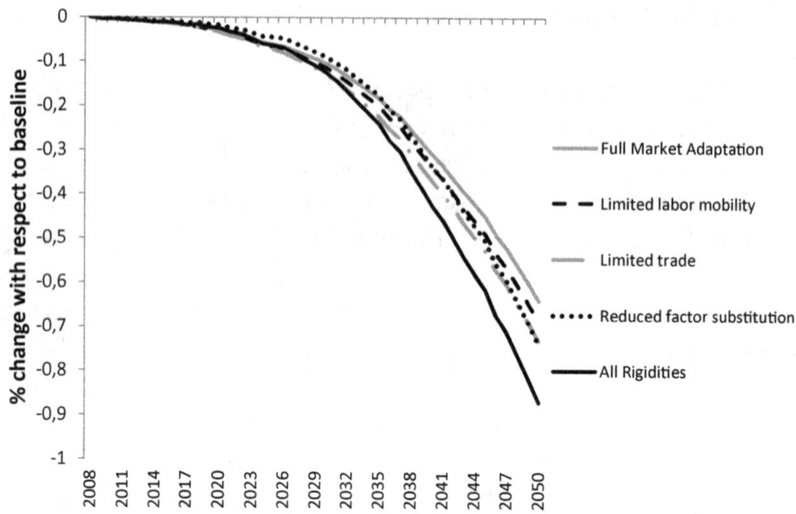

Fig. 9. Climate change impacts on global GDP with market rigidities (RCP 8.5).

0.73% of Global GDP in 2050, showing a very similar impact as reducing primary factor substitution, but has a stronger effect in the initial simulation years. Reduced labor mobility seems a minor determinant: it increases costs just by 0.04 percentage points of global GWP in 2050.

A quick inspection of the regional details (Fig. 10) confirms the asymmetric distribution of negative impacts which are much higher in developing countries. South Asia and India show losses of around 5% of GDP. Developed countries, albeit increasing their losses, are much less adversely affected: USA loses roughly 0.2% of GDP by "limited market adaptation"; GDP losses in European countries remain negligible. It is worth noting that rigidities in primary factor substitution and labor mobility turn the initial slight gains from climate change into a slight loss for northern European countries. Interestingly, some of the countries that in the case of full adaptation experienced net benefits from a changing climate (i.e., Russia, Canada, Japan, Russia, and Brazil) increase these gains in the limited adaptation scenarios. This last result depends upon two facts: First, the different elasticities produce a slightly different structural composition of the economic system. Therefore, notwithstanding that the GDP is the same across the

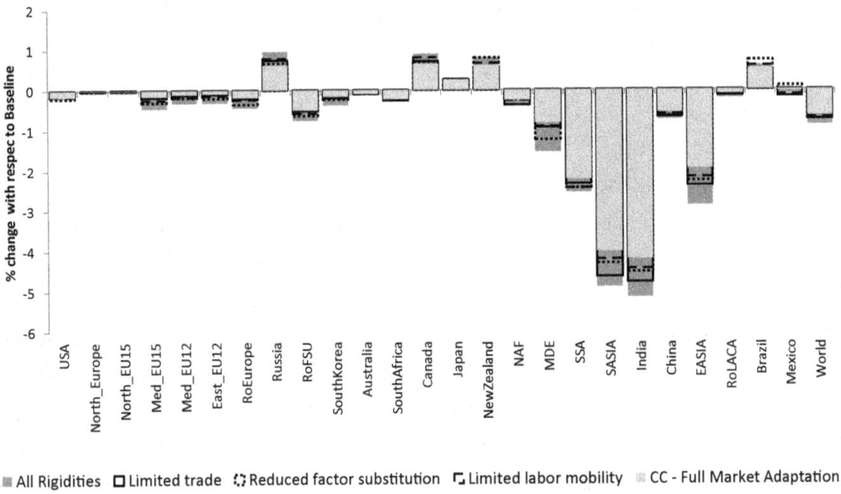

Fig. 10. Climate change impacts on regional GDP with market rigidities (RCP 8.5).

full and limited adaptation case, macro sectors weigh differently and this can amplify/smooth positive/negative effects. Second, there are interaction effects through international trade. Higher losses in some countries can induce higher gains in their competitors.

All in all, the exercise shows somewhat mixed results: On the one hand, relatively minor deviations from the basic parameterization of the model concerning input substitutability/intersectoral mobility are able to increase impacts by roughly 30% at the global level. In this sense, the modeling of market adjustments plays an important role in the determination of the final impacts. On the other hand, the main messages conveyed by the assessment do not change: without including catastrophic events, at least at the world level, and considering the limited range of temperature increase analyzed, GDP impacts of climate change remain limited. This seems to point out that the "apparently" low climate change costs emphasized by CGE models only marginally depend on autonomous market adaptation mechanisms. In fact, this seems mostly due to other impacts which are usually omitted due to their proven difficulty to be included in a regular CGE assessment such as extreme events, damages due to ecosystem services' losses, as well as major disruptions due to the existence of tipping points.

5.2. *Reduced-form climate change damage functions with "limited adaptation"*

For completeness, in this section, we extrapolate a reduced-form climate change damage function for the case of limited adaptation. The methodology followed is the same as Section 4.1. For the sake of comparability, we also include in the damage component catastrophic impacts from Nordhaus and Boyer (2000) and Nordhaus (2007). Figure 11 compares full and limited adaptation damage functions for the World, Europe, and China. As expected, limited adaptation results in higher damage for the world. Due to the quadratic specification of the damage function, the divergence of the two settings is particularly notable for higher temperatures: GWP losses are 20% higher than with full adaptation at a temperature of 5°C. Different regions also present different sensitivity to limits to adaptation. Europe is among the regions that register lower damages even in the presence of adaptation rigidities. Damages with limited adaptation increase only by 10% with respect to full adaptation at the same temperature increase. China

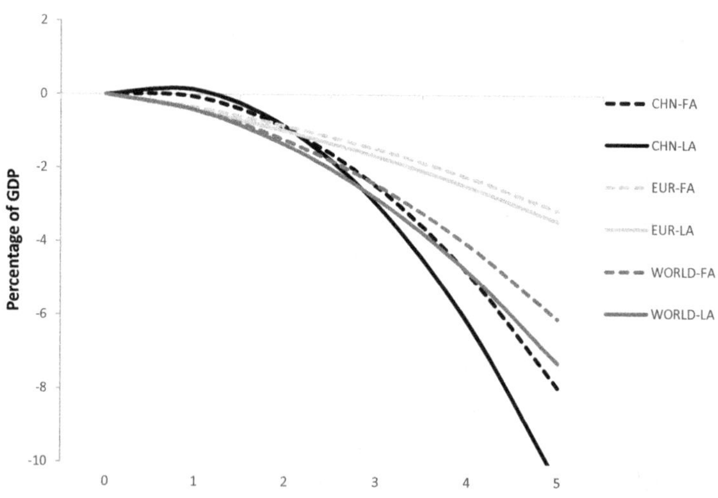

Fig. 11. Reduced-form damage functions with full and limited adaptation (FA and LA in figure).

provides instead a striking example of much higher damage in a scenario with limited adaptation: total impacts of climate change would increase by 32% at a temperature of 5°C.

6. Conclusions

The IA literature proposes two broad approaches for the economic quantification of climate change damages. One makes ample use of reduced-form climate change damage functions which translate temperature increases into GDP losses. Parameterization of these functions involves extrapolations from the impact literature, or data are directly taken from experts' opinions. The other, extensively used in impact assessments conducted with Computable General Equilibrium (CGE) models, consists in translating climate change pressures into changes in quantity/quality of factors of production and/or in agents' preferences driving demand and supply behavior in the models. GDP losses (climate change costs) are thus the direct outcome of the model simulation and do not derive from an explicit function and its ad hoc parameterization.

In this paper, we present a simple impact assessment exercise conducted with a CGE model with two purposes. First, we address a specific criticism raised against IAMs: that of "overly optimistic" representation of adaptation processes that brings, as a consequence, the implicit conclusion of a tendency to underestimate climate change damages. We show that by introducing rigidities in adaptation processes (a lower substitutability of primary input in the production function, a lower substitutability across domestic and imported intermediates, and finally an imperfect mobility of the labor force across sectors), the general results of the economic damage assessment performed did change, but not substantively. We conclude that a more difficult adaptation increases, as expected, the damages (in our specific case, globally by 20%, but at high-temperature levels). The most important driver of cost increases in the long term is the elasticity of input substitution, while, in the short term, it is the restriction in domestic and imported input substitution. However, this is not sufficient to drastically change the overall picture. On the one hand, this highlights the "robustness" of the results obtained with respect to adaptation processes. On the other hand, it shows that the autonomous market adaptation mechanisms embedded in CGE models explain only marginally low climate change costs. These are in fact due to omission of other impacts because of their proven difficulty to be modeled, such as extreme events, damages due to ecosystem services' losses, as well as major disruptions due to the existence of tipping points.

Second, we also verify if the assessments performed with CGE models produce lower climate change cost estimates than IA models using reduced-form climate change damage functions. We show that, in fact, when the same impact categories are considered across the two methodologies, damage estimates do not differ significantly at the global level. In particular, the major driver of differences in costs is the modeling of the catastrophic component. When this is introduced to correct the CGE-driven estimates, these are not significantly different from those used by some well-established hard-linked integrated assessment models.

We conclude with some more general considerations:

This exercise uses one specific CGE model and sensitivity is tested for a narrow spectrum of parameters. Although the model, the parameters, and their values have been chosen for their representativeness and relevance for adaptation, it has to be recognized that different outcomes might be obtained expanding upon all of them. Therefore, this analysis has to be considered preliminary and suggestive of further research.

Noting that the inclusion of "catastrophic events" is the major driver of change in the economic impact assessment suggests a general reflection on the contribution of CGE models to economic assessment of climate change. They can be particularly useful when moderate changes in economic conditions are involved, i.e., when impacts are low. This applies when temperature increases remain sufficiently "low," or when tipping points are not trespassed. Under these conditions, the model parameterization is not stretched too much and enables further sensitivity testing, for instance, on the role of adaptation as done here.

They are however much less informative when "large" transformations may occur. This is because catastrophic events can be only marginally captured by CGE models. The issue here is twofold: on the one hand, large negative impacts can be outside the simulation capability of the model. This applies to all model types; however, CGE models which are based on extensive calibration processes are particularly sensitive to large deviation from the baseline conditions. On the other hand, CGE models are mostly deterministic and catastrophic losses are typically accounted "deterministically." A typical procedure to include them, for instance, consists in upscale expected annual losses (say in factors of production). But, doing so spans over time a loss that would occur in one instant and, furthermore, neglects a proper modeling of risk and uncertainty aversion, which is an important dimension in cost determination.

All in all, results from these exercises are possibly a good representation of economic consequences of climate change at low range of temperature increases, but induce strong downward biases at high range of temperature increases. What "low" or "high" is can be defined by the probability to experience catastrophic outcomes or reaching a tipping point.

Considering that the full impact of extreme events is still not certain and it is increasing and that tipping points and catastrophic events are so important in cost determination, it clearly suggests the direction for further investigation.

Acknowledgments

We are highly indebted to many people and institutions that shared the results of their research and made the related data available for inclusion in the present report.

In particular, we thank Sally Brown, Robert Nicholls, Athanasios Vafeidis, and Jochen Hinkel who generated sea level rise impacts as part of the EU Seventh Framework Programme project ClimateCost and the Met Office who elaborated climate change scenarios for sea level rise within the same project.

We thank Silvana Mima who provided data on climate change impacts on energy demand elaborated during the EU Seventh Framework Programme project ClimateCost.

We thank Fraziska Piontek who provided data on climate change impacts on crop yields elaborated during the EU Seventh Framework Programme project Global IQ.

We thank Richard Tol who provided data on climate change impacts on tourism elaborated during the EU Seventh Framework Programme project ClimateCost as well as his elaborations on climate change impacts on mortality and morbidity.

Nevertheless, please consider that the values reported in this document are our elaborations based on these data, and accordingly the responsibility for any mistake or imprecision is ours alone.

Finally, the present paper has been produced as part of the research conducted under the European Union's Seventh Framework Programme (FP7/2007–2013) "Impacts Quantification of global changes (Global-IQ)" research project (Grant agreement no: 266992), whose financial support is gratefully acknowledged.

References

Aaheim, A., Amundsen, H., Dokken, T., Ericson, T., and Wei, T. (2009). A Macroeconomic Assessment of Impacts and Adaptation to Climate Change in Europe. *CICERO Report 2009.06*. CICERO.

Ackerman F. and Stanton E. A. (2012). Climate risk and carbon prices: Revising the social cost of carbon. *Economics: The Open-Access, Open-Assessment E-Journal*, 6(2012–10), 1–25.

Anthoff, D. and Tol, R. S. J. (2013). The uncertainty about the social cost of carbon: A decomposition analysis using FUND. *Climatic Change*, 117(3), 515–530.

Auffhammer, M. (2018). Quantifying economic damages from climate change. *The Journal of Economic Perspectives*, 32(4), 33–52.

Berrittella, M., Bigano, A., Roson, R., and Tol, R. S. J. (2006). A general equilibrium analysis of climate change impacts on tourism. *Tourism Management*, 25, 913–924.

Bigano, A., Bosello, F., Roson, R., and Tol, R. S. J. (2008). Economy-wide impacts of climate change: A joint analysis for sea level rise and tourism. *Mitigation and Adaptation Strategies for Global Change*, 13(8), 765–791.

Bigano, A., Hamilton, J. M., and Tol, R. S. J. (2007). The impact of climate change on domestic and international tourism: A simulation study. *Integrated Assessment Journal*, 7, 25–49.

Bigano, A., Hamilton, J. M., Maddison, D. J., and Tol, R. S. J. (2006). Predicting tourism flows under climate change — an editorial comment on Goessling and Hall. *Climatic Change*, 79, 175–180.

Bondeau A., Smith, P. C., Zaehle, S. O. N., Schaphoff, S., Lucht, W., Cramer, W., Gerten, D., Lotze-Campen, H., Müller, C., and Reichstein, M. (2007). Modelling the role of agriculture for the 20th century global terrestrial carbon balance. *Global Change Biology*, 13, 679–706.

Bosello, F., Nicholls, R. J., Richards, J., Roson, R., and Tol, R. S. J. (2012). Economic impacts of climate change in Europe: Sea-level rise. *Climatic Change*, 112, 63–81.

Bosello, F., Roson, R., and Tol, R. S. J. (2006). Economy wide estimates of the implications of climate change: Human health. *Ecological Economics*, 58, 579–591.

Bosello, F., Roson, R., and Tol, R. S. J. (2007). Economy wide estimates of the implications of climate change: Sea level rise. *Environmental and Resource Economics*, 37, 549–571.

Bosello, F., Roson, R., and Tol, R. S. J. (2008). Economy wide estimates of the implications of climate change: Human health — a rejoinder. *Ecological Economics*, 66, 14–15.

Bosetti, V., Carraro, C., and Galeotti, M. (2006). The dynamics of carbon and energy intensity in a model of endogenous technical change. *The Energy Journal, Endogenous Technological Change and the Economics of Atmospheric Stabilisation*, 27, 191–206 (special issue).

Bosetti, V., De Cian, E., Sgobbi, A., and Tavoni M. (2009). "The 2008 WITCH Model: New Model Features and Baseline," FEEM Note di Lavoro N. 85.2009.

Brown, S., Nicholls, R. J., Vafeidis, A., Hinkel, J., and Watkiss, P. (2011). The impacts and economic costs of sea-level rise on coastal zones in the EU and the costs and benefits of adaptation. Summary of results from the EU RTD climatecost project. In: Watkiss P (ed) The ClimateCost project. Final report. Volume 1: Europe. Stockholm Environment Institute, Sweden.

Burke, M., Hsiang, S. M., and Miguel, E. (2015). Global non-linear effect of temperature on economic production. *Nature*, 527(7577), 235–239.

Carleton, T. A. and Hsiang, S. M. (2016). Social and economic impacts of climate. *Science*, 353(6304), doi: 10.1126/science.aad9837.

Cheung, W. W. L., Close, C., Lam, V. *et al.* (2008a). Application of macroecological theory to predict effects of climate change on global fisheries potential. *Marine Ecology Progress Series*, 365, 187–197.

Cheung, W. W. L., Lam, V. W. Y., and Pauly, D. (2008b). "Dynamic bioclimate envelope model to predict climate-induced changes in distribution of marine fishes and invertebrates," in: Modelling Present and Climate-Shifted Distributions of Marine Fishes and Invertebrates. Fisheries Centre Research Reports 16(3) (eds Cheung WWL, Lam VWY, Pauly D), pp. 5–50. University of British Columbia, Vancouver.

Cheung, W. W. L., Lam V. W. Y., Sarmiento J. L., Kearney, K., Watson, R., Zeller, D. I. R. K., and Pauly D. (2010). Large-scale redistribution of maximum fisheries catch potential in the global ocean under climate change. *Global Change Biology*, 16, 24–35, doi: 10.1111/j.1365-2486.2009.01995.x.

Chima, R. I., Goodman, C. A., and Mills, A. (2003). The economic impact of malaria in Africa: a critical review of the evidence. *Health Policy*, 63, 17–36.

Ciscar, J. C., Iglesias, A., Feyen, L., Szabó, L., Van Regemorter, D., Amelung, B., Nicholls, R., Watkiss, P., Christensen, O. B., Dankers, R., Garrote, L., Goodess, C. M., Hunt, A., Moreno, A., Richards, J., and Soria, A. (2011). Physical and economic consequences of climate change in Europe. *Proceedings of the National Academy of Sciences of the United States of America*, 108(7), 2678–2683.

Criqui, P. (2001). POLES: Prospective Outlook on Long-term Energy Systems, Institut d'Economie et de Politique de l'Energie, available on line at: http://webu2.upmf-grenoble.fr/iepe/textes/POLES8p_01.pdf.

Criqui, P., Mima, S., and Menanteau, P. (2009). The trajectories of new energy technologies in carbon constraint cases with the POLES world energy model. *IOP Conference Series Earth and Environmental Science*, 6(21).

Darwin, R. F. and Tol, R. S. J. (2001). Estimates of the economic effects of sea level rise. *Environmental and Resource Economics*, 19, 113–129.

Deke, O., Hooss, K. G., Kasten, C., Klepper, G., and Springer, K. (2001). "Economic Impact of Climate Change: Simulations with a Regionalized Climate-Economy Model," Kiel Institute of World Economics Working Papers n. 1065.

Dellink, R., Lanzi, E., and Chateau, J. (2019). The sectoral and regional economic consequences of climate change to 2060. *Environmental and Resource Economics*, 72(2), 309–363, doi: 10.1007/s10640-017-0197-5.

Eboli, F., Parrado, R., and Roson, R. (2010). Climate change feedback on economic growth. *Environment and Development Economics*, 15(5), 515–533.

Edenhofer, O., Bauer, N., and Kriegler, E. (2005). The impact of technological change on climate protection and welfare: Insights from the model MIND. *Ecological Economics*, 54, 277–292.

EUROSTAT. (2013). Environmental protection expenditure by the public sector — % of GDP, Source of Data: Eurostat, update, 13.11.2013, accessed on 14 Nov 2013, hyperlink: http://epp.eurostat.ec.europa.eu/tgm/table.do?tab=table&init=1&plugin=1&language=en&pcode=ten00049.

Gerlagh, R. (2007). Measuring the value of induced technological change. *Energy Policy*, 35, 5287–5297.

Howard, P. H. and Sterner, T. (2017). Few and not so far between: A meta-analysis of climate damage estimates. *Environmental and Resource Economics*, 68(1), 197–225, doi: 10.1007/s10640-017-0166-z.

IEA (International Energy Agency). (2011). "World Energy Outlook — 2011," IEA, Paris.

IEA (International Energy Agency). (2012). "World Energy Outlook — 2012," IEA, Paris.

Ignjacevic, P., Botzen, W., Estrada, F., Kuik, O., Ward, P., and Tiggeloven, T. (2020). CLIMRISK-RIVER: Accounting for local river flood risk in estimating the economic cost of climate change. *Environmental Modelling & Software*, 132, 104784, doi: 10.1016/j.envsoft.2020.104784.

IWGSCC (Interagency Working Group on Social Cost of Carbon). (2010). Social Cost of Carbon for Regulatory Impact Analysis under Executive Order 12866. February. United States Government. http://www.whitehouse.gov/sites/default/files/omb/inforeg/for-agencies/Social-Cost-of-Carbon-for-RIA.pdf.

Jomini, P., Zeitsch, J. F., McDougall, R., Welsh, A., Brown, S., Hambley, J., and Kelly, J. (1991). SALTER: A General Equilibrium Model of the World Economy, Vol. 1. Model Structure, Data Base, and Parameters. Canberra, Australia: Industry Commission.

Link, P. M. and Tol, R. S. J. (2004). Possible economic impacts of a shutdown of the thermohaline circulation: An application of FUND. *Portuguese Economic Journal*, 3, 99–114.

Manne, A., Mendelsohn, R., and Richels, R. (1995). MERGE: A model for evaluating regional and global effects of GHG reduction policies. *Energy Policy*, 23(1), 17–34.

Manne, A. and Richels, R. (2004). MERGE an Integrated Assessment Model for Global Climate Change, on line documentation on the MERGE model, available at: http://www.stanford.edu/group/MERGE/GERAD1.pdf.

Martens, W. (1998). Health impacts of climate change and ozone depletion: An ecoepidemiologic modelling approach. *Environmental Health Perspectives*, 106(Suppl 1), 241–251.

Murray, C. J. L. and Lopez, A. D. (1996). *Global Health Statistics: A Compendium of Incidence, Prevalence and Mortality Estimates for Over 200 Conditions.* World Health Organization, World Bank & Harvard School of Public Health. https://apps.who.int/iris/handle/10665/41848.

Nakicenovic N. and Swart R. (eds). (2000). Special report on Emissions Scenarios, available at: http://www.ipcc.ch/pdf/special-reports/emissions_scenarios.pdf.

Narayanan, G. B., Aguiar A., and McDougall, R. (eds). (2012). Global Trade, Assistance, and Production: The GTAP 8 Data Base, Center for Global Trade Analysis, Purdue University.

Nordhaus, W. D. (2007). *The Challenge of Global Warming: Economic Models and Environmental Policy*, Yale University, New Haven, http://www.econ.yale.edu/~nordhaus/homepage/OldWebFiles/DICEGAMS/dice_mss_072407_all.pdf.

Nordhaus, W. D. (1991). To slow or not to slow: The economics of the greenhouse effect. *The Economic Journal*, 101(407), 920–937.

Nordhaus, W. D. and Boyer, J. (2000). *Warming the World: Economic Models of Global Warming*, MIT Press, Cambridge, MA.

Nordhaus, W. D. and Yang, Z. (1996). A regional dynamic general-equilibrium model of alternative climate-change strategies. *American Economic Review*, 86(4), 741–765.

O'Neill, B. C., Kriegler, E., Riahl, K., Ebi, K. L., Hallegatte, S., Carter, T. R., Mathur, R., and van Vuuren, D. (2014). A new scenario framework for climate change research: The concept of shared socio-economic pathways. *Climatic Change*, 122, 387–400.

Ortiz, R. A., Golub, A, Lugovoy, O, Markandya, A., and Wang, J. (2011). DICER: A tool for analyzing climate policies. *Energy Economics*, 33, S41–S49.

Parrado, R. and De Cian, E. (2013). Technology spillovers embodied in international trade: Intertemporal, regional and sectoral effects in a global CGE framework. *Energy Economics*, 41, 76–89.

Patt, A. G., van Vuuren, D., Berkhout F., Aaheim, A., Hof, A. F., Isaac, M., and Mechler, R. (2010). Adaptation in integrated assessment modelling: Where do we stand? *Climatic Change*, 99, 383–402.

Pindyck, R. S. (2017). The use and misuse of models for climate policy. *Review of Environmental Economics and Policy*, 11(1), 100–114.

Pindyck, R. S. (2019). The social cost of carbon revisited. *Journal of Environmental Economics and Management*, 94, 140–160.

Popp, D. (2004). ENTICE: endogenous technological change in the DICE model of global warming. *Journal of Environmental Economics and Management*, 48, 742–768.

Rogelj, J., Meinshausen, M., and Knutti, R. (2012). Global warming under old and new scenarios using IPCC climate sensitivity range estimates. *Nature Climate Change*, 2(4), 248–253, doi: 10.1038/NCLIMATE1385.

Roson, R. and Van der Mensbrugghe (2010), "Climate, Trade and Development," background paper for Round Table 1 on The Impact of Climate Change on Trade Patterns, at the "business-government-academic conference Climate Change, Trade and Competitiveness: Issues for the WTO." Geneva, 16th, 17th and 18th June, 2010.

Stern, N. (2013). The structure of economic modelling of the potential impacts of climate change: Grafting gross underestimation of risk onto already narrow science models. *Journal of Economic Literature*, 51(3), 838–859.

Szewczyk, W., Feyen. L., Matei, A., Ciscar, J. C., Mulholland, E., and Soria, A. Economic analysis of selected climate impacts, EUR 30199 EN, Publications Office of the European Union, Luxembourg, 2020, ISBN 978-92-76-18459-1, doi: 10.2760/845605, JRC120452.

Tol, R. S. J. (2002a). New estimates of the damage costs of climate change, Part I: Benchmark estimates. *Environmental and Resource Economics*, 21(1), 47–73.

Tol, R. S. J. (2002b). New estimates of the damage costs of climate change, Part II: Dynamic estimates. *Environmental and Resource Economics*, 21(1), 135–160.

Tol, R. S. J. (2014). Correction and update: The economic effects of climate change. *Journal of Economic Perspectives*, 28(2), 221–226.

Tol, R. S. J. and Dowlatabadi, H. (2001). Vector-borne diseases, climate change, and economic growth. *Integrated Assessment*, 2, 173–181.

Tsigas, M. E., Frisvold, G. B., and Kuhn, B. (1997). Global climate change in agriculture, in Thomas W. H. (ed.), *Global Trade Analysis: Modeling and Applications*, Cambridge University Press.

Vafeidis, A. T., Nicholls, R. J., McFadden, L., Tol, R. S. J., Hinkel, J., Spencer, T., Grashoff, P. S., Boot, G., and Klein, R. J. T. (2008). A new global coastal database for impact and vulnerability analysis to sea-level rise. *Journal of Coastal Research*, 24(4), 917–924.

Van Vuuren *et al.* (2012). A proposal for a new scenario framework to support research and assessment in different climate research communities. *Global Environmental Change*, 22(1), 21–35

Warren, R., Hope, C., Mastrandrea, M., Tol, R., Adger N., and Lorenzoni, I. (2006). "Spotlighting impacts functions in integrated assessment," WP 91, Tyndall Centre for Climate Change Research.

Weitzman, M. L. (2007). A review of the Stern Review on the economics of climate change. *Journal of Economic Literature*, 45(3), 703–724.

Weitzman, M. (2008). On modeling and interpreting the economics of catastrophic climate change. *The Review of Economics and Statistics*, 91(1), 1–19.

Weitzman, M. (2009). Additive damages, fat-tailed climate dynamics, and uncertain discounting. *Economics: The Open-Access, Open-Assessment E-Journal*, 3, 2009–2039, http://www.economics-ejournal.org/economics/journalarticles/2009-39.

Weitzman, M. (2010). What is the "Damages Function" for global warming — and what difference might it make? *Climate Change Economics*, 1(1), 57–69.

Annex

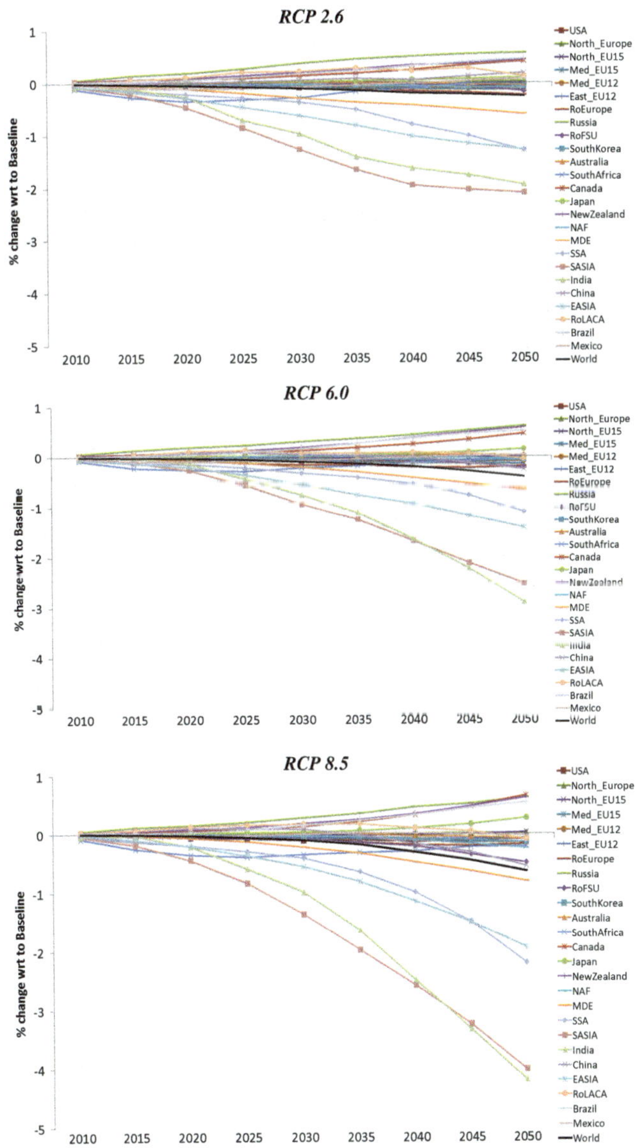

Fig. A.1. Climate change impacts on regional GDP by RCP (RCP 2.6 top; RCP 6.0 middle; RCP 8.5 bottom).

https://doi.org/10.1142/9789811240553_0007

Chapter 7

Agricultural TFP Under a Changing Climate: Evidence from High, Middle, and Low-Income Countries

Sevil Acar[*,‡] **and Simay Kızılkaya**[†,§]

*[*]Boğaziçi University,
Department of Tourism Administration Hisar Campus,
34342 Bebek, İstanbul*
*[†]Altınbaş University,
Department of International Trade,
Gayrettepe Social Sciences Campus, 34394 Şişli, İstanbul*
[‡]sevil.acar@boun.edu.tr
[§]simay.kizilkaya@altinbas.edu.tr

Climate change impacts are already visible in agriculture. In most parts of the world, exposure to climate extremes in the form of droughts, floods, heat spells, or storms has increased. This chapter aims to contribute to the literature by addressing climate change using a novel dataset for extreme weather events that include climate-related disasters and shocks such as floods, landslides, and wildfires as well as by examining temperature nonlinearities, and analyzes their impacts on agricultural TFP across country samples of varying income groups. The analysis is conducted for a total of 137 countries during the 1995–2015 period. The impacts of both climate change indicators are estimated to be negative only in the case of low- and middle-income countries. The relationship is proven to be robust to alternative specifications.

1. Introduction

In the process following the Industrial Revolution, the economic system established by humanity has undergone a radical change in the climate of our planet, incomparable to previous periods. Greenhouse gases (GHGs) such as carbon and methane in the atmosphere have increased significantly in the last two centuries and reached an unprecedented level. The atmospheric global carbon dioxide (CO_2) concentration, which was 280 parts per million (ppm) before industrialization, exceeded 350 ppm in the 1980s and is over 400 ppm today (NOAA, 2020).

The 4th Assessment Report (AR4) of the Intergovernmental Panel on Climate Change IPCC (2007) was based on the need to keep the global CO_2 concentration below 450 ppm and the global temperature rise below 2°C over pre-industrial levels, so as not to give rise to irreversible climate impacts. The same report relates the frequent changes in extreme climatic conditions, droughts, floods, rising ocean levels, and degradation of ecosystems with the radical change humanity has imposed on the planet's climate via increased GHG emissions. It emphasizes that the inability to stop the temperature rise and to implement adaptation mechanisms will inevitably exacerbate these conditions. A more recent (IPCC, 2018) report has shown that even limiting the temperature rise at 1.5°C instead of 2°C will bring severe climate impacts on ecosystems, crop yields, sea levels, etc. For instance, the report highlights that the reduction in maize harvests in the tropics could reach 3% under the scenario of 1.5°C, whereas the decline is 2.3 times worse under the 2°C scenario. Similarly, the decline in marine fisheries could reach 1.5 million tonnes under the 1.5°C scenario, while it would be twice this level under 2°C.

Climate change impacts are already visible in the agricultural sector. In most parts of the world, exposure to climate extremes in the form of droughts, floods, heat spells, or storms has increased (such as the frequency of droughts and floods in eastern and western Europe and in the Mediterranean region). The heat waves observed in Europe in the last two decades have had a significant impact on agricultural output as shown by several studies. For instance, Ciais *et al.* (2005) demonstrate that primary productivity reduction in eastern and Western Europe can be explained by rainfall deficit and extreme summer heat witnessed in 2003 in the region. In addition, rising temperatures, more frequent heat waves, and shifting precipitation patterns harm worker health and productivity, which poses issues for agricultural labor as well.

This chapter aims to contribute to the literature by addressing climate change using a novel dataset for extreme weather events that include climate-related disasters and shocks such as floods, landslides, and wildfires as well as by examining temperature nonlinearities, and analyzes their impacts on agricultural TFP across country samples of varying income groups. The flow of the chapter is as follows: The second section provides a review of the literature. The third section presents data diagnostics. The fourth and fifth sections undertake econometric analysis and robustness checks. The last section concludes.

2. Literature Review on the Effects of Climate Change and Global Warming on Agricultural Productivity

The inter-dependencies between climate change and agriculture have been frequently addressed in the previous literature. Climate change and global warming, which manifest themselves in the form of rising temperatures, decreasing and more volatile precipitation, extreme weather events, land degradation, sea level rise, and ocean acidification, influence agriculture in various ways. Climate change gives rise to the deterioration of agricultural systems through a range of diverse channels, including biodiversity loss, freshwater decline, pests, and droughts, which in turn affect agricultural productivity. Figure 1 from the FAO (2016) displays the cascading effects of climate change on agroecosystems and agricultural production, and hence, on food security and nutrition.

As far as agricultural productivity is concerned, one may take into account either the productivities of individual factors, such as land, labor, and capital, or the total factor productivity (TFP) of all inputs of production. Climate change might affect each factor as well as the technology of production at different levels and through various channels.

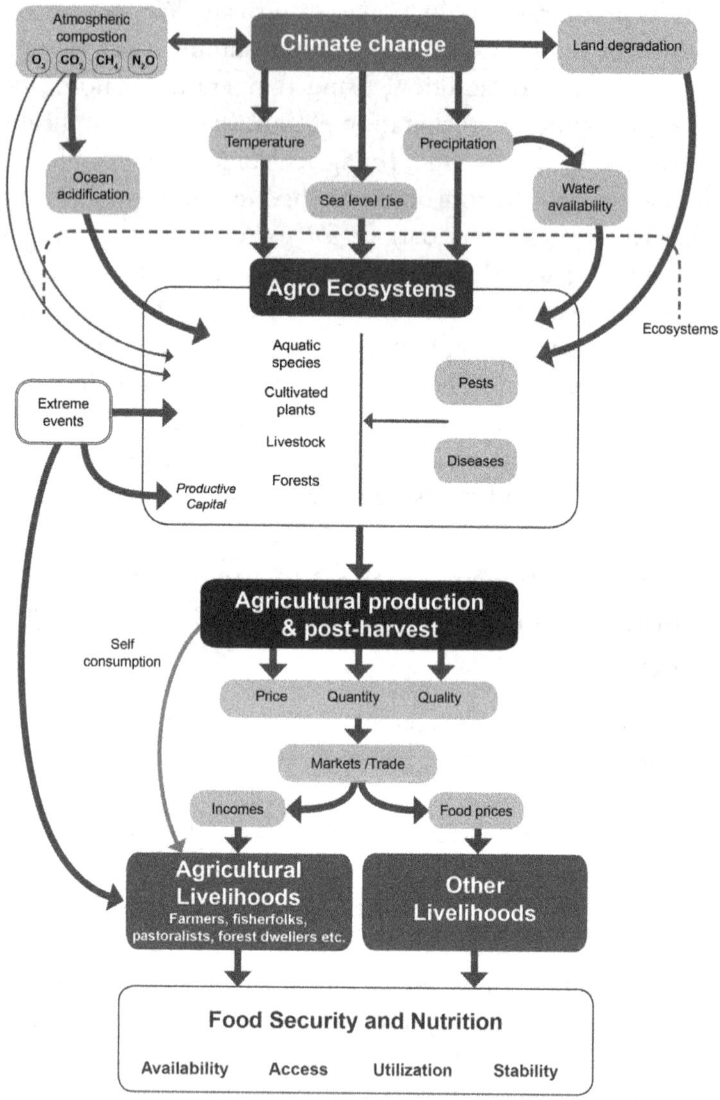

Fig. 1. Impacts of climate change on agriculture, food security, and nutrition.

Notes: A range of physical, biological, and biophysical impacts bear on ecosystems and agroecosystems, translating into impacts on agricultural production. This has quantity, quality, and price effects, with impacts on the income of farm households and on purchasing power of non-farm households (FAO, 2016).

Source: FAO (2016, 4).

This section provides a summary of the relevant literature focusing on at least one aspect of productivity or TFP in the agricultural sector (ATFP).

2.1. *Changes in temperature, precipitation, and seasonality*

To begin with, agricultural productivity is highly influenced by higher and more variable temperatures and lower and more variable rainfall as well as changes in seasonality due to climate change. At their reproductive and maturation stages, most crops become more sensitive to high temperatures. Although the effects will show variation across regions and crops, crop yields are prone to potential decline globally. For instance, in their analysis of European agricultural productivity, Olesen and Bindi (2002) find that warming is expected to result in expansion of suitable cropping areas to the north and reduced growing period of determinate crops (e.g., cereals), but an increase in indeterminate crops (e.g., root crops). Climate change in the northern regions of Europe can have positive impacts on agriculture by introducing new crop types and varieties, expanding areas suitable for higher crop production and crop cultivation. On the contrary, the disadvantages will be predominant in the southern regions. Kang *et al.* (2009) go through the implications of temperature and rainfall fluctuations for water availability, which determine crop water productivity. They conduct a review of the existing models and observe that an increase in precipitation implies an increase in crop yield, and additionally, crop yield is more sensitive to precipitation than temperature. When, due to climate change, temperature increases and precipitation fluctuates, water availability and crop production will potentially be lower in the future.

McCarl *et al.* (2009) hypothesize that varying climatic variables impair the effect of public agricultural research investments on ATFP and test this hypothesis utilizing annual data from 48 contiguous states of the United States (U.S.) from 1970 to 1999. They find that the effect of higher temperature on ATFP is positive for Southeast and Pacific regions, whereas it is negative for Southern Plains. Besides, total precipitation has a positive effect on ATFP, while the effect of intensity of precipitation is negative. According to the study, high-volume research investment should be expected by adapting to the foreseen climate conditions to maintain the current return rates of agricultural research.

OECD (2015) analyzes the impacts of exogenous climate-related yield shocks from changes in heat and water stress by water basin on productivity in the agricultural sectors. The OECD model produces a pathway between 2010 and 2050 by proportionally changing the effect of climate change on productivity without considering CO_2 fertilization effects on vegetation. The findings demonstrate that the consequences of climate change for agricultural productivity contribute most to diminished income growth in the examined regions (OECD (America-Europe-Pacific regions), rest of Europe and Asia, Latin America, Middle East and North Africa, South and South-East Asia, and Sub-Saharan Africa), which is mostly caused by labor productivity[1] losses from occupational heat stress (OECD, 2015, 58). Between 2040 and 2060, agricultural damages are found to increase threefold, while, by 2060, these damages (including those to fisheries) are expected to result in 0.8% GDP loss. Despite the fact that the share of agriculture in GDP is insubstantial in most regions, productivity impacts are estimated to be quite significant (OECD, 2015, 59).

Liang *et al.* (2017) investigate the impact of climate models on overall U.S. agricultural performance, based on long records of the most up-to-date data. The study uses the previous year's TFP change (TFPC) as an indicator of economic growth. The first step is analyzing the correlation of TFPC with seasonal and geographic distributions of climatic variables. Then, it defines a set of climatic variables at regional level that have statistically significant relationship with TFPC aiming to develop a model to capture aggregate agricultural TFP growth at national level. The potential results are presented in two models that focus on periods of 1951–1980 and 1981–2010. According to the

[1]The topic of labor productivity decline due to climate change is handled further in Section 2.3.

findings, these periods exhibit different TFPC–climate relationships. TFP of the latter period (1981–2010) seems to be more sensitive to climatic changes than the first period, which implies that, by time, sensitivity of agriculture to climate rises. Apart from other studies, Liang *et al.* (2017) differentiate between the response of crop production and livestock production to climatic variables. Productivity of crop production appears to be more sensitive to climatic variables than livestock production is, since crop production is more sensitive to adverse weather events than livestock production.

Sabasi and Shumway (2018) examine the changes in the components of ATFP (technical change, technical efficiency change, and scale and mix efficiency change) and the effect of the climatic variables for 48 U.S. states for the period 1961–2003. The study finds that climate change has the largest effect on the change in ATFP and its components, compared to effects of education, labor, health, and farm size variables. Current year precipitation positively affects ATFP. The study finds a positive impact of agro-temperature on ATFP change in the Northern band of states, but no impact in the Central or Southern bands. An increase in precipitation is found to be detrimental for productivity in the Central band of states, but beneficial in the warmer Southern band. Damaging degree days, which is a measure of adverse current year temperature, negatively affects ATFP change. Focusing on specific sectors of the 48 U.S. states over the period 1963–2016, Kahn *et al.* (2019) demonstrate that the agricultural sector is negatively impacted by a rise in temperature above its historical norm. Besides, precipitation above and below the historical norm is also found to exert negative pressure on agricultural output.

Monthly rainfall variability proliferates the predictability problem for agricultural productivity as feed availability and pasture conditions are highly seasonal and unpredictable depending on climatic changes (Jaber *et al.*, 2016). According to the analyses of Lafakis *et al.* (2019), agricultural productivity is expected to decrease in more regions than it will increase in the absence of adaptation, as long as the increase in average global temperature climbs up. The authors show that there will be a few countries, such as China and Russia, which will benefit from higher temperatures; however, these benefits in agricultural productivity will be offset by productivity losses in other sectors due to heat stress and worker health concerns. Similarly, according to a recent McKinsey Global Institute (2020) report, Canada's agricultural productivity may increase, or northern countries such as Sweden and Finland may not experience water stress or drought due to climate change on the horizon extending to 2050. However, the probability of more than 10% yield reduction in wheat, corn, soy, and rice will increase from 6% to 18% globally in any year. Besides, fish productivity will be reduced due to ocean warming, which will affect the livelihood and well-being of around 650 million–800 million people living on fishing around the world. According to the same report, Turkey and Egypt will be among the countries that will suffer the most from water stress due to climate change, along with Iran and Mexico. This will significantly risk the food systems associated with drought and the availability of freshwater resources along with agricultural lands.

Another regional study was conducted by Zhong *et al.* (2019), who evidence significant and negative effects of annual precipitation, average temperature in growing season, and evaporation intensity for 30 regions of China during the period 1993–2012, based on spatial panel data analysis.

Apart from their differences with respect to latitudes and dominating climate regimes, countries also display variation in regard to income levels and economic structure of their national economies while facing the impacts of temperature and precipitation changes on productivity levels. Letta and Tol (2019) provide support for this possible variation between low- and high-income countries for the period 1960–2006. They observe a negative impact of temperature shocks on total factor productivity (TFP) growth only in poor countries. They explain such a difference between rich and poor countries referring to the fact that "poor countries have a much larger share of their GDP in the agricultural sector, much more outdoor work and lower adaptive capacity" (Letta and Tol, 2019, 299). Apparently, the composition of agricultural TFP matters in its interplay with climate change as well.

In regard to impacts on specific crops, there are countless studies in the previous literature. Notable effects stand out especially when rain-fed crops or crops that require larger amounts of water during their growing seasons are considered. Iizumi *et al.* (2018) observe that climate change that was observed between 1981 and 2010 brought down crop yields on the global scale and led to production losses (especially for maize, wheat, and soybeans). Besides, climate adaptation, so far, has not succeeded in compensating for the negative impacts of global warming, specifically at lower latitudes. Reyer *et al.* (2017) investigate biophysical impacts for the future in five diverse regions of the world under various global warming scenarios. Apart from other factors such as flooding and sea-level rise, they detect temperature increase as a serious threat for agricultural productivity and crop yield in Latin America and the Caribbean, Middle East and Northern Africa, South Asia, Central Asia, and Sub-Saharan Africa. For instance, they argue that "water resources might increase during the first half of the century leading to higher flood risk and decline thereafter, amplifying the competition for water between hydropower generation and irrigation to avoid declining agricultural production" Reyer *et al.* (2017, 1566).

2.2. *Frequency of climatic shocks/extreme events*

Another way that climate change manifests itself is through increased frequency of extreme weather events, mainly droughts and floods. Climatic extremes are different from seasonality, i.e., seasonal temperature and rainfall fluctuations, as the former are highly unpredictable and generally give rise to irrevocable effects on farming and animal husbandry. As a result of the drought in the south of Africa in 2015, agricultural output was recorded to decrease by 15%. It is obvious that agriculture will suffer quite a lot if these events become more frequent.

Olesen and Bindi (2002) review previous studies regarding the effects of climate change on agricultural productivity in Europe and the results of policy and research. Accordingly, climate-related disadvantages will be dominant in the southern regions of Europe. Possible increase in water shortage and extreme weather events can result in less harvestable yields, higher yield variability, and a reduction in areas suitable for traditional crops.

Calculating the Global Climate Risk Index, which is a measure of the extent and effects of weather-related loss events such as storms, floods, and heatwaves on countries and regions, Eckstein *et al.* (2019) show that, of the ten countries and regions most impacted during the period 1999–2018, seven were developing countries in the low-income or low–middle-income category, two were listed as upper middle-income countries (Thailand and Dominica), and one as an advanced high-income economy (Puerto Rico). Although the index falls short of capturing indirect effects (such as drought and food shortages) and continuous changes of important climate parameters (such as a long-term decline in rainfall that was experienced in African countries, which influenced agricultural output substantially), it is useful for demonstrating how weather extremes can threaten life via direct effects on human beings and livestock, once more depending on the development levels of countries.

Cottrell *et al.* (2019) conduct an analysis of 134 countries for the period 1961–2013 and find that more than half of all shocks to crop production systems were a result of extreme weather events, which were mainly composed of droughts. Climatic shocks and weather extremes could also damage infrastructure, mainly transport systems, giving rise to losses and spoilage of agricultural inputs (Cho, 2018).

2.3. *Impacts on labor (via working hours at altered climatic conditions or extreme heat)*

According to a new report from the ILO (2019), heat stress adds to the other negative effects of climate change by leading to occupational health risk and lower labor productivity. Heat stress is defined as "heat in excess of what the body can tolerate without suffering physiological impairment" (ILO, 2019) and is one of the major consequences of global warming. The report projects that agriculture is the sector, which is expected to be worst affected, globally, such that 60% of global working hours will be lost due to heat stress by the year 2030.[2]

[2] The contribution of labor productivity losses from occupational heat stress to agricultural productivity decline is also evidenced in Roson and van der Mensbrugghe (2012) and Ciscar *et al.* (2014).

It is well known that climatic conditions help to shape labor productivity, especially when it comes to conventional outdoor agriculture. Loureiro (2009) evaluates Norway's agricultural productivity in terms of labor productivity focusing on health conditions of farmers. The article highlights that Norway's farmworkers are suffering from arctic and sub-arctic climatic conditions, designated by non-normal temperatures and bare growing seasons. Using stochastic production frontier regressions which include parameters related to the total worth of the farm, the total area of the farm, total working hours on the farm, stated health conditions, years of experience, and total output value, the study reveals that health conditions of farmers influenced by extremely low temperatures has a statistically significant role in explaining the variance of the inefficiency factor in Norway's agricultural production. Climate variability and temperature fluctuations add to such inefficiencies and uncertainties regarding labor productivity. Altinsoy and Yildirim (2015) aim to shed light on the direct and indirect impacts of climate change on workers' health and labor productivity in Turkey by demonstrating diminishing labor productivity as a consequence of decreased working hours. They use the climatic outputs of the Regional Climate Model (RegCM3) obtained from the ENSEMBLES Project to calculate the wet bulb globe temperature (WBGT) over western Turkey. Covering the period between 1971 and 2100, they forecast the total number of loss days for the critical regions and find that agricultural labor productivity is predicted to decline over Central Anatolia and parts of the Aegean and eastern Mediterranean coastal areas. The decline in labor productivity in agriculture in these regions reaches as high as 2–3% in the projected period, which is also reflected in the total economic loss of Turkey that is to be expected in the range of 5–8% between 2041 and 2100.

In low-income countries where a greater proportion of labor is concentrated in agricultural activity, the risk of the workers being exposed to excessive heat is greater than that of the higher income countries which rely more on services sectors. Thus, climate change effects on labor productivity vary widely between countries. For instance, according to the analysis of McKinsey Global Institute (2020), the slowdown in working hours and labor productivity due to heat stress will influence output in agriculture by 2050 especially in countries like India and Pakistan, where agriculture constitutes a significant share of GDP.

2.4. *Impacts on physical capital, including the loss in the value of capital assets and land*

Extreme rainfall and floods as well as hurricanes that are exacerbated with the effect of climate change can form damage on agricultural physical capital and infrastructure. Such climatic hazards might even destroy a whole farming system together with all types of assets it embodies such as farmland, harvesters, plows, and tractors. Some of these assets including farm machinery could be reproducible, whereas the others — such as land — might be non-reproducible.

Bezabih *et al.* (2011) analyze the economic effects of climate change on the performance of the Tanzanian economy, using a countrywide computable general equilibrium (CGE) model. The effect of overall climate change on agricultural productivity (indicated as decreasing land productivity) is estimated to be relatively limited until around 2030 and then it worsens. Simulation results show that, despite the predicted reduction in agricultural productivity, adverse effects on agricultural productivity may potentially be quite limited. Similarly, Ciscar *et al.* (2014) model the gains and losses of agricultural land use changes at the European level and under a climate change scenario which leads to a global temperature increase of 3.5°C compared to the pre-industrial level. They find that agricultural land is prone to more than around 60% total loss during the 2010–2030 period.

Differently from other applied studies conducted on agricultural productivity, Deschênes and Greenstone (2007) investigate the economic impacts of climate change on U.S. agriculture focusing on the impacts of temperature and precipitation volatility on agricultural profits. They utilize a hedonic cross-sectional farm value model in which the value of agricultural land per acre in units and time depends on a detectable vector of determinants of farmland values and a series of climate variables. The data used for the analysis cover production in agriculture, temperature, precipitation, and quality of soil. The results show that climate change will stimulate agricultural sector profits by around $1.3 billion or 4% during the period of 2070–2099. Furthermore, the authors find that anticipated rises in temperature and precipitation would bring together no significant effects on the yield of most crops. Besides, predicted climate change is estimated to change the value of agricultural land within a range of $200–$320 billion, which is argued to be wider than what the previous literature finds.

As displayed in Table 1, the previous literature has paid little attention to the effects of climate change on agricultural TFP. From this point of view, this research aims to find answers to the following questions: "What is the effect of climate change and global warming on agricultural productivity, mainly on agricultural TFP?" More specifically, this chapter tries to answer how increasing and more variable temperature, reduced and more variable rainfall, as well as the frequency of climatic shocks/extreme events affect agricultural total factor productivity.

3. Background Statistics and Data

In its simplest definition, ATFP is defined as the ratio of agricultural output to inputs. According to the related literature, the set of inputs generally comprises land, labor, physical capital, livestock, fertilizers, and pesticides. ATFP compares the total amount of crops and livestock, considering all land, labor, capital, and material resources used in farm production. If the growth rate of output is higher than the growth rate of total inputs, then ATFP of the factors of production increases. ATFP differs from measures such as crop yield per acre or agricultural value added per worker as it considers a larger set of inputs used in production.

We use ATFP data calculated by the USDA particularly for data availability reasons. The ATFP indices (base year 2005 = 100) are provided over the 1961–2015 period using primarily FAO and ILO data, supplemented in some cases by national statistics. For the calculation of ATFP, USDA prefers agricultural output represented by "gross agricultural output for each year at constant 2004–2006 average international prices, measured in thousands of dollars." Input series are composed

Table 1. Summary of the literature on climate change and agricultural TFP.

Climate change variables	Implications for agricultural productivity	Methodology	Region and time frame	References
Temperature, rainfall, changes in total seasonal precipitation, pattern of variability of precipitation, extreme meteorological events (spells of high temperature, heavy storms, or droughts)	Warming is expected to expand suitable cropping areas toward the north and reduced growing period of determinate crops (e.g., cereals), but an increase in indeterminate crops (e.g., root crops). Climate change in the northern regions can have positive impacts by introducing new crop types and varieties, expanding areas suitable for higher crop production and crop cultivation.	Review of consequences and policies	Regions of Europe	Olesen and Bindi (2002)

(*Continued*)

Table 1. (*Continued*)

Climate change variables	Implications for agricultural productivity	Methodology	Region and time frame	References
	Disadvantages will be dominant in the southern regions. Possible increase in water shortage and extreme weather events can result in less harvestable yields, higher yield variability, and a reduction in areas suitable for traditional crops.			
Mean annual temperature (°F), total yearly precipitation (inches), a measure of the intensity of yearly rain precipitation,	The effect of higher temperature on ATFP is positive for the Southeast and Pacific region, negative for Southern Plains.	Panel Error Correction Model (ECM)	48 U.S. states, 1970–1999	McCarl *et al.* (2009)

(*Continued*)

Table 1. (*Continued*)

Climate change variables	Implications for agricultural productivity	Methodology	Region and time frame	References
standard deviation of temperature and precipitation, Palmer Drought Severity Index	Total precipitation has a positive effect, whereas the effect of intensity of precipitation is negative.			
Temperature, precipitation	The effect of overall climate change on agricultural productivity (modeled as decreasing land productivity) is predicted as relatively limited until about 2030 and then it worsens.	Computable General Equilibrium(CGE) Model	Tanzania, 2010–2085	Bezabih *et al.* (2011)

(*Continued*)

Table 1. (*Continued*)

Climate change variables	Implications for agricultural productivity	Methodology	Region and time frame	References
Daily average surface temperature, daily cumulative precipitation anomalies	ATFP of 1981–2010 is more sensitive to climatic changes than that of 1951–1980. Impacts of climate change vary across regions. ATFP is correlated with both temperature and precipitation anomalies. Productivity of crops is more sensitive to climatic variables than livestock production is.	Panel Data Analysis, Lasso Regression Analysis	United States, 1951–2010	Liang *et al.* (2017)
Precipitation, growing degree days, damaging degree days, agro-temperature	The effects of climate variables are heterogeneous across states. Positive impact of climate warming on ATFP change.	Prais–Winsten parameter estimates	48 U.S. states, 1961–2003	Sabasi and Shumway (2018)

(*Continued*)

Table 1. (*Continued*)

Climate change variables	Implications for agricultural productivity	Methodology	Region and time frame	References
	Current year precipitation positively affects ATFP, whereas damaging degree days negatively affects it.			
Annual total precipitation, average temperature in growing season, evaporation intensity		Data Envelopment Analysis, Spatial Panel Data Analysis	30 Regions of China, 1993–2012	Zhong *et al.* (2019)

of land in terms of "total agricultural land in hectares of "rainfed cropland equivalents," irrigated cropland, and permanent pasture," agricultural labor represented by "the number of economically active adults in agriculture," livestock in the form of "total livestock capital on farms in "cattle equivalents" based on relative size and feeding requirements," machinery that covers "the total stock of farm machinery in 40 metric horsepower tractor equivalents," fertilizer referring to "metric tonnes of Nitrogen (N), Potassium (P_2O_5), Phosphate (K_2O) fertilizer consumption," and finally, feed covering "total metabolizable energy (ME) in animal feed from all sources, in 1000 mega calories" (USDA, 2020).

Figure 2 presents ATFP levels of countries in 2015 across their income levels (in logarithms). Accordingly, middle- and high-income countries display higher variation in their ATFP levels, whereas low-income countries' ATFP index does not manifest much variation. One should note here that the value of the index in any year is the level

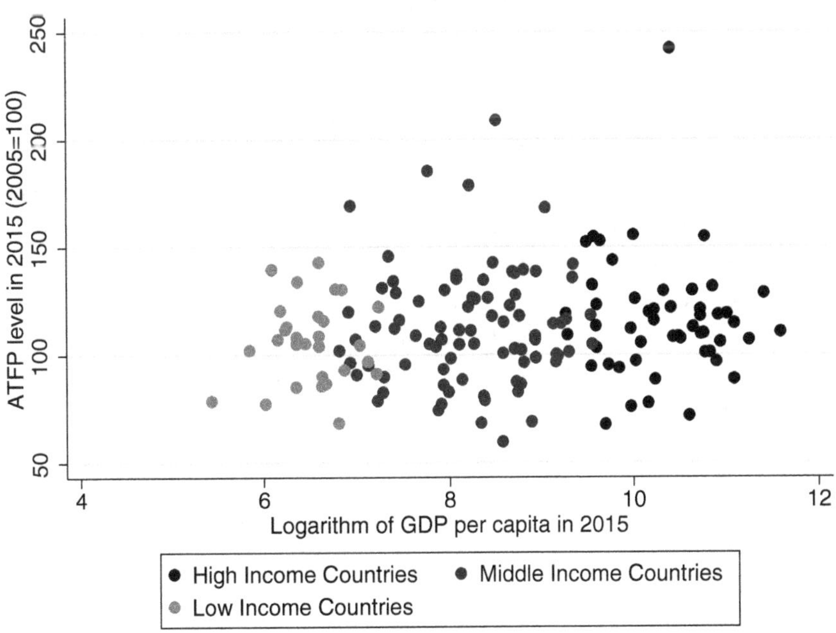

Fig. 2. ATFP levels and GDP per capita of countries in 2015.

of ATFP relative to 2005. Hence, comparing ATFP among countries demonstrates where ATFP is growing faster or more slowly in comparison to the base year, but it does not show where productivity levels are higher or lower.

Extreme weather events (*Weather_events*), which is our main climate change variable, are an indicator of climate extremes. It shows average annual weather-related disaster occurrence. We include average number of weather events classified as meteorological, hydrological, and climatologic under the natural disaster group. The meteorological disaster sub-group is defined as a hazard caused by short-lived, micro- to mesoscale extreme weather and atmospheric conditions that last from minutes to days, and includes extreme temperature, fog, and storm as the main types. Besides, the hydrological disaster sub-group is defined as a hazard caused by the occurrence, movement, and distribution of surface and subsurface freshwater and saltwater and includes flood, landslide, and wave action as the main types. Climatologic events are defined as a hazard caused by long-lived, meso- to macroscale atmospheric processes ranging from intra-seasonal to multi-decadal climate variability and include drought, glacial lake outbursts, and wildfire as the main types (EM-DAT, 2020).

Figure 3 displays the number of weather events with respect to income levels of countries for the years 1995, 2005, and 2015. Noticeably, low- and middle-income countries are prone to higher numbers of such weather extremes due to climate change. For the whole period, 1995–2015, median number of annual weather extremes exceeds three in the case of low-income countries, and is around one in middle-income countries, whereas it is close to zero for high-income countries. Large outliers, which are located outside the whiskers of the box plot, are plenty more in the case of middle-income countries (e.g., see Pakistan, Indonesia, Philippines, and Russia in the selected years in Fig. 3). The year 2005 appears to have hosted the highest numbers of weather extremes in low- and middle-income countries. Besides, 1995 and 2005 are likely to be noticeably different for the case of low-income countries since the median number of events in 2005 lies outside the 1995 box. In the case of high-income countries, more outliers were observed in the year 2015 than in 1995 and 2005, although the median

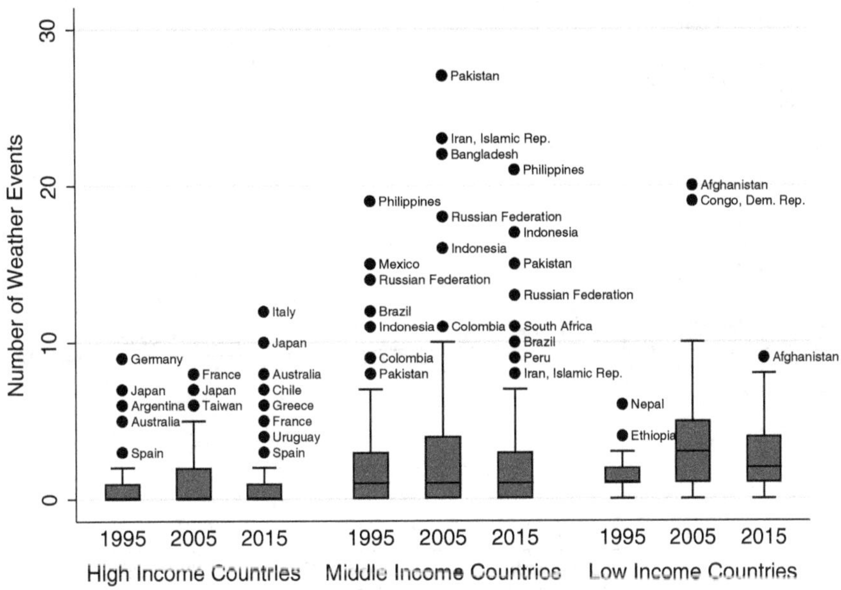

Fig. 3. Number of weather events with respect to income groups (1995, 2005, 2015).

Notes: Excluding China, India, Nigeria, and the U.S. as they are far outliers with more than 30 events in the selected years.

number of extreme weather events did not change much throughout the years.

Contrasting the number of weather extremes with average ATFP levels during the period of interest, Fig. 4 hints at a negative correlation. Countries that seem to have experienced higher numbers of extreme weather events (e.g., Russia, Philippines, and Nigeria) have lower ATFP levels on average relative to their base year levels, while countries that have experienced less weather extremes (e.g., Singapore and Brunei-Darussalam) have higher ATFP in comparison to their base year levels. It is observable that most countries have faced 1 to 6 weather extremes on average during the same period.

Alternatively, we plot period-average ATFP levels versus average temperature changes (in degrees Celsius) in Fig. 5. Temperature change (*Temp_ch*) data provided by the FAO (2020) stands here for annual (meteorological year) mean temperature anomalies for

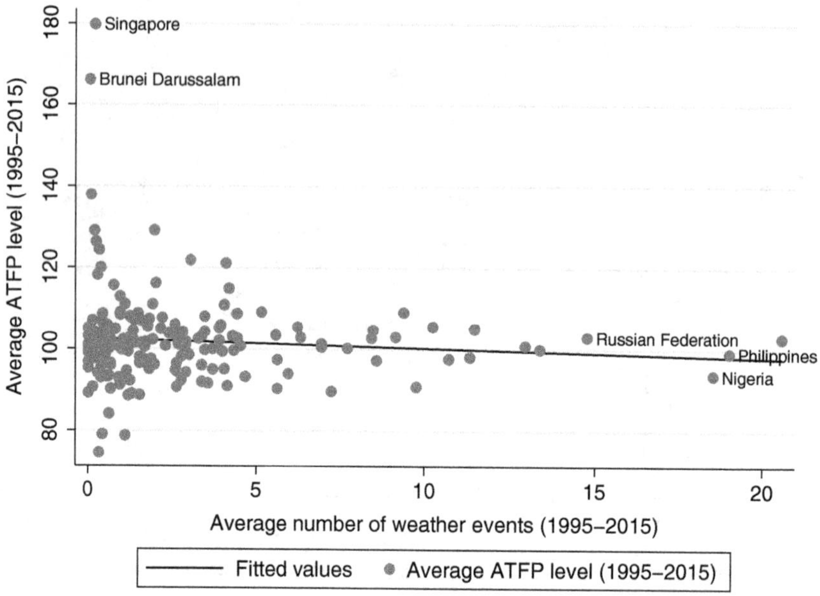

Fig. 4. Average ATFP levels and average number of weather events (1995–2015).

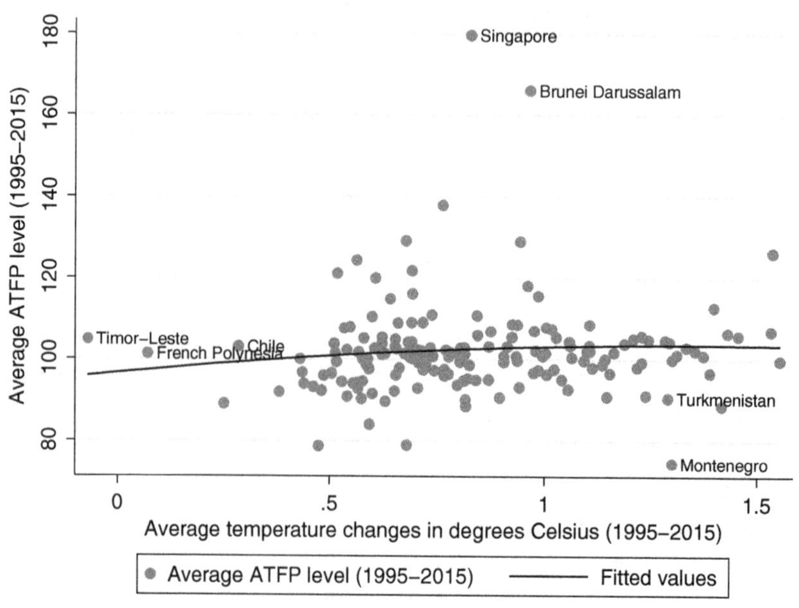

Fig. 5. Average ATFP levels versus average temperature changes in degrees Celsius (1995–2015).

the period 1995–2015 with respect to a baseline climatology corresponding to the period 1951–1980. The FAO uses the publicly available Global Surface Temperature Change data distributed by the National Aeronautics and Space Administration Goddard Institute for Space Studies (NASA-GISS). The baseline is chosen to be the 1951–1980 period primarily because it is considered a period of relatively stable global temperature before global warming accelerated in recent decades, as demonstrated by NASA's temperature analyses. It is noted that meteorological rather than calendar definitions were used for annual means of temperature change[3]. There seems to be a quadratic relationship between ATFP and *Temp_ch* during the investigated period. At lower levels of *Temp_ch*, ATFP levels are higher. As *Temp_ch* increases, ATFP levels get lower on average. The turning point for *Temp_ch* seems to be around 1 degree Celsius, which is tested econometrically in the following sections.

Our preliminary analysis based on the scatter diagrams and box plots signals that countries are eager to experience lower ATFP levels as they are more and more prone to climate change-related changes and shocks. In the next section, we formally analyze the climate change–ATFP relationship with the help of a set of explanatory variables that are hypothesized to be influential for determining ATFP.

4. Econometric Model and Results

Previous literature on the determinants of ATFP elaborates a number of factors ranging from technological progress and education of farmers to public and private investments in agriculture. Arnade (1998) uses the

---

[3]In the Northern Hemisphere, the seasonal mean "Dec-Jan-Feb" corresponds to the meteorological winter; Mar-Apr-May to the meteorological spring; Jun-Jul-Aug to the meteorological summer; Sep-Oct-Nov to the meteorological autumn. In the Southern Hemisphere, Dec-Jan-Feb corresponds to the meteorological summer; Mar-Apr-May to the meteorological autumn; Jun-Jul-Aug to the meteorological winter; Sep-Oct-Nov to the meteorological spring. For both hemispheres, annual mean temperature change data correspond to the meteorological year beginning on December 1st of the previous calendar year and ending on November 30th of the same calendar year (FAO, 2020).

Malmquist index to calculate ATFP and examines factors such as technological improvements, the use of traditional versus non-traditional inputs, and agricultural subsidies. He finds that the impacts differ with respect to the development levels of the countries investigated. For instance, technology improvement increases productivity in a developed country, while it decreases ATFP in a developing country. Besides, input subsidies are found to give rise to allocative inefficiency and, when abolished, might generate technical inefficiencies due to input wasting.

Fernandez-Cornejo and Shumway (1997) explore the long-term impact of research and technology diffusion on TFP in Mexican agriculture during the period 1940–1990. The article relates the increases in productivity to the Green Revolution, which brought together improved seeds and increase in modern inputs that were subsidized by the Mexican government. The results of cointegration tests indicate that there is a long-term relationship between Mexican ATFP, investment in agricultural research, and productivity of agriculture in the U.S. Fulginiti and Perrin (1997) investigate agricultural productivity changes for 18 developing countries from 1961 to 1985. According to their results, productivity in agriculture declines during the periods of 1961–1973 and 1974–1985 in many countries. The effect of the Green Revolution is confirmed in this article as well giving rise to a trend change. Positive effects of the Green Revolution were not observed in the initial periods, but came into effect later on. Countries such as Pakistan and the Philippines reflect the trend change after 1965.

Fuglie and Heisey (2007) present a review of the literature on the agricultural research expenditures and agricultural productivity nexus. The study concludes that agricultural research expenditures stimulate agricultural productivity and its components generating significant social returns. With a similar focus on agricultural research, Liu *et al.* (2011) examine ATFP growth and its convergence in the U.S. in the context of dynamic effects of health and knowledge spillovers at both inter-state and inter-industry levels by using panel data. They attempt to measure the impact of health capital, which is proxied by health care supply in rural areas, and the effect of R&D spillovers on ATFP and, next, examine the dynamic effects of policy variables on ATFP growth.

One of the main results is that TFP converges to a steady state for U.S. agriculture. Besides, in both the short and the long run, health care supply in rural areas and spillovers of research from other states and non-agricultural sectors have significant effects on ATFP growth. Furthermore, according to the results, rural health care supply and education levels of farmers stimulate ATFP growth in the long run. Rada *et al.* (2011) study the effects of government policies on agricultural productivity in Indonesia with stochastic output distance frontier modeling. Among the range of interventions that are examined in the study (namely, trade restrictions, subsidies, price supports and taxes, and public research), research appears to be least effective in boosting productivity growth. On the other contrary, the authors find that market liberalization efforts applying to agriculture in the late 1990s have a significantly positive impact on agricultural productivity.

Although our focus is on climate change here, the model constructed below also accounts for other explanatory variables such as gross fixed capital formation and energy use per capita. Besides, we control for the effects of average precipitation and average temperature levels in order to see the level effects of weather-related variables on ATFP. The variables that are included in the model, their abbreviations, descriptions, and data sources are as provided below:

Capital stock share in agriculture (*C_share*): Gross fixed capital formation in agriculture, forestry, and fishing as a share of value added [FAOSTAT]. A positive impact of capital stock additions to agriculture on ATFP is expected. Rada *et al.* (2011) elaborate the effect of agricultural capital expenditures mainly comprising spending on water resources and irrigation enhancement and expansion in their analysis of Indonesian ATFP and detect a positive impact of it.

Energy use per capita (*Energy_use*): Energy use (kg of oil equivalent per capita) refers to the use of primary energy before transformation to other end-use fuels, which is equal to indigenous production plus imports and stock changes, minus exports and fuels supplied to ships and aircraft engaged in international transport (IEA Statistics). USDA estimates TFP growth using labor and capital without treating energy as one of the inputs in the production process. However, we believe energy use is a factor that might alter agricultural TFP. Schurr (1982) and Jorgenson (2007) have explained the role of energy use in productivity growth. The use of energy always helps to make the production process more efficient through technology channels, which ultimately boosts total factor productivity growth (Moghaddasi and Pour, 2016). Therefore, examining the role of energy in determining ATFP is imperative. A better indicator of energy would be agricultural energy use. However, due to data unavailability, we choose energy use per capita as a proxy for that.

Average precipitation (*Avr_precip*): Average yearly rainfall derived from average monthly rainfall data, in mm (World Bank, Climate Change Knowledge Portal). The impact of precipitation might differ depending on timing and seasonal averages. Generally, we expect a positive impact of increased rainfall as water availability is key to agricultural production. However, although average annual rainfall quantity may be relatively unchanged, a major consequence of climate change is significant shifts in the timing of rainfall and its intra-year variability (Torres *et al.*, 2019).

Average temperature (*Avr_temp*): Average yearly temperature derived from average monthly temperature data, in degrees Celsius (World Bank, Climate Change Knowledge Portal). As in the case of rainfall, timing and seasonal averages of temperature matter for agricultural production. While low temperatures may prevent planting and seed growth, high temperatures and drought may also negatively affect growth of plants or might even give rise to plant death (if they happen during the growing season) and livestock damage. Schlenker and Roberts (2009) demonstrate that temperature nonlinearities such as days with over 30°C temperature, rather than a continuous temperature variable, have significant impacts on crop productivity. Yet, we would like to see the impact of mean temperature on productivity level.

Extreme weather events (*Weather_events*): Average annual weather-related disaster occurrence (EM-DAT, 2020). We use it as an indicator of climate extremes and include average number of weather events classified as meteorological, hydrological, and climatologic under the natural disaster group. We expect that the impact

Table 2. Summary statistics for the selected variables (1995–2015).

	Unit	Mean	SD	Min	Max	Obs
ATFP	Index (2005 = 100)	102.089	20.123	57.111	515.979	3,893
C_share	Percentage	.135	.139	−.060	2.340	3,947
Energy_use	kg of oil equivalent per capita	2484.188	3002.890	9.548	22120.370	2,943
Avr_temp	Celsius	19.2	8.6	−17.8	29.5	4,074
Avr_precip	Millimeters	104.550	81.299	.772	736.478	4,074
Weather_events	Number	2.854	6.448	0	101	4,851
Temp_ch	Celsius	.830	.511	−.993	3.030	3,870
Temp_ch_sq	Celsius	.950	1.084	0	9.180	3,870

Notes: Minimum value for *C_share* takes a negative value as gross fixed capital formation may include both positive and negative values. According to the OECD definition, negative values consist of disposals of fixed assets, e.g., of existing fixed assets, which can be either sold, surrendered in barter, or surrendered as capital transfers in kind. Disposals of fixed assets are recorded as negative acquisitions and exclude consumption of fixed capital and exceptional losses, such as those due to drought or other natural disasters.

of this variable on ATFP will be negative. To the best of our knowledge, this is the first study that utilizes EM-DAT data to analyze the impact of climate extremes on ATFP. Eckstein *et al.* (2019) use the Climate Risk Index (CRI), which shows the level of exposure and vulnerability that countries must understand as a warning to prepare for more frequent and/or more serious events in the future in a similar vein. Nevertheless, although the data reflect the direct effects (direct losses and deaths) of extreme weather events, indirect effects (such as drought and food shortages) are not accounted for.

Table 2 presents the descriptive statistics pertaining to the variables used in this study.

We use the fixed effects specification of panel data modeling in order to observe the impact of the climate variables on agricultural TFP for 137 countries in total for the period 1995–2015. Furthermore, in order to investigate heterogeneous effects of weather events, we interact the vector of weather events with income group dummies, which stand for "high-income" or "low- and middle-income" countries. Our base model is the following:

$$\begin{aligned} \mathrm{ATFP_{it}} &= \alpha_i + \beta \mathrm{C\_share_{it}} + \gamma \mathrm{Energy\_use_{it}} + \delta \mathrm{Avr\_temp_{it}} \\ &\quad + \zeta \mathrm{Avr\_precip_{it}} + \eta \mathrm{Weather\_events_{it}} + \varepsilon_{\mathrm{it}}, \end{aligned} \tag{1}$$

where $\mathrm{ATFP_{it}}$ represents annual agricultural TFP index (base year 2005 = 100), and $\mathrm{C\_share_{it}}$ is annual gross fixed capital formation as a share of value added. $\mathrm{Energy\_use_{it}}$ represents annual energy use per capita. $\mathrm{Avr\_temp_{it}}$ represents annual average temperature and Avr_precip_{it} is annual average precipitation. $\mathrm{Weather\_events_{it}}$ represents average annual disaster occurrence in terms of extreme weather events. α_i indicates fixed effects for each country, which are cross-section specific.

One point to take into consideration while working with panel data is the problem of unit roots. Standard regression models rest on the assumption that series are stationary. If series are trending rather than stationary, meaning that the dependent variable and the independent variable have an increasing or decreasing trend over time, the problem of spurious regression arises. When this is the case, there appears to be a relationship between the dependent variable and the independent variable, even if there is none. In such cases, panel unit root tests should be conducted. Fisher type unit root test (based on ADF tests) results can be found in Appendix A. Accordingly, none of the series, except energy use in some specifications of the test, have unit roots.

The results are presented in Table 3.

The findings suggest that *Weather_events* has a negative significant impact on ATFP for the overall sample. The impact becomes more obvious once the sample is classified as high-income countries and the rest. Taking into account the interaction of *Weather_events* and income dummies, it is observed that the total effect of climate extremes in high-income countries becomes insignificant, whereas that in the low- and middle-income group remains significant with a negative coefficient. The findings are in parallel with Olesen and Bindi (2002), Liang *et al.* (2017), and Eckstein *et al.* (2019). As also evidenced in

Table 3. Fixed effects estimation including extreme weather events as the climate indicator.

Dependent variable: Agricultural TFP index (base year 2005 = 100)	(1)	(2)	(3)	(4)
C_share	28.938***(5.821)	29.206***(5.857)	29.073***(5.859)	29.073***(6.829)
Energy_use	.006***(.000)	.006***(.000)	.006***(.000)	.006***(.001)
Avr_temp	2.759***(.742)	2.699***(.748)	2.711***(.748)	2.711**(.904)
Avr_precip	.035 (.025)	.039 (.025)	.039 (.025)	.039 (.032)
Weather_events		−.261*(.129)	−.210 (.139)	−.590*(.286)
Weather_events x High			−.379 (.379)	
Weather_events x Low_Mid				.379 (.321)
_cons	27.953*(13.532)	29.776*(13.608)	29.656*(13.609)	29.656(17.623)
N	2,518	2,498	2,498	2,498
R^2	.054	.056	.056	.056
F-test	34.33	28.06	23.55	7.91
Total effect in high-income countries			−.589	
Total effect in low- and middle-income countries				−.211

Notes: *High* is a dummy variable with value 1 for high-income countries. *Low_Mid* is a dummy variable with value 1 for low- and middle-income countries. Standard errors are in parentheses. Legend: $^{*}p < 0.05$; $^{**}p < 0.01$; $^{***}p < 0.001$. To exemplify goodness of fit, the residuals are plotted against the fitted values of ATFP for the case of low- and middle-income countries as shown in Appendix C.1.

Eckstein *et al.* (2019), income levels of countries play a differentiating role in the effect of climate extremes on agriculture.

Focusing on the other explanatory variables, it is detected that the coefficients of *Avr_temp* in all the four models are significant and positive, implying that higher average annual temperature leads to higher ATFP. On the contrary, the impact of *Avr_precip* is insignificant across all the four models.

The coefficients of *C_share* and *Energy_use* are all significant and positive as expected and are in line with the previous literature. Higher investments in agricultural capital stock and higher energy use per capita boost ATFP highly significantly.

5. Robustness Checks

We conduct a variety of regression analyses to ensure the robustness of the above results. The following model is performed with another climate change indicator alternative to our baseline specification:

$$\begin{aligned} \text{ATFP}_{\text{it}} = {} & \alpha_i + \beta \text{C\_share}_{\text{it}} + \gamma \text{Energy\_use}_{\text{it}} + \delta \text{Avr\_temp}_{\text{it}} \\ & + \zeta \text{Avr\_precip}_{\text{it}} + \eta \text{Temp\_ch}_{\text{it}} + \theta \text{Temp\_ch\_sq}_{\text{it}} + \varepsilon_{\text{it}}, \end{aligned} \tag{2}$$

where, in addition to the previous explanatory variables, $\text{Temp\_ch}_{\text{it}}$ represents temperature change and $\text{Temp\_ch\_sq}_{\text{it}}$ represents square of temperature change. In particular, we exclude $\textit{Weather\_events}_{it}$ from the regression to test the validity of our findings using an alternative climate change variable related to warming. Temperature change stands here for annual (meteorological year) mean temperature anomalies with respect to a baseline climatology, corresponding to the period 1951–1980 (FAO, 2020). As such, different from using average temperature levels, this indicator enables one to capture the temperature deviations from a historical benchmark average. As warming to some extent in some regions could become favorable or unfavorable for agricultural productivity, we include temperature change and its square simultaneously in the regression equation in order to detect potential nonlinear effects of warming after some threshold temperature change is reached.

Table 4. Fixed effects estimation including temperature change as an alternative climate indicator.

Dependent variable: Agricultural TFP index (base year 2005 = 100)	(1) All countries	(2) High-income countries	(3) Low- and middle-income countries
C_share	28.585*** (5.680)	26.082*** (7.566)	31.570* (13.402)
Energy_use	.006*** (.000)	.005*** (.000)	.017*** (.001)
Avr_temp	1.903 (1.128)	1.635 (1.622)	3.202 (1.834)
Avr_precip	.050(.027)	.076 (.065)	.044 (.025)
Temp_ch	3.135 (2.174)	−.798 (3.848)	5.480* (2.599)
Temp_ch_sq	−.778 (.898)	1.023 (1.560)	−2.606* (1.037)
_cons	41.042* (19.323)	43.526* (21.079)	7.340* (36.460)
N	2,437	935	1502
R^2	.058	.055	.097
F-test	23.8	8.69	25.4
Turning point for temperature change			1.05°C

Notes: Turning point for temperature change is calculated by the negative signed coefficient of the *Temp_ch* divided by the doubled coefficient of the *Temp_ch_sq* [i.e., $-\eta/2\theta$]. Standard errors are in parentheses. Legend: * $p < 0.05$; ** $p < 0.01$; *** $p < 0.001$. To exemplify goodness of fit, the residuals are plotted against the fitted values of ATFP for the case of low- and middle-income countries as shown in Appendix C.2.

The results are displayed in Table 4. Findings for the whole sample (1), high-income countries (2), and low- and middle-income countries (3) are presented separately.

Accordingly, *Temp_ch* and *Temp_ch_sq* occur in a significant manner only for the low- and middle-income country sample. In other words, climate change manifested in the form of surface temperature deviations from historical averages (with respect to the period 1951–1980) becomes harmful for low- and middle-income countries' agricultural productivity after some threshold *Temp_ch* is reached, but it does not affect high-income countries' ATFP. The threshold temperature change level is calculated as 1.05°C (using $-\eta/2\theta$), implying that up to this change in temperature, ATFP is positively affected by surface temperature rises, whereas afterward, once 1.05°C change is exceeded, ATFP starts to decline. The temperature change turning point is found to be within the temperature change range of low- and middle-income countries. For instance, middle-income countries, such as Albania, Bulgaria, Mongolia, Morocco, Nigeria, Serbia, Sri Lanka, Tunisia, and Turkey, have experienced temperature changes of above 1.05°C (in comparison to the historical averages) at least once within the investigated period. Low-income countries including Afghanistan, Benin, Ethiopia, the Syrian Arab Republic, and Tajikistan have also faced higher temperature changes than the threshold in several years during the same period. These countries' ATFP indices are likely to be affected negatively in those hotter years. These results support our findings on extreme weather events in the previous section.

6. Conclusion and Discussion

Impacts of climate change can be traced in agricultural productivity. In most parts of the world, exposure to climate extremes in the form of droughts, floods, heat spells, or storms has increased. Vulnerability of agriculture to such shocks rests on the sector's capacity to adapt, the scale, timing, and frequency of shocks, and its linkages with the other sectors, especially the sectors that provide inputs to it.

This study examines the relationship between climate change and agricultural TFP across income groups of countries during the 1995–2015 period by focusing on extreme weather events and temperature nonlinearities. We detect a negative impact of both climate change indicators only in low- and middle-income countries. The relationship is proven to be robust to alternative specifications, all of which we do not report here.

Our findings are generally coherent with but not directly comparable to the limited number of studies on ATFP and climate change in the previous literature. Reviewing the effects of temperature, rainfall, changes in total seasonal precipitation, pattern of variability of precipitation, and extreme meteorological events (spells of high temperature, heavy storms, or droughts), Olesen and Bindi (2002) argue that climate change is likely to increase productivity of European agro-systems in northern countries where warming will provide more favorable conditions for crop production, whereas in southern regions of the continent, productivity will be subject to decline especially due to extreme weather events and water shortage. In our analysis, we detect deterioration in ATFP as a result of extreme weather events in low- and middle-income countries, which consist of a few European countries such as Albania, Bulgaria, Kosovo, Montenegro, and Serbia; however, we do not find a significant impact of extreme weather events for the high-income country group, which includes most of the European countries. Using mean annual temperature (°F), total yearly precipitation (inches), a measure of the intensity of yearly rain precipitation, and standard deviation of temperature and precipitation, McCarl *et al.* (2009) also find differentiated impacts on climate change on ATFP in various regions of the U.S. for the period 1970–1999. For instance, the effect of higher temperature on ATFP is positive for the Southeast and Pacific region, but negative for Southern Plains. Bezabih *et al.* (2011) predict much worse effects of climate change through decreasing land productivity in Tanzanian agriculture after the year 2030. Looking at daily average surface temperature and daily cumulative precipitation anomalies, Liang *et al.* (2017) evidence lower productivity of crop production and livestock production for the U.S. in the 1951–2010 period. Sabasi and Shumway (2018) also evidence lower productivity due to higher damaging degree days in the U.S. states.

Schlenker and Roberts (2009) and Lambert (2014) investigate the effect of temperature nonlinearities opting for a different specification. They both take the days with over a certain level of temperature in order to capture the nonlinear impacts. The former finds the threshold temperature as 30°C (in the U.S.), whereas the latter finds it as 32.2°C (in Kansas), after which crop productivity decreases. Our analysis differs from them in the sense that we use temperature change anomalies instead of temperature level anomalies in order to show the nonlinear impacts of warming.

Previous findings together with our results imply that the timing and extent of climate-related changes or shocks matter for their consequences for ATFP. Besides, income levels of countries play a major role in how they cope with the effects of such changes or shocks in order to maintain their productivity levels. For instance, the impact of capital stock investments changes once we account for income differences between country groups. Gross fixed capital formation and energy use are more influential in the case of low- and middle-income countries.

Nevertheless, our study fails to address several aspects. First, our data series is restricted to the period 1995–2015, although climate-related extreme events and warming have accelerated further in the last few years. Second, we are aware of the fact that the data of weather extremes do not necessarily cover only climate change-related extremes. We use the EM-DAT database for the ease of availability for almost all countries and years and for the purpose of approximating such events for climate events. In fact, most events listed in Appendix B such as droughts, floods, and storms can be attributed to climate change and global warming.

Third, we are not able to capture all the possible factors that might explain ATFP. Inclusion of indicators such as agricultural research and development spending, the number of agricultural researchers, credit to agriculture, education and/or training of farmers, and agricultural subsidies in the analysis would enrich the models and improve the reliability of the findings. However, these indicators are not available for all countries and years at the same data quality.

Appendices

Appendix A. Panel Unit Root Test: Summary.

Fisher type unit root test (Based on ADF tests)	Constant		Time Trend	
	Statistics	*P*-value	Statistics	*P*-value
ATFP				
Inverse chi-squared(374) P	505.0782	0.0000	803.7638	0.0000
Inverse normal Z	0.3412	0.6335	−9.1221	0.0000
Inverse logit t(939) L*	0.1032	0.5411	−10.8419	0.0000
Modified inv. chi-squared Pm	4.7927	0.0000	15.7137	0.0000
C_share				
Inverse chi-squared(374) P	694.2404	0.0000	711.9306	0.0000
Inverse normal Z	−6.2946	0.0000	−7.9363	0.0000
Inverse logit t(939) L*	−7.5224	0.0000	−9.2651	0.0000
Modified inv. chi-squared Pm	11.3987	0.0000	12.0404	0.0000
Energy_use				
Inverse chi-squared(374) P	495.5186	0.0000	301.6169	0.9113
Inverse normal Z	3.8173	0.9999	1.6199	0.9474
Inverse logit t(939) L*	1.4965	0.9325	1.5531	0.9396
Modified inv. chi-squared Pm	6.1536	0.0000	−1.3264	0.9076
Avr_temp				
Inverse chi-squared(374) P	2126.5353	0.0000	2129.1998	0.0000

(*Continued*)

Appendix A. (*Continued*)

Fisher type unit root test (Based on ADF tests)	Constant		Time Trend	
	Statistics	*P*-value	Statistics	*P*-value
Inverse normal Z	−33.7232	0.0000	−33.7748	0.0000
Inverse logit t(939) L*	−41.7082	0.0000	−41.6604	0.0000
Modified inv. chi-squared Pm	62.4098	0.0000	62.5054	0.0000
Avr_precip				
Inverse chi-squared(374) P	2890.0951	0.0000	2303.8546	0.0000
Inverse normal Z	−43.0777	0.0000	−36.0593	0.0000
Inverse logit t(939) L*	−57.2855	0.0000	−45.4188	0.0000
Modified inv. chi-squared Pm	89.8200	0.0000	68.7752	0.0000
Weather_events				
Inverse chi-squared(374) P	3235.4369	0.0000	2698.0620	0.0000
Inverse normal Z	−44.9135	0.0000	−38.7511	0.0000
Inverse logit t(939) L*	−61.3258	0.0000	−50.7949	0.0000
Modified inv. chi-squared Pm	91.2394	0.0000	73.5610	0.0000
Temp_ch				
Inverse chi-squared(374) P	2395.5110	0.0000	2257.4800	0.0000
Inverse normal Z	−36.6725	0.0000	−35.1300	0.0000
Inverse logit t(939) L*	−47.2467	0.0000	−44.4339	0.0000
Modified inv. chi-squared Pm	72.3239	0.0000	67.3560	0.0000
Temp_ch_sq				
Inverse chi-squared(374) P	2524.0175	0.0000	2267.4099	0.0000
Inverse normal Z	−37.7079	0.0000	−35.0402	0.0000
Inverse logit t(939) L*	−49.7288	0.0000	−44.5828	0.0000
Modified inv. chi-squared Pm	76.9489	0.0000	67.7134	0.0000

Appendix B. Classification of Weather Events Data.

Disaster group	Disaster subgroup	Disaster main type	Disaster sub-type	Disaster sub-sub-type
Natural	Meteorological	Extreme temperature	Cold wave	
			Heat wave	
			Severe winter conditions	Snow/ice
				Frost/freeze
		Storm	Extra-tropical storm	
			Tropical storm	
			Convective Storm	Derecho
				Hail
				Lightning/ thunderstorm
				Rain
				Tornado
				Sand/dust storm
				Winter storm/blizzard
				Storm/surge
				Wind
				Severe storm
		Fog		
	Hydrological	Flood	Coastal flood	
		Riverine flood	Flash flood	
			Ice jam flood	
		Landslide	Avalanche (snow, debris, mudflow, rockfall)	
		Wave action	Rogue wave	
			Seiche	
	Climatological	Drought		
		Glacial Lake Outburst		
		Wildfire	Forest Fire	
			Land fire: Brush, bush, Pasture	

Source: EM-DAT (2020).

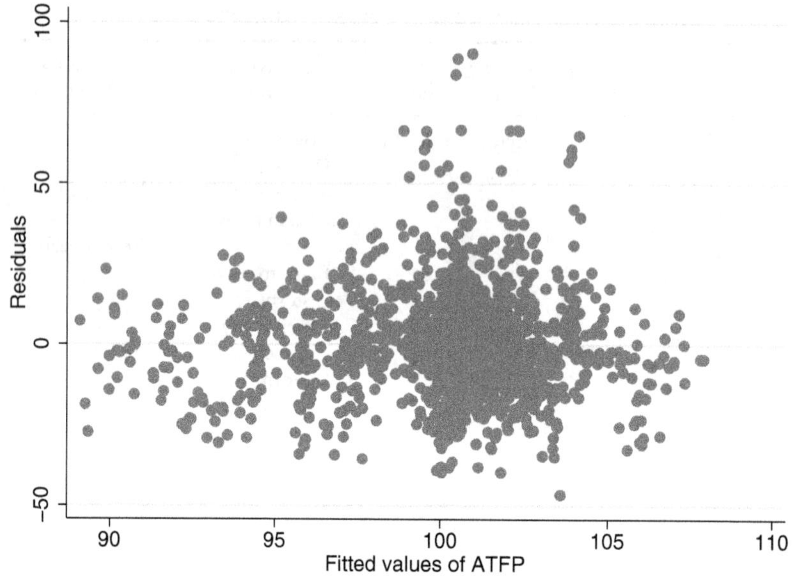

Appendix C.1. Analysis of residuals in the model with Weather Events for the case of Low- and Middle-Income Countries

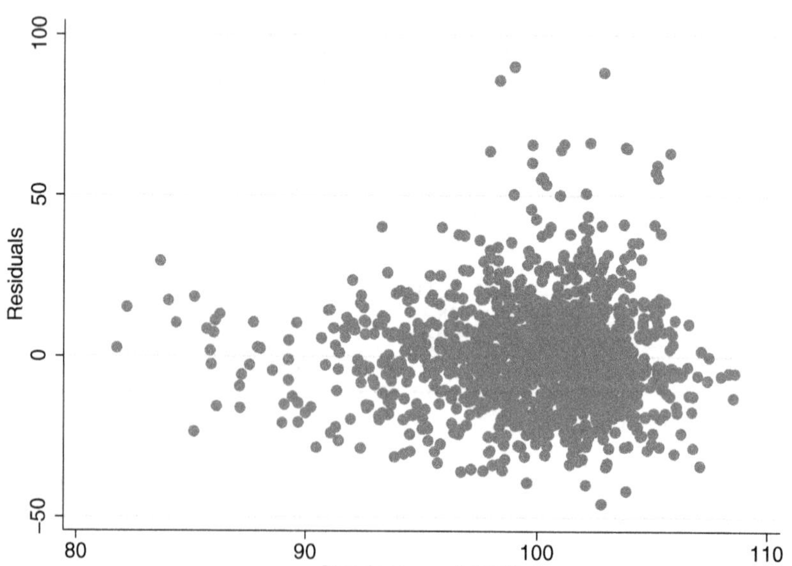

Appendix C.2. Analysis of residuals in the model with Temperature Change for the case of Low- and Middle-Income Countries

References

Altinsoy, H. and Yildirim, H. A. (2015). Labor productivity losses over western Turkey in the twenty-first century as a result of alteration in WBGT. *International Journal of Biometeorology*, 59(4), 463–471, doi: 10.1007/s00484-014-0863-z.

Arnade, C. (1998). Using a programming approach to measure international agricultural efficiency and productivity. *Journal of Agricultural Economics*, 49(1), 67–84.

Bezabih, M., Chambwera, M., and Stage, J. (2011). Climate change and total factor productivity in the Tanzanian economy. *Climate Policy*, 11(6), 1289–1302.

Cho, R. (2018). How Climate Change Will Alter Our Food, Columbia University Earth Institute. https://blogs.ei.columbia.edu/2018/07/25/climate-change-food-agriculture/.

Ciais, P., Reichstein, M., and Viovy, N. *et al.* (2005). Europe-wide reduction in primary productivity caused by the heat and drought in 2003. *Nature*, 437, 529–533, doi: 10.1038/nature03972.

Ciscar, J. C. *et al.* (2014). Climate impacts in Europe. The JRC PESETA II project, JRC scientific and policy reports, No. EUR 26586EN. *Report*. Luxembourg: Publications Office of the European Union.

Cottrell, R. S., Nash, K. L., Halpern, B. S., Remenyi, T. A., Corney, S. P., Fleming, A., and Blanchard, J. L. (2019). Food production shocks across land and sea. *Nature Sustainability*, 2(2), 130–137, doi: 10.1038/s41893-018-0210-1.

Deschěnes, O. and Greenstone, M. (2007). The economic impacts of climate change: Evidence from agricultural output and random fluctuations in weather. *American Economic Review*, 97(1), 354–385.

Eckstein, D., Künzel, V., Schäfer, L., and Winges, M. (2018). Global Climate Risk Index 2020. Who Suffers Most from Extreme Weather Events? Weather-Related Loss Events in 2018 and 1999 to 2018. Germanwatch Briefing Paper. https://germanwatch.org/sites/default/files/20-2-01e%20Global%20Climate%20Risk%20Index%202020_14.pdf.

EM-DAT (2020). The OFDA/CRED International Disaster Database.

FAO. (2016). *Climate Change and Food Security: Risks and Responses*. FAO, Rome, Italy. ISBN: 978-92-5-108998-9. http://www.fao.org/3/a-i5188e.pdf.

FAO. (2020). *FAOSTAT Temperature Change Dataset*. FAO, Rome, Italy. Available at: http://www.fao.org/faostat/en/#data/ET.

Fernandez-Cornejo, J. and Shumway, C. R. (1997). Research and productivity in Mexican agriculture. *American Journal of Agricultural Economics*, 79(3), 738–753.

Fuglie, K. O. and Heisey, P. W. (2007). Economic Returns to Public Agricultural Research. Economic Brief Number 10, U.S. Dept. of Agriculture, Economic Research Service. (September 2007) https://www.ers.usda.gov/webdocs/publications/42826/11496_eb10_1_.pdf?v=0.

Fulginiti, L. E. and Perrin, R. K. (1997). LDC agriculture: Nonparametric Malmquist productivity indexes. *Journal of Development Economics*, 53(2), 373–390.

Iizumi, T., Shiogama, H., Imada, Y., Hanasaki, N., Takikawa, H., and Nishimori, M. (2018). Crop production losses associated with anthropogenic climate change for 1981–2010 compared with preindustrial levels. *International Journal of Climatology*, 38(14), 5405–5417.

ILO. (2019). Working on a warmer planet: The impact of heat stress on labor productivity and decent work. International Labor Office, Geneva, ILO.

IPCC. (2007). *Climate change 2007: Synthesis report.* Contribution of Working Groups I, II and III to the Fourth Assessment Report of the Intergovernmental Panel on Climate Change [Core Writing Team, Pachauri, R.K and Reisinger, A. (eds.)]. *Report.* Geneva, Switzerland: IPCC, 104 pp.

IPCC. (2018). *Global Warming of 1.5° C. An IPCC Special Report on the impacts of global warming of 1.5° C above pre-industrial levels and related global greenhouse gas emission pathways, in the context of strengthening the global response to the threat of climate change, sustainable development, and efforts to eradicate poverty* (Masson-Delmotte, V., Zhai, P., Pörtner, H.-O., Roberts, D., Skea, J., Shukla, P. R., Pirani, A., Moufouma-Okia, W., Péan, C., Pidcock, R., Connors, S., Matthews, J. B. R., Chen, Y., Zhou, X., Gomis, M. I., Lonnoy, E., Maycock, T., Tignor, M., and Waterfield, T. (eds.)). *Reports.* Geneva, Switzerland: IPCC.

Jaber, L. S., Diehl, K. E., and Hamadeh, S. K. (2016). Livestock and food security in the Arab region: Policy framework. Food Security, 8, 899–908, doi: 10.1007/s12571-016-0608-4.

Jorgenson, D. W. (2007). The role of energy in productivity growth. *American Economic Review*, 74, 26–30.

Kahn *et al.* (2019). "Long-Term Macroeconomic Effects of Climate Change: A Cross-Country Analysis," IMF Working Paper No. WP/19/215.

Kang, Y., Khan, S., and Ma, X. (2009). Climate change impacts on crop yield, crop water productivity and food security — a review. *Progress in Natural Science*, 19(12), 1665–1674.

Lafakis, C., Ratz, L., Fazio, E., and Cosma, M. (2019). *The Economic Implications of Climate Change.* Moody's Analytics. https://www.moodysanalytics.com/-/media/ article/2019/economic-implications-of-climate-change.pdf

Lambert, D. (2014). Historical impacts of precipitation and temperature on farm production in Kansas. *Journal of Agricultural and Applied Economics*, 46(4), 439–456, doi: 10.1017/S1074070800029047.

Letta, M. and Tol, R. S. J. (2019). Weather, climate and total factor productivity. *Environmental and Resource Economics*, 73, 283–305. https: //doi.org/10.1007/s10640-018-0262-8.

Liang, X. Z., Wu, Y., Chambers, R. G., Schmoldt, D. L., Gao, W., Liu, C., ... and Kennedy, J. A. (2017). Determining climate effects on U.S. total agricultural productivity. *Proceedings of the National Academy of Sciences*, 114(12), E2285–E2292.

Liu, Y., Richard Shumway, C., Rosenman, R., and Ball, V. E. (2011). Productivity growth and convergence in US agriculture: New cointegration panel data results. *Applied Economics*, 43(1), 91–102.

Loureiro, M. L. (2009). Farmers' health and agricultural productivity. *Agricultural Economics*, 40(4), 381–388.

McCarl, B. A., Villavicencio, X., and Wu, X. (2009). The effect of climate change over agricultural factor productivity: Some econometric considerations (No. 319-2016-9762). 0

McKinsey Global Institute. (2020). Climate risk and response: Physical hazards and socioeconomic impacts. Report available at: https://www.mckinsey.com/business-functions/sustainability/our-insights/ climate-risk-and-response-physical-hazards-and-socioeconomic-impacts.

Moghaddasi, R. and Pour, A. A. (2016). Energy consumption and total factor productivity growth in Iranian agriculture. *Energy Reports*, 2, 218–220

NOAA [National Oceanic and Atmospheric Administration, U.S. Department of Commerce]. (2020). Climate Change: Atmospheric Carbon Dioxide, available at: https://www.climate.gov/news-features/understanding-climate/ climate-change-atmospheric-carbon-dioxide.

OECD. (2015). *The Economic Consequences of Climate Change*, OECD Publishing, Paris, doi: 10.1787/9789264235410-en.

Olesen, J. E. and Bindi, M. (2002). Consequences of climate change for European agricultural productivity, land use and policy. *European Journal of Agronomy*, 16(4), 239–262.

Rada, N. E., Buccola, S. T., and Fuglie, K. O. (2011). Government policy and agricultural productivity in Indonesia. *American Journal of Agricultural Economics*, 93(3), 867–884.

Reyer, C. P. O., Rigaud, K. K., Fernandes, E. *et al.* (2017). Turn down the heat: Regional climate change impacts on development. *Regional Environmental Change*, 17, 1563–1568, doi: 10.1007/s10113-017-1187-4.

Roson, R. and van der Mensbrugghe, D. (2012). Climate change and economic growth: Impacts and interactions. *International Journal of Sustainable Economy*, 4, 270–285.

Sabasi, D. and Shumway, C. R. (2018). Climate change, health care access and regional influence on components of U.S. agricultural productivity. *Applied Economics*, 50(57), 6149–6164.

Schlenker, W. and Roberts, M. J. (2009). Nonlinear temperature effects indicate severe damages to U.S. crop yields under climate change. *Proceedings of the National Academy of Sciences of the United States of America 106*, 37, 15594–15598.

Schurr, S. (1982), Energy efficiency and productive efficiency: Some thoughts based on American experience. *Energy Journal*, 3, 3–14.

Torres, M., Howitt, R., and Rodrigues, L. (2019). Analyzing rainfall effects on agricultural income: Why timing matters, *EconomiA*, 20(1), 1–14, doi: 10.1016/j.econ.2019.03.006.

USDA. (2020). USDA ERS International Agricultural Productivity Dataset, available at: https://www.ers.usda.gov/data-products/international-agricultural-productivity/. USDA, Washington, DC, United States.

Zhong, Z., Hu, Y., and Jiang, L. (2019). Impact of climate change on agricultural total factor productivity based on spatial panel data model: Evidence from China. *Sustainability*, 11(6), 1516, https://doi.org/10.3390/su11061516.

PART 2

PATHWAYS THROUGH WHICH CLIMATE CHANGE CAN CAUSE HARM (OR BENEFIT) TO DEVELOPMENT

https://doi.org/10.1142/9789811240553_0008

Chapter 8

The Climate–Conflicts Nexus and the Role of Geographical Spillovers

Federica Cappelli*[,¶], Valeria Costantini*[,||], Elena Paglialunga[†,], Giorgia Sforna[‡,††] and Anil Markandya[§,‡‡]**

**Roma Tre University, Rome, Italy*
[†]University of Urbino "Carlo Bo," Urbino, Italy
[‡]SEEDS — Sustainability Environmental Economics and Dynamics Studies, Ferrara, Italy
[§]BC3 — Basque Centre for Climate Change, Bilbao, Spain
[¶]federica.cappelli@uniroma3.it
[||]valeria.costantini@uniroma3.it
[**]elena.paglialunga@uniurb.it
[††]giorgia.sforna@enea.it
[‡‡]anil.markandya@bc3research.org

The chapter reviews the literature on the pathways through which climate change leads to armed conflict. These are pressures on agriculture, resource scarcity, factors that result in the resource curse, and migration. There is evidence, especially from Africa, that climate change has worked through all of these to varying degrees to increase armed conflict. The questions being addressed are as follows: what scale is appropriate for the analysis and over what time period do variations in climate make an impact? On the first, most studies focus on region- or country-specific case studies. Recent research has been shifting toward a much more geographically disaggregated level of analysis that captures local factors shaping conflict dynamics. This also allows an assessment to be made of the spillover effect of conflict in one locality on other localities nearby. Such spillovers are found to be important. On the time period over which climate change impacts are relevant, while most studies focus on yearly variations in temperatures and precipitation, some consider deviations from long-term averages and others take into account aspects like extreme temperature. Studies find links to conflict using all of these and as yet there is no conclusive view on what the right measure is.

1. Introduction

The nature of armed conflicts has changed substantially since the foundation of the United Nations 75 years ago, becoming on average less lethal (United Nations, 2020); despite that, the number of conflicts has risen over this period. The year 2016 registered the highest number of conflicts over the last 30 years (United Nations World Bank, 2018) and it is estimated that, by 2030, more than half of the world's population living in developing countries will be afflicted by acute violent episodes (OECD, 2015).

Armed conflicts are a serious threat to livelihoods and development, so much so that Collier *et al.* (2003) define them as "development in reverse," because of the costs they impose on societies and the lingering effects they have on the whole economy for several years after the conflict has ended. Collier (1999) argues that the disruptive effects of conflicts on the economies manifest themselves through several mechanisms, including the destruction of resources, social disorder, the shifting of public expenditure toward military purposes, and capital flight. Several other studies (Gates *et al.*, 2012, Fukuda-Parr *et al.*, 2011, Shemyakina, 2011, Cohen and Pinstrup-Andersen, 1999, Teodosijevic, 2003) report their effects in terms of exacerbation of food insecurity and development issues. Among these, results from an empirical work by Messer and Cohen (2004) show that civil conflicts in Africa from 1960 to 2000 caused losses amounting to $120 billion in agricultural production.

In the last few decades, the disruptive effects of climate change have been manifesting at a far hastier pace and with a stronger intensity (Hoegh-Guldberg *et al.*, 2018). In the same way as armed conflicts, climate change is a major security concern and affects crucial aspects of human life especially in developing countries, through its impacts on agriculture and food security, access to water, and other resources (Markandya *et al.*, 2017, Nordås and Gleditsch, 2007). This may exacerbate the social disorder and instability already present in those countries, likely fueling conflicts (Weir and Virani, 2011). Indeed, even though socio-economic and institutional circumstances are crucial in explaining the onset and evolution of conflicts (Buhaug, 2010), climate change and resource endowment may reasonably act as "threat multipliers." Doherty and Clayton (2011) find that, as a consequence of a 1.1°C (2°F) temperature increase in the USA, interpersonal violence and murders per year would rise by 24,000. In a study of 2013, Hsiang, Burke, and Miguel estimate the impact of a one standard deviation increase in either temperature or extreme rainfall on different typologies of conflicts. They find that deviations from normal values have a systematic effect on increasing conflict risk. In particular, such a 1-SD increase brings about an intensification of the frequency of interpersonal violence by 4% and of intergroup conflict by 14%. Furthermore, numerous studies (Gleick, 2014, King, 2015, Kelley *et al.*, 2015) have identified the hard drought conditions affecting Syria during the last few years as one of the factors contributing directly to the deterioration of the country's economic conditions and, accordingly, to the escalation of the still ongoing (although often forgotten) civil conflict.

Accordingly, both climate change and armed conflicts are major security concerns, jeopardizing human development and affecting, disproportionately, crucial aspects of human life. For this reason, during the last few years, a possible linkage between these two main issues has been widely debated to shed light on the possible role of climate change in inducing or aggravating armed conflicts. Hsiang and Burke (2014) review 50 independent studies examining the impacts of climate change on conflicts and find strong support for a causal link ranging across regions, time intervals, and spatial scales. However, because the mechanism through which climate change affects the onset of conflicts is not direct but mediated by other factors, a multitude of alternative explanations has emerged from the literature. In particular, four main channels are investigated: (i) the agricultural sector; (ii) the scarcity of resources; (iii) the resource curse; and (iv) migrations.

On a geographic dimension, empirical investigations in this strand of literature usually spotlight Africa (Burke *et al.*, 2009, Hendrix and

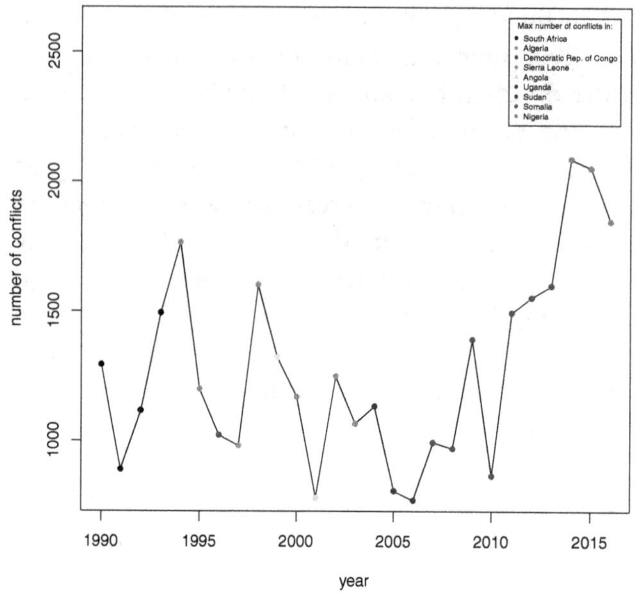

Fig. 1. Number of conflicts by year, 1990–2016 (peak country).

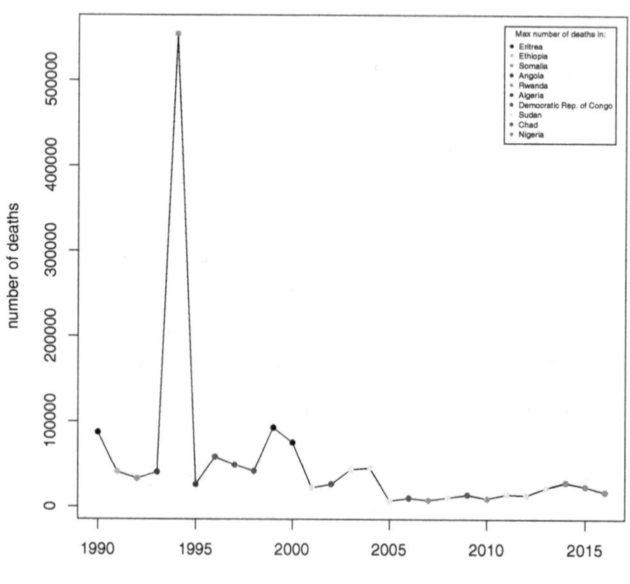

Fig. 2. Number of deaths by year, 1990–2016 (peak country).

Salehyan, 2012, Harari and La Ferrara, 2018; Breckner and Sunde, 2019; Scheffran *et al.*, 2019, van Weezel, 2020) for multiple reasons. First, as shown in Figs. 1 and 2, the African continent has hosted many and some of the bloodiest conflicts of the last decades (Croicu and Sunberg, 2017), including the Tutsi genocide in Rwanda in 1994; the Second Congo War, which took place between 1998 and 2003; and the Arab Spring, which involved Tunisia, Egypt, and Libya between 2010 and 2012.

Second, large areas of the continent are among the ones most heavily burdened with the adverse effects of climate change (Moore and Diaz, 2015), with ravaging desertification compromising food security of entire societies (Searchinger *et al.*, 2014). This is evident from Fig. 3 where, except for some localities along the coasts, the whole continent has experienced a dramatic surge in average temperatures in the period 2014–2016, compared to the average values registered in 1990–1992. In some regions, this warming effect has been so pronounced as to exceed the average of the initial period by 3°C. Figure 4 depicts a no less worrying situation: the Sahara desert, one of the less

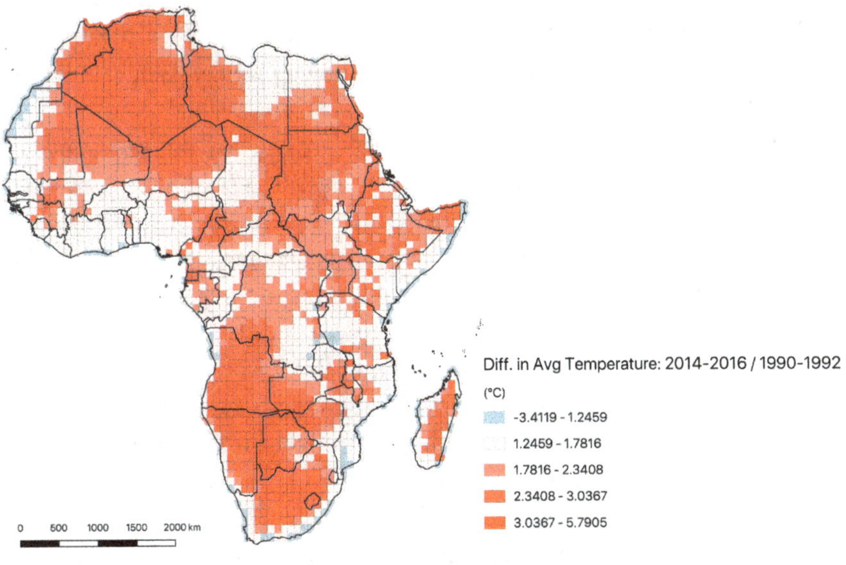

Fig. 3. Differences in average temperatures: 2014–2016/1990–1992.

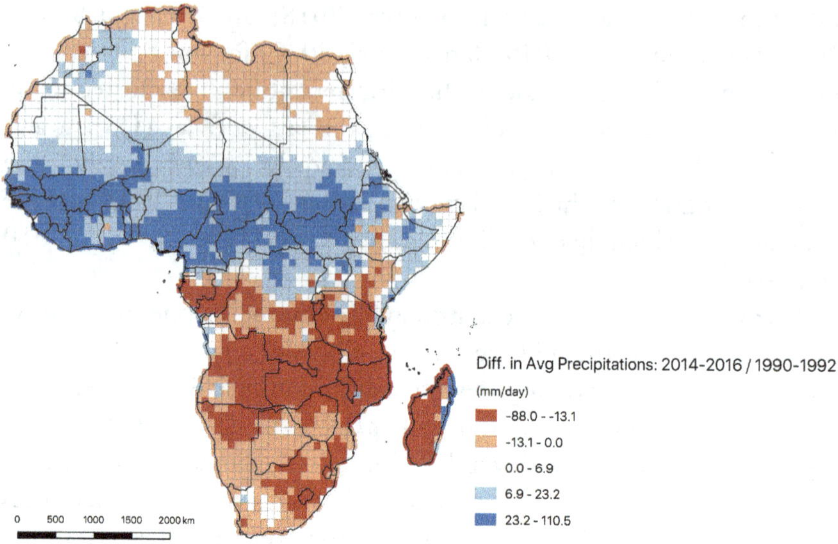

Fig. 4. Differences in average precipitations: 2014–2016/1990–1992.

populated areas of the continent, is the only region where the aridity has been somehow mitigated, while the rest of Africa has experienced a way more severe drought condition in 2014–2016, compared to 1990–1992.

Third, several African countries rank in the lowest positions in terms of human development (Conceição, 2019). Fourth, the economic structure of the vast majority of the African countries is mainly reliant on the primary sector. Fifth, some areas struggle to grow and the spatial inequality in income distribution and growth (shown in Fig. 5) may fuel political instability and undermine social cohesion (Lessmann, 2016). In addition, population dynamics, both in terms of demography and of migration flows, are not very stable, as evident from Fig. 6. In particular, in Fig. 5 we report the difference, for each cell, between the average GDP in the period 2014–2016 and the average GDP in the period 1990–1992. In Fig. 6, the benchmark is the cell's population number in 1990 and the map represents the percentage change that occurred in 2016 with respect to 1990.

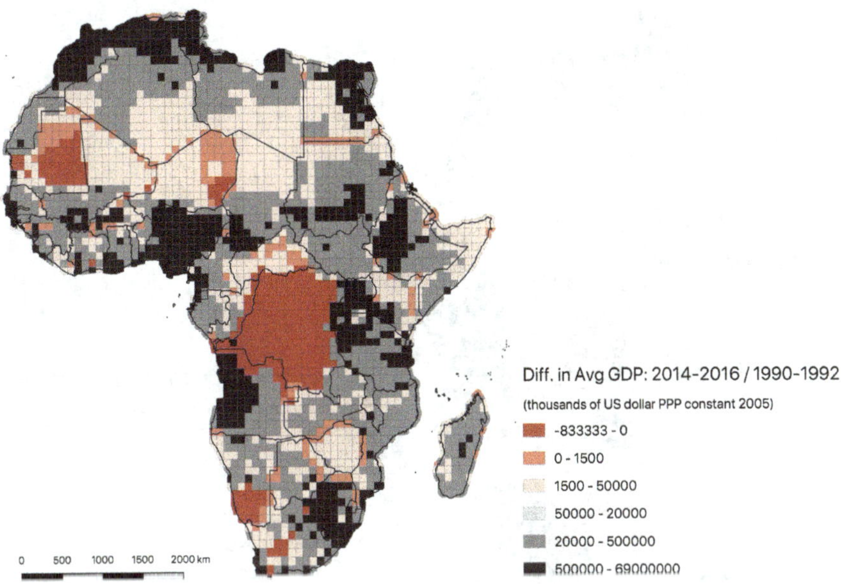

Fig. 5. Differences in average GDP: 2014–2016/1990–1992.

All of these factors contribute to making the continent very vulnerable to any external shock that undermines the fragile socio-political environment of African societies (Daccache *et al.*, 2015, Hendrix and Glaser, 2007, Marchiori *et al.*, 2012, Maystadt *et al.*, 2015).

The rest of this chapter is structured as follows: the next section investigates in detail the different channels through which this linkage is expressed. Section 3 gets to the heart of the methodological debate, especially focusing on the issue regarding the role of spatial spillovers. Section 4 concludes by providing some impulses for the future research agenda.

2. Backgrounds on the Climate–conflict Nexus

Four channels of investigation that emerged from the literature (Section 2.1) that aim to discern the mechanisms driving the linkage between climate change and armed conflicts are considered in this Section. This is followed by an examination of the role of institutions

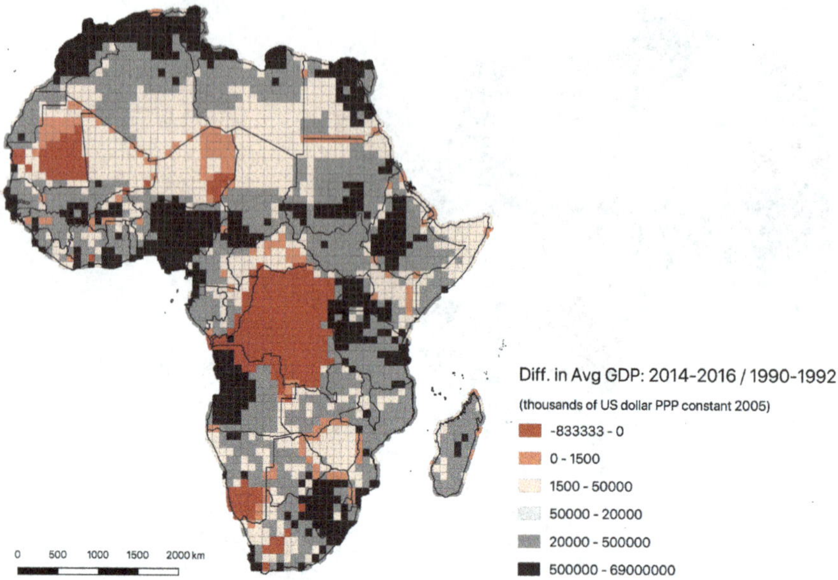

Fig. 6. Rate of population variation 1990–2016.

(Section 2.2) and the propagation of conflicts across time and space (Section 2.3).

2.1. *The main channels of investigation*

2.1.1. *The agricultural sector*

Several studies (Crost *et al.*, 2018, Harari and La Ferrara, 2018, Wischnath and Buhaug, 2014, Ang and Gupta, 2018) focus on the channel of agriculture because of its high exposure to climate variability, as more than 80% of world food production relies on rainfed irrigation, which depends critically on the variation of the spatial and temporal distribution of precipitation (Bates *et al.*, 2008). Climate change has devastating effects on crop yields, threatening food security for all its four components, i.e., food availability, food accessibility, food utilization, and food system stability (FAO, 2008). As stated by the FAO, "climate change influences biophysical factors (plant and animal growth, water cycles, biodiversity and nutrient cycling), and the ways in which these are managed through agricultural practices and land use for food production. Climate variables also have an impact on physical and human capital (roads, storage and marketing infrastructure, houses, productive assets, electricity grids, and human health), which indirectly changes the economic and socio-political factors that govern food access and utilization and can threaten the stability of food systems" (FAO, 2008, p. 11), intensifying the risk of competition for necessary but limited resources (Raleigh *et al.*, 2010, Wischnath and Buhaug, 2014). According to Burke *et al.* (2009), the effect of increasing temperatures on civil conflicts in Africa is driven by agricultural performance. Some authors, including Adano *et al.* (2010), Schilling *et al.* (2014), and Theisen (2012), consider pastoral communities as central actors in armed conflicts, which usually take the form of raids on neighboring areas. These communities are extremely dependent on pastures and water, whose availability is threatened by increased variability induced by climate change. Prolonged periods of droughts causing the death of herds alter the nature of relations between pastoral communities, from cooperative to competitive, inducing thefts from neighboring communities to replace lost cattle (Meier *et al.*, 2007). Furthermore, albeit perhaps counterintuitive, drought and water scarcity are not the only causes of inter-pastoralist conflicts, but an abundance of water, if experienced at the wrong times, can induce violence (Adano *et al.*, 2010, Eaton, 2008, Raleigh and Kniveton, 2012), too. The timing of extreme climatic events is a factor observed also by Harari and La Ferrara (2018), who concentrate on the growing season, the period in which crops are most sensitive to shocks.

Another source of conflicts in this sector is related to food prices. In this framework, Raleigh *et al.* (2015) observe the relationship existing among climate change, conflicts, and international food prices and find that all three aspects are interrelated at the local level. They find a bilateral relationship between international food prices and conflicts, while climate change fuels conflicts not only directly but also indirectly, by affecting food prices. Hence, there is a compelling need to enhance adaptation practices in this sector to build resilience and prevent conflicts in the face of climate change (Burke *et al.*, 2009, Fjelde and von

Uexkull, 2012). For instance, Jones *et al.* (2017) show how the presence of a low-vulnerable state can effectively mitigate both the effect of food insecurity and the likelihood of violent conflicts.

2.1.2. *The scarcity of resources*

One of the most debated aspects in the climatic conflict discourse concerns the contrast between two opposite strands of literature. On the one hand, some argue that the scarcity of basic resources, especially renewable ones, is the primary source of conflict; on the other hand, other scholars maintain that armed conflicts are triggered by (particularly non-renewable) resource abundance. Natural resources represent a crucial economic source and the competition for their control may increase the risk of conflicts. In the model proposed by Maxwell and Reuveny (2000), natural resources and armed conflicts are found to be interdependent: resource scarcity likely triggers the onset of conflicts and, at the same time, conflicts subtract and damage resources earmarked for population livelihood. This generates cyclical phases of conflicts that may last a long time, though not forever.

As for the role of climate change, one of its main effects is an increase in temperatures as well as changes in precipitation patterns that generally lead to more severe drought conditions. Moreover, there is also an increase in the frequency and magnitude of other extreme events (e.g., floods), which can bring about major damage in terms of destruction of cultivated land, villages, and infrastructures. Consequently, most countries, especially developing ones, suffer from a reduction of resources, above all cropland and water.

A crucial issue in this strand of literature is related to water access. Freshwater being an essential source of development, whose demand is dramatically increasing with the improvement of human societies' standards of living, several studies have investigated the link between conflicts and climate-induced water scarcity (Brochmann and Gleditsch, 2012, Mwiturubani, 2017). On the one hand, freshwater supply turns out to be scarcer and more uncertain owing to climate change and pollution (Gleick, 1993). On the other hand, the delay in the past in recognizing the risks posed by limited water availability and in decoupling economic development from water use, in both developed and transition economies, has made societies extremely water-dependent (Dinar, 2012). In particular, the risk of competition for access to freshwater is very high (Codjoe and Larbi, 2016). In this respect, DCs remain highly dependent on rain-fed agriculture for both employment and economic production, and the zones without an irrigation system are found to be the most exposed to the risk of conflicts as a consequence of climatic variations (Daccache *et al.*, 2015, von Uexküll, 2014). Such water dependency, heightened by climate change, has often led to the use of control over water resources as an instrument of war for both offensive and defensive purposes (Gleick, 1993, King, 2015).

According to Mwiturubani (2017), in addition to water access, conflicts over water also occur as a struggle to utilize the scarce resource.[1] This study argues that conflict for both water access and use may occur at the household level (e.g., gender issues), at the village level (e.g., members of a village can access water at a nearby village, intensifying water scarcity), and between livelihood systems (e.g., between people practicing different economic activities). Even though historical evidence reports that cooperation has been preferred over struggle in shared transboundary water basins (Kloos *et al.*, 2013), where the stipulated agreements on water use and allocation are questioned (e.g., by migrating population or unexpected changes in water demand), conflicts are likely to arise (Otto *et all*, 2017).

In this respect, Olsson *et all* (2014) point out that the exacerbation of critical geophysical and socio-economic conditions imposed by climate change may undermine social cohesion and reciprocity behaviors, boosting vulnerability of endangered groups. Figure 7 shows the spatial distribution of both armed conflicts that occurred in Africa from 1990 to 2016 and water resources. As we can see, the map confirms findings from the literature, as the vast majority of conflicts are located along the main watercourses and along the coast of water basins.

[1]Water-use conflicts occur when one water source is used for more than one use by different users and the uses are not complementary (Mwiturubani, 2017).

Variations in temperatures and precipitation patterns also influence the probability of conflicts through changes in features and properties of both water basins (De Stefano *et al.*, 2017, Onuoha, 2010) and pastoral zones (Meier *et al.*, 2007), thus altering fishing activities and pastoral livelihoods. Onuoha (2010) shows that the effects of climate change on Lake Chad have brought about both dynamics. The lake is located in a strategic position, crosscutting the borders of four African countries (namely, Chad, Cameroon, Niger, and Nigeria) and representing the main source of freshwater for both drinking and sanitation purposes for each of these countries. In addition, it is also crucial for economic activities, including agriculture, fishing, and pastoralism for several communities based along its coasts. During the last 40 years, climate change has compromised the availability of water

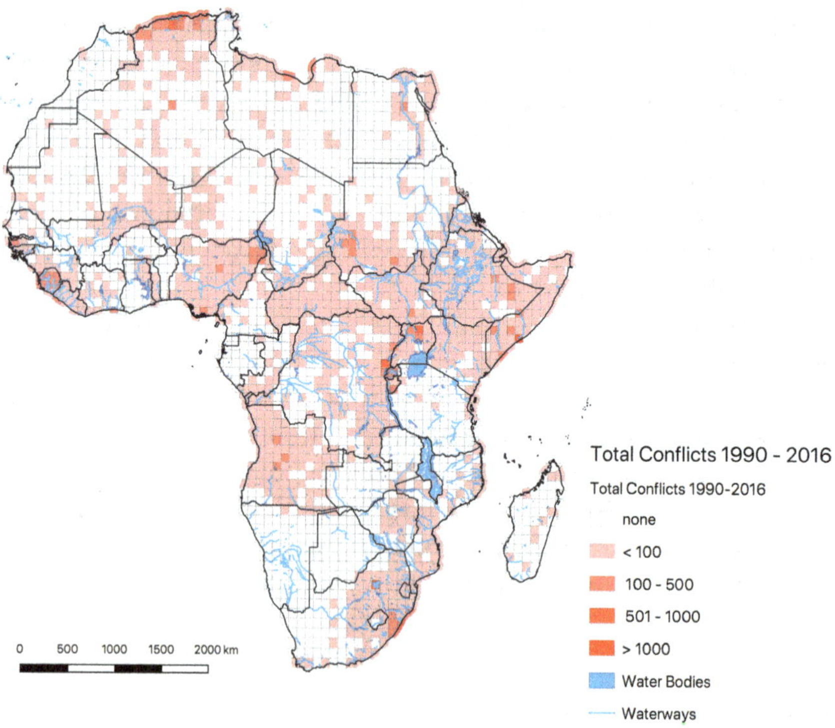

Fig. 7. Total conflicts 1990–2016 and water resources.

in the lake, which has lost over 50% of its water. The loss of water resources and, consequently, of fish stock, vegetation, and fertile land, has contributed to the eruption of violent conflicts over control of the remaining resources.

Finally, it is worth noting that climate change is characterized by a high level of uncertainty (Markandya, 2014, Mach *et al.*, 2019) that can determine unpredictability about the future availability of resources, representing a possible cause of conflict in the coming years. In this respect, Mwangi (2010) investigates the case of Lesotho, which is endowed with abundant water that it exports to South Africa. Nevertheless, scenarios indicate that the country will in the future suffer from water stress and scarcity as a result of climate change. This creates the potential for future interstate conflicts as Lesotho may be unable to supply adequate water to South Africa. The study concludes that the main challenge for Lesotho "currently lies in the management of its water resources." Accordingly, there is a need for strong institutions that would improve water management in order to reduce the degradation of water sources and enhance equitable access to and utilization of the resource (Mwiturubani, 2017).

2.1.3. *The Resource Curse Hypothesis*

The availability of natural resources alone does not necessarily prevent conflicts, but, on the contrary, sometimes triggers them. An example relates to a situation in which a large share of national wealth is derived from a few economic activities or industries connected with the exploitation of (abundant) natural resources. Indeed, this entails the risk of neglecting other sectors (Auty, 1993) or unfair distribution of the revenues derived from the exploitation of these resources, with the possibility of being trapped in the so-called resource curse. Among the several studies analyzing these dynamics, Cilliers (2009) and Holmberg (2008) show that in poor countries with high natural resources endowment, controlling and exploiting processes for those resources are likely to result in environmental crisis and civil conflicts.

According to Auty (2001) and Sachs and Warner (1995), the abundance of natural resources is often associated with poor economic growth and institutional quality, two important factors in fostering the onset of armed conflicts. Ayodele (2010) highlights how oil exploration in Nigeria has increased environmental degradation, due to gas flaring, oil and water pollution, bush burning, and CO2 emissions. This has led to severe consequences in terms of poverty and human development, as well as increasing the civil conflicts.

Collier (2000) argues that in countries relying economically on the export of natural resources, the risk of experiencing armed conflicts is higher. Ross (2004) reviews several studies on natural resource and civil war links and suggests that oil production and exports increase the likelihood of (the onset of) conflicts, due to further financial incentives resulting from the rent-seeking behavior. This is especially true in the case of capital-intensive processes, where the state and extraction firms gain more benefits than local unskilled workers. Although similar mechanisms may be expected to apply also in the case of non-fuel minerals, this issue has received much less attention, especially in quantitative terms. Figure 8 complements the previous figure by integrating the spatial distribution of fossil and mineral resources.

While most exhaustible resources are located close to water basins and waterways, thus adding another possible source of conflict, there are some oil-rich areas (for instance, in Angola and in the Central African Republic) that have hosted several conflicts and where no relevant water sources are present. However, from a policy perspective, caution must be used when trying to design measures to prevent excessive exploitation of resources in some areas or to overcome the resource curse. Parker and Vadheim (2017) present the US Dodd-Frank Act of 2010, Section 1502 as an emblematic example of the latter. This act, despite aiming at cutting off conflicts induced by large companies searching for profits from the extraction of tin, tantalum, and tungsten in the Democratic Republic of Congo, a country affected by the resource curse, unfortunately, had unexpected adverse outcomes (Parker and Vadheim, 2017). The authors demonstrated empirically that, by fostering competition among armed groups for controlling unregulated gold-mining areas, the act provoked an increase in the incidence of conflicts in the same territories.

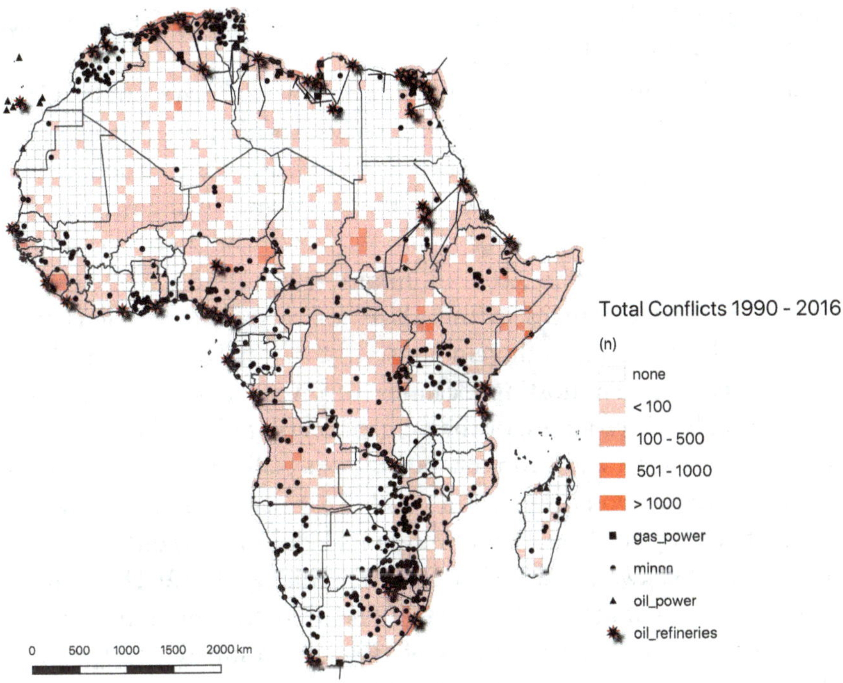

Fig. 8. Total conflicts 1990–2016 and resources.

2.1.4. *Migrations*

Another widely investigated channel in the climate–conflict research agenda is the climate change–migration–conflict nexus. The estimated number of people who may be forced to migrate because of climate change by 2050 ranges from 50 million to 1 billion people (Stern, 2006), and areas which are more dependent on environment-related activities, especially agriculture, will be the most affected (Reuveny, 2007, Cai *et al.*, 2016). Migration per se does not trigger conflicts, but may act as an aggravating factor of already critical situations, which can fuel violence because of the ethnic and socio-economic tensions it may pose (Olzak, 1992). In this context, a common explanation that has a foothold in the climate change–migration–conflict nexus is the so-called "neo-Malthusian" view, according to which the increased competition for resources, induced by climate change and population growth, and further exacerbated by migrations, gives rise to armed conflict (Hendrix and Glaser, 2007).

Severe drought conditions and subsequent soil barrenness (Gray and Mueller, 2012), as well as sudden climatic shocks provoking natural disasters, often induce forced mass migrations as a form of adaptation (McLeman and Smit, 2006, Tacoli, 2009), possibly giving rise to conflicts in the receiving regions or countries (Foresight, 2011, D'Andrea *et al.*, 2011, Theisen *et al.*, 2013, Ghimire *et al.*, 2015). While reducing pressure on resources in the places of origin, hence alleviating climate-induced conflicts therein (Bosetti *et al.*, 2018), migrant flows may alter equilibria in hosting localities. Motives include the increased pressure on local resources, or the perception of it (Brzoska and Fröhlich, 2016, Burrows and Kinney, 2016), especially when exploitation is not well regulated at the central level (Linke *et al.*, 2017), or social instability owing to the arrival of migrants belonging to different ethnic groups (Gaikwad and Nellis, 2017). Linke *et al.* (2018) analyze climate-induced migrations in Kenya and find that migrants are far more likely to be involved in acts of violence, compared to the ones who decide to remain in their homeland and, in most cases, who are the victims of such violence and not the perpetrators. Nonetheless, because of the scant availability of bilateral flows of migration data, these studies usually analyze single case studies (Burrows and Kinney, 2016, Linke *et al.*, 2017, 2018) or international migration flows at the country level (Cai *et al.*, 2016, Cattaneo and Bosetti, 2017, Marchiori *et al.*, 2012).

2.2. *The role of institutions*

All the aspects previously described can be aggravated by the absence of proper institutional settings. Good institutions are essential for effective use of resources as well as to cope with adverse socio-economic conditions and to implement adaptation policies limiting the vulnerability to climate change. The more a country is vulnerable to climate change, the more it is exposed to these risks, especially if the focus of the economy is on a few climate-dependent sectors, as is the case for many DCs. Many of them already suffer from food insecurity, lack of access to water, poor economic development, and political tensions. They are also characterized by a very high vulnerability to climate change (and, often, low adaptive capacity), together with scarce institutional quality and an economic structure mainly reliant on the primary sector. In these contexts, where the impacts of climate change represent a serious threat to the entire economic system and an obstacle for future development (Castells-Quintana *et al.*, 2017), the risk of escalation of tensions and hostilities can be particularly high. In the past, national states have often failed to address the security risks posed by climate change, by limiting their intervention to border management, humanitarian aid, and entrusting disaster management to military forces (Brzoska, 2012).

The presence of strong and effective institutions, implementing sound policies, and directing public expenditure toward social welfare systems can help to moderate social tensions and avoid the outbreak of conflicts. Bodea *et al.* (2016) investigate how different allocations of public expenditure may have a mitigating effect on the onset of civil conflicts. In particular, they consider the effect of an increase in general government expenditure, military expenditure, and welfare expenditure, differentiating between oil-rich and oil-poor countries. They find general government expenditure not to be statistically significant to explain conflict onset, while an increase in military expenditure is associated with a higher probability of conflict onset in oil-poor countries and a lower probability in oil-rich countries. On the contrary, a higher welfare expenditure, including health, social security, and education expenditure relative to GDP, always has a mitigating effect on conflict onset (Barnett and Adger, 2007).

However, Lai and Thyne (2007) find that, on average, during a civil war a state cuts its expenditure for education down by 3–4% points per year. Education enrolment is also reduced, likely producing a persistent effect on instruction outcomes even after the end of the conflict.

While there is common agreement in the literature about the mitigating effect of welfare expenditure, not everybody agrees on the role of military expenditure. Some authors, including Collier and Hoeffler (2002) and Taydas and Peksen (2012) posit that military expenditure is not robustly associated with increasing or decreasing risk of conflict, whereas Henderson and Singer (2000) contend that higher military expenditure crowds out welfare expenditure, thereby fueling conflicts.

Strong institutions should also ensure equitable access to resources and protection to vulnerable households and groups. The latter aspect relates to horizontal inequality, another factor deserving attention considering that, on the one hand, differences in the treatment of groups who are believed to face similar economic and social challenges may contribute to jeopardizing socio-political stability, thereby strongly increasing the likelihood for an area to experience violence and conflicts (Østby, 2005; Hillesund *et al.*, 2018). On the other hand, because different groups react differently to environmental stressors, the marginalized ones, as well as those overreliant on agriculture, have higher probabilities to be victims of violence (von Uexküll *et al.*, 2016).

2.3. *The conflict trap hypothesis and the probability of contagion*

In general, conflicts can occur more frequently in vulnerable communities. Indeed, not all societies and not all population groups within a society are equally exposed to environmental shocks. For instance, Raleigh *et al.* (2015) find that communities living in degraded environments, as well as in places where conflict rates are already high, are most likely exposed to new conflicts. The latter concept is what Collier *et al.* (2003) define as the "conflict trap" hypothesis: once a country has had a conflict, it is more at risk of experiencing further conflicts. This is the case, for instance, for Burundi, where the juxtaposition between the Hutu and the Tutsi ethnicities has led to several recurrent waves of civil conflicts since the Seventies (in 1972–1973, in 1988, from 1991 to 2005, and from 2015 until the present). The conflict trap often acts in tandem with the well-known poverty trap, as livelihoods and economic conditions plummet as a consequence of the devastation caused by wars, generating further social instability and creating the conditions for the outbreak of additional violent episodes (Collier and Hoeffler, 2002).

Hegre *et al.* (2016), by examining the four pathways that define the conflict trap, namely, the conflict-induced increase in the likelihood of continuation, recurrence, escalation, and diffusion of armed conflicts, find that previous studies have underestimated both its intensity and duration over time. To break this conflict trap, Wennmann (2011) suggests fostering investments in natural resources and sharing the revenues emerging from the exploitation of them more equitably, as the control of such resources is seen by the author as the primary source of armed conflicts.

According to Silve and Verdier (2018), from a theoretical point of view, there are at least two channels to be considered jointly. On the one side, regional clusters of civil wars result from the clustering of similar internal features (geographical or social characteristics, resource endowments, and climatic conditions). On the other, spatial spillovers between neighboring regions should be considered as a crucial determinant of the geographical distribution of civil wars. Empirical results on contagion based on quantitative analyses at a highly disaggregated level and embracing large datasets are few (Harari and La Ferrara, 2018), and regional interactions and feedback effects should be further investigated. Accordingly, the geographical dimension of spillover effects must be carefully shaped into the empirical setting.

3. Relevant Aspects within the Methodological Debate

Given the difficulties in identifying a direct mechanism of action, the debate about the direction and strength of the linkage between climate change and armed conflicts is still open (Koubi, 2019). However, as emphasized by Detges (2017), the absence of an agreement does not mean that evidence is lacking. From a theoretical perspective, major disagreement rests in the juxtaposition between those who assert the existence of a strong causal link between climate change and armed conflicts (Hsiang *et al.*, 2013, Hsiang and Burke, 2014) and those who dispute the direct connection and see in socio-political issues the main source of grievances (Buhaug, 2015, Ide *et al.*, 2014). In very recent years, the focus of the debate has shifted toward methodological aspects. One of these aspects questions what the most relevant geographic scale of analysis should be to better capture local-specific changes in climatic conditions and, accordingly, the kind of econometric model that best fits it (Ide, 2017). The next paragraph expands on this issue. Another controversial aspect concerns the correct representation of climate change. Hsiang (2016) provides a useful guide to the parametrization of the main aspects related to weather and climate. Most studies focus on yearly variations in temperatures and precipitations, while others take into account other aspects like extreme temperatures (O'Loughlin *et al.*, 2012), drought conditions (Fjelde and von Uexkull, 2012), usually represented by the Standardised Precipitations Index or the Standardised Evapotranspiration Index, or El Niño and La Niña oscillations (Hsiang *et al.*, 2011). Buhaug (2015) and Ide and Scheffran (2014) warn about the appropriate time-horizon length in order to correctly frame climate change, as opposed to climate variability, and the possible confusion between the two. While most studies focus on short-term variations, notable exceptions include the studies by Hendrix and Salehyan (2012), Koubi *et al.* (2012), Tol and Wagner (2010), Breckner and Sunde (2019), and van Weezel (2020), who consider climate deviations from long-term averages. Nonetheless, the evolution of human societies is rapid and, as such, justifies shorter periods of analysis, too. This unsolvable trade-off is defined by Hsiang and Burke (2014) as the "frequency–identification trade-off," because of the inability of current statistical techniques to simultaneously take into account both rates of change.

Finally, ambiguity is also driven by the interpretations of results (Mach *et al.*, 2019) because of the high sensitivity of conflicts' outcomes (Hegre and Sambanis, 2006), which explains the divergence in findings on the relevancy or not of the role played by climate change in triggering conflicts.

3.1. *Geographical spillovers as a way forward*

The controversy highlighted by Ide (2017) on the suitable geographical scale to adopt in this research field is motivated by concerns about the great variation in the size of the climate-induced effect on the onset of armed conflicts, depending on the spatial scale considered (Salehyan,

2014). Adopting one scale over another allows one to capture different aspects. At the national level, climate change appears to be a security issue since it affects indirectly the effectiveness of governments in several ways, including addressing the threatening of economic livelihood, worsening inequalities, factors affecting human health, and those imposing substantial costs on national economies (Barnett, 2003).

Further, environmental issues, as well as climate change impacts, are likely to fuel existing conflict dynamics and socio-political tensions between nation-states (Homer-Dixon and Percival, 1996, Wolf, 1999), while, at the subnational level, these factors are increasingly recognized to trigger the onset of armed conflicts (Barnett, 2003). In addition, conflicts often do not involve directly the entire population, especially in large countries (Buhaug and Gates, 2002, Buhaug and Rød, 2006, Raleigh *et al.*, 2010); thus, using country-level indicators to measure their impacts may underestimate the local effect of conflicts or neglect important local drivers (e.g., intrastate migration and resource distribution at the local level).

Most studies in the previous years have focused either on region- or country-specific case studies considering households as units of analysis (Meierding, 2013, Salick and Ross, 2009), or on country level studies, often with a global coverage, adopting administrative boundaries as meaningful statistical entities (Almer *et al.*, 2017, Maystadt *et al.*, 2015, Raleigh and Kniveton, 2012). Nonetheless, in more recent years, the research focus has been shifting toward a geographically disaggregated level of analysis that allows capturing local factors shaping conflict dynamics, which depend more on geographical and landscape characteristics rather than on administrative boundaries.

By this means, one can better disentangle the risk of exposure to physical hazards from the actual impact on the human population (Busby *et al.*, 2014). Within the African continent, most of the studies based on geo-referenced analysis have focused on East Africa with the literature largely accounting for variations in the precipitation patterns and, more recently, temperatures change. The units of analysis are usually represented by gridded cells of various dimensions and, in some cases (Schleussner *et al.*, 2016, von Uexküll *et al.*, 2016), by ethnic groups.

Raleigh and Kniveton (2012) gather data for Uganda, Ethiopia, and Kenya from 1997 to 2010. Their results show that with increasing rainfall variability (from monthly 2.5°grid data), the frequency of small-scale conflicts increases. Using a 1°gridded analysis covering precipitation and temperature anomalies, O'Loughlin *et al.* (2012) analyze several countries in East Africa (Burundi, Djibouti, Eritrea, Ethiopia, Kenya, Rwanda, Somalia, Tanzania, and Uganda) from 1990 to 2009. They highlight that higher temperature raises the risk of violence, while wetter precipitation deviations have a mitigating effect (on the conflict risk), but their results do not support the inverse relationships (that a lack of rain would raise conflict risk) and drier and normal periods show no effects on the risk of conflicts. They further highlight the relevance of contextual conditions as pastoralist and non-pastoralist agriculture and other geographic, socio-economic, and political factors. Ide *et al.* (2014) focus on Kenya and Uganda and try to answer the question of where the link between climate change and violent conflicts is most likely to occur. They consider three dimensions, exposure (higher temperatures and reduced precipitation), vulnerability (e.g., education, health, political instability, environmental dependence, population density, and soil degradation), and violent conflict risk (GDP and democracy level, population density, and previous conflicts), and combine them in a composite risk index (CRI) for 2008 with a spatial resolution of 0.5°. Maystadt *et al.* (2015) build a grid cell 0.5°resolution dataset for North and South Sudan from 1997 to 2009 to analyze the impact of precipitation and temperature anomalies on violent conflicts and find the link to temperature to be particularly strong. They also suggest that water scarcity (as an example of competition over natural resources) is an aggravating factor in the climate–conflict relationships, especially in pastoralism-dependent regions. Almer *et al.* (2017) rely on a fine geographical disaggregation with cells of $0.5° \times 0.5°$ and monthly data to investigate the relationship between water shocks (measured by the Standardised Precipitation-Evapotranspiration Index) and small social conflicts in Sub-Saharan Africa. Small social conflicts, as opposed to armed conflicts between organized groups, tend to be in place for very short periods and spatially confined in specific areas. They find that whatever the dependent variable considered — Days with riots (count variable), Incidence (binary variable), or Onset (binary variable) — a negative water shock brings about a higher conflict level, suggesting the presence of an effect of competition for water resources. In addition, this effect is stronger in cells affected more heavily by water scarcity or where there are a large number of groups competing for water (Almer *et al.*, 2017).

A more comprehensive analysis with respect to the geographical coverage is provided by Harari and La Ferrara (2018), Breckner *et al.* (2019), and van Weezel (2020), who focus on the entire African continent. Although there is large consensus on the motivations guiding the choice of focusing on Africa, some contest it inasmuch as subject to the so-called "streetlight effect" (Adams *et al.*, 2018). This term is used to describe selection bias that may affect the quantitative climate–conflict research focusing on Africa because of its "naturally" high propensity to violence. However, despite not being generalizable to the entire world, analyses based on grid representation of an entire continent and, thus, including both conflictual and non-conflictual cells, help to solve bias related to sample selection and to provide a rationale for all the factors determining a relatively higher propensity to conflicts. On the contrary, Ide and Scheffran (2014) warn about the limits of large N studies which, even at a highly disaggregated level, randomly select a number of cases with the aim to look for the existence of patterns in a large sample, but often at the expense of losing important information that may not be available in a measurable form for extremely large samples.

Harari and La Ferrara (2018) build a dataset at the sub-national level for Africa over the period 1997–2011 where the cross-sectional units are structured as a raster grid with 1° latitude and longitude resolution cells. They analyze the relationship between conflicts and climate change focusing on the role of agriculture as main channel in the link between weather shocks and the worsening of socio-economic conditions. In particular, they analyze the effect of variations in drought conditions during the growing season of main crops, by means of the Standardised Precipitation-Evapotranspiration Index (SPEI), which summarizes the effects of precipitations, evaporation, and temperatures on the soil. The spatial analysis is at the sub-national level where the incidence of civil conflicts in a cell is explained not only in terms of climate indicators from the cell itself but also controlling for spatial correlation in the covariates (with respect to neighboring cells) and autocorrelation in the dependent variable, both in time and space. This appears to be the first empirical study where the possibility of conflict spillovers across geographical units and the persistency in the occurrence of civil conflicts are accounted for, in line with the conflict trap hypothesis. The main results of their analysis can be summarized in two main points: first, they find that a shock in the SPEI index (expressed as units of standard deviation from the cell's historical average level) during the growing season increases the likelihood of conflict; second, they observe that conflicts present a high persistence both in time and space, as suggested by the conflict trap hypothesis. The pioneering study by Harari and La Ferrara (2018) paved the way to expand research in the same direction. Two very recent contributions are the ones by Breckner and Sunde (2019) and van Weezel (2020). Both focus on the entire African continent adopting a high-resolution spatial scale of analysis and look at long-term dynamics of climate change. The former paper represents climate change as the occurrence and the frequency and duration of extreme temperatures compared to long-run average conditions. Results from their study indicate the coexistence of mechanisms driving the influence of climate change on conflict outbreak. In particular, they point at population dynamics and agricultural productivity, both individually and the interaction between the two, providing evidence for a strong effect of extreme temperature events acting through both diminishing agricultural productivity, owing to land degradation, and migration flows. On the contrary, van Weezel (2020) directly links climate change to the onset of armed conflicts, without intermediate mechanisms mediating the two. The main contributions of his work are the characterization of climate change as yearly average temperature anomalies with respect to a benchmark period, and the use of Bayesian Model Averaging (BMA) as econometric strategy. The employment of BMA allows the model to be estimated without choosing a priori the independent variables to include, thus shedding light on concerns about the sensitivity of conflict outcomes raised by Hegre and Sambanis (2006).

4. Conclusions

As of today, despite the great advancements in climate–conflict research, the debate is still open. The scientific community seems, at least in large part, to have come to an agreement about the indirect nature of the linkage between climate change and armed conflicts. Such a linkage appears to be mediated by various socio-economic factors which often interact and respond to complex dynamics. In this chapter, we have taken into account the four main channels emerging from the climate–conflict literature, namely, the agricultural sector, resource scarcity, the resource curse hypothesis, and migrations. They apply in different degrees and with regional variations. Africa is a wide and variegated continent, and in different regions, some factors may prevail over others in driving the linkage. Recent advancements in spatial econometrics should help shed light on these diversities at the local level.

As for the methodological debate, numerous concerns related to both spatial and temporal dimensions, as well as to the interpretation of results, have been raised. In very recent years, some of them have been addressed, but there is still a long way to go. Indeed, at present, although research in this field is very prolific and proceeding at a fast pace, a comprehensive study addressing all of the issues discussed in Section 3 has not yet been produced. Future empirical research may follow the suggestions provided by Ide (2017), to integrate econometric techniques and qualitative analyses, as well as to extend the use of geographical information systems (GIS) to risk evaluation.

References

Adams, C., Ide, T., Barnett, J., and Detges, A. (2018). Sampling bias in climate–conflict research. *Nature Climate Change*, 8(3), 200–203.

Adano, W. R., Dietz, T., Witsenburg, K., and Zaal, F. (2012). Climate change, violent conflict and local institutions in Kenya's drylands. *Journal of Peace Research*, 49, 65–80.

Almer, C., Laurent-Lucchetti, J., and Oechslin, M. (2017). Water scarcity and rioting: Disaggregated evidence from Sub-Saharan Africa. *Journal of Environmental Economics and Management*, 86, 193–209.

Ang, J. B. and Gupta, S. K. (2018). Agricultural yield and conflict. *Journal of Environmental Economics and Management*, 92, 397–417.

Auty, R. (1993). Sustaining Development in Mineral Economies: The Resource Curse Thesis. Routledge.

Auty, R. (2001). *Resource Abundance and Economic Development*, Oxford University Press.

Ayodele, B. (2010). Silence on climate change and the natural resources conflict in Nigeria. The Niger Delta region experience, in Mwiturubani, D. A. and van Wyk, J. A. (eds), *Climate Change and Natural Resources Conflicts in Africa*, Institute for Security Studies Monographs, 2010(170), 105–121.

Barnett, J. (2003). Security and climate change. *Global Environmental Change*, 13(1), 7–17.

Barnett, J. and Adger, W. N. (2007). Climate change, human security and violent conflict. *Political Geography*, 26(6), 639–655.

Bates, B., Kundzewicz, Z. W., Wu, S., and Palutikof, J. P. (eds) (2008). *Climate Change and Water*, IPCC Secretariat, Geneva.

Bodea, C., Higashijima, M., and Singh, R. J. (2016). Oil and civil conflict: Can public spending have a mitigation effect? *World Development*, 78: 1–12.

Bosetti, V., Cattaneo, C., and Peri, G. (2018). Should they stay or should they go? Climate Migrants and Local Conflicts (No. w24447). Cambridge, MA: National Bureau of Economic Research.

Breckner, M. and Sunde, U. (2019). Temperature extremes, global warming, and armed conflict: new insights from high resolution data. *World Development*, 123, 104624.

Brochmann, M. and Gleditsch, N. P. (2012). Shared rivers and conflict — A reconsideration. *Political Geography*, 31(8), 519–527.

Brzoska, M. (2012). Climate change as a driver of security policy, in Scheffran, J., Brzoska, M., Brauch, H. G., Link, P. M., and Schilling, J. (eds), *Climate Change, Human Security and Violent Conflict*, Berlin Heidelberg, Germany: Springer, 165–184.

Brzoska, M. and Fröhlich, C. (2016). Climate change, migration and violent conflict: Vulnerabilities, pathways and adaptation strategies. *Migration and Development*, 5, 190–210.

Buhaug, H. (2010). Climate not to blame for African civil wars. *Proceedings of the National Academy of Sciences of the United States of America*, 107(38), 16477–16482.

Buhaug, H. (2015). Climate–conflict research: Some reflections on the way forward. *Wiley Interdisciplinary Reviews: Climate Change*, 6, 269–275.

Buhaug, H. and Gates, S. (2002). The geography of civil war. *Journal of Peace Research*, 39(4), 417–433.

Buhaug, H. and Rød, J. K. (2006). Local determinants of African civil wars, 1970–2001. *Political Geography*, 25(3), 315–335.

Burke, M. B., Miguel, E., Satyanath, S., Dykema, J. A., and Lobell, D. B. (2009). Warming Increases the Risk of Civil War in Africa. *Proceedings of the National Academy of Sciences of the United States of America*, 106(49), 20670–20674.

Burrows, K. and Kinney, P. (2016). Exploring the climate change, migration and conflict nexus. *International Journal of Environmental Research and Public Health*, 13(4), 443.

Busby, J. W., Smith, T. G., and Krishnan, N. (2014). Climate security vulnerability in Africa mapping 3.01. *Political Geography*, 43, 51–67.

Cai, R., Feng, S., Oppenheimer, M., and Pytlikova, M. (2016). Climate variability and international migration: The importance of the agricultural linkage. *Journal of Environmental Economics and Management*, 79, 135–151.

Castells-Quintana, D., Lopez-Uribe, M. del P., and McDermott, T. K. J. (2017). Geography, institutions and development: a review of the long-run impacts of climate change. *Climate and Development*, 9(5), 452–470.

Cattaneo, C. and Bosetti, V. (2017). Climate-induced international migration and conflicts. *CESifo Economic Studies*, 63, 500–528.

Cilliers, J. (2009). Climate change, population pressure and conflict in Africa. *Institute for Security Studies Papers*, 2009(178), 20.

Codjoe, S. N. A. and Larbi, R. T. (2016). Climate change/variability and schistosomiasis transmission in Ga district, Ghana. *Climate and Development*, 8(1), 58–71.

Cohen, M. J. and Pinstrup-Andersen, P. (1999). Food security and conflict. *Social Research*, 66(1), 375–416.

Collier, P. (1999). On the economic consequences of civil war. *Oxford Economic Papers*, 51(1), 168–183.

Collier, P. (2000). Economic Causes of Civil Conflicts and Their Implications for Policy. World Bank. Washington, DC.

Collier, P., Elliot, V. L., Hegre, H., Hoeffler, A., Reynal-Querol, M., and Sambanis, N. (2003). *Breaking the Conflict Trap: Civil War and Development Policy*, World Bank and Oxford University Press, New York.

Collier, P. and Hoeffler, A. (2002). Military Expenditure: Threats, Aid, and Arms Races. The World Bank.

Conceição, P. (2019). Human Development Report 2019, Beyond Income, Beyond Averages, Beyond Today: Inequalities in Human Development in the 21st Century. *Report.* United Nations Development Programme, 1.

Croicu, M. and Sundberg, R. (2017). UCDP GED Codebook version 17.1, Department of Peace and Conflict Research, Uppsala University.

Crost, B., Duquennois, C., Felter, J. H., and Rees, D. I. (2018). Climate change, agricultural production and civil conflict: Evidence from the Philippines. *Journal of Environmental Economics and Management*, 88, 379–395.

D'Andrea, W. J., Huang, Y., Fritz, S. C., and Anderson, N. J. (2011). Abrupt Holocene climate change as an important factor for human migration in West Greenland. *Proceedings of the National Academy of Sciences of the United States of America*, 108(24), 9765–9769.

Daccache, A., Sataya, W., and Knox, J. W. (2015). Climate change impacts on rain-fed and irrigated rice yield in Malawi. *International Journal of Agricultural Sustainability*, 13(2), 87–103.

De Stefano, L., Petersen-Perlman, J. D., Sproles, E. A., Eynard, J., and Wolf, A. T. (2017). Assessment of transboundary river basins for potential hydro-political tensions. *Global Environmental Change*, 45, 35–46.

Detges, A. (2017). Climate and Conflict: Reviewing the Statistical Evidence: A Summary for Policymakers. *Report.* Berlin, Germany: Climate Diplomacy Report.

Dinar, A. (2012). Economy-wide implications of direct and indirect policy interventions in the water sector: Lessons from recent work and future research needs. Policy Research Working Paper; No. 6068. World Bank, Washington, DC.

Doherty, T. J. and Clayton, S. (2011). The psychological impacts of global climate change. *American Psychologist*, 66(4), 265.

Eaton D. (2008). *Violence, Revenge and the History of Cattle Raiding along the Kenya-Uganda Border*, Dalhousie University, Halifax.

FAO. (2008). Climate Change and Food Security: A framework document. Interdepartmental Working Group On Climate Change Document. *Report.* Rome: FAO.

Fjelde, H. and von Uexkull, N. (2012). Climate triggers: Rainfall anomalies, vulnerability and communal conflict in Sub-Saharan Africa. *Political Geography*, 31(7), 444–453.

Foresight, U. K. (2011). Migration and Global Environmental Change: Final Project Report. *Report*. London: The Government Office for Science.

Fukuda-Parr, S., Ashwill, M., Chiappa, E., and Messineo, C. (2011). The conflict–development nexus: A survey of armed conflicts in Sub-Saharan Africa, 1980–2005, in *Security and Development*, Edward Elgar Publishing.

Gaikwad, N. and Nellis, G. (2017). The majority-minority divide in attitudes toward internal migration: Evidence from Mumbai. *American Journal of Political Science*, 61, 456–72.

Gates, S., Hegre, H., Nygård, H. M., and Strand, H. (2012). Development consequences of armed conflict. *World Development*, 40, 1713–1722.

Ghimire, R., Ferreira, S., and Dorfman, J. H. (2015). Flood-induced displacement and civil conflict. *World Development*, 66, 614–628.

Glcick, P. H. (1993). Water and conflict: Fresh water resources and international security. *International Security*, 18(1), 79–112.

Gleick, P. H. (2014). Water, drought, climate change, and conflict in Syria. *Weather, Climate, and Society*, 6(3), 331–340.

Gray, C. and Mueller, V. (2012). Drought and population mobility in rural Ethiopia. *World Development*, 40(1), 134–145.

Harari, M. and Ferrara, E. L. (2018). Conflict, climate, and cells: A disaggregated analysis. *Review of Economics and Statistics*, 100(4), 594–608.

Hegre, H., Buhaug, H., Calvin, K. V., Nordkvelle, J., Waldhoff, S. T., and Gilmore, E. (2016). Forecasting civil conflict along the shared socioeconomic pathways. *Environmental Research Letters*, 11(5), 054002.

Hegre, H. and Sambanis, N. (2006). Sensitivity analysis of empirical results on civil war onset. *Journal of Conflict Resolution*, 50(4), 508–535.

Henderson, E. A. and Singer, J. D. (2000). Civil war in the post-colonial world, 1946–92. *Journal of Peace Research*, 37(3), 275–299.

Hendrix, C. S. and Glaser, S. M. (2007). Trends and triggers: Climate, climate change and civil conflict in Sub-Saharan Africa. *Political Geography*, 26(6), 695–715.

Hendrix, C. S. and Salehyan, I. (2012). Climate change, rainfall, and social conflict in Africa. *Journal of Peace Research*, 49(1), 35–50.

Hillesund, S., Bahgat, K., Barrett, G., Dupuy, K., Gates, S., Nygård, H. M., Rustad, S. A., Strand, H., Urdal, H., and Østby, G. (2018). Horizontal inequality and armed conflict: A comprehensive literature review. *Canadian Journal of Development Studies*, 39, 463–480.

Hoegh-Guldberg, O., Jacob, D., Bindi, M., Brown, S., Camilloni, I., Diedhiou, A., ... Hijioka, Y. (2018). Impacts of 1.5°C global warming on natural and human systems. Global warming of 1.5°C. *Report.* An IPCC Special Report.

Holmberg, J. (2008). Natural resources in sub-Saharan Africa: Assets and vulnerabilities. Current Africa Issue 39/2008. Uppsala: Nordiska Afrikainstitutet.

Homer-Dixon, T. and Percival, V. (1996). *Environmental Scarcity and Violent Conflict: Briefing Book.* Princeton University Press, Princeton.

Hsiang, S. (2016). Climate econometrics. *Annual Review of Resource Economics*, 8, 43–75.

Hsiang, S. M. and Burke, M. (2014). Climate, conflict, and social stability: What does the evidence say? *Climatic Change*, 123(1), 39–55.

Hsiang, S. M., Burke, M. and Miguel, E. (2013). Quantifying the influence of climate on human conflict. *Science*, 341(6151).

Hsiang, S. M., Meng, K. C., and Cane, M. A. (2011). Civil conflicts are associated with the global climate. *Nature*, 476(7361), 438–441.

Ide, T. (2017). Research methods for exploring the links between climate change and conflict. *Wiley Interdisciplinary Reviews: Climate Change*, 8(3), e456.

Ide, T. and Scheffran, J. (2014). On climate, conflict and cumulation: Suggestions for integrative cumulation of knowledge in the research on climate change and violent conflict. *Global Change, Peace & Security*, 26(3), 263–279.

Ide, T., Schilling, J., Link, J. S. A., Scheffran, J., Ngaruiya, G., and Weinzierl, T. (2014). On exposure, vulnerability and violence: Spatial distribution of risk factors for climate change and violent conflict across Kenya and Uganda. *Political Geography*, 43, 68–81.

Jones, B. T., Mattiacci, E., and Braumoeller, B. F. (2017). Food scarcity and state vulnerability: Unpacking the link between climate variability and violent unrest. *Journal of Peace Research*, 54(3), 335–350.

Kelley, C. P., Mohtadi, S., Cane, M. A., Seager, R., and Kushnir, Y. (2015). Climate change in the Fertile Crescent and implications of the recent Syrian drought. *Proceedings of the National Academy of Sciences*, 112(11), 3241–3246.

King, M. D. (2015). The weaponization of water in Syria and Iraq. *The Washington Quarterly*, 38(4), 153–169.

Kloos, J., Gebert, N., Rosenfeld, T., and Renaud, F. (2013). Climate Change, Water Conflicts and Human Security. Regional Assessment and Policy Guidelines for the Mediterranean, Middle East and Sahel. CLICO Final Report. *Report.* United Nations University–Institute for Environment and Human Security (Report, 10).

Koubi, V. (2019). Climate change and conflict. *Annual Review of Political Science*, 22, 343–360.

Koubi, V., Bernauer, T., Kalbhenn, A., and Spilker, G. (2012). Climate variability, economic growth, and civil conflict. *Journal of Peace Research*, 49(1), 113–127.

Lai, B. and Thyne, C. (2007). The effect of civil war on education, 1980–97. *Journal of Peace Research*, 44(3), 277–292.

Lessmann, C. (2016). Regional inequality and internal conflict. *German Economic Review*, 17(2), 157–191.

Linke, A. M., Witmer, F. D. W., O'Loughlin, J., McCabe, J. T., and Tir, J. (2017). Drought, local institutional contexts, and support for violence in Kenya. *Journal of Conflict Resolution*, 62, 1544–1578.

Linke, A. M., Witmer, F. D. W., O'Loughlin, J., McCabe, J. T., and Tir, J. (2018). The consequences of relocating in response to drought: human mobility and conflict in contemporary Kenya. *Environmental Research Letters*, 13, 094014.

Mach, K. J., Kraan, C. M., Adger, W. N., Buhaug, H., Burke, M., Fearon, J. D., ... Roessler, P. (2019). Climate as a risk factor for armed conflict. *Nature*, 1, 193–197.

Marchiori, L., Maystadt, J. F., and Schumacher, I. (2012). The impact of weather anomalies on migration in subSaharan Africa. *Journal of Environmental Economics and Management*, 63(3), 355–374.

Markandya, A. (2014). Incorporating climate change into adaptation programmes and project appraisal: Strategies for uncertainty, in Markandya, A., Galarraga, I., and Sainz de Murieta, E. (eds), *Routledge Handbook of the Economics of Climate Change Adaptation*, Routledge, London 97–119.

Markandya, A., Costantini, V., Paglialunga, E., and Sforna, G. (2017). "Global and Regional Economic Damages from Climate Change," Oxford Encyclopaedia of Environmental Science. OUP: New York, doi:10.1093/acrefore/9780199389414.013.409.

Maxwell, J. W. and Reuveny, R. (2000). Resource scarcity and conflict in developing countries. *Journal of Peace Research*, 37(3), 301–322.

Maystadt, J. F., Calderone, M., and You, L. (2015). Local warming and violent conflict in North and South Sudan. *Journal of Economic Geography*, 15(3), 649–671.

McLeman, R. and Smit, B. (2006). Migration as an adaptation to climate change. *Climatic Change*, 76(1–2), 31–53.

Meier, P., Bond, D., and Bond, J. (2007). Environmental influences on pastoral conflict in the horn of Africa. *Political Geography*, 26, 716–735.

Meierding, E. (2013). Climate change and conflict: Avoiding small talk about the weather. *International Studies Review*, 15, 185–203.

Messer, E. and Cohen, M. J. (2004). Breaking the links between conflict and hunger in Africa (No. 26). International Food Policy Research Institute (IFPRI).

Moore, F. and Diaz, D. B. (2015). Temperature impacts on economic growth warrant stringent mitigation policy. *Nature Climate Change*, 5, 127–131.

Mwangi, O. G. (2010). Climate change, hydropolitics and security in Lesotho, in Mwiturubani, D. A. and van Wyk, J. A. (eds.), *Climate Change and Natural Resources Conflicts in Africa*, Institute for Security Studies Monographs, 170, 45–60.

Mwiturubani, D. A. (2017). Climate change and access to water resources in the Lake Victoria Basin, in Aall, P. and Crocker, C. A. (eds), *The Fabric of Peace in Africa: Looking Beyond the State*, McGill-Queen's Press-MQUP.

Nordås, R. and Gleditsch, N. P. (2007). Climate change and conflict. *Political Geography*, 26(6), 627–638.

O'Loughlin, J., Witmer, F. D. W., Linke, A. M., Laing, A., Gettelman, A., and Dudhia, J. (2012). Climate variability and conflict risk in East Africa, 1990–2009. *Proceedings of the National Academy of Sciences of the United States of America*, 109(45), 18344–18349.

OECD (Organisation for Economic Co-operation and Development). (2015). States of Fragility 2015: Meeting Post-2015 Ambitions. Paris: OECD.

Olsson, L., Opondo, M., Tschakert, P., Agrawal, A., Eriksen, S., Perch, L. N., and Zakeldeen, S. (2014). Livelihoods and Poverty. In: Field, C. B., Barros, V. R., Dokken, D. J. et al. (eds.) Climate change 2014: impacts, adaptation, and vulnerability. Part A: global and sectoral aspects. Contribution of Working Group II to the Fifth Assessment Report of the Intergovernmental Panel on Climate Change. Cambridge University Press, Cambridge.

Olzak, S. (1992). *The Dynamics of Ethnic Competition and Conflict*, Stanford University Press, Stanford.

Onuoha, F. (2010). Climate change, population surge and resource overuse in the Lake Chad area, in Mwiturubani, D. A. and van Wyk, J. A. (eds), *Climate Change and Natural Resources Conflicts in Africa*, Institute for Security Studies Monographs, 170, 23–44.

Østby, G. (2008). Inequalities, the political environment and civil conflict: Evidence from 55 developing countries, in Stewart F. (ed), *Horizontal Inequalities and Conflict*, Palgrave Macmillan, London, 136–159.

Otto, I. M., Reckien, D., Reyer, C. P., Marcus, R., Le Masson, V., Jones, L., ... Serdeczny, O. (2017). Social vulnerability to climate change: A review of concepts and evidence. *Regional Environmental Change*, 17, 1651–1662.

Parker, D. P. and Vadheim, B. (2017). Resource cursed or policy cursed? US Regulation of Conflict Minerals and Violence in the Congo. *Journal of the Association of Environmental and Resource Economists*, 4(1), 1–49.

Raleigh, C., Choi, H. J., and Kniveton, D. (2015). The devil is in the details: An investigation of the relationships between conflict, food price and climate across Africa. *Global Environmental Change*, 32, 187–199.

Raleigh, C. and Kniveton, D. (2012). Come rain or shine: An analysis of conflict and climate variability in East Africa. *Journal of Peace Research*, 49(1), 51–64.

Raleigh, C., Linke, A., Hegre, H., and Karlsen, J. (2010). Introducing ACLED: An armed conflict location and event dataset: special data feature. *Journal of Peace Research*, 47(5), 651–660.

Reuveny, R. (2007). Climate change-induced migration and violent conflict. *Political Geography*, 26(6), 656–673.

Ross, M. L. (2004). What do we know about natural resources and civil war? *Journal of Peace Research*, 41(3), 337–356.

Sachs, J. D. and Warner, A. M. (1995). Natural Resource Abundance and Economic Growth (Working Paper No. 5398). National Bureau of Economic Research.

Salehyan, I. (2014). Climate change and conflict: Making sense of disparate findings. *Political Geography*, 43, 1–5.

Salick, J. and Ross, N. (2009). Traditional peoples and climate change. *Global Environmental Change*, 19(2), 137–190.

Scheffran, J., Link, P. M., and Schilling, J. (2019). Climate and conflict in Africa. In Oxford Research Encyclopedia of Climate Science.

Schilling, J., Akuno, M., Scheffran, J., and Weinzierl, T. (2014). On raids and relations: Climate change, pastoral conflict and adaptation in northwestern Kenya. *Conflict-sensitive Adaptation to Climate Change in Africa*, 241.

Schleussner, C.-F., Dongesa, J. F., Donnera, R. V., and Schellnhuber, H. J. (2016). Armed-conflict risks enhanced by climate-related disasters in ethnically fractionalized countries. *Proceedings of the National Academy of Sciences of the United States of America*, 113, 9216–9221.

Searchinger, T., Hanson, C., Ranganathan, J., Lipinski, B., Waite, R., Winterbottom, R., ... Dumas, P. (2014). Creating a sustainable food future. A menu of solutions to sustainably feed more than 9 billion people by 2050. World resources report 2013–14: Interim findings. World Resources Institute.

Shemyakina, O. (2011). The effect of armed conflict on accumulation of schooling: Results from Tajikistan. *Journal of Development Economics*, 95(2), 186–200.

Silve, A. and Verdier, T. (2018). A theory of regional conflict complexes. *Journal of Development Economics*, 133, 434–447.

Stern, N. (2006). *Stern Review: The Economics of Climate Change*, Cambridge University Press, Cambridge, UK.

Tacoli, C. (2009). Crisis or adaptation? Migration and climate change in a context of high mobility. *Environment and Urbanization*, 21(2), 513–525.

Taydas, Z. and Peksen, D. (2012). Can states buy peace? Social welfare spending and civil conflicts. *Journal of Peace Research*, 49(2), 273–287.

Teodosijevic, S. B. (2003). Armed conflicts and food security. ESA Working Paper No. 03-11. FAO.

Theisen, O. M. (2012). Climate clashes? Weather variability, land pressure, and organized violence in Kenya, 1989–2004. *Journal of Peace Research*, 49(1), 81–96.

Theisen, O. M., Gleditsch, N. P., and Buhaug, H. (2013). Is climate change a driver of armed conflict? *Climatic Change*, 117(3), 613–625.

Tol, R. S. and Wagner, S. (2010). Climate change and violent conflict in Europe over the last millennium. *Climatic Change*, 99(1–2), 65–79.

United Nations. (2020). A new era of conflict and violence. UN75 — 2020 and Beyond Issue Brief. Access online https://www.un.org/en/un75/new-era-conflict-and-violence.

United Nations World Bank. (2018). *Pathways for Peace: Inclusive Approaches to Preventing Violent Conflict*. Executive Summary booklet. World Bank, Washington, DC.

van Weezel, S. (2020). Local warming and violent armed conflict in Africa. *World Development*, 126, 104708.

von Uexküll, N. (2014). Sustained drought, vulnerability and civil conflict in Sub-Saharan Africa. *Political Geography*, 43, 16–26.

von Uexküll, N., Croicu, M., Fjelde, H., and Buhaug, H. (2016). Civil conflict sensitivity to growing-season drought. *Proceedings of the National Academy of Sciences of the United States of America*, 113, 12391–12396.

Weir, T. and Virani, Z. (2011). Three linked risks for development in the Pacific Islands: Climate change, disasters and conflict. *Climate and Development*, 3(3), 193–208.

Wennmann, A. (2011). Breaking the conflict trap? Addressing the resource curse in peace processes. *Global Governance: A Review of Multilateralism and International Organizations*, 17(2), 265–279.

Wischnath, G. and Buhaug, H. (2014). Rice or riots: On food production and conflict severity across India. *Political Geography*, 43, 6–15.

Wolf, A. (1999). "Water Wars" and water reality: Conflict and cooperation along international waterways, in Lonergan, S. (ed), *Environmental Change, Adaptation and Security*, Kluwer Academic Publishers, Dordrecht, 251–265.

https://doi.org/10.1142/9789811240553_0009

Chapter 9

A Subscription vs. Appropriation Framework for Natural Resource Conflicts

Dripto Bakshi[*,‡] **and Indraneel Dasgupta**[†,§]

[*] *Institute of Economic Growth,*
University Enclave, Delhi, India
[†] *Indian Statistical Institute and IZA Bonn*
Economic Research Unit, Indian Statistical Institute,
203 Barrackpore Trunk Road, Kolkata 700108,
West Bengal, India
[‡] *bakshi.dripto@gmail.com*
[§] *indraneel@isical.ac.in*

We examine how cross-community cost or benefit spillovers, arising from the consumption of group-specific public goods, affect both inter-group conflicts over the appropriation of such goods and decentralized private provision for their production. Our model integrates production versus appropriation choices, vis-à-vis group-specific public goods, with their decentralized voluntary supply, against a backdrop of such cross-community consumption spillovers. Our flexible and general formulation of consumption spillovers incorporates earlier specifications as alternative special cases. We show that stronger negative (or weaker positive) consumption spillovers across communities may reduce inter-group conflict and increase aggregate income (and consumption) in society under certain conditions. Thus, stronger negative consumption spillovers may have socially beneficial consequences. We also identify conditions under which their impact will be both conflict-augmenting and income-compressing. Our general theoretical analysis offers a conceptual structure within which to organize investigation of feedback loops linking ethnic conflict and natural resource degradation in developing country contexts.

1. Introduction

Many forms of social conflict are rooted in the fact that certain kinds of collectively consumed environment-related items have the characteristics of group-specific public goods. Their consumption, use, or exploitation in some particular manner generates benefits that accrue in a non-rival manner to all members of one specific group. However, those benefits spill over to members of another group only to a lesser extent, or not at all. Indeed, in extreme cases, members of another group may all suffer some cost, so that what constitutes a public good within one community may constitute a public bad for another. In these situations, all members of either community benefit if a larger proportion of that item is reserved for exclusive use by their own community. Thus, there arises scope for inter-community conflict over environmental or natural resource policy and, more generally, modes of collective consumption.

To fix ideas, consider the case of cow protection in India. Orthodox Hindus consider the cow sacred. Hindu nationalist governments in many Indian states have drastically expanded the ambit of laws against cow slaughter and increased the penalty for their violation in recent years. At the same time, vigilante groups have engaged in violence against, and even murder of, cattle traders suspected of transporting cattle to other states and neighboring countries for slaughter. Consequently, farmers, unable to sell, have increasingly taken to abandoning their economically unproductive bullocks and older cows. This has led to a dramatic increase in the number of stray cattle, which in turn poses a serious threat to standing crops, imposes large fencing costs on farmers, degrades common grazing land, and increases methane emissions. Thus, the crackdown on cow slaughter, and its attendant restrictions on inter-state and inter-country cattle trade, may be seen as generating non-rival and non-excludable benefits for orthodox Hindus who are not farmers, but constituting a public bad for the farming community, with significant negative environmental consequences. Evidently, this creates scope for political conflict over the content and implementation of laws against cow slaughter between the two groups.[1]

Inter-group conflicts over sharing of group-specific public goods in general, and such conflicts with environmental implications in particular, often acquire greater salience in developing countries, due to traditional concentrations of particular ethnic groups in specific economic locations. For example, resource conflicts between pastoralists and cultivators in West Africa often acquire broader ethno-linguistic and religious colors, because of strong correlations between such identities and economic interests.[2] In India, laws governing hunting and exploitation of forest produce, and conversion of forest land for commercial forestry, mining, or industrial purposes, often bring traditionally forest-dwelling tribal communities into conflict with non-tribals (Aggarwal, 2020). Thus, cross-community spillovers with environmental implications (whether positive or negative) in the group-specific use of natural resources carry important implications for both social conflicts and overall economic well-being in many different, particularly in developing country, contexts. But, what exactly are those implications?

With a given stock of some natural resource, stronger negative spillovers, or greater exclusivity, across communities in its exploitation would imply stronger incentives for individuals to help appropriate that resource for exclusive use of their own community. This may be intuitively expected to increase conflict between competing communities and divert more resources overall to appropriation, rather than productive activities. But, what happens then to individual incentives to

---

[1]For detailed discussions, see Alavi (2019) and Chari (2019). Relatedly, in Sweden, while many nature lovers consider the Swedish wolf a public good, it constitutes a public bad for reindeer herders, whose livestock it preys on (Bostedt, 1999). As noted by Buchholz *et al.* (2018), similar examples involving costly preservation of different animals can be provided from around the world.

[2]See Shettima and Tar (2008) for a discussion of the vast literature on such conflicts. Dasgupta and Kanbur (2005a,b, 2007, 2011) develop the idea that intra-group sharing of group-specific public goods generates the cohesion of interest necessary to both make and maintain stable identity *communities* out of groups of individuals.

contribute to public goods necessary for the maintenance or expansion of that resource stock itself?

For example, if degradation of common village grazing land leads to more destruction of standing crops by stray cattle, conflicts between farmers and "cow protector" vigilante groups can be expected to increase. But, what would happen to decentralized individual incentives to contribute to local veterinary clinics or non-governmental organizations (NGOs) that undertake immunization and treatment programs for all local cattle, thereby maintaining its stock? If reduced rainfall due to climatic change alters migration patterns of pastoralists and thereby causes greater damage to cultivators, conflict between the two groups over control of local waterbodies would rise. But, what happens to individual incentives to contribute to the maintenance of local irrigation projects that replenish these contested waterbodies? If commercial afforestation involves planting trees that deplete groundwater more and thereby make both fruit trees and animal life less viable, conflict between hunter-gatherer communities and commercial planters, over what proportion of a given forest area should be allocated to commercial forestry, would rise. But, what happens then to individual incentives to participate in forest protection associations meant to resist timber smuggling (or land grab attempts by third parties such as cultivator communities and mining companies)?

If individual incentives to contribute to its maintenance decline sufficiently overall, the stock of the resource being contested over would fall. The dampening effect of that contraction would counteract the conflict-expanding effect of stronger negative spillovers. What are the conditions, then, that determine whether the net effect would turn out to be conflict-expanding? Is it possible that stronger cross-community negative spillovers would actually increase the deployment of resources to production rather than appropriation, and thus increase aggregate social output, instead of reducing both, as one might perhaps intuitively expect? The purpose of this paper is to develop a parsimonious theoretical framework to address these issues.

We develop a model of a society populated by individuals who are partitioned into two equal-sized groups, or communities. All individuals are endowed with one unit of some resource ("money" or "effort").

Individuals have to allocate their endowment among three alternative uses in decentralized manner. They can convert it to a privately consumed numeraire good, use it to subscribe to a society-wide common pool, or expend it on a Tullock (1980)-style appropriation contest between the two communities. The common pool, or fund, generated through individual subscriptions produces, according to a strictly concave and iso-elastic production technology, the item whose inter-group division is contested over. This item has the characteristics of a group-specific public good, in that, ceteris paribus, all members of either group are strictly better off if their own group achieves a larger share. The benefit received by members of either group from a given production of the contested good falls monotonically as the share achieved by its antagonist increases, according to a convex and iso-elastic *loss function.* A more elastic loss function implies a lower loss to a community from its antagonist achieving any given share, as does a fall in its scale parameter. Thus, the elasticity and scale parameters of the loss function capture the strength of consumption spillovers and externalities, whether positive or negative, impacting on either community in consequence of its antagonist exploiting any given share of the contested good accruing to it. All individuals allocate their respective endowments simultaneously.

Examining the properties of the Nash equilibrium, we find the following. Whether stronger cross-community negative consumption spillovers, modeled as either a fall in the elasticity of the loss function or an increase in its scale factor, will serve to increase group conflict depends critically on the production technology for the contested good. The total amount of resources wasted on appropriation will fall when the output elasticity of that production technology, which may vary over the open unit interval, is sufficiently close to unity. However, it will rise otherwise. A mean-preserving decrease in the spread of the scale parameters of the loss functions has the same effect. Given any elasticity of the production technology for the contested good, stronger cross-community negative consumption spillovers must reduce aggregate social income, measured in units of the numeraire good, when the numerical size of the communities exceeds a threshold value. In this very specific sense, stronger cross-community negative consumption spillovers may affect aggregate societal well-being adversely, as might be intuitively expected. Strikingly, however, given any arbitrary community size, and any arbitrary production elasticity for the contested good, there also exist parametric configurations under which the effect would be positive. Specifically, aggregate social consumption is likely to expand when the strength of negative spillovers increases further, from an already high initial level.

A large theoretical literature has developed, stemming from the seminal contributions by Hirshleifer (1991) and Skaperdas (1992), which investigates how, when property rights are not fully secure, appropriation opportunities impact production incentives, and vice-versa.[3] In these (so-called "production vs. appropriation") models, the magnitude of the item open to appropriation — the size of the prize — is endogenously determined. The item open to appropriation is typically one whose consumption is fully rival across individuals — a standard private good. Our analysis belongs to this tradition, in its focus on endogenous determination of the size of the prize, and, in consequence, mutual determination of production and appropriation. However, we extend this literature by highlighting inter-group appropriation conflicts over items which exhibit public good characteristics within groups, i.e., over group-specific public goods, whose size is endogenously determined through such interplay, via a process of society-wide voluntary subscriptions.

Parallel to the production vs. appropriation literature, and originating from Katz *et al.* (1990) and Ursprung (1990), a large theoretical literature has also developed to address inter-group contests over group-specific public goods. This literature originally developed to examine inter-community conflicts over the sharing of state investment in public goods of localized or jurisdiction-specific benefit like schools, roads, hospitals, security, public art, and local anti-pollution measures when the communities exhibit locational segregation, but

[3]See, for example, Murphy *et al.* (1993), Grossman and Kim (1996), Anderton *et al.* (1999), Noh (2002), Hausken (2005), Caruso (2010), Dal Bó and Dal Bó (2011, 2012), Mitra and Ray (2014), Cornes *et al.* (2019), and Bakshi and Dasgupta (2020).

subsequently incorporated many other applications.[4] Most recently, it has expanded to include investigations of ethno-linguistic and religious conflicts over identity goods and social norms.[5] These models however almost all belong to the "rent-seeking," rather than "production and appropriation," tradition, in that the size of the public good prize being contested over between groups is exogenously given, instead of being determined as an endogenous consequence of the interplay of production and expropriation.[6] Our model expands this literature precisely through such endogenization.[7]

Thus, like Bakshi and Dasgupta (2020), the present paper builds a bridge between the production and appropriation literature and that on inter-group contests over group-specific public goods. However, we depart fundamentally from that analysis by endogenizing the size of the public good prize being contested over between groups.[8]

---

[4]Contributions include Katz *et al.* (1990), Ursprung (1990), Gradstein (1993), Riaz *et al.* (1995), Baik (2008, 2016), Epstein and Mealem (2009), Nitzan and Ueda (2009), Esteban and Ray (2001, 2011a,b), Lee (2012), Kolmar and Rommeswinkel (2013), Chowdhury *et al.* (2013), Dasgupta (2017), Bakshi and Dasgupta (2018, 2020), Cheikbossian and Fayat (2018), Dasgupta and Guha Neogi (2018), Baik and Jung (2021), and Dasgupta and Pal (2021).

[5]Esteban and Ray (2011a), Dasgupta (2017), Bakshi and Dasgupta (2018, 2020), Dasgupta and Guha Neogi (2018), and Dasgupta and Pal (2021) are examples of such recent application.

[6]One partial exception is Gradstein (1993). See footnote 7.

[7]Gradstein (1993) examines endogenous determination of the size of a local public good prize in the context of inter-jurisdiction contests over location of that local public good. The local public good, whose size is determined according to the preferences of members of the winning jurisdiction, is however generated through taxation of the entire society in his model, not through society-wide voluntary subscriptions (as in ours). Another related contribution is Cheikbossian (2008), who focuses on the size of (uniform lump-sum) tax-funded government spending on public good provision, when two competing groups have differing preferences over that size and can lobby the government in Tullock (1980) fashion to reflect their respective preferences more closely. Neither voluntary private supply of public goods nor group-specificity in their consumption appears in that analysis. These however constitute critical elements of our model.

[8]The present paper also ignores both within-group conflict over sharing of private consumption and cross-territorial conflict spillovers — key features of the model in Bakshi and Dasgupta (2020).

The third dimension along which we expand the literature is by incorporating a quite general and flexible specification of cross-community consumption spillovers and externality effects with regard to the contested and group-specific public good. Ihori (2000) and Buchholz *et al.* (2018) formalize the idea that an item may be a public good for members of one group, but a public bad for members of another. They develop models where the benefits members of one group receive from an item generated by voluntary contributions on their part may be reduced by another item similarly generated by members of another group. We expand this idea to the domain of public good contests. In our model, the benefits received by all members of one group from its share of an item, acquired in consequence of contestation with another group (over a stock produced through voluntary contributions by members of *both* groups), may be reduced (or augmented) by the use its antagonist group makes of its own share. These inter-group spillover or externality effects may be asymmetric — the strength of the spillovers from, say, community A to community B may be different from that from B to A. This permitted asymmetry extends the formulation introduced by Dasgupta and Guha Neogi (2018), incorporating it as a special case. Indeed, we even permit the association of positive spillovers in one direction with negative spillovers in another. Furthermore, the strength of these spillovers may vary in a nonlinear fashion with the level of consumption. This last feature of our model extends it beyond the linear aggregative structure adopted by both Ihori (2000) and Buchholz *et al.* (2018), which constitutes a special, limiting case of our analysis.

Lastly, our contribution has relevance for the literature on voluntary contribution to public goods. This literature typically asks the following question: how would an exogenously supplied redistribution of income/wealth affect private supply of public goods?[9] The question

[9]This literature originates from Bergstrom *et al.* (1986). See, for example, Andreoni (1990), Cornes (1993), Cornes and Sandler (1994, 1996, 2000), and Buchholz *et al.* (2018) for subsequent developments. Dasgupta and Kanbur (2005a,b, 2007, 2011) analyze how private supply of public goods affects anti-poverty transfer policy, demand for income or wealth redistribution, and welfare inequality.

we address instead is as follows: how would inter-group conflict over their distribution affect private supply of public goods?

Section 2 sets up the model. Equilibrium outcomes are characterized in Section 3. Our main comparative static conclusions are presented in Section 4. Section 5 discusses some possible variants of our model. Section 6 concludes. Detailed proofs of propositions are provided in an appendix.

2. The Model

Consider a society partitioned into two mutually exclusive equal-sized groups or communities, H and M. Each community has n members, $n \geq 1$. Given any community $k \in \{H, M\}$, we shall use $-k$ to denote the other. Individuals are indexed by a pair $\langle i, k \rangle$, where $i \in \{1, 2, \ldots, n\}$ and $k \in \{H, M\}$. Every individual in this society is endowed with one unit of a numeraire good, C (intuitively, "money" or "effort") which she can directly convert to fully rival and non-contestable consumption (c_{ik}), contribute to a common fund for the production of some contestable good Υ (y_{ik}), or allocate to appropriation, i.e., inter-group conflict over division of that contestable good so produced (x_{ik}). Thus, each individual's budget constraint is as follows:

$$c_{ik} + y_{ik} + x_{ik} = 1 \tag{1}$$

with $c_{ik}, y_{ik}, x_{ik} \geq 0$. The size of the common fund for production of Υ, B, is given by the sum of individual contributions, so that

$$B = \sum_{i=1}^{n} y_{iH} + \sum_{i=1}^{n} y_{iM}; \tag{2}$$

and that good is produced according to a strictly concave and iso-elastic production function:

$$\tilde{\Upsilon} = B^{\alpha}, \tag{3}$$

where $\alpha \in (0, 1)$. The parameter α measures the output elasticity of Υ (i.e., $\frac{B d\tilde{\Upsilon}}{\tilde{\Upsilon} dB}$). Intuitively, the common fund B may be identified with either a pool of voluntary labor or a sum of money raised through decentralized and voluntary individual subscriptions that may be deployed to produce or maintain some collective good. The assumed strict concavity of the production function ascribed to Υ may be interpreted in standard fashion as a technological given. Evidently, the case of inter-group conflict over division of the common fund itself constitutes one limiting case of our model ($\alpha = 1$). We discuss a possible alternative formulation of the production technology for Υ in Section 5 below.

The good Υ is contestable at a community level — its division between competing user groups is determined by a political process involving group-specific resource investment in lobbying, bribery, and possibly violence. More formally, the proportion of any produced amount of that good unilaterally controlled, and exploited or utilized, by community k is given by the symmetric Tullock (1980) contest success function:

$$p_k = \frac{X_k}{X} \quad \text{if } X > 0, \quad \text{and } \frac{1}{2} \text{ otherwise,} \tag{4}$$

where the community conflict allocations are simply the sum of individual members' allocations, so that $X_k = \sum_{i=1}^{n} x_{ik}$, and total (society-wide) conflict allocation is defined as $X = X_H + X_M$.[10]

The consumption of Υ may, in effect, be less than or more than fully rival across communities due to cross-community consumption spillovers, which may be either positive or negative. This key feature of our model is captured via a distinction between a community's *control* share of that good, p_k, arrived at through a process of Tullock contestation, and the proportion that it would need to be able to use/exploit, in order to achieve the same benefit, in case its antagonist *did not* exploit or utilize its own control share, p_{-k}. We term this the community's

---

[10]One can generalize the model to permit inter-community differences in conflict efficiency, by replacing (4) with the following condition: $p_H = \frac{\vartheta X_H}{X_M + \vartheta X_H}$ if $[X_M + \vartheta X_H] > 0$, and $\frac{\vartheta}{1+\vartheta}$ otherwise, where $\vartheta > 0$. Then, ϑ captures the relative productivity of investment in appropriation by H. Evidently, (4) is simply the symmetric special case of this general formulation, where $\vartheta = 1$. This generalization would considerably increase the algebraic burden, but not add anything of substance to our comparative static conclusions.

effective share

$$g_k = \max\left\{1 - a_k\left(\frac{p_{-k}^{\rho}}{\rho}\right), 0\right\}, \tag{5}$$

where $a_k \in (0, 2)$ and $\rho \geq 1$. We shall provide a detailed explanation of the distinction between control and effective shares, and the various properties of the latter, once we finish specifying our model.

Consumption of Y is at least partly non-rivalrous within each community, so that each member of community k has, effectively, consumption access to $\frac{\tilde{Y} g_k}{n^{\theta}}$ amount of the good Y, with $\theta \in [0, 1)$. Y is a pure public good within either community when $\theta = 0$, and a pure intra-community private good in the limiting case of $\theta = 1$. For any individual i in community k, the payoff function is given by

$$u_{ik} = c_{ik} + \frac{T\tilde{Y}g_k}{n^{\theta}}, \tag{6}$$

where $T \in (0, 1]$. All individuals simultaneously choose their private consumption c_{ik}, production common fund subscription y_{ik}, and expropriation investment x_{ik} so as to maximize (6), subject to the constraints (1)–(5) above.

2.1. *Control vs. effective share*

We now proceed to lay out in detail the key features of the effective share function introduced in (5). To fix ideas, it is helpful to start with an illustrative example. Suppose pastoralists and cultivators both contribute voluntary labor for maintaining a network of drainage channels that feed rainwater into a reservoir. Through a process of political contestation, pastoralists (H) acquire exclusive access to the reservoir for p_H proportion of the year, and cultivators (M) the rest. Pastoralists use the reservoir as a water source for their herds, while cultivators use its water for irrigation. Then, the control shares of the two communities are, respectively, p_H and p_M. Suppose now that pesticides and chemical fertilizers used by the cultivators seep into the water of the reservoir, reducing the survival rate of the pastoralists' livestock, even as greater irrigation by the cultivators, by increasing their crops, allows the pastoralists' animals to forage better, increasing their survival rate. The proportion of the livestock which survives the year is then determined jointly by these two effects, as well as by the proportion of the year that the pastoralists can access the reservoir (their control share). This aggregate survival rate is captured by the pastoralists' effective share g_H. Notice that, by (5), any positive effective share on their part implies

$$g_H = p_H + \left[p_M - a_H\left(\frac{p_M^{\rho}}{\rho}\right)\right].$$

The second term on the right-hand side captures the aggregate effect on livestock survival stemming from the cultivators' mode of utilization of their (control) share of access to the reservoir (p_M) — the net spillover effect of their actions on the pastoralists. Suppose, for example, that access is equally shared, so that both control shares take the value ½. Suppose further that $a_H = \frac{4}{3}$. Then, if $\rho = 2$, the pastoralists' effective share takes the value $\frac{5}{6}$: greater than their control share ½. Pastoralists can access the reservoir only half the year, which, by itself, would let only half their livestock survive. However, the actions taken by cultivators while exploiting their access to the reservoir generate net positive spillovers for the pastoralists, which increase the survival rate of their livestock to $\frac{5}{6}$. In the absence of these actions, then, the pastoralists would need access to the reservoir for an additional four months per year to attain the same survival rate — for ten months instead of the assumed six.

Now, suppose, as before, that $p_H = \frac{1}{2}, a_H = \frac{4}{3}$ but $\rho = 1$. Then, $g_H = \frac{1}{3}$. In this case, negative spillovers from cultivators to pastoralists reduce the latter's effective share below their control share. Pastoralists can access the reservoir only half the year (as before), which, by itself, would let half their livestock survive. However, pesticides and chemical fertilizers applied by cultivators poison the water of the reservoir to such an extent that only a third of the pastoralists' livestock actually survive after drinking it. Clearly, this situation for the pastoralists is identical to one where cultivators do not poison the water, but permit others to access the reservoir only four months of the year, instead of the assumed six.

The general case of positive externalities and spillovers is captured by $g_k > p_k$.[11] Then, the use of its control share p_{-k} of the public good by its opponent augments the benefit k can receive from unilateral exploitation of its own control share, p_k, to the extent of $\tilde{\Upsilon}(g_k - p_k)$. If its antagonist were to stop exploiting its control share, community k's control share would need to be augmented by $(g_k - p_k)$, for it to be able to achieve the same benefit from Υ as before. In our example, such positive externalities and spillovers may be generated by cultivators for pastoralists if their farming practices generate grass or fodder that the pastoralists' herds can feed on.

Alternatively, $g_k > p_k$ may also capture a combination of imperfect rivalry and incomplete excludability in consumption across groups. Within this class, since $\lim_{a_k \to 0} g_k = \lim_{p \to \infty} g_k = 1$, fully non-rival and non-excludable (but spillover-less) consumption of Υ across communities constitutes one limiting case. In this case, the benefits that can be derived by a community, say M, from Υ does not depend on how much of that good is unilaterally exploited by H, instead of M. In terms of our example, this may capture a situation where (a) water from the reservoir seeps into and thereby replenishes aquifers which supply sufficient water for cultivators' needs throughout the year, and (b) cultivators can entirely prevent pastoralists' herds from destroying crops, say through fencing. Then, what proportion of the year the pastoralists (H) have exclusive access to the reservoir (their control share p_H) makes no difference to the cultivators (M), who can extract all the water they need from the aquifers which are replenished by water from the reservoir. The pastoralists cannot prevent this seepage regardless of the extent of their control over the surface of the reservoir, nor can their herds affect the cultivators' crops in any manner. Thus, regardless of their control share, the cultivators' effective share of the reservoir,

---

[11]Note that the symmetric specification introduced by Dasgupta and Guha Neogi (2018), viz., $[g_k = 1 - p_{-k}^{\rho}]$, with $\rho > 1$, falls in this class.

g_M, is 1. Notice that non-excludability may be asymmetric — it may be possible (though not rational) for cultivators to prevent pastoralists from accessing the reservoir. Similarly, there may be spillovers from the former to the latter — say through contamination of the reservoir water due to the use of pesticides. Hence, neither the control share nor the access share of the pastoralists needs to equal 1 even in this case.

As $g_k = p_k$ at $a_k = \rho = 1$, fully rival, excludable, and spillover-less consumption constitutes another special case of the effective share function g_k. In this case, each community can only benefit from the public good to the extent it comes to own or control it through the process of political contestation, so that control and access shares become identical. In other words, the actual unilateral use of its control share by, say, M does not impose any additional cost or benefit on H — only possession matters.[12] In the context of our example, this captures the case where (a) physical access to the reservoir alone determines water availability for either community, and (b) cultivators do not contaminate the water for pastoralists, nor do pastoralists' herds affect or benefit from cultivators' crops in any manner.

When $g_k < p_k$, not only does the use of its control share p_{-k} of the public good by its opponent imply a loss of access for community k by the same proportion but such use also imposes a net additional cost on k via negative externalities and spillover effects. The magnitude of this cost, measured in units of the contested good, is $\tilde{\Upsilon}(p_k - g_k)$. Thus, if its antagonist were to merely cease exploiting its own share, community k would receive this additional benefit, even with the same control share p_k. Intuitively, this may happen through an across-the-board decline in the productivity of k's stock of the good Υ, because of negative externalities and spillovers stemming from the actions its antagonist takes while unilaterally exploiting its own stock.[13] In our example,

[12]This particular special case of our model is the standard formulation adopted in the literature on contests over group-specific public goods.

[13]Ihori (2000) and Buchholz *et al.* (2018) use a linear aggregative structure for net benefits to capture the idea that an item may constitute a public good for one community, but a public bad for another. Since, given $\rho = 1$, $[g_k = 1 - a_k p_{-k}]$, translated to our framework, their formulation, in essence, falls out as a special case of our formulation when $a_k > 1$ and $\rho = 1$. When the contest success function is interpreted as providing the success probabilities, instead of the group *shares* as in

such negative externalities and spillovers are imposed on pastoralists by cultivators through their farming practices, which poison the reservoir water and thereby increase the mortality rate of the former's livestock. Conversely, foraging by such livestock, by destroying standing crops, generates negative spillovers from pastoralists to cultivators.

Notice that the effective share function in (5) is monotonically increasing in own control share. Thus, the inter-community contest over control shares remains salient, despite the effective share diverging from the control share. Recalling (5), let $L_k \equiv a_k(\frac{p_{-k}^{\rho}}{\rho})$. The term L_k can be thought of as a *loss* function, in that it specifies the loss (measured in terms of effective share) to k, that is generated in consequence of its antagonist exploiting any given control share. As noted above, $[L_k > p_{-k}]$ implies negative spillovers from its antagonist to community k, while $[L_k < p_{-k}]$ implies positive spillovers. Notice that spillovers must necessarily be positive if $\left[\left(\frac{a_k}{\rho}\right) < 1\right]$, and necessarily negative if $[\left(\frac{a_k}{\rho}\right) > 1$ and $\rho = 1]$. However, since

$$a_k\left(\frac{p_{-k}^{\rho}}{\rho}\right) - p_{-k} = p_{-k}\left[p_{-k}^{\rho-1}\left(\frac{a_k}{\rho}\right) - 1\right],$$

when $\left[\left(\frac{a_k}{\rho}\right), \rho > 1\right]$, spillovers will be negative at high values of p_{-k}, but positive at low values, reflecting non-monotone effects of its antagonist's actions on community k.[14]

---

our model, assuming risk neutrality, the expected utility of an individual must take the form $\left[Eu_{ik} = c_{ik} + \left(\frac{T\tilde{\Upsilon}}{n^{\theta}}\right)\left[p_k + (1 - p_k)\left(1 - \frac{a_k}{\rho}\right)\right] = c_{ik} + \left(\frac{T\tilde{\Upsilon}}{n^{\theta}}\right)\left[1 - a_k\left(\frac{p_{-k}}{\rho}\right)\right]\right]$. Hence, the individual pay-off function must always reduce to this special limiting form, regardless of the specification of the effective share function in (5). Thus, the linear aggregative structure considered by Ihori (2000) and Buchholz *et al.* (2018) can alternatively be derived as a special case of our formulation when (a) $\left(\frac{a_k}{\rho}\right) > 1$, (b) the contest success function is assumed to provide success probabilities instead of group shares, and (c) agents are assumed to be risk-neutral expected utility maximizers.

[14]Recall that an interpretation of the contest success function as generative of success probabilities leads to a reduced form linear aggregative structure for g_k (recall footnote 13). Under a linear aggregative structure, $\left[\left(\frac{a_k}{\rho}\right) > 1\right]$ must always imply negative spillovers, regardless of the value of ρ. In this specific sense, our interpretation of the contest success function, as generating group shares, yields a strictly richer set of

Changes in the parameters a_H, a_M, and ρ capture changes in cross-community spillovers. The effective share g_k is monotonically increasing in ρ and monotonically decreasing in a_k. The parameter ρ measures the *elasticity* of the loss function of either community with respect to its antagonist's control share. Higher loss elasticity implies a lower loss to either community from any positive control share accruing to its antagonist. It also implies a lower loss to either community from a marginal increase in its antagonist's control share. Thus, intuitively, a more elastic loss function implies, in effect, a *symmetric* decline in inter-group consumption rivalry with respect to Υ. In the context of our example, greater use by cultivators of non-contaminating farming methods, in conjunction with greater adoption by pastoralists of feeding practices which reduce foraging (and consequent crop destruction) by their herds, might be modeled through a rise in the loss elasticity. We ignore inter-group asymmetry in loss elasticity for the sake of simplicity and tractability — permitting such asymmetry greatly adds to the algebra, without much compensation in the way of substantive additional insights.

Since $\lim_{\rho \to 1} \frac{dL_k}{dp_{-k}} = \lim_{\rho - k \to 1} \frac{dL_k}{dp_{-k}} = a_k$, the scale parameter a_k provides the upper bound for the loss to k due to a marginal increase in its antagonist's control share. We shall accordingly call a_k the *marginal degradation* rate for community k. This is the channel through which we introduce spillover *asymmetry* in our model. The marginal degradation rates may vary across communities — a_H need not be equal to a_M. Thus, the spillover effect on H due to M's exploitation of its control share may differ from that flowing in the reverse direction, even under an equal division of control. It follows that equal control shares do not, in general, imply equal effective shares in our model.

Lastly, note that the lower bound of 0 imposed on effective shares in (5) implies that the effect of any negative spillovers from, say, H to M is confined to degrading the latter's stock of the contestable good.

possibilities than the alternative interpretation in terms of success probabilities (with risk-neutral expected utility-maximizing agents).

Such negative spillovers do not affect the benefits derived by members of M from their non-contested (and private) consumption. This assumption is made entirely for expositional clarity. As we shall establish in Section 3 below, equilibrium effective shares must be positive under our parametric restrictions. The lower bound of 0 will thus be non-binding in equilibrium. We can therefore eliminate it altogether and thereby relax (5) to $\left[g_k = 1 - a_k\left(\frac{p_{-k}^{\rho}}{\rho}\right)\right]$, without any consequences for our conclusions.

Figure 1 below illustrates the relationship between control and effective shares for the linear case of unit loss elasticity ($\rho = 1$), and for a given community, say H. The distance OA equals the distance OC, with both representing 1. The broken horizontal line AB represents the limiting case of perfectly non-rival, non-excludable, and spillover-less consumption of Υ by H (i.e., of $a_H = 0$). Here, the benefit received by members of H from Υ is entirely independent of its use by M, and thus of the proportion of Υ that H has exclusive control over (its control share p_H). EB represents the case of net positive spillovers flowing to H from its antagonist's consumption (or that of imperfect rivalry and incomplete excludability) — the case where $0 < a_H < 1$. Here, the effective share of H, g_H exceeds its control share whenever H has less than perfect control (i.e., whenever $p_H < 1$). The 45^0 line OB captures fully rival, excludable, and spillover-less consumption between the two communities; here, $a_H = 1$. Control and effective shares turn identical in this case. The schedule ODB represents net

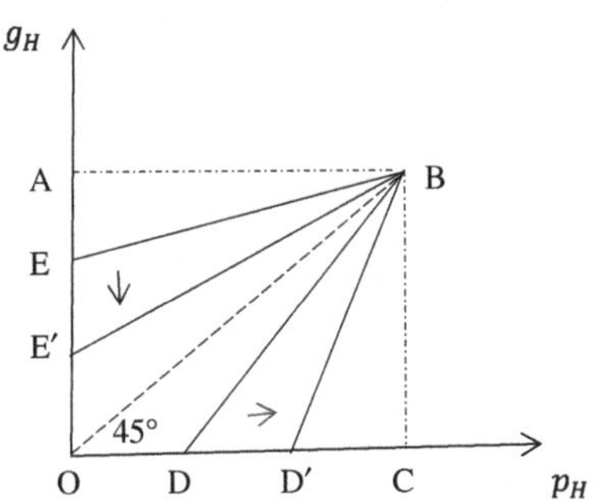

Fig. 1. Control share vs. effective share of H under $\rho = 1$.

negative spillovers due to M's actions degrading the stock of the contested good controlled by H (alongside perfect rivalry and complete excludability in consumption of the contested good across communities). Due to such degradation, the effective share of H falls short of its control share whenever H has less than perfect control over Υ. Here, $1 < a_H < 2$. Given the loss elasticity, weaker positive spillovers (or stronger negative spillovers) from M to H are captured by a rise in the latter's marginal degradation rate a_H, which swivels the effective share schedule of H downward. Such a change is depicted in Fig. 1, for the case of net positive spillovers from M to H, by the downward shift of EB to E′B. For the case of net negative spillovers from M to H, this change is depicted in Fig. 1 by the rightward shift of ODB to OD′B.

3. Equilibrium

We proceed now to characterize the equilibria of our model. In light of (1)–(6), remembering that $[p_k = 1 - p_{-k}]$, and assuming an interior solution, the first-order conditions yield

$$\text{for every } k \in \{H, M\} : X_{-k} T \tilde{\Upsilon} \left(\frac{dg_k}{dp_k} \right) = n^{\theta} X^2. \tag{7}$$

From (7), denoting equilibrium values of all variables by the superscript E, the relative marginal degradation rate by $A_k \left(A_k \equiv \frac{a_k}{a_{-k}} \right)$, noting (5), and that, by (4), $\frac{X_{-k}}{X_k} = \frac{p_{-k}}{p_k}$, we have the equilibrium control share ratio

$$\left(\frac{p_{-k}^E}{p_k^E} \right)^{\rho} = A_{-k}. \tag{8}$$

Equation (8) implies

$$p_k^E = \left(A_{-k}^{\frac{1}{\rho}} + 1 \right)^{-1}. \tag{9}$$

Together, (5) and (9) yield

$$g_k^E = g_{-k}^E = 1 - \frac{a_H a_M}{\rho \left(a_H^{\frac{1}{\rho}} + a_M^{\frac{1}{\rho}} \right)^{\rho}}. \tag{10}$$

Thus, the equilibrium control shares differ across communities when their marginal degradation rates differ. The community with the higher marginal degradation rate stands to lose more from its antagonist achieving any given control share. It consequently allocates more resources to appropriation — to the contest over sharing of Υ, and therefore receives the higher control share. In marked contrast, the equilibrium effective shares are always identical across communities. Thus, control shares provide a misleading picture of cross-community benefit disparity — any control advantage is completely compensated by a higher degradation rate — indeed, such control advantage comes about only as a compensatory response to higher negative spillovers, as captured by a higher degradation rate. Recall that $a_k \in (0,2)$ and $\rho \geq 1$ by assumption, which implies $\left[\frac{1}{\rho\left(a_H^{\frac{-1}{\rho}} + a_M^{\frac{-1}{\rho}}\right)^{\rho}} < 1\right]$. It then follows immediately from (10) that equilibrium effective shares must be positive, less than 1, increasing in the spillover (loss) elasticity and decreasing in the marginal degradation rates. These properties are stated more formally in Observation 1.

Observation 1. For all $k \in \{H, M\}$,

(i) $\lim_{\rho\to\infty} g_k^E = 1$ and $\left[1 > \lim_{\rho\to 1} g_k^E > 0\right]$;

(ii) $\frac{dg_k^E}{d\rho} > 0$;

and

(iii) $\frac{dg_k^E}{da_H}, \frac{dg_k^E}{da_M} < 0$.

Now, notice that, in light of (10), the first-order conditions also imply that, in an interior equilibrium,

$$T\left(\frac{\alpha}{B^{1-\alpha}}\right)\left(\frac{g_H}{n^{\theta}}\right) = T\left(\frac{\alpha}{B^{1-\alpha}}\right)\left(\frac{g_M}{n^{\theta}}\right) = 1. \qquad (11)$$

Together, (10) and (11) imply

$$B^E = \left(\left(\frac{T\alpha}{n^\theta} \right) \left(1 - \frac{a_H a_M}{\rho \left(a_H^{\frac{1}{\rho}} + a_M^{\frac{1}{\rho}} \right)^\rho} \right) \right)^{\frac{1}{1-\alpha}}. \tag{12}$$

The following conclusions may be then deduced about the equilibrium size of the subscription fund, B, dedicated to the production of the contested good Υ.

Observation 2.

(i) $B^E \in (0, 1)$;
(ii) $\frac{dB^E}{d\rho} > 0$ and $\frac{dB^E}{da_M}, \frac{dB^E}{da_H} < 0$;
(iii) there exists $\hat{\alpha} \in (0, 1)$ such that $\frac{dB^E}{d\alpha} > 0$ (resp. < 0) at every $\alpha < \hat{\alpha}$ (resp. $> \hat{\alpha}$).

Proof. See the appendix. □

Total subscription for production of Υ increases as the loss elasticity rises, reducing inter-community rivalry in its consumption and thereby increasing the effective shares of both communities. It decreases if either marginal degradation rate rises, reducing both effective shares. The effect of a marginal increase in the output elasticity of the contested good is however non-monotone. At low levels of such elasticity, total subscription rises as the elasticity increases, but it falls at output elasticities close to 1.

Since the equilibrium subscription fund expands as the loss function becomes more elastic, or as either marginal degradation rate declines, it is obvious from (3) that the amount of the contested good produced, $\tilde{\Upsilon}$, must correspondingly expand as well. More interestingly, it turns out that the latter necessarily declines as its production technology becomes more elastic, even when more input is forthcoming in response to such an increase (recall Observation 2(iii)).

Observation 3.

(i) $\tilde{\Upsilon}^E \in (0, 1)$;
(ii) $\frac{d\tilde{\Upsilon}^E}{d\rho} > 0$ and $\frac{d\tilde{\Upsilon}^E}{da_M}, \frac{d\tilde{\Upsilon}^E}{da_H} < 0$;
(iii) $\frac{d\tilde{\Upsilon}^E}{d\alpha} < 0$.

Proof. See the appendix. □

We now turn to characterizing aggregate conflict, measured in standard fashion by the total resource expended on appropriation, in equilibrium. Using (3) and (7), we get

$$X^E = \left(\frac{T}{n^\theta}\right)\left(B^E\right)^\alpha \left(\left(\frac{dg_H\left(p_H^E\right)}{dp_H}\right)^{-1} + \left(\frac{dg_M\left(p_M^E\right)}{dp_M}\right)^{-1}\right)^{-1}, \tag{13}$$

where $\frac{dg_H(p_H^E)}{dp_H}$ and $\frac{dg_M(p_M^E)}{dp_M}$ are the derivatives of the effective share functions in (5) with respect to the corresponding own control shares, evaluated at the equilibrium values of the latter. Combining (4), (9), and (13), we get the expressions for community conflict allocations:

$$\text{for every } k \in \{H, M\} : X_k^E = \left(\frac{T}{n^\theta}\right)\left(B^E\right)^\alpha \left(\left(\frac{dg_H\left(p_H^E\right)}{dp_H}\right)^{-1} + \left(\frac{dg_M\left(p_M^E\right)}{dp_M}\right)^{-1}\right)^{-1}\left(A_{-k}^{\frac{1}{\rho}} + 1\right)^{-1}. \tag{14}$$

By (4) and (5), recalling that $a_k \in (0, 2)$ by assumption, and that $p_H^E, p_M^E > 0$ by (9),

$$0 < \frac{dg_k(p_k^E)}{dp_k} = a_k(p_{-k}^E)^{\rho-1} < 2. \tag{15}$$

An explicit solution for X^E can be derived by combining (9), (12), (13), and (15), while those for X_H^E and X_M^E are derived by combining

(9), (12), (14), and (15). Note that, since, by assumption, $T \in (0, 1]$, $\alpha \in (0, 1)$ and $n^{\theta} \geq 1$; together, Observations 2(i), (13), and (15) imply that

$$X^E \in (0, 1). \tag{16}$$

Remark 9.1. Since each community must have resource endowment of at least 1 (as $n \geq 1$), Observation 2(i) and (16) imply that an interior Nash equilibrium must be feasible. Any interior equilibrium must satisfy (9) and (12)–(15), and satisfaction of these conditions guarantees the interiority of the equilibrium. It can be checked that, given our assumption $a_H, a_M \in (0, 2)$, every Nash equilibrium must satisfy Eqs. (9) and (12)–(15). Hence, our model uniquely characterizes total common fund subscription and group conflict allocations in equilibrium. However, individual consumption of the private good C, individual common fund subscription, and individual conflict contribution are all indeterminate, as are group private consumption and group common fund subscription levels. Thus, the model produces multiple Nash equilibria — essentially a consequence of the quasi-linearity of the reduced form of our preference specification.

4. Conflict, Aggregate Income, and Cross-community Spillovers

We are now ready to address our central questions. What happens to aggregate conflict as cross-community negative consumption spillover effects become stronger, leading to either a decline in the loss elasticity or an increase in the marginal degradation rates? Furthermore, how do such changes affect aggregate social income (or consumption), measured in units of the numeraire good, C?

Noting (1)–(6), define the total consumption of community $k \in \{H, M\}$, measured in terms of units of the numeraire good — the private consumption good C — as follows:

$$W_k^E = \sum_{i=1}^{n} (1 - x_{ik} - y_{ik}) + nT\tilde{\Upsilon}^E \left(\frac{g_k^E}{n^{\theta}} \right). \tag{17}$$

Total equilibrium consumption in society, measured in units of C, is, therefore,

$$W^E \equiv W_H^E + W_M^E = \left(2n - X^E - \left(\tilde{\Upsilon}^E\right)^{\frac{1}{\alpha}}\right) + \left(\frac{T}{n^{\theta-1}}\right)\tilde{\Upsilon}^E(\mathcal{g}_H^E + \mathcal{g}_M^E). \tag{18}$$

It is evident from (18) that cross-community spillovers affect aggregate social consumption in equilibrium, measured in units of the numeraire good, through three distinct, but inter-related, channels. These are aggregate conflict investment (X^E), magnitude of the contested good ($\tilde{\Upsilon}^E$), and size of the effective shares ($\mathcal{g}_H^E$ and $\mathcal{g}_M^E$).

Ceteris paribus, stronger negative spillovers from its antagonist increase the benefit, in terms of a gain in its effective share, to a community from a marginal increase in its control share (recall (15)). By itself, this effect will, clearly, incentivize greater conflict over control shares (note (13)). However, stronger cross-community negative spillovers, by effectively degrading more the stock of Υ controlled by either community, will also reduce the equilibrium effective shares (note (10)). Since this reduces the benefit to either community from contributing to the common pool for production of the contestable good, the common fund will shrink, correspondingly reducing the production of Υ (recall (12)). This fall in the size of the prize being contested over will dampen individual incentives to engage in appropriation. Thus, two contradictory effects obtain, which makes the net conflict consequence of stronger negative spillovers a priori ambiguous, and therefore non-trivial.

Is it possible, then, for stronger negative spillovers across communities to, somewhat counter-intuitively, reduce inter-community conflict? If so, noting (18), we have the intriguing possibility that greater negative consumption spillovers across communities may prove socially beneficial, in terms of their role in expanding the extent of social peace, and thus aggregate consumption. However, as already noted, they will reduce voluntary contributions to a common fund for production of a good whose consumption is at least partly non-rivalrous within a community. This effect may exacerbate the standard inefficiency associated with decentralized provision of any at least partly public good, as well as that due to less than full marginal benefit of its subscription accruing to either community. The fall in the effective shares brought about by stronger negative spillovers will depress the numeraire good measure of aggregate consumption as well. Can one then find parametric configurations under which the combination of these three effects is positive, so that, counter-intuitively, stronger negative spillovers end up expanding both peace and aggregate consumption (or, equivalently, production or income) in society?

To fix ideas, it is helpful to begin with an illustrative example.

Example 9.1. Suppose $T = 1, \theta = 0, \rho = 1, a_H = a_M = b \in (0,2)$. Then, from (12), (13), and (15),

$$B^E = (\alpha)^{\frac{1}{1-\alpha}} \left(1 - \frac{b}{2}\right)^{\frac{1}{1-\alpha}}; \tag{19}$$

$$X^E = (\alpha)^{\frac{\alpha}{1-\alpha}} \left(1 - \frac{b}{2}\right)^{\frac{\alpha}{1-\alpha}} \left(\frac{b}{2}\right). \tag{20}$$

(i) We have, from (20),

$$\left(\frac{b}{X^E}\right)\left(\frac{dX^E}{db}\right) = \left[1 - \left(\frac{\alpha}{1-\alpha}\right)\left(\frac{2}{b} - 1\right)^{-1}\right]. \tag{21}$$

By (21), any increase in the output elasticity reduces the elasticity of aggregate conflict with respect to the common degradation rate. Furthermore, $\frac{dX^E}{db} < 0$ (resp. > 0) when $\alpha >$ (resp. $<$) $\left(1 - \frac{b}{2}\right)$. Thus, starting from some initial level, say $\ddot{b}$, any increase in the common degradation rate will reduce aggregate conflict if the output elasticity is greater than $\left(1 - \frac{\ddot{b}}{2}\right)$. However, if the output elasticity falls below this threshold, a marginal increase in the common degradation rate will expand conflict. Thus, stronger negative spillovers depress conflict when the production technology for the contested good is relatively

elastic, but expand it otherwise. We shall generalize and expand this idea in Proposition 1.
(ii) Now, using (15) and (18)–(20),

$$W^E = 2n + \tilde{\Upsilon}^E \left[n(2-b) - \left(\frac{b}{2}\right)\right] - \left(\tilde{\Upsilon}^E\right)^{\frac{1}{\alpha}}. \tag{22}$$

Using (22), and recalling that, by (19), $\left[\tilde{\Upsilon}^E = (\alpha)^{\frac{\alpha}{1-\alpha}}\left(1-\frac{b}{2}\right)^{\frac{\alpha}{1-\alpha}}\right]$, we get

$$\frac{dW^E}{db} = -\tilde{\Upsilon}^E\left[\frac{1}{2} + n\left(\frac{1}{1-\alpha}\right) - \left(\frac{\alpha}{1-\alpha}\right)\left(\frac{1}{2-b}\right)\right]. \tag{23}$$

From (23),

$$\frac{dW^E}{db} < 0 \text{ iff } \left[n > \left(\frac{\alpha}{2-b}\right) - \frac{(1-\alpha)}{2}\right]. \tag{24}$$

By (24), a marginal increase in the common degradation rate will reduce aggregate social consumption when the common population size exceeds $\left[\left(\frac{\alpha}{2-b}\right) - \frac{(1-\alpha)}{2}\right]$, given $T = 1, \theta = 0$, and $\rho = 1$. For example, at $\left[b = 1, \alpha = \frac{1}{2}\right]$, $\frac{dW^E}{db} < 0$ for all $n \geq 1$, whereas, at $\left[b = \frac{19}{10}, \alpha = \frac{9}{10}\right]$, $\frac{dW^E}{db} < 0$ for all $n \geq 9$. These examples provide a concrete illustration of a general phenomenon that we shall identify and underline in Proposition 2.
(iii) Lastly, it follows from (24) that, given $T = 1, \theta = 0$, and $\rho = 1$, $\frac{dW^E}{db} > 0$ iff $\left[b > 2\left(\frac{1-2\alpha+2n}{1-\alpha+2n}\right)\right]$. Thus, any increase in the common degradation rate, b, over $\left(2\left(\frac{1-2\alpha+2n}{1-\alpha+2n}\right), 2\right)$ must increase aggregate social consumption. For example, when $n = 1$, $\alpha = \frac{1}{2}$, any increase in the common degradation rate over $\left(\frac{8}{5}, 2\right)$ must expand it. Thus, our example suggests that when negative spillovers are already at high levels (ρ is close to 1 and a_H, a_M are both close to 2), further increases in their strength might expand social consumption. Proposition 3 below formalizes and generalizes this idea.

Proposition 1. *Let* $\eta_b \equiv \left(\frac{bdX^E}{X^E db}\right)$.

(i) $\eta_\alpha < 0$.

(ii) *For every* $k \in \{H, M\}$: $(a) \frac{d(\eta_{a_k})}{d\alpha} < 0$ *and* (b) *there exists* $\breve{\gamma} \in (0,1)$ *such that:* $\eta_{a_k} > 0$ *(resp.* < 0*) if* $\alpha < \breve{\gamma}$ *(resp.* $> \breve{\gamma}$*).*

(iii) *Let* $a_H = a + \Delta$, *let* $a_M = a - \Delta$, *and suppose* $\Delta > 0$. *Then,* $\frac{d(\eta_\Delta)}{d\alpha} > 0$; *furthermore, there exists* $\delta \in (0,1)$ *such that:* $\eta_\Delta < 0$ *(resp.* > 0*) if* $\alpha < \delta$ *(resp.* $> \delta$*).*

(iv) $\frac{d(\eta_\rho)}{d\alpha} > 0$; *furthermore, there exists* $\gamma \in (0,1)$ *such that:* $\eta_\rho < 0$ *(resp.* > 0*) if* $\alpha < \gamma$ *(resp.* $> \gamma$*).*

Proof. See the appendix. □

Proposition 1 specifies the sign of the elasticity of aggregate conflict with respect to the different parameters of the model. This elasticity with respect to the production technology parameter (α) is negative, implying that conflict falls as the production technology becomes more elastic (Proposition 1(i)). This happens because an increase in the latter reduces the production of the contested good (Observation 3(iii)), but does not affect effective shares (recall (10)). The impact of changes in the spillover parameters is however more complicated. The conflict elasticity with respect to either marginal degradation rate declines monotonically as the output elasticity rises — it is positive at low output elasticities, but negative at high ones (Proposition 1(ii)). Thus, greater negative spillover from, say, M to H, due to a rise in the marginal degradation rate for H, will reduce aggregate conflict when the output elasticity is close to 1, but increase it when the latter is close to 0. A mean-preserving decrease in the spread of the marginal degradation rates has the same effect (Proposition 1(iii)), as does a reduction in the elasticity of the loss function (Proposition 1(iv)). Thus, in sum, stronger negative spillovers across communities, instead of increasing conflict, may indeed dampen it when the output elasticity is close to 1, as suggested by Example 1 (part (i)) earlier.

Intuitively, as already noted, stronger negative spillovers reduce subscriptions and thereby contract the size of the prize (i.e., the contested good, Υ). Such contraction reduces the incentive to invest resources in appropriation. Stronger negative spillovers however increase the incentive to invest in appropriation for any given level of the prize. When the output elasticity is close to 1, the first effect dominates. The second effect dominates when the output elasticity is close to 0.

We now turn to aggregate social consumption. From (18), we get the following conclusions.

Proposition 2.

(i) *There must exist* $\dot{n}$ *such that, if* $n > \dot{n}$, *then* (a) $\frac{dW^E}{da_H}, \frac{dW^E}{da_M} < 0$, *and* (b) *given* $(a_H + a_M)$, $\frac{dW^E}{d\Delta} > 0$, *whenever* $\Delta \equiv \frac{\|a_H - a_M\|}{2} > 0$.

(ii) *There must exist* $\overbrace{n}$ *such that, if* $n > \overbrace{n}$, *then* $\frac{dW^E}{d\rho} > 0$.

(iii) *There must exist* $\hat{n}$ *such that, if* $n > \hat{n}$, *then* $\frac{dW^E}{d\alpha} < 0$.

Proof. See the appendix. □

Proposition 2 essentially implies that, given the other parameters of the model, stronger negative cross-community spillovers unambiguously reduce aggregate social consumption when the communities are sufficiently numerous (parts (i) and (ii)). More rigorously, given the other parameters, one can always find a threshold community size with the following property: stronger negative cross-community spillovers, whether in the form of higher marginal degradation rates or a lower loss elasticity, must reduce aggregate social consumption whenever the communities are larger than this threshold size. A mean-preserving contraction in the spread of the marginal degradation rates and a rise in the output elasticity will both have the same effect when the communities are above this size threshold. The exact threshold size of the communities will of course depend on the parameters being held constant, as illustrated in Example 1 (part (ii)). All these conclusions essentially arise from the fact that the combined negative effect of any fall in the subscription fund and in effective shares must dominate any consumption gains from consequent lower expenditure on appropriation when the communities are sufficiently large.

Nonetheless, given any arbitrary community size, there always exist parametric configurations under which, at the margin, greater negative spillovers will increase aggregate consumption in society. This holds, in particular, under a combination of high marginal degradation rates and low loss elasticity (recall part (iii) of Example 1). This somewhat paradoxical possibility is presented formally in Proposition 3 below.

Proposition 3. *Suppose $a_H, a_M = a$. Then, given any $n \geq 1$, there exist $\breve{a} > 0, \check{b} > 1$ such that, whenever $[a \in (\breve{a}, 2)$ and $\rho \in [1, \check{b})]$,*

$$\left[\frac{dW^E}{da_H}, \frac{dW^E}{da_M}, \frac{dW^E}{d\alpha} > 0 \quad \text{and} \quad \frac{dW^E}{d\rho} < 0\right].$$

Proof. See the appendix. □

Proposition 3 implies the following. Given any community size and any elasticity of the production technology for the contested good, one can find a threshold level of the marginal degradation rate, say $\breve{a}$, and a threshold level of the loss elasticity, say $\check{b}$, with the following property. Consider any initial situation where (a) the two marginal degradation rates are identical and above $\breve{a}$, while (b) the loss elasticity is below $\check{b}$. This initial situation can be broadly interpreted as one characterized by negative cross-community spillovers that are strong enough to exceed a certain threshold level. Any increase of either degradation rate, from this initial situation, must improve aggregate social consumption (or equivalently, production or income) measured in units of the numeraire good. The same holds for a marginal increase in the output elasticity. Any decrease in the loss elasticity from this initial situation must improve aggregate social consumption as well. Thus, in sum, greater negative spillovers across communities may be aggregate consumption augmenting, and, in this specific sense, socially beneficial, irrespective of the size of the communities. Intuitively, this is likely when the strength of negative spillovers increases further, from an already high initial level.

Notice that a linear aggregative structure for the effective share function implies $\rho = 1$. It follows from Proposition 3 that, when the effective share function is assumed to have this form, there will always exist a threshold, beyond which stronger negative spillovers will be consumption augmenting.

5. Variants

We now identify and discuss two possible variants of our model in Section 3, one of which involves an alternative production technology for the contested good, and the other a more general specification of individual preferences.

(i) We have assumed, via (2) and (3), that the subscriptions of the two communities combine in summative fashion to generate the total input allocation for the contestable good. An alternative modeling strategy might be to assume that each community separately produces the contestable good using the total subscription of its own community members as the input pool: $\left[B_k = \sum_{i=1}^{n} y_{ik}\right]$. Letting $\tilde{\Upsilon}_k$ denote the amount of the contestable good produced by community k (i.e., $\tilde{\Upsilon}_k \equiv (B_k)^{\alpha}$), the total stock of Υ is then given as $[\tilde{\Upsilon} = \tilde{\Upsilon}_H + \tilde{\Upsilon}_M]$, instead of (3). Notice that the equations derived from the first-order conditions, (7) and (11), remain unchanged under this formulation (except that B is replaced, sequentially, by B_H and B_M in (11)). Since (7) remains unchanged, Eqs. (8)–(10) remain unchanged as well, as does Observation 1. The expression for total common pool subscription in (12) now comes to stand for that within either community, $B_H^E = B_M^E$, so that we have $B^E = 2B_H^E$, with B_H^E given by (12). It follows that we now get $B_k^E, \tilde{\Upsilon}_k \in (0, 1)$, so that $B^E, \tilde{\Upsilon}^E \in (0, 2)$, while the comparative static properties stated in Observation 2 ((ii) and (iii)) and Observation 3 ((ii) and (iii)) remain unchanged. Equation (13) now comes to take the form

$$X^E = 2\left(\frac{T}{n^{\theta}}\right)\left(B_H^E\right)^{\alpha}\left(\left(\frac{dg_H\left(p_H^E\right)}{dp_H}\right)^{-1} + \left(\frac{dg_M\left(p_M^E\right)}{dp_M}\right)^{-1}\right)^{-1},$$

and (14) is modified correspondingly. The claim in (15) remains unchanged, while that in (16) changes to $X^E \in (0, 2)$. The claims made in Remark 1 now come to hold under the assumption that $n \geq 3$, with the added proviso that each group's total contribution to the production of Υ, i.e., B_k^E, is now uniquely defined by (12). Thus, in this alternative formulation, for each group, total private consumption, total subscription to the production of the contestable good, and total expenditure on appropriation all come to be uniquely defined in equilibrium. However, individual private consumption, individual conflict allocation, and individual contribution to the production of Υ all remain indeterminate, as in our benchmark model (recall Remark 1). Since the expressions, respectively, for total spending on Υ in (12) and total conflict allocation in (13) change only by a multiplicative factor of 2, the comparative static results presented in Propositions 1–3 below remain unchanged. Thus, in sum, very little of substance changes if we replace the specification of the contestable good's production technology adopted in our benchmark formulation with the alternative specification discussed above. A further generalization, which permits the elasticity of that production technology to vary across communities (i.e., $\tilde{\Upsilon}_k = (B_k)^{\alpha_k}$, where α_H need not equal α_M), drastically complicates the algebra, but does not yield much additional insight.

(ii) The linear specification of the utility function adopted by us via (6) evidently constitutes a limiting case of the quasi-linear form

$$u_{ik} = c_{ik} + T\left(\frac{\tilde{\Upsilon} g_k}{n^\theta}\right)^\gamma,$$

where $\gamma \in (0,1)$. The assumed linearity of the utility function in the private consumption good, C, enables us to use that good as the numeraire commodity, and thereby arrive at aggregate measures of social consumption in terms of units of C (recall Propositions 2 and 3). We cannot consistently use the contestable group-specific public good, Υ, as the numeraire good because its marginal utility, even in our linear case of (6), cannot be defined independently of the endogenous variable g_k. Thus, we cannot dispense with the assumed linearity of our utility function in the private good. However, our comparative static conclusions, summarized by Propositions 1–3, are consistent with diminishing marginal utility from the contested good. Propositions 1–3 are derived implicitly for the limiting case ($\gamma = 1$) of the quasi-linear form defined above. Since all relevant functions are continuous, it follows that Propositions 1–3 must continue to hold when γ is less than 1, but sufficiently close to it (i.e., within some non-empty interval $(\varepsilon, 1)$). Thus, the assumed linearity of our utility function drastically simplifies the algebra, but is not necessary for our main conclusions to hold. However, it does appear an open question whether Propositions 1–3 hold for every value of γ in the $(0, 1)$ interval.

6. Concluding Remarks

This paper has developed a parsimonious theoretical framework to examine how cross-community cost or benefit spillovers, arising from the consumption or exploitation of group-specific public goods, affect both inter-group conflicts over the appropriation of such goods and decentralized private provision for their production. We have offered a model which integrates production versus appropriation choices, vis-à-vis group-specific public goods, with their decentralized voluntary supply, against a backdrop of such cross-community consumption spillovers. Our flexible and general formulation of consumption spillovers incorporates earlier specifications as alternative special cases. We have shown that, somewhat counter intuitively, stronger negative (or weaker positive) consumption spillovers across communities may serve to reduce inter-group conflict and increase aggregate income (and consumption) in society under certain conditions, which we have identified. Thus, stronger negative consumption spillovers, under certain conditions, may have socially beneficial consequences. Of course, their impact will be both conflict-augmenting and income-compressing, as may be intuitively expected, under other conditions. We have identified these latter conditions as well.

In many different developing country contexts, climate change and environmental degradation (as well as state policy, population growth, or market pressures) increase the costs imposed on one ethnic group due to another group's exploitation of some natural resource. This increases inter-group competition over natural resources and often triggers persistent and widespread social conflict. Such conflict in turn affects decentralized community-level mechanisms for the maintenance and augmentation of the contested natural resource, which feeds back into the original conflict. Our general theoretical analysis offers a broad conceptual structure within which to organize case studies of such feedback loops, linking ethnic conflict and natural resource degradation, in specific developing country contexts.

Dasgupta and Guha Neogi (2018) have examined how within-group fragmentation affects inter-group contests over group-specific public goods, while Esteban and Ray (2001), generalizing Olson (1965), have investigated how group size affects such conflicts under quite broad preference specifications. Analogous incorporation of within-group fragmentation and group size effects in suitably augmented versions of our model may generate useful insights. How income/wealth inequality and polarization affect social conflict (Esteban and Ray, 2011b) within our framework remains an open question. One may use alternatives to our perfect-substitutes summative specification for each community's aggregate group conflict effort, such as a constant elasticity of substitution aggregation (Kolmar and Rommeswinkel, 2013, Cheikbossian and Fayat, 2018), the best-shot specification (Chowdhury *et al.*, 2013), or the weakest-link formulation (Lee, 2012). Similar alternatives have also been applied to specify the public good's production technology in voluntary subscription models (Cornes, 1993). The consequences of cross-community spillovers with endogenous provisioning, in public good contests under such alternative specifications, whether of the conflict technology or the public good's production technology, constitute another promising avenue of future inquiry. We look forward to these and other extensions in future work.

Acknowledgment

We thank an anonymous referee for many helpful comments on an earlier version.

Appendix

Proof of Observation 2. From Observation 1 ((i) and (ii)), for all $k \in \{H, M\}$, $g_k^E \in (0, 1)$. By assumption, $T \in (0, 1]$ and $\alpha \in (0, 1)$, and $n \geq 1$. Then, part (i) of Observation 1 follows immediately from (12) in light of (10). Now, from (12), we get

$$B^E = \left(\left(\frac{T\alpha}{n^\theta}\right)\left(1 - \frac{1}{\rho\left(a_H^{\frac{-1}{\rho}} + a_M^{\frac{-1}{\rho}}\right)^\rho}\right)\right)^{\frac{1}{1-\alpha}}$$

$$= \left(\left(\frac{T\alpha}{n^\theta}\right)\left(1 - \frac{a_M}{\rho\left(1 + \left(\frac{a_M}{a_H}\right)^{\frac{1}{\rho}}\right)^\rho}\right)\right)^{\frac{1}{1-\alpha}}. \quad \text{(A.1)}$$

Without loss of generality, suppose $\left(\frac{a_M}{a_H}\right) \leq 1$. Then, part (ii) of Observation 2 follows immediately from (A.1). Now, from (A.1),

$$\ln B^E = \left(\frac{1}{1-\alpha}\right)\left[\ln\alpha + \ln\left(\left(\frac{T}{n^\theta}\right)\left(1 - \frac{a_H a_M}{\rho\left(a_H^{\frac{1}{\rho}} + a_M^{\frac{1}{\rho}}\right)^\rho}\right)\right)\right];$$

implying

$$\left(\frac{(1-\alpha)^2\alpha}{B^E}\right)\frac{dB^E}{d\alpha} = \left[(1-\alpha) + \ln\left(\left(\frac{T\alpha}{n^\theta}\right)\left(1 - \frac{a_H a_M}{\rho\left(a_H^{\frac{1}{\rho}} + a_M^{\frac{1}{\rho}}\right)^\rho}\right)\right)^\alpha\right]. \quad \text{(A.2)}$$

Let $Z \equiv \left[(1-\alpha) + \ln\left(\left(\frac{T\alpha}{n^\theta}\right)\left(1 - \frac{a_H a_M}{\rho\left(a_H^{\frac{1}{\rho}} + a_M^{\frac{1}{\rho}}\right)^\rho}\right)\right)^\alpha\right]$. Then,

$$\lim_{\alpha\to 0} Z = 1, \text{ and } \lim_{\alpha\to 1} Z = \ln\left(\left(\frac{T}{n^\theta}\right)\left(1 - \frac{a_H a_M}{\rho\left(a_H^{\frac{1}{\rho}} + a_M^{\frac{1}{\rho}}\right)^\rho}\right)\right) < 0.$$

Now, let $\tilde{Z} \equiv \alpha \ln\left(\left(\frac{T\alpha}{n^\theta}\right)\left(1 - \frac{a_H a_M}{\rho\left(a_H^{\frac{1}{\rho}}+a_M^{\frac{1}{\rho}}\right)^\rho}\right)\right)$. Then, $\frac{d\tilde{Z}}{d\alpha} = \ln\left(\left(\frac{T\alpha}{n^\theta}\right)\left(1 - \frac{a_H a_M}{\rho\left(a_H^{\frac{1}{\rho}}+a_M^{\frac{1}{\rho}}\right)^\rho}\right)\right) + 1$; implying $\frac{dZ}{d\alpha} = \ln\left(\left(\frac{T\alpha}{n^\theta}\right)\left(1 - \frac{a_H a_M}{\rho\left(a_H^{\frac{1}{\rho}}+a_M^{\frac{1}{\rho}}\right)^\rho}\right)\right) < 0$. Part (iii) of Observation 2 follows.

Proof of Observation 3. Parts (i) and (ii) of Observation 3 follow immediately from parts (i) and (ii), respectively, of Observation 2, in light of (3). Now, using (3) and (12),

$$\tilde{\Upsilon}^E = \left(\left(\frac{T\alpha}{n^\theta}\right)\left(1 - \frac{a_H a_M}{\rho\left(a_H^{\frac{1}{\rho}} + a_M^{\frac{1}{\rho}}\right)^\rho}\right)\right)^{\frac{\alpha}{1-\alpha}}. \tag{A.3}$$

Hence,

$$\ln \tilde{\Upsilon}^E = \left(\frac{\alpha}{1-\alpha}\right)\left[\ln\alpha + \ln\left(\left(\frac{T}{n^\theta}\right)\left(1 - \frac{a_H a_M}{\rho\left(a_H^{\frac{1}{\rho}} + a_M^{\frac{1}{\rho}}\right)^\rho}\right)\right)\right];$$

implying

$$\left(\frac{(1-\alpha)^2}{\tilde{\Upsilon}}\right)\frac{d\tilde{\Upsilon}^E}{d\alpha} = \left[(1-\alpha) + \ln\left(\left(\frac{T\alpha}{n^\theta}\right)\left(1 - \frac{a_H a_M}{\rho\left(a_H^{\frac{1}{\rho}} + a_M^{\frac{1}{\rho}}\right)^\rho}\right)\right)\right]. \tag{A.4}$$

Let $Z \equiv \left[(1-\alpha) + \ln\left(\left(\frac{T\alpha}{n^\theta}\right)\left(1 - \frac{a_H a_M}{\rho\left(a_H^{\frac{1}{\rho}} + a_M^{\frac{1}{\rho}}\right)^\rho}\right)\right)\right]$. Then, $\lim_{\alpha\to 0} Z = -\infty$, and $\lim_{\alpha\to 1} Z = \ln\left(\left(\frac{T}{n^\theta}\right)\left(1 - \frac{a_H a_M}{\rho\left(a_H^{\frac{1}{\rho}} + a_M^{\frac{1}{\rho}}\right)^\rho}\right)\right) < 0$. Furthermore, $\frac{dZ}{d\alpha} = -1 + \frac{1}{\alpha} > 0$. Part (iii) of Observation 3 follows.

Proof of Proposition 1. By (5) and (9), $\left(\left(\frac{dg_H(p_H^E)}{dp_H}\right)^{-1} + \left(\frac{dg_M(p_M^E)}{dp_M}\right)^{-1}\right)^{-1}$ is independent of α. Part (i) of Proposition 1 then follows directly from (13) in light of (3) and Observation 3(iii).

We shall prove parts (ii), (iii), and (iv) of Proposition 1 via the following lemma.

Lemma 1.

(i) *For every* $k \in \{H, M\}$, $\lim_{\alpha\to 0}\left(\frac{a_k dX^E}{X^E da_k}\right) = p_{-k}^E$, $\lim_{\alpha\to 1}\left(\frac{a_k dX^E}{X^E da_k}\right) = -\infty$, *and* $\frac{d\left(\frac{a_k dX^E}{X^E da_k}\right)}{d\alpha} < 0$.

(ii) *Let* $a_H = a + \Delta$, *let* $a_M = a - \Delta$, *and suppose* $\Delta > 0$. *Then,* $\lim_{\alpha\to 0}\left(\frac{\Delta dX^E}{X^E d\Delta}\right) = \Delta\left[\frac{p_M^E}{a_H} - \frac{p_H^E}{a_M}\right] < 0$, $\lim_{\alpha\to 1}\left(\frac{\Delta dX^E}{X^E d\Delta}\right) = \infty$, *and* $\frac{d\left(\frac{\Delta dX^E}{X^E d\Delta}\right)}{d\alpha} > 0$.

(iii) $\lim_{\alpha\to 0}\left(\frac{\rho dX^E}{X^E d\rho}\right) = K$, $\lim_{\alpha\to 1}\left(\frac{\rho dX^E}{X^E d\rho}\right) = \infty$, *and* $\frac{d\left(\frac{\rho dX^E}{X^E d\rho}\right)}{d\alpha} > 0$, *where*

$$K = \rho\left(\frac{\ln p_M^E + \left(\frac{p_H^E}{p_M^E}\right)\ln p_H^E}{1 + \left(\frac{p_H^E}{p_M^E}\right)}\right) < 0.$$

Proof of Lemma 1.

(i) Using (13),

$$\left(\frac{n^{\theta}}{T}\right)X^{E}=\tilde{\Upsilon}^{E}\left(\left(\frac{dg_{H}\left(p_{H}^{E}\right)}{dp_{H}}\right)^{-1}+\left(\frac{dg_{M}\left(p_{M}^{E}\right)}{dp_{M}}\right)^{-1}\right)^{-1}. \quad \text{(A.5)}$$

Hence,

$$\begin{aligned}&\left(\frac{n^{\theta}}{T}\right)\left(\left(\frac{dg_{H}\left(p_{H}^{E}\right)}{dp_{H}}\right)^{-1}+\left(\frac{dg_{M}\left(p_{M}^{E}\right)}{dp_{M}}\right)^{-1}\right)\left(\frac{dX^{E}}{da_{k}}\right)\\&=\frac{d\tilde{\Upsilon}^{E}}{da_{k}}-\tilde{\Upsilon}^{E}\left(\left(\frac{dg_{H}\left(p_{H}^{E}\right)}{dp_{H}}\right)^{-1}+\left(\frac{dg_{M}\left(p_{M}^{E}\right)}{dp_{M}}\right)^{-1}\right)^{-1}\\&\times\left[\left(\frac{\partial\left(\left(\frac{dg_{H}(p_{H}^{E})}{dp_{H}}\right)^{-1}+\left(\frac{dg_{M}(p_{M}^{E})}{dp_{M}}\right)^{-1}\right)}{\partial p_{H}}\right)\left(\frac{dp_{H}}{da_{k}}\right)\right.\\&\left.+\left(\frac{\partial\left(\left(\frac{dg_{H}(p_{H}^{E})}{dp_{H}}\right)^{-1}+\left(\frac{dg_{M}(p_{M}^{E})}{dp_{M}}\right)^{-1}\right)}{\partial a_{k}}\right)\right].\end{aligned} \quad \text{(A.6)}$$

Define $S\equiv\left(\frac{\partial\left(\left(\frac{dg_{H}}{dp_{H}}\right)^{-1}+\left(\frac{dg_{M}}{dp_{M}}\right)^{-1}\right)}{\partial p_{H}}\right)$. Then, noting that $p_H = 1 - p_M$, we get

$$S=-\left(\left(\frac{dg_{H}}{dp_{H}}\right)^{-2}\frac{d^{2}g_{H}}{dp_{H}^{2}}-\left(\frac{dg_{M}}{dp_{M}}\right)^{-2}\frac{d^{2}g_{M}}{dp_{M}^{2}}\right). \quad \text{(A.7)}$$

Recall that, from (5), $\frac{dg_k}{dp_k} = a_k p_{-k}^{\rho-1}$, $\frac{d^2 g_k}{dp_k^2} = -\left(\frac{\rho-1}{p_{-k}}\right)\frac{dg_k}{dp_k}$. Then, from (A.7), we have

$$S = \left(\frac{dg_M}{dp_M}\right)^{-1}(\rho-1)\left(\left(\frac{dg_M}{dp_M}\right)\left(\frac{dg_H}{dp_H}\right)^{-1}\left(\frac{1}{p_M}\right) - \left(\frac{1}{p_H}\right)\right).$$

Since $\left(\frac{dg_M}{dp_M}\right)\left(\frac{dg_H}{dp_H}\right)^{-1} = \left(\frac{a_M}{a_H}\right)\left(\frac{p_H}{p_M}\right)^{\rho-1}$, and, from (8), $\left[1 = \left(\frac{a_H}{a_M}\right)\left(\frac{p_M}{p_H}\right)^{\rho}\right]$ in equilibrium, we then have

$$S^E = \left(\frac{dg_M}{dp_M}\right)^{-1}(\rho-1)\left(\left(\frac{p_H}{p_M}\right)^{-1}\left(\frac{1}{p_M}\right) - \left(\frac{1}{p_H}\right)\right) = 0. \quad \text{(A.8)}$$

In light of (A.8), (A.6) reduces to

$$\left(\frac{n^\theta}{T}\right)\left(\left(\frac{dg_H\left(p_H^E\right)}{dp_H}\right)^{-1} + \left(\frac{dg_M\left(p_M^E\right)}{dp_M}\right)^{-1}\right)\left(\frac{dX^E}{da_k}\right)$$

$$= \frac{d\tilde{\Upsilon}^E}{da_k} - \tilde{\Upsilon}^E\left(\left(\frac{dg_H\left(p_H^E\right)}{dp_H}\right)^{-1} + \left(\frac{dg_M\left(p_M^E\right)}{dp_M}\right)^{-1}\right)^{-1}$$

$$\times\left(\frac{\partial\left(\left(\frac{dg_H\left(p_H^E\right)}{dp_H}\right)^{-1} + \left(\frac{dg_M\left(p_M^E\right)}{dp_M}\right)^{-1}\right)}{\partial a_k}\right). \quad \text{(A.9)}$$

Now recall that, by (5),

$$\left(\frac{dg_H}{dp_H}\right)^{-1} + \left(\frac{dg_M}{dp_M}\right)^{-1} = \left(\frac{1}{a_H p_M^{\rho-1}} + \frac{1}{a_M p_H^{\rho-1}}\right), \quad \text{(A.10)}$$

implying

$$\left(\frac{\partial\left(\left(\frac{dg_H}{dp_H}\right)^{-1} + \left(\frac{dg_M}{dp_M}\right)^{-1}\right)}{\partial a_k}\right) = -a_k^{-1}\left(\frac{dg_k}{dp_k}\right)^{-1}. \quad \text{(A.11)}$$

Combining (A.10) and (A.11), and recalling that $A_k = \frac{a_k}{a_{-k}}$, we get

$$\left(\left(\frac{dg_H}{dp_H}\right)^{-1} + \left(\frac{dg_M}{dp_M}\right)^{-1}\right)^{-1} \left[\left(\frac{\partial\left(\left(\frac{dg_H}{dp_H}\right)^{-1} + \left(\frac{dg_M}{dp_M}\right)^{-1}\right)}{\partial a_k}\right)\right]$$

$$= -\frac{a_k^{-1}}{\left(1 + A_k\left(\frac{p_{-k}}{p_k}\right)^{\rho-1}\right)}. \tag{A.12}$$

Hence, combining (A.9) and (A.12), we have

$$\left(\frac{n^\theta}{T}\right)\left(\left(\frac{dg_H\left(p_H^E\right)}{dp_H}\right)^{-1} + \left(\frac{dg_M\left(p_M^E\right)}{dp_M}\right)^{-1}\right)\left(\frac{dX^E}{da_k}\right)$$

$$= \frac{d\tilde{\Upsilon}^E}{da_k} + \frac{a_k^{-1}\tilde{\Upsilon}^E}{\left(1 + A_k\left(\frac{p_{-k}}{p_k}\right)^{\rho-1}\right)}. \tag{A.13}$$

By (13),

$$\left(\frac{n^\theta}{T}\right)\left(\left(\frac{dg_H\left(p_H^E\right)}{dp_H}\right)^{-1} + \left(\frac{dg_M\left(p_M^E\right)}{dp_M}\right)^{-1}\right)$$

$$= \tilde{\Upsilon}^E(X^E)^{-1}. \tag{A.14}$$

Since, by (3), $\left[\left(\frac{d\tilde{\Upsilon}^E}{da_k}\right) = \alpha\tilde{\Upsilon}^E\left(B^E\right)^{-1}\left(\frac{dB^E}{da_k}\right)\right]$, (A.13) and (A.14) together yield

$$a_k\left(X^E\right)^{-1}\left(\frac{dX^E}{da_k}\right) = \alpha a_k\left(B^E\right)^{-1}\left(\frac{dB^E}{da_k}\right)$$

$$+ \frac{1}{\left(1 + A_k\left(\frac{p_{-k}}{p_k}\right)^{\rho-1}\right)}. \tag{A.15}$$

Since, from (8), $\left[1 = \left(\frac{a_H}{a_M}\right)\left(\frac{p_M}{p_H}\right)^{\rho}\right]$ in equilibrium, (A.15) reduces to

$$a_k \left(X^E\right)^{-1} \left(\frac{dX^E}{da_k}\right) = \alpha a_k \left(B^E\right)^{-1} \left(\frac{dB^E}{da_k}\right) + p^E_{-k}. \tag{A.16}$$

Now, from (11),

$$B^E = \left(\frac{\alpha T g^E_k}{n^\theta}\right)^{\frac{1}{1-\alpha}}, \tag{A.17}$$

so that

$$\alpha \left(\frac{a_k}{B^E}\right) \frac{dB^E}{da_k} = a_k \left(\frac{\alpha}{1-\alpha}\right) \left(g^E_k\right)^{-1} \left(\frac{dg^E{}_k}{da_k}\right). \tag{A.18}$$

From (9) and (10),

$$\frac{dg^E_k}{da_k} = -\rho^{-1} \left(p^E_{-k}\right)^{(\rho+1)}. \tag{A.19}$$

Combining (A.16), (A.18), and (A.19), we get

$$a_k \left(X^E\right)^{-1} \left(\frac{dX^E}{da_k}\right) = p^E_{-k} \left(1 - a_k \left(\frac{\alpha}{1-\alpha}\right) \left(g^E_k\right)^{-1} \rho^{-1} \left(p^E_{-k}\right)^{\rho}\right). \tag{A.20}$$

Noting that, by (9) and (10), both p^E_{-k} and g^E_k are independent of α, part (i) of Lemma 1 follows.
(ii) From (A.20), recalling (10),

$$\begin{aligned}\Delta \left(X^E\right)^{-1} \left[\frac{dX^E}{d\Delta}\right] &= \Delta \left(X^E\right)^{-1} \left[\frac{dX^E}{da_H} - \frac{dX^E}{da_M}\right] \\ &= \left(\frac{\alpha}{1-\alpha}\right) \Delta \left(g^E_M\right)^{-1} \rho^{-1} \\ &\quad \times \left[\left(p^E_H\right)^{(\rho+1)} - \left(p^E_M\right)^{(\rho+1)}\right] \\ &\quad + \Delta \left[a_H^{-1} p^E_M - a_M^{-1} p^E_H\right].\end{aligned}$$

Since $\Delta > 0$, $a_H > a_M$. Hence, by (8), $p_H^E > p_M^E$, so that $[a_H^{-1} p_M^E - a_M^{-1} p_H^E] < 0$ and $[(p_H^E)^{(\rho+1)} - (p_M^E)^{(\rho+1)}] > 0$. Part (ii) of Lemma 1 follows.
(iii) From (A.5),

$$\left(\frac{n^\theta}{T}\right)\left(\left(\frac{dg_H\left(p_H^E\right)}{dp_H}\right)^{-1}+\left(\frac{dg_M\left(p_M^E\right)}{dp_M}\right)^{-1}\right)\left(\frac{dX^E}{d\rho}\right)$$

$$=\frac{d\tilde{\Upsilon}^E}{d\rho}-\tilde{\Upsilon}^E\left(\left(\frac{dg_H\left(p_H^E\right)}{dp_H}\right)^{-1}+\left(\frac{dg_M\left(p_M^E\right)}{dp_M}\right)^{-1}\right)^{-1}$$

$$\times\left[\left(\frac{\partial\left(\left(\frac{dg_H(p_H^E)}{dp_H}\right)^{-1}+\left(\frac{dg_M(p_M^E)}{dp_M}\right)^{-1}\right)}{\partial p_H}\right)\left(\frac{dp_H}{d\rho}\right)\right.$$

$$\left.+\left(\frac{\partial\left(\left(\frac{dg_H(p_H^E)}{dp_H}\right)^{-1}+\left(\frac{dg_M(p_M^E)}{dp_M}\right)^{-1}\right)}{\partial\rho}\right)\right]; \qquad \text{(A.21)}$$

which, in light of (A.7), (A.8), (A.10), and (A.14), reduces to

$$\left(X^E\right)^{-1}\left(\frac{dX^E}{d\rho}\right)=\tilde{\Upsilon}^{E-1}\left(\frac{d\tilde{\Upsilon}^E}{d\rho}\right)$$

$$-\left(\frac{1}{a_H\left(p_M^E\right)^{\rho-1}}+\frac{1}{a_M\left(p_H^E\right)^{\rho-1}}\right)^{-1}$$

$$\times\left(\frac{\partial\left(\left(\frac{dg_H}{dp_H}\right)^{-1}+\left(\frac{dg_M}{dp_M}\right)^{-1}\right)}{\partial\rho}\right). \qquad \text{(A.22)}$$

From (A.10),

$$\left(\frac{\partial\left(\left(\frac{dg_H}{dp_H}\right)^{-1}+\left(\frac{dg_M}{dp_M}\right)^{-1}\right)}{\partial\rho}\right)$$

$$= -\left(\left(\frac{dg_H}{dp_H}\right)^{-1}(\ln p_M)+\left(\frac{dg_M}{dp_M}\right)^{-1}(\ln p_H)\right). \quad \text{(A.23)}$$

Using (5), (A.22), and (A.23), we then get

$$(X^E)^{-1}\left(\frac{dX^E}{d\rho}\right) = \tilde{\Upsilon}^{E-1}\left(\frac{d\tilde{\Upsilon}^E}{d\rho}\right)$$
$$+\left(\frac{1}{a_H\left(p_M^E\right)^{\rho-1}}+\frac{1}{a_M\left(p_H^E\right)^{\rho-1}}\right)^{-1}$$
$$\times\left(\frac{\ln p_M^E}{a_H\left(p_M^E\right)^{\rho-1}}+\frac{\ln p_H^E}{a_M\left(p_H^E\right)^{\rho-1}}\right). \quad \text{(A.24)}$$

Since, by (3), $\left[\left(\frac{d\tilde{\Upsilon}^E}{d\rho}\right)=\alpha\tilde{\Upsilon}^E\left(B^E\right)^{-1}\left(\frac{dB^E}{d\rho}\right)\right]$, in light of (8), (A.24) reduces to

$$\rho\left(X^E\right)^{-1}\left(\frac{dX^E}{d\rho}\right) = \rho\alpha\left(B^E\right)^{-1}\left(\frac{dB^E}{d\rho}\right)$$
$$+\rho\left(\frac{\ln p_M^E+\left(\frac{p_H^E}{p_M^E}\right)\ln p_H^E}{1+\left(\frac{p_H^E}{p_M^E}\right)}\right). \quad \text{(A.25)}$$

Without loss of generality, suppose $A_M \geq 1$. From (A.17), we have

$$\rho\alpha\left(B^E\right)^{-1}\frac{dB^E}{d\rho} = \rho\left(\frac{\alpha}{1-\alpha}\right)\left(g_H^E\right)^{-1}\left(\frac{dg_H^E}{d\rho}\right). \quad \text{(A.26)}$$

Then, (A.25) reduces to

$$\rho\left(X^{E}\right)^{-1}\left(\frac{dX^{E}}{d\rho}\right)=\rho\left(\frac{\alpha}{1-\alpha}\right)\left(g_{H}^{E}\right)^{-1}\left(\frac{dg_{H}^{E}}{d\rho}\right)$$

$$+\rho\left(\frac{\ln p_{M}^{E}+\left(\frac{p_{H}^{E}}{p_{M}^{E}}\right)\ln p_{H}^{E}}{1+\left(\frac{p_{H}^{E}}{p_{M}^{E}}\right)}\right). \quad \text{(A.27)}$$

Now, from (5),

$$\frac{dg^{E}{}_{H}}{d\rho}=-a_{H}\left(\frac{p_{M}^{E\rho}}{\rho}\right)\left[\ln p_{M}^{E}-\left(\frac{\rho}{p_{M}^{E}}\right)\frac{dp_{H}^{E}}{d\rho}-\frac{1}{\rho}\right]. \quad \text{(A.28)}$$

From (9), $\frac{dp_H^E}{d\rho}=\left(A_M^{\frac{1}{\rho}}+1\right)^{-2}\left(\frac{A_M^{\frac{1}{\rho}}}{\rho^2}\right)\ln\left(A_M\right)\geq 0$, since $A_M\geq 1$ by assumption. Hence, from (A.28), $\frac{dg_H^E}{d\rho}$ is positive, finite, and independent of α. The terms g_H^E and p_H^E are both finite and independent of α as well. Lemma 1(iii) then follows from (A.27). □

Parts (ii), (iii), and (iv) of Proposition 1 follow immediately from parts (i), (ii), and (iii) of Lemma 1, respectively. □

Proof of Proposition 2.

(i) From (18),

$$\frac{dW^{E}}{da_{k}}=\left(-\frac{dX^{E}}{da_{k}}-\frac{dB^{E}}{da_{k}}\right)+\alpha\left(\frac{T}{n^{\theta-1}}\right)\left(B^{E}\right)^{\alpha-1}\left(\frac{dB^{E}}{da_{k}}\right)$$

$$\times(g_{H}^{E}+g_{M}^{E})+\left(\frac{T}{n^{\theta-1}}\right)\tilde{\Upsilon}^{E}\left(\frac{d\left(g_{H}^{E}+g_{M}^{E}\right)}{da_{k}}\right). \quad \text{(A.29)}$$

Together, (A.29) and (11) yield

$$\frac{dW^E}{da_k} = \left((2n-1)\left(\frac{dB^E}{da_k}\right) - \frac{dX^E}{da_k}\right) + \left(\frac{T}{n^{\theta-1}}\right)\tilde{\Upsilon}^E\left(\frac{d\left(g_H^E + g_M^E\right)}{da_k}\right). \tag{A.30}$$

In light of (A.16), (A.30) reduces to

$$\frac{dW^E}{da_k} = \left[(2n-1) - \alpha\left(B^E\right)^{-1}X^E\right]\left(\frac{dB^E}{da_k}\right) - \frac{X^E p_{-k}^E}{a_k} + \left(\frac{T}{n^{\theta-1}}\right)\tilde{\Upsilon}^E\left(\frac{d\left(g_H^E + g_M^E\right)}{da_k}\right). \tag{A.31}$$

From (11) and (13),

$$\alpha\left(\frac{X^E}{B^E}\right) = g_H^{-1}\left(\left(\frac{dg_H\left(p_H^E\right)}{dp_H}\right)^{-1} + \left(\frac{dg_M\left(p_M^E\right)}{dp_M}\right)^{-1}\right)^{-1}. \tag{A.32}$$

From (8) and (A.10),

$$g_H^{-1}\left(\left(\frac{dg_H}{dp_H}\right)^{-1} + \left(\frac{dg_M}{dp_M}\right)^{-1}\right)^{-1} = \frac{\rho a_H p_M^\rho}{\rho - a_H p_M^\rho}. \tag{A.33}$$

In light of (A.32) and (A.33), (A.31) yields

$$\frac{dW^E}{da_k} = \left[\frac{(2n-1)\left(\rho - a_H\left(p_M^E\right)^\rho\right) - \rho a_H\left(p_M^E\right)^\rho}{\rho - a_H\left(p_M^E\right)^\rho}\right]\left(\frac{dB^E}{da_k}\right) - \frac{X^E p_{-k}^E}{a_k} + \left(\frac{T}{n^{\theta-1}}\right)\tilde{\Upsilon}^E\left(\frac{d\left(g_H^E + g_M^E\right)}{da_k}\right). \tag{A.34}$$

Now, notice that, by (11), (A.18), and (A.19),

$$\frac{dB^E}{da_k} = -\left(\frac{\alpha}{1-\alpha}\right)\left(\tilde{\Upsilon}^E\right)\left(\frac{T}{n^\theta}\right)\rho^{-1}(p^E_{-k})^{(\rho+1)}. \tag{A.35}$$

From (10), $\left(\frac{dg^E{}_H}{da_k}\right) = \left(\frac{dg^E{}_M}{da_k}\right)$. Then, (A.19), (A.34), and (A.35) yield

$$-(\tilde{\Upsilon}^E)^{-1}\frac{dW^E}{da_k} = \left(\left[\frac{(2n-1)(\rho - a_H(p^E_M)^\rho) - \rho a_H(p^E_M)^\rho}{\rho - a_H(p^E_M)^\rho}\right]\right.$$
$$\left.\times\left(\frac{\alpha}{1-\alpha}\right) + 2n\right)\left(\frac{T}{n^\theta}\right)\rho^{-1}\left(p^E_{-k}\right)^{(\rho+1)}$$
$$+\frac{X^E p^E_{-k}}{\tilde{\Upsilon}^E a_k}. \tag{A.36}$$

Together, (A.5) and (A.36) yield

$$-\left(\tilde{\Upsilon}^E\right)^{-1}\left(\frac{n^\theta}{T}\right)\frac{dW^E}{da_k}$$
$$= \left(\left[\frac{(2n-1)\left(\rho - a_H\left(p^E_M\right)^\rho\right) - \rho a_H\left(p^E_M\right)^\rho}{\rho - a_H\left(p^E_M\right)^\rho}\right]\right.$$
$$\left.\times\left(\frac{\alpha}{1-\alpha}\right) + 2n\right)\rho^{-1}\left(p^E_{-k}\right)^{(\rho+1)}$$
$$+\left(\frac{p^E_{-k}}{a_k}\right)\left(\left(\frac{dg_H\left(p^E_H\right)}{dp_H}\right)^{-1} + \left(\frac{dg_M\left(p^E_M\right)}{dp_M}\right)^{-1}\right)^{-1}. \tag{A.37}$$

Consider the term $Z \equiv (2n-1)(\rho - a_H(p^E_M)^\rho) - \rho a_H(p^E_M)^\rho$. By Observation 1, $(\rho - a_H(p^E_M)^\rho) > 0$. Then, there must exist $\dot{n}$ such that, if $n > \dot{n}$, then $Z > 0$. Part (a) of Proposition 2(i) follows. Now, using (A.37), and noting (10), we have

$$
\begin{aligned}
&-\left(\tilde{\Upsilon}^{E}\right)^{-1}\left(\frac{n^{\theta}}{T}\right)\left(\frac{dW^{E}}{da_{H}}-\frac{dW^{E}}{da_{M}}\right)\\
&=\left(\left[\frac{(2n-1)\left(\rho-a_{H}\left(p_{M}^{E}\right)^{\rho}\right)-\rho a_{H}\left(p_{M}^{E}\right)^{\rho}}{\rho-a_{H}\left(p_{M}^{E}\right)^{\rho}}\right]\right.\\
&\quad\left.\times\left(\frac{\alpha}{1-\alpha}\right)+2n\right)\rho^{-1}\left[\left(p_{M}^{E}\right)^{(\rho+1)}-\left(p_{H}^{E}\right)^{(\rho+1)}\right]\\
&\quad+\left[\left(\frac{p_{M}^{E}}{a_{H}}\right)-\left(\frac{p_{H}^{E}}{a_{M}}\right)\right]\left(\left(\frac{dg_{H}\left(p_{H}^{E}\right)}{dp_{H}}\right)^{-1}+\left(\frac{dg_{M}\left(p_{M}^{E}\right)}{dp_{M}}\right)^{-1}\right)^{-1}.
\end{aligned}
\tag{A.38}
$$

Without loss of generality, suppose $a_H > a_M$. Then, from (8), $p_H^E > p_M^E$. Part (b) of Proposition 2(i) then follows from (A.38).
(ii) From (18),

$$
\begin{aligned}
\frac{dW^{E}}{d\rho}&=\left(-\frac{dX^{E}}{d\rho}-\frac{dB^{E}}{d\rho}\right)+\alpha\left(\frac{T}{n^{\theta-1}}\right)\left(B^{E}\right)^{\alpha-1}\\
&\quad\times\left(\frac{dB^{E}}{d\rho}\right)\left(g_{H}^{E}+g_{M}^{E}\right)+\left(\frac{T}{n^{\theta-1}}\right)\tilde{\Upsilon}^{E}\left(\frac{d\left(g_{H}^{E}+g_{M}^{E}\right)}{d\rho}\right).
\end{aligned}
\tag{A.39}
$$

Together, (A.39) and (11) yield

$$
\begin{aligned}
\frac{dW^{E}}{d\rho}&=\left((2n-1)\left(\frac{dB^{E}}{d\rho}\right)-\frac{dX^{E}}{d\rho}\right)\\
&\quad+n\left(\frac{B^{E}}{\alpha}\right)\left(g_{H}^{E}\right)^{-1}\left(\frac{d\left(g_{H}^{E}+g_{M}^{E}\right)}{d\rho}\right).
\end{aligned}
\tag{A.40}
$$

In light of (A.25), (A.40) reduces to

$$\frac{dW^E}{d\rho} = \left[(2n-1) - \alpha\left(B^E\right)^{-1} X^E\right]\left(\frac{dB^E}{d\rho}\right)$$
$$-X^E\left(\frac{\ln p_M^E + \left(\frac{p_H^E}{p_M^E}\right)\ln p_H^E}{1+\left(\frac{p_H^E}{p_M^E}\right)}\right)$$
$$+n\left(\frac{B^E}{\alpha}\right)\left(g_H^E\right)^{-1}\left(\frac{d\left(g_H^E + g_M^E\right)}{d\rho}\right). \tag{A.41}$$

Noting (A.32) and (A.33), (A.41) further reduces to

$$\frac{dW^E}{d\rho} = \left[\frac{(2n-1)\left(\rho - a_H\left(p_M^E\right)^\rho\right) - \rho a_H\left(p_M^E\right)^\rho}{\rho - a_H\left(p_M^E\right)^\rho}\right]\left(\frac{dB^E}{d\rho}\right)$$
$$-X^E\left(\frac{\ln p_M^E + \left(\frac{p_H^E}{p_M^E}\right)\ln p_H^E}{1+\left(\frac{p_H^E}{p_M^E}\right)}\right) + n\left(\frac{B^E}{\alpha}\right)\left(g_H^E\right)^{-1}$$
$$\times\left(\frac{d\left(g_H^E + g_M^E\right)}{d\rho}\right). \tag{A.42}$$

Together, (A.42), (A.26), and (10) yield

$$\left(\frac{\alpha g_H^E}{B^E}\right)\left(\frac{dW^E}{d\rho}\right) = \left(\left[\frac{(2n-1)\left(\rho - a_H\left(p_M^E\right)^\rho\right) - \rho a_H\left(p_M^E\right)^\rho}{\rho - a_H\left(p_M^E\right)^\rho}\right]\right.$$
$$\left.\times\left(\frac{\alpha}{1-\alpha}\right) + 2n\right)\left(\frac{dg_H^E}{d\rho}\right)$$
$$-\left(\frac{\alpha g_H^E X^E}{B^E}\right)\left(\frac{\ln p_M^E + \left(\frac{p_H^E}{p_M^E}\right)\ln p_H^E}{1+\left(\frac{p_H^E}{p_M^E}\right)}\right). \tag{A.43}$$

By (A.28), $\frac{dg_H^E}{d\rho}$ is positive. By Observation 1, $(\rho - a_H(p_M^E)^\rho) > 0$. Note that, by (12) and (13), $\frac{X^E}{B^E}$ is positive and finite, as is $\lim_{\alpha\to 1}\frac{X^E}{B^E}$. Then, there must exist $\widehat{n}$ such that, if $n > \widehat{n}$, then $[(2n-1)(\rho - a_H(p_M^E)^\rho) - \rho a_H(p_M^E)^\rho] > 0$. Proposition 2(ii) follows.
(iii) Combining (13) and (18) and using (10), we have

$$\frac{dW^E}{d\alpha} = g_H^E\left(\frac{T}{n^\theta}\right)\left[2n - g_H^{E^{-1}}\left(\left(\frac{dg_H\left(p_H^E\right)}{dp_H}\right)^{-1} + \left(\frac{dg_M\left(p_M^E\right)}{dp_M}\right)^{-1}\right)^{-1}\right]\frac{d\tilde{\Upsilon}^E}{d\alpha} - \frac{dB^E}{d\alpha}. \quad \text{(A.44)}$$

Together, (A.33) and (A.44) yield

$$\frac{dW^E}{d\alpha} = g_H^E\left(\frac{T}{n^\theta}\right)\left[2n - \frac{\rho a_H\left(p_M^E\right)^\rho}{\rho - a_H\left(p_M^E\right)^\rho}\right]\frac{d\tilde{\Upsilon}^E}{d\alpha} - \frac{dB^E}{d\alpha}. \quad \text{(A.45)}$$

Since $\left[\frac{dB^E}{d\alpha} = \left(\frac{B^E}{\alpha\tilde{\Upsilon}^E}\right)\frac{d\tilde{\Upsilon}^E}{d\alpha} - \left(\frac{B^E}{\alpha}\right)\ln B^E\right]$, (A.45) yields

$$\frac{dW^E}{d\alpha} = \left[g_H^E T\left[2n^{1-\theta} - \frac{\rho a_H\left(p_M^E\right)^\rho}{n^\theta\left(\rho - a_H\left(p_M^E\right)^\rho\right)}\right] - \left(\frac{B^{E^{1-\alpha}}}{\alpha}\right)\right]\frac{d\tilde{\Upsilon}^E}{d\alpha} + \left(\frac{B^E}{\alpha}\right)\ln B^E. \quad \text{(A.46)}$$

Noting that $B^E \in (0,1)$ by Observation 2(i), so that $[\ln B^E < 0]$, and recalling that $\frac{d\tilde{\Upsilon}^E}{d\alpha} < 0$ by Observation 3(iii), part (iii) of Proposition 2 follows from (A.46). □

Proof of Proposition 3.

Let $Z \equiv \frac{\rho a_H (p_M^E)^\rho}{\rho - a_H (p_M^E)^\rho}$. By (9), $\left[a_H (p_M^E)^\rho = \frac{1}{\left(a_H^{\frac{-1}{\rho}} + a_M^{\frac{-1}{\rho}}\right)^\rho}\right]$. Hence, when $a_H = a_M = a, \rho = 1$, we have $\left[a_H (p_M^E)^\rho = \frac{a}{2}\right]$, so that $\lim_{\rho \to 1, a \to 2} Z = \infty$. Proposition 3 then follows, by continuity, from (A.37), (A.43), and (A.46). □

References

Aggarwal, M. (2020). India is missing a clear forest policy and its jungle dwellers are the worst off, *Quartz India*, January 13, https://qz.com/india/1783965/indias-missing-forest-policy-is-hurting-tribals-the-most/.

Alavi, F. (2019). Stray cattle issue — a reality check, *The Indian Express*, June 29, https://indianexpress.com/article/opinion/columns/stray-cattle-issue-a-reality-check-cow-slaughter-india-livestock-5805684/.

Anderton, C., Anderton, R., and Carter, J. R. (1999). Economic activity in the shadow of conflict. *Economic Inquiry*, 37(1), 166–179.

Andreoni, J. (1990). Impure altruism and donations to public goods: a theory of warm-glow giving. *Economic Journal*, 100, 464–477.

Baik, K. H. (2008). Contests with group-specific public-good prizes. *Social Choice and Welfare*, 30, 103–117.

Baik, K. H. (2016). Contests with alternative public-good prizes. *Journal of Public Economic Theory*, 18(4), 545–559.

Baik, K. H. and Jung, H. M. (2021). Contests with multiple alternative prizes — public good/bad prizes and externalities. *Journal of Mathematical Economics*, 92, 103–116.

Bakshi, D. and Dasgupta, I. (2018). A model of dynamic conflict in ethnocracies. *Defence and Peace Economics*, 29(2), 147–170.

Bakshi, D. and Dasgupta, I. (2020). Identity conflict with cross-border spillovers. *Defence and Peace Economics*, 31(7), 786–809.

Bergstrom, T. C., Blume, L., and Varian, H. (1986). On the private provision of public goods. *Journal of Public Economics*, 29, 25–49.

Bostedt, K. G. (1999). Threatened species as public goods and public bads: An application to wild predators in Sweden. *Environmental and Resource Economics*, 13, 59–73.

Buchholz, W., Cornes, R., and Rübbelke, D. (2018). Public goods and public bads. *Journal of Public Economic Theory*, 20(4), 525–540.

Caruso, R. (2010). Butter, guns and ice-cream: Theory and evidence from sub-Saharan Africa. *Defence and Peace Economics*, 21(3), 269–283.

Chari, M. (2019). Hindutva paranoia about cow slaughter has given India a stray cattle problem that's here to stay, *Scroll.in*, January 13, https://scroll.in/article/908702/the-cow-and-bull-story-as-farmers-vent-anger-indias-stray-cattle-problem-is-here-to-stay.

Cheikbossian, G. (2008). Heterogeneous groups and rent-seeking for public goods. *European Journal of Political Economy*, 24, 133–150.

Cheikbossian, G. and Fayat, R. (2018). Group size, collective action and complementarities in efforts, *Economics Letters*, 168, 77–81.

Chowdhury, S. M., Lee, D., and Sheremeta, R. M. (2013). Top guns may not fire: Best-shot group contests with group-specific public good prizes. *Journal of Economic Behavior & Organization*, 92, 94– 103.

Cornes, R. (1993). Dyke maintenance and other stories: Some neglected types of public goods. *Quarterly Journal of Economics*, 108, 259–271.

Cornes, R. and Sandler, T. (1994). The comparative static properties of the impure public good model. *Journal of Public Economics*, 54, 403–421.

Cornes, R. and Sandler, T. (1996). *The Theory of Externalities, Public Goods and Club Goods* (2nd ed.), Cambridge University Press, Cambridge, UK.

Cornes, R., Hartley, R., and Tamura, Y. (2019). Two-aggregate games: Demonstration using a production–appropriation model. *The Scandinavian Journal of Economics*, 121(1), 353–378.

Cornes, R. and Sandler, T. (2000). Pareto-improving redistribution and pure public goods. *German Economic Review*, 1, 169–186.

Dal Bó, E. and Dal Bó, P. (2011). Workers, warriors, and criminals: Social conflict in general equilibrium. *Journal of the European Economic Association*, 9(4), 646–677.

Dal Bó, E. and Dal Bó, P. (2012). Conflict and policy in general equilibrium: Insights from a standard trade model, in Garfinkel, M. and Skaperdas, S. (eds), *The Oxford Handbook of The Economics of Peace and Conflict*, Oxford University Press, New York, 611–632.

Dasgupta, I. (2017). Linguistic assimilation and ethno-religious conflict, in Buchholtz, W. and Rübbelke, D. (eds), *The Theory of Externalities and Public Goods: Essays in Memory of Richard C. Cornes*, Springer, Berlin, 219–242.

Dasgupta, I. and Guha Neogi, R. (2018). Between-group contests over group-specific public goods with within-group fragmentation. *Public Choice*, 174 (3–4), 315–334.

Dasgupta, I. and Kanbur, R. (2005a). Community and anti-poverty targeting. *Journal of Economic Inequality*, 3(3), 281–302.

Dasgupta, I. and Kanbur, R. (2005b). Bridging communal divides: Separation, patronage, integration, in Barrett, C. (ed), *The Social Economics of Poverty: On Identities, Groups, Communities and Networks*, Routledge, London, 146–170.

Dasgupta, I. and Kanbur, R. (2007). Community and class antagonism. *Journal of Public Economics*, 91(9), 1816–1842.

Dasgupta, I. and Kanbur, R. (2011). Does philanthropy reduce inequality? *Journal of Economic Inequality*, 9, 1–21.

Dasgupta, I. and Pal, S. (2021). Touch thee not: Group conflict, caste power and untouchability in rural India. *Journal of Comparative Economics*, 49(2), 442–466.

Epstein, G. S. and Mealem, Y. (2009). Group specific public goods, orchestration of interest groups with free riding. *Public Choice*, 139, 357–369.

Esteban, J. and Ray, D. (2001). Collective action and the group size paradox. *American Political Science Review*, 95, 663–672.

Esteban, J. and Ray, D. (2011a). A model of ethnic conflict. *Journal of the European Economic Association*, 9, 496–521.

Esteban, J. and Ray, D. (2011b). Linking conflict to inequality and polarization. *American Economic Review*, 101(4), 1345–1374.

Gradstein, M. (1993). Rent-seeking and the provision of public goods. *Economic Journal*, 103, 1236– 1243.

Grossman, H. I. and Kim, M. (1996). Predation and accumulation. *Journal of Economic Growth*, 1, 333– 350.

Hausken, K. (2005). Production and conflict models versus rent-seeking models. *Public Choice*, 123, 59–93.

Hirshleifer, J. (1991). The paradox of power. *Economics & Politics*, 3(3), 177–200.

Ihori, T. (2000). Defense expenditures and allied cooperation. *Journal of Conflict Resolution*, 44, 854– 867.

Katz, E., Nitzan, S., and Rosenberg, J. (1990). Rent-seeking for pure public goods. *Public Choice*, 65, 49–60.

Kolmar, M. and Rommeswinkel, H. (2013). Contests with group-specific public goods and complementarities in efforts. *Journal of Economic Behavior and Organization*, 89, 9–22.

Lee, D. (2012). Weakest-link contests with group-specific public good prizes. *European Journal of Political Economy*, 28(2), 238–248.

Mitra, A. and Ray, D. (2014). Implications of an economic theory of conflict: Hindu-Muslim violence in India. *Journal of Political Economy*, 122(4), 719–765.

Murphy, K. M., Schleifer, A., and Vishny, R. W. (1993). Why is rent-seeking so costly to growth? *American Economic Review*, 83(2), 409–414.

Nitzan, S. and Ueda, K. (2009). Collective contests for commons and club goods. *Journal of Public Economics*, 93, 48–55.

Noh, S. J. (2002). Production, appropriation and income transfer. *Economic Inquiry*, 40(2), 279–287.

Olson, M. (1965). *The Logic of Collective Action: Public Goods and the Theory of Groups*, Harvard University Press, Cambridge, MA.

Riaz, K., Shogren, J. F., and Johnson, S. R. (1995). A general model of rent-seeking for pure public goods. *Public Choice*, 82, 243–259.

Shettima, A. G. and Tar, U. A. (2008). Farmer-pastoralist conflict in West Africa: Exploring the causes and consequences. *Information, Society and Justice*, 1(2), 163–184.

Skaperdas, S. (1992). Cooperation, conflict, and power in the absence of property rights. *American Economic Review*, 82, 720–739.

Tullock, G. (1980). Efficient rent seeking, in Buchanan, J. M., Tollison, R. D. and Tullock, G. (eds), *Toward a Theory of the Rent-seeking Society*, Texas A and M University Press, College Station, 97–112.

Ursprung, H. W. (1990). Public goods, rent dissipation, and candidate competition. *Economics and Politics*, 2, 115–132.

https://doi.org/10.1142/9789811240553_0010

Chapter 10

Climate and Migration

Katrin Millock[*,‡] and Cees Withagen[†,§]

[*]Paris School of Economics and CNRS, France
[†]Emeritus professor Vrije Universiteit Amsterdam, The Netherlands
[†] *millock@univ-paris1.fr*
[§] *cwithagen@feweb.vu.nl*

We review some of the recent estimates of the effect of weather and climate on migration, and articles examining the historical evidence of such links. We identify four issues that have received less attention in previous reviews on the topic. The first one is general equilibrium effects of climate change and migration. The second one concerns accounting for thresholds in the climate-migration relationship. Some of the articles that we review incorporate nonlinear effects, but only in the relation between income and migration, and in the relation between weather, climate, and migration. Other thresholds are not yet incorporated into the literature. A third issue where much work remains to be done relates to climate change and conflict, and their influence on migration. Finally, we conclude with some reflections on the implications of the results for economic development.

1. Introduction

Environmental migration, in particular migration induced by climate change, has become an urgent policy concern. Migration is increasingly seen as a means of adaptation to climate change (Black *et al.*, 2011), both as a response to gradual changes in temperature and precipitation and slow-onset processes such as land degradation, drought, and desertification, but also to rapid-onset events, such as tropical storms and floods. The image of huge migration flows across international borders being driven by climate change has been tempered somewhat, as most migration across borders are costly and surrounded by policy barriers (see, e.g., Beine and Parsons, 2015). Human mobility is normal and takes many forms, including both international and internal migration, either temporary or permanent, circular migration (Findley, 1994), and also involuntary displacement or immobility. Indeed, Boas *et al.* (2019) call for reframing the research on climate-induced migration to ask how and to what extent climate change affects established patterns of mobility.

There is much evidence though, both historically and currently, of internal and regional migration due to climatic events. Hugo (1996) discusses the millions displaced by the extreme droughts that occurred in Sub-Saharan Africa from 1968 to 1973 and from 1982 to 1984. The World Bank's Groundswell Report, issued in 2018, quantified the number of projected internal migrants in Sub-Saharan Africa, South-East Asia, and Latin America as 145 million by 2050 in the worst-case scenario (Rigaud *et al.*, 2018). These numbers, although impressive, have to be put in perspective with actual migration patterns. In 2019, there were 272 million international migrants, representing 3.5% of the world population. In addition, at the end of 2018, there were 25.9 million refugees displaced involuntarily across international borders. A small part of internationally displaced persons constitutes asylum seekers, who can seek legal protection from the government of the destination country on the basis of recognized motives for leaving and not being able to return to their country of origin. The International Organization for Migration (2020) counted 3.5 million asylum seekers at the end of 2018, mainly from a small set of conflict-ridden origin countries. Given the costs of crossing international borders, most migration is internal, though, and has been estimated to at least twice the number of international migrants. Whereas migration is seen as a voluntary choice, displacement captures involuntary mobility. The Internal Displacement Monitoring Center (IDMC) estimates the stock of internally displaced people to 41.3 million people at the end of 2018 (Internal Displacement Monitoring Centre, 2020). Disasters have always been linked with human displacement, in the best case of a temporary nature

(Perch-Nielsen *et al.*, 2008; Berlemann and Steinhardt, 2017). In 2018 alone, 28 million people were displaced within national borders, of which 17.2 million were linked with disasters and 10.8 million linked with conflict (abstracting from any potential link between the two).

In addition to these absolute estimates of future migration flows, the empirical literature on climate change and migration gives estimates on the share of past migrants that can be inferred to weather shocks or climate variability, as well as projections of future flows. Marchiori *et al.* (2012) estimate that temperature and rainfall anomalies caused a total displacement of 5 million people in Africa during the period 1960–2000, i.e., a minimum of 128,000 people every year. The projections based on their estimations predict 11.8 million additional migrants in Sub-Saharan Africa by 2099. For India, Dallmann and Millock (2017) find that an increase in the frequency of droughts leads to an increase in the bilateral inter-state migration rate of 1.5% on average, and by 1.7% in agricultural states. Applying these estimates to past migrant flows over 5 years, they find 11.96 million additional migrants due to drought, or a yearly mean of 2.4 million displaced by drought alone from 1996 to 2001. For comparison, the IDMC states that 3.7 million people were displaced due to natural disasters in India in 2015 alone.

International studies give estimates of the changes in current migration rates that may be expected from increases in temperature. Cai *et al.* (2016) estimate that each 1°C increase in temperature implies a 4.7% increase in out-migration from the top 25% of agricultural countries, whereas Backhaus *et al.* (2015) estimate that a 1°C higher average temperature in the countries of origin is associated with a 3.3% increase in migration flows between a country pair over one year. This estimate is a one-year elasticity and only for countries with a large share of value-added in agriculture. Cattaneo and Peri (2016) separate the response by income status and estimate that each 1% increase in temperature increases international migration rates by 4% in middle-income countries, whereas it decreases emigration rates in poor countries by 16%, ceteris paribus. These numbers imply that the migration rate from middle-income countries would increase from 4.2 to 5%, whereas the migration rate from poor countries would decrease from 1.8 to 0.4%. When assessing these numbers, it is useful to recall that the current migrant stock constitutes 3.5% of the world's population (International Organization for Migration, 2020). Finally, Missirian and Schlenker (2017), who use UNHCR data on asylum demands specifically, project an increase of 28% in asylum applications to the European Union by 2099 (98,000 additional applications) under Representative Concentration Pathway (RCP) scenario 4.5 and by 188% (660,000 more) under RCP 8.5.

Following this overview of some of the estimates of the role of past weather variability and climatic factors in migration and the projected future migration flows, we will devote this chapter to reviewing and discussing a few issues that have not received much attention in the literature so far, and that have not been covered in reviews such as Millock (2015), Berlemann and Steinhardt (2017), or Cattaneo *et al.* (2019). These include general equilibrium effects of migration in destination and source countries, and implications for economic growth, the issue of nonlinearities in response and thresholds, and the links between climate-induced migration and conflict. We start by briefly recalling some of the conclusions that can be drawn based on historical evidence.

2. Historical Evidence

Learning from major climatic events or disasters in the past is one way to assess human mobility responses to climate change. Some studies use historical data from ancient China to better understand human responses to extreme events. Bai and Kung (2011) argue that low rainfall may have induced nomadic tribes from the steppes to invade Han Chinese regions. The nomadic economies relied heavily on rainfall and in normal circumstances their society was sustainable. However, with shocks in rainfall, their economy could be severely hit, leading them to invade China's central planes, the "old" agricultural China. The study of Bai and Kung (2011) covers the period 220 BC till 1839 AD. The main finding is a positive correlation between nomadic invasions and incidence of droughts. Hence, more invasions with more severe droughts. Another historic example concerns the fall of the Roman Empire, which has been argued to be related to the same causes (Brooke, 2014, Harper, 2017). The fall of Rome, from 700,000 people living there in 400 AD to 20,000 a few decades later, has fascinated many historians. Many hypotheses have been proposed to explain this disaster and the further decline of the Roman Empire, but more and more attention is given to natural changes as well as pandemics. Volcanic eruptions made the years 536–545 very cold, and there were also severe droughts that drove the Huns toward the West and South. In addition, there were pandemics, that could relatively easily spread through the network of roads. See also Büntgen *et al.* (2011).

Using population data from pre-industrial Iceland, Turner *et al.* (2012) estimate that adverse climate change reduced steady-state population levels during the 18th and 19th centuries by 10–26% for every 1°C temperature. Boustan *et al.* (2020) gathered centennial data from the USA on disasters and estimated that the effect of a severe disaster entails a 1.5% point increase in the net county migration rate. They find further that these effects differ across disaster categories. On the one hand, floods induce net in-migration, consistent with their early work (Boustan *et al.*, 2012), probably because an infrastructure of levees and storage reservoirs had been developed for floods. On the other hand, wildfires and hurricanes lead to net out-migration, which would be consistent with the lack of protection infrastructure in the form of early warning systems at the time. Less severe disasters have no such effects. Still, these numbers are much smaller than those found for some well-known extreme events, such as the 1927 Great Mississippi flood. The 1927 Mississippi flood followed heavy rainfall and failure of the levee system. The disaster led to large out-migration of black Americans from flooded states to the North, in part because it affected the existing labor structures at plantations but other mechanisms could also have been important. Using county-level data from 1900 to 1970, and individual data from the years around the flood, Hornbeck and Naidu (2014) show that flooded counties experienced more out-migration than non-flooded counties compared to a base year of 1925 or 1920. They also find that in the following decades, landowners in flooded countries use more capital-intensive production methods compared to similar landowners in non-flooded counties. Although this consequence cannot be characterized as a labor-saving technological change, it is evidence of disaster-induced migration having major impacts on the agricultural sector and its production technology. As for general equilibrium effects, which we discuss in the next section, the authors find very small local spillovers of this major flood.

Another more recent example in history comes from analyses of changes in mobility patterns and on-farm adaptation during the American Dust Bowl experienced in the Midwest counties of the USA in the 1930s (Hornbeck, 2012, Long and Siu, 2018). In an analysis of agricultural adaptation in the short and long run to this major event of soil erosion, Hornbeck (2012) found little on-farm adjustment in the form of capital investments. This limited on-farm adaptation may be evidence of important adjustment costs, and of severe credit constraints following the Great Depression, which limited capital investment. Instead, population seems to have been the main margin of adjustment. In an analysis using historic county migration rates from the 1920s up to the 1950s, Long and Siu (2018) decompose the net decrease in population rates to show that it stems mainly from lower in-migration rates into affected counties rather than from higher out-migration rates. They also find marked differences in the destination choices and in the characteristics of the migrants that left the counties affected by the Dust Bowl compared to the migrants who left the same counties before the Dust Bowl. Compared to migrants from the same counties in the decades before the Dust Bowl, the Dust Bowl migrants had children and worked in non-farm occupations. Instead of migrating far away (for example to California), most migrants moved to nearby counties, probably reflecting the relative costs of different moves. This detailed analysis of the historical data thus pokes holes in some of the myths surrounding the typical Dust Bowl migrants and their destinations. It provides relevant evidence of how major extreme events can reshape existing migration patterns in different directions.

3. Climate-Induced Migration and its Effects on the Economy

In this section, we review several general equilibrium models of the relationship between climate change and the economy. General equilibrium models are not widely used in the climate-migration nexus literature. Most models found in the literature are of a partial equilibrium nature, where migration is mainly driven by wage differentials between rural and urban regions, or between low-income and high-income countries and these differentials are taken as given. However, so-called general equilibrium effects can be relevant. The following are some examples. Migration has an impact on the labor market in the region from where migration takes place as well as on the labor market in the region where migrants move to. Also the housing market in both regions or countries can be affected. The same holds for agricultural production in the regions from where people leave. Many more examples exist. Hence, these effects can have feedback on the decisions to migrate, and they should not be neglected if one wants to provide a full picture.

First, we briefly sketch some of the theoretical models that provide additional insight. Then, we mention some applied general equilibrium models and their empirical findings. A broad distinction can be made according to governments being active or inactive in promoting the welfare of their residents.

One of the first papers on migration and transboundary environmental problems was by Hoel and Shapiro (2003). They consider a given number of countries or regions that all emit a pollutant that is uniformly mixing. Production in each region is higher the larger is the population, and production is also increasing in emissions. Preferences are identical across all agents and depend on consumption and (country-specific) damages from aggregate emissions. The model is static in nature. Governments aim to maximize the welfare of their residents, including migrants. Clearly, with fixed populations in the countries, a non-cooperative equilibrium has higher emissions levels than Pareto-efficiency would dictate. However, if there is unrestricted population mobility and if migration is costless, then an equilibrium will entail equal utilities for all agents in all countries. It is shown by Hoel and Shapiro that there exists a Nash equilibrium that is Pareto-efficient, in which the individual governments use environmental policy and transfers. This is a strong result. However, the game can have multiple Nash equilibria, so that coordination is needed to pick the right Nash equilibrium. Moreover, the efficiency result no longer holds if interregional transfers are ruled out. All in all, the study offers an optimistic view on migration and welfare, but only under special conditions. Also, Silva (1997) and Wellisch (1994, 1995, 2000) reason along the same lines.

However, Haavio (2005) argues that optimism is no longer warranted in the presence of migration costs and if dynamics are introduced into the model. These are important and relevant generalizations. In Haavio's model, a country's emissions are proportional to consumption with factor of proportionality equal to unity. The consumer good is produced by environmental commodities only. Individual welfare depends on per capita consumption and local environmental quality, which is decreasing in the pollution stock (since our focus is on climate change, we assume here that the pollution stock is global and we will call it CO_2). The atmospheric CO_2 stock decays at a constant rate. Migration is costly. The cost of migrating from one country to another depends on the number of people who are also leaving the (origin) country and on the number of people entering the (destination) country. The last part of this cost captures the fact that the new labor market cannot immediately absorb all supply, whereas the first part may be motivated by, e.g., the fact that selling a house that is left behind is more difficult when more people leave. Governments maximize social welfare of their residents, and they do so at all instants of time, given the state of the economy. With perfect (=costless) mobility, the Nash equilibrium produces a social optimum, as before. But, with constant re-optimizing, based on the current state, and with costly migration, there is too much pollution in the steady state, even more than without migration. With perfect commitment, imperfect mobility is better than perfect mobility. These results are important, also because they show that thinking in general equilibrium terms may shed new light on issues like migration.

The work by Mason (2017) adds several interesting insights to this literature. In his model, local governments only care about the welfare of their "own" citizens (hence not about the welfare of the migrants). The North is emitting CO_2, the South is not. Most damages from emissions are suffered by the South. The difference, if large enough to compensate for the migration cost, may induce Southern citizens to move to the North. A special feature of the model is that immigration may not be appreciated by the more industrialized country. In this setting, it is shown that the Northern government has an incentive to set a policy to reduce CO_2 emissions, and hence damages in the South. Hence, this presents another example where the option of migration may give rise to a climate policy that turns out to be beneficial, in this case because of a crowding externality that creates a disutility for the population in the North and that is the driving force for climate policy. Interestingly, such policy trade-offs have been tested in economic experiments by Marotzke *et al.* (2020), who find that wealthy subjects in the experiment may want to limit migration by increasing their mitigation efforts (see also Kline, 2020).

Another general equilibrium approach couples migration to the New Economic Geography (see e.g., Fujita *et al.*, 2001). This issue has been largely ignored. To our knowledge, Eppink and Withagen (2009) were the first to use such an approach to the environment. Although their article does not directly address climate change, it can be reinterpreted in that way. They assume perfect costless migration, where migration is steered by individual welfare considerations. In each country, there is agricultural production by means of a fixed amount of unskilled immobile labor. Also land available for agriculture is given. Industrial production requires skilled labor and land which competes with land, e.g., afforestation (biodiversity in the paper). The central idea is that more domestic industrial production may lead to positive agglomeration effects, but it also leads to less land for combating climate change. Industrial production is made up of a large number of varieties. This set-up leads to new views on the equilibrium in the two countries. One conclusion is that a Nash equilibrium may be the first-best. However, as we have seen before, here too multiple Nash equilibria exist. The analysis leads to the conclusion that mobility and environmental welfare considerations can drastically alter the general equilibrium characteristics.

Marchiori and Schumacher (2011) develop a two-country (North and South) general equilibrium model to explain international migration. The novelty of their model concerns overlapping generations, but most of their results only hold in the long-run steady-state. In each country, there is a representative firm using capital and labor in a

Cobb–Douglas production function. Total factor productivity (TFP) is constant in the North, whereas in the South, TFP decreases with higher temperatures above some threshold (see also the threshold models in the following section). The production elasticities of capital and labor are identical across countries. Preferences are log-linear in present and future consumption, where future utility is discounted by a common rate of time preference. We omit for the time being the distinction between countries. The analysis is restricted to the steady state so that initial endowments do not count. Utility maximization given lifetime income yields demand for consumption when young and demand for consumption when old. Suppose in the steady state, a certain fraction of the agents live and are employed in the South and the others live in the North. Some of the residents in the North are migrants. Upon migration, when they were young, they had to bear a cost which constituted a fraction of their (labor) income. Since we are in the steady state, no new migrants enter. If capital is immobile, then for the North as well as for the South, we have that total savings must equal available capital. Moreover, the interest rate follows from the optimal input of capital. It follows that the interest rates are the same in the North and South. If capital is mobile, then of course the same holds. This yields as an equilibrium condition that marginal products of capital are equal across both regions. In a steady state, a Southern resident must be indifferent between staying in the South and moving to the North. A couple of assumptions are made: TFP in the South is decreasing in temperature and initially TFP is larger in the North. Moreover, initially, the South is more populated than the North. The main conclusion is that climate change, if substantial enough to trigger migration, leads to migration and is detrimental to welfare in the North as well as the South. Because of higher temperature, TFP in the South is getting small, which leads to more migration and more inequality. This is another channel than the channel described by Mason (2017), where immigration *per se* has a negative impact on welfare in the North. In addition, here, each government cares for the welfare of each resident.

A general (spatial) equilibrium is also used as a vehicle in an empirical paper by Oliveira and Pereda (2020) who study internal migration in Brazil. They convincingly show that in practice general equilibrium forces are relevant. They put forward that "ignoring these (general equilibrium) effects leads to overestimation of the overall impact of climate change on internal migration." Let us, therefore, go into the model in some detail. The country has a given number of locations, each with two types of activities: agriculture and non-agriculture. All individuals have identical preferences and they inelastically supply one unit of homogeneous labor. The initial distribution of people over the regions is given. Preferences are Cobb–Douglas and they depend on consumption of the agricultural good and housing with the sum of the elasticities of marginal utility equalling unity. Preferences are exponential in local amenities, consisting of climate and non-climate features, and amenities depending on the sector of employment. Living in a particular location that is not the original location and working in a sector bring along migration costs. Moreover, every agent has a stochastic taste shock that is time-, location-, and sector-dependent. Given these characteristics, one can calculate the probability of an agent in a certain region having a particular occupation to move to another region with, possibly, a different occupation. Production uses only labor and the technology is sector- and region-specific, with a TFP that depends on climate in the region (not for the non-agricultural sector). Then, equilibrium in the housing market is established by demand and supply, where supply is driven by the interest rate. The effect of climate change can be identified and general equilibrium effects through labor and housing markets are shown to be significant and region- and sector-specific shocks. Workers choose the location as well as the type of work. The conclusion is that the Northeast of Brazil, a poor region, will lose population and welfare, whereas the Southeast, that is already more prosperous, will gain in population size and welfare.

Desmet *et al.* (2021) study sea level rise in a spatial general equilibrium world model based on Desmet *et al.* (2018). Agents have preferences over consumption and (local) amenities. They derive income from supplying labor and land. The existing technology allows for technological progress giving rise to agglomeration effects. The model is dynamic and allows for agents to move from one region to another. The existence of a general equilibrium is established. The model is calibrated for the world economy and the effects of (exogenous) sea level rise are investigated. These effects vary widely across the globe. The projected sea level rise will lead to a considerable loss in world GDP. These are upper bound estimates, though, since no adaptation efforts are accounted for in the model. In particular, coastal countries or cities are hit economically: Vietnam, Shanghai, and Hong Kong. Another striking outcome of this general equilibrium model is that the outcomes would be far worse if there were no mobility possible whatsoever, even though migration is costly.

Shayegh (2017) is one of the few papers to account for the fact that demography may be an important endogenous variable in migration decisions. The model describes an economy with overlapping generations. The young generation decides on current consumption and future consumption. Future consumption is related to the number of children each agent decides on and their expected wages. These wages depend on whether the children are skilled or unskilled and on where they are employed: in the home country or abroad, which is an endogenous decision which in turn depends on climate (temperature) and the cost of moving (surprisingly, foreign wages do not play a role). Young households can decide on whether they have a skilled or an unskilled child. The likelihood of migration depends on whether children are skilled or unskilled. Skilled children require more time to educate than unskilled children. Given the model structure, total time to be devoted to children is exogenous. Hence, the household faces a trade-off between many low-skilled children and a few high-skilled children. Production includes agriculture, requiring less-skilled workers, and manufacturing, requiring skilled workers, with the production functions linear in labor and also depending on temperature and exogenous technological progress. Temperature itself is not endogenous. This model cannot be solved analytically, even in the steady state (or a state of steady growth), because it results in a complicated set of differential equations. Simulations with a calibrated model show that there is a strong general equilibrium effect: the possibility of migration decreases fertility, but agents choose to have more skilled children. Skilled children have better opportunities to migrate and will therefore earn more in equilibrium. The author also claims that migration may alleviate negative impacts of climate change. At a minimum, if the channel described in the model operates, income inequalities will be reduced in the country of origin.

Finally, Burzynski *et al.* (2018) develop an overlapping generations model that is in some regards similar to the one studied by Shayegh (2017). There are two generations: children and adults (the retirement period is neglected). A distinction is made between low-skilled and high-skilled adults to account for the fact that their migration probabilities are different. Labor is the only input in production. Each economy has two sectors: agriculture and non-agriculture, producing the same good (contrary to what Shayegh assumes). Changes in relative prices are thus not accounted for in the model. Moreover, each region has two areas (flooded or non-flooded). The size of these areas is endogenous. TFP depends on temperature (exogenous) and the average schooling level of employed workers. There is also a skill bias in technology. The distinction between flooded and non-flooded areas is important, and one of the advantages of this model is its ability to distinguish between forced displacement, following flooding through sea level rise, and voluntary migration driven by economic incentives. Finally, the study advocates more coherent policies when it comes to migration, development, and the environment. The study produces a prediction of voluntary and forced migration of about 200 million people. But the largest part will move internally and only 19% will want to move to OECD countries. These figures are in the interval of the estimates of internal migration by Rigaud *et al.* (2018), and again, they project mainly internal migration rather than mass migration to OECD countries. The main reason behind this result is the existing barriers to migration in high-income countries. The model also accounts for conflict-driven migration and shows that climate-related conflicts are an important channel which can increase future international migration pressures to OECD countries to a large extent, although current migration flows do not reflect it to the same extent.

To conclude, general equilibrium models give more insight. They are also useful in developing testable hypotheses. Moreover, it turns out that general equilibrium effects are prevailing and may be significant. More is to be done. In particular, since most existing general equilibrium models are essentially static in nature, and since migration is essentially a dynamic phenomenon, much work is waiting. This also concerns policy. Migrants have an effect on the destination country, positively or negatively. In both cases, this has an impact on policy. For example, climate policy can account for the migration flow from countries affected by climate change. Also, the functioning of labor markets may require extra attention.

4. Climate-induced Migration and Thresholds

Climate-change-induced migration has been shown to react differently to slow-onset events such as gradual changes in temperature and precipitation, and to sudden-onset events, such as disasters and other extreme events. In the latter case, one typically sees a sudden increase in migration (see e.g., Cattaneo *et al.*, 2019). However, an issue that has received less attention so far is the fact that large parts of the globe could become uninhabitable if recent trends in temperature increases continue, and then mass migration may occur. If the average temperature in the Sahel region reaches above the limit of human life, this would induce involuntary displacement because people are obliged to move for survival. The heatwaves in India and in Pakistan during the summers of 2018 and 2019, with temperatures around 50°C, present another example that reminds us that some regions may become uninhabitable, either because temperatures exceed the limits for health or because drought decreases water supply below subsistence levels. In this section, we will discuss how thresholds are taken into account in the literature, using some empirical examples.

McLeman (2018) surveys the issue of thresholds in climate migration. McLeman makes a distinction between six types of thresholds with, in our interpretation, increasing damages from climate change, summarized as follows: adaptation becomes necessary; adaptation becomes ineffective; substantive changes in land use/livelihood become necessary; *in situ* adaptation fails, migration ensues; migration rates become nonlinear, and, finally, rates cease to be nonlinear. All these thresholds are time-specific and space-specific, but the prevalence of the thresholds applies to many circumstances. McLeman (2018) gives several interesting examples. With a low severity of climate hazard, no adaptation may be necessary and no migration takes place. However, if the severity increases, e.g., more drought and higher temperatures in Canada's Prairie provinces in the 1930s, agricultural activities come under pressure because the crop may fail, so that irrigation becomes necessary. However, drought and high temperatures may be so persistent that irrigation becomes ineffective (Adger *et al.*, 2009). In that case, irrigation is no longer eligible as an adaptation measure and farmers may rely on other measures such as adopting drought-resistant crops. Still, no migration needs to take place. The next threshold becomes relevant in case the climate conditions get so hard that wheat production is no longer possible, whatever measures are taken. In that case, the farmer must look for other means of earning an income, which depends on market conditions, the farmer's skills, *etc.* This is what the third threshold is about: the necessity of finding other types of land use or economic activity. One way to be prepared for and realize such alternatives is to develop resilient systems. This can obviously be very challenging, as illustrated by the case of communities heavily depending on coral reefs (for fishing or tourism), but that can hardly change the conditions under which coral reefs are "productive." The next threshold is the condition under which mass migration takes place. Migration can be permanent or temporary, and it can apply to entire communities or families or just to parts of it, in which case one or two family members leave. McLeman describes the conditions under which migration took place from the Canadian Prairies in the 30s: the collapse in agricultural market prices, the collapse of financial institutions, and lack of off-farm employment. However, this threshold is not absolute, in the sense that now all agents would move. This may be due to a lack of financial means to move. This aspect of migration plays a key role in early work by Stark (1984) and Stark and Bloom (1985), two of the seminal papers of the new economics of migration. It concerns the necessity of being above a certain threshold of income to sustain the cost of migration. Because not all agents move, some nuance is needed here. For example, migration may be seasonal, over short distances (in case of flooding), and temporary. Thus, much depends on the nature of the climate hazard.

We now discuss a few recent studies on migration where thresholds are relevant. The first relevant nonlinearity in existing migration studies is the U-shaped relationship between migration and income.

The study by Bazzi (2017) on Indonesian temporary international migration flows provides detailed evidence of income-related thresholds. He finds that, overall, more out-migration takes place for higher incomes in villages with a larger share of small landowners. These are relatively poor communities. The increase in migration is due to the fact that the real cost of migration becomes smaller. But, migration decreases as there is a positive income shock, due to subsidies on rice, in richer communities. This suggests that there is a critical income level for an increase or a decrease in migration. The trade-off between opportunity cost (the cost of giving up income) and liquidity cost (direct migration cost) explains this difference.

In the specific context of climate-induced migration, Cattaneo and Peri (2016) estimate a reduced form model of how international migration responds to temperature and rainfall. They include 115 countries in the analysis. They start out with the observation that agricultural productivity is inverted U-shaped as a function of temperature (as established inter alia in Schlenker and Roberts, 2009). Therefore, since agriculture is an important source of income and employment in many poor countries, there is likely a nonlinear relationship between income and temperature. The main finding then is that in terms of migration poor countries react differently to temperature change: in poor countries, liquidity constraints will worsen and migration will decrease with higher temperatures. These predictions are confirmed by the empirical analysis.

Cai *et al.* (2016) also study international migration flows, taking into account the bilateral ties between countries, with data from 42 destination countries and 163 origin countries. They find a statistically significant positive relationship between out-migration and temperature, but only in countries that depend heavily on agriculture. A policy implication would be that in order to reduce migration flows, policy should be directed specifically to countries that depend on agriculture.

Recently, Peri and Sasahara (2019) explored the issue further, following up on Cattaneo and Peri (2016). Both studies consider multiple countries. Peri and Sasahara cover the whole world with grids of 0.5×0.5 square degrees. They fit population data, temperature, and precipitation data to each cell for the period 1970–2000 at 10-year intervals. The model employed is in a sense neoclassical in that it exploits differences in (random) productivity and therefore in wages. Moreover, an increase in temperature decreases productivity, mainly in agricultural activities. In order for an individual to migrate, two conditions need to be satisfied. First, her productivity must be high enough so that net earnings after migrating to an urban area are higher than before, including the cost of migration itself. Second, the earnings must be high enough to pay the migration cost out of the previous earnings in the rural area. The authors make a distinction between poor, lower-middle-income, and upper-middle-income countries. The findings extend and confirm earlier results (see also Cattaneo and Peri (2016)) for rural-urban migration. Migration from rural to urban mainly takes place in countries that are at an intermediate level of economic development. The reason is that the rural population in low-income countries lacks the means to migrate, whereas the rural population can afford the cost of migration in higher-income countries. Peri and Sasahara (2019) predict that a large group of people will get trapped in poverty if temperature increases persist.

The other specific feature related to climate-induced migration is nonlinearities in the climatic variables. Depending on the type of weather data that are used, most empirical studies in reduced form test for quadratic terms in temperature and precipitation, or, if daily data are available, by using degree days, that is, counting the number of days with temperature within a certain range, and then creating variables for each range ("bins"). In one major study of permanent (full) household migration between Indonesian provinces over a 15-year period, Bohra-Mishra *et al.* (2014) find a U-shaped relationship between temperature and rainfall on the one hand and permanent migration on the other hand, with the threshold being at about 25°C. For natural disasters, there are either no or relatively small effects on permanent migration. Bohra-Mishra *et al.* (2014) also find that the effect of rainfall is nonlinear. In originally dry circumstances less rainfall increases migration, whereas with wetter initial conditions more rainfall increases migration.

This seems to contradict the presence of migration costs, but given that it is internal migration that is estimated, with relatively low migration costs, the direct effect of temperature may dominate.

Another standard way of accounting for non-linearities is to use a dummy variable to account for extreme temperatures and precipitation or use the quartiles of the distribution of the variables. In this manner, for example, Mueller *et al.* (2014) find that male internal migration in rural Pakistan increases when temperatures are in the fourth quartile only, with no statistically significant effect of other temperature intervals.

In another country study, focusing on internal rural-urban migration in Mexico, Nawrotzki *et al.* (2017) explore nonlinearities and thresholds. They find a non-linear relationship between cumulative exposure to drought and rural-urban migration. For moderate temperature increases (and sufficient rainfall), they find a decrease in migration. It is only when a threshold for temperature is reached that rural-urban migration increases (as in Bohra-Mishra *et al.*, 2014). In another country-level study, focusing on rapid-onset hydrometeorological disasters and emergencies in Costa Rica, Robalino *et al.* (2015) show that less severe disasters have a positive effect on rural migration. Large disasters (in terms of the number of lives lost) decrease rural migration, and may thus actually impede people from migrating. This result is consistent with earlier results on migration following earthquakes (Halliday, 2006) and may indicate that disasters limit households' wealth so much that they can no longer defray the costs of migration.

Earlier works on environmental migration also reflects such non-linearities but less precisely measured. Gray and Bilsborrow (2013) find that large-distance domestic migration is non-monotonic in severity and that only high temperatures drive migration. Few studies have explored the role of income variability itself, though (stemming from increases in climatic variability). Marchiori *et al.* (2015) provide an exception. They find, however, that, for migration between 39 Sub-Saharan countries, it is not significant as a driver for migration. They also find that agricultural dependence interacts with temperature and precipitation to explain international migration.

It would be difficult to assess all thresholds mentioned by McLeman (2018) in one single empirical model. The studies conducted so far and mentioned above, mainly address the income threshold for migration and (strongly related) the non-linear dependence of agriculture on precipitation and temperature.

5. Climate, Migration, and Conflict

The relationship between climate change, migration, and conflicts can be seen from different angles. First, climate change may lead to invasions and, therefore, conflict, for instance, water wars. There exists appealing anecdotal evidence for the link between climate and conflict through migration. The two historic events considered in Section 2, the migration into China and the one into the Roman Empire (Brooke, 2014, Harper, 2017), caused major disruptions as a consequence of climatic changes. Second, climate change may lead to conflicts, without there being a violent invasion. The causal link between climate change, migration, and conflict can occur on smaller scales than international. They can be local or regional, as described in detail by, e.g., Reuveny (2007). We will go into this in due course. In the case, we have in mind here, the conflict is mainly within the country or the region where climate change and its negative effects occur. A third way to look at the link is where the deterioration of environmental circumstances and the subsequent migration give rise to conflicts in countries that receive the displaced persons. One example was already mentioned when we discussed the negative externality caused by immigration in the work by Mason (2017). In this section we will briefly go into all three aspects of the link, acknowledging that some of them are politically sensitive and delicate.

Reuveny (2007) lists a number of reasons for conflicts. He mentions competition for resources, especially in the absence of well-defined property rights. There might also be ethnic tensions. Another driver might be what Reuveny calls distrust: a receiving country might be afraid of penetration and the origin country might think migrants are mistreated. Reuveny also mentions fault lines. For example, migrants and residents may compete over jobs. Finally, he mentions that if the receiving country is poor and migrants cannot be offered acceptable living standards, they may join rebel groups. Reuveny argues that "environmental migration crosses international borders at times and plays a role in conflict."

Reuveny also lists a large number of environmentally induced migrations that led to conflicts. In most cases, the driving environmental forces have to do with water (droughts, floods, and ownership) and concern ethnic conflict, or conflicts between nomads and farmers. Hsiang *et al.* (2013) review 60 quantitative studies and find a strong causal relationship between climate and human conflicts, many of which have to do with migration of groups of people. Salehyan (2014) also stresses the potential importance of the relationship. There exist other studies (e.g., Bhavnani and Lacina (2015) and Salehyan and Gleditsch (2006)) that suggest that the presence of refugees could enhance conflict in the receiving country. This could even be the case if such refugees are not admitted to the country they want to settle in, the argument being that they will end up in a less preferred country where a conflict may arise that can spread to the original country. However, the evidence is mixed.

When testing the hypothesis on international bilateral migration data for 117 countries over the period 1970–2000, Cattaneo and Bosetti (2017) find no significant relationship between climate-induced migrants and civil conflict in the destination countries, however. They use a measure of high-level conflict, accounting for more than 25 deaths, and also find the same results when testing for civil war, but they do not test the possibilities of low-level social conflict. The recent paper by Bosetti *et al.* (2020) tests two hypotheses: (a) whether there are more climate-driven conflicts in countries with low migration propensity, and (b) whether the presence of climate-induced migrants leads to conflict in the destination country. To do so, they use the same long-run data on migration as in Beine and Parsons (2015) and Cattaneo and Peri (2016) over the period 1960–2000, together with the UCDP/PRIO dataset, as in Cattaneo and Bosetti (2017), but here the focus is on low-level conflict. The estimation accounts for endogeneity in the relation by predicting migration using typical gravity equations for climate-induced migration as an instrumental variable. They use a dummy for a low stock of migrants in 1960 to assess the effect of having a lower propensity of migration on the conflict probability in the country of origin. The empirical results indicate that poor countries with a low stock of external migrants in 1960 are more likely to experience climate-driven conflict, compared to other poor countries, an effect that the authors interpret as migration acting as a safety valve. As in Cattaneo and Bosetti (2017), they find no statistically significant effect of inflows of migrants on the probability of conflict in the destination country.

Hence, further research seems necessary here. The findings of such research are important for policymaking as is described by Mason (2017), discussed earlier, and by Prieur and Schumacher (2016). Both contributions stress the fact that climate policy and migration policy should be coupled. Prieur and Schumacher consider two conflicts in their theoretical model. One is the internal conflict arising when refugees are accepted in the region, and one is called external conflict, arising when refugees are not allowed in. They find support in the work by Reuveny (2007) who argues that "environmental migration crosses international borders at times and plays a role in conflict." In order to control the flow of migrants and to contain conflicts, it might then be instrumental to have a climate mitigation policy in place.

Some studies address asylum seeking directly. Abel *et al.* (2019) consider yearly bilateral asylum seeking flows (these are not identical to refugees) between a large group of countries (157) covering the years 2006–2015. They also have climate data (drought conditions) as well as conflict data (battle-related deaths) for many countries. Other variables that play a role include GDP, ethnic polarization measures, level of democratization, distance between country of origin and country of destination (the model is a gravity model), and whether these share a common language. The authors claim that their model in principle allows for a causal interpretation. The main conclusions read as follows: Drought episodes may enhance conflict and consequently out-migration, particularly in a specific period of time, namely, 2010–2012 (Arab spring), in countries with some form of democracy. The authors claim that conflict in such countries may arise from a government not adequately reacting to climate change. There is also another possible link, namely, that immigration may, through the competition over resources, lead to conflict in the receiving regions. Abel *et al.* (2019) argue, however, that the empirical evidence for these narratives is scarce.

We agree that one should be very careful with anecdotal evidence and ad hoc modeling. Current work has started to test hypotheses carefully on real data. More work is definitely to be done. It maybe goes too far to say that adequate climate policies, at least in (semi-) democratic countries may help to avoid conflicts. In addition, high-income countries can effectively do something against forced migration, and its negative consequences, by helping more vulnerable countries with adaptation to climate change or by mitigating their own emissions (although the latter will only work in the long run).

An alternative view is presented by Boas *et al.* (2019). In policy circles it is widely assumed that climate change will be a major driver of mass migration, which needs to be averted because it may lead to aggravating conflicts (UN Security Council). The authors say that predicting large numbers of climate refugees may be a false narrative. Research programs are now developed that should try to contain migration "at the source." There is also a call, e.g., within the EU to strengthen border control. All this can be interpreted as examples of "securitization" policies. The authors argue that a new research agenda should be developed, one that recognizes that there are other reasons for migration than climate change and that migration is part of the general phenomenon of globalization.

6. Implications for Economic Growth

It is widely recognized that poverty and climate change are the two main challenges for policy (Stern, 2016). It is also well known from the literature that rural-urban migration plays a key role in economic growth. Understanding the indirect implications of climate change-induced migration on growth is thus crucial in the context of accelerating climate change.

A well-known conjecture attributed to Thomas Schelling indicates that economic growth may be the best means of adaptation for developing countries (Schelling, 1992). What has been termed the Schelling conjecture has since been questioned, as even poor countries may be relatively better off by investing in small levels of adaptation capital (Millner and Dietz, 2015), although the optimal mix of investment in productive capital and adaptation capital investments depends on the adaptation efficiency and the initial amount of adaptation capital.

As discussed in the review, several mechanisms explain the economic effects of climate change: conflicts, rural-urban migration, and food security. These may spur migration, but climate-induced migration will in its turn have consequences for the possibilities for economic growth and human development. Despite measurement problems, the empirical evidence attests to a lower productivity of workers employed in the agricultural sector compared to the non-agricultural sector (Gollin *et al.*, 2014). If we add to this that capital is unequally allocated geographically between rural areas and urban areas, especially in developing countries, it implies that climate change will affect growth not only directly but also through the indirect channel of internal and international migration. In the past, lower rainfall tended to increase urbanization, in particular in Sub-Saharan Africa (Barrios *et al.*, 2006). Henderson *et al.* (2017) show that the attraction of urban areas for climate-induced migrants depends on the capital structure and possibilities of manufacturing jobs to substitute for lost productivity in agriculture. In areas with manufacturing, rural-urban migration increases following increases in temperature, whereas such migration decreases in urban areas that are essentially agricultural market towns, which also suffer the direct impact of the shock to agriculture. Recent work building on this literature shows that higher temperatures may reduce the possibilities of sectoral reallocation through rural-urban migration. On long-term data over six decades from India, Liu *et al.* (2020) show that higher temperatures reduce rural-urban migration, and that this effect is not present in rural areas with dense road networks. The authors argue that the evidence, in the long run, would imply that such possibilities of sectoral reallocation by geographic mobility are limited unless policy measures reduce the potential barriers to rural-urban migration by, for example, strengthening transport networks. Without such policy measures, climate change would only reinforce the role of barriers to sectoral re-allocation that occurs spatially. Poor countries that are also more vulnerable to climate change because of their geographic location may thus be susceptible to indirect effects leading to poverty traps.

7. Conclusion

This review has pointed to some of the areas of recent research which are relevant for the policy discussion around climate-induced migration. In a world where climate-induced migration is increasingly becoming a political topic of security concern, it is important to replace the discussion in the larger context of the new economics of migration. Such migration shares the same characteristics as other forms of migration in involving trade-offs in expected improvements in living conditions compared to relative costs of mobility according to distance. Hence, natural responses may include sheltering in place, for the very poor, and short-distance internal migration, sometimes of a temporary nature. Climate-induced migration has some novel features though, that include nonlinear effects from increases in temperature and changes in precipitation patterns. We have reviewed some examples of how such threshold effects have been taken into account in recent analyses.

Whereas the link between climate change-induced conflicts and migration is still a matter of intense scientific debate, we have reviewed some of the recent work on this topic. It is surely one of the mechanisms between climate change and migration that will develop further over time.

Another issue that is largely absent from the literature is the existence of tipping points which make some areas uninhabitable. The current literature incorporates nonlinear responses to climatic variables, which establish thresholds (in terms of temperature, for example) for migration of some groups of individuals, but not really the existence of tipping points where entire geographic areas become uninhabitable. Current work on sea level rise and mobility captures this phenomenon to some extent, but more modeling of this issue would be useful. This is one of the future risks that could change current predictions and lead to mass migration.

Acknowledgments

We thank Ingmar Schumacher and an anonymous reviewer for their helpful comments.

References

Abel, G., Brottrager, M. J., and Muttarak, R. (2019). Climate, conflict and forced migration. *Global Environmental Change*, 54, 239–249.

Adger, W., Lorenzini, I., and O'Brien, K. (2009). Adaptation now, in Adger, W., Lorenzoni, I., and O'Brien, K. (eds), *Adapting to Climate Change: Thresholds, Values, Governance*, Cambridge University Press, Cambridge, pp. 1–22.

Backhaus, A., Martinez-Zarzoso, I., and Muris, C. (2015). Do climate variations explain bilateral migration? A gravity analysis. *IZA Journal of Migration*, 4(3), 1–15.

Bai, Y., and Kung, J. (2011). Climate shocks and sino-nomadic conflict. *Review of Economics and Statistics*, 93, 970–981.

Barrios, S., Bertinelli, L., and Strobl, E. (2006). Climatic change and rural-urban migration: The case of Sub-Saharan Africa. *Journal of Urban Economics*, 60, 357–371.

Bazzi, S. (2017). Wealth heterogeneity and the income elasticity of migration. *American Economic Journal: Applied Economics*, 9, 219–255.

Beine, M. and Parsons, Ch. (2015). Climatic factors as determinants of international migration. *Scandinavian Journal of Economics*, 117, 723–767.

Berlemann, M. and Steinhardt, M. (2017). Climate change, natural disasters and migration — A survey of the empirical evidence. *CESIfo Economic Studies*, 63, 353–385.

Bhavnani, R. and Lacina, B. (2015). The effects of weather-induced migration on sons of the soil riots in India. *World Politics*, 67, 760–794.

Black, R., Bennett, S., Thomas, S., and Reddington, J. (2011). Migration as adaptation. *Nature*, 478, 447–449.

Boas, I., Farbotko, C. Adams, H., Sterly, H., Bush, S., Geest, van der, K.,Wiegel, H., Ashraf, H., Baldwin, A., Bettini, G., Blondin, S., Bruijn, de M., Durand-Delacre, D., Frohlich, C., Gioli, G., Guaita, L., Hut, E., Jarawura, F., Lamers, M., Lietaer, S, Nash, S., Piguet, E., Rothe, D.,

Sakdapolrak, P., Smith, L., Furlong, B., Turhan, E., Warner, J., Zickgraf, C., Black, R., and Hulme, M. (2019). Climate migration myths. *Nature Climate Change*, 9, 901–903.

Bohra-Mishra, P., Oppenheimer, M., and Hsiang S. (2014). Nonlinear permanent migration response to climatic variations but minimal response to disasters. *Proceedings of the National Academy of Sciences*, 111, 9780–9785.

Bosetti, V., Cattaneo, C., and Peri, G. (2020). Should they stay or should they go? Climate migrants and local conflicts, forthcoming in *Journal of Economic Geography*, doi:10.1093/jeg/lbaa002.

Boustan, L., Kahn, M., and Rhode, P. (2012). Moving to higher ground: Migration response to natural disasters in the early twentieth century. *American Economic Review*, 102, 238–244.

Boustan, L., Kahn, M., Rhode, P., and Yanguas, M. (2020). The effect of natural disasters on economic activity in US counties: A century of data. *NBER Working Paper 23410.*

Brooke, J. (2014), *Climate Change and the Course of Global History: A Rough Journey*, Cambridge University Press, Cambridge.

Büntgen, U., Tegel, W., Nicolussi, K., McCormick, M., Frank, D., Trouet, V., Kaplan, J., Herzig, F., Heussner, K., Wanner, H., Luterbacher, J., and Esper, J. (2011). 2500 years of European climate variability and human susceptibility. *Science*, 331, 578–582.

Burzynski, M., Deuster, C., Docquier, F., and Melo, de J. (2018). Climate Change, Inequality and Migration. *Discussion Paper 2019-14* UCL Louvain.

Cai, R., Feng, S., Oppenheimer, M., and Pytlikova, M. (2016). Climate variability and international migration: The importance of the agricultural linkage. *Journal of Environmental Economics and Management*, 79, 135–151.

Cattaneo, C. and Bosetti, V. (2017). Climate-induced international migration and conflicts. *CESIfo Economic Studies*, 63(4), 500–528.

Cattaneo, C. and Peri, G. (2016). The migration response to higher temperatures. *Journal of Development Economics*, 122, 127–146.

Cattaneo, C., Beine, M., Fröhlich, C., Kniveton, D., Martinez-Zarzoso, I., Mastrorillo, M., Millock, K., Piguet, E., and Schraven, B. (2019). Human migration in an era of climate change. *Review of Environmental Economics and Policy*, 13, 189–206.

Dallmann, I. and Millock, K. (2017). Climate variability and inter-state migration in India. *CESIfo Economic Studies*, 63(4), 560–594.

Desmet, K., Nagy, D., and Rossi-Hansberg, E. (2018). The geography of development. *Journal of Political Economy*, 126, 903–983.

Desmet, K., Kopp, R., Kulp, S., Nagy, D., Oppenheimer, M., Rossi-Hansberg, E., and Strauss, B. (2021). Evaluating the economic cost of flooding. *American Economic Journal: Macroeconomics*, 13(2), 444–486.

Eppink, F. and Withagen, C. (2009). Spatial patterns of biodiversity conservation in a multiregional general equilibrium model. *Resource and Energy Economics*, 31, 75–88.

Findley, S. (1994). Does drought increase migration? A study of migration from rural Mali during the 1983–1985 drought. *International Migration Review*, 28, 539–553.

Fujita, M, Krugman, P., and Venables, A. (2001), *The Spatial City: Cities, Regions and International Trade*, The MIT Press, Cambridge.

Gollin, D., Lagakos, D., and Waugh, M. (2014). The agricultural productivity gap. *Quarterly Journal of Economics*, 129(2), 939–993.

Gray, C. and Bilsborrow, R. (2013). Environmental influences on human migration in rural Ecuador. *Demography*, 50, 1217–1241.

Haavio, M. (2005). Transboundary pollution and household mobility: Are they equivalent? *Journal of Environmental Economics and Management*, 50, 252–275.

Halliday, T. (2006). Migration, risk, and liquidity constraints in El Salvador. *Economic Development and Cultural Change*, 54, 893–925.

Harper, K. (2017), *The Fate of Rome, Climate, Disease, and the End of an Empire*, Princeton University Press, Princeton.

Henderson, V., Storeygard, A., and Deichmann, U. (2017). Has climate change driven urbanization in Africa?. *Journal of Development Economics*, 124, 60–82.

Hoel, M. and Shapiro, P. (2003). Population mobility and transboundary environmental problems. *Journal of Public Economics*, 87, 1013–1024.

Hornbeck, R. (2012). The enduring impact of the American dust bowl: Short and long-run adjustments to environmental catastrophe. *American Economic Review*, 102, 1477–1507.

Hornbeck, R. and Naidu, S. (2014). When the levee breaks: Black migration and economic development in the American South. *American Economic Review*, 104(3), 963–990.

Hsiang, S., Burke, M., and Miguel, E. (2013). Quantifying the influence of climate on human conflict. *Science*, 341, 1235367.

Hugo, G. (1996). Environmental concerns and international migration. *International Migration Review*, 30, pp. 105–131.

Internal Displacement Monitoring Centre. (2020). Global report on internal displacement 2020. *Report.* Geneva, Switzerland: IDMC.

International Organization for Migration (2020). World migration Report 2020. *Report.* Geneva, Switzerland: IOM.

Kline, R. (2020). Where mitigation and migration meet. *Nature Climate Change*, 10, 493–494.

Liu, M., Shamdasani, Y., and Taraz, V. (2020). Climate change, structural transformation, and infrastructure: Evidence from India, *Preprint.*

Long, J. and Siu, H. (2018). Refugees from dust and shrinking land: Tracking the dust bowl migrants. *The Journal of Economic History*, 78, 1001–1033.

Marchiori, L., and Schumacher, I. (2011). When nature rebels: International migration, climate change and inequality. *Journal of Population Economics*, 24, 569–600.

Marchiori, L., Maystadt, J.-F., and Schumacher, I. (2012). The impact of weather anomalies on migration in sub-Saharan Africa. *Journal of Environmental Economics and Management*, 63, 355–374.

Marchiori, L., Maystadt, J-F., and Schumacher, I. (2015). Is environmentally induced income variability a driver of human migration? *Migration and Development*, 6, 33–59.

Marotzke, J., Semmann, D., and Milinski, M. (2020). The economic interaction between climate change mitigation, climate migration and poverty. *Nature Climate Change*, 10, 518–525.

Mason, C. (2017). Climate change and migration: A dynamic model. *CESifo Economic Studies*, 63, 421–444,

McLeman, R. (2018). Thresholds in climate migration. *Population and Environment*, 39, 319–338.

Millner, A. and Dietz, S. (2015). Adaptation to climate change and economic growth in developing countries. *Environment and Development Economics*, 20, 380–406.

Millock, K. (2015). Migration and environment. *Annual Review of Resource Economics*, 7, 35–60.

Missirian, A. and Schlenker, W. (2017). Asylum applications respond to temperature fluctuations. *Science*, 358, 1610–1614.

Mueller, V., Gray, C., and Kosec, K. (2014). Heat stress increases long-term human migration in rural Pakistan. *Nature Climate Change*, 4, 182–185.

Nawrotzki, R., De Waard, J., Bakhtsiyarava, M., and Trang Ha, J. (2017). Climate shocks and rural-urban migration in Mexico: Exploring nonlinearities and thresholds. *Climatic Change*, 140, 243–258.

Oliveira, J. and Pereda, P. (2020). The impact of climate change on internal migration in Brazil. *Journal of Environmental Economics and Management*, 103, 102340.

Perch-Nielsen, S., Bättig, M., and Imboden, D. (2008). Exploring the link between climate change and migration. *Climatic Change*, 91, 375–393.

Peri, G. and Sasahara, A. (2019). The impact of global warming on rural-urban migrations: Evidence from global big data. NBER Working Paper 25728.

Prieur, F. and Schumacher, I. (2016). The role of conflict for optimal climate and immigration policy. *Toulouse School of Economics*, Working Paper TSE 663.

Reuveny, R. (2007). Climate change-induced migration and violent conflict. *Political Geography*, 26, 656–673.

Rigaud, K., de Sherbinin, A., Jones, B., Bergmann, J., Clement, V., Ober, K., Schewe, S., Adamo, S., McCusker, B., Heuser, S., and Midgley, A. (2018), *Groundswell: Preparing for Internal Climate Migration*, World Bank, Washington, DC.

Robalino, J., Jimenez, J., and Chacón, A. (2015). The effect of hydro-meteorological emergencies on internal migration. *World Development*, 67, 438–448.

Salehyan, I. (2014). Climate change and conflict: Making sense of disparate findings. *Political Geography*, 43, 1–5.

Salehyan, I. and Gleditsch, K. (2006). Refugees and the spread of civil war. *International Organization*, 60, 335–366.

Schelling, Th. (1992). Some economics of global warming. *American Economic Review*, 82, 1–14.

Schlenker, W. and Roberts, M. (2009). Nonlinear temperature effects indicate severe damages to U.S. crop yields under climate change. *Proceedings of the National Academy of Sciences*, 106, 15594–15598.

Shayegh, S. (2017). Outward migration may alter population dynamics and income inequality. *Nature Climate Change*, 7, 828–832.

Silva, E. (1997). Decentralized and efficient control of transboundary pollution in federal systems. *Journal of Environmental Economics and Management*, 32, 95–108.

Stark, O. (1984). Rural-to-urban migration in LDCs: A relative deprivation approach. *Economic Development and Cultural Change*, 32, 475–486.

Stark, O. and Bloom, D. (1985). The new economics of labor migration. *American Economic Review*, 75, 173–178.

Stern, N. (2016). Current climate models are grossly misleading. *Nature*, 530, 407–409.

Stern, N., Peters, S., Bakhshi, V., Bowen, A., Cameron, C., Catovsky, S., and Crane, D. (2006). *Stern Review: The Economics of Climate Change*, Cambridge University Press, Cambridge.

Turner, M. A., Rosenthal, J. S., Chen, J., and Hao, C. (2012). Adaptation and to climate change in preindustrial Iceland. *American Economic Review Papers and Proceedings*, 102(3), 250–255.

Wellisch, D. (1994). Interregional spillovers in the presence of perfect and imperfect household mobility. *Journal of Public Economics*, 55, 167–184.

Wellisch, D. (1995). Can household mobility solve basic environmental problems?. *International Tax and Public Finance*, 2, 245–260.

Wellisch, D. (2000), *Theory of Public Finance in a Federal State*, Cambridge University Press, Cambridge, UK.

Further Reading

Baez, J., Caruso, G., Mueller, V., and Nui, C. (2017). Heat exposure and youth migration in Central America and the Caribbean. *American Economic Review Papers and Proceedings*, 107(5), 446–450.

Benonnier, T., Millock, K., and Taraz, V. (2019). Climate change, migration, and irrigation. Paris School of Economics Working Paper 2019-21.

Black, R., Adger, W., Arnell, N., Dercon, S., Geddes, A., and Thomas, D. (2011). The effect of environmental change on human migration. *Global Environmental Change*, 21, S3–S11.

Bohra-Mishra, P., Oppenheimer, M., Cai, R., Feng, S., and Licker, R. (2017). Climate variability and migration in the Philippines. *Population and Environment* 38, 286–308.

Colmer, J. (2020). Temperature, labour reallocation, and industrial production: Evidence from India. forthcoming in *American Economic Journal: Applied Economics*.

Dell, M., Jones, B., and Olken, B. A. (2009). Temperature and income: Reconciling new cross-sectional and panel estimates. *American Economic Review*, 99, 198–204.

Dell, M., Jones, B., and Olken, B. (2012). Temperature shocks and economic growth: Evidence from the last half century. *American Economic Journal: Macroeconomics*, 4, 66–95.

Dillon, A, Mueller, V., and Salau, S (2011). Migratory responses to agricultural risk in northern Nigeria. *American Journal of Agricultural Economics*, 93, 1048–1061.

Drabo, A., and Mbaye, L. (2015). Natural disasters, migration and education: An empirical analysis in developing countries. *Environment and Development Economics*, 16, 767–796.

Feng, S., Krueger, A., and Oppenheimer, M. (2010). Linkages among climate change, crop yields and Mexico-US cross-border migration. *Proceedings of the National Academy of Sciences*, 107, 14257–14262.

Gray, C. and Mueller V.(2012a). Drought and population mobility in rural Ethiopia. *World Development*, 40, 134–145.

Gray, C. and Mueller, V. (2012b). Natural disasters and population mobility in Bangladesh. *Proceedings of the National Academy of Sciences*, 109, 6000–6005.

Gray, C. and Wise, E. (2016). Country-specific effects of climate variability on human migration. *Climatic Change*, 135, 555–568.

Herrendorf, B. and Schoellman, T. (2018). Wages, human capital and barriers to structural transformation. *American Economic Journal: Macroeconomics*, 10, 1–23.

Henry, S., Schoumaker, B., and Beauchemin, C. (2004). The impact of rainfall on the first out-migration: A multi-level event-history analysis the impact of rainfall on the first out-migration: A multi-level event-history analysis in Burkina Faso. *Population and Environment*, 25, 423–460.

Hirvonen, K. (2016). Temperature changes, household consumption, and internal migration: evidence from Tanzania. *American Journal of Agricultural Economics*, 98, 1230–1249.

Hunter, L., Murray, S., and Riosmena, F. (2013). Rainfall patterns and U.S. migration from rural Mexico. *International Migration Review*, 47, 874–909.

Kaczan, D. and Orgill-Meyer, J. (2020). The impact of climate change on migration: A synthesis of recent empirical insights. *Climatic Change*, 158, 281–300.

Kleemans, M. (2015). Migration choice under risk and liquidity constraints. *Working Paper*, University of Illinois, Urbana-Champaign.

Koubi, V., Stoll, S., and Spilker, G. (2016). Perceptions of environmental change and migration decisions. *Climatic Change*, 138, 439–451.

Mastrorillo, M., Licker, R., Bohra-Mishra, P., Fagiolo, G., Estes, L., and Oppenheimer, M. (2016). The influence of climate variability on internal migration flows in South Africa. *Global Environmental Change*, 39, 155–169.

Miguel, E., and Satyanath, S. (2011). Re-examining economic shocks and civil conflict. *American Economic Journal: Applied Economics*, 3, 228–232.

Miguel, E., Satyanath, S., and Sergenti, E. (2004). Economic shocks and civil conflict: An instrumental variables approach. *Journal of Political Economy*, 112, 725–753.

Munshi, K. (2003). Networks in the modern economy: Mexican migrants in the U.S. labor market. *The Quarterly Journal of Economics*, 118, 549–599.

Munshi, K. and Rosenzweig, M. (2016). Networks and misallocation: Insurance, migration and the rural-urban wage gap. *American Economic Review*, 106, 46–98.

Naudé, W. (2010). The determinants of migration from sub-Saharan African countries. *Journal of African Economies*, 19, 330–356.

Nawrotzki, R. and DeWaard, J. (2016). Climate shocks and the timing of migration from Mexico. *Population and Environment*, 38, 72–100.

Nawrotzki, R. Riosmena, F., and Hunter L. (2013). Do rainfall deficits predict U.S.-bound migration from rural Mexico? Evidence from the Mexican census. *Population Research and Policy Review*, 32, 129–158.

Neumann, B., Vafeidis, A., Zimmermann, J., and Nicholls, R. (2015). Future coastal population growth and exposure to sea-level rise and coastal flooding — a global assessment. *PLoS One*, 10, e0118571.

Rosenzweig, M. and Stark, O. (1989). Consumption smoothing, migration, and marriage: Evidence from rural India. *Journal of Political Economy*, 97, 905–926.

Saldaña-Zorrilla, S. and Sandberg, K. (2009). Impact of climate-related disasters on human migration in Mexico: A spatial model. *Climatic Change*, 96, 97–118.

Stapleton, S., Nadin, R., Watson, C., and Kellett, J. (2017). Climate change, migration, and displacement: The need for a risk-informed and coherent approach. *Overseas Development Institute and United Nations Development Programme*, New York.

Suhrke, A. (1993). *Pressure Points. Environmental Degradation, Migration and Conflict*, Academy of Arts and Sciences, Cambridge.

Withagen, C. (2014). The climate change, migration and conflict nexus. *Environment and Development Economics*, 19, 324–327.

PART 3

HOW CLIMATE POLICY CAN BE DESIGNED TO AID DEVELOPMENT?

https://doi.org/10.1142/9789811240553_0011

Chapter 11

Smart and Sustainable Cities in the MENA Countries: Combining Sustainable Growth and Climate Adaption?

Jan Friesen[*,‡,§] **and Marc Ringel**[†,‡,¶]

[*]Department of Catchment Hydrology, Helmholtz Centre for Environmental Research GmbH — UFZ, Permoserstraße 15, 04318 Leipzig, Germany

[†]Nuertingen Geislingen University and Vrije Universiteit Brussels, Parktstr. 4, 73312 Geislingen, Germany

[‡]Arab-German Young Academy of Sciences and Humanities (AGYA), Berlin-Brandenburg Academy of Sciences and Humanities, Berlin, Germany

[¶]jan.friesen@ufz.de

[‖]marc.ringel@hfwu.de

Cities and urban areas will play an increasing role in mitigating and adapting to global warming. Combining this role with the overall concept of smart city development can lead to solutions that deliver on economic growth and climate protection at the same time. Our contribution aims to analyze the combination of economic, technological, and climate action in smart city projects in the Middle East and North Africa (MENA) region. We focus on five MENA cities and juxtapose these to a comparison group of European cities with the aim to put our assessment results into an international perspective. We apply a staged methodology of analyzing external factors based on the Global Human Settlement (GHS) dataset and on an internal assessment by means of surveys in which representatives of cities responsible for smart city activities were interviewed.

We find that regional context plays a clear role in the design and the governance of many of these projects. Whereas we can identify some interplay between the contextual factors, we need to stress that these are not one-to-one relationships: Usually, multi-factor causalities prevail. Governance of smart city projects is a pivotal aspect, which deserves further examination.

1. Introduction

Urban spaces will play a leading role for both the use of resources and the options to combat global warming. As the Intergovernmental Panel on Climate Change (IPCC) points out, taking action in urban centers with a high density of population and the concentration of key economic activities will be pivotal for effective adaptation to global climate change (Revi *et al.*, 2014).

At present, some 3.5 billion people live in urban areas (Mauree *et al.*, 2019). Cities and urban agglomerations represent about two third of global energy demand and cause roughly 70% of global greenhouse gas (GHG) emissions (IEA, 2014). 2050 estimates of the United Nations (United Nations DESA, 2018) show a persisting global trend for urbanization. This will lead to over 80% of the European population and over 50% of the Middle East and North Africa (MENA) population living in cities and urban areas. Already now, population pressure and overly high resource consumption have acted as strong drivers for investigating the redesign of city concepts in Europe and the MENA region (Griffiths, 2017, Eurostat, 2019).

In contrast to the high vulnerability of cities and agglomerations, these drivers can act as a point of departure for applying technical and non-technical solutions to address global warming. This enabling function of cities is discussed under the umbrella of "smart and sustainable cities." Perspectives on the transformational potential of cities vary strongly between disciplines and regions.

Interestingly, the MENA region, specifically Masdar City (UAE), has pioneered the real-life application of smart and sustainable cities (Reiche, 2010). Yet, concepts in the fields of resource use (energy, mobility, water), governance, and business models have been largely analyzed in European countries (Allam and Newman, 2018,

Bouzguenda *et al.*, 2019, Desdemoustier *et al.*, 2018, Fraunhofer-Gesellschaft, 2019, Kramers *et al.*, 2014, Mora and Deakin, 2019). Information on smart and sustainable city concepts in the MENA region remains overall scarce (Asif, 2016, Griffiths, 2017, Ramady, 2012, Saxena and Al-Tamini, 2018). Furthermore, most of the present analyses miss out on combining regional context with the "inner workings" of smart city projects: their governance, drivers, and needs within this context, as perceived by decision-makers.

Our present contribution aims to close this gap, based on a staged approach to investigate MENA smart city projects. First, we analyze the external framing conditions for smart city development, based on the Global Human Settlement (GHS) dataset (population, GDP, CO_2 emissions, and others). Second, we contrast these external factors with an analysis of the inner workings of smart city development, based on surveys in which representatives of cities responsible for smart city activities were interviewed. We will focus on five key MENA projects. In order to assess these projects, we will compare them to European smart city projects of five German cities that place their smart city activities in the context of climate policies and in the framework of the European research funding Horizon 2020.

In our contribution, we use the definition of a "smart city" as advanced by the World Bank: This concept defines a smart city as a technology-intensive city that delivers "intelligent" energy and mobility solutions in cooperation with its citizens (Muente-Kunigami and Mulas, 2015). We enlarge this definition with the notion of a "sustainable city." This implies maximizing resource streams and environmental impacts, as well as adapting to global climate change (Toli and Murtagh, 2020).

The remainder of this contribution is organized as follows: In Section 2, we will outline our overall methodology. Section 3 presents the regional context of MENA cities in terms of their regional and socio-demographic features. Section 4 shifts the focus from this external to the internal view. We assess key policy-maker views on the value of smart city projects for climate adaptation and the governance options to bring about these adaptation activities. Section 5 draws conclusions on our analysis.

2. Methodology

In order to contextualize the surveyed cities to urban centers in the whole study region, data from the European Commission's GHS initiative were utilized (Florczyk *et al.*, 2019). The GHS Urban Centre Database (GHS-UCDB v.1.2) compiles a set of multi-temporal attributes for urban centers around the world, such as population, area, gross domestic product (GDP), green spaces, as well as CO_2 emissions for different time steps ranging from 1975 to 2015.

The internal dimension of our review rests on direct stakeholder interviews, which we retrieved based on a semi-structured questionnaire. Our interview grid contained overall 75 items, systemized in several question batteries and took about 60 to 90 minutes to complete. The survey covers the following areas: (i) factors that motivated initiating a smart city project (e.g., adaptation concerns, economic interest, societal pressure); (ii) adaptation and technology choices (e.g., renewable energies, energy efficiency, mobility solutions); and (iii) governance and the importance of key stakeholders (e.g., research institutions, local or central government). Questions were formulated based on existing smart city assessment grids (Nilssen, 2019, Addanki and Venkataraman, 2017, Fraunhofer-Gesellschaft, 2019, Giffinger *et al.*, 2007) to make them comparable to existing studies. They concerned Likert-scale ratings of motivations, options, and governance choices to deliver climate-proof smart cities. We applied even scale rating. Scales ranged from one to six, with one representing the lowest rating and six the highest.

Our sampled population targeted expert stakeholders of MENA smart city projects. Based on government and city website screening as well as contacts via international chambers of trade and commerce, we identified 67 expert stakeholders overall and retrieved feedback from 22 of them. The sampled cities are Cairo (Egypt), Doha (Qatar), Dubai/Ras Al Khaimah (UAE), Kuwait City (Kuwait), and Masdar City/Abu Dhabi (UAE). As a comparison group, we use the average ratings of a set of German cities (Berlin, Bremen, Cologne, Hamburg, and Munich). This choice is motivated by several reasons: First, smart city initiatives in all of these cities have been kick-started by participating in projects run within the European Horizon 2020 research program, which makes these cities exemplary for European smart city development. Second, all cities operate in one jurisdiction, enabling a sharper comparison to the national projects in the MENA region.

The relatively small number of interviewees is explained by the fact that many government interlocutors operate in a hierarchical structure and refer to the "one" responsible person for the project. Still, we made sure to countercheck government positions by systematically including associated research and university representatives to obtain a balanced feedback.

3. Regional Context

According to the GHS-UCDB, the study region comprises 954 urban centers from the 23 MENA countries[1] and Germany ranging from about 50,000 to 20 million inhabitants. Within MENA, we further specify the Gulf Cooperation Council (GCC) countries as a subset as the GCC has substantially different economic and governance settings (Bertelsmann, Stiftung, 2020).

In view of the regional context, Cairo, as a global megacity, is a clear outlier for most parameters (Tables 1 and 2). Despite its size, being situated in a lower GDP region compared to the comparison group (Germany) and to the GCC cities can be clearly seen.

The comparison group indicates the lowest population densities (built-up area per capita). Interestingly, Doha (Qatar), with a similar population density, and the cities of the comparison group are the only cities that indicate declining fossil CO_2 emissions per capita (Tables 1 and 2).

[1]Within this study, we used the following list as MENA countries: Algeria, Bahrain, Comoros, Djibouti, Egypt, Iraq, Jordan, Kuwait, Lebanon, Libya, Mauritania, Morocco, Oman, Palestina, Qatar, Saudi Arabia, Somalia, Sudan, Syria, Tunisia, United Arab Emirates, Western Sahara, and Yemen.

Table 1. City overview of population built-up area per capita, and GDP for 2015.

Cities	Population in metropolitan area in millions	Build-up area per capita [m^2]	GDP per capita [US$ (2007)]
Comparison group[a]	1.67 ± 1.03	173 ± 38	26302 ± 5293
Cairo	19.73	32	7060
Kuwait City	3.17	96	51740
Doha	1.56	163	80750
Dubai	4.91	59	29734
Ras Al Khaimah	0.18	77	25981

Note:[a]The comparison group involves the German cities Berlin, Bremen, Cologne, Hamburg, and Munich.

Table 2. Growth per year [%] for population, average green spaces, and fossil CO_2 emissions.

Cities	Population growth (1975–2015)	Green area change per capita (1990–2014)	Fossil CO_2 emission change (1975–2015) per capita
Comparison group	0.6% ± 0.5	0.4% ± 0.7	−1.3% ± 0.5
Cairo	1.9%	−1.0%	2.7%
Kuwait City	3.3%	−0.3%	1.0%
Doha	6.5%	−4.5%	−2.3%
Dubai	8.2%	−5.3%	0.7%
Ras Al Khaimah	5.0%	−2.1%	2.5%

In order to contextualize the sampled cities, Fig. 1 visualizes all cities with regard to population change (1975–2015) and GDP (2015) in their regional subgroup (GCC, MENA, Germany). In general, it can be seen that the sampled cities represent their regions well, with the exception of Cairo, which, as mentioned earlier, is a regional and global outlier, being a megacity.

Considering the abatement of fossil CO_2 emissions as one driver of smart and sustainable cities (Löbsinger-Kägi *et al.*, 2016), Fig. 2

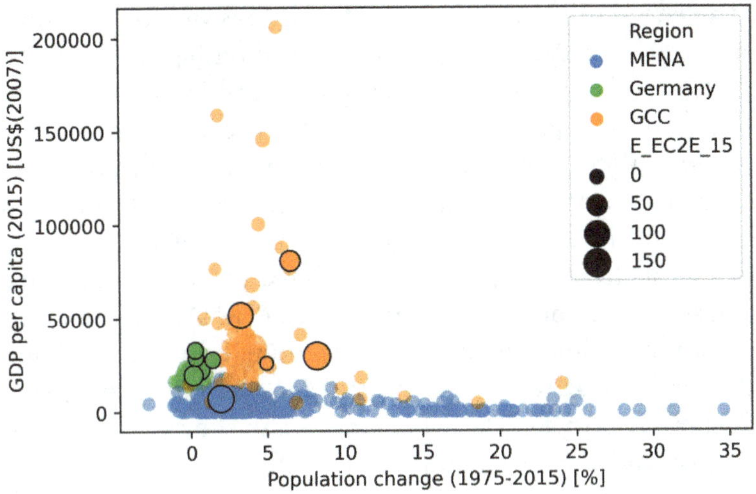

Fig. 1. Population growth (1990–2015) vs. GDP per capita (2015). The bubbles are scaled by total fossil CO_2 emission (2015). E_EC2E_15 are total fossil CO_2 emissions in million tons per annum (MTPA).

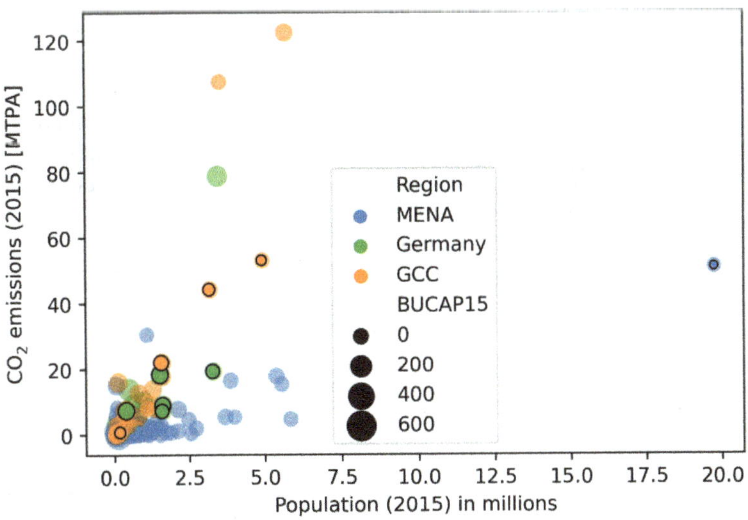

Fig. 2. Population (2015) vs. total fossil CO_2 emission (2015). The bubbles are scaled by built-up area per capita (2015). BUCAP15 is built-up area per capita in m^2.

shows a general increase of fossil CO_2 emissions with population size. Regarding the surveyed focus cities, this relationship is obvious.

Looking at greenness change, being another driver of smart and sustainable cities, both in terms of increased living conditions (Löbsinger-Kägi *et al.*, 2016) as well as a planning option for adaption, taking advantage of the natural cooling or water storage functions (Salmeri, 2014, Govindarajulu, 2014, Anguluri and Narayana, 2014), Fig. 3 shows a clear decrease with population growth, that is also depicted with most cities in the three regions, GCC, MENA, and Germany. At the same time, within the comparison group, only Munich shows a negative green area growth. Despite the trend, all other cities (MENA, GCC) show a green area decline. Figure 3 also shows that regionally a majority of cities seem to follow the same trend.

Considering fossil CO_2 emissions and average greenness as smart and sustainable city motivation, no clear relationship is distinguishable (Fig. 4).

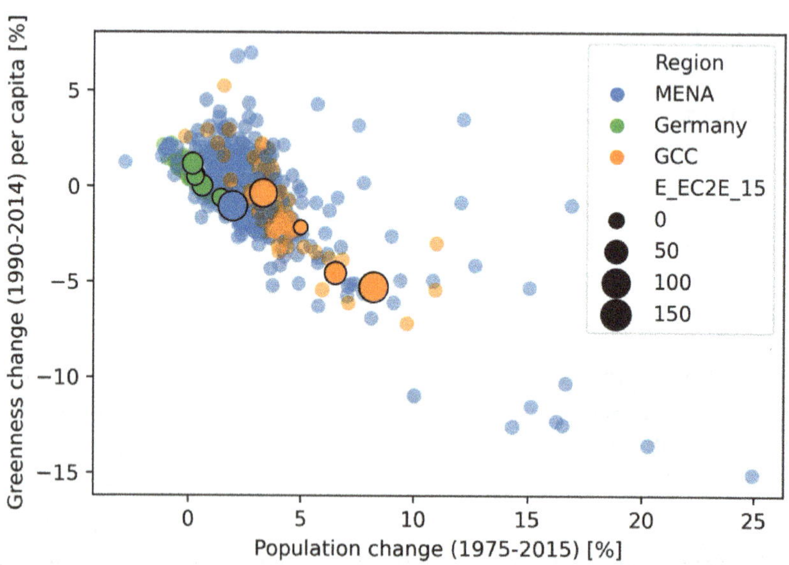

Fig. 3. Population growth (1990–2015) vs. green area growth (1990–2014). The bubbles are scaled by total fossil CO_2 emission (2015). E_EC2E_15 are total fossil CO_2 emissions in million tons per annum (MTPA).

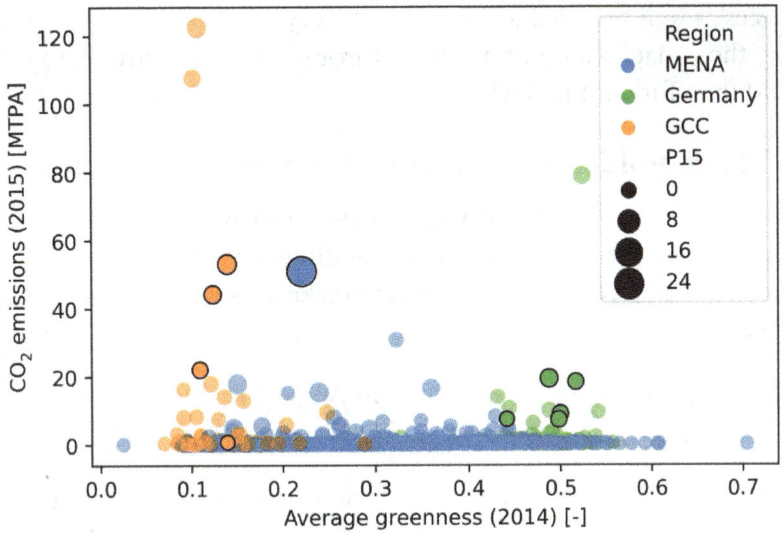

Fig. 4. Green area (2014) vs. CO_2 emissions (2015). The bubbles are scaled by population (2015). P15 is population in millions.

The regional context shows that the sampled cities represent their regions rather well with the exception of yet again Cairo (Fig. 1).

Looking at smart and sustainable city drivers and motivation, fossil CO_2 emissions and average greenness are parameters that are most promising in view of the detailed surveys. Both have also been identified to play a role in smart and sustainable city motivation (Löbsinger-Kägi *et al.*, 2016, Govindarajulu, 2014). For fossil CO_2 emissions (with population) and greenness change (with population change), relationships can be distinguished (cf. Figs. 2 and 3).

In addition, greenness as a proxy for impervious surfaces and green spaces as well as fossil CO_2 emissions as a proxy for air quality are both visible by citizens and provide a clear motivation for political decision-makers to adopt and develop smart and sustainable city measures. Contextualization of the detailed surveys with global databases such as GHS-UCDB therefore allows us to put a limited number of detailed surveys into a regional context. The limitations of such databases are, however, the completeness of these datasets throughout the region. The GHS-UCDB, for example, also includes data on renewable energy sources as well as a distinction of fossil CO_2 emissions by sector; however, those data were not available throughout our study region and could therefore not be included.

4. Stakeholder Assessment of Smart City Projects

Having discussed the contextual factors for adaptation and smart city development, we now turn to our findings concerning the "inner" motivation of city officers and policy-makers to engage in smart city projects.

4.1. *Adaptation as motivator for starting smart city projects*

A literature search renders a multitude of motivations to engage in smart city activities. Overall, authors converge on the fact that information and communication technologies (ICT) can be used to the benefits of citizens (Abellá-García *et al.*, 2015, Joshi *et al.*, 2016), to improve living conditions (Monfaredzadeh and Krueger, 2015), urban management, (Jedliński, 2014), and act as a solution to energy and climate problems (Letnik *et al.*, 2018, Pincetl, 2017, Sicilia *et al.*, 2017).

Based on the literature and on the existing evaluation of studies on smart city developments (see Section 2), we retained five key factors that motivate city planners and policy-makers to engage in smart city activities. These concern the following:

(i) Societal pressure such as growing urban population.
(ii) Economic motivations such as increasing local economic attractiveness and competitiveness of a city and its surrounding region.
(iii) Resource and energy concerns, notably the provision of clean water, safe and clean energy, or adequate treatment of waste in an urban area as well as mobility concerns.
(iv) Adaptation and climate proofing of cities, including the possibility to engage in mitigation activities in parallel to adaption and
(v) Mitigating environmental pollution, such as local air pollutants.

One particularity of the smart city projects that we investigated is the fact that an overwhelming majority of them are greenfield projects — cities or city quarters built from scratch. The underlying

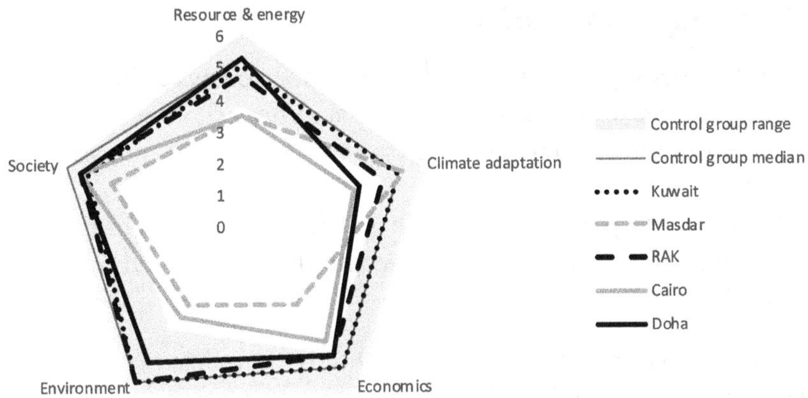

Fig. 5. Motivation to engage in smart city projects.

motivation for the project therefore has a considerably stronger influence on the design output than in European cities where large parts of the infrastructure have to be taken as existing framework conditions.

Figure 5 shows the results of our expert assessments. The internal assessment of city experts and policy-makers confirms the key role of societal pressure to engage in smart city projects. All MENA cities with the slight exception of Abu Dhabi's Masdar City as a pilot sustainable city rate societal drivers (population pressure, growing middle class with the need for decent living) as "very high" (MD = 5.0). Only the comparison group (MD = 6.0) shows higher ratings, but confirms the importance of this driver. Energy and resource concerns somewhat mirror this observation with Doha, Kuwait City, and Ras Al Khaimah (RAK) mirroring the comparison group's high rating (MD around 5.0). Interestingly, the other groups of motivators already show a more diverse picture: Regarding climate adaptation, stakeholders from Kuwait City, Masdar, and the comparison group assess this as a "very important" aspect (MD = 5.0), with RAK closely following. In Doha and notably Cairo, the appreciation of this aspect is somewhat lower ("rather important" or MD around 3). This picture is mirrored concerning the assessment of the economic and environmental aspects, demonstrating clear local disparities between the individual smart city projects.

4.2. *Adaptation options*

Further to investigating the overall motivation to engage in smart city projects, we asked our interviewees to rank the technological options in the energy and mobility fields to bring about climate mitigation and adaptation.

We presented policy-makers with a choice of 15 items in the technology field. These items were subsequently consolidated into three overall groups:

(i) Renewable energies (centralized and de-centralized).
(ii) Energy efficiency (building insulation, consumption reduction).
(iii) Mobility (public transport, smart logistics).

Given that many actors perceive smart cities as applying ICT options to address climate policies, we added two dedicated ICT aspects in this field:

(i) Smart grids, which optimize energy consumption from the supply side of the energy provision chain.
(ii) Prosumers (production and consumption), actively influencing energy provision from the demand side, for example, by off-grid solar installations.

The results of expert assessments of these groups are presented in Fig. 6.

The assessment of experts in the surveyed MENA cities is striking in several ways. First, note the strong alignment of actors on smart grid solutions as very important (MD = 5.0 or higher). This suggests that experts and policy-makers consider ICT solutions as a central aspect for energy provision. As all projects are greenfield projects, which suggests the strong will to engage in best available technologies for the set-up of a new city or city quarter. The interest, however, strongly mirrors the comparison group's interest in supply-side optimization of electricity provision.

Next, stakeholders in MENA cities and the comparison group closely align around the topic of energy efficiency. Whereas the comparison group of cities ranks this item as "very important" (MD = 5.0),

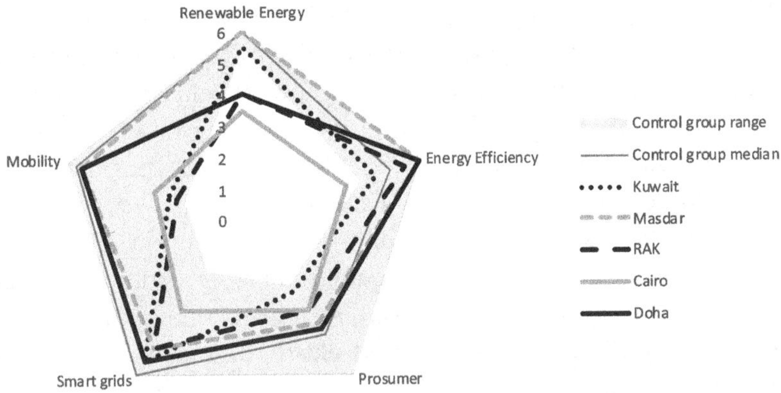

Fig. 6. Energy choices for climate policies in smart cities.

the UAE (RAK, Masdar) and Qatar (Doha) stakeholders see this topic as extremely important (MD = 6.0). The reasons behind this are as follows: First is the key link between saving energy and reducing greenhouse gas emission. Second is the strong interest to reduce domestic energy consumption. For example, Qatar is among the most energy- and carbon-intensive countries in the world (Charfeddine *et al.*, 2018). A similar argument was advanced by Kuwait City's policy-makers and experts (Jaffar *et al.*, 2018, Gelan, 2018, Alotaibi, 2011).

Doha and Masdar also stand out in terms of their assessment of sustainable mobility options such as promoting public transport or electric vehicles. Their assessment of this technology group (MD = 6.0 or "extremely important") is in line with the assessment of the European comparison group. It is also in stark contrast to the other surveyed city projects, where experts assess this aspect as being of only secondary importance.

Turning to the deployment of renewable energies, both for provision of electricity as well as heating and cooling, no clear picture emerges. Renewable energies have been the centerpiece of the Masdar project (Lau, 2012, Masdar Company, 2016, Masdar Institute, 2014, Shelton *et al.*, 2015, Tok *et al.*, 2014) and as such are rated as "extremely important" (MD = 6.0) there, which mirrors our comparison group. Next follows the appreciation of Kuwait City experts

(MD = 5.0 or "very important"), which has been the subject of a dedicated review (Alsayegh *et al.*, 2018). The other cities seem to take a moderate view on the integration of renewable energies into future city projects. Still, it might also be the case that renewable energies are already seen as a "classic" for future city development (Binamer, 2019) and as such do not raise strong enthusiasm any more.

A slightly closer alignment can be witnessed around the option to integrate consumers into energy production via "prosumer" models. Here, a majority of MENA city projects seem to align with the comparison group in rating this option as clearly interesting, but not of central importance.

4.3. *Governance*

A last battery of questions helped us gain insights into governance aspects of smart city development. First and foremost, city planning is a key task of local governments and local authorities. As a particularity with especially MENA countries, a strong national government influence is noted in the literature (Phondani *et al.*, 2016, Sodiq *et al.*, 2019, Ben Letaifa, 2015).

Our surveyed experts mirror these findings (Fig. 7). Concerning local government support, all experts rate this aspect as "extremely important" (MD = 6.0), mirroring yet again the European comparison group. The only noteworthy exception is Masdar City, which followed

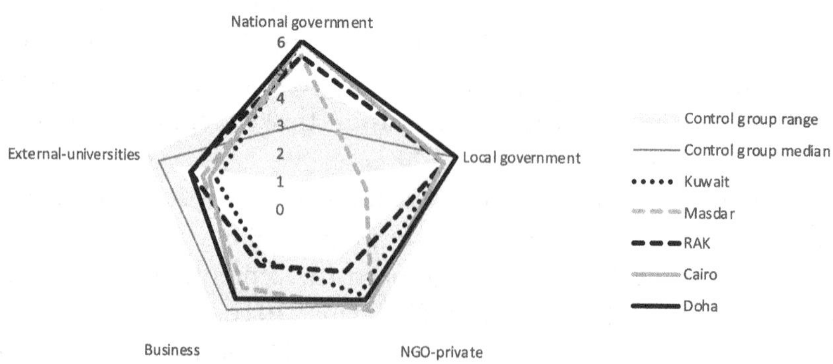

Fig. 7. Importance of actors in smart city development.

national rather than local planning (Wachsmuth and Angelo, 2018, Cugurullo, 2018).

The role of national governments for smart city projects is clearly confirmed. Experts from all surveyed MENA projects rate the importance of central governments as "extremely important" to "very important" (MD = 6.0 or 5.0, respectively). This is in stark contrast to the comparison group: European cities such as the sample of our five German cities tend to regard smart cities mainly as local projects without national government intervention. This difference will need to be taken account of when designing global exchanges on smart city policies.

Business sector and non-governmental organizations seem to hold a somewhat secondary importance in contrast to the public sector actors, albeit with differences between the individual MENA city projects.

Finally, another noteworthy difference shows up when analyzing the assessment of the role of external smart city partners such as universities. In the European comparison group, universities and research institutions play a very strong role in terms of shaping projects (MD = 5.5 or "very important"). As all projects were kick-started as research projects and with European research funding, this rating of EU stakeholders is hardly surprising. In contrast, the assessment of the importance of research institutions in the MENA projects shows that, here, research plays a somewhat subordinate role. One explanation for this could be the fact that often these projects are planned and designed with the support of international consortia (*The Economist*, 2017, PMR, 2019). It follows that they aim to install global best practices rather than advancing and testing research, as seems to be one aim of the European projects (Fraunhofer-Gesellschaft, 2019).

5. Conclusions

Our contribution aimed at analyzing the combination of economic, technological, and climate action in MENA smart city projects. We focused on five key MENA projects and contrasted these to a comparison group of European cities to put our assessment results into an international perspective.

We find that, unsurprisingly, regional context plays a clear role in the design and the governance of many of these projects. Whereas we could identify some interplay between the contextual factors, we need to stress that these are not one-to-one relationships. Rather than finding one explanatory factor for addressing climate policy issues in a city context, usually multi-factor causalities prevail.

The comparison of the surveyed focus cities to cities in the study region was done by using data from the GHS Urban Centre Database. Overall, this allowed a contextualization of the survey cities into the study region. Prominent drivers for smart and sustainable city motivation, such as CO_2 emissions and greenness, show how the link to global databases can be used (a) to show how the survey cities correspond to other cities in the region and (b) given that strong relationships are identified may even allow one to extrapolate detailed survey findings to the regional level.

Our sampling of policy-makers and implementing experts confirmed the focal intention to use the potential of smart city projects for climate proofing, both in terms of mitigation and adaptation. The survey confirmed the importance of overall four key pillars: (i) ICT and smart network infrastructure, (ii) energy efficiency, (iii) renewable energies, and — to a lesser extent — (iv) sustainable mobility. All these fields seem promising options to engage into an international benchmarking and good practice exchange.

Governance at the local and national level is confirmed as pivotal for the success of a smart city project. Regarding national governments and universities, clear differences between the MENA projects and the European comparison group are shown. These differences will have to be kept in mind when engaging in a stakeholder dialogue. Taking into consideration the enormous potential for climate adaptation and decreasing climate vulnerability of cities, this dialogue clearly should be further fostered.

References

Abellá-García, A., Ortiz-de-Urbina-Criado, M., and De-Pablos-Heredero, C. (2015). The ecosystem of services around smart cities: An exploratory analysis. *Procedia Computer Science*, 64, 1075–1080, doi: 10.1016/j.procs.2015.08.554.

Addanki, S. C. and Venkataraman, H. (2017). Greening the economy: A review of urban sustainability measures for developing new cities. *Sustainable Cities and Society*, 32, 1–8, doi: 10.1016/j.scs.2017.03.009.

Allam, Z. and Newman, P. (2018). Redefining the smart city: Culture, metabolism and governance. *Smart Cities*, 1(1), 4–25, doi: 10.3390/smartcities1010002.

Alotaibi, S. (2011). Energy consumption in Kuwait: Prospects and future approaches. *Energy Policy*, 39(2), 637–643, doi: 10.1016/j.enpol.2010.10.036.

Alsayegh, O., Saker, N., and Alqattan, A. (2018). Integrating sustainable energy strategy with the second development plan of Kuwait. *Renewable and Sustainable Energy Reviews*, 82, 3430–3440, doi: 10.1016/j.rser.2017.10.048.

Anguluri, R. and Narayana, P. (2014). Role of green space in urban planning: Outlook towards smart cities. *Urban Forestry & Urban Greening*, 25, 58–65, doi: 10.1016/j.ufug.2017.04.007.

Asif, M. (2016). Growth and sustainability trends in the buildings sector in the GCC region with particular reference to the KSA and UAE. *Renewable and Sustainable Energy Reviews*, 55, 1267–1273, doi: 10.1016/j.rser.2015.05.042.

Ben Letaifa, S. (2015). How to strategize smart cities: Revealing the SMART model. *Journal of Business Research*, 68(7), 1414–1419, doi: 10.1016/j.jbusres.2015.01.024.

Bertelsmann, S. (2020). Bertelsmann Stiftung's Transformation Index (BTI) 2020. Gütersloh: Bertelsmann Stiftung, http://www.bti-project.org.

Binamer, A. O. (2019). Al-Abdaliya integrated solar combined cycle power plant: Case study of Kuwait, part I. *Renewable Energy*, 131, 923–937, doi: 10.1016/j.renene.2018.07.076.

Bouzguenda, I., Alalouch, C., and Fava, N. (2019). Towards smart sustainable cities: A review of the role digital citizen participation could play in advancing social sustainability. *Sustainable Cities and Society*, 50, 101627, doi: 10.1016/j.scs.2019.101627.

Charfeddine, L., Al-Malk, A., and Al Korbi, K. (2018). Is it possible to improve environmental quality without reducing economic growth: Evidence from the Qatar economy. *Renewable and Sustainable Energy Reviews*, 82, 25–39, doi: 10.1016/j.rser.2017.09.001.

Cugurullo, F. (2018). Exposing smart cities and eco-cities: Frankenstein urbanism and the sustainability challenges of the experimental city. *Environment and Planning A*, 50(1), 73–92, doi: 10.1177/0308518X17738535.

Desdemoustier, J., Crutzen, N., and Giffinger, R. (2018). Municipalities' understanding of the Smart City concept: An exploratory analysis in Belgium. *Technological Forecasting and Social Change*, 142, 129–141, doi: 10.1016/j.techfore.2018.10.029.

Eurostat (2019). Greenhouse gas emission statistics — emission inventories. Luxembourg, Eurostat.

Florczyk, A., Corbane, C., Schiavina, M., Pesaresi, M., Maffenini, L., Melchiorri, M., Politis, P., and Sabo, F. (2019). GHS Urban Centre Database 2015, multitemporal and multidimensional attributes, R2019A. European Commission, Joint Research Centre (JRC) [Dataset]. Online verfügbar unter https://data.jrc.ec.europa.eu/dataset/53473144-b88c-44bc-b4a3-4583ed1f547e.

Fraunhofer-Gesellschaft (2019). Morgenstadt — City of the future. Innovation areas. Online verfügbar unter https://www.morgenstadt.de/en.html (abgerufen am 15.07.19).

Gelan, A. U. (2018). Kuwait's energy subsidy reduction: Examining economic and CO_2 emission effects with or without compensation. *Energy Economics*, 71, 186–200, doi: 10.1016/j.eneco.2018.02.014.

Giffinger, R., Fertner, C., Kramar, H., Kalasek, R., Pichler-Milanovic, N., and Meijers, E. (2007). Smart cities – Ranking of European medium-sized cities. Final report. http://www.smart-cities.eu/download/smart_cities_final_report.pdf (accessed 09 July 2021).

Govindarajulu, D. (2014). Urban green space planning for climate adaptation in Indian cities. *Urban Climate*, 10(1), 35–41, doi: 10.1016/j.uclim.2014.09.006

Griffiths, S. (2017). A review and assessment of energy policy in the Middle East and North Africa region. *Energy Policy*, 102, 249–269, doi: 10.1016/j.enpol.2016.12.023.

IEA (2014). *World Energy Outlook 2014*, OECD Publishing, Paris, France.

Jaffar, B., Oreszczyn, T., Raslan, R., and Summerfield, A. (2018). Understanding energy demand in Kuwaiti villas: Findings from a quantitative household survey. *Energy and Buildings*, 165, 379–389, doi: 10.1016/j.enbuild.2018.01.055.

Jedliński, M. (2014). The position of green logistics in sustainable development of a smart green city. *Procedia — Social and Behavioral Sciences*, 151, 102–111, doi: 10.1016/j.sbspro.2014.10.011.

Joshi, S., Saxena, S., Godbole, T., and Shreya (2016). Developing smart cities: An integrated framework, *Procedia Computer Science*, 93, 902–909, doi: 10.1016/j.procs.2016.07.258.

Kramers, A., Höjer, M., Lövehagen, N., and Wangel, J. (2014). Smart sustainable cities — exploring ICT solutions for reduced energy use in cities. *Environmental Modelling & Software*, 56, 52–62, doi: 10.1016/j.envsoft.2013.12.019.

Lau, A. (2012). Masdar City: A model of urban environmental sustainability. *Social Sciences* (09), 77–82. Online verfügbar unter https://ugc.futurelearn.com/uploads/files/a5/9f/a59f7a08-d066-4090-93b2-17d80312d5f2/Masdar_City.pdf (Accessed on January 19, 19).

Letnik, T., Marksel, M., Luppino, G., Bardi, A., and Božičnik, S. (2018). Review of policies and measures for sustainable and energy efficient urban transport. *Energy*, 163, 245–257, doi: 10.1016/j.energy.2018.08.096.

Löbsinger-Kägi, Weiss S. *et al.* (2016). Treiber und Barrieren auf dem Weg zu einer Smart City. Erkenntnisse aus Theorie und Praxis. In: ZHAW School of Management and Law (Hg.). Energy Governance Working Paper, 1–31.

Masdar Company. (2016). A Decade of Delivering. Sustainability Report 2016. *Report.* Online verfügbar unter https://masdar.ae/-/media/corporate/downloads/about-us/masdar-annual-sustainability-reports/sustainability_report_2016.pdf (Accessed on January 19, 19).

Masdar Institute. (2014). Masdar Sustainability Report 2014. *Report.*

Mauree, D., Naboni, E., Coccolo, S., Perera, A. T. D., Nik, V. M., and Scartezzini, J.-L. (2019). A review of assessment methods for the urban environment and its energy sustainability to guarantee climate adaptation of future cities. *Renewable and Sustainable Energy Reviews*, 112, 733–746, doi: 10.1016/j.rser.2019.06.005.

Monfaredzadeh, T. and Krueger, R. (2015). Investigating social factors of sustainability in a smart city. *Procedia Engineering*, 118, 1112–1118, doi: 10.1016/j.proeng.2015.08.452.

Mora, L. and Deakin, M. (2019). Smart city development as an ICT-driven approach to urban sustainability, in *Untangling Smart Cities*, Elsevier, 19–55.

Muente-Kunigami, A. and Mulas, V. (2015). Smart Cities. Online verfügbar unter https://www.worldbank.org/en/topic/digitaldevelopment/brief/smart-cities (Accessed on July 15, 2019).

Nilssen, M. (2019). To the smart city and beyond? Developing a typology of smart urban innovation. *Technological Forecasting and Social Change*, 142, 98–104, doi: 10.1016/j.techfore.2018.07.060.

Phondani, P. C., Bhatt, A., Elsarrag, E., Alhorr, Y. M., and El-Keblawy, A. (2016). Criteria and indicator approach of global sustainability assessment system for sustainable landscaping using native plants in Qatar. *Ecological Indicators*, 69, 381–389, doi: 10.1016/j.ecolind.2016.05.003.

Pincetl, S. (2017). Cities in the age of the Anthropocene: Climate change agents and the potential for mitigation. *Anthropocene*, 20, 74–82, doi: 10.1016/j.ancene.2017.08.001.

PMR — Persistence Market Research Pvt. Ltd. (2019). Global Smart Cities Market. Online verfügbar unter https://www.prnewswire.com/news-releases/global-smart-cities-market-to-reach-us-3482-trillion-by-2026-a pej-to-outpace-north-america-609626355.html (Accessed on July 15, 2019).

Ramady, M. A. (2012). *The GCC Economies*, Springer New York, New York, NY.

Reiche, D. (2010). Renewable energy policies in the Gulf countries: A case study of the carbon-neutral "Masdar City" in Abu Dhabi. *Energy Policy*, 38(1), 378–382, doi: 10.1016/j.enpol.2009.09.028.

Revi, A., Satterthwaite, D., and Aragón-Durand, J. (2014). Climate Change 2014: Impacts, Adaptation, and Vulnerability. Part A: Global and Sectoral Aspects. Contribution of Working Group II to the Fifth Assessment Report of the Intergovernmental Panel on Climate Change. *Report*. Cambridge: Cambridge University Press.

Salmeri, C. (2014). Urban Greening management in the framework of Smart City Development. Conference: 8th Study Day of INU — Policies for Italian Cities At: Napoli Volume: Urbanistica Informazioni 257(3): 158–162, ISSN n. 0392-5005.

Saxena, S. and Al-Tamini, T. (2018). Visioning "smart city" across the Gulf Cooperation Council (GCC) countries. *Foresight*, 20(3), 237–251, doi: 10.1108/FS-11-2017-0068.

Shelton, T., Zook, M., and Wiig, A. (2015). The "actually existing smart city." *Cambridge Journal of Regions, Economy and Society*, 8(1), 13–25, doi: 10.1093/cjres/rsu026.

Sicilia, Á., Madrazo, L., Massetti, M., Plazas, F. L., and Ortet, E. (2017). An energy information system for retrofitting smart urban areas. *Energy Procedia*, 136, 85–90, doi: 10.1016/j.egypro.2017.10.291.

Sodiq, A., Baloch, A. A. B., Khan, S. A., Sezer, N., Mahmoud, S., Jama, M., and Abdelaal, A. (2019). Towards modern sustainable cities: Review of sustainability principles and trends. *Journal of Cleaner Production*, 227, 972–1001, doi: 10.1016/j.jclepro.2019.04.106.

The Economist (2017). Government releases New Kuwait 2035 strategic plan. Online verfügbar unter http://country.eiu.com/article.aspx?articleid=1675084151 (Accessed on July 17, 2019).

Tok, E., Al Mohammed, F., and Al Merrekhi, M. (2014). Crafting smart cities in the Gulf region: A comparison of Masdar and Lusail. *European Scientific Journal*, (Special Issue), 130–140.

Toli, A. M. and Murtagh, N. (2020). The concept of sustainability in smart city definitions. *Frontiers in Built Environment*, 6, 3, https://doi.org/10.3389/fbuil.2020.00077.

United Nations DESA (2018). World Urbanization Prospects 2018. New York, NY, UN.

Wachsmuth, D. and Angelo, H. (2018). Green and gray: New ideologies of nature in urban sustainability policy. *Annals of the American Association of Geographers*, 108(4), 1038–1056, doi: 10.1080/24694452.2017.1417819.

https://doi.org/10.1142/9789811240553_0012

Chapter 12

Negative Emissions in Climate Policy — Scenarios, Governance, and Challenges

Joahnnes Pfeiffer* and Karen Pittel†

IFO Institute – Leibniz Institute for Economic Research at the University of Munich Poschinger Str. 5, 81679 Munich, Germany
**pfeiffer@ifo.de*
†pittel@ifo.de

Negative emissions play an increasingly important role in climate policy scenarios. As a consequence, the scientific literature on carbon removal technologies has been expanding quickly in recent years. This literature focuses, however, predominantly on technical aspects, potentials for deployment, and costs. Still, the level of uncertainty associated with some of these technologies, especially those that go beyond ecosystem-based approaches, remains high. This chapter gives an overview of this literature, but especially addresses questions regarding (a) impacts of negative emissions technologies on sustainable development that go beyond carbon dioxide (CO_2) removal and (b) the design of climate policy frameworks needed to foster the deployment of CDR (especially with respect to net-negative emissions). Despite the attention devoted recently to negative emissions, the latter aspect in particular has so far been often neglected in academic as well as political discussions.

1. Introduction

Negative emissions were, until a short while ago, often dismissed in the public and political debate on climate policy. Thinking of not only reducing emissions but also actually removing carbon dioxide (CO_2)

from the atmosphere in larger quantities was thought to be a rather theoretical exercise that was rooted more in academics than in the real world. At the same time, negative emissions became more and more important for scenarios describing pathways to reach the goals set out in the Paris Climate Agreement. It is by now widely agreed that the implementation of the objectives of the Paris Agreement is likely to depend to some extend on the use of negative emission technologies (NETs). Yet, it was primarily the translation of the Paris goals into actual political targets, as, for example, the 2050 net-zero emission target of the EU, due to which negative emissions and CO_2 removal became increasingly discussed outside expert circles.

Overall, net-zero or climate neutrality targets, understood as a balance between emissions and absorption into sinks, have been gaining considerably in importance in the climate policy debate of recent years. Climate neutrality is explicitly formulated as an objective in the Paris Agreement. By 2020, 126 countries that account for about 51% of global GHG (greenhouse gas) emissions have either formally adopted or announced net-zero goals or are considering setting up such goals (UN, 2020).

The relevance of negative emissions, however, does not end with reaching net-zero emissions. For the implementation of the Paris temperature targets, achieving climate neutrality is only sufficient if emissions are reduced sufficiently fast globally. If this is not accomplished, CO_2 must be removed from the atmosphere via net-negative emission balances in order to compensate for earlier emissions and reduce CO_2 concentrations. For this reason, large amounts of negative emissions are part of many scenarios describing pathways to implement the goals of the Paris Agreement. Relying on negative emissions at a large scale as a backstop type of technology should, however, be viewed with caution.

In general, NETs expand the possibilities for the design of climate protection paths if available and realizable at reasonable social costs: on the one hand, carbon dioxide removal (CDR) allows one to more aggressively reduce gross emissions toward carbon neutrality and to compensate for emissions which are generally held to be difficult to abate (but at the same time result from goods, services, or behavior that are still socially desirable).[1] This "compensatory" function is especially relevant in the first half of the 21st century and can help to keep cumulative emissions closer to or within the remaining carbon budgets and thereby to limit or avoid overshooting. On the other hand, NETs create flexibility in the allocation of climate protection efforts over time as they allow one to correct for past failures in climate policy by removing earlier emissions from the atmosphere at a later date. Put differently, one can think of the compensatory role of CDR as intersectoral compensation, whereas achieving net-negative emissions function by use of CDR allows for an intertemporal compensation of emissions (Fuss *et al.*, 2018, p. 3).

Due to their potential to compensate for emissions that cannot be avoided or only at very high cost, negative emissions play an important — albeit often not entirely transparent — role in many announcements of companies and states to achieve "climate neutrality" by a certain date. A climate neutrality target can, for example, address CO_2 emissions only instead of all GHG emissions, thereby not really targeting climate but rather carbon neutrality.[2] Even more importantly, adopting a climate neutrality target generally leaves open the amount of negative emissions that is intended to compensate for residual emissions. For example, the EU aims for GHG neutrality by the middle of the century. Still, EU climate policy communication often remains silent, or is at least rather intransparent, about the necessary role of CDR for climate neutrality (Geden and Schenuit, 2020). The associated long-term scenarios (EU Commission, 2018) rely on negative emissions from land use, land use change, and forestry (LULUCF) to offset residual emissions. However, in deriving these residual emissions,

---

[1]Some process emissions in industry (e.g., in cement production) or GHG (non-CO_2) emissions in agriculture are technically unavoidable according to current knowledge (Luderer *et al.*, 2018). In some other areas, mitigation is only possible at extremely high costs, so that NETs can promise savings in the costs of climate protection.

[2]Schreyer *et al.* (2020), for example, look at CO_2 neutrality instead of a broader notion of climate neutrality. Even for CO_2 neutrality, they show that carbon dioxide removal (CDR) from land use change and bioenergy with carbon capture and storage (BECCS) is required to compensate for residual emissions in all major industrialized countries.

the scenarios already include an additional substantial use of carbon capture (amounting to 239–606 Mt CO_2eq in 2050) not only for geological storage but also for further processing and use in synthetic fuels or materials. So, the overall contribution of CDR approaches in 2050 is substantially larger than the compensation of 6–9% of emissions by LULUCF might suggest.

Existing studies on climate neutrality differ with respect to the technologies they consider to be viable and competitive. While the European Commission, for example, includes direct air capture and storage (DACCS) (see for example Fuss *et al.*, 2018) in their 2050 scenarios and Fuhrmann *et al.* (2020) even assume DACCS to make substantial climate protection contributions in 2035, Schreyer *et al.* (2020) does not see DACCS to be competitive by 2050. At which point in time specific technologies become competitive and to which extend they are used in climate neutrality scenarios depend inter alia on assumptions about their role-out (scale effects) but also on natural conditions that allow, for example, bioenergy with carbon capture and storage (BECCS) and re-/afforestation or the generation of the large amounts of cheap, renewable electricity needed for DACCS. This is also illustrated by the large differences in the structure of CDR and emissions reductions which Schreyer *et al.* (2020) find for carbon neutrality in different industrialized countries.[3]

Despite their widespread use especially in 1.5°C climate pathways, relying on CDR in the second half of the century to correct for past failures to reduce emissions fast enough is also seen critically. First, as argued for example by Rogelj *et al.* (2019), focusing on temperature targets at the end of the 21st century would not be compatible with the Paris Agreement if global warming were to overshoot in the meantime. It can be shown that the implementation of a maximum warming to be tolerated for the entire 21st century leads to significantly stronger emission reductions and earlier use of NETs. Second, some sustainability risks associated with NETs depend strongly on the scaling of

---

[3]They also show that, without CDR, future CO_2 prices are expected to be higher, illustrating the potential for cost reduction through negative emissions.

their application, thus calling for a more evenly distributed use across time rather than a fast, large-scale deployment in the second half of the century (Obersteiner *et al.*, 2018).

In Section 2, we will first provide some background on the use of negative emissions in the Intergovernmental Panel on Climate Change (IPCC) special report on a global warming of 1.5°C (IPCC, 2018). Section 3 gives an overview of different NETs, their CDR potential, and costs. Implications from NETs for sustainability that go beyond the aspect of carbon removal from the atmosphere are addressed in Section 4. Finally, Section 5 discusses the governance of NETs. This comprises a general conceptual discussion as well as an overview of the status quo in Europe and internationally.

2. Negative Emissions in Scenarios Assessed in IPCC SR 1.5°C

The IPCC special report on a global warming of 1.5°C (IPCC, 2018) shows very clearly that the implementation of the objectives of the Paris Agreement will most likely depend on the use of NETs. In the reported scenarios, all of the calculated 1.5°C paths rely on NETs. NETs are also often used in the scenarios to compensate for high emissions and slower emission reductions in the first half of the century in order to stabilize the temperature increase in the long term at the set target of 1.5°C or 2°C. The critical factors in this context are the question of how quickly and ambitiously the global CO_2 emissions can be reduced in the short term in the 2020s.

Even under optimistic assumptions, it is expected that over the course of the 21st century at least 500 $GtCO_2$ from fossil sources will cumulatively be emitted to the atmosphere. Taken together with emissions from the AFOLU (agriculture, forestry, and other land use) sector, the IPCC therefore projects cumulative emissions of 650 to 1.270 $GtCO_2$ until the year 2100 (IPCC, 2018).

At the same time, starting in 2018, humankind should not emit more than 420 $GtCO_2$ to the atmosphere to have a 66% chance to limit global warming to 1.5°C (IPCC, 2018). Given emissions of about 42 $GtCO_2$ per year and no significant change in global emission trends

(Peters *et al.*, 2010), this remaining carbon budget has already shrunk substantially. To stay within this carbon budget, it would be necessary to reduce carbon emissions to net zero in about 20 years (IPCC, 2018) in order to avoid relying on negative emissions. For a 2°C target, the corresponding carbon budget is 1.170 $GtCO_2$, so that net-zero emissions would have to be reached in about 30 years starting in 2018.[4]

However, according to the IPCC, there are no scenarios with socio-economic development paths for reducing emissions fast enough to limit global warming to 1.5°C without at least some negative emissions from AFOLU (IPCC, 2018). Moreover, due to significant socio-economic barriers to reduce carbon emissions in the short term and barriers to quickly scale up the deployment of CDR, cumulative emissions substantially exceed the remaining carbon budget in most IPCC pathways. This implies a temporary overshoot of CO_2 concentrations in the atmosphere over the given carbon budget and of temperatures over the set warming target (IPCC, 2018). There are only a rather limited number of scenario pathways which keep global warming below 1.5°C permanently, i.e., for which peak warming is 1.5°C or lower over the entire 21st century. Whenever negative emissions play a role in the scenarios, they usually contribute to reaching the targets in the two ways already alluded to in the introduction: through intersectoral as well as intertemporal compensation, although intersectoral compensation in the IPCC scenario pathways is usually limited by the constrained scalability of CDR approaches.

Comparing 1.5°C with 2°C scenarios shows that 1.5°C pathways have to entail a much more aggressive reduction in gross CO_2 emissions from fossil fuels and industry processes until 2030. For no or limited overshooting pathways, global CO_2 emissions should not only peak before 2030 but should also be reduced to 25–30 $GtCO_2eq$/year by 2030 (in contrast to emissions projections based on NDCs which lead to 52–58 GtCO2eq/year in 2030; IPCC, 2018). This implies a reduction of global net anthropogenic CO_2 emissions by about 45%

[4]Note that there is substantial scientific uncertainty regarding the derivation of these budgets (for a discussion, see Rickels *et al.*, 2019).

from 2010 levels by 2030 and toward net zero around 2050, or on average a 3–7% per year reduction in CO_2 emissions between 2030 and 2050 compared to 2030 according to Fuss *et al.* (2018). These 1.5°C pathways are also characterized by a sustained period of net-negative emissions of 1.3 to 29 $GtCO_2$/year in the period 2050 to 2100. Moreover, emissions from AFOLU are reduced significantly so that AFOLU already delivers some carbon removal from 2030 onward.

Overall, cumulative deployment projected spans a wide range of 100–1000 $GtCO_2$ of CDR in 1.5°C pathways with no or limited overshooting. Some overshooting pathways require an even larger cumulative CDR deployment to compensate for carbon emissions from the first half of the 21st century (IPCC, 2018). In these scenarios, the upper end of (annual) deployment rates of BECCS and AFOLU-CDR measures toward mid-century exceeds corresponding deployment potentials per year derived in the literature (around 5 $GtCO_2$/year for BECCS and 3.6 $GtCO_2$/year for afforestation; IPCC, 2018). Those 1.5°C pathways in IPCC (2018) that limit the deployment of CDR to 100–200 $GtCO_2$ even for 1.5°C global warming are characterized by rather optimistic assumptions regarding the potentials to drastically reduce energy demand and/or rapid shifts in socio-economic development paths, for example, implying rapid shifts to sustainable food systems (i.e., low meat consumption) (see also Grubler *et al.*, 2018, van Vuuren *et al.*, 2018).

In the 2°C pathways, most scenarios project a 25% carbon emission decline by 2030 and net-zero emissions at around 2070 (see IPCC, 2018). From 2030 to 2050, this translates into net emissions reductions of 1–4% annually according to Fuss *et al.* (2018) who also point out that even most 2°C pathways rely on substantial amounts of negative emissions toward 2100, ranging from 5 to 21 $GtCO_2$/year at the end of the 21st century. AFOLU contributes to negative emissions in these scenarios in the second half of the 21st century Jia *et al.* (2019). Cumulative deployment of CDR in 85% of 2°C pathways reaches 300 $GtCO_2$ or more, compared to a cumulative removal of about 500 $GtCO_2$ in many 1.5°C scenarios (Hilaire *et al.*, 2019). 2°C scenarios without any deployment of CDR are still theoretically viable if aggressive emission reductions in the short term are assumed. However, as

Strefler *et al.* (2018) point out, significant transitional challenges have to be overcome if emissions reductions at this scale are to be realized in the near term. In general, if international climate policy fails to break current global emission trends until 2030, "the negative emissions characteristic of 2°C scenarios become increasingly similar to the 1.5°C scenarios with immediate action" (Hilaire *et al.*, 2019).

Note that in the IPCC projections, the annual deployment levels of BECCS do not differ much between 1.5°C and 2°C pathways until around 2050, reflecting the challenges of a more rapid upscaling and deployment of BECCS (IPCC, 2018). Still, according to Fuss *et al.* (2018) between 5 $GtCO_2$/year and 15 $GtCO_2$/year of NETs are deployed in most 1.5°C scenarios between 2030 and 2050, removing on average 0.1–0.8 $GtCO_2$/year additionally as compared to most 2°C scenarios. While economic rationales are the dominant drivers of CDR deployment in 2°C mitigation scenarios, CDR deployment in 1.5°C scenarios is seen to be primarily driven by geophysical requirements, i.e., by the requirement to compensate for emissions exceeding the remaining carbon budgets (Fuss *et al.*, 2018, p. 5; Hilaire *et al.*, 2019).

Despite or perhaps due to their intensive use in IPCC (2018), there is also widespread critique of the scenario assumptions that give rise to high and especially late CDR deployment. Obersteiner *et al.* (2018), Rogelj *et al.* (2019), and Schultes *et al.* (2020), for example, point out that CDR deployment and emissions pathways of the scenarios assessed in IPCC (2018) are strongly driven by the underlying scenario framework, i.e., cost minimization over the entire 21st century with a focus on temperature outcomes in 2100. They argue that this framework does not adequately consider climate damages and impacts from even modest global warming which supports temporary overshooting of global warming/peak warming over the course of the 21st century, and leads to a rather late deployment of CDR with large annual deployment rates toward the end of the 21st century. According to Schultes *et al.* (2020), applying a so-called least total cost perspective, which aims to derive mitigation pathways by minimizing social costs for a set temperature target, would result in much more stringent reductions in (net) emissions in the short term and significantly higher carbon prices (in 2030, the median carbon price reaches $115 compared to $61 for a cost effectiveness framework). Similarly, limiting peak global warming not only for 2100 but over the entire 21st century would exclude overshooting of temperatures and lead to much more ambitious reductions in global net GHG emissions (Rogelj *et al.*, 2019).

However, using CDR primarily later in time is also seen critically due to potential externalities and risks associated with large-scale deployment concentrated over a short period of time. Obersteiner *et al.* (2018) point out that in order to, for example, limit the impacts of BECCS on land use, ecosystems, and food prices and to achieve substantial carbon removal over the entire century, it is important to deploy BECCS early and more evenly over the century so that annual deployment rates can be more modest (see also Chapter 4).

Whether or along which paths temperature targets in 2100 as well as the climate neutrality target in 2050 can be reached of course also depends on the assumptions about the scalability and short-term availability of NETs. Especially regarding BECCS and DACCS, these assumptions are sometimes viewed critically. For example, Fuhrmann *et al.* (2020) consider a rather large-scale early deployment of DACCS in the order of up to 3 $GtCO_2$ per year in 2035 in low overshooting scenarios with limits on peak warming. In the scenarios of Schreyer *et al.* (2020), in contrast, high costs hinder DACCS to contribute to reaching carbon neutrality in 2050.

3. Overview of NETs

While there are a number of technologies and routes available to remove CO_2 from the atmosphere, a standard categorization of these approaches is still missing. Field and Mach (2017), for example, distinguish between "improved ecosystem stewardship" to enhance the carbon sink function of ecosystems, biomass-based technological approaches, and a third category of pure technological approaches entailing non-biological techniques to capture CO_2 like DACCS or enhanced weathering. Rickels *et al.* (2020) consider the options to integrate NETs into the EU Emission Trading System and thereby more broadly distinguish between "technical" and "ecosystem-based" processes for CDR, given that the current EU climate policy architecture separates emissions and removals from land use, land use change and forestry (LULUCF) from mitigation measures in other sectors (covered by the EU ETS and the Effort Sharing Regulation).

The CDR approaches mostly included in the scenarios of integrated assessment models (IAMs) are BECCS and re-/afforestation, mainly due to reasons of practicability in the modeling process but also due to other CDR technologies still being less far in their development and associated with higher uncertainty regarding their potential, side effects, and costs. Yet, it is widely recognized that if negative emissions are to play an important role in the future, a portfolio of approaches will likely be used. Within such a portfolio of NETs/CDR, there are trade-offs and synergies between different approaches, for example, with respect to biomass or energy demand, demand for land, or (geological) storage capacities. In the course of the last years, some contributions to the scientific literature have started to assess the CDR potential and input requirements (e.g., water and electricity) for different NETs. As different studies are often based on different assumptions, the results are, however, often difficult to compare. Nevertheless, the assessments of some recent studies for a non-exhaustive number of different approaches are presented in Table A1. Potential trade-offs and synergies between different NETs imply that CDR potentials indicated in Table A1 generally cannot be aggregated. In the following, this chapter only describes basic characteristics of some technologies, while potentially associated risks to sustainability are primarily discussed in Chapter 4.

Af-/Reforestation of unwooded areas and of deforested forest areas is central to many mitigation scenarios and probably the most prominent and discussed means to remove carbon from the atmosphere. Atmospheric CO_2 is bound in the biomass of trees or wood products. The overall impact of forestry activities on global warming, however, largely also depends on the induced changes in surface albedo. For example, afforestation in boreal zones is widely seen as counterproductive due to the low albedo of boreal forests (Fuss *et al.*, 2018). The distinction between afforestation and reforestation is fluid and partly dependent on which time horizons are used as a basis. In principle, both offer substantial potential for CO_2 removal, whereby the literature shows large ranges (see Table A.1). Besides re-/afforestation itself, improved forest management can also contribute to increased carbon sequestration in forests and forest soils. CDR via the renaturation of ecosystems is, of course not restricted to forests: the renaturation of wetlands, including peatlands, also offers significant carbon sequestration potentials of about 1.7 $GtCO_2eq$/year.

BECCS is a rather diverse concept which includes a range of different technologies (Bui *et al.*, 2018). The basic BECCS process always consists of capturing CO_2 from the atmosphere in biomass, using the biomass to produce energy (electricity and/or heat) or liquid biofuels, capturing the carbon when the biomass is burned or converted, and finally geologically storing the carbon underground (Fajardy *et al.*, 2019). The carbon is stored either in gaseous state or in long-term mineralized form, i.e., by binding in the rock, when stored in appropriately reactive rock layers (Climeworks, 2020). Sometimes, capturing CO_2 from biogenic industrial processes in the paper or pulp industry is also subsumed under BECCS (Fajardy *et al.*, 2019, IEA, 2020). Technical potential limits of BECCS (as well as DACCS see below) result from the limited availability of land for biomass growth and of suitable geological storage sites.

Due to potential emissions from biomass supply and the operation of applications to sequester and pump CO_2 to geological formations, a life cycle analysis of BECCS processes is important to assess whether a specific BECCS application actually removes CO_2 from the atmosphere or not (Hanssen *et al.*, 2020). In addition, emissions induced by direct and/or indirect land use changes in principle have to be accounted for. However, particularly indirect land use changes and resulting emissions are often difficult to monitor (Fuss *et al.*, 2018).

BECCS mostly consists of known and available components and is therefore seen as one of the more mature CDR approaches (Bui *et al.*, 2018) even though there are currently only about 13 BECCS plants globally in operation according to IEA (2020), with often limited CO_2 capturing capacities/mostly at a demonstration level.

DACCS, in contrast to BECCS, does not rely on burning fossil or renewable energy resources first and capturing the resulting CO_2 emissions afterward. DACCS allows for direct sequestration of CO_2 from the air with the help of technical filters. The filtering of CO_2 from the air is carried out via chemical sorbents, either via liquid chemical solutions or via special air filters with chemical binding effect. Energy is then required in both processes to extract the CO_2 from the chemical binding agents (IEA, 2020). Using liquid chemical solutions is the technically more mature process, but it requires higher temperatures and thus more energy and is less suitable for smaller systems (Gambhir and Tavoni, 2019, Realmonte *et al.*, 2019).

The fundamental challenge for DACCs is not the filtration per se as this has been done with CO_2-intensive exhaust gases already for a longer time. What is challenging is rather the filtration of large amounts of carbon without costs becoming prohibitively high when the concentration of CO_2 in the air is low. Large-scale deployment of DACCS is still associated with a number of questions regarding, e.g., the potential for further cost reductions, infrastructure for transport of CO_2, and the production capacity for chemical binding agents. Due to these uncertainties, several authors assume the scalability potential of DACCS to be limited at least until 2050 (Realmonte *et al.*, 2019, Gambhir and Tavoni, 2019, Bui *et al.*, 2018) while expecting significantly higher potentials toward the end of the 21st century (Fuss *et al.*, 2018).

Enhanced weathering builds on the natural but normally very slow process of rock weathering and the (bio-)chemical reactions between atmosphere and the rock surface that bind CO_2 from the air. Through targeted crushing of rocks, the reactive surface and thus the CO_2 binding are increased (WBGU, 2021). Like DACCS, enhanced weathering requires a lot of energy (in the rock crushing process). Spreading the rock powder on soils can improve soil quality and thereby help to raise the productivity of agricultural land or restore degraded soils (Fuss *et al.*, 2018). Yet, uncertainty exists with regard to possible pollution of water systems and the release of heavy metals (Beerling *et al.*, 2020).

Soil carbon sequestration employs a number of different land use practices such as adapted harvest cycles, water management, or nutrient management to increase the carbon content of the soil and thus remove CO_2 from the atmosphere (Fuss *et al.*, 2018). Soil carbon sequestration practices can be used on different types of land such as pasture, arable land, or forest areas. Soil carbon sequestration also improves overall soil quality, i.e., the nutrient content, and reduces vulnerability to erosion (Smith *et al.*, 2019a, p. 264).

Biochar is produced by the heating of biomass under almost complete exclusion of oxygen (incomplete combustion). The storage of the original biomass carbon in biochar is generally considered as more resistant to decomposition than carbon stored in untreated biomass (The Royal Society, 2018). The potential use of biochar differs depending on the manufacturing process with some uses binding carbon in the longer run and others leading to a release of the bound carbon to the atmosphere. Biochar can be used, for example, to replace fossil fuels, to filter exhaust air and wastewater, or to produce electrodes (Röhrdanz *et al.*, 2019). Mixtures of biochar and inorganic clay result in an energy-efficient insulating material (Lee *et al.*, 2019). When applied to soils, biochar supports the formation of soil carbon stocks and thereby provides an approach for long-term carbon sequestration in soils with a range of co-benefits, for example, by raising soil fertility (The Royal Society, 2018, Teichmann, 2014).

Ocean fertilization aims to bind more atmospheric CO_2 in the oceans by increasing its nutrient content (especially with respect to iron) and fostering plankton growth. As Geden and Schenuit (2020) point out, the long-term effectiveness and potential side effects of ocean fertilization are subject to high uncertainty. "How permanently the removed CO_2 could be stored is a controversial issue, since only a small part of the additionally absorbed CO_2 would be stored in sea floor sediment" (Geden and Schenuit, 2020, p. 12). Ocean fertilization can also result in a number of side effects that led Gnanadesikan *et al.* (2003) to question its overall usefulness and induced Geden and Schenuit (2020) to suggest that it is rarely treated as a serious option nowadays.

4. CO_2 Removal and Sustainable Development

Given their prominent role in many climate change mitigation scenarios, NETs can substantially contribute to more sustainable development paths by mitigating risks and impacts from more severe climate change. These impacts would have to be borne by future generations, in particular in less developed countries (IPCC, 2018). The interlinkage between sustainable development and CDR is, however, more complex and more ambiguous. Particularly, CDR and its integration in long-term sustainable mitigation strategies involve a broad range of questions about how costs and risks of climate change, climate change mitigation, and CDR deployment itself are distributed geographically between different countries and intertemporally between different generations. Risks, distributional implications, and trade-offs of CDR deployment typically cannot directly be observed from aggregate, global mitigation scenarios and pathways, but are highly relevant from a sustainable development perspective. In the following, we first discuss the side effects of CDR and the risks they pose for sustainable development. We then consider the distribution of effects between regions and the risks of relying on uncertain future CDR.

4.1. *Side effects of CDR*

CDR can provide co-benefits in addition to its contribution to climate change mitigation, but generally also comes with negative external costs (Dietz *et al.*, 2018). Co-benefits and costs differ substantially between CDR approaches, for example, between ecosystem-based and more technical approaches, and with the rate of deployment of the respective approach, but are so far not fully understood. Potential co-benefits are numerous (Smith *et al.*, 2019a): Ecosystem-based approaches like the restoration of wetlands or forests combine the generation of CDR with the protection of biodiversity, for example, while the application of biochar and methods of soil carbon sequestration can contribute to soil fertility and an increase in food security. Af-/reforestation may positively affect local temperature and precipitation patterns and improve local water systems. Even more technical approaches like BECCS have positive co-benefits, for example, by providing energy services or fostering local (rural) employment and income (Fuss *et al.*, 2018).

Substantial negative external costs of CDR can arise from the demand for water (e.g., for forest plantations), the increased use of fertilizers for the fast growth of biomass (for bioenergy or biochar generation), or indirectly via large energy demand (e.g., for DACCS or enhanced weathering; Fuss *et al.*, 2018, Smith *et al.*, 2019a). Another major sustainability concern arises from the land area which NETs like BECCS and af-/reforestation require for generating significant amounts of CDR. The land area used for these land-intensive CDR methods in 1.5°C-mitigation pathways (with low overshooting) exceeds 5 M[illion]km^2 which would correspond to over 25% of current global cropland area or over 50% of the land area of the United States (Fuhrmann *et al.*, 2020). Conducting a life cycle assessment for BECCS, Hanssen *et al.* (2020) conclude that the cumulative CDR deployment in the 1.5°–2°C-pathways assessed by the IPCC could approximately be met from a biophysical perspective, but would require up to 16% of the total global land area by the end of the century.

Dedicating these vast amounts of land to BECCS and/or afforestation, or generally to land-intensive CDR deployment at scale, either comes at the expense of natural forests and grassland, thereby increasing the anthropogenic pressure on ecosystems and risking further biodiversity losses (Dooley *et al.*, 2020), or comes at the expense of agricultural land for food crop production, thereby threatening food security and raising food prices (Roe *et al.*, 2019). Fuhrmann *et al.* (2020), for example, project a sevenfold increase of food prices at the end of the century compared to 2010 (for mitigation pathways with low overshooting and with CDR from BECCS and afforestation only). This drastic increase is due to the strict constraints on commercial land use which they impose for the protection of natural lands and ecosystems and the thereby induced shift from food to bioenergy crop production on agricultural land. Without such a constraint, studies find more modest albeit still substantial increases in food prices due to the expansion of land-intensive CDR and the corresponding reduction in global pasture land and cropland for food (Fajardy *et al.*, 2020, Jia *et al.*, 2019). In fact, the expansion of land-intensive CDR in mitigation paths could profoundly reshape global land use structures at an unprecedented scale and speed (Jia *et al.*, 2019).

Applying a broader portfolio of NETs could reduce the most severe land use conflicts induced by land-intensive NETs, and generally external costs of NETs. The reason is that negative side effects of NETs strongly depend on their scale of deployment (Fuss *et al.*, 2018, Smith *et al.*, 2019a). In fact, more recent scenario results illustrate that including DACCS as a third, less land-intensive option for large-scale CDR can attenuate the land use implications of NET deployment in ambitious climate change mitigation pathways, but would raise energy demand significantly (Realmonte *et al.*, 2019). Regarding the implications for food markets, an early and rapid market scale-up of DACCS leads to a more moderate increase in global food prices in the scenario analysis of Fuhrmann *et al.* (2020), although prices still triple compared to 2010.

The complexity of the interaction between different NETs as well as CDR and mitigation in ambitious emission reduction scenarios can also be illustrated by the "rebound effect" on water demand pointed out by Fuhrmann *et al.* (2020): while generally less water-intensive than BECCS, the inclusion of DACCS in their scenario increases water demand because overall emissions and therefore overall CDR deployment also rise strongly when DACCS is included. So far, the complex implications of portfolios of NETs, i.e., the synergies and potential trade-offs between different NETs, and their implications on markets, livelihoods, and sustainable development, are not well understood and an important topic for future research (Smith *et al.*, 2019a).

An important insight from the literature is also that the negative external costs of NETs strongly depend on the overall socio-economic development path. This is illustrated by comparisons between different shared socioeconomic pathways (SSPs), which describe and define the more general framework conditions and socio-economic developments underlying climate mitigation scenarios. Overall, more sustainable development pathways generally reduce the need for large-scale CDR deployment and thereby corresponding sustainability risks, for example, due to decreasing energy demand or less meat-intensive diets (Roe *et al.*, 2019). Since such pathways often involve less land-intensive consumption and production patterns, they are also generally less prone to severe land use conflicts arising from the deployment of CDR (Lenzi, 2018; Smith *et al.*, 2019b, p. 687).

4.2. *Distributional effects between regions*

The burden of the (social) costs of large-scale CDR deployments is rather unevenly distributed between regions. Fajardy *et al.* (2020) point out that over 80% of BECCS capacities in global 1.5°C mitigation pathways are deployed in developing countries, due to favorable natural conditions to grow biomass (but often also driven by lower opportunity costs of land use). In fact, such a global cost minimizing deployment of CDR substantially deviates from a "fair" allocation of costs when countries' historical responsibility for climate change or their economic capability to bear mitigation costs is used as a concept of fairness (Fyson *et al.*, 2020). Under such fairness concepts, industrialized countries or regions like the United States or the EU with high historical emissions and strong economic capabilities would have to significantly increase CDR efforts, either via local deployment or via providing financial resources. Similarly, different local conditions for CDR as well as different emission intensities of infrastructures also raise questions about the distribution of burdens between industrialized countries, for example, when pursuing a climate neutrality target within the EU (Geden and Schenuit, 2020, Schreyer *et al.*, 2020).

On a global level, the geographically heterogeneous deployment of land-intensive CDR also implies that regions are differently affected by local external costs. Local external costs of CDR deployment — for example, water scarcity or decreasing water quality — would predominantly accrue in developing countries along pathways minimizing global mitigation costs. Also, as illustrated, for example, by Fajardy *et al.* (2020), there are substantial differences in food price increases between different regions of the world depending on the regional shift in agricultural production induced by the deployment of BECCS (and afforestation). Fuhrmann *et al.* (2020) similarly point out that in their scenarios food price increases are concentrated in Sub-Saharan Africa. These distributional implications are exacerbated by the fact that the social consequences of such changes in commodity prices, and food prices in particular, are generally much more severe in poorer regions than richer industrialized countries.

4.3. *Intertemporal risk and uncertainty*

CDR, in principle, allows one to reduce transitional challenges of aggressive emissions reductions, especially for generations living in the first half of the 21st century. This is true for using CDR as an additional mitigation option compensating for (residual) emissions which are generally held to be difficult to abate, as well as for using CDR to achieve net-negative emissions in the medium or long term. Relying on CDR, however, comes with various risks. These risks on the one hand arise from the potential large external costs of vast CDR deployment which future societies would have to bear and which increase in the scale of necessary CDR deployments per period, as discussed before (Smith *et al.*, 2019a). On the other hand, technological uncertainties, the limited permanence of carbon storage, and/or our current limited understanding of the carbon cycle and geophysical uncertainties give rise to a substantial risk that relying on CDR will fail to limit global warming in the end.

Technological uncertainty arises mainly with respect to NETs whose large-scale deployment has not yet been proven to be (technically, economically, and politically) viable. Relying heavily on the future availability of such unproven technologies, like BECCS and DACCS, is therefore often criticized as a risky bet on the future (Lenzi, 2018). The optimistic, rapid scale-up of BECCS and DACCS in many scenarios should accordingly be treated with caution. Currently, only a small number of BECCS facilities are dedicated to storing CO_2 underground, and only 15 DACCS facilities are in operation, often for demonstration purposes and at small scales (IEA, 2020). For comparison, a "typical 2°C climate scenario requires the funding, construction and operation of as many as 16,000 plants that combine biomass burning with carbon capture and storage by 2050" (Lenzi *et al.*, 2018, p. 304). High average deployment growth rates of about 20–30% per year, which would be required along some scenario mitigation pathways, have been observed historically, for example, for solar photovoltaics.

Yet, it is still an open question whether a similarly dynamic deployment over time is realistic for less modular CDR technologies like BECCS (Nemet *et al.*, 2018, Realmonte *et al.*, 2019, Creutzig *et al.*, 2019).

Apart from uncertainty about the future development and costs of at least some NETs, the removal of carbon from the carbon cycle by CDR is not necessarily permanent, and mostly seen to be less permanent and safe than leaving carbon bound in fossil resources underground (Fuss *et al.*, 2018). Permanence of storage and the risk of reversibility differ between CDR approaches depending on the storage process and medium used. Ecosystem-based CDR approaches, while more readily available and less prone to incur severe negative external costs, are typically seen to provide less permanent storage as they saturate rather quickly and are mostly highly susceptible to external influences, either natural influences like droughts or fire or anthropogenic pressure (Hurlbert *et al.*, 2019). In particular, the biogenic storage option is also affected by ongoing climate change, potentially giving rise to additional feedback effects. In contrast, geological storage, for example, as used with BECCS or DACCS, is mostly seen as a more resilient and permanent storage approach with large storage volumes available even though the risk of leakage, especially from large reservoirs, requires a reliable and comprehensive monitoring system (Fuss *et al.*, 2018, Bui *et al.*, 2018, WBGU, 2021). In either case, ensuring long-term monitoring and managing of storage sites poses major governance challenges which call for stable institutional and political conditions that, at least today, seem not to be present in all regions with high CDR deployment potentials.

Finally, geophysical limits of negative emissions and the reversibility of a temporary overshoot of CO_2 emissions and temperatures by use of CDR are still not fully understood and subject to scientific debate (Fuss *et al.*, 2018, Steffen *et al.*, 2018). Moreover, it is unclear how much CDR would be necessary to compensate for a temporary overshooting of CO_2 concentrations and temperatures and to return to a lower temperature equilibrium due to carbon cycle feedbacks (Lenzi, 2018).[5]

[5] Of course, there are also negative external costs from larger CO_2 emissions in earlier periods of time arising, for example, by an increased acidification of oceans.

In integrated assessment model scenarios, the inclusion of NETs, or even an increase in the NETs portfolio, typically leads to a reduction in short-term abatement efforts (Realmonte *et al.*, 2019).[6] This widely noted effect is due to the discounting of future costs and the basic model framework with a strong focus on achieving end-of-century temperature at lowest costs (Hilaire *et al.*, 2019), which is increasingly criticized as already pointed out in Section 2.

However, there is also the ethical concern that the mere presence or expected availability of NETs induces policy makers and societies to obstruct short-term mitigation and to take excessive risks at the expense of future generations (Lenzi, 2018). Even though such moral hazard was probably not the dominant cause for the insufficient and slow climate policy progress in the past, it might become more relevant with the increasing awareness of CDR in the future (Fuss *et al.*, 2020). Moreover, it is important to note that excessive risk taking and overly relying on CDR also have strong distributional implications between poorer and richer countries in the future if global warming cannot be controlled: "It is ethically significant that the potential losers of a failed gamble upon NETs are future generations, and especially the poorest among them, who would be most vulnerable if it failed, and who could not possibly consent" (Minx *et al.*, 2018, p. 21).

5. Governance of CO_2 Removal

To some extent, the discussion of governance NETs and CDR is still in its first stages with many open questions remaining on a general, national as well as international climate policy level.

Among the general questions is not only how negative emissions should be treated in relation to conventional mitigation but also how to incentivize emitters to conduct CDR and how to deal with sustainability risks that arise from CDR deployment (see Chapter 4).

[6]For example, in mitigation scenarios assessed by the IPCC, the inclusion of CDR raises fossil emissions in 2030 by about 9 $GtCO_2$ compared to scenarios without CDR (Lenzi *et al.*, 2018, p. 304).

Dealing with both questions calls for an integrated governance system that considers mitigation as well as CDR and includes additional governance provisions to account for negative side effects of CDR. In practice, a number of challenges arise in the implementation of such a system. First, monitoring and quantification of the external costs have to be possible at all. Second, sufficiently strong governance systems for these external costs have to be established despite potential resistance, given that there is increasingly strong economic pressure to use more seemingly cheap CDR options when carbon prices rise or emissions caps are tightened. Also, CDR is not one uniform technology but includes a wide range of technologies and approaches with different challenges and external costs. So, not only do trade-offs and differences between mitigation and negative emissions have to be considered but also trade-offs and differences between different CDR methods (e.g., ecosystem based vs. technological approaches).

On the international level, it is unclear which countries should generate (net) negative emissions, how much, and when. In a discussion that is similar to the discussion about the allocation of mitigation efforts and the distribution of mitigation burdens, it has to be determined what efficient as well as "fair" contributions for different countries are. To what extent should differences with respect to the starting points toward climate neutrality and, in general, between countries with different conditions for realizing CO_2 removal be considered? And, to which extent should countries be allowed to meet negative emissions obligations by investments abroad (e.g., in developing countries) or by buying negative emissions credits?

On a national level (or equivalently within the EU), challenges arise from the implementation and operationalization of climate neutrality targets. On a fundamental level, the role of negative emissions in reaching climate neutrality has to be discussed, i.e., what is the optimal ratio between negative emissions and emissions reduction, how can this ratio be determined, and which sectors are "allowed" to emit under climate neutrality.

Many of these questions arise if climate policy treats CDR and conventional mitigation separately which is sometimes suggested to address sustainability risks of CDR directly and to hinder seemingly cheap CDR approaches to undermine mitigation incentives (e.g., McLaren *et al.*, 2019). A fully integrated approach like an EU-wide ETS with full coverage of all sectors over a sufficiently long period of time with credits for negative emissions, however, comes with its own challenges. These include potentially limited time horizons of emitters, difficulties of regulators to credibly commit to long-term regulation and targets, and how to deal with seemingly cheap negative emissions options (like afforestation) which are, however, much less permanent and, in particular, more susceptible to external damage and climate change.

In the following, we provide an overview of the challenges of setting incentives for CDR deployment building upon carbon pricing and briefly summarize the current state of CDR incentives, especially in Europe.

5.1. *Establishing incentives to develop and invest in CDR via carbon pricing*

As generating negative emissions is costly and represents a public good provision by mitigating global warming, private emitters will usually only engage in CDR if they have financial incentives to do so. Such incentives can, for example, be created by CDR-specific governance and finance systems, i.e., by setting CDR-specific targets and requiring emitters to contribute to these targets according to some criteria. Including CDR into a carbon pricing system is a second option. Pricing carbon emissions, however, creates an incentive for CDR deployment only if emitters can use CDR to offset their emissions and thereby avoid payments for emissions. By allowing for the generation of carbon credits that can be used by emitters instead of engaging in CDR themselves, incentives are not limited to emitters with installations which could be equipped with components to capture and store carbon from emissions. In this case, there is demand for CDR, or an incentive to invest in CDR, as long as marginal CDR costs, or the price of CDR for emitters, are lower than the carbon price and as long as there is at least one emitter with positive net emissions at the same time.

Incentivizing CDR via strictly positive carbon prices, however, can result in a corner solution at net-zero emissions, if CDR is sufficiently cheap. The reason is that carbon pricing establishes a (financial) liability of emitters for their (current) emissions only and does not create any incentive to deploy CDR independent from emissions. Thus, incentives to deploy CDR disappear for each individual emitter as soon as the emitter achieves net-zero emissions from mitigation and CDR. This discontinuity of incentives to deploy CDR at net-zero emissions has been pointed out by Lemoine (2020), and holds true for the individual emitter as well as economy-wide. A carbon price with CDR offsetting, therefore, does not generate an incentive to achieve net-negative emissions, irrespective of the carbon price level or how severe (marginal) climate damages are. Such a corner solution therefore implies less than first-best CDR even if the carbon tax rate is set equal to the social cost of carbon (SCC).

Let us illustrate this scenario in Fig. 1 for the example of a carbon tax (the general reasoning holds equally for the case of carbon pricing through a cap and trade system). Confronted with a carbon tax τ, cost minimizing emitters with initial emission level e_t^0 choose mitigation level m_t^{tax} such that marginal abatement costs MAC equal the carbon tax if CDR is not available or eligible under the carbon tax scheme. If CDR offsetting is admissible, emitters use the additional option to reduce emissions and thereby avoid tax payments. Equilibrium deployment, or investments in CDR is characterized by the condition that marginal CDR costs MCR equal marginal abatement costs: mitigation efforts are somewhat reduced (by B), but overall the reduction of emissions increases (by A) due to the compensatory CDR deployment.

In the scenario depicted in Fig. 1, emission abatement and CDR are so cheap that emitters reach overall net-zero emissions at marginal abatement (and CDR) costs below the carbon tax. Net-zero emissions represent, however, a suboptimal equilibrium in this scenario. Given that the carbon tax rate reflects the SCC, the removal of an additional ton of carbon from the atmosphere would be less costly than the damages arising from that ton of carbon (as represented by the SSC). Thus, optimal deployment of CDR would require net-negative emissions in the amount of $C + B$ and larger mitigation efforts $m_t^{\text{tax}} > m_t^{\text{off}}$, so that CDR compensating for residual emissions would be reduced to the amount A.

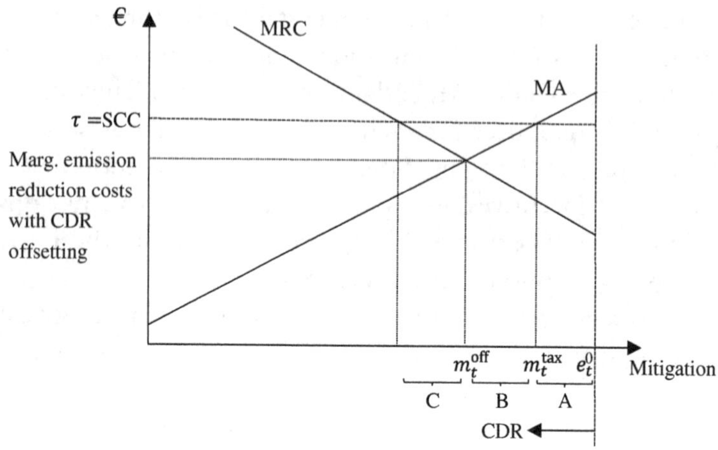

Fig. 1. Mitigation and CDR for low CDR costs.

Equivalently to a scenario with a carbon tax, in an emission trading system, incentives for CDR deployment are created as soon as emitters can comply with the cap not only by purchasing certificates or conventional mitigation but also by offsetting emissions with CDR credits. In this case, the price inelastic supply of emission certificates becomes effectively price elastic for certificate prices above (marginal) CDR costs (Rickels *et al.*, 2020). There would be positive demand for CDR (credits) from emitters as soon as the marginal abatement costs, or the certificate price in a competitive certificates market, would rise above the price of CDR credits (or, again assuming a competitive market, marginal CDR deployment costs). In the equilibrium, prices of emission certificates and of CDR credits would be equalized and the resulting level of residual (uncompensated) emissions would still be equal to the cap on emissions.

Of course, in principle, it is also possible to set a negative cap on period emissions. However, for a static perspective with a one-period emissions cap without borrowing or banking (i.e., intertemporal trading of certificates), the aforementioned discontinuity of CDR deployment incentives would not disappear even if such a negative (period emissions) cap was set. The reason again is that the (financial) liability of carbon emitters in such an emission trading system is limited to their emissions within the period of time to which the emissions cap applies. The emissions trading scheme generally does not introduce a liability, or incentive, to deploy CDR independent of emissions which would be necessary to generate net-negative emissions.

One might argue that the discontinuity of CDR deployment incentives is a more long-term problem and that in the short- to medium-term setting, pursuing a climate neutrality target is sufficiently ambitious. In fact, for climate neutrality, the familiar carbon pricing approaches, either via taxing carbon emissions or control of carbon emissions' quantities, create sufficient incentives for CDR if the use of CDR for offsetting carbon emissions is introduced. However, transforming carbon-intensive economies to states in which these economies are not only carbon neutral but possibly even carbon negative is a highly dynamic process due to various path dependencies (infrastructure, R&D). Thus, the question is whether operationalizing and pursuing a carbon neutrality target without considering the possibility or requirement to achieve net-negative emissions later will lead to a long-term/dynamically efficient development path.

Rickels *et al.* (2020) suggest that in order to overcome the net-zero discontinuity, an adjustment in the trading proportion of emissions certificates vs. CDR credits could be introduced, e.g., to offset one ton of carbon an emitter would have to hand in, for instance, two CDR credits. Such a system could be based on the additional risks with which CDR is associated compared to mitigation (regarding, for example, the durability of the carbon removal and potential side effects).[7]

An emissions trading system, however, can also generate incentives for CDR deployment beyond net-zero emissions if the trading period is extended so that the cap defines cumulative emissions not only over one

---

[7]Alternatively, the regulator could require emitters to contribute to CDR beyond reaching net-zero emissions, e.g., based on past emissions. From an economic point of view, this could only be justified if these past emissions were either not priced or priced too low compared to the social cost of carbon. Such a system would extend the overall liability of emitters to past or historic emissions, as often requested, for example, by developing countries.

but over several periods, and (perfect) intertemporal trading of emission certificates and CDR credits is allowed (banking and borrowing). In this case, it can be optimal for firms to offset emissions exceeding the cap in, e.g., early periods (when certain mitigation and/or CDR technologies are still expensive) by deploying additional CDR in later periods. This can help to not only lower the overall costs of reaching climate neutrality but also to implement stricter carbon budgets compared to a "static" trading system with a more limited temporal scope. Put differently, such an extended trading system not only creates an incentive for intersectoral compensation but also for intertemporal compensation which both typically can be observed along scenario pathways (see Chapter 1, or (Fuss *et al.*, 2018, p. 3)). In fact, in a perfect foresight world with credible government commitments, one could think of a large-scale emissions trading system translating the remaining carbon budget for the 21st century into a regulatory cap on cumulative emissions over the entire century, so that the trading system would more or less directly translate the modeling approach taken in integrated assessment models into actual regulation. The incentives to generate period net-negative emissions in such a system, of course, strongly depend on the cumulative (intertemporal) carbon budget. If the climate targets were only achievable by cumulatively reducing carbon stocks in the atmosphere from now on, even such an intertemporal emission trading system would not provide the sufficient economic incentives without further establishing a liability of participants to invest in CDR.

More importantly, from a welfare economics perspective, it must particularly be taken into account that the criticism raised with respect to pure cost-minimizing mitigation scenarios analogously applies to such an intertemporal system which would increase the chances for a temporal overshoot of emissions and temperatures. Also, it might induce large deployments of CDR in later periods that induce risks for sustainability (see Chapter 4).

Another option to deal with the corner solutions at net-zero emissions would be to introduce a separate remuneration scheme for CDR. This system could either just set a price paid for CDR, for example, equal to the carbon tax rate, or use an auction mechanism to better align remuneration payments to private CDR deployment costs, which are expected to change over time due to technological progress, for example (Burke *et al.*, 2019). Such a separate CDR remuneration system would be possible for both a carbon tax and an emissions trading system.

A separate CDR remuneration system either entails that offsetting would have to be abolished or, if the possibility to purchase CDR credits to reduce carbon price payments were still possible in such a public procurement system, that the system would have to be designed in a way that does not allow for double counting of CDR (e.g., a unit of CDR that the regulator is paying for via subsidies cannot be sold to as a CDR credit to a private emitter later). In such a system, the CDR demand from the regulator would simply serve to increase the CDR demand from emitters substituting conventional mitigation for CDR. Net-negative emissions in such a mixed public procurement and CDR offsetting approach would result from the regulator purchasing "additional" CDR credits beyond net-zero emissions (Rickels *et al.*, 2020).

A public CDR procurement system would allow the regulator to exclude a scenario as depicted in Fig. 1. For example, by paying a CDR subsidy equal to the carbon tax and excluding offsetting at all (or as soon as CDR is financed by the subsidy), emitters would mitigate m_t^{tax} in market equilibrium (so that level $\tau = \text{MAC}$), while CDR is deployed up to point at which marginal deployment costs equal the subsidy set by the regulator. In the economy-wide carbon emission accounting system, CDR would still offset residual emissions and may or may not generate net-negative emissions, depending on the carbon tax and the subsidy chosen by the regulator.

In contrast to the integrated approach of carbon pricing with CDR offsetting, such a system of separate incentives for CDR and mitigation entails an increase in government spending, which at least to some extent could be refinanced by the larger carbon tax revenues (larger compared to the offsetting case, because emitters no longer have the possibility to deduct CDR offsets from tax payments). However, in particular when there is a need for large CDR deployment so that net-negative emissions are achieved, carbon tax revenues in that period may no longer be sufficient to finance CDR remuneration completely (Bednar *et al.*, 2019; especially when only intratemporal cross-financing from revenues from carbon pricing to CDR expenditures is considered).

Instead of separate CDR remuneration, Lemoine suggests an "atmospheric rental policy" (Lemoine, 2020) which basically taxes the use of the atmosphere at each point in time rather than emissions. The aim of this system is to create incentives for emitters to deploy CDR even beyond individual net-zero emissions. The logic is to determine the overall carbon tax an emitter has to pay in a specific period based on the damages that result from past and current emissions of the emitter in that same period. Each emitter then has an incentive to consider not only the reduction of current emissions but possibly also of past emissions in each period, i.e., the individual financial liability in each period is extended to past emissions and thereby to the continuous use of the atmosphere as a carbon deposit.

In this system, the time structure of tax payments, i.e., the fact that the carbon tax has to be paid not only once but continuously as long as the respective ton of carbon stays in the atmosphere, directly reflects the stock pollutant nature of the global warming externality. First-best mitigation incentives are established if the tax rate corresponds to the current external costs of emitting another ton of carbon to the atmosphere, i.e., current (marginal) social damages. In contrast, under the standard approach of carbon taxation, the stock pollutant nature is reflected by the tax rate and not by the time structure of tax payments. With a one-time tax payment, to internalize the full externality of global warming, the tax rate has to be set equal to the present value of aggregated climate damages from the time of emission onward (e.g., also Dietz and Venmans, 2019). The liability of the emitter, and thereby any incentive to mitigate climate damages from that ton of carbon later, then ends with paying the tax. Of course, a one-time carbon tax set at the (cumulative) SCC is obviously much higher than a periodic carbon tax which equals just the current marginal damages of carbon in the atmosphere.

With an infinite time horizon and a private discount rate equal to the social discount rate (and perfect foresight), the present value of overall tax burdens from both approaches to tax carbon, i.e., one-time payment of cumulative SCC and the periodic payment of instantaneous social costs/damages of carbon over time, should be equivalent. By distributing the payment over time, the periodic carbon tax (or, atmospheric rental policy) extends the liability of the emitter over time thereby creating a permanent incentive to consider CDR. To mimic the same incentive structure under the more familiar approach of a one-time carbon tax (optimally set at a rate equal to the SCC), the regulator would have to make the (credible) announcement to repay (parts of) the tax burden as soon as the ton of carbon will be removed from the atmosphere again. This repayment should then equal the SCC at that moment in time when the ton of carbon is removed from the atmosphere. The emitter then also effectively pays "only" for the external costs incurred over that period of time the ton of carbon stayed in the atmosphere (of course, again assuming an infinite time horizon, perfect foresight, and that the regulator and the private emitter use the same discount rate to assess future costs/damages). However, a carbon tax design following the "atmospheric rental policy" would require a number of strong, highly stylized assumptions to hold due to the long-term nature of the policy.

For example, for such a policy, based on an extended, long-term liability of emitters, the emitting firms must survive sufficiently long, preferably forever, without going bankrupt. Otherwise, their liability for past emissions would end. This problem is also pointed out by Lemoine (2020) who suggest "carbon shares" as a way to preserve optimal CDR incentives even with positive possibility of firms going bankrupt. These carbon shares are attached to past emissions and turn these emissions into valuable assets which can be traded. Their value derives from the option to get a payment from the regulator (parts of the original carbon fee) if the ton carbon is removed from the atmosphere at some point in time.

The same problem, of course, arises in a long-term (intertemporal) emissions trading system with an aggregate emission cap. If these caps were allocated to individual firms and these firms would go bankrupt, they would not be able to redeem excessive past emissions with negative emissions in the future. Also, emitters must have perfect foresight about the availability and cost of CDR and trust in firms deploying

CDR in the future. They have to believe in the regulatory announcement that the emissions budget and the trading system overall will not be changed by the regulator even over long periods of time (which might also be undermined by strategic behavior of the firms). That a regulatory commitment over a time horizon of several decades is possible and credible seems to be a rather unrealistic assumption. Similarly, assuming perfect foresight about the future availability and costs of CDR is not plausible given the current status of CDR projects, the high technological uncertainty involved, and the uncertainty with respect to social acceptance and side effects of large-scale CDR deployment.

Beyond the problems of long-term carbon pricing schemes, other challenges arise in the context of combining carbon pricing and carbon offsetting:

- Offsetting ensures that marginal (private) mitigation costs and marginal (private) costs of CDR deployment are equalized. While this contributes to cost efficiency in a static perspective, deviations from relying solely on carbon pricing might be justified from a more dynamic perspective. On the one hand, there is a widely noted, large need for further research and to gather experience with larger-scale CDR deployments, especially of technical approaches like BECCS and DACCS, to bring down deployment costs and learn more about side effects and external costs of CDR (Fuss *et al.*, 2018; Nemet *et al.*, 2018). On the other hand, pure reliance on carbon pricing might lead to large-scale CDR deployment in later decades when emitters trade-off mitigation and CDR efforts intertemporally. A more evenly distributed deployment over the 21st century could, however, reduce side effects and external costs (Obersteiner *et al.*, 2018).
- The integration of relatively cheap CDR options for offsetting emissions, like afforestation, into an emissions trading system directly reduces the certificates' price and thereby mitigation incentives. If this leads to a delay of investments in mitigation technologies and infrastructure, the costs of more ambitious emission

reduction targets in the longer run could rise given missing technological developments, cost reductions from learning-by-doing, and/or problems to speed up building capital-intensive facilities and infrastructure over shorter transition periods. The price dampening effect in an emissions trading scheme reflects the broader "moral hazard" concern with expectations over the future availability of CDR (which seems to be particularly relevant on the political level by easily providing political arguments for delaying costly mitigation efforts in the short term, see also Section 4.3).

- Offsetting, depending on which methods of CDR are included, can link different sectors with substantially different "economic capacities": there can be strong demand for seemingly cheap ecosystem CDR from "strong" economic sectors like the industry or energy sector which could heavily increase the anthropogenic pressure on ecosystems (e.g., by strong economic incentives to (re-)plant "CDR-optimized" instead of natural forests). The crucial question then is whether it is possible to effectively set regulatory limits to these economic incentives within an integrated carbon pricing approach with CDR offsetting (Honegger and Reiner, 2018).
- Even if readily available like mitigation, CDR might not be fully equivalent to mitigation with respect to its contribution to climate protection (Hurlbert *et al.*, 2019). As pointed out in Chapter 4, CDR involves a risk of reversibility. In particular, ecosystem-based CDR approaches are not only less verifiable but also less reliable and resilient in climate change mitigation than conventional abatement measures which they might substitute under offsetting (Minx *et al.*, 2018).
- If instead of an integrated system a governance approach is pursued that keeps mitigation and CDR largely separated, the regulator explicitly has to plan the respective contributions from mitigation and CDR, not only for a net-negative emissions target. Thereby, familiar regulatory problems of missing/asymmetric information about current and future private mitigation and CDR costs arise which can lead to inefficiencies and unjustified producer rents.

5.2. *Incentives for CDR in the status quo*

Current climate policy frameworks create only few financial incentives to invest in the deployment or development of CDR approaches and technologies. When CDR is addressed, this is often limited to ecosystem-based approaches as will be shown for examples from the UNFCCC and the EU.

REDD+, for example, constitutes the most important framework to foster CDR on a global scale. It was established under the UNFCCC in 2007 to reduce emissions from deforestation and forest degradation and to enhance forest carbon stocks in developing countries (Maniatis *et al.*, 2019). REDD+ represents a transfer scheme from industrialized countries to developing countries to protect and enhance carbon sinks in forests which generally should also include private sector contributions. While explicitly addressed in the Paris Agreement, the role of REDD+ in the future climate policy architecture and future carbon international market(s) currently negotiated under Art. 6 Paris Agreement is rather unclear. So far, REDD+ strongly depends on public funding from a rather small number of governments, and, not least because of that, did not scale up as originally intended (Duchelle *et al.*, 2019). Moreover, REDD+ is restricted to CDR from re-/afforestation projects in developing countries and does therefore not represent a systematic, integrated approach to internationally finance different types of CDR.

Honegger and Reiner (2018) argue that the market mechanism under Article 6.4 of the Paris Agreement, also called "Sustainable Development Mechanism," could play a vital role for mobilizing funds for CDR, in particular from industrialized countries. Such international carbon market mechanisms were also considered to be an important source of financing projects under REDD+. However, they are still under negotiation within the UNFCCC, in particular due to the question of how projects financed via these market mechanisms should be credited toward the NDCs.

Honegger and Reiner (2018) also point out that relying on market mechanisms to support CDR deployment would require at least initially that countries were allowed to pay premiums for CDR or support

CDR otherwise as not all CDR technologies are competitive so far. With respect to ecosystem-based approaches, the introduction of these markets would have to be accompanied by the development of reliable monitoring and accounting systems, international oversight, and low transaction costs. Also, as we already pointed out before in the more general discussion of offsetting, the market mechanism would have to be supplemented by effective social and environmental safeguards which guarantee that CDR activities within these market mechanisms do not conflict with sustainable goals — which is an ambitious goal as similar approaches for such safeguards have yielded at best mixed results (see Honegger and Reiner, 2018).

In the European climate policy architecture, ecosystem-based approaches to remove GHG from the atmosphere are primarily addressed by the LULUCF regulation which represents the third climate policy pillar next to sectors covered by the EU ETS and those under the ESR. While generally strictly separated, the ESR allows member states (under the conditions specified in Art. 7 (1) ESR) to compensate for emissions by credits generated in the LULUCF sector, e.g., from reforestation. This flexibility is, however, capped at about 262 Mt CO_2eq for all Member States over the period from 2021 to 2030.

The demand from the ESR sectors for LULUCF credits creates some financial incentives to invest in the enhancement of land-based carbon sinks. These incentives are, however, limited and hardly sufficient to incentivize additional investments compared to the reference development of the LULUCF sector. This conclusion is drawn by the EU Commission itself in its recent impact assessment: "Given that [the] flexibility to the ESR is fixed per Member State and cannot be traded between Member States, it is unlikely that the full 262 Mt flexibility will be used over the 10 year period. As such the incentive signal provided by the current climate policy architecture to take increased action in the LULUCF sector is limited ..." (EU Commission, 2020, p. 113).

The EU ETS, or the ETS Directive as its legislative foundation, currently provides only incentives for capturing emissions from fossil sources by CCS applications, but not for a net removal of carbon from the atmosphere. The reason is that the ETS Directive only applies to processes and applications which lead to the release of greenhouse gases in the atmosphere. For GHG emissions that do not reach the atmosphere because they are captured and transported for permanent storage, no emission certificates have to be surrendered (EU Parliament and EU Council, 2003). Moreover, given that under the European climate policy architecture, emissions from biomass use completely fall under the LULUCF regulation, bioenergy generation is climate neutral from the EU ETS perspective. The EU ETS, therefore, also does not provide incentives for the deployment of BECCS even though carbon capture and storage, in principle, would be eligible as a mitigation option (Rickels *et al.*, 2020). As Rickels *et al.* (2020) note, this does not leave scope for ecosystem-based removals.

Finally, the Common Agricultural Policy sets some incentives for more ecological farming in the agricultural sector which can, for example, enhance soil carbon formation and thereby lead to CDR. These incentives for "green" farming are, however, widely held to be insufficient (Pe'er *et al.*, 2019, Simoncini *et al.*, 2019), not only with respect to CDR but in particular with respect to overall external environmental costs of agricultural production, and generally do not systematically address ecosystem-based CDR.

6. Conclusions

We have shown that while negative emissions and CO_2 removal play an increasingly important role in climate policy scenarios, many questions remain. This concerns not only the design of climate policy frameworks needed to foster the deployment of CDR (especially with respect to net-negative emissions) but also questions where, when, and at which pace CDR should be conducted. Uncertainty about potentials and (private as well as external) costs is still high. This holds especially for technologies that go beyond ecosystem-based approaches with some technologies either still being in the development phase or, at least, not having been rolled out at scale. Existing CDR-related policies are very likely not sufficient to deliver negative emissions at a level needed to reach the 1.5°C temperature target of the Paris Agreement — especially with global GHG emissions still being on an upward trajectory.

It is therefore hardly surprising that the German Council on Global Change (WBGU) found considerable need for research and development with respect to (a) the integration of CDR into the climate protection architecture, (b) individual technologies, and (c) the extent to which a portfolio of CDR measures can achieve a resilient, sustainable contribution to climate protection without compromising, for example, biodiversity conservation and food security (WBGU, 2020).

Appendix A

Table A.1. CDR technologies.

	Fuss *et al.* (2018)[a]	IEA (2020)	IPCC (2019)*	NAP (2019)	The Royal Society (2018)
BECCS					
Cost	100–200 USD/tCO_2	15–85 USD/tCO_2		Middle = 20–100 USD/tCO_2	140–270 USD/tCO_2 (without long-term monitoring cost)
Potential	0.5–5 GtCO_2/year (in 2050)	100–1,170 GtCO_2[b]	0.4–11.3 GtCO_{2eq}/year	3.5–5.2 GtCO_2/year[c]	up to 10 GtCO_2/year
			DACCS		
Cost	In 2050: 100–300 USD/tCO_2 In 2100: 25–1,000 USD/tCO_2	135–345 USD/tCO_2		High => 100 USD/tCO_2	200–600 USD/tCO_2 (without storage)
Potential	In 2050: 0.5–5 GtCO_2/year In 2100: 10–40 GtCO_2/year	108–1,000 GtCO_2[b]		0[d]	about 900 GtCO_2 storage capacity in depleted oil and gas fields only
			Forests		
Cost	5–50 USD/tCO_2	5–50 USD/tCO_2		Low = 0–20 USD/tCO_2	0.4 GtCO_2 for under 3 USD/tCO_2 1.2 GtCO_2/year for under 30 GtCO_2 In 2100: 15–30 USD/tCO_2

(*Continued*)

Table A.1. (*Continued*)

	Fuss *et al.* (2018)[a]	IEA (2020)	IPCC (2019)*	NAP (2019)	The Royal Society (2018)
Potential	Af-/Reforestation: 0.5–3.6 $GtCO_2$/year	80–260 $GtCO_2$[b]	Af-/reforestation: 0.5–10.1 $GtCO_2$eq/year Forest management: 0.4–2.1 $GtCO_2$eq/year	Af-/reforestation: 1 $GtCO_2$/year[c] Forest management: 1.5 $GtCO_2$/year[c]	Af-/reforestation and forest management: 3–18 $GtCO_2$/year[e] Forest management: 1–2 $GtCO_2$/year by 2030
			Enhanced Weathering		
Cost	50–200 USD/tCO_2	50–200 USD/tCO_2		Middle–High = 20– > 100 USD/tCO_2	52–480 USD/tCO_2
Potential	2–4 $GtCO_2$/year	100–367 $GtCO_2$[b]	0.5–4 $GtCO_2$/year	unknown	0.5–4 $GtCO_2$/year by 2100[f]
			Soil Carbon Sequestration		
Cost	0–100 USD/tCO_2			Low–Middle = 0–100 USD/tCO_2	−12 – 3 USD/tCO_2
Potential	2–5 $GtCO_2$/year		0.4–8.6 $GtCO_2$eq/year	Agricultural practices to enhance soil carbon storage: 3 $GtCO_2$/year[c]	1.1–11.4 $GtCO_2$/year

(*Continued*)

Table A.1. (*Continued*)

	Fuss *et al.* (2018)[a]	IEA (2020)	IPCC (2019)*	NAP (2019)	The Royal Society (2018)
			Biochar		
Cost	30–120 USD/tCO_2	30–120 USD/tCO_2			18–166 USD/tCO_2
Potential	0.5–2 $GtCO_2$/year	78–1,468 $GtCO_2$[b]	0.03–6.6 $GtCO_2$eq/year		2.1–4.8 tCO_2 per ton of biochar on a life cycle basis 1.8–4.8 $GtCO_2$/year
			Ocean Fertilization		
Cost	No authors' assessment; 0–460 USD/tCO_2 range in literature				10–500 USD/tCO_2
Potential	Extremely limited; 0.5–44 $GtCO_2$/year range in literature				Max. CDR of 3.7 $GtCO_2$/year for ocean iron fertilization Total capacity until 2100: 70–300 $GtCO_2$

(*Continued*)

Table A.1. (*Continued*)

	Fuss *et al.* (2018)[a]	IEA (2020)	IPCC (2019)*	NAP (2019)	The Royal Society (2018)
			Wetland and Peatland Restoration		
Cost					10–100 USD/tCO_2[g]
Potential			Coastal wetland restoration: 0.2–0.84 $GtCO_2eq$/year Peatland restoration: 0.15–0.81 $GtCO_2eq$/year		Wetland restoration: 0.4–18 tCO_2/year per ha[f]

References

Bednar, J., Obersteiner, M., and Wagner, F. (2019). On the financial viability of negative emissions. *Nature Communications*, 10, 1783, doi: 10.1038/s41467-019-09782-x.

Beerling, D. J., Kantzas, E. P., Lomas, M. R., Wade, P., Eufrasio, R. M., Renforth, P., Sarkar, B., Andrews, M. G., James, R. H., Pearce, C. R., Mercure, J.-F., Pollitt, H., Holden, P. B., Edwards, N. R., Khanna, M., Koh, L., Quegan, S., Pidgeon, N. F., Janssens, I. A., Hansen, J., and Banwart, S. A. (2020). Potential for large-scale CO_2 removal via enhanced rock weathering with croplands. *Nature*, 583(7815), 242–248, doi: 10.1038/s41586-020-2448-9.

Bui, M., Adjiman, C. S., Bardow, A., Anthony, E. J., Boston, A., Brown, S., Fennell, P. S., Fuss, S., Galindo, A., Hackett, L. A., Hallett, J. P., Herzog, H. J., Jackson, G., Kemper, J., Krevor, S., Maitland, G. C., Matuszewski, M, Metcalfe, I. S., Petit, C., Puxty, G., Reimer, J., Reiner, D. M., Rubin, E. S., Scott, S. A., Shah, N., Smit, B., Trusler, J. P. M., Webley, P., Wilcoxx, J., and Mac Dowell, N. (2018). Carbon capture and storage (CCS): the way forward. *Energy & Environmental Science*, 11, 1062–1176, doi: 10.1039/c7ee02342a.

Burke, J., Byrnes, R., and Fankhauser, S. (2019). How to price carbon to reach net-zero emissions in the UK, London: Grantham Research Institute on Climate Change and the Environment and Centre for Climate Change Economics and Policy, London School of Economics and Political Science.

Climeworks (2020). *Direct Air Capture. A Technology to Reverse Climate Change*. https://www.climeworks.com/page/co2-removal, Climeworks, Zürich.

Creutzig, F., Breyer, C., Hilaire, J., Minx, J. C., Peters, G. P., and Socolow, R. (2019). The mutual dependence of negative emission technologies and energy systems. *Energy & Environmental Science*, 12, 1805–1817, doi: 10.1039/c8ee03682a.

Dietz, S., Bowen, A., Doda, B., Gambhir, A., and Warren, R. (2018). The economics of 1.5°C climate change. *Annual Review of Environment and Resources*, 43, 455–480, doi: 10.1146/annurev-environ-102017-025817.

Dietz, S. and Venmans, F. (2019). Cumulative carbon emissions and economic policy: In search of general principles. *Journal of Environmental Economics and Management*, 96, 108–129, doi: 10.1016/j.jeem.2019.04.003.

Dooley, K., Harrould-Kolieb, E., and Talberg, A. (2020). Carbon-dioxide removal and biodiversity: A threat identification framework. *Global Policy*. doi: 10.1111/1758-5899.12828.

Duchelle, A. E., Seymour, F., Brockhaus, M., Angelsen, A., Larson, A. M., Moeliono, M., Wong, G. Y., Pham, T. T., and Martius, C. (2019). *Forest-Based Climate Mitigation: Lessons from REDD+ Implementation*, World Resources Institute (WRI), Washington, DC.

EU Commission (2018). In-depth analysis in support on the COM(2018) 773: A Clean Planet for all — A European strategic long-term vision for a prosperous, modern, competitive and climate neutral economy, https://knowledge4policy.ec.europa.eu/publication/depth-analysis-support-com2018-773-clean-planet-all-european-strategic-long-term-vision_en.

EU Commission (2020). Impact assessment – Stepping up Europe's 2030 climate ambition investing in a climate-neutral future for the benefit of our people, https://ec.europa.eu/clima/sites/clima/files/eu-climate-action/docs/impact_en.pdf.

EU Parliament and EU Council (2003). Directive 2003/87/EC of the European Parliament and of the Council, https://eur-lex.europa.eu/legal-content/EN/TXT/?uri=CELEX%3A02003L0087-20200101.

Fajardy, M., Köberle, A., Mac Dowell, N., and Fantuzzi, A. (2019). BECCS deployment: a reality check, Grantham Institute Briefing paper No 28, Imperial College London.

Fajardy, M., Morris, J., Gurgel, A., Herzog, H., Mac Dowell, N., and Paltsev, S. (2020). The economics of bioenergy with carbon capture and storage (BECCS) deployment in a 1.5°C or 2°C world, MIT Joint Program on the Science and Policy of Global Change Report 345.

Field, C. and Mach, K. J. (2017). Rightsizing carbon dioxide removal. *Science*, 356(6339), 706–707, doi: 10.1126/science.aam9726.

Fuss, S., Canadell, J. G., Ciais, P., Jackson, R. B., Jones, C. D., Lyngfelt, A., Peter, G., and Van Vuuren, D. P. (2020). Moving toward net-zero emissions requires new alliances for carbon dioxide removal. *One Earth*, 3(2), 45–149, doi: 10.1016/j.oneear.2020.08.002.

Fuss, S., Lamb, W. F., Callaghan, M. W., Hilaire, J., Creutzig, F., Amann, T., Beringer, T., de Oliveira Garcia, W., Hartmann, J., Khanna, T., Luderer, G., Nemet, G. F., Rogelj, J., Smith, P., Vicente, J. L. V., Wilcox, J., del Mar Zamora Dominguez, M., and Minx, J. C. (2018). Negative emissions — Part 2: Costs, potentials and side effects. *Environmental Research Letters*, 13, doi: 10.1088/1748-9326/aabf9f.

Fuhrmann, J. McJeon, H., Patel, P., Doney, S. C., Shobe, W. M., and Clarens, A. F. (2020). Food-energy-water implications of negative emissions technologies in a +1.5°C future. *Nature Climate Change*, 10, 920–927, doi: 10.1038/s41558-020-0876-z.

Fyson, C. L., Baur, S., Gidden, M., and Schleussner, C.-F. (2020). Fair-share carbon dioxide removal increases major emitter responsibility. *Nature Climate Change*, 10, 836–841, doi: 10.1038/s41558-020-0857-2.

Gambhir, A. and Tavoni, M. (2019). Direct air carbon capture and sequestration: How it works and how it could contribute to climate-change mitigation. *On Earth*, 1(4), 405–409, doi: 10.1016/j.oneear.2019.11.006.

Geden, O. and Schenuit, F. (2020), Unkonventioneller Klimaschutz – Gezielte CO2-Entnahme aus der Atmosphäre als neuer Ansatz in der EU-Klimapolitik, SWP-Studie 10, Stiftung Wissenschaft und Politik, Berlin.

Gnanadesikan, A., Sarmiento, J. L., and Slater, R. D. (2003). Effects of patchy ocean fertilization on atmospheric carbon dioxide and biological production. *Global Biogeochemical Cycles*, 17(2), doi: 10.1029/2002GB001940.

Grubler, A., Wilson, C., Bento, N., Boza-Kiss, B., Krey, V., McCollum, D. L., Rao, N. D., Riahi, K., Rogelj, J., and De Stercke, S. (2018). A low energy demand scenario for meeting the 1.5 C target and sustainable development goals without negative emission technologies. *Nature Energy*, 3(6), 515–527.

Hanssen, S. V., Daioglou, V., Steinman, Z. J. N., Doelman, J. C., Van Vuuren, D. P., and Huijbregts, M. A. J. (2020). The climate change mitigation potential of bioenergy with carbon capture and storage. *Nature Climate Change*, 10, 1023–1029, doi: 10.1038/s41558-020-0885-y.

Hilaire, J., Minx, J. C., Callaghan, M. W., Edmonds, J., Luderer, G., Nemet, G. F., Rogelj, J., and Zamora, M. (2019). Negative emissions and international climate goals – learning from and about mitigation scenarios. *Climate Change*, 157, 189–219, doi: 10.1007/s10584-019-02516-4.

Honegger, M. and Reiner, D. (2018). The political economy of negative emissions technologies: Consequences for international policy design. *Climate Policy*, 18(3), 306–321, doi: 10.1080/14693062.2017.1413322.

Hurlbert, M., Krishnaswamy, J., Davin, E., Johnson, F. X., Mena, C. F., Morton, J., Myeong, S., Viner, D., Warner, K., Wreford, A., Zakieldeen, S., and Zommers, Z. (2019). Chapter 7: Risk management and decision making in relation to sustainable development. In: Shukla, P. R., Skea, J.,

Buendia, E. C., Masson-Delmotte, V., Pörtner, H.-O., Roberts, D. C., Zhai, P., Slade, R., Connors, S., Diemen, R. v., Ferrat, M., Haughey, E., Luz, S., Neogi, S., Pathak, M., Petzold, J., Pereira, J. P., Vyas, P., Huntley, E., Kissick, K., Belkacemi, M., and Malley, J. (Hrsg.): *Climate Change and Land: An IPCC Special Report on Climate Change, Desertification, Land Degradation, Sustainable Land Management, Food Security, and Greenhouse Gas Fluxes in Terrestrial Ecosystems.* Intergovernmental Panel on Climate Change (IPCC), Genf, pp. 673–800.

International Energy Agency (IEA, 2020). Energy Technologies Perspectives 2020: Special Report on Carbon Capture Utilisation and Storage – CCUS in clean energy transitions, September 2020.

IPCC (2018). Global Warming of 1.5°C. An IPCC Special Report on the impacts of global warming of 1.5°C above pre-industrial levels and related global greenhouse gas emission pathways, in the context of strengthening the global response to the threat of climate change, sustainable development, and efforts to eradicate poverty [V. Masson-Delmotte, P. Zhai, H.-O. Pörtner, D. Roberts, J. Skea, P. R. Shukla, A. Pirani, W. Moufouma-Okia, C. Péan, R. Pidcock, S. Connors, J. B. R. Matthews, Y. Chen, X. Zhou, M. I. Gomis, E. Lonnoy, T. Maycock, M. Tignor, and T. Waterfield (eds.)]. In Press.

Jia, G., Shevliakova, E., Artaxo, P., Noblet-Ducoudré, N. D., Houghton, R., House, J., Kitajima, K., Lennard, C., Popp, A., Sirin, A., Sukumar, R., and Verchot, L. (2019). Chapter 2: Land–climate interactions. In: Shukla, P. R., Skea, J., Buendia, E. C., Masson-Delmotte, V., Pörtner, H.-O., Roberts, D. C., Zhai, P., Slade, R., Connors, S., Diemen, R. v., Ferrat, M., Haughey, E., Luz, S., Neogi, S., Pathak, M., Petzold, J., Pereira, J. P., Vyas, P., Huntley, E., Kissick, K., Belkacemi, M., and Malley, J. (Hrsg.): *Climate Change and Land: An IPCC Special Report on Climate Change, Desertification, Land Degradation, Sustainable Land Management, Food Security, and Greenhouse Gas Fluxes in Terrestrial Ecosystems*, Intergovernmental Panel on Climate Change (IPCC), Genf, pp. 131–247.

Lee, H., Yang, S., Wi, S., and Kim, S. (2019). Thermal transfer behavior of biochar-natural inorganic clay composite for building envelope insulation. *Construction and Building Materials*, 223, 668–678.

Lemoine, D. (2020). Incentivizing negative emissions through carbon shares, NBER Working Paper No. 27880, http://www.nber.org/papers/w27880.

Lenzi, D. (2018). The ethics of negative emissions. *Global Sustainability*, 1(e7), 1–8, doi: 10.1017/sus.2018.5.

Lenzi, D., Lamb, W. F., Hilaire, J., Kowarsch, M., and Minx, J. C. (2018). Weigh the ethics of plans to mop up carbon dioxide. *Nature*, 561(7723), 303–305.

Luderer, G., Vrontisi, Z., Bertram, C., Edelenbosch, O. Y., Pietzcker, Ro. C., Rogelj, J., De Boer, H. S., Drouet, L., Emmerling, J., Fricko, O., Fujimori, S., Havlík, P. Iyer, G., Keramidas, K., Kitous, A., Pehl, M., Krey, V., Riahi, K., Saveyn, B., Tavoni, M., Van Vuuren, D. P., and Kriegler, E. (2018). Residual CO_2 emissions in 1.5–2°C pathways. *Nature Climate Change*, 8, 626–633, doi: 10.1038/s41558-018-0198-6.

Maniatis, D., Scriven, J., Jonckheere, I., Laughlin, J., and Todd, K. (2019). Toward REDD+ implementation. *Annual Review of Environment and Resources*, 44, 373–398, doi: 10.1146/annurev-environ-102016-060839.

McLaren, D. P., Tyfield, D. P., Willis, R., Szerszynski, B., and Markusson, N. O. (2019). Beyond "Net-Zero", a case for separate targets for emissions reduction and negative emissions. *Frontiers in Climate*, 1(4), 1–5, doi: 10.3389/fclim.2019.00004.

Minx, J. C., Lamb, W. F., Callaghan, M. W., Fuss, S., Hilaire, J., Creutzig, F., Amann, T., Beringer, T., de Oliveira Garcia, W., Hartmann, J., Khanna, T., Lenzi, D., Luderer, G., Nemet, G. F., Rogelj, J., Smith, P., Vicente, J. L. V., Wilcox, J., and del Mar Zamora Dominguez, M. (2018). Negative emissions – Part 1: Research landscape and synthesis. *Environmental Research Letters*, 13, doi: 10.1088/1748-9326/aabf9b.

NAP: National Academies of Sciences, Engineering, and Medicine 2019. *Negative Emissions Technologies and Reliable Sequestration: A Research Agenda*, The National Academies Press, Washington, DC, doi: 10.17226/25259.

Nemet, G. F., Callaghan, M. W., Creutzig, F., Fuss, S., Hartmann, J., Hilaire, J., Lamb, W. F., Minx, J. C., Rogers, S., and Smith, P. (2018). Negative emissions – Part 3: Innovation and upscaling. *Environmental Research Letters*, 13(6), doi: 10.1088/1748-9326/aabff4.

Obersteiner, M., Bednar, J., Wagner, F., Gasser, T., Ciais, P., Forsell, N., Frank, S., Havlik, P., Valin, H., Janssens, I. A., Peñuelas, J., and Schmidt-Traub, G. (2018), How to spend a dwindling greenhouse gas budget. *Nature Climate Change*, 8, 2–12, doi: 10.1038/s41558-017-0045-1.

Pe'er, G., Zinngrebe, Y., Moreira, F., Sirami, C., Schindler, S., Müller, R., Bontzorlos, V., Clough, D., Bezák, P., and Bonn, A. (2019). A greener path for the EU Common Agricultural Policy. *Science*, 365 (6452), 449–451, doi: 10.1126/science.aax3146.

Peters, G. P., Andrew, R. M., Canadell, J. G., Friedlingstein, P., Jackson, R. B., Korsbakken, J. I., Le Quéré, C., and Peregon, A. (2020). Carbon dioxide emissions continue to grow amidst slowly emerging climate policies. *Nature Climate Change*, 10, 2–10, doi: 10.1038/s41558-019-0659-6.

Realmonte, G., Drouet, L., Gambhir, A., Glynn, J., Hawkes, A., Köberle, A. C., and Tavoni, M. (2019). An inter-model assessment of the role of direct air capture in deep mitigation pathways. *Nature Communications*, 10, 3277, doi: 10.1038/s41467-019-10842-5.

Rickels, W., Merk, C., Honneth, J., Schwinger, J., Quaas, M., and Oschlies, A. (2019). Welche Rolle spielen negative Emissionen für die zukünftige Klimapolitik? *Perspektiven der Wirtschaftspolitik*, 20(2), 145–158, doi: 10.1515/pwp-2018-0034.

Rickels, W., Proelß, A., Geden, O., Burhenne, J., and Friedahl, M. (2020). The Future of (Negative) Emissions Trading in the European Union, Kiel Working Paper No. 2164, Kiel Institute for the World Economy.

Roe, S., Streck, C., Obersteiner, M., Frank, S., Griscom, B., Drouet, L., Fricko, O., Gusti, M., Harris, N., Hasegawa, T., Hausfather, Z., Havlík, P., House, J., Nabuurs, G., Popp, A., Sanz Sánches, M. J., Sanderman, J., Smith, P., Stehfest, E., and Lawrence, D. (2019). Contribution of the land sector to a 1.5°C world. *Nature Climate Change*, 9, 817–828, doi: 10.1038/s41558-019-0591-9.

Rogelj, J., Huppmann, D., Krey, V., Riahi, K., Clarke, L., Gidden, M., Nicholls, Z., and Meinshausen, M. (2019). A new scenario logic for the Paris Agreement long-term temperature goal. *Nature*, 573, 357–363, doi: 10.1038/s41586-019-1541-4.

Röhrdanz, M., Pannemann, F., Dittrich, K., Klenke, T., Buchwald, R., and Wark, M. (2019). Erweiterung der Verwertungs-Kaskaden von Reststoff-Biomassen durch die Herstellung von HTC-Biokohle am Beispiel unterschiedlicher Güllearten. In: Marx Gómez, J., Solsbach, A., Klenke, T., and Wohlgemuth, V. (Hrsg.): *Smart Cities/Smart Regions — Technische, wirtschaftliche und gesellschaftliche Innovationen*, Springer, Heidelberg, Berlin, pp. 755–763.

Schreyer, F., Luderer, G., Rodrigues, R., Pietzcker, R. C., Baumstark, L., Sugiyama, M., Brecha, R. J., and Ueckerdt, F. (2020). Common but differentiated leadership: Strategies and challenges for carbon neutrality by 2050 across industrialized economies. *Environmental Research Letters*, 15(11), https://doi.org/10.1088/1748-9326/abb852.

Schultes, A., Piontek, F., Soergel, B., Rogelj, J., Baumstark, L., Kriegler, E., Edenhofer, O., and Luderer, G. (2020). Economic damages from on-going climate change imply deeper near-term emission cuts, MPRA Paper 103655, University Library of Munich, Germany.

Simoncini, R., Ring, I., Sandström, C., Albert, C., Kasymov, U., and Arlettaz, R. (2019). Constraints and opportunities for mainstreaming biodiversity and ecosystem services in the EU's Common Agricultural Policy: Insights from the IPBES assessment for Europe and Central Asia. *Land Use Policy*, 88, 104099, doi: 10.1016/j.landusepol.2019.104099.

Smith, P., Adams, J., Beerling, D. J., Beringer, T., Calvin, K. V., Fuss, S., Griscom, B., Hagemann, N., Kammann, C., Kraxner, F., Minx, J. C., Popp, A., Renforth, P., Vicente Vicente, J. L., and Keesstra, S. (2019a). Land-management options for greenhouse gas removal and their impacts on ecosystem services and the sustainable development goals. *Annual Review of Environment and Resources*, 44(1), 255–286, doi: 10.1146/annurev-environ-101718-033129.

Smith, P., Nkem, J., Calvin, K., Campbell, D., Cherubini, F., Grassi, G., Korotkov, V., Hoang, A. L., Lwasa, S., McElwee, P., Nkonya, E., Saigusa, N., Soussana, J.-F., and Taboada, M. A. (2019b). Chapter 6: Interlinkages between desertification, land degradation, food security and greenhouse gas fluxes: synergies, trade-offs and integrated response options. In: Shukla, P. R., Skea, J., Buendia, E. C., Masson-Delmotte, V., Pörtner, H.-O., Roberts, D. C., Zhai, P., Slade, R., Connors, S., Diemen, R. v., Ferrat, M., Haughey, E., Luz, S., Neogi, S., Pathak, M., Petzold, J., Pereira, J. P., Vyas, P., Huntley, E., Kissick, K., Belkacemi, M. and Malley, J. (Hrsg.): *Climate Change and Land: An IPCC Special Report on Climate Change, Desertification, Land Degradation, Sustainable Land Management, Food Security, and Greenhouse Gas Fluxes in Terrestrial Ecosystems*, Intergovernmental Panel on Climate Change (IPCC), Genf, pp. 551–672.

Steffen, W., Rockström, J., Richardson, K., Lenton, T. M., Folke, C., Liverman, D., Summerhayes, C. P., Barnosky, A. D., Cornell, S. E., Crucifix, M., Donges, J. F., Fetzer, I., Lade, S. J., Scheffer, M., Winkelmann, R., and Schellnhuber, H. J. (2018). Trajectories of the Earth system in the anthropocene. *Proceedings of the National Academy of Sciences*, 115(33), 8252–8259, doi: 10.1073/pnas.1810141115.

Strefler, J., Bauer, N., Kriegler, E., Popp, A., Giannousakis, A., and Edenhofer, O. (2018). Between Scylla and Charybdis: Delayed mitigation narrows the passage between large-scale CDR and high costs. *Environmental Research Letters*, 13(4), doi: 10.1088/1748-9326/aab2ba.

Teichmann, I. (2014). Klimaschutz durch Biokohle in der deutschen Landwirtschaft: Potentiale und Kosten, *DIW-Wochenbericht*, 81(1/2), 3–13.

The Royal Society (2018). *Greenhouse Gas Removal*, The Royal Society, London.

UN (2020). Emissions Gap Report 2020, https://www.unenvironment.org/emissions-gap-report-2020.

van Vuuren, D. P., Stehfest, E., Gernaat, D. E. H. J., Van Den Berg, M., Bijl, D. L., De Boer, H. S., Daioglou, V., Doelman, J. C., Edelenbosch, O. Y., and Harmsen, M. (2018). Alternative pathways to the 1.5 C target reduce the need for negative emission technologies. *Nature Climate Change*, 8(5), 391–397.

WBGU (2021). Rethinking Land in the Anthropocene: from Separation to Integration. Berlin: WBGU. https://www.wbgu.de/de/publikationen/publikation/landwende.

https://doi.org/10.1142/9789811240553_0013

Chapter 13

Can Blue Carbon Initiatives Help Conserve Mangroves in Developing Countries?

Christa Brunnschweiler[*,‡] **and Tiziana Luisetti**[†,§]

**University of East Anglia,*
School of Economics and Centre for Behavioural and Experimental Social Science (CBESS) NR4 7TJ Norwich, UK
†Centre for Environment Fisheries & Aquaculture Science (Cefas) Pakefield Road, Lowestoft, Suffolk NR33 0HT, UK
‡c.brunnschweiler@uea.ac.uk
§tiziana.luisetti@cefas.co.uk

Mangrove forests are important global carbon sinks, and offer other, local ecosystem services such as fish nurseries and sources of firewood and building materials. Most mangroves are located in developing countries, where — despite widespread legal protection — they are in severe decline mainly due to human pressure. We investigate whether and how blue carbon initiatives can help conserve and restore mangroves in developing countries. We focus on financing and stakeholder involvement through the lens of scalability, and discuss which designs are likely to be successful for the rapid, large-scale projects needed to face the current climate change emergency. We make three suggestions: First, in the design phase, large-scale projects should combine the use of qualitative, participatory methods, which have proved effective for stakeholder involvement in small projects, with more quantitative, survey, and experimental methods for faster, evidence-based solutions. Second, the financial product chosen for a blue carbon project must be supported by local communities if it is to be successful in the long term. And, third, bundling ecosystem services together is more likely to achieve financial returns that are high enough to facilitate the crucial stakeholder support at community and higher levels.

1. Introduction

Coastal ecosystems act as crucial buffer zones between sea and inland areas; they are also rich habitats for flora and fauna and important natural carbon sinks (Rogers *et al.*, 2019). Unfortunately, estimates show that nearly half of global coastal ecosystems (including saltmarshes, mangroves, and seagrass meadows) have been lost over the past century, mostly because of human pressure, e.g., urban encroachment and wetland conversion, pollution, and the effects of climate change (Li *et al.*, 2018). A recent IPCC Special Report on the Ocean and Cryosphere in a Changing Climate states that conservation and restoration of these so-called "coastal blue carbon ecosystems" could help mitigate global carbon emissions and, perhaps even more important, have positive knock-on effects for the resilience of coastal ecosystems and communities (Pörtner *et al.*, 2019).

One blue carbon ecosystem is mangrove forests; because these grow in warm waters, they are located mainly in developing countries (see, e.g., Jakovac *et al.*, 2020). These coastal wetland forests provide vital ecosystem services for local communities, for example, through their function as fish nurseries, sources of firewood and building material, and sea defenses. And, though they account for less than half a percent of global forest cover, they are a remarkable global carbon sink: estimates show that mangroves store more carbon than land-based forests Atwood *et al.* (2017). This is why, even with their limited global coverage, their destruction and conversion into pastureland would release three times more CO_2 into the atmosphere than the deforestation of the entire Amazon forest (Kauffman *et al.*, 2016).

Although most countries legally protect mangroves from deforestation and degradation, for example, through coastal management plans and explicit bans on mangrove destruction, these traditional top-down conservation tools have been unable to stem the decline in global mangrove forest cover (Herr *et al.*, 2017). Unfortunately, despite their importance as global carbon sinks, mangrove forests are still not systematically included in established policy frameworks such as the UNFCC's Reducing Emissions from Deforestation and Forest Degradation (REDD+) scheme and the Clean Development Mechanism (CDM), both of which rely on the creation of verified carbon credits that are sold on a carbon market. The reasons for this include uncertainties around mangrove forests' extent, carbon stocks, monitoring possibilities, the legal definition of mangrove forests (they need to be officially classified as forest cover by a country seeking REDD+ financing, for example), and the lengthy (national) processes involved when complying with a UNFCC mechanism (Wylie *et al.*, 2016). The past five years have seen a slow increase in the inclusion of mangroves in these mechanisms, but there are also other initiatives for mangrove conservation and restoration.

In this chapter, we examine whether and how blue carbon initiatives can help conserve and restore mangrove forests in the developing world. We focus on two interlinking aspects of blue carbon initiatives that are particularly important: the financing scheme and the involvement of stakeholders in the design and implementation. Concerning the first aspect, protecting and managing an ecosystem requires a substantial budget not only during project implementation but also later during the long-term management. Some funding schemes have already proved to be successful for small-scale projects, but here we focus on the new emerging ideas that could be more suitable on a larger scale, and promise more rapid success of blue carbon financing. An important point to remember when designing a financing scheme is that if a blue carbon ecosystem is protected, it cannot be used for something else for which it has previously been, or could be, profitable — i.e., it carries an opportunity cost. Therefore, the temporal scale of the project and of the trade-offs involved, that is, for how long the economic benefits will be provided, is important not only for the environmental pillar of sustainability but also for the social pillar (Purvis *et al.*, 2019).

The second aspect is linked to the social pillar of sustainability, and addresses the competing uses and values by local communities in particular that need to be reconciled in any mangrove conservation and restoration initiative. Strong stakeholder involvement has emerged as the key ingredient in successful REDD+ projects, and first experiences show that it is similarly important for specific blue carbon initiatives. However, a majority of already implemented projects have been on a relatively small scale, with a participatory, trial-and-error approach to involving stakeholders in a limited number of local communities. Unfortunately, climate change has arrived at a stage that requires large-scale action within the next ten years. Because of this urgency, our analysis is performed through the lens of scalability: Which approach to designing a blue carbon initiative can be applied to large-scale mangrove conservation and restoration projects?

Our findings lead to three suggestions for designing and implementing blue carbon initiatives involving mangrove forests. First, in the project design phase, we propose combining qualitative, participatory approaches for stakeholder involvement with more quantitative approaches — i.e., representative surveys, lab-in-the-field experiments, or randomized control trials — that offer strong data-driven evidence on which (limited number of) strategies are most likely to produce the desired ecosystem conservation and restoration results on a large scale. The combination of methods would allow for more timely evidence on the viable ecosystem management options, and for an understanding of the underlying behavioral mechanisms that would ease the adaptation of a project design to a different context. In general, we believe that it is important for scientists and practitioners to maintain a flexible approach, and to be open to combining insights from practice-based reports, from environmental science, environmental economics and finance, behavioral economics, and sociology.

Second — and linked to the first suggestion — the choice of the financial product to be developed for the conservation of a specific coastal ecosystem should take into account not just the market potential of that ecosystem based on its environmental characteristics but also the buy-in and acceptability of the product by the local communities. And, third, bundling the many ecosystem services of mangrove forests together can help achieve sufficient financial return to facilitate the crucial stakeholder buy-in not only at the community level but also at the donor and investor level. Ultimately, the aim should be the rapid realization of mangrove conservation and restoration projects that enjoy strong stakeholder support and have a strong financial backing.

Note that although our focus in this chapter is on mangrove conservation and restoration in developing countries, these suggestions could readily be adapted to other types of ecosystem or to developed countries.

The rest of the chapter is organized as follows. Section 2 gives a brief overview of the literature on blue carbon initiatives, Sec. 3 examines the financing aspect, and Sec. 4 the stakeholder involvement aspect of blue carbon initiatives. Section 5 discusses the findings and puts forward our suggestions for the design of blue carbon initiatives, and Sec. 6 concludes.

2. A Brief Review of the Literature on Blue Carbon

The CO_2 sequestered from the atmosphere by coastal vegetated ecosystems, such as saltmarshes, mangroves, and seagrasses, and locked down in the sediment beneath them is called "blue carbon" (Macreadie *et al.*, 2019). Carbon sequestration helps mitigate climate change and is an important ecosystem service. It is only since the term blue carbon was conceived about a decade ago that blue carbon ecosystems have been getting some recognition as key players in the mitigation of climate change, as advocated by da Silva Copertino (2011). An increasing number of scientists have been showing the significance of the carbon sinks in mangroves and saltmarshes since the beginning of the new millennium (Macreadie *et al.*, 2019), and the IPCC Special Report on the Ocean and Cryosphere in a Changing Climate (Pörtner *et al.*, 2019) summarizes scientific contributions around blue carbon so far. Since then, policy advocacy in several countries has led to governments' consideration of these ecosystems in their Nationally Determined Contributions (NDCs) — the voluntary emission-reduction pledges in fulfillment of the 2015 Paris Agreement (see Gallo *et al.*, 2017). Similarly, non-governmental organizations are also taking these ecosystems' carbon storage capacity into account (see Ullman *et al.*, 2013). For the purposes of this chapter, two main blue carbon literature reviews are considered: Macreadie *et al.* (2019) and Thomas (2014).

"The Future of Blue Carbon Science" (Macreadie *et al.*, 2019) shows where we are with the blue carbon science, encompassing natural sciences and social sciences alike, including the challenges of economic valuation and management of blue carbon. The paper uses a less traditional definition of blue carbon so as to include the Ocean and its role in carbon sequestration. We summarize their major findings about mangroves. Macreadie *et al.* (2019) report that mangroves are mostly located in developing countries as they are found in areas of tropical and sub-tropical climate, and that they have been declining at an estimated annual rate between 1% and 3% since the 1950s. Blue carbon ecosystems, especially mangroves and seagrasses, can be directly affected by urban development and coastal infrastructures and indirectly by climate change, for example, due to the negative effects of ocean acidification on marine ecosystems. The authors report that of the three blue carbon ecosystems, mangrove forests are the ones which we know more about in terms of areal extension, although the use of different methodologies to map them can provide a different spatial extent. However, even though we have a better carbon budget for mangroves than for seagrasses and saltmarshes, this is still surrounded by uncertainties, especially with reference to the estimates of net carbon burial. The latter refers to the quantity of carbon sequestered compared to the quantity of greenhouse gases — including methane and nitrous oxide — emitted during carbon sequestration and storage (see also Oreska *et al.*, 2020). Such data are crucial, for example, for the calculation of the NDCs, or for other climate change mitigation mechanisms that have begun to consider blue carbon ecosystems as important contributors in reducing the effects of climate change. However, Macreadie *et al.* (2019) highlight the fact that technical, financial, and policy barriers still remain in the scaling-up of local blue carbon projects around the globe; we will look at the challenges of broadening the scale of blue carbon projects in the next sections.

Carbon market mechanisms and public and private carbon finance more generally are the objective of Thomas (2014) review. The whole carbon finance issue revolves around the opportunity costs of blue carbon, in particular mangrove forest conservation. Picking up on this, Jakovac *et al.* (2020) investigate the carbon price needed to conserve and restore mangroves around the world. They find that different carbon break-even prices are needed in different countries, depending on the opportunity costs involved. For example, to conserve 90% of existing mangroves (in 2017), in Cameroon, in a scenario of 25% of CO_2 stored in the living biomass and up to one meter in the soil released in the atmosphere because of deforestation, a carbon break-even price of 6.5 US$/t$CO_2$ is required. However, in the United States, this price could be about 22 US$/t$CO_2$. Therefore, the authors suggest broadening the scope and looking at the co-benefits provided by mangroves to combine carbon-based mechanisms with sustainable management for those areas where high-profit alternative land uses are involved.

Thomas (2014) discusses the suggestion that, within private finance remit, offsetting schemes such as the European Union Emissions Trading Scheme (EU ETS) are the most promising for blue carbon (see also Ullman *et al.*, 2013). However, there are examples of the use of other carbon offsetting mechanisms, such as Verified Carbon Standards (VCS), which trade carbon credits in voluntary markets. REDD+, which is an international public finance mechanism, has also been suggested as an option for blue carbon. The REDD+ initiative, focused originally on land-based deforestation, and launched in 2008, promised financing for projects that would have an impact on a global scale. It is worth noting that offsetting schemes can be based both on restoration and avoided deforestation in developed and developing countries, whereas the basics of REDD+ are of avoiding emissions from deforestation in developing countries only (Thomas, 2014).

Payments for ecosystem services (PESs) that consider the carbon sequestration provision alongside other benefits provided by blue carbon ecosystems are another possibility. However, in this case, concerns regarding equity around who the beneficiaries are and how the access to the benefits is managed exist (Thomas, 2014). Insurance products are also becoming more common. For example, parametric insurance mechanisms are considered with regard to climate change-related damages (e.g., hurricanes) and Thomas's review suggests that these could also be applied to blue carbon ecosystems for the provision of carbon sequestration.

Finally, Thomas (2014) also highlights the possibilities for blue carbon using micro-finance and climate green bonds. The author reports that bonds are the only mechanism able to capture both public and private finance. Recent financing suggestions leverage financial markets in order to conserve and/or restore coastal vegetated ecosystems, termed "blue capital" (Roth *et al.*, 2019). Blue bonds (BB), originally set in the Seychelles to support sustainable fishing, could also be a way forward, and we discuss these in more detail below.

3. The Financing of Blue Carbon Schemes for Mangrove Conservation and Restoration in Developing Countries

As we have seen in Section 2, there are several opportunities for financing blue carbon, some already a reality of ongoing projects, others a possibility. Thomas (2014) lists public and private financing opportunities, separating those available in developing and developed countries, and which are domestic or international mechanisms. Among the "other finance opportunities," green bonds are mentioned. However, a more appropriate opportunity for blue carbon conservation and restoration comes from a new finance instrument, the "blue bonds" (BBs).

3.1. *The new kid on the financing block: Blue bonds*

BBs are a new debt-for-nature mechanism — so new that we have to turn to the grey literature[1] to find a description of the mechanism and its initial implementations. At the heart of the definition of BBs for conservation is the opportunity of converting national debt to secure funding for conservation of a nation's marine and coastal environment that also benefits their blue economy. The emission of BBs and the restructuring of the nation's sovereign debt allow the country to realize some savings based on a lower interest rate and a longer

[1]A simple and effective explanation of blue bonds is provided by The Nature Conservancy, available at: https://www.nature.org/en-us/what-we-do/our-insights/perspectives/an-audacious-plan-to-save-the-worlds-oceans/.

repayment period for their national debt. Part of those savings will then be invested in the conservation activities the country has committed to, such as new marine protected areas. In 2016, The Nature Conservancy (TNC), a U.S. environmental NGO, led the first BB negotiations between the Republic of Seychelles, a third party that purchased the country's debt at a discount from its Paris Club creditors, and an independent public–private trust fund called the Seychelles Conservation and Climate Adaptation Trust (SeyCCAT).

BBs are an example of merged private and public interests. Donors allow the process to start providing initial necessary funds. Intermediaries, such as TNC, lead the negotiations between a coastal nation and the other key players such as the World Bank, commercial investors, and public funders. At the same time, the negotiator provides scientific advice and links with local stakeholders (more on this in Section 4) to set up the necessary plan, policies, and regulations needed for the implementation. The coastal nation is asked to commit to protect at least 30% of its inshore areas. This means that blue carbon, and therefore mangroves, is included. Host governments are also asked to commit to other environmentally sustainable initiatives such as improving fisheries management and reducing pollution.

BBs are a promising new financial mechanism for environmental conservation, and private financial institutions are taking an interest in them. For example, the informational material released by Morgan Stanley in September 2019 suggested a broader use of BBs in the context of the World Bank initiative on plastic waste to support the SDGs.[2]

3.2. *Other financing options for blue carbon projects*

Given the initial results reported by TNC, BBs seem to be a very positive initiative for island nations, and in fact BB projects are currently being developed for Caribbean, Pacific, and West Indian Ocean Island

[2]Informational material about the future of blue bonds prepared by Morgan Stanley in 2019 can be found, available at: https://www.morganstanley.com/content/dam/msdotcom/ideas/blue-bonds/2583076-FINAL-MS_GSF_Blue_Bonds.pdf.

states.[3] However, if we want to go for big projects with big results for blue carbon, Ullman *et al.* (2013) suggest the use of regulated market mechanisms like the EU ETS. We find several challenges that limit the implementation of such regulated markets for carbon credits for blue carbon. From a natural science point of view, Thomas (2014) mentions that we still lack appropriate monitoring and evidence for blue carbon ecosystems: he considers the measurement of environmental assets a fundamental condition for blue carbon financial products. Natural capital and ecosystem services accounting is proving a useful supporting tool in providing these data (Luisetti *et al.*, 2020).

However, other evidence is still lacking. For example, for blue carbon offsetting mechanisms to be considered, it would be better to have the estimates of net carbon sequestration rates (Oreska *et al.*, 2020), because the methane and nitrous oxide released in the carbon sequestration process can partially offset the blue carbon benefit. From a policy point of view, the same challenges common to the terrestrial ecosystems of additionality (i.e., without the project, there would not have been any carbon emissions reduction), leakage (i.e., the carbon emissions problem just changes geographical area), and permanence (i.e., minimizing the risk that the carbon emissions problem is only temporarily solved) still remain for blue carbon offsetting mechanisms (Ullman *et al.*, 2013).

Finally, we have the well-established PESs. The main criticisms that PESs receive are with regard to the human side of a project: the ethics, equity, and the measurement of the human–nature relationship (Thomas, 2014). In terms of ethics, there is the risk that if the financial value of the PES is too low, perverse incentives might arise; this is why knowing the break-even price is important (Jakovac *et al.*, 2020). For these reasons, it is crucial to engage with the local communities from an early stage of the development of the blue carbon

[3]Information on the ongoing (as of 2020) The Nature Conservancy blue bonds projects can be found, available at: https://www.nature.org/en-us/what-we-do/our-insights/perspectives/an-audacious-plan-to-save-the-worlds-oceans/.

financing mechanism — to have their buy-in and their involvement in the management of the blue carbon resource.

4. The Importance of Stakeholder Support for Mangrove Conservation and Restoration Projects

We outlined above the potential of new financing schemes for blue carbon initiatives in developing countries and pointed out the importance of local stakeholder support. We can draw similar lessons for the content design and implementation of these initiatives.

Traditional, top-down command-and-control tools for mangrove conservation rely on regulatory regimes such as coastal protection, strict fishery laws, and penal provisions in case of contraventions. Most countries have been legally protecting mangroves and other coastal wetlands in this way for decades.[4] Yet, the fact that these habitats are currently acknowledged to be under threat across the world attests to the scarce success of these measures. In general, the failures can be attributed to human activity — land use change, urbanization, and overexploitation of the natural resources account for 62% of global mangrove loss between 2010 and 2016 — and increasingly also to natural causes, including the effects of climate change (Goldberg *et al.*, 2020). Looking in more detail at the underlying issues, (Herr *et al.*, 2017) point at poor enforcement and conflicts between top-down protection measures and the needs of local communities — including historical tenure claims — as the main culprits.

These failures have shaped the current thinking, which places the long-term success of mangrove conservation and restoration initiatives on the support of local stakeholders, from the initial understanding of the use, benefits, and future preferences for mangroves to the development and implementation of a long-term mangrove conservation plan.

[4]For example, Indonesia's Forestry Code of 1999 prohibits the cutting of all trees along coasts and waterways, and Ecuador has banned mangrove destruction specifically since the 1970s. Nevertheless, both countries have seen large human-driven declines in mangroves in the past two decades (Goldberg *et al.*, 2020). For more details and examples, see Herr *et al.* (2017) and references therein.

Key concepts in this approach are using "local knowledge" and creating a sense of "ownership" among the stakeholders directly affected by a project. Recent blue carbon conservation and restoration efforts have implemented the approach mainly through qualitative, participatory methods in small-scale projects.[5] We first discuss some of these experiences, and then examine their scalability to large-scale projects.

4.1. *Experiences of stakeholder involvement in small-scale blue carbon projects*

There are now a good number of mostly small-scale blue carbon projects in developing countries that include strong elements of stakeholder involvement, though most of them have yet to begin trading carbon credits.[6] We describe three small projects in developing countries that reflect the best practice for community engagement (see Herr *et al.*, 2017 and Wylie *et al.*, 2016, for more examples), before turning our focus to larger-scale projects.

The first community-led mangrove conservation and restoration project in the world to successfully begin trading carbon credits is *Mikoko Pamoja* in Gazi Bay, Kenya. The project was implemented in 2013 through a collaboration between the Kenya Marine Fisheries Institute, Napier Edinburgh University, and Earthwatch Institute. It covers an area of 117 ha of mangroves and involves nearly 500 households in two local communities. Carbon credits are sold through Plan Vivo on the voluntary market, trading around 3,000 tCO_2-equivalent per year. The *Mikoko Pamoja* project was born from long-term research and community engagement in the area. Participatory consultative community meetings were used to decide on the use of the profits from carbon credit sales, and the mangroves are managed by a community organization. The profits are reinvested in the community, to

[5] The term "participatory" refers to the active and influential involvement of the end users of a project, usually from the planning to the implementation phase.

[6] For example, Plan Vivo — a main certification body for community land use and forestry projects — currently lists only one mangrove project (*Mikoko Pamoja* in Kenya, described below) that is selling carbon credits, or Plan Vivo Certificates (PVCs), on the voluntary market, in addition to two coastal rainforest projects (see planvivo.org).

supply clean water access, school materials, and safeguard the mangrove forest. The project also set up a small ecotourism initiative managed by local women, which is proving a model for other parts of Kenya and other countries UNDP (2020). In 2017, the project won the UNDP Equator Prize (see equatorinitiative.org). UNEP and CIFOR (2014) link the success of *Mikoko Pamoja* to the strong community support, the wealth of research into mangroves in the region, supportive regulation and knowledgeable government agencies, and the (serendipitous, we note) presence of an individual in Gazi Bay who is one of the project founders.

Rakotomahazo *et al.* (2019) discuss a project in southwestern Madagascar that used two participatory methods (public participation geographic information systems (GIS) and concept modeling workshops) in ten coastal communities to help set up a sustainable management strategy, funded through PESs, for approximately 1,507 ha of mangroves. The project, called *Tahiry Honko*, is designed to integrate into the national REDD+ strategy, and was jointly implemented by the UK-based NGO Blue Ventures and the managers of the local coastal protected area. The aims of the participatory approach here were to understand the spatial distribution of land and resource use for the development of a mangrove zoning plan, and the pressures faced by the mangrove forests in the area for the development of a "concept model," which included listing the threats to the mangroves, their origins, and possible long-term management strategies. Though the project was initiated by a foreign NGO, the approach tried to deliver not only good-quality data on the site but also create a sense of ownership by the local communities through their involvement in the actual decision-making. The NGO is currently designing the funding model for the generation and sale of carbon credits through Plan Vivo on the voluntary carbon market, to implement the mangrove management strategies that emerged from the participatory work.

Thompson and Friess (2019) study mangrove conservation and restoration schemes in two sites in Thailand. Both sites had ongoing mangrove restoration projects funded through the corporate social responsibility scheme of a Thai association, as well as complementary efforts by the Thai government. In common with the Malagasy example above, a participatory approach was used both for research purposes and to involve stakeholders in the choice of the long-term mangrove management strategy. The authors used a combination of initial high-level (i.e., national) stakeholder interviews to identify the full selection of national, regional, and local stakeholders, and a participatory multi-criteria decision analysis (MCDA) to compile a final ranking of preferred mangrove management options and understand the underlying reasons. The results suggested strong stakeholder support for the top-ranked option of PESs in both sites. However, the actual implementation of the mangrove management strategy is still uncertain.

4.2. *The scope for stakeholder involvement in large-scale mangrove conservation and restoration projects*

The projects described so far illustrate the small scope and often early implementation stage of blue carbon initiatives focusing on mangroves and coastal wetlands. The question is whether the best practices for stakeholder involvement emerging from these small projects are scalable to the type of large-scale projects that we are in urgent need of. To answer this question, the lack of experience to date means that we need to look beyond mangroves. We first describe the stakeholder involvement aspects of two large-scale terrestrial forest conservation and restoration initiatives under REDD+, and then turn to the pioneering blue bond project in the Seychelles mentioned in Section 3.

The REDD+ facility has included several hundred mainly small projects in over thirty developing countries, financed by a limited number of national development agencies. There have been failures and successes (see, e.g., Bayrak and Marafa, 2016), and a push is now underway in the donor community for action on a larger scale. A recent World Bank (2019) report provides a useful guideline for best practices gained from established, large-scale, results-based land use projects from around the developing world, including PES, community forest management, and REDD+ programs. For example, Nepal launched a nationwide community forestry management program in 1989 (World

Bank, 2019). Building on this, more recently, a series of meetings with local stakeholders was held over the course of a year to develop subnational REDD+ action plans that were tailored to the local requirements and, where possible, integrated into existing community forestry management approaches (UN-REDD, 2018). The example shows how stakeholder involvement from the design phase onward can help reconcile the needs of heterogeneous communities across one country under one unified program; it also shows that approaches that worked at a small scale can be scaled up. This is a model that could be adopted for large mangrove conservation and reforestation projects, too, though the timeframe and maturity of existing management structures in Nepal hinder rapid replication in other contexts.

While the Nepalese program is still at the advanced development stage, the World Bank's $900 million Carbon Fund (part of the Forest Carbon Partnership Facility or FCPF) has already begun making results-based payments to countries that have qualified for REDD+ financing. To date, four countries (Chile, DRC, Ghana, and Mozambique) have signed payment agreements with the Carbon Fund; another 18 qualifying countries are expected to do so by November 2020 (Nepal is not among them), bringing the area of avoided deforestation to roughly half the size of India.[7] In September 2020, Ghana became the first of the qualifying countries to receive an advance of US$1.3 million out of the $50 million agreement signed in 2019. The funding is for the Ghana Cocoa Forest REDD+ Program (GCFRP), which covers an area of 1.2 million hectares of forest reserves and national parks and is part of the country's NDCs under the UNFCCC. Over its full 20-year horizon, the GCFRP is estimated to produce a total 294,395,567 million tCO_2 emission reductions (Forestry Commission, 2020).

Stakeholder engagement is a key component of the Ghanaian program, and the country made use of the FCPF's guidance for designing

[7]Shaanti Kapila, "We need innovative tools for a resilient recovery; luckily, we have them and know how to use them," World Bank Blogs, August 31 2020, accessed 10 September 2020 at: https://blogs.worldbank.org/climatechange/we-need-innovative-tools-resilient-recovery-luckily-we-have-them-and-know-how-use.

benefit-sharing agreements,[8] which closely reflects the earlier World Bank (2019) and puts stakeholder involvement at all stages — from design to implementation, and evaluation of programs — squarely in the center of good practice. The Ghanaian program is based on a unique public–private partnership between cocoa companies, traditional authorities, cocoa farmers, members of local communities, the Ghana Cocoa Board, and the Forestry Commission. For the program design, fieldwork included focus group discussions and key informant interviews, followed by stakeholder consultations at the local and national levels, and expert reviews. The initial six-year stage of the program that is currently being funded includes six geographical areas that were selected due to the "presence and commitments of key stakeholders" for the implementation (Forestry Commission, 2020, p. 7). The first independent verification of emission reductions is expected in 2021. From a policy-making point of view, the selection criteria for the pilot areas is likely to make a clear understanding of the mechanisms leading to (lack of) success of the program more difficult. There was no randomization involved; instead, areas believed most likely to succeed were given precedence.

The REDD+ examples show that stakeholder involvement is indeed possible on a large scale, at least in the early project development and design phases. However, these projects have not yet been fully implemented. We need to turn to the pioneering blue bond initiative in the Seychelles, mentioned in Section 3, to see whether stakeholder involvement is possible and even desirable in all stages of a large project. The Seychelles debt transaction launched in 2018 aims at funding a Marine Spatial Plan for sustainable fisheries in the whole Seychelles Exclusive Economic Zone. Available sources suggest that participatory stakeholder involvement was crucial for the plan, from the initial phases of gathering information on the issues the fishers faced, through early

[8]See the news article "Reaping the Rewards of Sustainable Land Use," World Bank, August 26, 2020, Accessed 10 September 2020 at: https://www.worldbank.org/en/news/feature/2020/08/26/reaping-the-rewards-of-sustainable-land-use.

consultations, to gathering suggestions and feedback on the management strategies. We note that the Seychelles have a small and relatively homogenous population, which likely facilitated this strong qualitative approach to stakeholder involvement.

The Marine Spatial Plan is set to include various "co-management" plans to cover different areas of the archipelago. The main island of Mahé, where three-quarters of the less than 100k population live, has been the first to develop a sub-plan (Seychelles Fishing Authority, 2019). It allows us to gain an insight into whether and how stakeholder involvement continues during the implementation phase of the sustainable fisheries management plan. The Mahé co-management plan sets out the aims and management steps for fisheries, and details the various stakeholders and how they are included in the implementation in numerous places. For example, at the second meeting of the Co-management Plan Implementation Committee in March 2019, "the concerns of stakeholders" that had arisen at the first meeting in January were "addressed and resolved" (Seychelles Fishing Authority, 2019, p. 3). In order to fully address and adapt to the challenges that will arise for fishers during the implementation, the latter is scheduled to happen in two phases, separated by two years. The highest priority issues identified by stakeholders are to be tackled first, using the management strategies suggested by stakeholders. The implementation is thus seeing sustained stakeholder involvement.

5. Moving Forward: Design Suggestions for Future Blue Carbon Projects for Mangrove Conservation

Following the discussion above, we put forward three suggestions on how to design a large-scale blue carbon initiative. The first regards how to involve local stakeholders in the project design. The evidence on the ground strongly suggests that greater stakeholder involvement can lead to more successful long-term, sustainable mangrove management — with the climate change mitigation and adaptation benefits this entails — than the traditional, top-down regulatory approach. The iterative, qualitative approach to stakeholder involvement of the Seychelles fisheries' management plan outlined above is very much in line with the best practices collected by the World Bank, for example, and suggests that stakeholder engagement is possible in large-scale blue economy projects.

However, we cannot ignore that the long-term success of blue carbon projects, and mangrove management projects especially, that are founded on strong stakeholder support is still unproven. In this context, it is interesting that the "best practices" proposed by the World Bank and other donors — and the case studies they build upon — do not include any of the quantitative or behavioral methods (i.e., large survey analysis, lab-in-the-field, or field experiments) that have become standard tools to guide policy-making in environmental and development economics. We believe that this omission can be explained at least in part by the small scale of most projects to date: there is no scope for large surveys, and experiments may not seem a cost-efficient approach to finding a solution to a small ecosystem management problem. Nevertheless, the lack of rigorous, data-driven proof does leave an open door for remaining skeptics of the stakeholder involvement approach: might not a clear top-down method be faster and lead to a similar end result?

There is no need for large-scale field experiments to test the benefits of a top-down vs. a stakeholder involvement approach to mangrove conservation. Time is of the essence, and the case study evidence clearly favors the latter approach. We do believe, however, that there are good reasons to include more quantitative methods in the content design stage of mangrove conservation plans. For example, how should we decide which ecosystem management strategy for a large stretch of coastal mangrove forest should be chosen from many suggestions by stakeholders in numerous heterogeneous communities? The best-practice approach of developing an overarching plan and then finding community-specific strategies through participatory methods can lead to lengthy trial-and-error processes and potential inefficiencies through a large number of solutions, where a more streamlined process from the start could have led to quicker results. Survey and experimental findings based on a randomly selected, representative subsample of a large population can give timely, important insights into the potential for acceptance and support for a strategy to conserve and restore mangroves.

In addition, it is difficult to disentangle causal effects of different interventions over time where a trial-and-error approach is adopted, or where non-random criteria have been applied to select the intervention areas. Experimental methods in particular would allow causal inference for a large sample, as well as a greater understanding of the underlying behavioral mechanisms and heterogeneous effects. The experimental approach has become the norm in impact evaluation, but why wait until well into the project implementation phase to gather causal evidence on what is likely to work best for mangrove conservation?

We therefore suggest integrating the best practices on qualitative, participatory stakeholder involvement with more quantitative approaches that can deliver well-founded, timely evidence on which (limited number of) strategies are most likely to produce the desired ecosystem conservation and restoration results on a large scale. Participatory methods may be best suited for relatively small projects without large differences between communities, e.g., regarding land tenure rights, use of mangroves, or existing stakeholders and decision-making structures. Where projects are larger and there is a necessity for a unified framework or a reduced set of mangrove management options, e.g., where different communities have different current use but face similar challenges of degradation and deforestation, more quantitative methods may be better suited to find an optimal solution. The quantitative methods we have in mind include large, representative surveys, lab-in-the-field experiments, or field experiments (i.e., randomized control trials or RCTs). For example, the local uses and benefits, and preferences for future management strategies, of a sizable area of coastal mangroves could be explored with a representative survey. The likely success of the top-ranked strategies could then be tested experimentally through an RCT. Qualitative and quantitative methods can be combined to exploit complementarities, e.g., using participatory meetings instead of a survey to initially understand uses of and preferences for mangroves, and/or to explain how an experiment led to the final selection of the top strategy(ies) that will be implemented. As a final note, the complementary use of participatory and quantitative/experimental methods could also help build societal outcomes, such as social learning on the role of mangroves for the local economy, and greater support for investment in the conservation and restoration of the ecosystem.

Although a large-scale blue carbon initiative using a unique financial instrument may be desirable (e.g., a global carbon market), from our analysis it seems that, for now, different solutions and mechanisms for different contexts are still more appropriate for swift implementation. However, several innovations can be suggested, which could lead to a more intense frequency of project occurrence, and/or a scaled-up local project that may equal the outcomes of a large-scale initiative. We saw in Secs. 3 and 4 that for the first BB project realized so far, TNC strongly engaged with the stakeholders in the Seychelles. These are fundamental activities for the realization of a truly sustainable blue economy, and can also address the potential ethical concerns of environmental conservation and restoration projects in developing countries. Our second suggestion is therefore linked to the first one: the choice of the financial product to be developed for the conservation of a coastal ecosystem should take into account not only just the market potential of that ecosystem based on its environmental characteristics but also the buy-in and acceptability of the product by the local communities.

Third, it is worth expanding the notion of ecosystem services that a blue carbon ecosystem such as mangroves offers, and taking a holistic perspective, valuing all the benefits provided as a bundle — not "just" the value of carbon sequestered — to offer incentives for conservation and restoration in the long term (see Oreska *et al.*, 2020, Jakovac *et al.*, 2020). Oreska *et al.* (2020) name them "co-benefits" credits. Considering a bundle of ecosystem services for "ecosystem credits" may allow the price for PESs to be competitive enough with alternative uses of the blue carbon ecosystem. Achieving sufficient financial returns for conservation would in turn facilitate that crucial stakeholder buy-in just mentioned, and become more attractive to prospective investors. BBs may be a welcome way forward to conserve mangroves and blue carbon ecosystems in general, as they can be structured to consider a bundle of ecosystem services. However, bundling the value of ecosystem services can help realize even smaller-scale projects and maintain success in the long term.

6. Conclusions

Mangrove forests play an important role globally as carbon sinks, and locally as sources of fuel and building materials, as fish nurseries, and as defenses against sea level rises and coastal erosion. Most mangroves are located along the coasts of developing countries in the tropics, and have been protected by law from deforestation and degradation. Nevertheless, their extent has been shrinking dramatically, mainly due to human activities, and mangrove conservation and restoration has been slow to take hold.

In this chapter, we offer three inter-related suggestions on the design of mangrove conservation and restoration projects. First, in the project design phase, we propose combining qualitative approaches to stakeholder involvement with more quantitative ones in order to obtain timely evidence on the potential success of ecosystem management options. Second — linked to the first suggestion — the financial product that supports the ecosystem conservation should consider both the ecosystem's market potential and the buy-in and acceptability of the product by the local communities. Third, bundling the many ecosystem services of mangrove forests together can help achieve sufficient financial return to facilitate the crucial stakeholder buy-in not only at the community level but also at the donor and investor level.

We believe that it is important to maintain a flexible approach, and to be open to combining insights from practice-based reports, from environmental science, environmental economics and finance, behavioral economics, and sociology. Ultimately, the aim should be the rapid realization of mangrove conservation and restoration projects that enjoy strong stakeholder support and have a strong financial backing.

Acknowledgement

We thank Dirk Rübbelke, Lisa Benson, and an anonymous reviewer for helpful comments and suggestions.

References

Atwood, T. B., Connolly, R. M., Almahasheer, H., Carnell, P. E., Duarte, C. M., Ewers Lewis, C. J., Irigoien, X., Kelleway, J. J., Lavery, P. S., Macreadie, P. I., Serrano, O., Sanders, C. J., Santos, I., Steven, A. D. L., and Lovelock, C. E. (2017). Global patterns in mangrove soil carbon stocks and losses. *Nature Climate Change*, 7, 523–528.

Bayrak, M. M. and Marafa, L. M. (2016). Ten years of REDD+: A critical review of the impact of REDD+ on forest-dependent communities. *Sustainability*, 8, 620.

da Silva Copertino, M. (2011). Add coastal vegetation to the climate critical list. *Nature*, 473, 255.

Forestry Commission (March 2020). Final benefit sharing plan: Ghana Cocoa Forest REDD+ Programme, Climate Change Directorate/National REDD+ Secretariat, Forestry Commission of Ghana.

Gallo, N. D., Victor, D. V., and Levin, L. A. (2017). Ocean commitments under the Paris agreement. *Nature Climate Change*, 7, 833–840.

Goldberg, L., Lagomasino, D., Thomas, N., and Fatoyinbo, T. (2020). Global declines in human-driven mangrove loss. *Global Change Biology*, 26, 5844–5855.

Herr, D., von Unger, M., Laffoley, D., and McGivern, A. (2017). Pathways for implementation of blue carbon initiatives. *Aquatic Conservation: Marine and Freshwater Ecosystems*, 7(S1), 116–129.

Jakovac, C. C., Latawiec, A. E., Lacerda, E., Leite Lucas, I., Korys, K. A., Iribarrem, A., Abreu Malaguti, G., Turner, R. K., Luisetti, T., and Baeta Neves Strassburg, B. (2020). Costs and carbon benefits of mangrove conservation and restoration: A global analysis. *Ecological Economics*, 176, 106758.

Kauffman, J. B., Trejo, H. H., Garcia, M. D. C. J., Heider, C., and Contreras, W. M. (2016). Carbon stocks of mangroves and losses arising from their conversion to cattle pastures in the Pantanos de Centla, Mexico. *Wetlands Ecology and Management*, 24(2), 203–216.

Li, X., Bellerby, R., Craft, C., and Widney, S. E. (2018). Coastal wetland loss, consequences, and challenges for restoration. *Anthropocene Coasts*, 1, 1–15.

Luisetti, T. Ferrini, S., Grilli, G., Jickells, T. D., Kennedy, H., Kröger, S., Lorenzoni, I., Milligan, B., van der Molen, J., Parker, R., Pryce, T., Turner,

R. K., and Tyllianakis, E. (2020). Climate action requires new accounting guidance and governance frameworks to manage carbon in shelf seas. *Nature Communications*, 11, 4599.

Macreadie, P. I., Anton, A., Raven, J. A., Beaumont, N., Connolly, R. M., Friess, D. A., Kelleway, J. J., Kennedy, H., Kuwae, T., Lavery, P. S., Lovelock, C. E., Smale, D. A., Apostolaki, E. T., Atwood, T. B., Baldock, J., Bianchi, T. S., Chmura, G. L., Eyre, B. D., Fourqurean, J. W., Hall-Spencer, J. M., Huxham, M., Hendriks, I. E., Krause-Jensen, D., Laffoley, D., Luisetti, T., Marbà, N., Masque, P., McGlathery, K. J., Megonigal, J. P., Murdiyarso, D., Russell, B. D., Santos, R., Serrano, O., Silliman, B. R., Watanabe, K., and Duarte, C. M. (2019). The future of Blue Carbon science. *Nature Communications*, 10, 3998.

Oreska, M. P. J., McGlathery, K. J., Aoki, L. R. *et al.* (2020). The greenhouse gas offset potential from seagrass restoration. *Scientific Reports*, 10, 7325.

Pörtner, H.-O., Roberts, D. C., Masson-Delmotte, V., Zhai, P., Tignor, M., Poloczanska, E., Mintenbeck, K., Alegría, A., Nicolai, M., Okem, A., Petzold, J., Rama, B., and Weyer, N. M. (eds). (2019). *IPCC Special Report on the Ocean and Cryosphere in a Changing Climate.* IPCC.

Purvis, B., Mao, Y., and Robinson, O. (2019). Three pillars of sustainability: In search of conceptual origins. *Sustainability Science*, 14, 681–695.

Rakotomahazo, C., Aigrette Ravaoarinorotsihoarana, L., Randrianandrasaziky, D., Glass, L., Gough, C., Boleslas Todinanahary, G. G., and Gardner, C. J. (2019). Participatory planning of a community-based payments for ecosystem services initiative in Madagascar's mangroves. *Ocean and Coastal Management*, 175, 43–52.

Rogers, K., Kelleway, J. J., Saintilan, N., Megonigal, J. P., Adams, J. B., Holmqist, J. R., Lu, M., Schile-Beers, L., Zawadzki, A., Mazumder, D., and Woodroffe, C. D. (2019). Wetland carbon storage controlled by millennial-scale variation in relative sea-level rise. *Nature*, 567, 91–95.

Roth, N., Thiele, T., and von Unger, M. (2019). Blue Bonds: Financing Resilience of Coastal Ecosystems. Key Points for Enhancing Finance Action. Blue Natural Capital Financing Facility: Technical guideline prepared for IUCN GMPP.

Seychelles Fishing Authority (March 2019). Mahé Plateau trap and line fishery co-management plan, Seychelles Fishing Authority.

Thomas, S. (2014). Blue carbon: Knowledge gaps, critical issues, and novel approaches. *Ecological Economics*, 107, 22–38.

Thompson, B. S. and Friess, D. A. (2019). Stakeholder preferences for payments for ecosystem services (PES) versus other environmental management approaches for mangrove forests. *Journal of Environmental Management*, 233, 636–648.

Ullman, R., Bilbao-Bastida, V., and Grimsditch, G. (2013). Including Blue Carbon in climate market mechanisms. *Ocean & Coastal Management*, 83, 15–18.

UNDP. (2020). Mikoko Pamoja, Kenya, Equator Initiative Case Study Series, New York, NY.

UNEP and CIFOR. (2014). Guiding principles for delivering coastal wetland carbon projects. United Nations Environment Programme, Nairobi, Kenya and Center for International Forestry Research, Bogor, Indonesia.

UN-REDD. (2018). 10th Consolidated Annual Progress Report of the UN-REDD Programme Fund, UN-REDD, Geneva.

World Bank. (2019). *Benefit Sharing at Scale: Good Practices for Results-based Land Use Programs*, The World Bank, Washington, D.C.

Wylie, L., Sutton-Grier, A. E., and Moore A. (2016). Keys to successful blue carbon projects: Lessons learned from global case studies. *Marine Policy*, 65, 76–84.

https://doi.org/10.1142/9789811240553_0014

Chapter 14

The Fight Against Deforestation of Tropical Forests — The Contribution of the Blockchain-Based Contract Management Method to Minimize Illegal Logging

Elena Mechik[*,‡] **and Michael von Hauff**[†,§]

[*]Research Unit Sustainability and Global Change, University of Hamburg, Grindelberg 5, 20144 Hamburg, Germany
[†]Department of Economics, Technical University of Kaiserslautern, Gottlieb-Daimler-Straße 42, 67663 Kaiserslautern, Germany
[‡]elena.mechik@inhubber.com
[§]hauff@wiwi.uni-kl.de

Tropical forests play a distinctive role in climate and atmospheric gas balance stabilization. They store carbon in their biomass, support biodiversity, and provide ecosystem services such as protection of watersheds or reduction of soil erosion. Forests act as sources for timber and non-timber forest products and are the habitat of forest communities' inhabitants. Despite the importance of tropical forests, they continue to be devastated, causing 17% of global carbon emissions, loss of biodiversity, and climate change. Decades of efforts by governmental, non-governmental, and international organizations to reduce illegal deforestation worldwide have had limited success. In this paper, we analyze the opportunities to develop administrative methods for forest conservation based on the blockchain technology in combination with the economic activities of forest communities. The aim is to reduce the sale of illegally logged timber, to contribute to the reduction of illegal logging, and thereby to the mitigation of climate change. Based on this analysis, we propose a concept for tropical forest preservation through a blockchain-based contract management platform. This concept is based on field research of economic activities in Brazilian, Indian, and Thai forest communities.

1. Introduction

Governments of tropical forest countries and the international community, with the participation of the World Bank and INTERPOL, are engaged in efforts to reduce destructive unauthorized forest deforestation and degradation. Despite administrative and even military actions, tropical forests continue to be devastated by estimated 10 million hectares per year (FAO and UNEP, 2020). During the United Nations' Climate Summit in 2014, more than 150 partners signed the "Forest Declaration," which calls for "halving forest loss by 2020 and halting illegal logging by 2030" (UN Climate Change Summit, 2014). By 2020, these goals were not met yet.

In September 2019, New York hosted the Climate Action Summit. The goal of this summit was, as UN Secretary General António Guterres said, not negotiations, but actions. The summit was attended by representatives of 195 countries, who presented their plans for climate protection in the coming years related to the Paris Agreement of 2015. The German delegation to the Climate Action Summit was led by German Chancellor Angela Merkel (23 September 2019). The World Bank and Germany announced the launch of PROGREEN, a new global partnership, designed to accelerate efforts to stop deforestation, restore degraded land, improve livelihoods in poor rural communities, and reduce greenhouse gas emissions in order to save the Amazon and African and Asian rainforests and combat illegal logging (Worldbank, 2019). As the outcome, Germany intends to invest US$250 million to save tropical forests, with a total plan to raise US$1 billion (Worldbank, 2019).

Technical progress and industrial development result in negative effects for the climate which are undisputed and up till now unabated. Simultaneously, there are people whose economic activities are consciously directed toward stabilizing the environment and the climate.

These include forest-dwelling people, who live together in forest communities. Such communities have for generations lived on the basis of traditional knowledge, customs, rules, and beliefs, which predestine them to preserve tropical rainforests (FAO, 2016b, p. 2). They therefore benefit directly from the sustainable management of forests, and thereby make an important contribution to climate protection for the world population.

Forest communities are, however, being displaced from their traditional living environment to an increasing extent. One explanation offered for this is that the growing world population needs more agricultural land to produce enough food, and that in many cases this justifies deforestation. On the contrary, various studies have demonstrated that with a more efficient use of farming land, deforestation can at least be mitigated. Nevertheless, particularly in South America and the Amazon region, as well as in some Asian and African countries, tropical forests are still being converted into agricultural or pasture land.

Geological investigations are carried out in the tropical forest areas as well. In case of a natural resource discovery, the decision is mostly made in favor of establishing a mining and processing industry. Mining is often tolerated or supported by governments, often disregarding their national legislation. The increasing demand for these resources leads to the planning of additional mines, which in this context also leads to the deforestation of tropical rainforests. The frequently unrelenting depletion of resources has far-reaching consequences for ecological balance, for example, the negative climatic impact on water cycles and other environmental services.

The different causes of deforestation require different approaches to solving these challenges. In this paper, we will show possibilities for regulation of the timber industry. It makes sense, however, first to point out the consequences of deforestation in general. This can be explained by the fact that there is a partial overlap of causes. Some deforestation is initiated by the extraction of wood by the timber industry or resources such as raw materials. After that, deforestation occurs to gain agricultural land or pasture.

In general it can be said that increasing deforestation jeopardizes not only the livelihoods of forest communities but also the population of the countries affected and the world community, since the function of the carbon sinks is weakened: "Acting as carbon sinks, they absorb the equivalent of roughly 2 billion tonnes of carbon dioxide each year" (FAO, 2018, p. xi). Furthermore, 17% of global anthropogenic greenhouse gas emissions are attributable to deforestation and agricultural emissions from livestock, soil and nutrient management, and are mainly caused by the deforestation of tropical rainforests (Nellemann, 2014, p. 5). The Intergovernmental Panel on Climate Change even postulates a percentage of around 25%. This accelerates climate change and complicates adherence to the global warming target level of 1.5°, and maximum of 2°, as set out in the Paris Agreement of 2015.

Such developments also fail to achieve Sustainable Development Goal (SDG) 13 of Agenda 2030, i.e., combatting climate change, to which the community of states committed in 2015. Therefore, indigenous forest communities in particular play a crucial role: "Indigenous peoples are recognized for their role as protectors of biodiversity and key actors in the implementation of sustainable development and land management. This connection is a central component of their collective identity as peoples" (IWGIA, 2019, p. 10).

In the following section, there is first a consideration of the climatic effects resulting from the loss of tropical forests. Section 3 represents the ineffectiveness of tropical forest conservation based on the research in forest communities of Brazil, India, and Thailand. The next section suggests a blockchain-based contract management platform as an option for a transparent timber supply chain and a possibility to minimize illegal logging.

2. Loss of Tropical Forests and Climatic Impacts

The following observations first present an overview of the 10 most highly forested countries, in which there are very divergent losses and gains of forest areas as a result of deforestation and reforestation (Table 1). Subsequently, there is an analysis of the different types of forests which have varying relevance for climatic trends.

Table 1. Top ten forest areas in 2015 by country.

	Country	Forest area [thousand ha]	% of land area	% of global forest area
1	Russia	814,931	50	20
2	Brazil	493,538	59	11
3	Canada	347,069	38	9
4	USA	310,095	34	8
5	China	208,321	22	5
6	Congo	152,578	67	4
7	Australia	124,751	16	3
8	Indonesia	91,010	53	2
9	Peru	73,973	58	2
10	India	70,682	24	2
	Total	**2,686,948**		67

Source: FAO (2016a, p. 17).

Between 1990 and 2015, there was an overall net decrease in global forest area from 4,128 million ha to 3,999 million ha (3%). Natural deforestation and deforestation caused by human activities were, however, offset by an increase in forest area. The annual rate of net forest loss halved over this period of 25 years and fell from 7.3 million ha in the 1990s to 4.6 million ha between 2000 and 2005, to 3.4 million from 2005 to 2010, and to 3.3 million ha from 2010 to 2015 (FAO, 2016a). Although this represents a positive trend, the climatic impacts are not sufficiently clear and a more detailed analysis of tropical forests is necessary.

2.1. *Tropical forests*

There are significant regional variations in deforestation. First, an analysis of the regions with the highest forest losses reveals that the tropical forest regions suffer most. As shown in Table 2, countries particularly affected include Brazil, Indonesia, Myanmar, the Democratic Republic of Congo, and Nigeria.

It is striking that subtropical and tropical forest regions in particular suffer the highest loss of forest area as a result of deforestation. This

Table 2. Top ten countries by annual net loss to forest, 2010–2015.

	Country	Annual net loss to forest: Forest area [thousand ha]	Rate [%]
1	Brazil	984	0.2
2	Indonesia	684	0.7
3	Myanmar	546	1.8
4	Nigeria	410	5.0
5	Tanzania	372	0.8
6	Paraguay	325	2.0
7	Zimbabwe	312	2.1
8	DR Congo	311	0.2
9	Argentina	297	1.1
10	Bolivia	289	0.5

Source: FAO (2016a), p. 17.

has very negative consequences in terms of both regional and global climatic trends. Back in the 1990s, Otto established that tropical evergreen rainforests with a 500 tonnes phytomass per hectare and year have a significantly higher net primary production of phytomass — and therefore also carbon storage — than deciduous forests in the cool temperate zone (400) and boreal coniferous forests (200) (Otto, 1994). Therefore, the clearing or loss of forest areas in tropical regions has a much more serious climatic effect than in temperate and boreal regions. The preservation of subtropical and tropical forests must therefore be a top priority in climate change policy (FAO and UNEP, 2020). Table 3 shows the trend for the period from 1990 to 2015.

However, as shown in Fig. 1, the effects on climate cannot simply be explained in terms of forest areas. This requires a comparison of the loss of forest areas as a proportion of the gain in agricultural areas in the four climatic domains for the period between 2000 and 2010. A very heterogeneous picture emerges. In the boreal and temperate climatic domains, the forest area has increased, whereas in the tropics, there is evidence of a huge decrease in tropical forest areas and a strong increase in agricultural land, including pasture land.

Table 3. Net rates of change in the areas of forest and other wooded land from 1990 to 2015 in different global climatic domains.

Forest	1990–2000	2000–2005	2005–2010	2010–2015
Boreal (incl. polar)	0.051	−0.193	1.204	−0.084
Temperate	2.290	3.657	2.851	2.208
Subtropical	−0.064	−0.173	−0.860	0.089
Tropical	−9.543	−7.863	−6.608	−5.520

Source: FAO (2016b, p. 13).

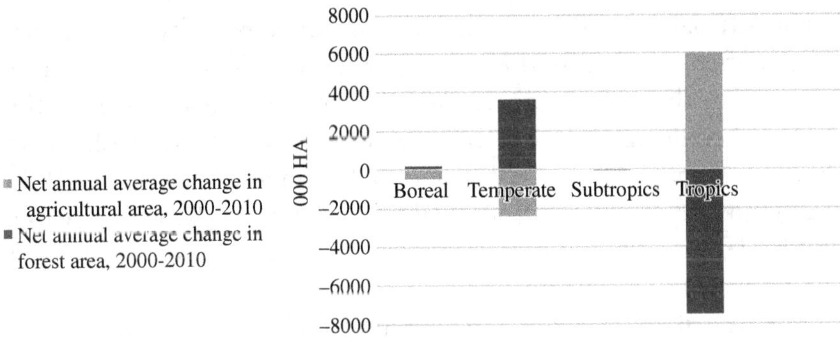

Fig. 1. Net annual average change in forest and agricultural land, by Climatic Domain 2000–2010.

Source: FAO (2016b, p. 13).

If this trend is classified according to regions, for the period from 2000 to 2010, there are great differences between the net annual average change in forest area and the net annual average change in agricultural area. In some regions, the decrease in forest area is almost identical to the increase in agricultural area. This applies particularly to South America — especially Brazil — as well as to Western, Central, Eastern, and Southern Africa (FAO and UNEP, 2020). It is striking that in South and Southeast Asia, there has been a significant increase in agricultural area and only a relatively slight loss of forest area. But, there are (also) many examples of illegal deforestation in African countries.

Addendum: With regard to illegal timber production, Ghana can be cited as an example. Although rosewood is already facing extinction in many regions of Western Africa, Ghana is a major center of destruction. According to statutory government requirements, it is strictly forbidden to cut down trees of the Dalbergia species, from which rosewood is produced. However, research carried out by the Environmental Investigation Agency (EIA) has revealed how illegal rosewood trade is conducted in Ghana through corruption and fraudulent agreements (Behrend, 2019).

For example, more than 540,000 tonnes of rosewood (corresponding to around 6 million trees) has been illegally exported to China since 2012. This has been made possible by Ghanaian and Chinese dealers forging official documents and falsely declaring types of wood. Confiscated timbers are then sold by corrupt officials at sham auctions. It is striking that the Chinese government records official statistics on the rosewood trade, although such trade is in breach of the Washington Convention on International Trade in Endangered Species of Wild Fauna and Flora and the national legislation in Ghana (Behrend, 2019). This has led to a disastrous crisis in Ghana because a large area of forest was destroyed and not reforested.

The described poaching and corruption scheme is possible due to the lack of reliable scientific-based state administrative and international control. The organization of such a control system may be possible on the basis of blockchain technology.

Blockchain technology is an immutable storage of information through a simultaneous recording of the same information at distributed nodes. It allows transactions to be processed without the necessity of a trusted third party. As a result, trust between business partners can be achieved as it is nearly impossible to tamper any transactions stored in blockchains and all the historical transactions are auditable and traceable.

2.2. *Climate change: The effects of deforestation of tropical forest areas*

The above observations have shown that the increasing deforestation of tropical forest areas has a dual climatic impact: negative climatic impacts are on the one hand caused by the reduction of the carbon sink through deforestation, and on the other hand by the increase in agricultural and pasture land. A rise in temperature above the limits agreed in Paris, for example, a rise of 4° as is widely feared, would have serious and irreparable consequences which the world population would have to suffer with varying intensity depending upon their geographical location. In any event, future generations would be harshly affected, which would be incompatible with the sustainability goal of intergenerational justice as called for in the Brundtland Report (Brundtland, 1987).

It has also been clearly proven that, according to the Climate Change Vulnerability Index, many countries in the southern hemisphere are at high risk. This applies in particular to several countries in South America, Africa, and in South and Southeast Asia, i.e., to many developing countries. Two key components of this risk are heat and the resulting drought, which also often exacerbate water shortages and decrease agricultural yields. Floods and storms also negatively impact the living conditions of those affected, adding to the problems of poverty, food supply, and health in the countries affected.

The relevance of forests for climate can be demonstrated by citing several key indicators. As already mentioned, they serve as a natural carbon sink for carbon, storing an estimated 296 gigatonnes of carbon in the above- and below-ground biomass. Thus, they store around half of the earthbound carbon in their vegetation, as well as absorbing around 2 billion tonnes of carbon dioxide annually (Muller *et al.*, 2018). Once again, a distinction should be made between the various types of forest: whereas in the living biomass, tropical forests store around 120 tonnes of carbon per hectare, the global average is 74 tonnes/hectare.

As a result of the conversion of forest areas into agricultural land and other degradations of forest areas, for example, through the depletion of raw materials, over the past 25 years the carbon storage in the forest biomass has fallen by around 11.1 tonnes/hectare, corresponding to a reduction of 442 million tonnes of carbon dioxide per year (FAO, 2015, p. 30). It is noteworthy that the net losses of 0.5 gigatonnes per year in the 1990s fell to 0.3 gigatonnes per year during the period 2010–2015. This decline in the loss rate is particularly linked to developments in countries in South and Central America, as well as Asia, as

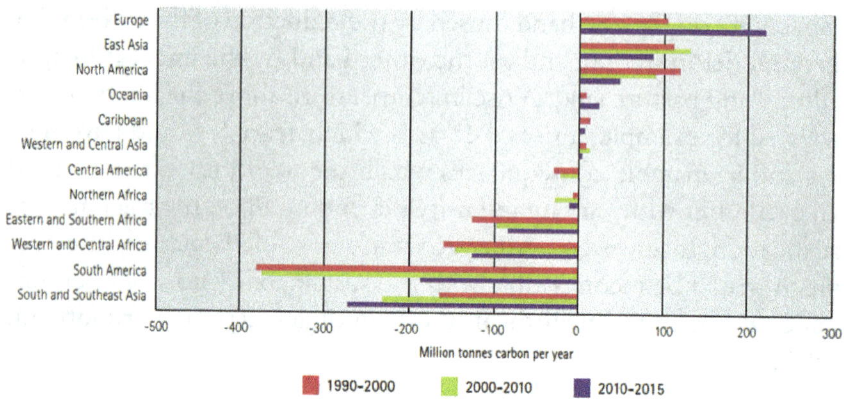

Fig. 2. Changes in carbon storage in forest biomass by region, 1990–2015.
Source: FAO (2016a, p. 31).

shown in Fig. 2. For example, in Brazil alone, the annual carbon loss in the above- and below-ground biomass fell from 240 million tonnes of carbon per year in the 1990s to around 80 million tonnes per year in 2010–2015 (FAO, 2016a, p. 31).

In terms of climatic impact, the question arises as to what are the major drivers of conversion from forest to agriculture, an area of study which has not yet been sufficiently explored. From the perspective of human intervention directly affecting forests, the following reasons are important: the expansion of agricultural land, extension of pasture land, the growth of cities and settlements, enlargement of the infrastructure, and mining.

According to estimates, there is a broad consensus that agricultural expansion is the major driver of deforestation worldwide (Skutsch and Esther, 2020). In this connection, there are geographical variations, since in the use of additional agricultural areas a distinction is to be made between commercial or industrial agriculture, which is strongly export-oriented, and small-scale subsistence farming as carried out in many African countries. For example, as drivers of deforestation, commercial agriculture accounts for 40% and local subsistence farming for around 33%.

An additional differentiation reveals that the expansion of cities and settlements is responsible for 10%, infrastructural expansion 10%, and mining 7% (Hosonuma *et al*, 2012). Furthermore, one particular factor should be mentioned: to some extent, this land-use change starts with illegal timber production, and is only then followed by the agricultural use of the previously forested land. In this case, such change cannot therefore be classified as a direct link between timber production and agricultural use. Finally, it should be mentioned that after 1990, agribusiness production in the Amazon region for international markets, such as livestock farming, soybean production, and oil palm plantations, has been specifically identified as the principal driver of deforestation (Boucher *et al.*, 2011).

The following summary presents the major drivers of climate change in regard with forest loss and its effects (FAO, 2016b):

- In the period from 1990 to 2020, the global forest area decreased by 420 million hectares (FAO and UNEP, 2020).
- Many people have a direct or indirect share of responsibility, for example, through their consumptional behavior, i.e., through the increasing demand for soya or meat produced on the newly acquired agricultural land.
- Although the annual forest loss rate has slowed down, the persistent loss of global forest area is in view of climate change one of the major problems for the world population.
- The loss of forest area particularly affects the poor population, whose livelihoods depend on forest goods.
- Climate change, which causes exceptional suffering for the poor population in many regions worldwide through droughts, floods, and storms, intensifies the negative consequences at least for SDG 1 (reduction of poverty) and SDG 2 (reduction of hunger).
- The protection of the habitats for 75% of terrestrial species in the world and the resilience of ecosystems is diminishing.
- The major part of forest area loss in the last 25 years has affected the tropical climatic domain, where the population — including in agricultural areas — is still growing, and predominantly impacts

the poor population. This also has a negative effect on the income trend for the low-income population.

3. Reasons for the Ineffectiveness of Tropical Forest Conservation

In addition to environmental and economic challenges, tropical forests are socially important as they are inhabited by approximately 1,300 million people. The inhabitants of forest communities are characterized by severe poverty including lack of jobs and employment problems, as well as lack of accessible social packages: health care, education, and modern means of communication. Our research (2010–2015) focused on the challenges of maintaining tropical forests through administrative, economic, and social means, with the participation of local people in forest communities in Brazil, India, and Thailand (Mechik *et al.*, 2017, Mechik and von Hauff, 2016).

Our studies have shown that an effective method of tropical forest conservation is an integrated administrative and institutional approach. The essence of these activities is to create employment opportunities in forest communities which depend on sustainable forest use. At the same time, economic and methodological assistance in organizing this employment is needed. Monitoring the state of the forest in the community's area of economic activities and informing the nature conservation organizations are integral parts of economic and methodological assistance.

One of the main social reasons for the destruction of the tropical forest is the lack of legal rights to use the forest by local inhabitants interested in tropical forest conservation. At the same time, the economic method of tropical forest conservation is to grant forest management rights to local communities and to provide them with financial and methodological assistance for production development and job creation. Such solutions will address the demographic situation, mainly the aging population through the migration of young people to megacities. The solution is not comprehensive, but it will preserve forest communities and keep the forest within those communities' range of forest use. The social responsibility of the international community must be supported by external investment in infrastructure and job creation in forest communities.

Our studies have noted that tropical forest protection issues are currently being addressed by force (police), as well as economic and administrative methods.

The reality shows that despite forceful, administrative, and economic efforts of the states, the INTERPOL, and the international community, the destruction of the tropical forest continues:

(1) for timber
(2) for livestock farming, agricultural plantations, etc.
(3) for the development of mining and processing industry, road construction, or power plant development.

The main drawbacks of the administrative control capabilities of supervising bodies are insufficient awareness or lack of reliable information. The control problem is also the inability to verify the reliability of documents submitted in real time.

In our opinion, society can counteract savage forest management with a solution to this multifaceted problem by organizing an end-to-end control system that provides real-time information from the felling of a particular tree to its sale to a particular consumer. Based on real time information with the necessary feedback, the effectiveness of police and economic measures can be significantly improved.

4. Structure of Contracts Requiring Transparency and Systematic Supervision

Modern approaches with blockchain-based contract management techniques open up new opportunities for administrative methods of tropical forest protection, based on the organization of the end-to-end control, starting with obtaining permission for felling until the sale of finished products to the end consumer. The use of such methods allows monitoring in real time of each organizational and technological process with a system of verification and feedback. As an innovative technology, blockchain is only starting to evolve in regard to the aim of raw resources' supply chain transparency. However, this new technology brings hope into the fight against long-lasting world challenges such as deforestation.

The European Union (EU) Timber Regulation aims to reduce illegal logging by ensuring that no illegal timber or timber products can be sold into the EU. It was created as part of the EU's Forest Law Enforcement, Governance and Trade (FLEGT) Action Plan.

EU Regulation No 995/2010 of the European Parliament and the Timber Council (EUTR) discourages the trade of illegally harvested timber and requires traceability of origin in timber trading. Traders in this part of the supply chain are obliged to keep records of their suppliers and customers. In Germany, the Bundesanstalt für Landwirtschaft und Ernährung (BLE) is responsible for implementing the Timber Regulation.

The regulation was developed in 2010 and entered into force on the 3rd of March 2013. However, its full implementation has not been possible until now. The blockchain technology can be an option to fully control the origin of each timber piece in real time starting from a felling license and ending with its sale to the end customer.

All information starting with the felling company till the end customer in accordance with the contracts is entered into the blockchain platform on which all parameters are recorded for each log in automatic mode. The information is accessed by the authorized supervisory authorities. Moreover, the list of responsible persons is approved, and each access to information is automatically recorded with a confirmed electronic signature.

The proposed blockchain-based contract management system confirmed by electronic signature provides feedback between the final sale, the timber supplier, and the regulatory authorities. Each tagged log sold is recorded with feedback on the felling permit. When using the proposed feedback system, it is not possible to sell a "duplicate" at any point of time.

The proposed system provides transparency of customs payments and income taxation of firms involved in the blockchain — from the cutter to the end consumer. At the same time, payments to budgets of all levels are made automatically in accordance with contracts at a given time. The seller and the buyer do not have the opportunity to sell or buy products not included in the blockchain-based contract management system.

5. Blockchain-Based Contract Management Platform for Timber

In the supply chain from licensing and felling to the end user, there are a large number of firms and contracts providing management of material and information flows. The complex system approach to the organization of all cycles and the control over all volumes of the information — from allowing documents on cutting down to the end consumer of finished goods — is possible on the basis of a blockchain-based contract management platform. The technology allows one to organize real administrative and technical control over reception of the license for cutting, control over volumes of the felled timber in conformity with the license, transportation, export, storage, sale, payments to budgets of all levels, processing, and the whole supply chain till the final consumer.

The task of controlling the compliance of documentary permits and actual felling, transportation, and final sale is reduced to the task of contract management.

Those interested in the control system described are as follows:

- government agencies that issue permits for cutting and control over the execution of contracts;
- budgets of all levels, including tax authorities, customs services;
- bidders in tenders for felling, including companies producing works and logistics companies;
- insurance companies that control the fulfillment of contract terms and cover losses in case of violation of insurance terms.

On the example of Ghana (see Section 2.1), we can see how corruption and fraudulent agreements can be extinguished in the future.

According to CNBC Africa, the price of 1 tonne of rosewood equals US$17,000. As mentioned in Section 2.1., 540,000 tonnes of rosewood has been illegally exported from Ghana to China since 2012 which equals US$9.18 billion alone for one kind of timber for one region. The proposed blockchain-based contract management provides an option on how this environmental and economic piracy can be minimized and how corruption can be mitigated.

5.1. *Organization of end-to-end timber monitoring*

Obtaining a felling permit is conditioned by the collection and development of documents in accordance with the legislation in each country (Fig. 3). All countries have common principles for obtaining a felling permit and selection of the contractor and felling company. An important issue is the prevention of corruption in obtaining a permit to clear a forest. International experience shows that the best way to select a company to receive a felling permit is to hold a tender.

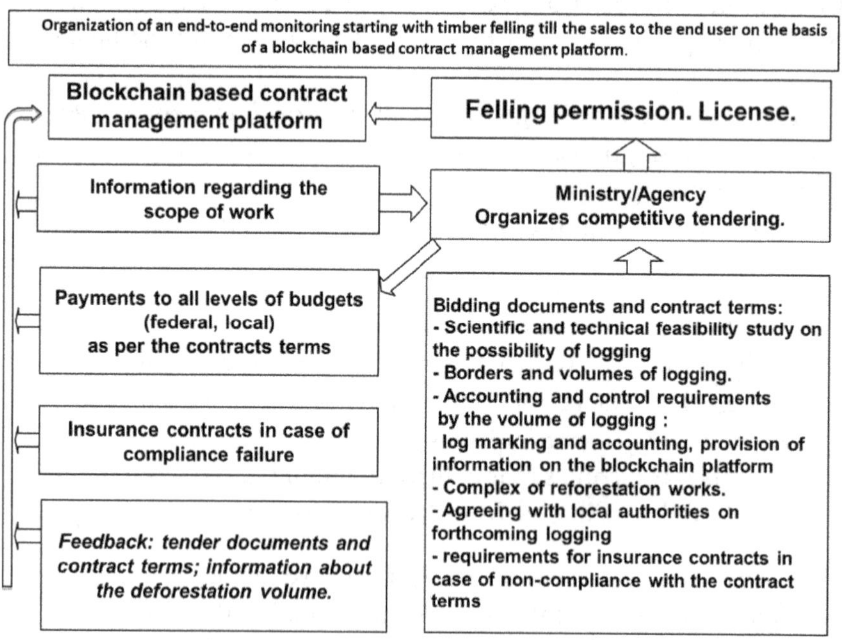

Fig. 3. Organization of an end-to-end timber monitoring.

Source: Own research results.

Selection of a contractor by means of competitive bidding is carried out after announcement of tender conditions, which are published in mass media and on the Internet. After that, a more favorable price and terms offer from the participants is accepted. Competitive bidding expands the range of contractors providing felling conditions. The tendering process identifies strategic and potential partners interested in cooperation and gives the most suitable proposal. After the tender, companies are given a guarantee of fulfilling their obligations and enter into a contract.

The Ministry publishes a list of tender documents provided by law including the following:

- Scientific and technical substantiation of the possibility of cutting down.
- Borders and volumes of cuttings.
- Requirements for accounting and control of felling volumes: timber labeling and accounting and obligation to provide information on the blockchain platform.
- Complex of reforestation works and requirements for insurance contracts in case of non-fulfillment of contract terms.
- Approval of information on forthcoming felling with local authorities.

The information about these documents and the source of their origin shall be stored in a blockchain, which provides transparency regarding the decisions carried out on the tender, which considerably reduces expenses and raises efficiency of supervising organizations (forest guards, tax bodies, customs service), and also provides protection for platform users from fraud.

The use of the blockchain platform provides feedback to monitor contractors' compliance with their obligations. An important component involves the insurance contracts in case of non-fulfillment of contract terms and conducted transactions with a series of operations for rapid information exchange, as a result of which changes are made to the system. The blockchain platform allows online modification of existing documents and contracts with a confirmed electronic signature.

5.2. *Supply chain transparency*

State legislative acts stipulate that timber of valuable timber species, the harvesting of which is allowed in accordance with the issued licenses, shall be subject to mandatory marking on a piece-by-piece basis by manufacturers of works by legal entities and entrepreneurs engaged in felling and transportation. The information on marking of timber by the companies which are carrying out export of such timber should be provided to the state automated information system of the accounting of timber and transactions in the form of the electronic document signed by an electronic signature, using information and telecommunication networks.

Labeling of timber ensures the possibility to apply and read information about timber using a scanner and other technical means. The timber marking contains information about the date of marking; the name of the company official; information about the company involved in felling, harvesting and exporting timber; the volume of timber in cubic meters, on which the label is attached when marking on a piece-by-piece basis. The use of the blockchain platform makes it possible to monitor in real time the changes of existing documents and contracts with a confirmed electronic signature.

Feedback allows one to receive information on each log: where it has been logged, where and how it was transported, and whom it was sold to as it is not possible to forge or duplicate the information stored on the blockchain technology (Fig. 4).

5.3. *Timber transportation and control of the timber supply chain*

An important part of felling control is the transport of timber by any means of transport. Careful operational control is required at this stage. Transportation shall be carried out on the basis of a transportation contract and an accompanying document that includes information on the shipper and consignee, the carrier of the wood, its volume,

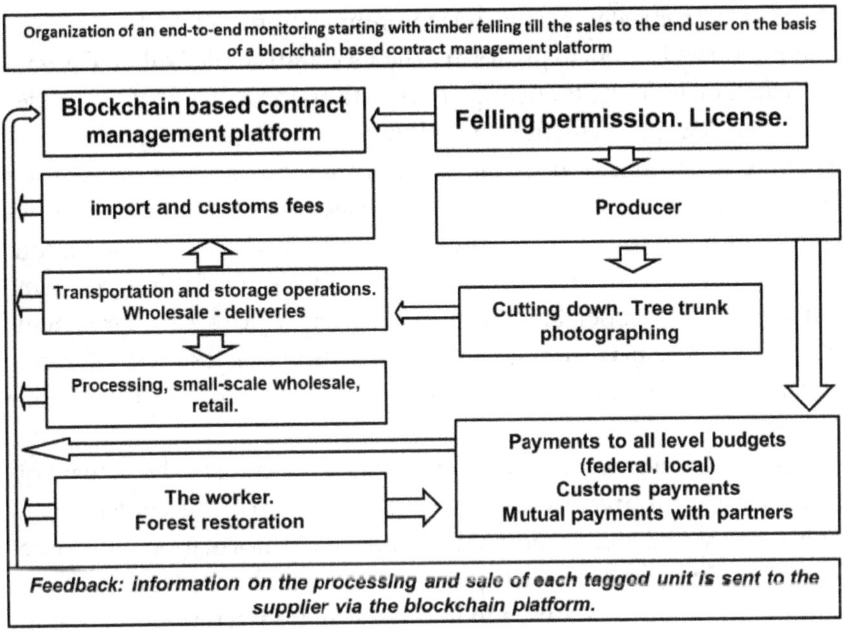

Fig. 4. Supply chain transparency.

Source: Own research results.

type (species) and assortment composition, points of departure and destination, the number of the declaration of timber transactions, as well as an indication of the vehicle in which the transportation is made. The accompanying document shall be executed by the owners of the wood. The corruption component is high, as paper documents can be forged and falsified. It is difficult and time consuming to check them in the field.

The use of the blockchain-based contract management platform allows one to check instantly in real time the authenticity of documents and the presence of mandatory payments made. In addition, the electronic signature will record the time of verification and the official performing the verification. This will exclude checks by non-authorized persons in order to obtain bribes and other abuses.

Entrepreneurs who have traded with timber should submit a single timber transaction declaration in the form of an electronic document signed electronically, using telecommunication networks and the Internet on a blockchain platform. The Declaration of Timber Transactions shall include the following: information on timber owners, parties to timber deals; information on volume of timber, type (species), and assortment composition of timber; information on documents used for harvest: information on forest site lease agreement or other document on provision of forest site, its location and date of conclusion, and number of this cutting permit, term of validity of this agreement, and volume of timber harvested in accordance with this agreement; information on place of harvest; information on location of forest site; and information on timber harvesting in accordance with this agreement.

The declaration on timber transactions may change the actual volume of timber transportation during the term of the agreement in which the stated declaration was submitted. Information on timber felling, marking and volumes, purchase and sale, transportation, warehousing, export operations, and in general all transactions shall be concentrated on the blockchain platform. All financial flows, such as import and export customs duties, income tax, payments on all contracts in all structures, and with all partners, are automatically monitored on the blockchain platform. All information is automatically transmitted to the organizations interested in receiving payments. A blockchain platform distributed on many nodes stores information, and tampering or falsification is impossible. Every change confirmed by an electronic signature is recorded and saved.

5.4. *Contract liability insurance, restoration of the felled areas*

An important component of the forest conservation problem is the work on restoration and use of felled areas. Reforestation of a forest after felling is included in the scientific and technical substantiation of the possibility of felling, which should be included in the tender documents and should be stipulated in the contracts terms.

The project shall take into account the characteristics of forest vegetation conditions of the forest site, including all important parameters like relief, hydrological conditions, soil, areas of the forest felling site suitable for restoration and use of land, the projected method of forest restoration (artificial, combined, natural restoration of forests), species composition of the restored forests, terms and technologies (methods) of work on forest restoration. Requirements and the form of the project on forest restoration shall be stipulated by the legislation.

The composition of the forest regeneration project and the procedure for its development shall be controlled by the authorized bodies of state authority and local self-government. The project shall necessarily calculate the volume and cost of the work to be done. These calculations shall be the basis for determining insurance amounts or deposits guaranteeing forest restoration.

Lumberjacks often avoid forest restoration work. These actions are a corruption component. To ensure that the contract is fulfilled, the bidder determines the method of security. This is one of three options: bank guarantee, liability insurance under the contract, or pledging money to the customer. Liability insurance under the state contract is the most advantageous way for the bidder to secure the contract performance, because the bank guarantee is much more expensive than insurance and it is rather difficult to obtain it, and it is not profitable to withdraw money from the turnover for the duration of the contract.

Under the insurance contract, the Insurer undertakes to reimburse the party of the state or municipal contract in favor of which the insurance contract has been concluded for the payment (insurance premium) stipulated in the contract upon occurrence of the events (insured events) stipulated in the contract, losses and/or penalty due to non-fulfillment, or improper fulfillment of obligations under the forest restoration contract. The insurance contract shall be concluded before the end of the guarantee period of forest restoration works.

In order to calculate the insurance rate quickly and accurately, the insurance questionnaire shall be usually filled in and the relevant documents shall be provided: the tender documentation, the draft contract, and the tender participant questionnaire. After the insurance terms and conditions are agreed upon with the tender committee, the contract shall be prepared.

The use of the blockchain platform makes it possible to monitor online in real time and, if necessary, make changes to existing documents and contracts with a confirmed electronic signature.

6. Conclusion

6.1. *Blockchain technology as an option for minimizing illegal logging*

The conservation of tropical forests from illegal logging, control of the subsequent restoration of forests, and legal use of forest land can be carried out by administrative methods based on the highest possible protection from falsification and counterfeiting of operational information. Real administrative control is necessary at every stage (Figs. 3 and 4) from obtaining a permit for felling to selling timber and its products to the end user.

The control shall include scientific justification of the possibility of felling and subsequent restoration of the forest and land-use project. The possibility of such control makes it possible to promptly involve law enforcement (prosecutor, judicial, and police) methods of regulating forest protection and combating corruption in case of non-compliance with contract terms. Modern technologies provide opportunities for continuous consistent control of the whole chain of blocks (Figs. 1 and 2) containing necessary information on the basis of the blockchain technology. Communication between blocks is ensured by the fact that each block contains not only its own data processing result (hashes) but also the hashes of the previous block (Iansiti and Lakhani, 2017).

Reliable storage of information is provided by the fact that in order to change the information in the block, one will have to also edit all subsequent blocks. Copies of chains of blocks are placed by different computers independent of each other. This makes it extremely difficult to make changes in the information already included in blocks (5) [2] (Fortney, 2020).

Reliability of information storage is provided by the fact that to change the information in the blockchain, you will have to modify the information on every node. The copies of information are placed by different computers independent of each other. It makes it extremely difficult and almost impossible to make changes in the information which is already contained on the blockchain.

6.2. *Potential effectiveness of the blockchain-based contract management platform*

Accounting, control, and administration of the forestry industry include large databases and can be converted to the blockchain technology. The blockchain system concept uses smart contracts, which are a kind of "honesty enforcement," eliminating legal delays, and the "electronic notary" uses blockchain technology to certify transactions with a certified electronic signature. This contract management platform with an included digital signature makes it difficult, if not impossible, to manipulate corrupt practices.

The blockchain technology ensures transparency of all technological processes. It enables real-time monitoring of the entire supply chain.

In the development and the use of the blockchain technology, taking into account the movement of timber from felling to the end user, the most interested parties are, first and foremost, the state financial, environmental, and regulatory organizations.

The feedback provided in the described technology allows controlling of all kinds of payments to the budget. The corruption component in obtaining permits for felling is reduced.

In case of poachers involved in the felling, it is impossible to export illegally extracted timber. For law-abiding timber traders, the use of the platform optimizes participation in competitive bidding and protects against corruption attacks by officials. At the same time, it reduces the volume of document circulation and facilitates the execution of all kinds of contracts, customs, and transport documents.

For miners who are involved in illegal logging and evasion of payments to the budget, it becomes impossible to falsify and forge permits and transport documents.

Environmental protection agencies have the opportunity to control the use of land and the restoration of felled areas. The basis of the administrative and economic approach is the control of forest use at all stages starting from timber logging (felling) and ending with the sale to the end customer. For the state, such control will ensure transparency of economic components and create conditions for all types of taxation.

References

Behrend, R. (2019). Stoppt den kriminellen Holzhandel mit China! in: Rettet den Regenwald e.V. 29. November.

Boucher, D., Elias, P., Lininger, K., May-Tobin, C., Roquemore, S., and Saxon, E. (2011). *The Root of the Problem: What's Driving Tropical Deforestation Today?* Union of Concerned Scientists, Cambridge, Massachusetts, USA.

Brundtland, G. (1987). Report of the World Commission on Environment and Development: Our Common Future. United Nations General Assembly document A/42/427.FAO (2015). Global Forest Resource Assessment, 2nd ed., Rome 2015. New source of literature.

FAO. (2016a). Global Forest Resources Assessment 2015, How are the World's Forests Changing? 2nd ed. *Report.* Rome.

FAO. (2016b). The State of the World's Forests: Forests and Agriculture: Land-use Challenges and Opportunities. *Report.* Rome.

FAO. (2018). The State of the World's Forests — Forest Pathways to Sustainable Development. *Report.* Rome.

FAO and UNEP. (2020). *The State of the World's Forests 2020: Forests, Biodiversity and People*, FAO and UNEP, Rome, Italy, doi: 10.4060/ca8642en.

Fortney, L. (2020). Blockchain Explained, https://www.investopedia.com/terms/b/blockchain.asp.

Hosonuma, N. *et al.* (2012). An assessment of deforestation and forest degradation drivers in developing countries. *Environmental Research Letters* 7, S. 44009, doi: 10.1088/1748-9326/7/4/044009.

Iansiti, M. and Lakhani K. R. (2017). The Truth About Blockchain // Harvard Business Review: Magazine. January–February 2017 issue. P. 118–127.

IWGIA. (2018). International Work Group for Indigenous Affairs. Yearbook 2018. Copenhagen.

Mechik, E. and von Hauff, M. (2016). Requirements for the sustainable development of economic activities in tropical forest communities. *European Journal of Sustainable Development*, 5(4), 107–120, doi: 10.14207/ejsd.2016.v5n4p107.

Mechik, E., von Hauff, M., De Moura, L. H. L., and Held, H. (2017). Analysis of the changes in economic activities of Brazilian forest communities after methodical support and provision of pre-financing capital. *Journal of Tropical Forest Science*, 29(2), 227–237.

Muller, E. U. *et al.* (2018). The State of the World's Forests: Forest Pathways to Sustainable Development. *Report.* Rome: Food and Agriculture Organization of the United Nations.

Nellemann, C. (2014). Green Carbon, Black Trade: Illegal Logging, Tax Fraud and Laundering in the World's Tropical Forests: A Rapid Response Assessment. *Report.* Arendal, Norway: Grid-Arendal.

Otto, H. J. (1994). Wald6kologie. Verlag Eugen Ulmer Stuttgart.

Paris Agreement to the UN Framework Convention on Climate Change Art. 4.4. (2015). T.I.A.S. No. 16-1104.

Skutsch, M. and Esther, T. (2020). REDD+: If communities are the solution, what is the problem? *World Development*, 130, (1. Juni 2020): 104942, doi: 10.1016/j.worlddev.2020.104942.

UN Climate Change Summit (2014). https://www.un.org/press/en/2014/sgsm16186.doc.htm.

Worldbank (2019). https://www.worldbank.org/en/programs/progreen.

https://doi.org/10.1142/9789811240553_0015

Chapter 15

Impact of Germany's Phase Out of Coal Power Plants on Developing Countries

Stefan Vögele[*,‡] and Kristina Govorukha[†,§]

[*]Forschungszentrum Jülich GmbH, Institute of Energy and Climate Research - Systems Analysis and Technology Evaluation (IEK-STE), 52425 Jülich, Germany

[†]TU Bergakademie Freiberg, Schloßplatz 1, 09596 Freiberg, Germany

[‡]s.voegele@fz juelich.de

[§]Kristina.Govorukha@vwl.tu-freiberg.de

In this chapter, we analyze the effects of a phase out of hard coal-fired power plants in Germany on developing countries. Besides impacts on economic factors, we take a closer look at related social and environmental impacts. The impacts are assessed by applying the list of Sustainable development goals (SDGs) of the UN. This enables us to assess the broad range of indirect effects in a systematic way. As key developing countries, which are affected by a phase out of coal-fired power plants in Germany, we identified Colombia and South Africa as important coal suppliers. We also pay attention to China as a supplier of PV modules that will partially substitute coal-fired power plants. Our study shows that coal mining is to a great extend linked with environmental and social problems. Hence, a reduction of mining activities due to phase out of coal-fired power plants could be helpful in reaching SDGs in developing countries. However, since Germany is less important (has relatively small share of countries' coal exports) for these coal exporting countries, the phase out of coal-fired power will not have significant impacts on their mining industries, as well as for the PV industry of China. Hence, the ancillary effects of the phasing out policy in Germany on SDGs in developing countries will be low.

1. Introduction

At the 21st Conference of the Parties (COP) of the UNFCCC in Paris, the participating countries stressed the need for more action with respect to the reduction of greenhouse gas (GHG) emissions. They claimed that the international community should try to limit the increase of the global temperature by 1.5°C. In response to the Paris Agreement on the limitation of the increase of temperature, at the COP23 in Bonn in 2017, together with 23 other partners, Canada and UK underpinned their willingness to decarbonize their energy systems by declaring phasing out of coal-fired power plants and launched the Powering Past Coal Alliance. Currently, the alliance consists of 33 national governments, 27 sub-national governments, and 37 businesses or organizations. The decision of Germany to join the alliance in 2019 was shaped by the recommendation of a coal exit commission, proposing a phase out of coal-fired power generation by 2038 at the latest and a climate action package.

In Germany, currently 57 TWh (9%) in 2019 of the electricity is produced by means of hard coal-fired power plants (BMWi, 2020). The amount of hard coal for electricity generation, which is imported, amounts to 32 M tonnes. The hard coal is imported from industrialized countries (e.g., USA), countries in transition (Russia), as well as from developing countries like Colombia and South Africa. In principle, it can be expected that a phase out of coal-fired power plants in Germany will affect these countries. Besides changes in revenues and employment, a drop in the demand for coal could impact the development of these countries with respect to sustainable development goals.

In the following, we analyze the effects of a phase out of hard coal power plants in Germany on developing countries. Besides impacts on economic factors, we emphasize impacts on social and environmental factors. In particular, we assess ancillary benefits of the phase out of coal-fired power plants on the sustainable developments goals (SDGs) of the UN. Following the list of the SDGs, the analysis includes, e.g., an assessment of aspects like reduction of poverty, improvement of health and well wellbeing, use and release of water, responsible consumption and production, changes in biodiversity, and decent jobs and economic growth.

The phase out of coal-fired plants is strongly related with lower coal imports, which thus lower activities in coal mining in foreign countries. For some countries, coal mining is a sector of prominent meaning for the economy as a whole and in particular for the society and the environment (see, e.g., Spencer *et al.*, 2018). Besides value added and generation of income, mining is related to perceived impacts on wellbeing (Poudyal *et al.*, 2019) and lifestyle (Cardoso, 2015). Regarding impacts of mining on the environment, Sinha *et al.* (2017), Park *et al.* (2020), and Mudd (2010) listed the extraction of finite resources, massive interventions in water regime and in the landscape as examples of the environmental impacts of mining. Monteiro *et al.* (2019) focused on mining in general and reviewed articles employing the SDG approach of the UN. Challenges for the coal sector resulting from the transition of the energy system are highlighted in an aggregated way by, e.g., Oei and Mendelevitch (2019) and Haftendorn *et al.* (2012). In contrast to these studies, we take a closer look at individual countries and relate developments in the selected countries to the coal phase out in Germany.

The Chapter is organized as follows: In Section 2, we give an overview of Germany's hard coal imports and key characteristics of the selected coal exporting countries. In Section 3, we describe the approach we applied for the assessment of the impacts being related to the hard coal trade. Results are presented and discussed in Section 4. Section 5 concludes.

2. Method

2.1. *Impacts of phase out of coal-fired power plants on the electricity supply system*

For the assessment of the impacts of phasing out of coal-fired power plants in Germany, it is important to take a closer look at the impact of phasing out of coal power plants in general. The "Act on the Phase-out of Coal-fired Power Plants," which was adopted by the German

Cabinet in January 2020, defined a timeline for the phase out of coal-fired power plants ending in 2038. By 2022, the installed capacity of coal-fired power plants will be reduced from 53 GW to around 30 GW (15 GW lignite and 15 GW hard coal-fired plants). In the next eight years, the installed capacity of the hard coal-fired power plants will be reduced by another 8 GW. By 2038, the last hard coal-fired plant will be closed. Similar phasing out strategies exist for other European countries (e.g., Italy by 2025, the Netherlands by 2029, and Sweden by 2022). Hence, Germany can serve as an example for other countries. For assessing the impacts of the phase out of coal-fired power plants, we compare scenarios focusing on the year 2040 with Germany's current electricity system. In principle, decreases in installed capacities are linked to lower demand for coal. Table 1 shows how the demand for coal will develop, assuming the constant rate of utilization. Correspondingly, the demand for coal will sharply drop in the next few decades.

It is expected that PV, wind, and gas-fired power stations will fill the supply gap that results from phasing out of coal-fired power plants. According to Gierkink *et al.* (2019), there will be a demand of 3 GW per year for PV, 4.8 GW per year in the next year. In the period 2025 to 2030, the demand for PV will increase to 5 GW/year and the demand for wind power plant to 5.6 GW. After 2030, the demand will drop to 1.0 GW/year (PV) and 1.5 GW/year (wind) (Table 1).

While wind power plants being installed in Germany are mainly produced in Germany, about 80% of the installed PV modules originated from China (Fraunhofer ISE, 2020). Assuming that there will be no major changes in the distribution of market shares, it is to be expected that certain countries like China will profit from phasing out of coal in Germany.

2.2. *Classification of impacts*

According to Buchholz *et al.* (2020), policy measure can be linked with manifold kinds of ancillary benefits. In this study we focus on the extent to which the phasing out of coal-fired power plants in Germany is related to the impacts on SDGs in developing countries. To assess

Table 1. Development of the demand for coal for coal-fired power plants in Germany.

	COAL						PV	WIND	GAS
	Installed capacity[a] [GW]		Demand for imports used for total electricity and heat sector[b] [Million tonnes/year]						
	Hard coal	Lignite	Steam coal	Coking coal	Lignite	Total	Market for new PV modules[c] [GW/year]	Market for new wind power plants[c] [GW/year]	Market for new gas-fired power plants[c] [GW/year]
2020	21.4	20.9	26.3	2.5	0.03	28.8	2.8 (2015–2020)	4.1 (2015–2020)	0.0 (2015–2020)
2022	15	15	18.4	1.8	0.02	10.2	3.0 (2020–2025)	4.8 (2020–2025)	0.4 (2020–2025)
2030	8	9	9.8	0.9	0.01	10.7	4.0 (2025–2030)	5.6 (2025–2030)	0.2 (2025–2030)
2040	0	0	0.0	0.0	0.00	0.0	1.0 (2030–2040)	1.5 (2030–2040)	0.7 (2030–2040)

Sources: [a](Federal Government, 2020); [b]Own calculation based on (BMWi, 2020); [c](Gierkink *et al.*, 2019).

the effects of the phasing out of coal-fired power plants in a systematic way, we employ the SDG approach of the UN (United Nations, 2020a). The UN distinguishes between 17 different sustainable categories and specified goals for each category (Fig. 1). The first category focuses on poverty aspects. The goal is defined as the end of poverty in its all forms. Sub-targets include, for example, reducing the number of people living on less than $1.25 a day and ensuring that each person has equal rights to economic resources and other forms of property. The second target is the end of hunger and achieving food security. The third goal focuses on "Good health and wellbeing" that includes, e.g., reduction of maternal mortality ratio, of premature mortality from non-communicable diseases as well as reduction of the number of deaths and illnesses from hazardous chemicals, and air, water, and soil pollution and contamination. "Quality Education" is listed as the fourth SDG. This goal includes, e.g., equal access for all women and men to affordable and quality technical, vocational, and tertiary education, eliminating gender disparities in education, and ensuring equal access to all levels of education and training.

"Gender equality" is defined as SDG 5. The goal comprises, e.g., the end of discrimination and violence against all women and girls as well as promotion of women's full and effective participation and equal opportunities for leadership at all levels of decision-making. SDG 6 focuses on access to water and sanitation for all. Among the sub-targets are, e.g., access to safe and affordable drinking water and improvement of

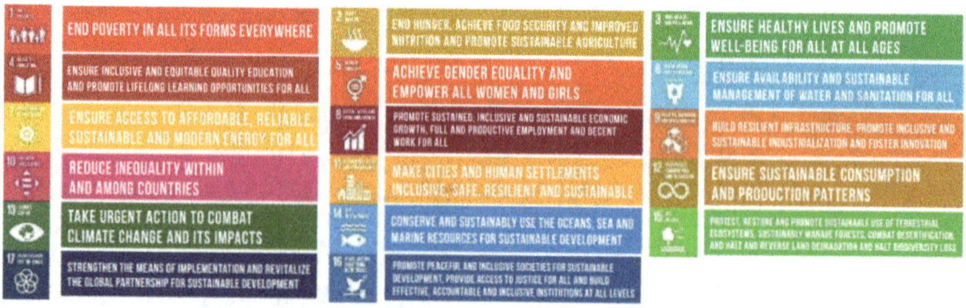

Fig. 1. Sustainable Development Goals.

Source: United Nations (2020a).

water quality by reducing pollution and minimizing the release of hazardous chemicals. Access to affordable, reliable, sustainable, and modern energy is defined in SDG 7. SDG 8 focuses on sustainable economic growth and employment for all. SDG 9 emphasizes the construction of resilient infrastructure and promotion of sustainable industrialization. Reduction of inequality within and among countries the aim of SDG 10 (DSDG, 2020).

In principle, the SDGs aim at developments at national and international levels. However, individual sectors foster or prevent developments toward reaching these goals. In the following, we employ the classification of the UN for a systematic assessment of the ancillary impact of phasing out of coal-fired power plants on the developing countries.

3. Impacted (developing) Countries

3.1. *Preliminary remarks — Definition "Developing countries"*

A widely used classification of countries is the "developed economics," "developing economies," and "economies in transition" approach. This classification aims to take into account differences in the basic economic conditions of countries under consideration (see, e.g., United Nations, 2020b). Developing economies are defined as nations with the relatively low gross domestic product (GDP) per capita, low living standards, undeveloped industrial base, and a low Human Development Index (HDI) (UNDP, 2018).

Since this classification is very rough and linked with some problems, the World Bank, in particular, uses an alternative approach. Focusing on income, the World Bank differentiates between high-income, upper-middle-income, lower-middle-income, and low-income countries. High-income countries are countries in which the benchmark for the gross national income (GNI) per capita is above $12,375. Upper-middle-income economies are those in which the GNI per capita is between $3,996 and $12,375, lower-middle-income economies with a

Table 2. Classification of countries.

	Developed economies	Economies in transition	Developing economies
High-income economies	Germany, USA, Australia		
Upper-middle-income economies		Russian Federation	China, Colombia, South Africa, Turkey
Lower-middle-income economies			Congo, India
Low-income economies			Niger, Rwanda

Sources: United Nations (2020b), World Bank (2019).

GNI per capita between $1,025 and $3,995, and low-income countries with a GNI per capita less than $1,025 (World Bank, 2019). Table 2 shows some examples of countries that fall under the different types of classifications. According to this table, the "income" classification allows differentiation between groups of developing countries.

For instance, Colombia and South Africa are classified as developing economies, whereas Russia counts in the Economies in transition (United Nations, 2020b).

3.2. *Countries being relevant for the utilization of coal-fired power plants*

In Germany, the installed capacity of coal-fired power plants accounts for more than 53 GW. 44 % of the coal-fired power plants use lignite as fuel and 56 % hard coal. With closing of the last hard coal mine in 2018, only imported coal is used in hard coal-fired power plants. Currently, coal imports account for 46 Mio. tonnes in production. Verein der Kohlenimporteure (2019), which corresponds to a value of 4,800 Mio.

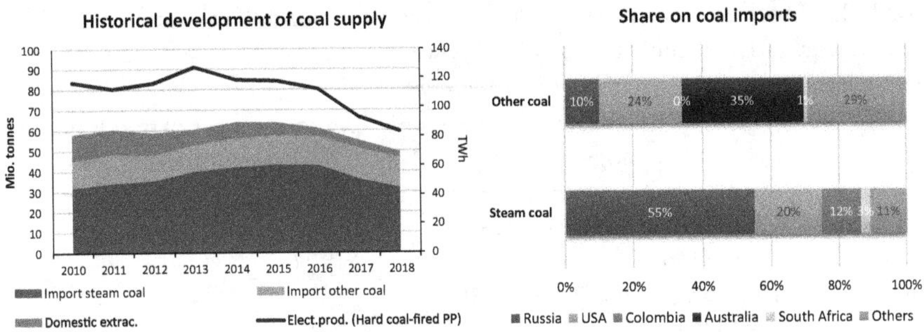

Fig. 2. Structure of Germany's coal imports.

Source: Verein der Kohlenimporteure (2019).

Euro.[1] Nearly 70% of the imported coal is steam coal, which is mainly used for electricity and heat production (Verein der Kohlenimporteure, 2019). Hence, imports of steam coal strongly depend on the activities of hard-coal fired power plants (Correlation coefficient: 0.93[2]). More than 55% of the steam coal originates from Russia, 20% from USA, 17% from Colombia, and 3% from South Africa (Fig. 2).

3.3. *Countries being relevant for substitute technologies*

According to the scenarios of Gierkink *et al.* (2019), a phase out of coal-fired power plants will result in an increase of the demand for wind and PV power stations as well as in greater use of gas-fired power plants. Hence, there is a need to take a closer look at which countries will be affected by changes in the increase in the demand for PV, wind, and gas-fired power plants. Table 3 gives an overview of foreign countries involved in the construction of these types of power stations with their operation.

According to Table 3 China and Malaysia, as well as Russia, will profit from the phasing out of coal-fired power plants in Germany.

[1]The value of imported coal is calculated by using data of VdKi (Verein der Kohlenimporteure, 2019) on imported volumes of coal and average prices.
[2]Own calculation based on (BMWi, 2020).

Table 3. Involvement of foreign countries in construction and utilization of Renewable Energy (RE) technologies/gas-fired power plants.

	Construction (technology exporter)	Utilization (export of goods needed for utilization incl. fuels)
PV	China, Malaysia, Japan (HS 854150)	—
Wind	Denmark, China, Turkey (HS 850231)	—
Gas-fired power plants	USA, France, United Kingdom, Canada (gas turbine HS 841182)	Russia, Norway (natural gas)

Notes: HS 854150: Diodes, transistors, and similar semiconductor devices; photosensitive semiconductor devices, including photovoltaic cells whether or not assembled in modules or made up into panels; HS 850231: Wind-Powered Generators.
Sources: BMWi (2020), UN (2020).

Hence, the list of developing countries which will become more important for the German electricity system differs from the list of developing countries which are currently involved in the operation of coal-fired power plants.

4. Impact Assessment

4.1. *Colombia*

4.1.1. *Preliminary remarks*

In the set of indicators used by the World Economic Forum for assessing the competitiveness of countries, Colombia ranks 57th out of 141 countries. Colombia has disadvantages with respect to "Institutions" (incl. security aspects such as organized crime as well as the burden of government regulation), "Infrastructure," "Skills" (including, e.g., years of schooling, staff training, and pupil to teacher ratio as sub-criteria), "Labor market," and "Innovation capability." Regarding "Macroeconomic stability" and "Health," Colombia shows less deficits (World Economic Forum, 2019). Regarding the Sustainable Development Goals, Colombia ranks 67th out of 162 countries. In particular, regarding the targets "Reduced inequality" and "Peace,

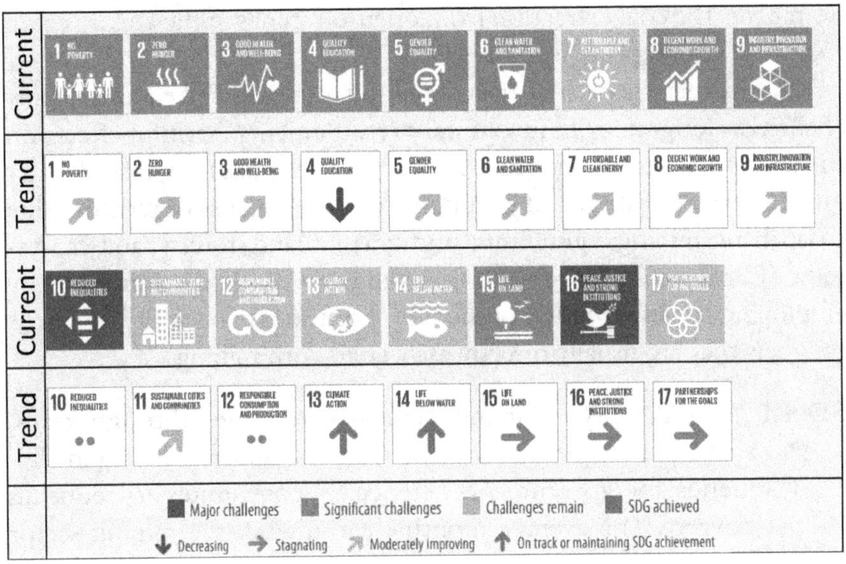

Fig. 3. Assessment of SDGs on the national level (Colombia).

Source: Sachs *et al.* (2019).

justice and strong institutions," other countries perform better than Colombia. "Quality education" shows a strong negative trend.

In past few years, the access to electricity and to clean fuels & technology for cooking has been improved, whereas the share of the population who feel safe walking alone at night in the city or area has dropped. All in all, the SDG performance is moderately improving (Fig. 3).

As mentioned, with respect to the steam coal supply within the group of developing countries, Colombia is the largest coal exporter globally: With exports of more than 80 Mio. tonnes of steam coal per year, Colombia ranks fourth on the list of the largest coal exporting countries (IEA, 2019).

4.1.2. *Contribution of coal mining to SDGs*

The coal fields in Colombia are mainly located in the north and middle of Colombia. The coal mine in La Guajira is one of the biggest open-pit coal mines in the world. Drummond Ltd is the company which dominates the coal extraction from open-pit mines in the Cesar region (National Mining Agency, 2019).

The extraction of coal from open-pit mines is linked with many challenges ranging from involuntary resettlements, harmful effects on the environment and on local communities, air pollution, loss of water quality, river deviation and groundwater damage, loss of territory due to open-pit mining, agricultural and grazing land, forests, and ecosystems (Cardoso, 2015). In the following, we assess these impacts by employing the list of SDGs of the UN. For the sake of clarity, we focus on goals that are usually directly associated with mining.

SDG 1 "No Poverty": Mining generates revenues through taxes, social protection systems for workers, and royalties and dividends for governments. Hence, it contributes to reducing poverty. The average monthly earnings in the mining sector remain above the average earnings across all economic sectors, thus benefitting goals like reduction of "Working poverty rate (percentage of employed living below US$1.90 PPP)" (Fig. 4).

SDG 2 "Zero Hunger": Since mining activities are linked with a) restrictions on the possibilities for farming, hunting, and

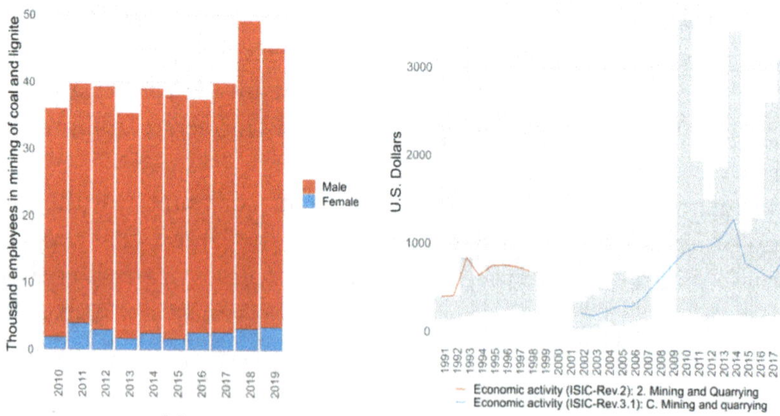

(a) (b)

Fig. 4. Employment data for Colombia.

Source: International Labour Organisation (ILOSTAT).

fishing, with b) losses of land which can be used for agriculture and c) since the huge water withdrawals of the mines in combination with chemical waste lower quality of soil, the mining activities are not in line with the SDG 2 (Vattenfall, 2017; EnBW, 2019).

SDG 3 "Good Health and Well-being": Usually, poor working conditions in the mines are stressed as an additional factor, which fosters resistance against the mines. According to a study by Vattenfall, mining activities impacted living conditions in a negative way. Besides, deterioration with respect to water use and the access to drinkable water with the mining activities were listed as challenges for reaching SDG 3 (Vattenfall, 2017; EnBW, 2019).

SDG 5 "Gender Equality"
As in many resource-dependent countries, in the Colombian mining sector, women workers remain underrepresented (see Fig. 3), although the trend is gradually increasing.

SDG 6 "Clean Water and Sanitation": A key characteristic of mining is the need for management of huge amounts of water. Studies highlighted that the water sources in the mining areas have been significantly impacted by the withdrawal of water and the release of hazardous chemicals and materials (Cerrejon, 2017, DSDG, 2020, Vattenfall, 2017). Hence, mining has to be classified as an activity with a negative impact on the SDG "Clean Water and Sanitation."

SDG 7 "Affordable and Clean Energy": Since coal is comparably a cheap and flexible energy carrier, in principle, coal mining helps to extend access to affordable energy. However, the use of coal is linked with high emissions. Thus, mining contributes in a positive and negative way to SDG 7.

SDG 8 "Decent Jobs and Economic Growth": As mentioned above, the mining industry supports economic growth. In Colombia, nearly 130.000 people are employed in the mining sector (Agencia Nacional, del Mineria, 2017) with nearly 45.000 directly in the mining of coal see (Fig. 3, International Labour Organisation (ILOSTAT)). Besides jobs in the mining industries, mining activities are linked with indirect effects. Low health and safety standards in combination with hostility to labor unions by the mining companies and conflicts between guerilla groups and the government affect working conditions (BetterCoal and Cerrejon, 2019, Diaz, 2016, Vattenfall, 2017). Violations in a safe and secure working environment increase social liabilities of coal mining and transportation (Cardoso, 2015). All in all, it could be assumed that there are more positive impulses with respect to SDG 8 than negative.

SDG 9 "Industry, Innovation and Infrastructure": Both for the transport of coal and for the transport of materials, infrastructure such as road, rail, and shipping networks and communication systems are necessary and have already been deployed. Since coal mining needs products from other industries and since the value added generated in the mining industry fosters the demand for other goods, mining contributes to SDG 9.

SDG 10 "Reduced Inequalities": Diaz (Diaz, 2016) highlights that with respect to resettlements and possibilities for farming, hunting, and fishing, in particular, indigenous people were discriminated against. Mining has, therefore, not reduced inequalities in the society (SDG 10).

SDG 11 "Sustainable Cities and Communities": In principle, royalties and taxes from mining help cities to improve their infrastructure and foster their economic development. However, despite high royalties and taxes from mining, the municipals in the coal regions are still poor and have problems to ensure minimum living standards for the majority of their population (BetterCoal and Cerrejon, 2019). The proximity of coal mines to the cities and communities affects the mean levels of fine particulate matter (PM 2.5, PM 10) in the air, producing adverse per capita environmental impact on health in the 23-km radius around the open-pit mines in Northern Colombia hosting 92% of bituminous coal production (Arregocés *et al.*, 2018).

SDG 12 "Responsible Consumption and Production": Regarding the SDG "Responsible Consumption and Production," it has to be highlighted that mining is linked with huge water withdrawals, water bodies affected by water discharges and/or runoff, and with significant interference with the landscape and levels of mining waste. Regarding environmental effects, increased dust and particulate air emissions, as well as water pollution resulting from coal mining operations, are reported.

SDG 13 "Climate Action": As coal is linked with high CO_2 emissions, activities aiming to promote coal as energy carrier counteract measures to combat climate change.

SDG 15 "Life on Land": Many studies mention negative impacts of mining on habitats and biodiversity (Cerrejon, 2017, EnBW, 2019, Vattenfall, 2017). In particular, deforestation and changes in quantity and quality of water resources are pointed out as main sources of losses in biodiversity.

SDG 16 "Peace and Justice — Strong Institutions": In Colombia, involuntary resettlements, health problems resulting from air pollutions and inferences in water bodies (i.e., changes in groundwater level, lower access to drinking water), and inappropriate working conditions have resulted in many complaints and conflicts (Niebank and Utlu, 2017, Anwaltskollektiv José Alvear Restrepo (Cajar), 2019). Currently, the International Trade Union Confederation listed Colombia as one of the 10 worst countries in the world for working people (ITUC, 2019). According to Vattenfall (Vattenfall, 2017), mining in Colombia has been strongly linked with corruption. Accordantly, the mining regions are the most corrupt regions in Colombia. In the last few years, measures have been introduced aiming to lower corruption. However, the corruption in Colombia is still on a high level (OECD, 2019, Transparency International, 2019) (Transparency International rank: 99 out of 180).

All in all, the assessment of coal mining in Colombia by using the UN list of sustainable development goals indicates that the mining sector in Colombia still hampers/decelerates Colombia's way to sustainability.

According to Table 4, the activities of the mining sector are not helpful for reaching the SDGs where Colombia performs below average. In the last few years, a lot of measures have been implemented to improve the situation (Bettercoal, 2019, Cerrejon, 2017). However, as Table 4 shows, there is still much to be done.

4.1.3. *Meaning of Germany's phase out of coal-fired power plants for Colombia*

About 25% of the coal exports of Colombia are destined for Europe (EU-28). Since the year 2011, the share of Germany in the exports has declined from 14% to 5%. Exports to the Netherlands show a similar trend. All in all, the difference between coal production at world prices and their total costs (weighted by production) accounts directly for almost 0.8 % of the GDP. Coal exported to Germany contributes 0.05% to Colombia's GDP.

According to Fig. 5, it has to be expected that the phase out of coal-fired power will not have significant impacts on the mining industry in Colombia. Hence, the ancillary effects of the phasing out policy in Germany on SDGs in Colombia will be negligible.

4.2. *South Africa*

4.2.1. *Preliminary remarks*

With respect to SDGs, South Africa shows weakness, e.g., in the goals "Poverty," "Good Health and Wellbeing," "Clean water Sanitation," "Decent Work and Economic Growth," and "Climate Action" (Fig. 6). In the last few years, South Africa has made some progress with respect to most of the goals; however, all in all, South Africa still ranks 113th on the list of 162 countries (Sachs *et al.*, 2019).

South Africa's economic development significantly dependents on export of resources. According to the World Bank, the difference between the coal production at world prices and their total costs (weighted by production) corresponds to 2.0 % of the GDP (World

Table 4. Assessment of contribution of coal mining for SDGs.

SDGs*	Contribution of coal mining sector**
1 No poverty	Mining generates revenues through taxes, royalties, and dividends for governments
2 Zero hunger	Reduction in availability of land and quality of soil for agriculture
3 Good health and well-being	Hard working conditions, release of hazardous chemicals and materials
4 Quality education	—
5 Gender equality	—
6 Clean water and sanitation	Water sources significantly impacted by the withdrawal of water, release of hazardous chemicals and materials
7 Affordable and clean energy	Coal can contribute to a cheap energy supply. Since coal is linked with high emissions, it is not a "clean" carrier
8 Decent jobs and economic growth	Creation of direct and indirect jobs, creation of economic values, partially, low health and safety standards, infringement of labor rights
9 Industry, innovation and infrastructure	Commission of new infrastructure for transport, supply industries benefit from development in the mining sector
10 Reduced inequalities	Discrimination of indigenous peoples
11 Sustainable cities and communities	Royalties as means for improvements on the community level
12 Responsible consumption and production	Water withdrawals, water bodies affected by water discharges and/or runoff, interference with the landscape, air, and water pollutions
13 Climate action	Promotion of coal (CO_2-intensive energy carrier)
14 Life below water	—
15 Life on land	Negative impacts on habitats and biodiversity, deforestation
16 Peace and justice — strong institutions	Social conflicts (e.g., with respect to labor and human rights as well as to resettlements), incidents of violations involving rights of indigenous peoples, corruption
17 Partnerships for the goals	—

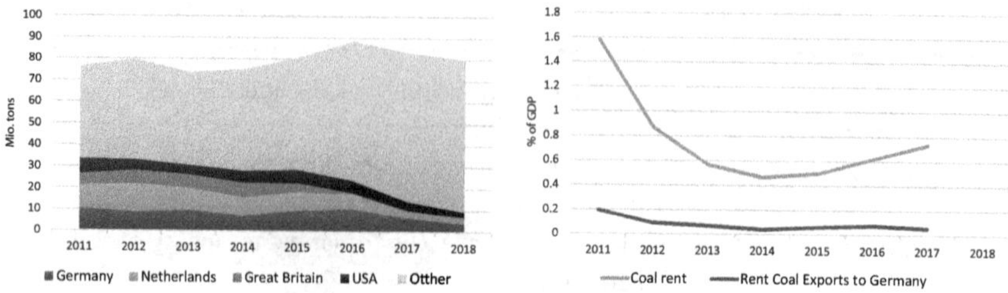

Fig. 5. Development of coal export and coal rents (Colombia).

Source: Verein der Kohlenimporteure (2017, 2019), World Bank (2020).

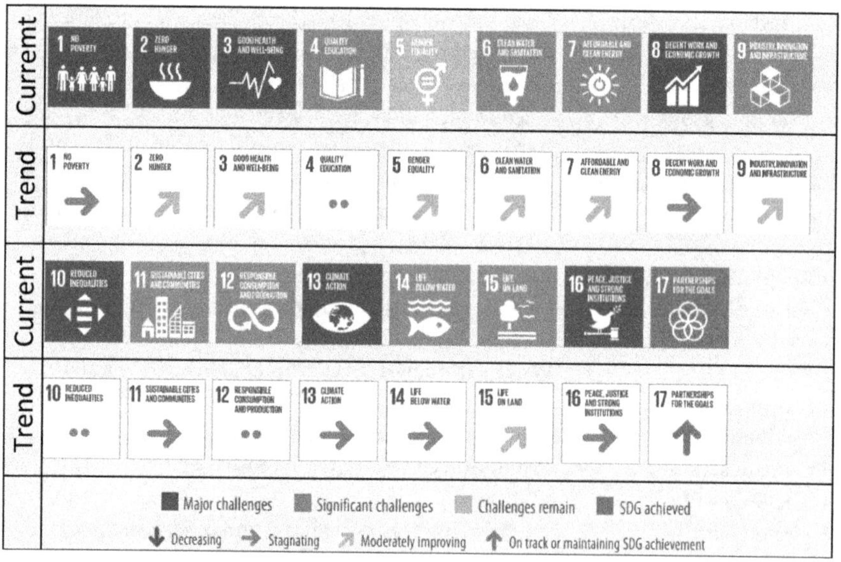

Fig. 6. Assessment of SDGs on the national level (South Africa).

Source: Sachs *et al.* (2019).

Bank, 2020). Each year, South Africa exports about 80 Mio. tonnes of coal. The mineral council of South Africa reported that currently 92.000 persons are employed in the coal sector, producing 259 Million tonnes of coal (Mineral Council Of South Africa, 2020).

4.2.2. *Contribution of coal mining to SDGs*

In South Africa, coal is mainly mined in open-cast mines located in Mpumalanga and Limpopo. Again, the extraction of coal is linked with a broad range of social and environmental impacts including resettlements, increasing emissions, on the use of water, and on local communities. Regarding SDGs, we get the following picture:

SDG 1 "No Poverty": All in all, the sales add up to more than 6.7 billion Euro (Mineral Council Of South Africa, 2020). With a share of 2% of the national gross domestic product, the mining sector contributes significantly to increase of welfare in South Africa. It offers decent, higher-than-average wages for employees in mining when compared to other economic sectors (in grey bars) (see Fig. 7).

SDG 2 "Zero Hunger": Like in Colombia, losses of agriculture land have to be mentioned as a negative impact of mining (Centre For Environmental Rights *et al.*, 2016). In combination with shortages of water, food production is threatened.

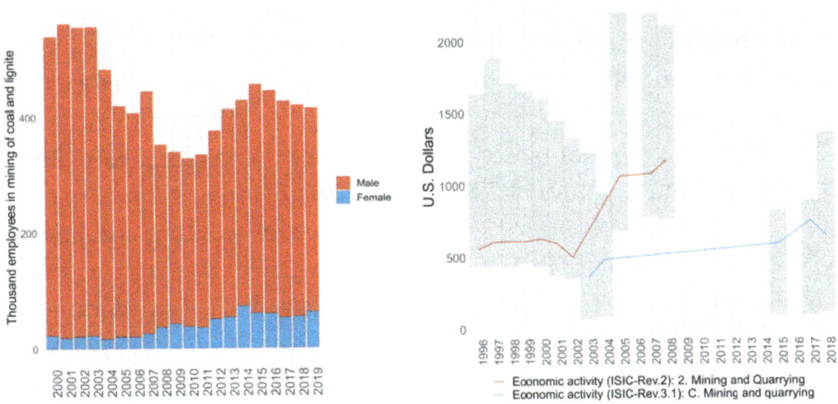

(a) (b)

Fig. 7. Employment data for South Africa.

Source: InternationaL Labour Organisation (ILOSTAT).

SDG 3 "Good Health and Well-being": Besides mine accidents and a high death rate, silicosis as well as other lung diseases, hearing loss, and illness caused by toxic air pollution are mentioned as characteristics of mining in South Africa (Bloch *et al.*, 2018, Utembe *et al.*, 2015, Munnik, 2010). Comparing to other industries, the mining sectors has to be considered as one that has a negative impact on reaching the SDG "Good Health and Well-being."

SDG 6 "Clean Water and Sanitation": Problems with respect to water quality are emphasized by Centre For Environmental Rights (2019) and Naidoo (2015): The authors emphasize, e.g., failures on the regulatory level, incorrect compliance ratings and statistics, and lacking quality control. Hence, e.g., acid mine drainage from coal mines polluted surface and groundwater. This, in turn, affects human health, livestock, crop production, and aquatic ecosystems. Centre For Environmental Rights *et al.* (2016) highlight that groundwater extraction by mines decreases the amount of water available to local communities.

SDG 7 "Affordable and Clean Energy": As mentioned above, coal is a comparably cheap and flexible energy carrier. Hence, in principle, coal mining helps to extend access to affordable energy. Since coal combustion is linked with high emissions, coal cannot be considered as clean energy. Thus, the mining industry does not contribute anything to reach the target "Clean Energy."

SDG 8 "Decent Jobs and Economic Growth": With more than 92000 jobs and revenues of 7.5 billion Euro, the mining industry contributes to economic growth. Dangerous working conditions, health impacts (incl. tuberculosis), accidents, fatalities, as well as lack of freedom in organizing trade reduce positive impulses with respect to reaching SGG8 (Coulson *et al.*, 2019, Stewart *et al.*, 2020, MHSI, 2018).

SDG 9 "Industry, Innovation and Infrastructure": Like the mining industry in other countries, the one in South Africa is directly and indirectly linked with improvements in infrastructure.

The industry spends money on R&D, focusing in particular on mining and is interested in reducing cost. Again, the industry is embedded in the overall economic system. Hence, the activities of the mining industry support developments of other sectors.

SDG 10 "Reduced Inequalities": Mining is a male-dominated industry. For a long time, mining in South Africa was fraught with extreme racial and gender discrimination. A lot of regulations and laws have been enacted to reduce discrimination. However, in particular, racism and violence against migrants from other African countries and white people can be observed (Laterza and Sharp, 2017).

SDG 11 "Sustainable Cities and Communities": Again, royalties and taxes from mining help cities to improve their infrastructure and foster their economic development. According to Centre For Environmental Rights *et al.* (2016), pollution from mines destroys ecosystems, which are essential for communities with respect to cultural and spiritual practices.

SDG 12 "Responsible Consumption and Production": As mentioned above, mining is linked with huge interventions in water regime and in the landscape. Acid mine drainage, spontaneous combustion, increased erosion and siltation of surface waters, as well as contamination of local groundwater are additional factors that indicate that the mining sector does not belong to the sectors with "responsible consumption and production" (Department Of Energy: Republic Of South Africa, 2020).

SDG 13 "Climate Action": Since coal is linked with high CO_2 emissions, activities aiming to promote coal as the energy carrier counteract measures to combat climate change.

SDG 15 "Life on Land": (Department Of Environmental Affairs, 2013) highlighted that losses and/or degradation or conversion of land, alteration of ecological processes (e.g., disruption of species movement patterns, disruption of the local hydrological cycle, and permanent alteration of flow), and pollution (including noise and light pollution) had resulted in losses of biodiversity.

SDG 16 "Peace and Justice — Strong Institutions": Violation of human rights, intimidation and violence against mining opponents, and lack of community participation in the development of social and labor plans associated with mining approvals are aspects why the mining industry in South Africa is still not among the industries that are at the forefront of SDG 16 (Spohr, 2016).

Regarding the SDGs where South Africa performs worse, the mining industry supports the achievement of SDG 1 and SDG 9, whereas SDGs 3, 7, 12, and 16 are not supported by activities of the mining industry; on the contrary, it contributes to jeopardizing the achievement of the objectives (Table 5).

Of course, it has to be mentioned that several improvements are on the way: OECD (OECD, 2013), for example, highlighted that some of the global mining companies introduced environmental management systems that included biodiversity issues in order to avoid negative impacts on their reputations. With the "Vision 2020: A globally competitive, sustainable and meaningfully transformed mining and minerals sector" and other initiatives, the government supports the transformation process of the mining sector (Macfarlane, 2018, Strambo *et al.*, 2019).

4.2.3. *Meaning of Germany's phase out of coal-fired power plants for South Africa*

About 98% of the exported coal is steam coal (IEA, 2019, Verein der Kohlenimporteure, 2019). The main destination countries for the coal are India, Pakistan, South Korea, and the Netherlands (Nicholas and Buckley, 2019). The exports to Germany are less critical for South Africa (see Fig. 8). Hence, a phase out of coal-fired electricity generation in Germany, as in the case of Colombia, will not have a significant impact on the mining industry in South Africa. Correspondingly, ancillary effects from reaching SDG in South Africa will be negligible.

Table 5. Contribution of mining in South Africa with respect to SDGs.

SDGs*	Contribution of coal mining sector**
1 No poverty	Mining generates revenues through taxes, royalties, and dividends for governments
2 Zero hunger	Reduction in availability of land and quality of soil for agriculture
3 Good health and well-being	Hard working conditions, release of hazardous chemicals and materials
4 Quality education	—
5 Gender equality	—
6 Clean water and sanitation	Water sources significantly impacted by the withdrawal of water, release of hazardous chemicals and materials
7 Affordable and clean energy	Coal can contribute to a cheap energy supply. Since coal is linked with high emissions, it is not a "clean" carrier
8 Decent jobs and economic growth	Creation of direct and indirect jobs, creation of economic values, partially, low health and safety standards, infringement of labor rights
9 Industry, innovation and infrastructure	Commission of new infrastructure for transport, supply industries benefit from development in the mining sector
10 Reduced inequalities	Racism and violence against migrants from other African and white people
11 Sustainable cities and communities	Royalties as means for improvements on the community level Pollution from mines destroys ecosystems, which are essential for communities with respect to cultural and spiritual practices
12 Responsible consumption and production	Water withdrawals, water bodies affected by water discharges and/or runoff, interference with the landscape, air, and water pollutions
13 Climate action	Promotion of coal (CO_2-intensive energy carrier)
14 Life below water	—
15 Life on land	Negative impacts on habitats and biodiversity, deforestation
16 Peace and justice — strong institutions	Social conflicts (e.g., with respect to labor and human rights as well as to resettlements)
17 Partnerships for the goals	

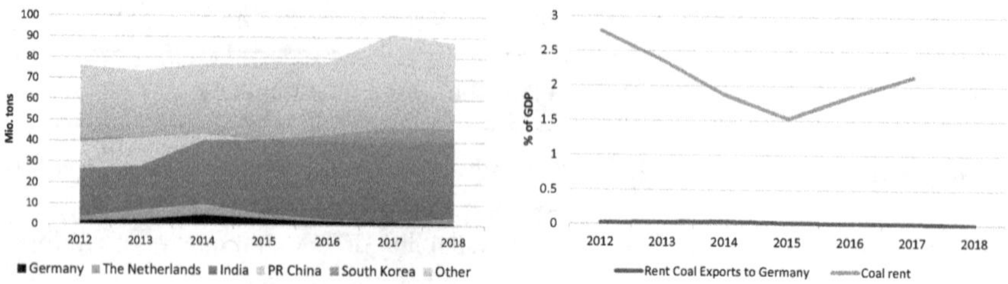

Fig. 8. Development of coal exports and coal rents (South Africa).

Source: (Verein der Kohlenimporteure, 2017, 2019, World Bank, 2020).

4.3. *China*

4.3.1. *Preliminary remarks*

According to the World Economic Forum (World Economic Forum, 2019), the competitiveness of China has increased due to progress in information and communications technology (ICT). Currently, China ranks 28th out of 141 countries. China profits from macroeconomic stability and from its innovation capability. Insufficient workers' rights protection, rigidities in wage determination and redundancy, conflictual industrial relations, low participation of women, high tax on labor, and lack of internal mobility are factors that lower the overall competitiveness and performance.

For China, the assessment of the SDGs gives an uneven picture: "Education" and "Decent work and economic growth" are the topics where China shows its strengths. China performs less in the SDGs "Reduce inequality," "climate action," and "Peace, justice and strong institutions" (Fig. 9). With ranking of 39th of 162, China is only 4 ranking points below the USA (Sachs *et al.*, 2019).

4.3.2. *Contribution of solar industry to SDGs*

In the following, we assess the contribution of the PV-module industry to the SDGs:

SDG 1 "No Poverty": With more than 2.2 million employees on their payroll, China's PV industry's wages contribute to an increase in income and hence to reduction of poverty (IRENA, 2019).

Fig. 9. Assessment of SDGs on the national level (China).

Source: Sachs *et al.* (2019).

SDG 2 "Zero Hunger": In contrast to mining, the production of PV modules is not linked with significant losses of agriculture land. Hence, PV does not impact SDG 2 directly.

SDG 3 "Good Health and Well-being": The PV-module industries use a lot of toxic chemicals including cadmium telluride, copper indium selenide, cadmium gallium (di)selenide, copper indium gallium (di)selenide, hexafluoroethane, lead, and polyvinyl fluoride (Nkuissi *et al.*, 2020). Some of the by-products of production can endanger human health. There are concerns regarding appropriate protection for all workers. Silicosis, in particular, is mentioned as a health issue (Mulvaney, 2014).

SDG 6 "Clean Water and Sanitation": Like other industries, the PV industry depends on the use of water and chemicals (Qi and Zhang, 2017). Infective control systems made accidents possible: Regarding production of PV modules, an incident in Hongxiao Village can serve as an example. In this example, polluted wastewater resulted in fish-kill in a nearby river (ICTA, 2020).

SDG 7 "Affordable and Clean Energy": PV counts as "clean energy." Thus, with the production of PV modules and with the aim of the industry to reduce the production cost, the PV industry helps to reach SDG 7.

SDG 8 "Decent Jobs and Economic Growth": According to IRENA (2019), more than 2.2 million persons are employed in the PV industry. It is expected that the demand for PV modules will increase in the next few decades. Hence, PV-module production supports reaching SDG 8.

SDG 9 "Industry, Innovation and Infrastructure": The production of PV modules is supported by the Chinese government. An example of industrial policy is the establishment of manufacturing clusters in the Yangtze River Delta. The presence of suppliers from sectors such as the glass industry enables solar firms to develop new technologies in close cooperation and to buy inputs inexpensively. With fostering innovation and industrialization in general, the PV industry contributes to reaching SDG 9.

SDG 10 "Reduced Inequalities": The PV industry is mainly located it the populated western part of China. Hence, only a part of the country profits directly from the economic activity of the sector. However, since PV modules can be used for the decentralized energy system, the deployment of PV modules helps to reduce inequalities (Zhang *et al.*, 2020).

SDG 11 "Sustainable Cities and Communities": Since PV production is linked to tax revenues, the industry supports the development of nearby cities and communities. Releases of toxic waste limit positive impulses on SDG 11.

SDG 12 "Responsible Consumption and Production": As mentioned, the production of PV modules is linked with the use of lot of chemicals and with toxic by-products (Xu *et al.*, 2018). There are concerns that toxic by-products are not always handled correctly and sometimes wastes are not disposed properly.

SDG 13 "Climate Action": The PV industry supports Climate Action by providing a "clean" technology. Even if the production of this technology is indirectly linked with emissions, as a (partial) substitute for coal-fired power plants, it contributes to the reduction of GHG emissions.

SDG 15 "Life on Land": In principle, the PV industry is not directly linked to major changes in biodiversity. However, the extrac tion of rare earth materials linked to the production of PV could be harming ecosystems, biodiversity, and habitats (Yang *et al.*, 2013).

SDG 16 "Peace and Justice — Strong Institutions": There have been several incidents with chemical use in the solar industries, which resulted in protests against companies. ICTA (ICTA, 2020) listed as examples the antipollution protests against JinkoSolar Company in 2011 and Apollo Precision (Fujian) Ltd. in 2015 with more than a thousand local residents joining the protests. All in all, the protests have been relevant at the local level for a relatively short period and have not impacted the society to a greater extend. The impact of the PV industry on SDGs is summarized in Table 6.

4.3.3. *Meaning of Germany's phase out of coal-fired power plants for China*

With JinkoSolar, JA Solar, Trina Solar, LONGi Solar Technology, Risen Energy, GCL Systems Integration Technology, and Shunfeng Photovoltaic International, 7 of the 10 biggest Solar modules manufactures are located in China. According to Jäger-Waldau (Jäger-Waldau,

Table 6. Contribution of SDGs by PV industry in China.

SDGs*	Contribution of PV industry**
1 No poverty	Generation of income
2 Zero hunger	No impact
3 Good health and well-being	Use of hazard chemicals
4 Quality education	—
5 Gender equality	—
6 Clean water and sanitation	Sporadic pollution of wastewater
7 Affordable and clean energy	Cost reductions and learning effects foster diffusion of PV as clean technology
8 Decent jobs and economic growth	PV will be an important dominant technology in the energy systems. Thus, the industry will create sustainable jobs
9 Industry, innovation and infrastructure	PV industry fosters R&D. The industry is linked with activities of other sectors
10 Reduced inequalities	PV industry is mainly located in populated areas. Thus, the industries does not contribute to reduce inequalities between poor and rich regions. PV modules can help to increase access to electricity
11 Sustainable cities and communities	Generation of taxes being related to PV industry helps cities to grow. PV can contribute to a clean electricity supply
12 Responsible consumption and production	Production of PV is linked with the use of toxic chemicals
13 Climate action	Support of "climate action" by providing a clean technology
14 Life below water	—
15 Life on land	—
16 Peace and justice — strong institutions	Sporadic protest against solar industries
17 Partnerships for the goals	—

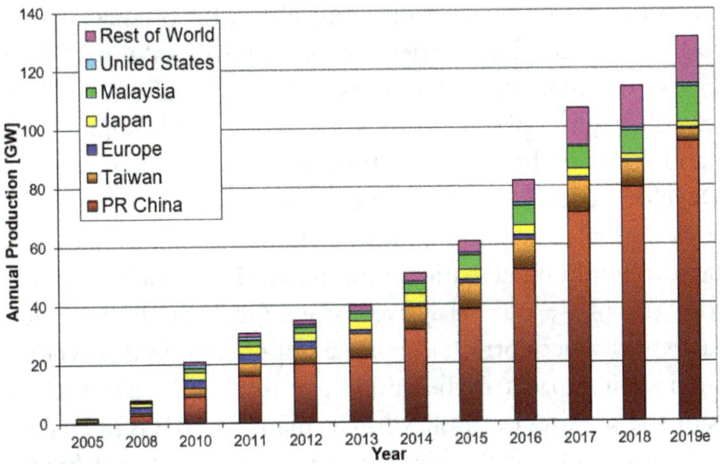

Fig. 10. World PV cell/module production from 2005 to 2019.

Source: Jäger-Waldau (2020).

2020), the annual production of PV cell/modules in China accounts for more than 90 GW (Fig. 10).

The Chinese module manufacturer GCL System Integration announced that in the next four years they will build a 60-GW solar module factory in eastern China. Hence, it can be expected that the PV industry in China will still continue to grow.

Assuming that the share of PV modules imported by Germany from China will stay at 80% (Fraunhofer ISE, 2020), the PV exports from China to Germany will account for 1 to 3 GW. In comparison to the production of PV modules in China, the exports to Germany are very small. Hence, it is unlikely that the demand from Germany for PV affects the PV industry in China (and indirectly SDGs) significantly.

5. Conclusion

For decades, the use coal-fired power plants was supported by the German government. The decision to phase out this technology means a paradigm shift. However, without phasing out coal-fired power plants, the ambitious emissions reduction targets cannot be reached. Like every policy measure, the phase out policy has not only primary effects (i.e., reduction of CO_2 emissions) but also a lot of ancillary benefits and costs. Since third countries are involved in value chains, it has to be expected that other countries will also be affected. There are concerns that developing countries, which currently supply coal, will suffer and could be hampered in their attempt to reach their Sustainable Development Goals. Our study shows that coal mining is to a great extend linked with environmental and social problems. Hence, a reduction in mining activities could mean that some SDGs will benefit from the phase out. However, since Germany is less important for coal exporting countries, the phase out of coal-fired power will not have significant impacts on their mining industries. Hence, the ancillary effects of the phasing out policy in Germany on SDGs in coal exporting countries will be negligible. Since phasing out of coal-fired power will result in a higher demand for other power plant technologies, we analyze to which extend China will benefit from ancillary effects with respect to SDGs. Taking China's huge capacity for PV, we conclude that China's SDGs will not be affected by Germany's increase in demand for PV.

References

Agencia Nacional Del Mineria (2017). *Coal, the Mining Godfather of Colombia*. https://www.anm.gov.co/?q=carbon_el_padrino_minero_de_colombia_boletin_prensa. (Accessed on April 22, 2020).

Anwaltskollektiv José Alvear Restrepo (Cajar) (2019). *Menschenrechtsverletzungen durch den Kohleabbau in El Cerrejón*, Bogota, Misereor.

Arregocés, H. A., Rojano, R., Angulo, L., and Restrepo, G. (2018). Intake fraction of PM10 from coal mine emissions in the North of Colombia. *Journal of Environmental and Public Health*, 2018, 8532463.

Bettercoal, C. (2019). *Bettercoal Assessment Public Report: Cerrejón Coal Company*. London.

Bloch, K., Johnson, L. F., Nkosi, M., and Ehrlich, R. (2018). Precarious transition: A mortality study of South African ex-miners. *BMC Public Health*, 18(1), 862.

BMWI (2020). *Energy Data: Complete Edition*. https://www.bmwi.de/Redaktion/EN/Artikel/Energy/energy-data.html, (Accessed on February 22, 2020).

Buchholz, W., Markandya, A., Rübbelke, D., and Vögele, S. (2020). *Ancillary Benefits of Climate Policy*, Springer International Publishing, Cham.

Cardoso, A. (2015). Behind the life cycle of coal: Socio-environmental liabilities of coal mining in Cesar, Colombia. *Ecological Economics*, 120, 71–82.

Centre For Environmental Rights (2019). *The Truth about Mpumalanga Coal Mines Failure to Comply with their Water Use Licences.* Johannesburg.

Centre For Environmental Rights, Centre For Applied Legal Studies, Groundwork, South Durban Community Environmental Alliance, Vaal Environmental Justice Alliance, Highveld Environmental Justice Network, Earthjustice (2016). *The threats to human rights from mining and coal-fired power production in South Africa.*

Cerrejon (2017). *Sustainability Report 2017.* Albania.

Coulson, N., Stewart, P. F., and Saeed, S. (2019). South African mineworkers' perspectives on the right to refuse dangerous work and the constraints to worker self-regulation. *Journal of the Southern African Institute of Mining and Metallurgy*, 119, 21–30.

Department of Energy: Republic Of South Africa (2020). *South African Coal Sector Report.* Department of Energy: Republic of South Africa. http://www.energy.gov.za/files/publications_frame.html, (Accessed on April 1, 2020).

Department of Environmental Affairs, Department of Mineral Resources, Chamber of Mines, South African Mining And Biodiversity Forum, South African National Biodiversity Institute (2013). *Mining and Biodiversity Guideline: Mainstreaming Biodiversity into the Mining Sector.* Pretoria.

Diaz, A. C. (2016). *Social-Environmental Liabilities of Coal Mining in Colombia: A Politcal Ecology Approach to the Global Coal Chain.* Barcelona.

DSDG (2020). *Sustainable Development Goals - Knowledge Platform.* Division for Sustainable Development Goals in the Department of Economic and Social Affairs. https://sustainabledevelopment.un.org/. (Accessed on April 21, 2020).

ENBW (2019). *Buying Coal from Colombia.* Karlsruhe.

Federal Government (2020). *Ending coal-generated power.* https://www.bundesregierung.de/breg-en/news/kohleausstiegsgesetz-1717014. (Accessed on April 22, 2020).

Fraunhofer ISE (2020). *Recent Facts about Photovoltaics in Germany.* Freiburg, Fraunhofer Institute for Solar Energy Systems ISE.

Gierkink, M., Lencz, D., and Arnold, F. (2019). *Auswirkungen einer Beendigung der Kohleverstromung bis 2038 auf den Strommarkt, CO2-Emissionen und ausgewählte Industrien*. Cologne, Energiewirtschaftliches Institut an der Universität zu Köln gGmbH (EWI).

Haftendorn, C., Kemfert, C., and Holz, F. (2012). What about coal? Interactions between climate policies and the global steam coal market until 2030. *Energy Policy*, 48, 274–283.

ICTA (2020). *EJAtlas - Global Atlas of Environmental Justice*. Institute of Environmental Science and Technology (ICTA), Universitat Autonoma de Barcelona. https://ejatlas.org/. (Accessed on April 5, 2020).

IEA (2019). *Coal Information 2019*. Paris.

International Labour Organisation (ILOSTAT). *Labour statistics*. https://ilostat.ilo.org/data/, 03.2020.

IRENA (2019). *Renewable Energy and Jobs – Annual Review 2019*. Abu Dhabi.

ITUC (2019). *ITUC Global Rights Index*. Brussels, International Trade Union Confederation (ITUC).

Jäger-Waldau, A. (2020). *PV Status Report 2019*. Luxembourg, Publications Office of the European Union.

Laterza, V. and Sharp, J. (2017). Extraction and beyond: People's economic responses to restructuring in southern and central Africa. *Review of African Political Economy*, 44(152), 173–188.

Macfarlane, A. S. (2018). Presidential Address: Towards the future: African Mining Vision, Mining Phakisa and the SAIMM. *Journal of the Southern African Institute of Mining and Metallurgy*, 118, 899–916.

MHSI (2018). *Annual Report 2017/2018*. Sunnyside, Pretoria, Mine Health and Safety Inspectorate.

Mineral Council Of South Africa (2020). *Facts and Figures Pocketbook 2019*. Johannesburg.

Monteiro, N. B. R., Da Silva, E. A., and Moita Neto, J. M. (2019). Sustainable development goals in mining. *Journal of Cleaner Production*, 228, 509–520.

Mudd, G. M. (2010). The environmental sustainability of mining in Australia: Key mega-trends and looming constraints. *Resources Policy*, 35:2, 98–115.

Mulvaney, D. (2014). Solar's green dilemma. *Spectrum, IEEE*, 51, 30–33.

Munnik, V. (2010). *The Social and Environmental Consequences of Coal Mining in South Africa*. Cape Town, Environmental Monitoring Group.

Naidoo, S. (2015). An assessment of the impacts of acid mine drainage on socio-economic development in the Witwatersrand: South Africa. *Environment, Development and Sustainability*, 17(5), 1045–1063.

National Mining Agency (2019). *Coal.* http://mineriaencolombia.anm.gov.co/index.php/en/colombia-a-privileged-country, (Accessed on February 26, 2020).

Nicholas, S. and Buckley, T. (2019). *South African Coal Exports Outlook.* Institute for Energy Economics and Financial Analysis (IEEFA), Cleveland.

Niebank, J.-C. and Utlu, D. (2017). *Closing Gaps in Protection - Transnational Cooperation on Human Rights: The Case of the Extractive Sector in Colombia.* German Institute for Human Rights, Berlin.

Nkuissi, H. J. T., Konan, F. K., Hartiti, B., and Ndjaka, J.-M. (2020). Toxic materials used in thin film photovoltaics and their impacts on environment, reliability and ecological aspects of photovoltaic modules. *IntechOpen.* https://www.intechopen.com/books/reliability-and-ecological-aspects-of-photovoltaic-modules/toxic-materials-used-in-thin-film-photovoltaics-and-their-impacts-on-environment.

OECD (2013). *OECD Environmental Performance Reviews: South Africa 2013.*

OECD (2019). *OECD Economic Surveys: Colombia 2019.*

Oei, P.-Y. and Mendelevitch, R. (2019). Prospects for steam coal exporters in the era of climate policies: A case study of Colombia. *Climate Policy*, 19(1), 73–91.

Park, J., Kwon, E., Chung, E., Kim, H., Battogtokh, B., and Woo, N. C. (2020). Environmental sustainability of open-pit coal mining practices at Baganuur, Mongolia. *Sustainability*, 12(1), 20.

Poudyal, N. C., Gyawali, B. R., and Simon, M. (2019). Local residents' views of surface mining: Perceived impacts, subjective wellbeing, and support for regulations in southern Appalachia. *Journal of Cleaner Production*, 217, 530–540.

Qi, L. and Zhang, Y. (2017). Effects of solar photovoltaic technology on the environment in China. *Environmental Science and Pollution Research*, 24, 1–10.

Sachs, J., Schmidt-Traub, G., Kroll, C., Lafortune, G., and Fuller, G. (2019). *Sustainable Development Report 2019.* Bertelsmann Stiftung and Sustainable Development Solutions Network (SDSN), New York.

Sinha, S., Chakraborty, S., and Goswami, S. (2017). Ecological footprint: an indicator of environmental sustainability of a surface coal mine. *Environment Development and Sustainability*, 19(3), 807–824.

Spencer, T., *et al.* (2018). The 1.5 degrees C target and coal sector transition: At the limits of societal feasibility. *Climate Policy*, 18(3), 335–351.

Spohr, M. (2016). *Human Rights Risks in Mining: A Baseline Study.* German Federal Institute for Geosciences and Natural Resources (BGR) and Max-Planck-Foundation for International Peace and the Rule of Law (MPFPR), Hannover.

Stewart, P., Bezuidenhout, A., and Bischoff, C. (2020). Safety and health before and after Marikana: subcontracting, illegal mining and trade union rivalry in the South African mining industry. *Review of African Political Economy*, 47(163), 27–44.

Strambo, C., Burton, J., and Atteridge, A. (2019). *The end of coal? Planning a "just transition" in South Africa.* Stockholm Environment Institute, Stockholm.

Transparency International (2019). *Corrpution Perception Index 2019.* Berlin.

UN (2020). *UN Comtrade Database.* https://comtrade.un.org/, (Accessed on February 18, 2020).

UNDP (2018). *Human Development Indices and Indicators – 2018 Statistical Update.* United Nations Development Programme (UNDP), New York.

United Nations (2020a). *The Sustainable Development Goals Report 2019.* New York, UN.

United Nations (2020b). *World Economic Situation and Prospects (WESP).* New York.

Utembe, W., Faustman, E., Matatiele, P., and Mary, G. (2015). Hazards identified and the need for health risk assessment in the South African mining industry. *Human & Experimental Toxicology*, 34, 1212–1221.

Vattenfall (2017). *A Human Rights Risk Assessment in Colombia.* Stockholm.

Verein Der Kohlenimporteure (2017). *Annual Report.* Berlin.

Verein Der Kohlenimporteure (2019). *Annual Report.* Berlin.

World Bank (2019). *New Country Classifications by Income Level: 2019-2020.* https://datatopics.worldbank.org/world-development-indicators/stories/the-classification-of-countries-by-income.html. (Accessed on February 24, 2020).

World Bank (2020). *World Development Indicators.* https://databank.worldbank.org/source/world-development-indicators, (Accessed on February 26, 2020).

World Economic Forum (2019). *The Global Competitiveness Report 2019.* Geneva.

Xu, L., Zhang, S., Yang, M., Li, W., and Xu, J. (2018). Environmental effects of China's solar photovoltaic industry during 2011–2016: A life cycle assessment approach. *Journal of Cleaner Production*, 170, 310–329.

Yang, X. J., Lin, A., Li, X.-L., Wu, Y., Zhou, W., and Chen, Z. (2013). China's ion-adsorption rare earth resources, mining consequences and preservation. *Environmental Development*, 8, 131–136.

Zhang, H., Wu, K., Qiu, Y., Chan, G., Wang, S., Zhou, D., and Ren, X. (2020). Solar photovoltaic interventions have reduced rural poverty in China. *Nature Communications*, 11(1), 1969.

https://doi.org/10.1142/9789811240553_bmatter

Index

A

abatement, 38, 63
adaptation, 309
adaptation and climate proofing, 354
adaptation processes, 139
adaptation to climate change, xxiv, 119
adjusted net national income per capita, 77, 80, 85
adjustment cost, 129
af-/reforestation, 380–381
afforestation, xxii, 317
Africa, xvii, xix, 222–223, 226, 229, 231, 233, 241–242, 245
Agenda 2030, 70, 85
agglomeration effects, 319
agricultural area, 445
agricultural capital stock, 206
agricultural expansion, 448
agricultural labor, 179, 195
agricultural land, 441, 444
agricultural output, 178, 183, 185–186, 189
agricultural production, 202
agricultural productivity, 324
agricultural sector, xvii
agriculture, xix, 222, 228, 231–232, 235, 238, 243
agriculture, forestry, and other land use (AFOLU), 371–373
annual forest loss, 449
appropriation, 275, 283, 287
armed conflicts, 222–223, 227, 229–231, 234, 239–240, 242, 244
Asia, xvii
asylum, 312, 329
atmospheric CO_2, 316
atmospheric rental policy, 394–395
average temperatures, 124

B

behavioral mechanisms, 418, 433
behavioral methods, 432
benchmark indicator, 67, 69, 73, 77
benefit-sharing agreements, 430
biochar, 379, 381
biodiversity, xxi, xxiii, 380–381, 401, 439
bioenergy with carbon capture and storage (BECCS), xxii, 370, 373–377, 380–381, 383–385, 396, 400
blockchain, 439, 442, 451, 455
blockchain platform, 455–456, 458, 460

blockchain technology, xxiii, 446, 452, 456, 460–461
blockchain-based, 461
blockchain-based contract management, 451–453
blockchain-based contract management platform, 457
blue bond, 422–423, 430, 434
blue carbon, 416, 419–420, 423, 426
blue carbon ecosystem, 434
blue carbon financing, 417, 422
blue carbon initiative, 417–418, 428, 431, 434
blue carbon projects, xxii
bottom-up partial-equilibrium exercises, 143
bribes, 457
broken window fallacy, 8

C

carbon budget, 372, 374, 392
carbon credits, 424, 426–427
carbon cycle, 384–385
carbon dioxide (CO_2) emissions, 69
carbon dioxide removal (CDR), xxi
carbon finance, 420
carbon fund, 429
carbon market, 434
carbon sequestration, 419
carbon sinks, 416
carbon storage, 447
carbon tax, 389, 393–395
catch potential, 145
causal inference, 433
CDR approaches, 397
CDR credits, 387, 390–391, 393, 399
chapters, 76, 375
China, xxiii
circumstance solidarity, 51, 53, 58–61
cities, xx
city planning, 358
civil war, 328
clean development mechanism (CDM), 417
clean energy investments, 82
climate, 7, 309
Climate Action (SDG 13), 67, 77, 85
climate action summit, 440
climate adaptation, xx, 185
climate and development, 67–69, 73, 77, 80, 82, 87
climate change, xiii, 8, 12, 38, 40, 62, 115, 222–223, 225, 227–232, 235–236, 239–240, 242, 244, 287, 420, 446, 449
climate change damages, 138
climate change impacts, 143
climate change mitigation and adaptation, 431
climate change mitigation scenarios, xxi
climate change policy, 444
climate events, 210
climate extremes, 177–178, 196, 202–204, 206, 208
climate mitigation and adaptation, 356
climate neutrality, 368–370, 375, 387, 391
climate policy, 63, 68, 85
climate scenarios, xvii
climatic hazards, 188
climatic impact, 448
climatic shocks, 186, 189
climato-economic livability, xvi
climato-economic theory of culture, 91, 93, 97–100, 102, 104–107, 109
climatologic events, 196
CO_2 emissions, 67, 72–73, 77, 80–81, 86
co-benefits credits, 434
co-benefits, xxi
co-benefits of CDR, 380
coal-fired power plants, xxiii
coastal ecosystems, 416
Cobb–Douglas, 121, 123, 319
Colombia, xxiii
combating corruption, 460
command-and-control tools, 425
Common Agricultural Policy, 400
community engagement, 426
competitive bidding, 455

computable general equilibrium (CGE), xviii, 122, 138
conflict, 282, 309
conflict investment, 279
constant elasticity of substitution (CES), 121–122
constant prices, 119
consumer behavior, 130
consumer price index, 126, 131
consumers' demand, 121
consumption spillovers, 261
content design, 432
contested good, 279
contract liability insurance, 458
contract management, 442, 453, 461
control share, 266, 271, 275
conventional outdoor agriculture, 187
corner solution at net-zero emissions, 388, 392
corruption, 446, 453, 457, 459, 461
cost minimization over the entire 21st century, 374
COVID-19 pandemic, 69, 80, 85
cow protection in India, 258
crop cultivation, 181
crop production, 181, 183, 209
crop productivity, 202, 209
crop yield, 146, 178, 181, 185, 189
cross-community consumption spillovers, 257, 264, 287
cross-community negative consumption spillovers, 261
cross-community negative spillovers, 260
cross-community spillovers, 279
cultivators, 267
cultural creativity, 99, 102–103, 114
cultural tightness, 99–101

D

DACCS, 375, 378, 381–382, 384–385, 396
damage estimates, xvii
damage functions, 116
decentralized private provision, 257, 287
decentralized provision, 280
declaration of timber transactions, 458
decrease in forest area, 445
deforestation, 416, 421, 441–443, 447–448
deforestation of tropical forests, 439
degradation rate, 275
demand structures, 124
democratization, 22
demographic transition, 21
desertification, 309
developing countries, 383, 387, 398
development, xiv, 222–223, 226, 230, 234, 237
Diamond, Jared, 105, 111
digital signature, 461
disasters, 326
discontinuity of CDR deployment incentives, 389–391
discount factor, 43–45, 52–53, 55–56, 58, 61
discount rate, 38, 40, 61
discounting, 39, 43, 45, 62
diseases, xiii
displacement, 311
distribution of income, 5
droughts, 177–179, 184–186, 196, 202–203, 208–210, 309

E

econometric approaches, 139
economic and social stability, xviii
economic capability, 383
economic damage, 127, 129, 132
economic damage assessments, xviii
economic damages of climate change, 126
economic development, xvii, 6, 91–92, 106, 108, 110, 309
economic growth, xvii, 4, 16, 312
economic impacts, 117, 132
economic motivations, 354
economic system, 124

ecosystem conservation and restoration, 433
ecosystem management strategy, 432
ecosystem services, 84, 147, 416, 418, 434–435
ecosystem-based, 397
ecosystem-based CDR approaches, 380, 385, 398–400
ecosystems, 375
effective share, 267, 275, 271
effort sharing regulation (ESR), 399
elasticities of substitution, 126
elasticity of marginal utility, 43, 52, 61
electronic signature, 452, 456
emigration, 311
emissions trading system, 390–391, 392, 395–396
employment opportunities, 450
employment problems, 450
end-to-end timber monitoring, 454
energy efficiency, xxi, 356
energy use, 201–202, 204, 206, 210
enhanced weathering, 378, 381
environmental degradation, 287
environmental determinism, 4
environmental goals, 76, 85–86
Environmental Investigation Agency, 446
environmental migration, 309
equity, 38–39, 83, 87
ethnic conflict, 257, 288
ethno-linguistic and religious, 263
European climate policy architecture, 399
European Emissions Trading Scheme (EU ETS), 399, 424
European Union (EU) Timber Regulation, 452
evidence-based solutions, xxii
excessive savings, 38, 48, 61
execution of contracts, 453
expert stakeholders, 348
external costs, xxi
external costs of CDR, 380 385, 387, 396
external costs of NETs/CDR, 382
extreme events, 189
extreme poverty, 69, 72, 81, 84
extreme temperatures, 326
extreme weather events, xiii, xviii, 177, 179, 185–186, 196–197, 203–204, 208–209

F

farm machinery, 188, 195
feed, 183, 195
felling permit, 454
fertilizer, 189, 195
financial liability of emitters, 389, 392, 394–395
financial liability of emitters for CDR, 390
fixed capital stock, 118
flexibility, 48
flood, 185
floods, 177–179, 188, 208, 210, 310
food insecurity, 222, 230, 236
food prices, 375, 381–382, 384
food security, xxii, 222, 228, 380–381, 401
forced displacement, 321
forecasted freedom, 105, 107
forest area loss, 449
forest areas, 443–444
forest communities, 440–441, 450–451
forest conservation, 458
forest losses, 443
forest management, 377
forest produce, 259
forest protection, 460
forest regeneration, 459
forest restoration, 459
forests, xxi
fossil fuel subsidy swap, 82–83
freedom, xvi
fundamental freedoms, 92–94, 97, 110
future generations, xiv

G

general equilibrium, 309
geography, xiv, 7
geological storage, 370, 385
geological storage (of carbon), 377
Germany, xxiii
Ghana, 429
Global Climate Risk Index, 185
global cooling, 91–92, 109–110
global economy, 77, 80
Global Responses to Anthropogenic Changes in the Environment, 122
Global Trade Analysis Project (GTAP), 122
global warming, 91–93, 105–106, 108–110
governance, 347, 358, 360
government spending, 393
GRACE, 124
greenhouse gas (GHG) emissions, 69
greenhouse gas emissions, 440
greenhouse gases, xiii
Greenland Norse, 93, 104
gross complements, 51
gross domestic product (GDP), 117, 133
gross fixed capital formation, 201, 204, 210
gross substitute, 52
group conflict, 261
group-specific public goods, 257–258, 261–262, 287–286

H

heat spells, 177–178, 208
heatwaves, 322
Hicksian neutral technology, 120
historical evidence, xxiii, 309
historical responsibility for climate change, 383
human health, 149
hunger, xiii
hurricanes, 188

I

IAMs, 115, 131
illegal deforestation, 445
illegal logging, xxii, 439, 460
illegal timber, 449
illegal timber or timber products, 452
illegal timber production, 446
imperfect rivalry and incomplete excludability, 269
in-migration, 313
income and migration, 309
India, 259
industrial agriculture, 448
industrialized countries, 383, 398
inelastic demand, 130
inequality, 39, 55, 58, 226, 238
inequality aversion, 43, 50, 52, 58, 61
information and communication technologies (ICT), xxi
information exchange, 455
infrastructural expansion, 449
infrastructure availability, xix
institutional determinism, 4
institutions, xiv, 233, 236, 238
insurance, 459
integrated assessment models, xvii, 138
inter-community conflict, 258, 279
inter-community contest, 271
inter-group conflicts, 257, 287
inter-group contests, 262
inter-state migration, 311
intergenerational distribution, xv
internal migration, 310
international carbon market mechanisms, 398
international development policies, 87
International Institute for Sustainable Development, 83
international migrants, 310
intersectoral compensation, 369, 372
intersectoral compensation of emissions, 369, 392
intertemporal compensation, 372
intertemporal compensation of emissions, 392

intertemporal evaluation, 40, 62–63
intertemporal social welfare function, xv
involuntary mobility, 310
IPCC, 106, 109, 111
irrigation, 323

K

Kenya, 426

L

labeling of timber, 456
labor productivity, 186–187
lack of legal rights, 450
Lagrange method, 44, 49
land, 195
land and water resources, xviii
land degradation, 179, 309
land productivity, 209
land use, 375, 377–378, 381, 383
land use, land use change, and forestry (LULUCF), 369–370, 399
land-intensive CDR, 381, 383
least total cost perspective, 374
legislation, 454
Leontief, 121, 123
liability insurance, 459
livelihoods of forest communities, 441
livestock, 183, 189, 195, 202
livestock production, 183, 209
living conditions, 447
local stakeholder, 425
local stakeholders, 423, 426, 429, 431
location of forest site, 458
loss elasticity, 272, 284
loss function, 271
low- and middle-income economies, 83
low-income countries, xvi, 67, 69, 72–73, 76–77, 79–82, 84–87

M

machinery, 195
Madagascar, 427
Malthusian equilibrium, 17
mandatory payments, 457
mangrove, 417–418, 425–426, 428–429, 431, 435
mangrove conservation, 417, 432–433
mangrove conservation and restoration, 435
mangrove conservation plan, 425
mangroves, xxii, 416, 420, 427
marginal degradation rate, 272, 284
marginal productivity, 55, 57, 119–120
marginal rate of substitution, 49, 53, 55
marginal rate of transformation, 41–42, 54, 57, 59–60
maximin criterion, 46, 62
megacity, 349
Middle East and North Africa (MENA) region, xx, 345, 360
middle-income countries, 311
migration, xix, xx, 226, 235, 241, 244, 309
migration across borders, 310
migration cost, 316
military expenditure, 237
minimizing illegal logging, 460
mining industries, xxiii
mitigating environmental pollution, 354
mobility, 356
moral hazard, 397
moral hazard of CDR deployment, 386
more difficult market-driven adaptation, 160

N

Nash equilibrium, 278, 315
Nationally Determined Contributions (NDCs), 82, 420
natural climate solutions (NCSs), 82, 84, 87
natural disasters, xiii, 8
natural resource, xix, 287
natural resource degradation, 257, 288
negative cross-community spillovers, 283–284
negative emissions technologies, xxi
negative external costs, xxii

negative externalities, 270
negative spillovers, 262, 271, 275, 280, 282
Nepal, 428
net carbon burial, 420
net carbon sequestration, 424
net welfare gain, 67, 80, 85
net-negative emissions, xxi
nomadic, 312
non-farm occupations, 314
nonlinearities, 312
North American, 130

O

ocean fertilization, 379
offsetting emissions, 369, 388–391, 393
offsetting emissions with CDR credits, 393, 396, 399
on-farm adjustment, 314
one-time payment of cumulative SCC, 395
optimum climate, 19
out-migration, 313
output of grain, 125
overshoot of CO_2 emissions and temperatures, 372–375, 385, 392

P

2015 Paris Agreement, 81
1.5° pathways, 370
1.5°C pathways, 371–374, 381
2ºC pathways, 373–374
pandemics, 313
Paris Accord, xiv, xxi
Paris Agreement, 368, 371, 398
participatory approaches, 418
participatory methods, 426–428, 430, 432–433
pastoralists, 267
pastoralists and cultivators, 259
pasture conditions, 183
payments for ecosystem services (PESs), 421, 424, 428, 434
per capita welfare change, 67, 85
periodic payment of instantaneous social costs, 395
permanence of carbon storage, 384–385
physical conflict, xviii
physical damage, 116, 127, 129
poaching, 446
policy, 234
policy analysis, 122
policy-maker views, 347
policy-makers, 356, 360
poor countries, 311
population, 317
population density, 18
population growth, 18
portfolio of NETs/CDR, 376, 382, 386
portfolios of NETs, 382
positive externalities, 269
positive spillovers, 271
post-COVID recovery, 81, 86
poverty, 234, 238
poverty traps, 16
precipitation, 179, 181–182, 188, 201–202, 208–209, 228, 230, 232, 241
price change effect, 118, 126
price-inelastic, 118
prioritarianism, 43, 62
private supply of public goods, 264
production versus appropriation, 257, 287
production vs. appropriation, 262
productivity, 39–40, 44, 45, 47–48, 50, 57–60, 63
productivity of land, 116, 120, 125
prosumer, 356, 358
protection level, 48–50, 52–53, 58–59
public bad, 258, 264
public good contests, 264
purchasing power parities (PPP), 115, 131, 133
pure time preference, 43

Q

quantitative approaches, 418
quantitative assessment, 72–73
quantitative methods, 432–433

R

rainfall, 179, 181, 183, 185–186, 188–189, 202, 208
rainfed crops, 184
rainforests, 441
re-/afforestation, 373, 376, 398
real price change effect, 127
reallocation of resources, 118
REDD+, 398, 417–418, 421, 428–429
reduced-form climate change damage function, 138, 164
reforestation, xxii, 458
refugees, 328
regional welfare, 126
relative prices, 131
reliable storage of information, 460
renaturation of ecosystems, 377
renewable energies, xxi, 356
rent-seeking, 263
representative concentration pathway, 125, 143
representative SDG indicators, 72, 73
residential energy demand, 148
residual, 390
residual emissions, 369, 389–390
resource, 223, 230–231, 233–234, 239, 241, 245
resource and energy concerns, 354
restoration of ecosystems, 380
risk of reversibility, 385, 397
rural and urban regions, 315
rural communities, 440
rural-urban migration, 330

S

scalability, 418
scalability of CDR/NETs, 372, 375, 378
scarcity of water, xix
schooling level, 321
SDG 1 No Poverty, 73
SDG 13 Climate Action, 69–70, 73, 76, 80, 85
sea level rise, 145, 320
security, 332
separate CDR remuneration scheme, 393
separate remuneration scheme for CDR, 392
Seychelles, 423, 430–431, 434
smart and sustainable cities, 346
smart contracts, 461
smart grids, 356
smart network infrastructure, xxi
social choice theory, 40, 51, 63
social conflict, xix, 287
social cost of carbon (SCC), 116, 389, 394
social discount rate, xv
social evaluation, 39–41, 43–45
social indifference curve, 43, 46, 52, 55
social learning, 434
social peace, 279
social preferences, 39–40
societal pressure, 354
socio-economic development path, 373, 382
soil carbon sequestration, 378, 380
Solowian growth, 21
South Africa, xxiii
sovereign debt, 422
spatial, 223, 226–228, 231, 234, 239–240, 242–243, 245
spillovers, 227, 239–240, 244
SSP2, 141
stakeholder buy-in, 434
stakeholder engagement, 429, 432
stakeholder interviews, 348
stakeholder involvement, xxii, 418, 430–431, 433
stakeholders, 356–357, 417, 428
static numerical model, 121
statistical model, 125
steady state, 316, 318, 320
steady-state, 313

Stern Review, xv
stochastic frontier, 24
stock pollutant nature of the global warming externality, 394
storms, 177–178, 185, 208–210
subsistence farming, 448
substitution elasticity, 123
supply chain, 453
supply chain transparency, 451, 456
surface albedo, 376
sustainabilitarian, 62–63
sustainability, 38–39, 44–45, 47, 50, 57–58, 62
sustainability risks, 370
sustainability risks of CDR, 376, 381–382, 387, 392
sustainable development, xxi, 39, 41, 68, 69, 82, 87, 442
sustainable development goals (SDGs), xvi, 67–68
sustainable growth, xx
sustainable mobility, xxi
synergies, 69
system, 393

T

1.5°C target, 371–372
2°C target, 371–372
taste shock, 319
technological improvement, 51, 58, 60–61
technological progress, 320
technological uncertainties, 384
temperature, 177–178, 181, 185, 188–189, 197, 199, 201, 206, 208–209, 223, 242, 244
tender conditions, 455
terrestrial and marine ecosystems, xxii
Thailand, 427
The Nature Conservancy (TNC), 423
thermometer for livability, 91, 93–95, 100, 105–106
thresholds, 309
timber monitoring, 454
timber supply chain, 456
timber transactions, 457
timber transportation, 458
tipping points, xviii, 332
tourism flows, 148
trade-offs, 69, 76–77, 80, 85
trade-offs and complementarities, 69
trade-offs and synergies, 67–69, 73, 76
transboundary environmental problems, 315
transformation curve, 41–43, 45–47, 52, 54–55
transparency, 452, 461–462
tropical carbon tax, 82, 84, 87
tropical forest, 440
tropical forest conservation, 442, 450
tropical forest protection, 451
tropical forests, xxiii, 444, 447
tropical regions, 444
tropical storms, 309
Tullock contestation, 266

U

UN Climate Conference of the Parties (COP 26), 82
UNFCC, 417
urbanization, 331
utilitarian social welfare function, 40, 42, 44–45, 48, 55–56, 61–62
utilitarianism, 62
utility function, xv, 121, 132

V

verified carbon credits, 417
verified carbon standards (VCS), 421
violence, xviii, 223, 229, 235, 238, 242–243
violent invasion, 327
volume of timber, 458
voluntary carbon market, 427
voluntary contribution to public goods, 264
voluntary contributions, 279
voluntary market, 426
voluntary subscriptions, 262
vulnerability, 231, 237, 242

W

water scarcity, 229, 231, 242–243
water shortage, 209
water stress, 182, 184
water supply, 322
weather extremes, 186, 196–197, 210
weather shocks, 12
welfare analysis, 78
welfare effect, 76
welfare effects, 69
well-being, xiii
West Africa, 259
wetlands, xxi
wildfire, 177, 179, 196
willingness to pay (WTP), 76
World Bank, 423, 432
World Bank's World Development Indicators, 72

Y

yield shocks, 182

CPSIA information can be obtained
at www.ICGtesting.com
Printed in the USA
LVHW051248031221
705026LV00001B/7

9 789811 240546